Rockies

THOMAS COOK

On 5 July 1841 Thomas Cook, a 32-year-old printer from Market Harborough, in Leicestershire, England, led a party of some 500 temperance enthusiasts on a railway outing from Leicester to Loughborough which he had arranged down to the last detail. This proved to be the birth of the modern tourist industry. In the course of expanding his business, Thomas Cook and his son, John, invented many of the features of organised travel which we now take for granted. Over the next 150 years the name Thomas Cook became synonymous with world travel.

Today the Thomas Cook Group employs over 13,000 people across the globe and its Worldwide Network provides services to customers at more than 3000 locations in over 100 countries. Its activities include travel retailing, tour operating and financial services – Thomas Cook is a world leader in traveller's cheques and foreign money services.

Thomas Cook believed in the value of the printed word as an accompaniment to travel. His publication *The Excursionist* was the equivalent of both a holiday brochure and a travel magazine. Today Thomas Cook Publishing continues to issue one of the world's oldest travel books, the *Thomas Cook European Timetable,* which has been in existence since 1873. Updated every month, it remains the only definitive compendium of European railway schedules.

The *Thomas Cook Touring Handbook* series, to which this volume belongs, is a range of comprehensive guides for travellers touring regions of the world by train, car and ship. Other titles include:

Touring by train

On the Rails around France and Benelux (Published 1995)

On the Rails around the Alps (Published 1996)

On the Rails around Eastern Europe (Published 1996)

On the Rails around Europe (Third Edition Published 1998)

On the Rails around Britain and Ireland (Second Edition Published 1998)

Touring by car

On the Road around California (Second Edition Published 1996)

On the Road around Florida (Second Edition Published 1997)

On the Road around Normandy, Brittany and the Loire Valley (Published 1996)

On the Road around the Capital Region (Published 1997)

On the Road around the South of France (Published 1997)

On the Road around the Pacific Northwest (Published 1997)

On the Road around England and Wales (Published 1998)

Touring by car, train and bus

Touring Australia (Published 1997)

Touring Southern Africa (Published 1997)

Touring by ship

Greek Island Hopping (Published annually in February)

For more details of these and other Thomas Cook publications, write to Passport Books, at the address on the back of the title page.

TOURING THE

Canadian
Rockies

Fly-drive holidays and
rail journeys in Alberta
and British Columbia

PASSPORT BOOKS
NTC/Contemporary Publishing Group

Fred Gebhart
and Maxine Cass

A THOMAS COOK TOURING HANDBOOK

Published by Passport Books, a division of
NTC/Contemporary Publishing Company
4255 West Touhy Avenue,
Lincolnwood (Chicago),
Illinois 60646-1975 USA.

Text:
© 1998 The Thomas Cook Group Ltd
Maps and diagrams:
© 1998 The Thomas Cook Group Ltd

ISBN 0-8442-9998-7
Library of Congress Catalog Card
    Number: 98-65238

Published by Passport Books in conjunction
with The Thomas Cook Group Ltd.

Managing Editor: Stephen York
Project Editor: Leyla Davies
Map Editor: Bernard Horton
Route diagrams: Caroline Horton
Maps drawn by RJS Associates
Typesetting: Tina West

Cover illustration by Tina West
Copy-editor: Pauline Smith
Text design by Darwell Holland
Text typeset in Bembo and Gill Sans using
    QuarkXPress for Windows
Maps and diagrams created using Macromedia
    Freehand and GSP Designworks
Printed in Great Britain by Fisherprint Ltd,
    Peterborough

Written and researched by
Fred Gebhart
Maxine Cass

Additional research by
Helena Zukowski

ABOUT THE AUTHORS

Fred Gebhart has lived in the West for more than 40 years, interrupted by extended sojourns in Europe and West Africa. He travelled Western Canada as a teenager as well as an adult. A freelance photojournalist for 16 years, Fred covers Western North America and Australasia between collaborations on *Thomas Cook Touring Handbook* titles with his wife, Maxine Cass. He has also contributed to other books and written computer software manuals. Fred's passion is scuba diving, a love that is more happily consummated in tropical climes than in the chilly waters of British Columbia.

Maxine Cass, born in California, has studied Medieval History at the University of California, lived in Greece and Senegal, and become a widely-published photojournalist and author in the fortysome years she has lived in the West. Maxine contributes to travel and business publications between book collaborations with her husband, Fred Gebhart. *Touring the Canadian Rockies* is their fourth *Thomas Cook Touring Handbook*. Others include *On the Road around California, On the Road around the Pacific Northwest* and *On the Road around Florida* (with Eric and Ruth Bailey), as well as her own *A AAA Photo Journey to San Francisco*. Between research trips around the world, Maxine gardens and shares a love of animals with her series co-author at their home in San Francisco.

Helena Zukowski is a full-time travel writer who was born in Alberta but moved as a child to British Columbia, which she insists is the true site of the Garden of Eden. Helena travels extensively from her base near Vancouver and her stories have been published in magazines and newspapers in Canada, the United States and abroad.

PHOTOGRAPHS

The photographs on the back cover and in the colour sections opposite p. 32 (except (i) Royal Hudson: Leisurail; and (ii) black bear: F Gebhart) and p. 128 were taken by Maxine Cass. All other photographs (except Emerald Lake: M Cass) were taken by Fred Gebhart.

ACKNOWLEDGEMENTS

The authors and publishers would like to thank the following people and organisations for their assistance during the preparation of this book:
The spirit and inspiration of Lloyd F. Gebhart, the buffalo who roamed the Plains and the salmon who swam the rivers; John Bateman, Super, Natural British Columbia; Eric Bélanger, Rocky Mountaineer Railtours; Big Country Tourist Association, Drumheller, AB; Shannon Birnie, Brewster Transportation & Tours; Black Knight Inn, Red Deer, AB; Monica Campbell-Hoppé, Canadian Consulate General, Los Angeles; Sgt Wayne Carroll and Cpl Gilles Moreau, RCMP; Jennifer Case, Cariboo Tourism Association, BC; Heather Chapman, Immedia Management, Inc; CMH Heli-hiking; Convention Inn, Edmonton, AB; Karen Cook, Rocky Mountain Tourism, BC; Jean Cullen, BC Rail; Maureen Cumming, British Columbia Ferry Corporation; Marla J Daniels, Edmonton Tourism, AB; ; Patsy Duggan, Tourism British Columbia, BC; Scott Eady, Jasper Raft Tours Ltd, AB; Jill & Neil Fenton, The Glass House, AB; Lou Gebhart; Samantha Geer, Jasper Park Lodge, AB; Sarah Geddes, Chateau Lake Louise, AB; John Gilchrist, Glenbow Museum, Calgary, AB; Mike Gregory, Canmore Regency, AB; Jurassic Inn, Drumheller, AB; Karim Karim, Bayshore Inn, AB; Jan Kozlowski, Kootenay Country Tourism, BC; Stephanie Kuxdorf, Rocky Mountain Tourist Destination Region, AB; Shannon Langley & Barry Rogers, Wild Rose Ranch & Resort, BC; Mona LeDuc, Canadian Pacific Hotels; Patricia M Lee; Freda Lentz, Red Deer Visitor & Convention Bureau, AB; George Mack, Mack Limosine, Vancouver, BC; Lisa Mackintosh, Alberta South Tourism Destination Region, AB; Paul & Virginia McCarthy; Murray Morgan, Jasper Adventure Centre Ltd, AB; Johanne & Lloyd O'Toole, Wicklow Bed & Breakfast, BC; Parks Canada; Poi; Tom & Ruth Powell; Prince Royal Suites, Calgary, AB; Mary Ellen Quesada; Paul Raynor, VIA Rail Canada Inc; Remington-Alberta Carriage Centre, Cardston, AB; Jan Repp, Fort Edmonton Park, AB; Reynolds-Alberta Museum, Wetaskawin, AB; Kevin Ridgeway, Vancouver, Coast & Mountains Tourism, BC; Karen Robinson, Leone & Leone Ltd; Krista Rodger, Jasper Tourism, AB; Royal British Columbia Museum Victoria, BC; Sandman Hotel, Lethbridge, AB; Laura Serena, Tourism Vancouver, AB; Paula Diakiw Smith, Jasper Park Lodge, AB; Cameron Spence, Rocky Mountain Tourist Destination Region, AB; Shaun Stevenson, North by Northwest, BC; Terri Stevenson; Dode Stiles, Calgary Convention & Visitors Bureau, AB; Super 8 Motel, Drumheller, AB; The Crossing, AB; Travel Alberta; Travelodge Macleod Trail, Calgary, AB; Linda Trudeau, Okanagan Similkameen Tourism Association, BC; Waterfront Centre Hotel, Vancouver, BC; West Harvest Inn, Edmonton, AB; Anne Winters, High Country Tourism, BC; Holly J Wood, Banff Springs Hotel, AB.

5

CONTENTS

ROUTES AND CITIES

*In alphabetical order. For indexing purposes, routes are listed in both directions – the reverse direction
to which it appears in the book is shown in italics.
See also the Route Map, p. 8, for a diagrammatic presentation of all the routes in the book.
To look up towns and other places not listed here, see the Index, p. 348.*

7

REFERENCE SECTION

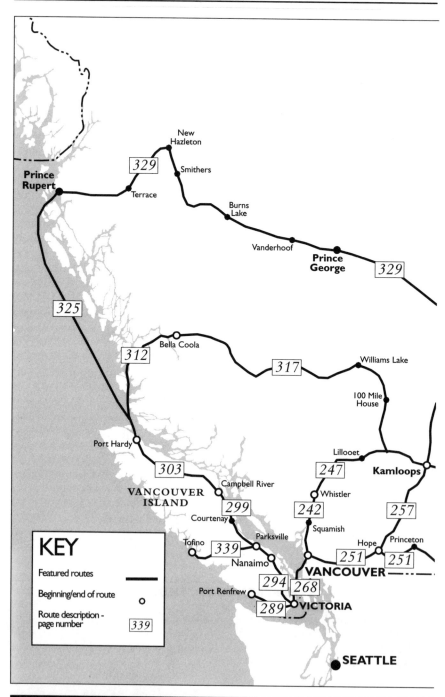

New Hazleton

Prince Rupert

329

Smithers

Terrace

Burns Lake

Vanderhoof

Prince George

329

325

312

Bella Coola

317

Williams Lake

100 Mile House

Port Hardy

Lillooet

303

247

Kamloops

VANCOUVER ISLAND

Campbell River

Whistler

242

257

299

Courtenay

Squamish

Tofino

339

Parksville

Hope

Princeton

251

251

Nanaimo

VANCOUVER

294

268

Port Renfrew

289

VICTORIA

SEATTLE

KEY

Featured routes

Beginning/end of route   O

Route description - page number   339

8

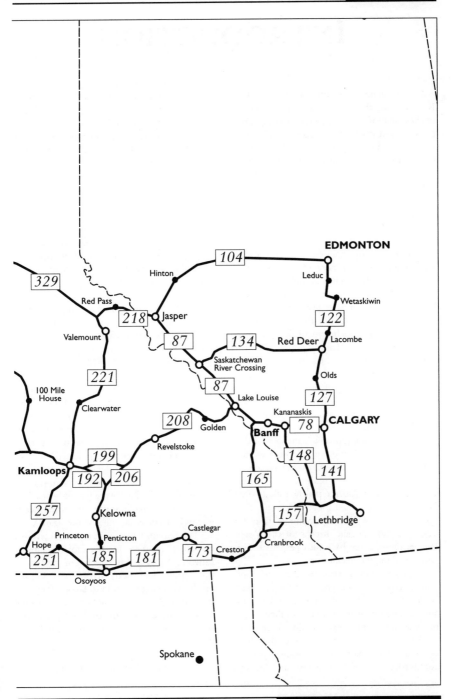

INTRODUCTION

Awe is the dominant emotion in the Canadian Rockies, awe that time, water, snow and ice could sculpt mountains into such soaring ramparts cloaked with icy blue glaciers and punctuated by thundering cataracts. There's awe, too, that such wild, untamed beauty survives daily onslaughts of tour coaches, cars, RVs, helicopters and hikers in search of solitude.

There's a tension in the Canadian Rockies, a ceaseless struggle for dominance between nature and humanity. That the majestic splendour of snow-clad peaks and deep forests chronicled by early explorers even exists today seems miraculous. It's more a testament to the avarice of businessmen and politicians who conspired to turn immense tracts of crown lands into semi-private playgrounds called national parks. Created for the enjoyment of the rich and the enrichment of the Canadian Pacific Railway, Banff, Jasper, Yoho, Kootenay and Glacier National Parks have instead become spiritual retreats for the masses. Together with dozens of provincial parks in Alberta and British Columbia, the natural wonders of Western Canada lure visitors by the millions each year.

Calgary, Edmonton and Vancouver have become vibrant urban gateways to the world, but nature remains the overriding presence. The icy grip of winter continues to exact its annual toll. The Alberta prairie rolls to the horizon like an undulating table-top. The inland forests of British Columbia turn to desert behind the rain shadow of the Coast Range, then plunge back into perpetual mist and rain along the Pacific coast.

Explored and settled in the name of commercial profit and pressured by an overweening neighbour to the south, the Rockies and the two provinces that contain them have become one of the most socially progressive corners of the continent and one of the most politically conservative. First Nations, systematically deprived of land, liberty and life by government policies that put White settlers first, have re-emerged as a potent political, economic and cultural force.

The birthplace of Greenpeace remains heavily dependent upon the exploitation of rapidly disappearing natural resources. Dense rain forests that stretched unbroken for thousands of kilometres are being reduced to scattered patches inside protected parklands. The seemingly limitless runs of silvery salmon are dwindling to yearly trickles in the wake of overfishing and overzealous timber cutting.

Jasper, and especially Banff, National Parks, created to preserve the tranquil beauty of pristine peaks and glimmering aquamarine lakes, are clogged with mid-summer traffic that creeps as slowly as any urban rush hour. At the same hour, highways in nearby Yoho and Kootenay National Parks, never as heavily publicised as their eastern neighbours on the Icefield Parkway, stand invitingly empty.

It's not the first time that change has altered the face of the Rockies. A new world overtook First Nations in the form of traders and fur hunters in the 18th century, themselves displaced by lumbermen and farmers in the 19th. Nature plays her own role in the perpetual tug-of-war, sometimes defeated with the damming of the once-mighty Columbia River into a string of lake, sometimes victorious as when railway builders were forced to abandon the surface of Rogers Pass to tunnel nearly 400 m beneath avalanching winter snows.

The tension between using resources now or conserving them for the future is already bringing change and the passing of ways of life that many hold dear. If Western Canada breaks with long tradition to favour conservation, it will preserve the awesome natural scenery that has been the stuff of legend since humans first set eyes on it more than 10,000 years ago.

Fred Gebhart and Maxine Cass

HOW TO USE THIS BOOK

ROUTES AND CITIES

Touring the Canadian Rockies provides you with an expert selection of over 30 recommended routes between key cities and attractions of Alberta and British Columbia, each in its own chapter. Smaller cities, towns, attractions and points of interest along each route are described in the order in which you will encounter them. Additional chapters are devoted to the major places of interest which begin and end these routes, and some circular routes explore regions of particular interest. These route and city chapters form the core of the book, from page 64 to page 343.

Where applicable, an alternative route which is more direct is also provided at the beginning of each route chapter. This will enable you to drive more quickly between the cities at the beginning and end of the route, if you do not intend to stop at any of the intermediate places. To save space, each route is described in only one direction, but you can follow it in the reverse direction, too.

The arrangement of the text consists of a chapter describing a large city or region of interest first, followed by chapters forming a larger circuit, taking in other major destinations before returning to the starting point. The first city to be covered is Calgary (pp.64–74), followed by Calgary Circuit circular drive (pp.75–77) and then routes leading away from Calgary: Calgary to Banff (pp.78–86), Banff to Jasper (pp. 87–103), Jasper to Edmonton (pp.104–107). Edmonton is described in the next two chapters, and routes following those take you back to Calgary. The routes then head south and then east into British Columbia, consecutive route chapters forming a longer circular tour. The order of chapters thus follows the pattern of your journey, beginning in a gateway or major town or city, forming a circuit that takes in the other major tourist centres.

The overall pattern of the routes runs west from Calgary in Alberta, heading into British Columbia to Vancouver Island and the western coast of Canada, then turning north to Prince Rupert and finally east back to Alberta. To find the page number of any route or city chapter quickly, use either the alphabetical list on the **Contents** pages, pp. 6–7, or the master **Route Map** on pp. 8–9.

The routes are designed to be used as a kind of menu from which you can plan an itinerary, combining a number of routes which take you to the places you most want to visit.

WITHIN EACH ROUTE

Each route chapter begins with a short introduction to the route, followed by driving directions from the beginning of the route to the end, and a sketch map of the route and all the places along it which are described in the chapter. This map, intended to be used in conjunction with the driving directions, summarises the route and shows the main intermediate distances and road numbers; for a key to the symbols used, see p.13.

DIRECT ROUTE

This will be the fastest, most direct, and sometimes, predictably, least interesting drive between the beginning and end of the route, usually along major highways.

SCENIC ROUTE

This is the itinerary which takes in the most places of interest, usually using ordinary highways and minor roads. Road directions are specific; always be prepared for detours due to road construction, adverse weather conditions, etc. The driving directions are followed by sub-sections describing the main attractions and places of interest along the way. You can stop at them all or miss out the ones which do not appeal to you. Always ask at the local tourist information centre (usually the Convention & Visitors Bureau or Chamber of Commerce) for more information on sights, lodgings and places at which to eat.

 SIDE TRACK

This heading is occasionally used to indicate departures from the main route, or out-of-town trips from a city, which detour to worthwhile sights, described in full or highlighted in a paragraph or two.

CITY DESCRIPTIONS

Whether a place is given a half-page description within a route chapter or merits an entire chapter to itself, we have concentrated on practical details: local sources of tourist information; getting around in city centres (by car, by public transport or on foot as appropriate); accommodation and dining; post and phone communications; entertainment and shopping opportunities; and sightseeing, history and background interest. The largest cities have all this detail; in smaller places some categories of information are less relevant and have been omitted or summarised. Where there is a story to tell which would interrupt the flow of the main description, we have placed **feature boxes** on subjects as diverse as 'The Royal Canadian Mounted Police' and 'The Naming of Kicking Horse'.

Although we mention good independently owned lodgings in many places, we always also list the hotel chains which have a property in the area, by means of code letters to save space. Many travellers prefer to stick to one or two chains with which they are familiar and which give a consistent standard of accommodation. The codes are explained on p. 346, and central booking numbers for the chains are also given there.

MAPS

In addition to the sketch map which accompanies each route, we provide maps of major cities (usually the downtown area), smaller towns, regions, national parks, and so on. At the end of the book is a section of **colour road maps** covering the Canadian Rockies and Western Canada, which is detailed enough to be used for trip planning and on the road. The **key to symbols** used on all the types of map in this book is shown on p. 13.

THE REST OF THE BOOK

The use of the **Contents** and **Route Map** pages has already been mentioned above. **Background Western Canada** gives a concise briefing on the history and geography of this fascinating region. **Travel Essentials** is an alphabetically arranged chapter of general advice for the tourist new to the Canadian Rockies, covering a wide range subjects such as accommodation and safety or how much to tip. **Driving in Western Canada** concentrates on advice for drivers on the law, rules of the road, and so on. **Rail Essentials** details the rail routes that cross Alberta and British Columbia (with further description of rail travel in Western Canada on pp. 138–140). **Cruise Essentials** gives the background to ferry and cruise services for those thinking of taking to the water. **Touring Itineraries** provides ideas and suggestions for putting together an itinerary of your own using the selection of routes in this book, and lists the pick of the National and Provincial Parks. At the back of the book,

Driving Distances is a tabulation of distances between main places, to help in trip planning, and the **Conversion Tables** decode metric sizes and measures for those more used to imperial measures. Finally the **Index** is the quick way to look up any place or general subject. And please help us by completing and returning the **Reader Survey** at the very end of the text; we are grateful for both your views on the book and new information from your travels in the Canadian Rockies.

KEY TO MAP SYMBOLS

Route diagrams

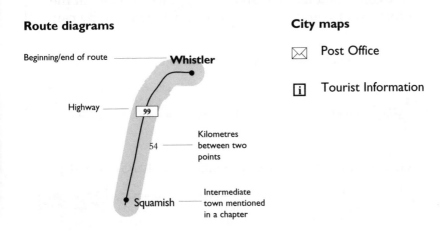

City maps

✉ Post Office

ⓘ Tourist Information

13

KEY TO PRICE DESCRIPTIONS

It is impossible to keep up to date with specific tariffs for lodging and accommodation or restaurants, although we have given some general advice under 'Cost of Living' in the Travel Essentials chapter p.28). Instead, we have rated establishments in broad price categories throughout the book, as follows:

Accommodation (per room per night)
Budget — Under $35
Moderate — Under $90
Expensive — Under $150
Pricey — $150 and higher

Meal (for one person, excluding drinks, tip or tax)
Cheap — Under $5
Budget — Under $10
Moderate — Under $20
Pricey — Over $20

ABBREVIATIONS USED IN THE BOOK
(For hotel chains, see p. 346)

Bldg	Building (in addresses)	min(s)	minute(s)
Blvd	Boulevard	Mon, Tues	Monday, Tuesday, etc.
Dr.	Drive (in addresses)	OTT	*Overseas Timetable* (see p. 46)
hr(s)	hour(s)	Rd	Road (in addresses)
Hwy	Highway, e.g. Hwy 1	St	Street (in addresses)
Jan, Feb	January, February, etc.	$	Canadian Dollars

BACKGROUND WESTERN CANADA

Western Canada is a triumph of politics over geography. Both Alberta and British Columbia traditionally had more in common with their American neighbours than with each other or with the rest of Canada. Until the Canadian Pacific Railway arrived in 1885, the only viable commercial routes through the Rocky Mountains lay in the United States. As far as the rest of Canada was concerned, Alberta and BC were somewhere on the other side of the British Empire.

Transportation, timber, mining and petroleum have turned both provinces into major international players. But geography and history have left them little more in tandem than the Rocky Mountains themselves.

GEOGRAPHY

The Land
British Columbia developed with abundance. The first humans who migrated into the region from Asia 10,000–20,000 years ago prospered. Coastal and interior rainforests supported a diversity of life seldom seen outside the tropics.

From 25-cm banana slugs to 3-m tall grizzly bears and 100-m tall trees, everything that lived was useful. Drier valleys supported immense fields of camas lilies. Desert rivers teemed with salmon and trout, the plains with game.

Life changed dramatically at the Rocky Mountains. The jumble of peaks rising to nearly 4000 m wrings moisture-laden clouds dry as they move eastward, creating a land of parched plains. The first formal survey of Alberta, conducted by Capt John Palliser in 1858 at the behest of the Royal Geographic Society, dismissed the Plains Indians' badlands territory as desert that could never be settled.

However, the Assiniboine, Stoney, Sarcee, Blackfoot and other tribes that called the plains home had herds of buffalo that ran tens of thousands strong, supplying clothing, food and most other necessities. Many bands also traded widely. Early White explorers who expected to traverse a forbidding, empty land instead found networks of trails criss-crossing every mountain range. When Simon Fraser journeyed down the river which bears his name in 1808, tribes that guided him through the Rockies knew the annual trading schedules of sailing vessels visiting Vancouver Island.

Nature provided little leisure or wealth on the Plains. BC bands, however, buoyed by annual salmon runs and more reliable rainfall, had the leisure to develop hugely complex societies. Ritual and art were highly varied and valued. White traders complained that the First Nations were the sharpest bargainers they had encountered.

HISTORY

Early Explorers
When the outside world first saw BC isn't

clear. A Chinese manuscript from 217 BC tells of an accidental voyage west to a land of towering trees and red-faced men. Sir Francis Drake may have touched Vancouver Island on his 1577 round-the-world voyage. Juan de Fuca, a Greek sailing for Spain in 1592, gets credit as the first European to visit Western Canada, but few cared before Danish captain Vitus Bering sailed east from Russia to Alaska in the early 1700s.

China prized the thick, silky fur of the sea otter. When Bering discovered huge populations of sea otters in Alaska, Russian merchants rushed to trade with Alaskan Natives for pelts. Spain sailed from Mexico in 1774 to claim the Queen Charlotte Islands and Nootka Sound, on the west coast of Vancouver Island. The next year, Bruno de Heceta and Juan Francisco de la Bodega y Quadra returned. Heceta noted, but didn't explore, 'the mouth of some great river', the Columbia, which rises in eastern BC near Fairmont Hot Springs.

The British Parliament had a standing reward of £20,000, a considerable fortune, for the discovery of a northern sea route to Asia. The fabled Northwest Passage remained undiscovered from the Atlantic side, so James Cook went looking from the Pacific side.

While anchored in Nootka Sound in 1778, Cook bought sea otter pelts for warm clothing and bedding. He was killed in Hawaii the next year without ever finding the route east. Neither did Cook's second-in-command, Charles Clark, who sailed for England by way of Macau. The well-worn otter skins fetched such high prices that the crew nearly mutinied to return to Nootka, but the expedition sailed home. Accounts of Cook's voyage set off a fur rush. Merchants from the newly-independent United States of America sailed as soon as war with England ended in

1783. British traders made the trip as well. Competition nearly brought war between England and Spain, but diplomacy prevailed. Both countries mounted expeditions to map the coast in preparation for a final settlement.

Spain sent Bodega y Quadra. Britain sent George Vancouver, who had visited Nootka as a midshipman under Cook. Vancouver missed the Columbia River, first charted by American trader Robert Gray in 1792, thus establishing US claims to the Pacific Coast. But as war consumed Europe and overhunting gutted the otter trade, England and Spain lost interest. In 1819, Spain ceded its Pacific Northwest claims to the United States.

The Columbia River

The inland fur trade was more successful. British traders had been dealing furs in Eastern Canada for two centuries. In 1670, the Hudson's Bay Company (HBC) obtained rights to Rupert's Land, essentially all of Canada from Hudsons Bay west to the Rocky Mountains. In 1754, Anthony Henday paddled up the North Saskatchewan River from Hudsons Bay, and became the first White to enter what is now Alberta. He returned the next spring, his canoes loaded with furs and his journals filled with accounts of unbelievable snow-capped mountains. Other traders followed, including the HBC's new competitor, the North West Company (NWC), formed in 1787.

The next year, Norwester Peter Pond opened Fort Chipewyan on Lake Athabasca, the first White settlement in Alberta. HBC built its first Alberta post, Buckingham House, adjacent to NWC's Fort George on the North Saskatchewan River. Growing European demand for beaver pelts spurred competition between the HBC, the NWC and US fur traders.

All three were searching frantically for the source of the Columbia River, the only practicable transportation link.

NWC partners Alexander Mackenzie, Simon Fraser and David Thompson pioneered northern routes from Alberta to the Pacific Coast from the 1790s to the 1810s; Americans Meriwether Lewis and William Clark explored west from American territory 1804–1806. Mackenzie reached the mouth of the Bella Coola River in 1793, the first outsider to cross the continent north of Mexico. Fraser fought through treacherous rapids to the sea at present-day Vancouver in 1808, realising that he, also, was too far north and that the Fraser River was too perilous to become a major trade route. In 1811, Thompson finally made his way downstream to the mouth of the Columbia, only to discover American traders already building Fort Astoria.

The NWC took over Astoria during the War of 1812, then built Fort Vancouver 170 km upriver at the confluence of the Columbia and Willamette Rivers. At war's end, the 49th Parallel divided US and British America east of the Rockies; the two powers jointly occupied what would become the states of Oregon and Washington and the province of British Columbia. When the HBC absorbed the NWC in 1821, England had an economic monopoly spanning North America, but nobody yet controlled the West.

Manifest Destiny and the HBC

Four years later, Britain and America accepted Russian authority south to 54°40'. The HBC established and expanded posts at Spokane, Okanagan, Nisqually, Langley and elsewhere to block American expansion. Manifest Destiny, the idea that God had ordained America to occupy the continent, was gaining strength in the United States. Missionaries filtered west to 'civilise the savages'. Their reports of rich farmland began to attract attention.

The HBC was also expanding. The company opened farms along the Columbia River and Puget Sound to supply inland forts and export to Russian Alaska, Hawaii and Asia. Dr John McLoughlin, HBC's chief factor at Fort Vancouver, directed American settlers south into the Willamette Valley, hoping to maintain HBC control of the Columbia River, the route to its most profitable fur territories in present-day BC. But just in case, HBC governor George Simpson moved to Fort Victoria, on the southern tip of Vancouver Island, in 1841. It was a prescient move.

The US Navy visited the Pacific Northwest in 1841, ostensibly on a goodwill mission, as US Army surveyors quietly surveyed a wagon route over the Rockies. In 1843, the US Senate declared Oregon Territory to be American and urged American settlers west. The lure was free land, 259 hectares for every white male US citizen plus 130 hectares for his wife.

The Gold Rush

US–British tensions escalated when James Polk swept America's 1844 presidential election on the slogan of '54°40' or Fight!'. Britain, which had reaped few profits from the West, agreed to extend the US boundary along the 49th Parallel to the coast, then through the Strait of Juan de Fuca to the Pacific. The HBC lost nearly the entire Columbia River, though the company survived. Furs from interior BC could still be transported by horseback over the Yellowhead Pass through the Northern Rockies and shipped downriver with Alberta furs. In more accessible coastal areas, the company turned to commerce.

In 1849, Britain leased Vancouver Island to the HBC to create a colony. The California gold rush promptly boosted

17

lumber exports. Commercial shipping and Royal Navy yards at Esquimalt supported coal mining at Nanaimo. Worldwide demand kept salmon canneries busy. But the HBC was unsuccessful at attracting settlers. The only practical access was a brutal, five-month voyage from England around the tip of South America. Would-be settlers preferred Oregon and Washington, where acreage was far cheaper and easily accessed by land. Even Victoria, HBC's Vancouver Island capital, remained a small, if prosperous, town in a vast forest.

Gold changed everything. The HBC had suppressed news of gold discoveries since at least 1850 to maximise profits and discourage further American expansion. When word of gold finds on the Fraser River got out in 1858, hordes of American miners flooded north, raising fears that America would annex territory that was British on paper but outside all control in practice. The fears were warranted. The mostly American mining population promptly called for changes to mining regulation and government practice. A special US commissioner sent to protect American interests in the gold fields reported that it was only a matter of time until both Vancouver Island and the mainland became American by force of population – unless Washington preferred to act sooner.

Territorial Claims

London moved first. In June 1858, the House of Commons created the mainland colony of New Caledonia. Queen Victoria changed the name to British Columbia and dispatched key officials. On Nov 19, a provisional government was installed at Fort Langley. Royal Engineers moved the capital to New Westminster (now part of Greater Vancouver), a site more defensible against American invasion. Gold Commissioners imposed strict order in the gold

fields, a sharp contrast to pervasive lawlessness in US gold camps.

The colony offered settlers 65 hectares at bargain prices. The entire Fraser Valley was under cultivation within nine years. Cattle ranches sprang up even as drovers brought thousands of head north from Washington State. Merchants prospered, but every economic downturn brought renewed calls to join the United States, the nearest economic power.

BC and Vancouver Island colonies were combined in 1866, but calls for a State of British Columbia increased when the US purchased Alaska from Russia in 1867. The US even tried to claim BC as compensation for British support of the Confederacy during the US Civil War.

Political leaders were firmly British in persuasion, but BC lived by business decisions made in San Francisco. The working population were American immigrants or Canadian-born with little love for Britain or rule from afar. It wasn't until BC joined the new Dominion of Canada in 1870 that pro-American feelings subsided, assuaged by promises of a trans-Canada railway and economic links to the east. When the railway finally arrived in 1885, a lumber town terminus called Vancouver blossomed into Western Canada's most cosmopolitan city.

First Nations

Dominion also sparked the first signs of growth in Rupert's Land, re-purchased from the HBC and re-christened the Northwest Territories. The HBC had discouraged settlement to preserve its fur resources, but trade was declining. Buffalo hunting was on the rise, but outside Fort Edmonton, permanent settlements were few and far between.

Most of the hunting was done by First Nations bands or itinerant Métis (mixed-blood) hunters. Unfortunately for the First

Nations, the Métis were experts. By the early 1870s, buffalo were becoming scarce and Indians were going hungry. At the same time, their tribal relatives in the United States were being coerced onto reservations to make way for White settlers. Bands which revolted or resisted were hunted by US Army troops.

Part of the US effort was a crackdown on traders dealing whisky and firearms to the Indians. Relishing the total absence of law north of the 49th Parallel, American whisky traders opened a network of forts and trading posts in Southern Alberta. If Canada was to settle the Northwest Territories, it would first have to control them.

The solution was the North West Mounted Police (NWMP), a force of 300 men sent west in 1874. The red-coated Mounties intimidated most whisky traders into legitimate lines of merchandise and imprisoned the few who resisted. NWMP success at bending Whites to the law pushed the First Nations' into accepting Dominion-drafted treaties without the bloody violence that had stalked America's westward expansion. The treaties deprived the region's original inhabitants of nearly all of their lands with minimal compensation, terms which are being challenged with a degree of success in modern courts.

The Railway and the 20th Century

The NWMP also kept the peace when the Canadian Pacific Railway (CPR) crossed the prairies in the 1880s. By the time the first wave of settlers rode the rails into Alberta, the West had already been won. But it hadn't been tamed. The immediate problem lay due south. Manifest Destiny remained popular in America, a political reality that moved even the CPR. The railway, which intended to pass through Fort Edmonton and the low Yellowhead Pass, instead took a more southerly route through Fort Calgary and the higher, far more expensive, Kicking Horse Pass in order to discourage US railway builders. The BC government had already commissioned the Dewdney Trail (now Hwy 3) to link existing towns with new mineral strikes eastward to Fort Steele and discourage similar US economic incursions.

Climate could also be gruelling, from drought-ridden 40°C summers to blizzard-whipped -40°C winters. With the buffalo all but exterminated, the First Nations on reserves and the CPR in operation, settlers began arriving in growing numbers. The prairies seemed too dry for dependable farming, but ranching offered great promise. Railway transport made Calgary Alberta's pre-eminent cattle town.

Cattle were largely displaced by homesteaders growing cash crops, but farming the plains was not easy. Ranchers who turned to grain discovered that crops were equally subject to frost, drought and disease. It wasn't until the development of new strains of wheat and other grains in the early 20th century that the prairie became one of the world's great bread baskets.

Oil is Alberta's top business. First discovered in the Turner Valley near Calgary in 1914, petro-dollars have pulled the province into the 20th century. The major oilfields are north of Edmonton, but the financial foundations of the industry remain in Calgary. Tourism is the region's third money spinner. The CPR created Rocky Mountain tourism to build business, sponsoring Banff, Jasper and Glacier National Parks, building elegant hotels and touting the Rockies as a fitting holiday for the rich, the famous and the royal. The hoi polloi quickly followed, turning the Canadian Rockies into a household icon even in households that had never seen the soaring peaks, surging waterfalls and teal-blue lakes except on postcards.

TRAVEL ESSENTIALS

The following is an alphabetical listing of helpful tips and advice for those planning a holiday in Western Canada and the Rockies.

ACCOMMODATION

Western Canada offers accommodation of every price level imaginable, from five-star hotels and posh resorts to youth hostels and campsites. *Alberta Accommodation and Visitors' Guide, Travel Alberta, Box 2500, Edmonton, AB T5J 2Z4; tel: (800) 661-8888* or *(403) 427-4321; fax: (403) 421-0867; web: http://www.AlbertaHotels.ab.ca*, lists hundreds of lodging possibilities, though Travel Alberta does not make bookings. *Alberta Campground Guide*, from Travel Alberta, lists campsites throughout the province. The *Alberta Bed & Breakfast Association* distributes a map and guide to its members around the province through Travel Alberta offices. *High Country Bed and Breakfast Association, Box 772, Turner Valley, AB T0L 2A0; tel: (403) 933-4174; fax: (403) 933-2870*, lists two dozen members in south-western Alberta. *Alberta Country Vacations, Box 396, Sangudo, AB T0E 2A0; tel/fax: (403) 785-3700*, lists guest ranches. *Hostelling International, 10926 88 Ave, Edmonton, AB T6G 0Z1; tel: (403) 432-7798; fax: (403) 433-7781*, maintains 17 hostels in Alberta.

British Columbia Accommodations, Tourism British Columbia, 1117 Wharf St, Victoria, BC V8W 2Z2; tel: (800) 663-6000 or *(604) 663-6000; web:http://www.travel.bc.ca/accom/index.html*, makes free bookings for lodging across the province; have a credit card ready to confirm advance bookings by telephone. *B&B Inns of BC*,

Western Canada Bed & Breakfast Inns Association, Box 74534, Vancouver, BC V6K 4P4; tel: (604) 255-9199, lists WCB-BIA-approved members in BC. *Best Canadian Bed & Breakfast Network, 1090 W. King Edward Ave, Vancouver, BC V6H 1Z4; tel: (604) 738-7207*, lists Bed and Breakfasts across Western Canada. *British Columbia Bed & Breakfast Directory, 1609 Blanshard St, Victoria, BC V8W 2J5; tel: (250) 382-6188; fax: (250) 382-6014*, lists Bed and Breakfasts throughout BC. *Hostelling International, 134 Abbott St, Suite 402, Vancouver, BC V6B 2K4; tel: (604) 684-7111; fax: (604) 684-7181*, have 15 hostels in BC.

Local Tourist Offices also provide lodging lists, but generally cannot make bookings. Where available, local lodging services are noted in the text.

Accommodation can be extremely hard to find in major tourist destinations during high season (usually mid May–early Sept – Labour Day weekend), plus weekends and major public holidays. Exceptions are Vancouver and Victoria, where high season runs from early May through September to match the Alaska cruise ship season; and ski resorts, where high season prices arrive with the first good snowfall.

Alberta charges a 5% **room tax**. BC levies 3% plus a 7% **provincial sales tax**, and local lodging taxes in some areas. **Goods & Service Tax, GST,** is an additional 7% national levy.

Expect to pay as much as 60% over low season rates during the high season. It is sometimes possible to avoid higher tariffs by travelling during the shoulder season, one or two weeks before or after high season, when crowds are smaller and rates lower. It is also possible to travel during low season, but many attractions, especially in rural areas, close at the end of high season. Weather can be marginal.

Thomas Cook or any other good travel agent can handle room bookings when purchasing air tickets and car or other local transportation. All-inclusive fly-drive arrangements, and 'do-it-yourself packages' such as Thomas Cook's American Fly-Drive and American Options programmes, can provide hotel coupons, exchangeable at a range of hotel chains, which guarantee a pre-paid rate at participating chains, although they do not guarantee rooms – you have to phone ahead as you go, or take a chance on availability, problematic during the full-up summer season. It is particularly important to pre-book the first and last nights' stay to avoid problems when connecting with international air flights.

It is also important to confirm pre-booked rooms by telephone if you expect to arrive after 1800. Many hotels and motels automatically cancel bookings at 1800, especially during high season, even if rooms have been guaranteed with a credit card. The best time to reconfirm the booking is 1300–1800 the day of the late arrival.

Throughout the book, we have indicated prices of accommodation in a comparative way by using terms such as 'moderate' and 'pricey'; see 'How to Use', pp. 11–13, for an explanation of what these descriptions mean. Prices are quoted in Canadian dollars unless otherwise noted.

Hotels and Motels

Hotel rates are quoted for single or double occupancy; children usually stay cheaply or for free with parents.

Once in Canada, you will find that most chain hotels and motels have toll-free reservation telephone numbers. The list on p. 346 gives a selection of these, along with the abbreviations used in the text to indicate which chains are present in the town or city being described.

Advance bookings generally require a voucher or credit card number to guarantee the booking. Ask for discounts if you're disabled, a senior, a motoring club member, or travelling off season. When checking in, always ask if there's a cheaper room rate than the one you pre-booked. It's often cost-effective to find lodging day by day, especially in off-peak seasons.

Motels are often the best bet. Literally, 'motor hotels', motels are one- to three-storey buildings with a modest version of a hotel's accommodation and facilities. Most belong to nationwide chains which enforce service and safety standards.

Independent motels may not be quite as fancy, but offer even lower prices. Motels fill up fast during high season, but last-minute rooms are usually available off season, especially during the week. The *CAA TourBook* for Western Canada and Alaska lists thousands of motels and hotels; thousands more are just as comfortable and affordable. Motels that line major highways entering most cities and towns often have special prices, noted on a roadside sign.

Bed and Breakfast

Bed and Breakfast can be a homely alternative to institutional-seeming hotels and motels, but they are seldom the bargain lodgings of their English cousins, especially in major cities. They *may* be appropriate for budget travellers in more rural areas. The accent is more often on luxury than on value, particularly in Vancouver and Victoria. The typical urban Bed and Breakfast is a refurbished room in a Victorian mansion, complete with chintz curtains, down comforter, fireplace and private facilities. If 'Victorians' are in short supply, any ordinary mansion will do, even a converted garage or barn, so long as it's properly luxurious. Bed and Breakfast accommodation in smaller towns and rural areas is much closer to the original concept, and may be in a ranch house. In some remote areas, it may be the only choice other than camping. Breakfasts vary, but the standard includes fruit juice, coffee or tea, an egg dish, home-made bread and a sweet. Pricier Bed and Breakfasts provide a huge gourmet breakfast.

Camping

Camping means a tent or a recreational vehicle (RV) in a rural campsite. KOA, Kampgrounds of America, is a private chain of RV parks that also accept tents. Commercially-operated campsites often offer electrical and water hook-ups, bathrooms with showers, restaurants, a grocery store, petrol and recreational facilities.

Many other campsites are public, most operated by federal or provincial authorities. Overnight fees range from $7 to more than $20, depending on location and season. Standard facilities include a food storage locker, fireplace, tent site, nearby showers/toilets and, during high season, daytime guided hikes and evening educational programmes around a large campfire.

The latest wrinkles in camping: the **yurt**, a permanent, round tent modelled on traditional Mongolian nomad tents; **tepees** and **covered wagons**. All are available at selected parks and guest ranches.

Many provincial park campsites can be reserved in advance. In popular parks, they must be. For Alberta parks, check the *Alberta Accommodation and Visitors' Guide; tel: (800) 661-8888* or *(403) 427-4321; fax: (403) 427-0867;* individual provincial parks take reservations May 1–Labour Day, or contact **Alberta Environmental Protection**, *9920 108 St, Main Floor,*

Edmonton, AB T5K 2M4; tel: (403) 944-0313. For BC parks, Discover Camping; tel: (800) 689-9025 or (604) 689-9025, makes bookings Mar 1–Sept 15.

Youth Hostels

Hostelling International was created for tight budgets, **Hostelling International Canada**, *205 Catherine St, Suite 400, Ottawa, ON K2P 1C3; tel: (613) 237-7884; web: http://www.HostellingIntl.ca/Alberta* and *e-mail: bchostel@axionet.com.* Most hostels provide a dormitory-style room and shared bath for $9–$22.50 per night. Some have family or private rooms, outdoor saunas, recreation programmes; all offer discounts to local attractions. The downside: there are an extremely limited number of hostels in the region. And when two or more people are travelling together and can share a room, cheap motels may be even cheaper than hostels.

AIRPORTS

Airport information booths and touch-screen information kiosks cover airport facilities, airport-to-city transport and local accommodation. For flight information and bookings, contact individual airlines.

All major airports have foreign exchange and banking services as well as car hire facilities. Secondary airports have automatic cash dispensers (ATMs) and car hire desks, but seldom currency exchange facilities. Public transportation to the nearest city is usually available, but seldom practical in terms of routes or time. Luggage trolleys are generally free for international arrivals; elsewhere, there is usually a $1–1.50 charge. Be prepared for long walks through terminals on arrival – moving walkways are few and far between, even at the largest airports.

Airport Improvement Fees, from $5–$10, are levied at Vancouver, Calgary and Edmonton International Airports, paid before boarding a flight.

Specific airport arrival information is given in the chapters dealing with the major airport gateway cities.

BICYCLES

Cycling is popular for countryside day touring – less so for overnight trips, due to geography. Bikes can be hired by the hour or the day in most wine country and urban areas as well as in major parks. Major Canadian cities have extensive bike lane systems throughout the urban area; downtown parkades (car parks) and lots generally have free bike racks.

For serious bikers (as cyclists are called in Western Canada), biking tours are available at all levels, from easy day trips to arduous pulls over the Rockies. On-your-own bike tours are also possible, but beware of unexpected distances and mountains between towns. Many abandoned railway rights of way have been reborn as cycling and walking trails. One of the most popular is the Kettle Valley Railroad in south-central BC.

Request a free **Alberta Cycling Information Map**, *Alberta Transportation and Utilities, Public Communications Branch, 1st Floor, Twin Atria Building, 4999 98 Ave, Edmonton, AB T6B 2X3; tel: (403) 427-7674,* which indicates routes.

Many highways have narrow or non-existent verges, which can make cycling nerve-wracking as well as dangerous in heavy traffic. Provincial laws require cyclists to wear protective helmets.

BORDERS

Customs and Immigration officials are paid to take their jobs very seriously. Canada has had problems with illegal immigration, most often visitors who overstay tourist and student visas. Canadian and US citizens need only proof of identity and citizenship to cross the border in either direction, but a passport remains the easiest documentation. Non-US citizens need a valid passport to enter; check if a visa is required as regulations change.

Customs and Immigration have *carte blanche* to ask any question, search anyone or anything, and do it in any manner they see fit. In reality, most inspectors are polite to a fault, but the only defence against an inspector who got up on the wrong side of the bed is to have passport, visa, proof of support and return ticket in order.

A car or RV can be a liability when crossing the border: the diligent search can extend to your vehicle. Canadian officials are especially diligent checking US-registered vehicles for firearms, weapons and self-defence sprays which are legal in the US but banned in Canada. They also show a keen interest in Canadian-registered vehicles which may have ventured south on a shopping spree and could well owe customs duties.

Duties levied on alcohol in excess of the duty-free allowance are very high, up to double the original purchase price.

Most animals, except dogs and cats, must be issued a Canadian Import Permit prior to entry. Pets must have an official Vaccination Certificate Against Rabies.

The importation of weapons, narcotics and non-approved pharmaceutical products is prohibited. Carry doctors' prescriptions with documentation (such as a doctor's letter) to prove that medications are legitimate.

BUSES

Greyhound Lines of Canada, *Customer Service, 877 Greyhound Way S.W., Calgary, AB T3C 3V8; tel: (800) 661-8747 or (403) 265-9111,* provide information on long-distance bus services between major cities.

23

There are discounts for seniors (over 55), disabled travellers, helpers, children (under 12) riding with a full-fare adult and travellers not resident in North America. Greyhound passes are obtainable through Thomas Cook travel shops in the UK.

If you're buying tickets locally ask for the **Canada Pass**, which, depending on distance travelled, may be more economical. Local transportation companies listed in the telephone directory under individual cities and towns provide local services. Thomas Cook publishes bi-monthly timetables of Canadian buses in the *Thomas Cook Overseas Timetable*. A special edition devoted to US and Canadian buses and trains, containing much additional travel information, is published annually under the title *Thomas Cook North American Rail and Bus Guide* (full details of these and other publications on p. 46).

CAMPERS AND RVs

It's the freedom of the open road, housekeeping on wheels, a large machine hurtling down slopes and ploughing up grades. An RV, caravan, or motorhome provides a kitchen, sleeping and bathroom facilities, all integrated atop a lorry chassis.

Fly-drive holiday packages usually offer the option of hiring an RV. The additional cost of hiring an RV can be offset by the economics of assured lodging for several people, space for meal preparation and eating, plus the convenience of comfort items and souvenirs stored nearby. RVs are cramped, designed to stuff you and your belongings into limited space. The economics work only if advance planning assures that the pricey spur-of-the-moment allure of a hotel shower or unplanned restaurant meal doesn't overcome RV campers! Factor in the cost of petrol – an RV guzzles 3–4 times more gas than a medium-sized car.

Always get operating manuals for the vehicle and all appliances before leaving the hire lot, and have someone demonstrate how *everything* works. Systems may be interdependent, or more complex than anticipated. Be prepared to pre-plan menus and allow additional time each morning and afternoon/evening to level the RV (perfect levelling is essential for correct operation of refrigerators), hook up or disconnect electricity, water and sewer hoses and cable television plugs. Some basic house cleaning must be done; also allow time for laundry at RV parks.

Buy a pair of sturdy rubber washing gloves to handle daily sewer chores. Pack old clothes to wear while crawling under the vehicle to hook up and disconnect at each stop – many RVers carry a pair of overalls. Without hook-ups, water and electricity are limited to what you carry with you from the last fill-up or battery charge. If you camp in a park without hook-ups, locate the nearest restrooms before dark. Using showers and toilets in RV parks or public campsites will save time cleaning up the RV shower space and emptying the toilet holding tank. Have a strong torch (flashlight) handy.

When you move out on the road, expect anything that's not secured to go flying, or to shake, rattle and roll. Quickly get into a routine of allotted tasks and assign a quick-grab spot for maps, snacks, cameras and valuables.

RV travel information: **Recreation Vehicle Industry Association (RVIA)**, *Dept RK, PO Box 2999, Reston, VA 22090-0999; tel: (703) 620-6003*. To plan RV camping, request: **Go Camping America**, Camping Vacation Planner video, *PO Box 2669, Reston, VA 22090-0669; tel: (888) GO-RVING*, covering Canada and the US.

Camping clubs offer RV information

for members; some, including the **Good Sam Club**, *PO Box 6060, Camarillo, CA 93011; tel: (805) 389-0300*, offer roadside assistance for breakdowns and tyre changing. Many camping clubs publish magazines or newsletters with tips on operating and driving an RV.

Campsite directories and provincial Tourist Office guides list private RV park locations, directions, size, number of pitches, hook-ups, laundry, on-premises convenience stores and showers. Directories cover parks in Canada and the US. Popular directories include: *Trailer Life Campground & RV Services Directory, TL Enterprises, 2575 Vista del Mar Dr., Ventura, CA 93001; tel: (805) 667-4100*, (US$19.95); *Woodall's Campground Directory (Western Edition), 13975 W. Polo Trail Dr., Lake Forest, IL 60045; tel: (800) 823-9076*, (US$13.95); *Wheelers RV Resort & Campground Guide, 1310 Jarvis Ave, Elk Grove Village, IL 60007; tel: (847) 981-0100*, (US$14.95); *Kampgrounds of America (KOA) Directory, PO Box 30558, Billings, MT 59114-0558; tel: (406) 248-7444* (US$3 or free at KOA campsites). The **CAA** have directories and maps for Western Canadian campsites. See 'Parks Information' in this chapter for campsites on provincial or federal land.

CHILDREN

Western Canada, with its many natural attractions, is both ideal for travelling with children and welcoming. Check for student or child rates, often segmented by age, e.g. under 3 years free, 6–12 years $3, 12–18 years $4. A student card must be shown to use student rates.

Travelling with children is never easy, but preparation helps. *Travel with Children,* by Maureen Wheeler (Lonely Planet) is filled with useful tips. Kids get bored and cranky on long drives. Pack favourite

games and books, and pick up a book of travel games. A traditional favourite is to count foreign, i.e. non-local, licence plates. The winner – always a child – gets a special treat later in the day. If the children are old enough, suggest that they keep a detailed travel diary. It will help them focus on the trip instead of what they might be missing back home. A diary also helps them remember details later to impress friends and teachers. Collecting anything, from postcards to admission tickets, adds a new dimension to travel.

Any driving destination in the region is equipped for children of all ages, from nappies to video games. Most hotels and motels can arrange for baby-sitters, though the price may be steep. Many motel chains allow children under 12, 14, and sometimes up to 18, to stay free in their parents' room. A rollaway child's bed, often called a cot, usually comes at no or low cost.

Meals can be difficult, but picnic lunches offer flexibility. It's also a good idea to carry a small cooler filled with ice, cold drinks and snacks, especially in hot weather. Most towns have coffee shops with long hours, children's menus and familiar fast-food names. If the children like McDonalds at home, they'll like Big Macs in Western Canada; and many McDonalds have elaborate children's play areas.

CLIMATE

Weather can change abruptly in or on either side of the mountains. Rain and snow are most likely Oct–Apr, but don't be surprised at a downpour or even snow in May or Aug – or any other month in the Rockies. Both provinces have days with sunshine, fog, drizzle, snow, hail and rainbows, sometimes all within a few hours.

In British Columbia, expect grey skies west of the Coastal Range and blue skies to the east, but fog is common along the coast

25

all year. Vancouver is known for cloudy skies and rain the year round, but the sun shows itself for at least a few minutes May–Sept, and many days in a row July–Sept. The Gulf Islands and Victoria, sheltered by the Olympic Mountains of Washington State and the mountainous spine of Vancouver Island, are much drier and sunnier.

The Pacific Ocean moderates coastal temperatures. Expect greater extremes inland, colder in winter and hotter in summer. Much of interior BC is semi-desert; the southern end of the Okanagan Valley is a genuine desert, complete with cactus and rattlesnakes in unirrigated areas.

In winter, warm **Chinook winds** push from the Pacific over the Rockies at the Continental Divide to meet a frigid mass from Alberta's plains, leaving Calgary thawing in their wake. The plains are hot and flat in summer, white, bitter cold and unprotected in winter. The badlands near Drumheller and in Dinosaur Provincial Park are as harsh as any desert.

Summer brings forest fires which may be allowed to burn unchecked unless

human lives or major property damage are threatened. Regular burning is a natural renewal mechanism and necessary for the regeneration of many forest species. If a patch of forest has not burned in several years, deliberate fires, called controlled burns, are set during wet weather to burn out accumulated dead growth and prevent later conflagrations. Smokejumpers, airborne fire-fighters who parachute into remote areas, and water bombers are at their busiest in late summer.

Summer also means lightning storms and very occasional tornadoes (twisters), particularly on the plains. See sections below for different precautions to be taken if out in either climatic condition.

Fall foliage colour is usually at its peak around Thanksgiving (mid Oct). Winter temperatures vary widely, from -50°C on the Alberta plains and the interior plateaux of BC to an occasional dip around -5°C in downtown Vancouver. Local cars are the best indicator of winter weather. If most have electrical plugs bouncing on the front bumper, expect a significant number of

26

Average Temperatures

	Calgary	Edmonton	Banff	Vancouver	Victoria
JANUARY					
Highest	26°F/14°C	16°F/-11°C	23°F/-5°C	43°F/6°C	43°F/6°C
Lowest	16°F/-31°C	0°F/-19°C	5°F/-15°C	34°F/1°C	36°F/2°C
APRIL					
Highest	51°F/10°C	52°F/10°C	48°F/9°C	59°F/15°C	55°F/13°C
Lowest	28°F/-24°C	30°F/-1°C	27°F/-3°C	43°F/6°C	43°F/6°C
JULY					
Highest	74°F/23°C	73°F/23°C	72°F/22°C	75°F/24°C	68°F/20°C
Lowest	49°F/10°C	56°F/12°C	45°F/7°C	55°F/13°C	52°F/11°C
OCTOBER					
Highest	55°F/-1°C	54°F/11°C	50°F/10°C	59°F/15°C	57°F/14°C
Lowest	13°F/-30°C	32°F/0°C	30°F/-1°C	44°F/7°C	46°F/8°C

nights at -20°C or below. The plugs connect electrical heaters that keep auto engine blocks from freezing solid.

CLOTHING

Summers can be blisteringly hot in the interior and shivery in coastal fog or mountain precipitation. Winters are cold to frigid. In any season, take plenty of choices, from shorts for the beach to jumpers and jackets for the mountains. Cotton and wool are the region's favourite fibres, although synthetics are gaining ground quickly. Natural or synthetic, dress in layers: one layer is cool, several layers are warm. Adding and removing layers makes it easier to stay comfortable no matter how many times the weather changes in a single day. Umbrellas and lightweight rain gear are indispensable along the coast.

Conservative informality is the norm throughout Western Canada, with the exception of a handful of elegant city restaurants which require jackets and ties for men. Runners, sandals and hiking boots are far more common than wingtips and high heels, even in fancy hotels. When in doubt, leave it at home. Clothing prices are cheaper than almost anywhere outside the Third World, especially in Alberta, which does not have a sales tax. But do take good, broken-in walking shoes.

COFFEE

Coffee has become something closer to a religious experience than a hot drink. Espresso carts are a way of breakfast, tiffin and tea time on city pavements from Drumheller to Tofino. In urban areas, motorists stuck in traffic jams jump out for a quick shot of espresso to speed the drive home while petrol stations sell cappuccino and latte alongside the motor oil and tyre chains. Even McDonalds restaurants have installed espresso machines.

The caffeine craze began when three University friends in Seattle named a 1971 coffee shop for the steadfast first mate of the *Pequod* in Herman Melville's *Moby Dick*. **Starbucks** introduced espresso to the masses and became the largest coffee roastery in Canada as well as America.

Urban residents are fiercely loyal to their chosen brand. Expect descriptions such as 'strong', 'nutty', etc. **Espresso** is the basic brew, black and thick. **Cappuccino** is espresso mixed with hot milk, topped with milk foam and a dusting of chocolate or cinnamon. **Latte** is similar to cappuccino, without the foam or the spice dusting. Most coffee bars offer more than a dozen flavoured coffees, from vanilla and hazelnut to coconut. The latest wrinkle is iced coffee drinks, often whipped.

CONSULATES

Australia: *World Trade Complex, 999 Canada Place, Suite 602, Vancouver, BC V6C 3E1; tel: (604) 684-1177; fax: (604) 684-1856.*

New Zealand: *888 Dunsmuir, Suite 1200, Vancouver, BC V6C 3K4; tel: (604) 684-7388.*

Republic of Ireland: *(Embassy) 170 Metcalfe St, Ottawa, ON K2P 1P3; tel: (613) 233-6281.*

South Africa: *3 Bentall Centre, 595 Burrard St, Suite 3023, Box 49096, Vancouver, BC V7X 1G4; tel: (604) 688-1301; fax: (604) 688-8193.*

UK: *1111 Melville, Suite 800, Vancouver, BC V6E 3V6; tel: (604) 683-4421; fax: (604) 681-0693.*

US: *1075 W. Pender St, Vancouver, BC V6E 2M6; tel: (604) 685-4311; fax: (604) 685-5285; and 615 Macleod Trail S.E., Suite 1000, Calgary, AB T2G 4T8; tel: (403) 228-8900; fax: (403) 264-6630.*

COST OF LIVING

Alberta does not have a local sales tax, although British Columbia does (7%). There is a 7% national Goods and Services Tax (GST) as well as hotel/lodging taxes. The combined levy, however, is less than the VAT charged in most of Europe. Prices are almost always marked or quoted *without tax,* which is added at time of purchase (see p. 41). Motel rooms cost $30–$70 per night; hotels from $50 up. Restaurant meals, including soup or salad, main course, dessert, beverage, and tax are about $10–$20 per person for lunch; $20–$25 for dinner. National, state and provincial parks charge $4–$20 per vehicle entrance; most museums charge $2–$6 per person.

CURRENCY

Canadian dollars ($) are the only legal currency in Alberta and BC. *Some* shops and restaurants accept US dollars, but only at a substantial discount in converted value.

Canadian banknotes come in $1, $2, $5, $10, $20 and $100 denominations, all the same size but different colours. $1 and $2 bills, now replaced by coins, are rarely seen. $1 coins are popularly called 'loonies' for the image of a loon, a type of duck, on the original issue. $2 coins, a small silvery disk surrounded by a golden disk, are occasionally called 'toonies' for the two metals.

There are 100 cents to the dollar: coins include the copper 1-cent piece, 5-cent nickel, 10-cent dime and 25-cent quarter. Size and weight of US and Canadian coins are slightly different and seldom work in vending machines or coin-operated telephones in the other country.

Banks and most larger hotels can exchange foreign currency or traveller's cheques. **Traveller's cheques** from well-known issuers such as Thomas Cook are accepted everywhere and can be used like cash or changed easily. To report Thomas

Cook travellers cheque losses and thefts; *tel: (800) 223-7373* (toll-free, 24-hr service).

For security reasons, avoid carrying large amounts of cash. The safest forms of money are traveller's cheques and credit or debit cards. Both can be used almost everywhere. If possible, bring at least one, preferably two, major credit cards, such as Access (MasterCard), American Express or Visa. Most urban locations accept MasterCard and Visa, but rural shops may accept only one of the two. Plastic is the only acceptable proof of fiscal responsibility. Car hire companies require either a credit card imprint or a substantial cash deposit before releasing a vehicle, even if the hire has been fully prepaid. Hotels and motels also require a credit card imprint or a cash deposit.

Some shops, cheaper motels, small local restaurants and low-cost petrol stations require cash. Automated teller machines, or **ATMs**, are a ubiquitous source of cash through withdrawals or cash advances authorised by debit or credit card. **Star** and **CIRRUS** are the most common international systems used in the region, but check terms, availability and PIN (personal identification number) with the card issuer before leaving home. Expect to pay transaction fees to the bank that owns the ATM and to your own bank for each transaction.

CUSTOMS ALLOWANCES

Personal duty-free allowances which can be taken into Canada by visitors are 1.14 litres of spirits or wine or 8.5 litres of beer or ale, 50 cigars, 200 cigarettes and 200 g of loose tobacco. On your return home you will be allowed to take in the following: **Australia**: goods to the value of A$400 (A$200 for those under 18) plus 250 cigarettes or 250 g tobacco and 1 litre alcohol. **New Zealand**: goods to the value of NZ$700. Anyone over 17 may also take 200 cigarettes or 250 g tobacco or 50

cigars or a combination of tobacco products not exceeding 250 g in all plus 4½ litres of beer or wine and 1.125 litres spirits.
South Africa: Goods to the value of 500 Rand. Anyone over 18 may also take 400 cigarettes and 50 cigars and 250 g tobacco plus 2 litres wine and 1 litre spirits, plus 50 ml perfume and 250 ml toilet water.
UK: The allowances for goods bought outside the EU and/or in EU duty-free shops are: 200 cigarettes or 50 cigars or 100 cigarillos or 250 g tobacco plus 2 litres still table wine, plus 1 litre spirits or 2 litres sparkling wine plus 60 ml perfume plus 250 ml toilet water.
US: US$400 worth of goods, including 1 litre spirits or wine and 200 cigarettes or 100 (non-Cuban) cigars.

Street prices for alcohol, tobacco, perfume and other typical duty-free items beat most duty-free shops, especially in Alberta. Shop at chain supermarkets and drug stores (e.g. Safeway, IGA, Overwaitea/Save-On Foods), discount stores (The Great Canadian Superstore, Zellers, K-Mart and Wal-Mart are most common) and Liquor Stores.

DISABLED TRAVELLERS

Access is the key word. Physically challenged is synonymous with disabled. Federal and provincial laws generally require that businesses, buildings and services used by the public be accessible by disabled persons, including those using wheelchairs, though not all are.

Access Canada, *Ministry of Small Business, Tourism and Culture, 1117 Wharf St, Victoria, BC V8W 2Z2,* is a Canada-wide programme that inspects and certifies disabled-accessible lodging on four levels of disability impairment: agility, vision, hearing and mobility. New hotels, restaurants, offices, shops, cinemas, museums, post offices and other public buildings should have access ramps and toilets designed for wheelchairs, but older structures may or may not be accessible. Disabled parking spots, always closest to an entrance, are painted with a blue wheelchair symbol.

Most cities and towns have ramps built into street crossings and most city buses have some provision for wheelchair passengers. Many parks have installed paved pathways. However, disabled facilities aren't always what they're meant to be. Older buildings often have barriers such as stairways or high door sills. Museums and public buildings are usually accessible, but special automobile controls for disabled drivers are seldom an option on hired vehicles. Kerbs may not be ramped.

Airlines are particularly hard on disabled passengers. Carriers can prevent anyone who is not strong enough to open an emergency exit (which weighs about 21 kg) or has vision/hearing problems from sitting in that row of seats – even if it means bumping them from the flight. Commuter airlines sometimes deny boarding to passengers with mobility problems on the grounds that they may block the narrow aisle during an emergency.

Some public telephones have special access services for the deaf and disabled. Broadcast television may be closed-captioned for the hearing impaired, indicated by a rectangle around a double 'cc' in a corner of the screen.

North American Information: SATH (Society for the Advancement of Travel for the Handicapped), *347 5th Ave, Suite 610, New York, NY 10016; tel: (212) 447-7284; sathtravel@aol.com.* The *Travelin' Talk Directory, PO Box 3534, Clarksville, TN 37043-3534,* is a North America guidebook of services and emergency contact information for disabled travellers, with newsletter updates. **UK Information**: RADAR, *12 City Forum, 250 City Rd, London, W1N 8AB; tel: (0171) 250 3222,* publish a useful annual guide, *Holidays and Travel Abroad,* which gives details of disabled facilities in different countries.

DISCOUNTS

Reductions and concessions on entrance fees and public transport for senior citizens, children, students and military personnel are common. Some proof of eligibility is usually required. For age, a passport or driving licence is sufficient. Military personnel should carry an official identification card. Students should carry an International Student Identity Card (ISIC) from their local student union, or a college ID.

The most common discount is for automobile club members. Touring guides from CAA (Canadian Automobile Association) and AAA (Automobile Association of America) affiliates list hundreds of member discounts throughout Western Canada. Always ask about CAA discounts at attractions, hotels, motels, car parks and car hire counters. Most recognise reciprocal membership benefits. Some cities will send discount booklets on request, good for shops, restaurants or lodging.

DRINKING

You must be 18 years old to purchase or to drink any kind of alcoholic beverage in Alberta, 19 in BC. Beer, wine and spirits are sold in government-licensed Liquor Stores in Alberta and provincially-owned Liquor Stores in BC. Both provinces allow the sale of beer and wine in specially licensed Beer and Wine Stores at slightly higher prices. Beer is also sold at some breweries and wine at nearly all wineries.

Opening hours for licensed establishments, usually called bars, lounges, pubs, saloons or taverns, vary by locale, but it is seldom difficult to find a drink between 0800 and 0200 except on election day, when liquor stores are closed.

Laws against drinking and driving are very strict, and very strictly enforced with fines and imprisonment. If stopped under suspicion of Driving Under the Influence (DUI), the police will ask you to choose between one of three tests: breath, blood or urine. Refusing to submit to a sobriety test is tantamount to admitting that you are drunk. Any liquor, wine or beer container in a vehicle (RVs excepted) must be full, sealed and unopened – or in the boot.

EARTHQUAKES

Earthquakes are less frequent in Western Canada than in California and Alaska, but not unknown. Archaeological evidence, First Nations accounts and settler diaries all record major quakes in BC, although not in recent years.

If you feel a mild earthquake, treat it like an amusement park ride. If items start falling from shelves, lamps sway or it becomes difficult to walk, take cover. Crawl under the nearest solid table for protection. If there's no table handy, brace arms and legs in an interior doorway. Stay away from windows, bookcases, stairs or anything else that could fall or break. *Don't* run outside. Glass, masonry and live power lines could be falling.

If driving, pull off the road and stop – it's almost impossible to control a vehicle when the road won't hold still.

Once the quake is over, make sure everyone is safe and provide all help possible to the wounded. And get ready for the next shake. There are always aftershocks.

ELECTRICITY

Canada uses 110 volt 60 hertz current. Two- or three-pin electrical plugs are standard. Electrical gadgets from outside North America require plug and power converters. Both are difficult to obtain in Canada because local travellers don't need them, although tourist hotels may have a supply of converters for their UK clientele.

Beware of buying electrical appliances for the same reason. Few gadgets on the North American market can run on 220 volt 50 hertz power. Exceptions are battery-operated equipment such as radios, cameras and portable computers. Tape cassettes, CDs, computer programmes and CD-ROMs sold in Canada can be used anywhere. Some radios and computers come with a switch to allow dual voltages, but plug converters may be needed.

North American video equipment, which uses the NTSC format, is *not* compatible with the PAL and SECAM equipment used in most of the rest of the world. *Pre-recorded* video tapes sold in Canada will not work with other equipment unless specifically marked as compatible with PAL or SECAM. *Blank* video tapes purchased in Canada, however, *can* be used with video recorders elsewhere in the world. Discount store prices on blank video cassettes are very reasonable, especially in Alberta, which has no sales tax.

EMERGENCIES

In case of emergency, ring *911,* free from any telephone. Ambulance, paramedics, police, fire brigades or other public safety personnel will be dispatched immediately. See also under 'Health'.

If you lose Thomas Cook traveller's cheques; tel: *(800) 223-7373* (toll-free, 24-hour service).

FOOD

Eating in most of Western Canada has revolved around salmon and berries for centuries. To a large degree, it still does. It's hard to find a fine restaurant in the region, even well onto Alberta's prairies, that does not have salmon on the menu. Chum, coho, chinook, dog, pink, silver and other types of salmon are seen more as a birthright than just another fish.

Increasing overfishing, combined with rampant habitat destruction from logging, land reclamation and housing construction, has decimated natural fish stocks. There's a growing likelihood that the fillet on your plate came from a fish farm. The same is true of oysters, clams, mussels, delicious rainbow trout, rarer Arctic char and many other types of seafood.

Berries have fared better in the modern world. More raspberries, blackberries, blueberries and gooseberries are grown and consumed in Western Canada than almost anywhere else in the world. The top of the berry heap belongs to the huckleberry, a kind of tart wild blueberry that has so far resisted every attempt at domestication. Slightly tart Saskatoon berries are an Alberta summertime treat. Add apples, peaches, pears, cherries, hazelnuts, wine grapes, hops, rhubarb and dozens of other introduced crops, and Western Canadian cooks are faced with a bounty that much of the world can only dream about.

Frontier traditions demand huge portions and hearty appetites, especially where Alberta's beef, famed for flavour and leanness is concerned. Caribou, venison, elk and buffalo are traditional game from the Rockies to the Arctic (Northwest Territories), well-garnished with a wide range of wild mushroom soups, crepes and sauces and nut-flavoured wild rice. Guinea fowl in birch bark, Northern Alberta lake fish and wild rice collected by First Nations people may be on the menu.

Breakfast may include fried fish or thinly-sliced bacon and eggs cooked to order (fried, boiled, poached), with hash browns (shredded fried potatoes) or chips. Toast, a flat 'English' muffin with butter and jam, or a bagel with cream (farmer's) cheese and lox (smoked salmon slices) may

31

be served alongside. Variations or additions include pancakes, French toast (bread dipped in egg batter and lightly fried) and waffles. Fresh fruit and yogurt, cereal and porridge are other possibilities. A 'continental breakfast' is juice, coffee or tea and some sort of bread or pastry.

Hotels and some restaurants offer Sunday brunch, usually 1100–1400, with all-you-can-eat self-service buffets heaped with hot and cold dishes. The economical Sunday brunch also includes coffee, tea, orange juice and sometimes cheap 'champagne' (sparkling wine).

Menus offer similar choices for lunch and dinner, the evening meal. Dinner portions are larger and more costly. Most menus offer appetisers (starters), salads, soups, pastas, entrées (main courses) and desserts. Urbanites expect salads to be fresh and crisp and sauces light and tasty. Cooking oils are not light on the palate, so avoid fried fish and ask instead for grilled seafood. Ice cream or sherbet is a lighter dessert choice.

For hearty eating, try a steak house where salad, baked potato and beans accompany a thick steak, be it beef or salmon. Italian restaurants serve pizza, pasta, seafood and steaks, with heavy doses of tomato and garlic. Ukrainian food has hearty cabbage rolls, home-made sausages, pierogies and borscht. Mexican cooks use thin wheat or corn tortillas as the base for beans, rice, cheese, tomatoes, spicy sauce and other ingredients.

The Chinese cuisine offered in Chinatowns is Cantonese with bean sprout chow mein and fried rice. More authentic Chinese dishes can be found in urban areas with regional variations, from spicy Hunan to rich, meaty Mandarin. Bite-size dim sum (filled dumplings) or any variety of won ton soup make a filling lunch. Japanese, Vietnamese and Thai food are other Asian cuisines. The culinary melting pot in major cities includes Basque, French, German, Spanish, Ukrainian, Cuban, Ethiopian, Salvadoran, Indian and a hundred others.

Fast food is quick and economical, be it a Big Mac, a buffalo burger or a bowl of Chinese noodles. Food is ordered, paid for and picked up from a service counter, all within a few minutes. Some fast-food outlets have a drive-through service, where the driver pulls up to a window, orders from a posted menu, pays and gets the meal, all without leaving the vehicle. Hamburgers, hot dogs, tacos, fried chicken and barbecue beef are common offerings. McDonalds' golden arches and KFC's grinning chubby colonel are easy to spot. Other fast-food chains include A & W, Arby's Roast Beef, Burger King, Domino's Pizza, Panagapolous Pizza Place, Subway and Taco Bell. All are cheap.

The budget rung of the price ladder includes chain restaurants such as Denny's (common along freeways and usually open 24 hours), Sizzler and White Spot.

Most cities have large covered Farmers Markets selling produce, meat, cheese and bakery goods. Many farms have 'U-pick' fruits and vegetables, where you pick up a bucket and harvest the quantity you desire. A new movement throughout the region is certification of organically grown (without pesticides) produce. Be prepared to pay a premium for these fruits and vegetables.

Colour section (i): Touring the Rockies: on the open road; inset, The Royal Hudson train.

(ii): Rocky Mountain Animals: black bear, elk (wapiti) and buffalo (see p.92–93).

(iii): Calgary (pp.64–74): view from Scottsman's Hill and Prince's Island with Canada geese.

(iv): Calgary Stampede (p.72): dressed for the Stampede; a First Nations dancer; Cow roping; and inset, White hats, the Calgary symbol.

GAMBLING

Gambling is illegal in Canada, but only under the wrong circumstances. Alberta and BC have highly advertised lotteries, casinos on and off First Nations reservations and bingo in church halls everywhere.

HEALTH

Hospital Emergency Rooms are where to go in the event of life-threatening medical problems. If a life is truly at risk, treatment will be swift and top notch, with payment problems sorted out later. For more mundane problems, 24-hour walk-in health clinics are available in urban areas and many rural communities.

Government-run programmes provide health care for all, including visitors. Non-Canadians must pay for treatment, but prices for routine care are a bargain compared to other industrialised countries. More serious illness, particularly emergency treatment for traffic and other accidents, can be hazardous to your financial health. Most travel agents who deal with international travel will offer travel insurance that covers medical costs in Canada – at least $1 million of cover is essential.

Bring enough prescription medication to last the entire trip, plus a few extra days. It's also a good idea to carry a copy of the prescription in case of emergency. Because trade names of drugs vary from country to country, be sure the prescription shows the generic (chemical) name and formulation of the drug, not just a brand name.

Western Canada is basically a healthy place to visit. No innoculations are required and common sense is enough to avoid most health problems. Eat and drink normally (or at least sensibly) and avoid drinking water that didn't come from the tap or a bottle. Most ground water, even in the high mountains, is contaminated with *giardia* and other intestinal parasites.

If travelling in or over the mountains, be alert for some symptoms of altitude sickness: lightheadedness, severe headache, disorientation, nausea and/or shortness of breath. If affected, get to lower altitude quickly and safely, and *do not drink alcohol.*

Sunglasses, broad-brimmed sun hats and sunscreen help prevent sunburn, sun stroke and heat prostration. Be sure to drink plenty of non-alcoholic liquids, especially in hot weather or at higher altitudes. Too little water is a particular problem when travelling from the coast to the dry interior.

AIDS (Acquired Immune Deficiency Syndrome) and other sexually transmitted diseases are endemic in Canada as they are in the rest of the world. The best way to avoid sexually transmitted diseases (STDs), is to avoid promiscuous sex.

In anything other than long-term, strictly monogamous relationships, the key phrase is 'safe sex'. Use condoms in any kind of sexual intercourse – they're *very* strongly encouraged by prostitutes plying the sex trade throughout the region. Condoms can be bought in drug stores, pharmacies and supermarkets, and from vending machines in many public toilets.

Rabies is another endemic disease. It's most likely to afflict those who try to hand feed the squirrels and chipmunks that haunt many parks, but end up being bitten instead. If bitten by an animal, try to capture it for observation of possible rabies, then go to the nearest emergency medical centre. You must seek *immediate* treatment – if left too late, rabies is untreatable and fatal. Squirrels and chipmunks also carry fleas that might transmit bubonic plague.

Don't wear shorts for hikes through the grasslands, forests and mountains. Cover up with long trousers, long-sleeved shirts and insect repellent. The risk of contracting **Lyme Disease** from ticks which thrive in moist climates, especially where deer are

33

present, is rising by the year. Lyme Disease is frequently misdiagnosed, usually mistaken for rheumatoid arthritis. Typical symptoms include temporary paralysis, arthritic pain in the hand, arm or leg joints, swollen hands, fever, fatigue, headaches, swollen glands, heart palpitations and a circular red rash around the bite up to 30 days later. Early treatment with tetracycline and other drugs is nearly 100% effective; late treatment often fails. Symptoms may not appear for three months or longer after the first infected bite, but the disease can be detected by a simple blood test.

Canadian ticks, travelling on elk, deer and ground squirrels also carry **Rocky Mountain spotted fever**, **Colorado tick fever** and **tularemia**. All are treatable, but it's easier to just avoid the diseases. Cover up while hiking and check skin all over the body, especially where clothing is tight, for ticks at midday and again in the evening. Look for tiny dark dots, 2–5.5 mm long, about the size of a full stop on this page. A tick likes to hide in hair on the head and at the back of the neck, drinking a blood meal while all but its mouth hangs loose. Ticks may be tweezed out and the area cleaned with antiseptic (even drinking alcohol will do in a pinch). If swelling or dizziness occur, *see a doctor immediately.*

HIKING

Walking is a favourite outdoor activity, especially in park areas. The same cautions that apply anywhere else are good in Western Canada: know the route; carry a map, compass and basic safety gear; carry food and water. It's also wise to stay on marked trails. Wandering off the trail, easy to do in the forest, adds to erosion damage.

Tick-borne diseases (see above) can usually be avoided by wearing long trousers and sleeves. The most common hiking problem is **Poison Ivy**, found throughout the region. This ivy-like plant is usually a shrub, sometimes a vine and always a trailside hazard. Variable leaf shapes make the plant difficult to identify, although the leaves always occur in clusters of three and usually look like rounded ivy leaves. Leaves are bright, glossy green in spring and summer, bright red in fall, and dead in winter – but not forgotten.

All parts of the plant, leaves, stems and flowers, exude a sticky sap that causes an intense allergic reaction in most people. The most common symptoms are red rash, itching, burning and weeping sores. The best way to avoid the problem is to avoid the plant. Second best is to wash skin or clothing that has come into contact with the plant immediately in hot, soapy water. If you are afflicted, drying lotions such as Ivy Block, calamine or products containing cortisone provide temporary relief, but time is the only cure. Don't burn it – smoke can burn, too.

Wildlife can also be a problem when an animal's territory is invaded, its young threatened or food temptingly left within range. In national parks, harassment of wildlife, including close approach, is forbidden. If animals roar, growl, charge, raise or swipe paws, swat tails, or have hair rising on the back, it's a 'no trespassing' signal.

Cougars (also called bobcats, mountain lions and pumas) would rather run than fight, but can be vicious if defending a den or accidentally cornered. Avoid hiking alone and never let small children run ahead or fall far behind. If you meet a cougar, *never* try to run or hide – you won't escape and either behaviour signals that you're prey. Instead, be aggressive. Stand your ground. Try to appear larger by raising your arms or opening up a jacket. Should the cougar approach, shout and throw sticks or stones. Show that you're ready to fight. And if attacked, fight with all you've got. Pummel, kick, hit with anything hard, and try to scratch the cat's eyes. Prove that you're not an easy target, and the cougar will probably look elsewhere.

Bears are a more serious threat, both black bears (which can be brown or cinnamon-coloured) and the larger grizzly bear. Grizzly bears have long, straight front claws and a shoulder hump. Both species are large, strong, fast-moving, always hungry and smart enough to connect humans with food. Parks and campsites have detailed warnings on how to safely store food to avoid attack. When possible, hang anything edible (including toothpaste) in bags well above the ground or store in metal lockers. *Never* feed bears, they won't know when the meal is over. Shouting, banging pots and throwing stones usually persuades bears to look somewhere else for a meal. Hikers and bikers in bear country often wear bells, called 'bear bells', around their ankles to warn bears of their presence.

Coyotes are common, if somewhat shy, inhabitants of the region. About the size of a small German Shepherd dog, coyotes prey on small rodents. You're most likely to see them hunting in open fields or meadows early and late in the day, or near cleared roads in winter. **Wolves** are also common in more remote areas. *Do not leave animals or small children outside at night when coyotes, wolves or cougars may be around.*

Larger animals, including **elk**, called **wapiti**, **moose**, **deer**, especially bucks with antlers, and **bison** (Elk Island National Park, Alberta) roam wild, especially in national parks. The elk, moose and deer go into overdrive during breeding season, or the rut, and are more aggressive than usual in turf defence. Females, does, will defend young vigilantly. Stay in vehicles, or, if hiking, be aware of scat (animal droppings) and give these animals, including the wild elk herds around Jasper, a wide berth.

Few people in Western Canada ever see **snakes** outside a zoo. The only poisonous snake native to the region is the **rattlesnake**, found only in desert sections of the Okanagan Valley. Only a handful of people each year across North America die from rattlesnake bites, usually while trying to catch them. 'Rattlers' are harmless if left alone (as all snakes should be). The markings vary, but all have diamond-shaped heads and rattles in their tails. Most, but not all, rattle a warning. In the wild, look where you're walking; don't put hands or feet on ledges which you can't see; and before sitting down, make sure a rattler hasn't already claimed the spot.

HITCH-HIKING

In an earlier, more trustful era, hitch-hiking was the preferred mode of transportation for budget travellers. Hitch-hiking remains popular in Canada, though there are many places where signs are posted to indicate that it is illegal. These days, drivers and riders are wary. Hitch-hiking or picking up hitch-hikers is too often asking for violent trouble, from theft to physical assault and murder. *Don't do it.*

HOLIDAYS

New Year's Day (Jan 1); **Alberta Family Day** (third Mon in Feb); **Good Friday** (Mar/Apr); **Easter Monday** (Apr); **Victoria Day** (mid May); **Canada Day** (July 1); **Alberta Heritage Day**, **BC Day** (first Mon in Aug); **Labour Day** (early Sept); **Thanksgiving** (mid Oct); **Remembrance Day** (Nov 11); **Christmas Day** (Dec 25); **Boxing Day** (Dec 26).

INSURANCE

Experienced travellers carry insurance that covers their belongings and holiday investment as well as their bodies. Travel insurance should include provision for cancelled or delayed flights and weather problems, as well as immediate evacuation home in the case of medical emergency. Thomas Cook and other travel agencies offer comprehensive policies. Medical cover should be high – at least $1 million. Insurance for drivers is covered on p. 56.

LANGUAGE

English and French are the official languages in Alberta and BC, but for more than a century, immigrants have added languages to the spoken mix. Spanish, Chinese (Cantonese and Mandarin), Tagalog, Vietnamese, Punjabi, Hindi and Korean are spoken widely in urban areas. Ukrainian and Polish are common near Edmonton. First Nations' languages add yet another layer of complexity.

English, the common tongue, creates its own difficulties. Canadian English is a hybrid of British spelling and grammar with American vocabulary and usage. The Queen's English is universally understood and occasionally spoken, but Canadians read, hear and use more Americanisms than Briticisms, e.g. 'taking a vacation' rather than 'taking a holiday', and buying 'gas' rather than 'petrol'. A selection of commonly encountered terms which may be unfamiliar or have a different meaning in Western Canada are set out in the box on pp. 38–39. Driving in Western Canada, p. 55, provides a glossary of motoring terms.

LIGHTNING STORMS

Each second between the visible flash and clap of thunder is 300 m distance between you and the storm's centre. Take shelter if the storm is less than 5 seconds away, staying away from metal objects, appliances, high spots and trees which could be struck.

If in your car, pull away from trees and higher objects – but *stay in the car*. Hair standing on end means lightning is about to strike – especially if you're alone in a flat area. Don't be tempted to lie on the ground, but drop to your knees, head down, hands on knees until the follicle-raising effect is well past.

LUGGAGE

Less is more where luggage is concerned. Porters don't exist outside the most expensive hotels and luggage trolleys (baggage carts) are rare outside airports. Trolleys are free for international arrivals in Calgary, Edmonton, Vancouver and Victoria, but must be hired almost everywhere else. Luggage has to be light enough to carry. The normal luggage allowance is 2 pieces each of 32 kg maximum. Luggage must also fit in the car or other form of transport. Canadians buy the same cars as Europeans, Australians and the rest of the world, not the enormous 'boats' of the 1960s. If it won't fit in the boot at home, don't count on cramming it into a Canadian rental car.

MAPS

The best all-round maps are produced by the **Canadian Automobile Association** (CAA) and distributed through their local affiliates. Provincial, regional and city maps are available free at all association offices, but only to members. Fortunately, most motoring clubs around the world have reciprocal agreements with CAA to provide maps and other member services. Show a membership card to obtain service.

Rand McNally road maps and atlases are probably the best known of the ranges available outside Canada, in the travel section of bookshops and more specialist outlets. Once in Canada, the **Up-Close®** series from **Gem Trek Publishing**, *Box 1618, Cochrane, AB T0L 0W0; tel: (403)* *266-2523; fax: (403) 932-4893*, provide excellent touring maps, some with 3-dimensional topographic detail, for Banff, Jasper and Lake Louise-Yoho National Park, among others. **MapArt**, *70 Bloor St E., Oshawa, ON L1H 3M2; tel: (905) 436-2525; fax: (905) 723-6677,* produce clear Calgary and Edmonton city maps.

Logging companies often provide the most accurate and up-to-date off-road maps through travel infocentres and timber industry information centres, but getting lost in the wilderness is a genuine possibility even with the best of maps in hand. If you are thinking of driving off the beaten track, always carry a topographic map (50,000:1 or better) and compass in addition to any other maps and guides.

Before leaving civilisation behind, compare every available map, even city maps, for discrepancies, then check with forest or park personnel. Most are experienced backcountry enthusiasts themselves, and since they're responsible for rescuing lost hikers, they have a vested interest in dispensing the best possible advice.

MEETING PEOPLE

Canadians are friendly. As in much of the world, asking for directions, map in hand, is a useful 'icebreaker'. Friendliness does not extend to inviting new acquaintances to their homes, however. A Bed and Breakfast is a good place to meet 'locals' on holiday. Sports events, casual restaurants and bars can be meeting places, but most local people are wary of approaches by strangers. Professional associations, sports or interest clubs welcome visitors from abroad; contact well in advance for meeting times and venues. Check Fri, Sun or weekly newspapers for listings of events. Street fairs and Farmers Markets, increasingly popular throughout Canada, bring out crowds with a variety of interests.

37

How to talk Canadian

Back Country The bush.

Back Bacon Known as Canadian Bacon in the USA and as Peameal Bacon elsewhere.

Bannock A deep-fried bread usually eaten with such trail 'delicacies' as moose stew.

Beaver Fever Giardiasis Severe diarrhoea and fever from drinking untreated ground water infected with *Giardia lamblia*.

Beer Parlour Pub.

Big Smoke Vancouver.

Block heater An electric engine heater attached to the other end of the plug dangling from the front bumper of most Canadian cars. The heater is plugged in on cold nights (-10°C or colder) to prevent the engine coolant and oil from freezing and cracking the engine block.

Brew A beer, either in bottle or on draught.

Buffalo Chip Dried bison or buffalo droppings, once used by First Nations people and early White settlers as fuel.

Canadian Cuisine Anything the chef wants it to be, usually based on local food such as maple syrup, fiddleheads (immature fern sprouts), venison, caribou, buffalo, salmon and berries. In budget restaurants, more often fried eggs, fried steaks and mystery meat egg foo young.

Canuck A Canadian or a member of the Vancouver Canucks ice hockey team.

Chinook A warm wind from west of the Rockies that melts winter snows as it passes over the mountains, warming Calgary and south-west Alberta. Also the trade jargon spoken throughout North-western North America in the last century and a Native American tribe from Washington State.

Cow pie Cattle droppings, a hazard to walkers on open grazing lands.

Cowtown Calgary.

Donair, Donner Kebab A sandwich made of shaved meat (usually lamb) wrapped in pita bread, sometimes called a *gyro* or *schwarma*.

Downtown City or town centre.

Flapjacks Pancakes.

Flat A case of 24 bottles or cans of beer.

Freedomite A member of the Sons of Freedom sect of the Doukhobors. Freedomites have engaged in nude parades and mass burning of all their property.

Fries Chips, usually, but not always, made of potatoes.

Galapagos of Canada The Queen Charlotte Islands, also called Haida Gwaii.

Gas Petrol.

Goeduck Pronounced 'gooey duck', a large clam with a thick neck, usually used for soup.

Gorbie Someone not from the area, a tourist, usually someone asking questions such as 'How much does that mountain weigh'?

Holiday A public holiday, such as Christmas or Boxing Day, not a private holiday, which is more often a *vacation*.

Hoodoo Pinnacle or column of rock,

38

OPENING HOURS

Office hours are generally Mon–Fri, 0900–1700, although some Tourist Offices also keep Saturday hours. Most banks and other financial institutions open Mon–Fri 1000–1600 and Sat mornings. Automatic cash dispensers (ATMs) are open 24 hours.

Small shops keep standard business hours. Large shops and shopping centres open Mon–Sat 0900/1000–2000/2100. Opening hours are slightly shorter on Sun.

Many restaurants, museums and legitimate theatres close on Mon, but most tourist attractions are open daily in summer. Many tourist attractions are closed Sept (after Labour Day)–May (opening Victoria Day or the last weekend).

PARKS INFORMATION

Much of Western Canada is publicly owned. The degree of protection and the type of uses varies, but camping is only

frequently capped by a flat disk. They are generally formed by erosion.

Hooter A species of blue grouse – really.

Hoser A term used by men to tease one another, implying the person being needled is none too bright.

Ice Fog Fog composed of ice crystals instead of water vapour.

Lodging The usual term for accommodation.

Loonie $1 coin, named for the Canadian Loon on the original issue.

Métis A person of mixed aboriginal and white ancestry, constitutionally recognised as one of three First Nations entities.

Ogopogo Mythical beast similar to the Loch Ness Monster believed to lurk beneath the waters of Okanagan Lake.

Organic Foods and other products grown and processed without artificial fertilisers or other synthetic chemical products.

Outlet shopping Shopping at large stores specialising in factory over-runs at reduced prices. In many cases, factory outlets are simply low-priced retail stores selling direct from the factory.

Parkade A parking garage.

Parking lot A car park or parking garage.

Poutine A French Canadian delicacy of French fries smothered in white sauce and melted cheese.

Raging Grannies Older women who appear at peace movement and environmental events to sing protest songs.

Road Apple Cattle or buffalo droppings on the road.

Road Kill Literally animals killed by passing automobiles, but also used to describe bad restaurant food.

Sasquatch Bigfoot, the legendary man-like hairy giant of the woods.

Shooter A raw oyster, usually swallowed whole. Originally a small glass, or 'shot' of whisky drunk in one swallow.

Shredding Snow boarding.

Sundog Ring around the sun formed by ice crystals in the upper atmosphere.

Talking Stick Originally a carved staff used in First Nations gatherings to signify that the holder was entitled to speak to the group, now used in non-Native meetings to focus attention on the speaker.

Texas Gate or *Cattle Gate* A grate of widely separated metal pipes set in the roadway to keep cattle and horses at bay.

Toque A winter hat, pronounced like 'spook'.

Toonie The $2 bi-metal coin.

Vamping Van camping.

Voyageur Canoe A canoe used by fur traders for long voyages, paddled by eight men.

Wapiti Elk.

Whisky Domestic spirit distilled from rye grain, often mixed with ginger ale for Canada's favourite libation, a rye and ginger.

Whisky Jay Canadian jay or gray jay, a small grey bird noted for stealing food and other small items from camps, tables and homes. Similar to the Clark's nutcracker, also known for snatching food.

Wrinkle Trend.

39

permitted in marked campsites. For specific parks and protected monuments and seashores, see the appropriate description among the routes throughout this book.

For general information on national parks and historic sites in Alberta and BC, contact **Parks Canada Service Centre**, **Calgary:** *220 4 Ave S.E., Room 552, Calgary, AB T2P 3H8; tel: (800) 748-7275* or *(403) 292-4401; fax: (403) 292-6004;* or **Vancouver:** *300 W. Georgia St, Suite 300, Vancouver, BC V6B 6C6; tel: (604) 666-0176; fax: (604) 666-3508; web: http://parkscanada.pch.gc.ca.* Request the excellent workbook, *Parks Canada Vacation Planner: A Year-Round Guide to the National Parks and National Historic Sites of Alberta and the B.C. Rockies.*

There is a per person, per day 'personal use fee' for entry to National Parks and Historic Heritage Sites. Daily or economical group (2–10 people) permits are sold at park gates and visitor centres. Parks Canada has the **Western Canada Annual Pass**, $35 per person or $70 per family, sold at parks and heritage sites, which includes most parks and historic sites, a bargain if you're planning to stay in or drive through parks as well as avoiding summer lines at park entrance booths.

Travel Alberta, *Box 2500, Edmonton, AB T5J 2Z4; tel: (800) 661-8888 or (403) 427-4321; fax: (403) 427-0867*, has information on **Alberta Provincial Parks**. For **BC Provincial Parks**, contact **BC Parks**, *800 Johnson St, Victoria, BC V8V 1X4; tel: (250) 387-5002*.

PASSPORTS AND VISAS

All non-US citizens must have a valid full passport (not a British Visitor's Passport) and, in some cases, a visa. Citizens of most countries must obtain a visa from the Canadian Embassy in their country of residence in advance of arrival. Documentation regulations change frequently and are complex for some nationalities; confirm your requirements with the nearest Canadian Embassy or consulate at least 90 days before you plan to depart.

POLICE

To telephone police in an emergency, ring *911*. There are many different police jurisdictions within Western Canada, but the Royal Canadian Mounted Police – the RCMP – or 'Mounties', provide police services for most areas outside greater Calgary, Edmonton, Vancouver and Victoria. Mounties only wear their famous red dress uniform for formal functions and occasional public appearances.

POSTAL SERVICES

Every town has at least one central post office. Hours vary, although all are open Mon–Fri, morning and afternoon.

Canada Post branches may be open Saturday or even Sunday. Some hotels sell stamps through the concierge; large department stores may have a post office; many chemists/drug stores have post office counters at the back of the store; and supermarkets and tourist gift shops often sell stamps at the checkout counter. Stamp machines are installed in some stores, but a surcharge may be included in the cost. For philatelic sales, check major city telephone directories under Canada Post.

Mail everything going overseas as Air Mail (surface mail can take weeks just to cross the US border). If posting letters near an urban area, mail should take about one week to international destinations. Add a day or two if mailing from remote areas.

Poste Restante is available at any post office, without charge. Mail should be addressed in block lettering to your name, Poste Restante/General Delivery, city, state, postal code, Canada (do not abbreviate). Mail is held for 15 days at the post office branch that handles General Delivery, usually the main office. Identification is required for mail pick up.

PUBLIC HOLIDAYS

Canada's love affair with the road extends to jumping in the automobile for holiday weekends. Local celebrations, festivals, parades, or neighbourhood parties can disrupt some or all activities in town. Post offices and government offices close on public holidays. Some businesses take the day off, though department and discount stores hold huge sales, well advertised in local newspapers. Petrol stations remain open. Small shops and some grocery stores close or curtail hours.

Call in advance before visiting an attraction on a public holiday as there are frequently special hours. National and state/provincial park campsites and lodging must be reserved in advance for all holidays. Easter, Thanksgiving and Christmas are family holidays, where accommodation is available and may even be discounted. Other holidays are 'mobile', so book early.

SALES TAXES

Canada levies a national 7% sales tax (the Goods & Services Tax, or GST) on nearly every product and service. In addition, BC has its own 7% provincial sales tax (PST). Alberta has no PST. Both provinces have local taxes on accommodation. There may also be special taxes or fees on rental cars.

SECURITY

Throwing caution to the winds is foolhardy at anytime, and even more so on holiday. Canada prides itself on a law-abiding tradition. Dial *911* on any telephone for free emergency assistance.

You can travel in perfect safety in Western Canada if you take the following common-sense precautions.

Travelling Safely

Never publicly discuss travel plans or money or valuables you are carrying. Drive, park and walk only in well-lit areas. If unsure of roads or weather ahead, stop for the evening and find secure lodging. Sightsee with a known companion, or in a group. Solo travel, in urban areas or in the countryside, is not recommended.

The best way to avoid becoming a victim of theft or injury is to walk with assurance and try to give the impression that you are not worth robbing (e.g. don't wear or carry expensive jewellery or flash rolls of banknotes). Use a hidden money-belt for your valuables, travel documents and spare cash. Carrying a wallet in a back pocket or leaving a handbag open is an invitation to every pickpocket in the area. In all public places, take precautions with anything that

is obviously worth stealing – use a handbag with a crossed shoulder strap and a zip, wind the strap of your camera case around your chair and place your handbag firmly between your feet under the table while you eat.

Never leave luggage unattended. At airports, security officials may confiscate unattended luggage as a possible bomb. In public toilets, handbags and small luggage items have been snatched from hooks, or from under stalls. Airports, bus and train stations usually have lockers. Most work with keys; guard the key and memorise the locker number. Hotel bell staff may keep luggage for one or more days on request, sometimes for a fee – get receipts for left luggage before surrendering it.

Concealing a weapon is against the law. Physical assault, by individuals or by gangs, is more of a problem in the US than in Canada. If you are attacked, it is safer to let go of your bag or hand over the small amount of obvious money – as you are more likely to be attacked physically if the thief meets with resistance. *Never resist.* Report incidents immediately to local police, even if it is only to get a copy of their report for your insurance company.

Driving Safely

Have car hire counter personnel recommend a safe, direct route on a clear map before you leave with the vehicle. Lock all valuables and luggage in the boot or glove box so that nothing is visible to passers-by or other drivers. Don't leave maps or guidebooks in evidence – why advertise that you're a stranger in town?

Always keep car doors and windows locked. Do not venture into unlit areas, neighbourhoods that look seedy, or off paved roads. *Do not stop* if told by a passing motorist or pedestrian that something is wrong with your car, or if someone signals

41

for help with a broken-down car. If you need to stop, do so only in well-lit or populated areas, even if your car is bumped from behind by another vehicle. If your car breaks down, turn on the flashing emergency lights. If it is safe to get out, raise the bonnet and return to the vehicle. Do not split passengers up. Emergency vehicle lights are red or red and blue, so do not stop for flashing white lights or flashing headlights. Ask directions only from police, at a well-lit business area or at a service station.

At night, have keys ready to unlock car doors before entering a parking lot. Check the surrounding area and inside the vehicle before entering. Never pick up hitch-hikers, or leave the car with the engine running. Take all valuables with you.

Sleeping Safely

When sleeping rough, in any sort of dormitory, train or open campsite, the safest place for your small valuables is at the bottom of your sleeping-bag. In train sleeping carriages, padlock your luggage to the seat, and ask the attendant to show you how to lock a compartment door at night. If in doubt, take luggage with you.

In hotels, motels and all other lodging, lock all door locks from the inside. Check that all windows are locked, including sliding glass doors. Ground-floor rooms mean easier access by molesters intent on breaking in. Never leave the room at night without leaving a light on. Lights deter prowlers and when you return, any disturbance to room contents will be visible.

Use a door viewer to check before admitting anyone to your room. If someone claims to be on the hotel staff or a repair person, do not let the person in before phoning the office or front desk to verify the person's name and job. Money, cheques, credit cards, passports and keys should be with you, or secured in your hotel's safe deposit box. When checking in, find the most direct route from your room to fire escapes, elevators, stairwells and the nearest telephone.

Documents

Take a few passport photos with you and photocopy the important pages and any visa stamps in your passport. Store these safely, together with a note of the numbers of your traveller's cheques, credit cards and insurance documents (keep them separate from the documents themselves). If you are unfortunate enough to be robbed, you will at least have some identification, and replacing the documents will be much easier. Apply to your nearest consulate (see p. 27 for addresses and phone numbers).

SHOPPING

Canadian souvenirs include BC wines; dried, tinned or smoked salmon; apples, cherries and other dried fruits; honey; berry jams and syrups (maple syrup is from Eastern Canada); prepared mustards, oils and condiments; and the ubiquitous T-shirts. Clothing can be a bargain, particularly at discount or factory outlet stores. Cameras and other photo equipment can be a fraction of UK prices, but do your homework on prices before you go, and shop around when you arrive.

First Nations products include wood, stone and soapstone carvings, paintings, rugs, masks, baskets, jewellery incorporating silver and gold, and hand-made grey or white Cowichan sweaters with traditional designs. Souvenirs depicting Mounties (RCMP) are ubiquitous.

Tape cassettes, blank video tapes, CDs, computer programmes and CD-ROMs sold in Canada can be used anywhere in the world. For more information on electrical goods, see 'Electricity', p. 30.

SMOKING

Lighting up is out in public buildings and on public transportation. All plane flights in North America are non-smoking. Some hire cars are designated as non-smoking. Most hotels/motels set aside non-smoking rooms or floors; Bed and Breakfast establishments are almost all non-smoking. Restaurant dining regulations vary by locality; some forbid all smoking; others permit it in the bar or lounge only; some have a percentage of the eatery devoted to smokers. Smoking is prohibited in most stores and shops. Always ask before lighting a cigarette, cigar or pipe. When in doubt, go outside to smoke. Smoking is more common in rural areas than in larger cities.

TAX REFUNDS

Canada imposes a 7% **Goods & Services Tax**, or **GST**, on nearly all purchases, including accommodation and meals. In addition, BC imposes a **Provincial Sales Tax**, or **PST**, of 7%. There is no PST in Alberta. Visitors may apply for a **refund** of GST paid on most products taken out of Canada and on accommodation of less than 30 days. To qualify for a refund, total purchases must be a minimum of $200 ($14 in tax), you must have *original receipts* and each individual receipt must show a minimum of $3.50 in tax (a $50 minimum purchase).

The refund application may be obtained from Canadian Customs and tourism offices, department stores, hotels and tourist InfoCentres. Refunds can also be obtained at duty-free shops adjacent to most vehicle border crossings, at some foreign exchange bureaux in Victoria, or by post: *Visitor Rebate Programme, Revenue Canada, Summerside Tax Centre, Summerside, PE C1N 6C6; tel: (800) 668-4748 or (902) 432-5608.* Duty-free shops and Revenue Canada return the entire rebate, but only after you've already left the

country. Currency exchange bureaux pay cash on the spot, but charge a commission, usually $5 or 15%, whichever is more. Unless you're planning a quick return to Canada, it's usually simpler to pay the commission and get the cash to spend before you leave.

TELEPHONES

The Canadian telephone system is divided into local and long-distance carriers. Depending on the time of day and day of the week, it may be cheaper to call Toronto than to call 50 km away. After 1800, Mon–Fri, and on weekends, rates are lower and are discounted further after 2300. Alberta's area code is *403;* BC has two area codes, *604* and *250.* In Jan 1999, Northern Alberta, including Edmonton, Jasper, Elk Island National Park and Wetaskawin, switch to area code *780.*

Public telephones are indicated by a sign with a white telephone receiver depicted on a blue field. Enclosed booths, wall-mounted, or free-standing machines are all used. If possible, use public phones in well-lit, busy public areas.

Dialling instructions are in the front of the local white pages telephone directory. For all long-distance calls, precede the area code with a *1.* In emergencies, call *911* for police, medical, or fire brigade response. *0* reaches an operator. For local number information, dial *411.* For long-distance phone information, dial *1,* the **local area code**, then *555-1212.* There is a charge for information calls.

Pay phones take coins; local calls cost $0.25. An operator or computer voice will come on-line to ask for additional coins if needed. Most hotels and motels add a stiff surcharge to the basic cost of a long-distance call, so use a public telephone in the lobby. Some public phones accept credit cards and calling cards. Prepaid

43

phone cards are widely available at grocery and convenience stores. Before you travel, ask your local phone company if your phone card will work in Canada. Most do, and come with a list of contact numbers. A credit card may be convenient, but only economical if you pay the bill immediately.

800, 877 and *888* numbers are toll-free. Like all long-distance numbers, the *800/ 877/888* area code must be preceded by a *1*, e.g. *1-888-123-4567*. Some telephone numbers are given in letters, i.e. *1-800-VAN-RIDE*. Telephone keys have both numbers and letters, so find the corresponding letter and depress that key. A few numbers have more than seven letters to finish a business name. Not to worry, Canadian phone numbers never require more than seven numerals, plus three for the area code.

Dial an international operator on *0* for enquiries or assistance.

For international dialling, dial *011-country code-city code* (omitting the first *0* if there is one)-*local number*; e.g., to call Great Britain, Inner London, from Canada, dial: *011-44-171-local number*. Country codes:

Australia 61
New Zealand 64
Republic of Ireland 353
South Africa 27
United Kingdom 44

Calls to the USA are preceded by a *1*, then the *area code* and *number,* i.e. *1-415-123-4567.*

In both provinces, the **Talking Yellow Pages**, *(local area code) 299-9000,* is a free source of information on weather, road conditions, time, international news and entertainment.

TIME

Most of British Columbia is on Pacific Standard Time (PST), GMT -8 hrs. Alberta and a small portion of south-eastern BC are

Time in the Canadian Rockies (MST)	9 a.m.	1 p.m.	6 p.m.	1 a.m.
Time in				
Auckland	4a.m.	8a.m.	1p.m.	8p.m.
Cape Town	6p.m.	10p.m.	3a.m.	10a.m.
Dublin	4p.m.	8p.m.	1a.m.	8a.m.
London	4p.m.	8p.m.	1a.m.	8a.m.
Perth	Midnt	4a.m.	9a.m.	4p.m.
Sydney	2a.m.	6a.m.	11a.m.	6p.m.
Toronto	11a.m.	3p.m.	8p.m.	3a.m.

on Mountain Standard Time (MST), GMT -7 hours. From the first Sun in Apr until the last Sun in Oct, clocks are advanced one hour to Pacific Daylight Time (PDT), GMT -7 hrs and Mountain Daylight Time (MDT), GMT -6 hrs.

TIPPING

Acknowledgement for good service should not be extorted. That said, tipping is a fact of life, to get, to repeat, or to thank someone for service.

Service charges are not customarily added to restaurant bills. Waiters and waitresses expect a tip of 15% of the bill before taxes are added on. In luxury restaurants, also be prepared to tip the maitre d' and sommelier a few dollars, up to 10% of the bill. Bartenders expect the change from a drink, up to several dollars. Hotel porters generally receive $1 per bag; a bellperson who shows you to the room expects several dollars; in luxury properties, tip more. Room service delivery staff should be tipped 10–15% of the tariff before taxes, unless there's a service charge indicated on the bill. Expect to hand out dollars for most services that involve room delivery. Some hotels have a chambermaid name card placed in the room: it's a hint for a tip of a few dollars upon your departure, but never required.

Taxi drivers are usually tipped $1 for fares under $4, or 15% of the charge for higher fares. Ushers in legitimate theatres, arenas and stadiums are not tipped; cinemas seldom have ushers, nor are tips expected. Do not tip petrol station attendants.

TOILETS

Washroom is the common term in Canada; *toilet*, *bathroom* and *WC* are acceptable. Whatever the term, most are marked with a figure for a male or a female; *men* and *women* are the most common terms. Occasionally, a washroom may be used by both sexes. Facilities may be clean and well-equipped or filthy. Most businesses, including bars and restaurants, reserve washrooms for clients. Petrol stations often provide keys for customers to access washrooms. Public toilets are sporadically placed, but well-marked. Parks and roadside rest stops have toilet facilities.

TORNADOES

When driving Alberta's plains May–Sept, you may see a tapering funnel cloud moving from the south-west to the north-east. Thunder-induced, twisters may come with lightning, downpour, hail and winds up to 450 kph! Listen for the tornado's loud roar. If audible, drive away from its 50–70 kph path at a right angle, and get safely out of the car if possible. Find shelter, even a ditch below ground level, or a tree to hang onto until it has passed.

TOURIST INFORMATION

Each province is responsible for its own tourism promotion. Address requests for information well in advance. **Travel Alberta**, *Box 2500, Edmonton, AB T5J 2Z4; tel: (800) 661-8888 or (403) 427-4321* (Mon–Fri 0900–1630); *fax: (403)*

427-0867; web: http://discoveralberta.com. **Tourism British Columbia**, *802–865 Hornby St, Vancouver, BC V6Z 2G3; tel: (800) 663-6000 or (604) 663-6000; fax: (604) 660-3383; UK: tel: (0891) 715000; fax: (0171) 389-1149; Germany: (06181) 45178; fax: (06181) 497558; web: http:// travel.bc.ca.*

Three well-stocked **Travel Alberta Visitor Information Centres** cover the province and Rockies: **Canmore:** *Canmore Service Rd, off TransCanada Hwy 1;* **Crowsnest Pass:** *8 km west of Coleman, AB and 6 km east of the BC border;* and **Field:** *south side of TransCanada Hwy 1 in Field, BC.* BC-wide information is available in **Vancouver Visitor Information Centres** at **Greater Vancouver Convention & Visitors Bureau/Tourism, Vancouver,** *200 Burrard St, Vancouver; tel: (604) 682-2222;* **Vancouver International Airport** *International Arrivals Area;* and at **Pacific Centre**.

Canada also has an active federal tourism promotion office, usually located in Canadian Consulates around the world.

The **Alberta Heritage SuperPass**, with substantial discounts to most provincial museums and historic sites, is available where honoured or from **Alberta Community Development**, *Cultural Facilities & Historical Resources Division, 8820 112 St, Old St Stephen's College, Edmonton, AB T6G 2P8; tel: (403) 431-2300; fax: (403) 427-5598.*

TRAINS

VIA Rail handles national passenger traffic; *tel: (888) 842-7245; web: http://www. viarail.ca.* Primary routes run east from Vancouver to Kamloops and onward across the Rockies and westward from Edmonton to Prince Rupert. **BC Rail**, *1311 West 1st St, North Vancouver, BC V7P 1A6; tel: (800) 663-8238 or (604) 984-*

5246; fax: (604) 984-5505; web: http:www. bcrail.com/bcr, operates passenger services in BC, including Vancouver–Whistler–Lillooet–Prince George lines. Trains do not stop at each town en route, so check if there is a stop at your destination. **Rocky Mountaineer**, *1150 Station St, 1st Floor, Vancouver, BC V6A 2X7; tel: (800) 665-7245 or (604) 606-7245; fax: (604) 606-7250; web: http:www.rkymtnrail.com,* provides a tourist service May–mid Oct on selected scenic runs between Vancouver, Banff, Jasper and other destinations.

Train times for many VIA Rail, BC Rail and local services are published in the *Thomas Cook Overseas Timetable* (see next column).

TRAVEL ARRANGEMENTS

Given the fact that most of the world's international airlines fly into Calgary or Vancouver, and the ease of hiring cars at airports, Western Canada is an ideal destination for independently-minded travellers. However, the many types of air ticket and the range of temporary deals available on busy routes make it advisable to talk to your travel agent before booking to get the best bargain.

Taking a fly-drive package such as one of Thomas Cook's own, or one of the many others offered by airlines and tour operators, is usually more economical than making all your own arrangements. All include the air ticket and car hire; some also follow set itineraries which enable them to offer guaranteed and prepaid en route accommodation at selected hotels. Programmes such as Thomas Cook's America for the Independent Traveller or Canada and Alaska allow the flexibility of booking the airline ticket at an advantageous rate and then choosing from a 'menu' of other items, often at a discounted price, such as car hire, hotel

coupons (which prepay accommodation but do not guarantee availability of rooms) and other extras such as excursions.

USEFUL READING

Most British and international colour-illustrated guidebook series feature one or more volumes on Western Canada. The *Handbook of the Canadian Rockies,* cited below, is the revered and entertaining field guide to natural history and issues affecting the region. If you are considering using trains for any part of your trip, the *Thomas Cook Overseas Timetable* (published every 2 months, £8.40 per issue) is indispensable, and referred to throughout this book as the OTT. Available from any UK branch of Thomas Cook or by phoning *(01733) 503571/2.* In North America, contact the **Forsyth Travel Library Inc.,** *226 Westchester Ave, White Plains, New York 10604; tel: (800) 367 7984 (toll-free).*

If you are arranging your own accommodation as you travel, a comprehensive guide such as the *CAA TourBook for Western Canada and Alaska* can often be obtained through specialist travel bookshops outside North America. Books you can buy in Western Canada include:

The Alberta Fact Book, Mark Zuehlke, 1997, Whitecap Books, Vancouver; *Alberta History Along the Highway,* Ted Stone, 1996, Red Deer College Press, Red Deer, AB; *Alberta Wildlife Viewing Guide,* by Alberta Forestry, Lands and Wildlife, 1990, Lone Pine Publishing, Edmonton; *Backroads of Southern Alberta,* Joan Donaldson-Yarmey, 1992, Lone Pine Publishing, Edmonton; *Backroading Vancouver Island,* Rosemary Neering, 1996, Whitecap Books, Vancouver; *The B.C. Fact Book,* Mark Zuehlke, 1995, Whitecap Books, Vancouver; *Canadian Rockies SuperGuide,* Graeme Pole, 1992, Altitude Publishing Canada Ltd., Canmore, AB; *Handbook of* the Canadian Rockies, Ben Gadd, 1995, Corax Press, Jasper; *Just East of Sundown: The Queen Charlotte Islands*, Charles Lillard, 1995, Horsdal & Schubart, Victoria; *Kananaskis SuperGuide*, Ward Cameron, 1996, Altitude Publishing Canada Ltd., Canmore, AB; *The Land Before Us: The Making of Ancient Alberta*, by the Royal Tyrrell Museum of Palaeontology, 1994, Red Deer College Press, Red Deer, AB; *Leaning on the Wind*, Sid Marty, 1995, HarperCollins Publishers Ltd., Toronto; *Looking at Indian Art of the Northwest Coast*, Hilary Stewart, 1979, Douglas & McIntyre, Vancouver/Toronto; *More English than the English: A Social History of Victoria*, Terry Reksten, 1986, Orca Book Publishers, Victoria; *Native Peoples and Cultures of Canada*, Alan D McMillan, 1995, Douglas & McIntyre, Vancouver; *Native Peoples of the Northwest: A Traveler's Guide to Land, Art, and Culture*, Jan Halliday & Gail Chehak, 1996, Sasquatch Books, Seattle; *Native Sites in Western Canada*, Pat Kramer, 1994, Altitude Publishing Canada Ltd., Canmore, AB; *Northwest Indian Travel Guide and Map*, Affiliated Tribes of Northwest Indians, *825 N.E. 20th Ave, Suite 310, Portland, OR 97232; tel: (503) 230-0293; fax: (503) 230-0580; Northwest Trees: Identifying & Understanding the Region's Native Trees*, Stephen F Arno, 1977, The Mountaineers, Seattle; *Official Guide to Pacific Rim National Park Reserve*, JM MacFarlane et. al., 1996, Blackbird Naturgraphics, Inc., Calgary; *The Spiral Tunnels and The Big Hill: A Canadian Railway Adventure*, Graeme Pole, 1995, Altitude Publishing Canada Ltd., Canmore, AB; *Totem Poles*, Pat Kramer, 1995, Altitude Publishing Canada Ltd, Canmore, AB; *A Traveller's Guide to Aboriginal B.C.*, Cheryl Coull, 1996, Whitecap Books, Vancouver; *A Traveller's Guide to Historic British Columbia*, Rose-

mary Neering, 1993, Whitecap Books, Vancouver; *Walks and Easy Hikes in the Canadian Rockies*, Graeme Pole, 1996, Altitude Publishing Canada Ltd., Canmore, AB; *The West Beyond the West: A History of British Columbia*, Jean Barman, Revised Edition 1996, University of Toronto Press, Toronto; *Yoho National Park*, Kathryn Cameron, Lisa Chevalier, 1997, Kicking Horse Publications, Field, BC.

WEIGHTS AND MEASURES

Canada is metric. Officially. In everyday conversation, miles and kilometres, gallons (US gallons and quarts are five-sixths of their Imperial equivalents) and litres, Celsius and Fahrenheit may be used interchangeably, partially reflecting the non-metric system still used in the USA. Canada has long since joined the metric majority of the world.

WHAT TO TAKE

Absolutely everything you could ever need is available, so don't worry if you've left anything behind. In fact, most North American prices will seem low to overseas visitors: competition and oversupply keeps them that way. Pharmacies (chemists), also called drug stores, carry a range of products, from medicine to beach balls. Prepare a small first-aid kit before you leave home with tried and tested insect repellent, sunscreen cream and soothing, moisturising lotion. Carry all medicines, glasses and contraceptives with you, and keep duplicate prescriptions or a letter from your doctor to verify your need for a particular medication.

Other useful items to bring or buy immediately upon arrival are a water bottle, sunglasses, a hat or visor with a rim, an umbrella and light rain gear, an electrical travel adapter, string for a washing line, an alarm clock and a camera

47

DRIVING IN WESTERN CANADA

This chapter provides hints and practical advice for those taking to the road in the Rockies and the rest of Western Canada, whether in a hire car or RV, or in their own vehicle.

ACCIDENTS AND BREAKDOWNS

Holidays should be trouble-free, yet **break-downs** can occur. Signal and pull off to the side of the road where visibility is good and you are out of the way of traffic. Turn on hazard flashers or indicators and, if it is safe, get out and raise the bonnet and tie a white cloth to the radio antenna. Use flares or a torch (flashlight) at night. Change a tyre only when safely out of the traffic flow.

For emergencies; *tel: 911* (toll-free) from any telephone to reach the appropriate police, fire or medical services. Emergency call boxes are placed every 2–5 km on some highways and can be used to report breakdowns or a need for petrol. Give your phone number, location, problem and need for assistance.

Earthquakes and tornadoes (Alberta) are rare but potentially devastating driving hazards – see p. 30 and p. 45 for specific advice.

If involved in a **collision** or an **accident**, stop immediately and always stay at the scene until legal formalities have been taken care of or until police give you permission to leave. Telephone the nearest police agency without delay if there are injuries, deaths or physical damage to vehicles or other property exceeding $1000

($600 if the accident involves a motorcycle). Be sure to write down the names and contact information for any witnesses. Outside Calgary, Edmonton, Vancouver and Victoria, the RCMP (Royal Canadian Mounted Police) usually provide police services. Alberta and BC require drivers to provide their own driver's licence number, vehicle licence number, vehicle registration number, insurance carrier and policy number and contact information to the other driver(s) involved in the accident. It's also wise to obtain contact information for any passengers in the other vehicle. You will also have to provide full information to the police if an official investigation is required.

Accidents must also be reported to your car hire company and your own insurance carrier. Accidents involving vehicles registered in British Columbia must *also* be reported to the provincial-owned Insurance Corporation of British Columbia (ICBC); *tel: (800) 663-3051 or (604) 520-8222,* which insures all BC vehicles.

Fly-drive travellers should bear in mind the effects of **jet lag** on driver safety. This can be a very real problem. The best way to minimise it is to spend the first night after arrival in a hotel near the airport or in the nearest city and pick up your hire vehicle the next day, rather than picking up the car and setting out on a long drive shortly after walking off the plane.

CAR HIRE

Hiring a car or RV (camper) gives you the freedom of the road with a vehicle you can leave behind after a few weeks. Whether booking a fly-drive package with an agency or making independent arrangements, plan well in advance to ensure that you get the type and size of vehicle your heart desires. Free, unlimited kilometres is common with cars, less so with RVs.

Sheer volume in airport rental car turnover means that it is almost always cheaper to pick up the vehicle from an airport than from a downtown site, and to return it to the airport. A surcharge, called a *drop fee,* may be levied if you drop the vehicle off in a different location from the place of hire. When considering an RV, ask about one-way and off-season rates.

You will need a valid credit card as security for the vehicle, even if the rental is prepaid or is being paid for in cash. Before you leave the hire agency, ensure that you have all documentation for the hire, that the vehicle registration is in the glove box and that you understand how to operate the vehicle and all of its accessories.

For RVs, also get instruction books and a complete demonstration of all systems and appliances and how they affect each other. Using a microwave oven, for example, can interfere with other electrical appliances in some RVs. On other RVs, it is possible to exhaust the engine battery by running the refrigerator or other appliances unless you first trip a special safety switch.

Try to avoid hiring a car that exhibits the hire company name on a window sticker, on the fender (bumper) or licence plate frames. The company name is advertising for criminal attention.

Car size terminology varies, but general categories range from small and basic to all-frills posh: sub-compact, compact, economy, mid-size or intermediate, full-size or standard and luxury. Sub-compacts are often over-subscribed. Expect to choose between two- and four-door models. The larger the car, the faster it accelerates and the faster it consumes petrol. Some vehicles are equipped with four-wheel drive (4WD or 4x4), unnecessary except for off-road driving, which is not covered in this book.

Standard features on Canadian hire cars usually include automatic transmission, air conditioning (a necessity for summer driving) and cruise control, which sets speeds for long-distance highway cruising, allowing the driver to take his or her foot off the accelerator. Even with cruise control engaged, it is necessary to pay constant attention to steering, however. Current hire cars in Canada come with headlamps that remain lit while the vehicle is running.

DIFFICULT DRIVING

Fog

Fog is frequent along the Pacific coast, in the mountains and by lakes all year. It can be treacherous to drive in, resulting in several chain-reaction mass collisions each year. Never use bright headlamps in fog: the high beams blind oncoming drivers, the driver ahead of you and reflect back in your own eyes like a mirror. Use low beam headlamps instead. In British Columbia, when fog is intense, fog lamps may be used instead of headlamps.

Winter

The Coastal Range, the Columbia Mountains and the Rocky Mountains are formidable barriers, and never more so than during winter snowstorms. Visibility can be nil due to high winds and blowing snow; total white-out is not uncommon in the mountains and on Alberta's prairies.

Some roads simply close for the season, e.g. Alberta Hwy 40 between the north end of Peter Lougheed Provincial Park and Highwood House (closed Dec 1–June 14).

49

To check road conditions; *tel: (800) 663-4997* (British Columbia only). Auto club members in Alberta can call **AMA (Alberta Motoring Association)**; *tel: (800) 642-3810*. **Talking Yellow Pages**, listed in phone directories, also give current road information.

The speed limit when using chains or other traction devices such as snow tyres or studded tyres is generally 40–50 kph. Chains (tyre traction devices), good snow tyres or all-weather tyres are required on mountain passes Nov 1–Apr 30. Studded tyres are prohibited between May 1–Sept 30. Even if chains are not needed, snow and adverse conditions often require caution and slower-than-normal driving speeds.

Allow extra time to get to and through mountain areas. Local radio stations broadcast weather information. Lorry drivers and truck stops are also excellent sources of information for conditions ahead. *Never* drive where snow has fallen, or is anticipated, without carrying chains or other traction devices and knowing how to install them. Vehicles with flashing amber and red lights are snow plows, which will pull over about every 8 km to let traffic behind pass.

Accelerating or braking sharply when roads are wet, snowy, icy, or covered with nearly invisible black ice where water has frozen suddenly is almost certain to throw your vehicle into a skid. If your car goes into a skid, ease off the petrol, stay off the brakes and steer in the direction you want to go.

If only the vehicle's rear is skidding, accelerate gently and steer in the direction of the skid. Heavy rain can cause hydroplaning, when a film of water builds up between the tyre and road surface causing uncontrolled sliding.

When meeting oncoming traffic on narrow roads, the driver going uphill always has the right of way – if one vehicle has to back up to a wider spot in the road, it is safer to back uphill than downhill. If you get stuck in snow or mud, don't spin the wheels, but rock the car gently backward and forward by changing from forward to reverse gears until you begin to move. Accelerate and brake gently.

When hiring a vehicle for winter mountain driving, be sure that chains or other traction devices are included. Rental cars generally are not equipped with snow tyres or studded tyres. After a snowfall, authorities post signs at checkpoints indicating that chains are required. Failure to install chains can result in a fine – or in getting stranded. In mountain areas, petrol station attendants and independent entrepreneurs will install chains for a fee, but only if you already have a set. Pull over for installation and get a receipt for the service as well as the installer's badge or identification number. The speed limit when chains are required is 40–50 kph.

Apart from Coastal British Columbia, hired cars should be equipped with an electrical plug at the front engine compartment. When temperatures fall to -10°C or below, look for parking where the car can be plugged in and the engine block heater turned on to prevent engine freeze-up.

Useful items for winter driving are an ice scraper, a small shovel for digging out, warning flares, a rope for towing, sand, petrol anti-freeze and warm sleeping bags, extra clothing, food and water in case of long delays. Keep the petrol tank at least half-filled so you'll be able to go back should a road close unexpectedly. Keep warm and conserve fuel if you have stalled, but keep the car ventilated inside.

DISTANCES

Point-to-point distances can be vast in

Western Canada. To estimate driving time, plan on an average speed of 85 kph, without stops, slower in cities and mountains. CAA maps include charts with approximate driving times between major points. Use the sample driving distances and times on p.345 as guidelines, but allow for traffic or road construction delays and stops, especially in summer.

DRIVING AGE

Legal driving age is 16 in both provinces. Car hire agencies usually require drivers to be 25 years old.

DOCUMENTATION

Your home country driving licence is valid in Alberta and British Columbia, but most car rental companies require that drivers be at least 25 years of age. Some companies accept younger drivers, but only upon payment of an additional fee. Both jurisdictions require that drivers carry driving licences with them at all times while operating a vehicle. An **International Driving Permit** is helpful if your own driving licence is not in English, but is not required. If using your own automobile insurance, be sure to carry proof of cover and ownership (see Vehicle Insurance, p. 56).

INFORMATION

Automobile or motoring club membership in your home country can be invaluable. CAA clubs provide members of corresponding foreign clubs travelling to North America the reciprocal services that CAA members are eligible to receive abroad. Auto club services include emergency road service and towing; maps, tour guidebooks and specialist publications; touring services; road and camping information; discounts to attractions and accommodation. In general, if it is free to you at your home club, it should be free to you at CAA offices.

The CAA may charge for some services, such as maps and tour books. Emergency breakdown road service may not be available to some non-North American club members. For information on reciprocal clubs and services, contact your own club before leaving home. Carry your own club membership card with you at all times.

MOTORCYCLES

If *Easy Rider* is still your idea of North America, so be it. Motorcycles provide great mobility and a sense of freedom. Luggage space is limited, however; vast distances can make for long days in the saddle; and potholes, gravel, poor roads, dust, smog and sun are constant touring companions.

Hire motorcycles locally by finding a telephone directory listing. Helmets are required by law for both driver and passenger. By custom, most motorcyclists turn on their headlamps even in the daytime to increase their visibility.

PARKING

Public parking garages, parking lots and parkades (car parks) are indicated by a blue sign showing a 'P' with a directional arrow. Prices are posted at the entrance. Some city centre lots charge per half hour to disguise higher rates. Many urban car parks accept credit cards as well as cash. Most parking lots do not have attendants and require either credit cards, $1 or $2 coins.

In civic centres, shopping and downtown areas, coin-operated parking meters govern kerbside parking. The charge and time limit vary with the location. Compare parking garages against meter charges for the more economical choice.

Kerbs are colour-coded throughout Canada: *Red* means no stopping or parking

51

for any reason at any time; *Blue* is for disabled parking, permitted only with a special permit; *White* is for passenger pick-up and drop-off only, no parking; *Green* is for limited-time parking as indicated on the kerb (usually 10 mins); *Yellow* is a commercial zone for lorries and delivery vehicles with commercial number plates. White, green and yellow zones may be enforced only during specific hours such as Mon–Fri 0800–1800; check the kerb or nearby signs.

No parking is allowed within 5m of a fire hydrant, near a disabled person pavement ramp, in bus stop areas, in an intersection or zebra crossing (crosswalk), on the pavement, blocking a driveway or on a freeway except in emergencies.

If you park in violation of times and areas posted on kerb signs or on signposts nearby, expect to be issued with a citation – a ticket that states the violation, amount of the fine and how to pay it. If you do not pay, the car hire company will charge the ticket amount, plus any penalties for late payment, against your credit card. Fines range from a few dollars to several hundred dollars, depending on the violation and the locality.

Valet parking at garages, hotels, restaurants and events may be pricey. The parking attendant will expect an additional tip of $1–$5 when returning the car. Leave the car keys with the valet attendant, who will return them with the car.

PETROL/GAS

Petrol (gas) is sold in litres in Canada. Posted prices include taxes. Prices tend to be higher in some urban areas like Vancouver and lower in BC suburban areas and oil-producing Alberta, as well as on the US side of the US–Canada border. Prices can be astronomical in remote parts of Vancouver Island and in mountainous

areas, particularly in the Rocky Mountain National Parks.

Some stations offer full service – filling the petrol tank, washing the windscreen and checking motor oil, nearly always for the same price as self-serve. Full service attendants do not expect a tip, but a few may suggest 'topping off', or filling, the motor oil unnecessarily. Non-brand-name petrol stations in BC sometimes offer discounted prices at the pump even though prices posted on advertising signs match the prevailing rate in town. Most motorists use the more common self-service.

Nearly all Canadian cars and RVs require unleaded petrol. Leaded petrol is generally unavailable due to environmental controls. The three fuel grades are regular, super and premium. Use regular unless the car hire company recommends otherwise. A few vehicles use diesel fuel.

When petrol stations are more than a few kilometres apart, road signs usually indicate the distance to the next services. Open petrol stations are very well-lit at night; many chain stations are open 24 hours. Most stations accept cash, credit cards and traveller's cheques in local currency. Some stations accept only cash and may require payment before filling the tank. Many stations, especially in urban areas, do not accept $100 bank notes because of security concerns.

POLICE

Police cars signal drivers with flashing red or red and blue lights, and sometimes a siren. Respond quickly, but safely by moving to the right side of the road. Roll the driver's side window down but stay in the vehicle unless asked to get out. You have the right to ask an officer – politely – for identification, though it should be shown immediately. Have your driver's licence and car registration papers ready for inspection when requested. Officers normally check computer records for vehicle registration irregularities and the driver for theft, criminal records, or other driving violations. If cited for a violation, arguing with the officer will only make a bad situation much worse.

ROAD SIGNS

International symbols are used for directional and warning signs, but many are different from European versions. Most, but not all, highway signs are English/French bilingual. Signs may be white, yellow, green, orange, red, brown or blue. (A selection of signs is included in the Planning Maps colour section at the back of this book.)

Stop, give way, do not enter and wrong way signs are *red* and *white*. *Yellow* is for warning or direction indicators; yellow surrounded by yellow and black cross-hatch is warning of upcoming hazards like sharp blind curves. *Orange* is for roadworks or detours (temporary route changes sometimes called *diversions*). *Green* indicates freeway directions. *Brown* is an alert for parks, campsites, hiking, etc. *Blue* gives non-driving information, such as radio station frequencies for traffic or park information, or services in a nearby town.

Speed limits and distances are shown in kilometres. Dual metric/English-system signage is occasionally posted near the US border. Speed limit signs are *white* with black letters.

Traffic lights are red, yellow and green. Yellow indicates that the light will turn red; stop, if possible, before entering the intersection. A steady green arrow means you may turn in the arrow's direction. A flashing green light or arrow means you may turn in the direction of the arrow if the intersection is clear.

A favourite (and highly illegal) trick is to jump the red light, that is, enter the intersection when the signal is yellow and about to turn red. Major cities have installed red light cameras which photograph the licence plate of cars running a red light. Tickets are then mailed to the registered owner of the vehicle. Car hire companies automatically charge renters with red light violations and other traffic tickets.

Police can also cite you if you enter an intersection and you will not be clear of the intersection before the light turns red.

It is permitted to turn right at a red traffic light if there is no traffic coming from the left, i.e. as if it were a 'give way' sign, unless there is a sign specifically forbidding it ('No Turn on Red'). It is also permitted to turn left from a one way street onto another one way street on a red light after stopping completely, if traffic permits.

A flashing yellow light, or hazard warning, requires drivers to slow down; a flashing red light means stop, then proceed when safe.

SPEED LIMITS

The general highway speed limit is 80 kph in Alberta; 90 kph in BC. Some freeways are posted for 100 or 110 kph. The speed limit in towns and cities is 50 kph unless otherwise posted. In school zones, the speed limit is 30 kph. Many drivers exceed the speed limit on both highways and in urban areas by about 10 kph.

Police in both Alberta and BC use photo radar, a camera linked to a radar speed detector. If the radar detects a car exceeding the speed limit, the camera takes a photo and the speeding ticket is mailed to the vehicle's owner. Car rental agencies bill photo radar tickets, like other traffic citations, to the renter's credit card for payment.

53

ROAD SYSTEM

Freeways, often called expressways elsewhere in Canada, are motorways with controlled access. **Highways** have cross traffic interrupting the flow. East–west roads generally have even numbers, e.g., Hwy 20; north–south roads are odd, e.g. Hwy 99. The numbering system is not consistent, however. Hwy 3, the Crowsnest Highway, travelling east–west across southern BC and Alberta, and Hwy 1, the TransCanada Highway, crossing the entire country from the Pacific to the Atlantic, are major exceptions.

Highway rest areas commonly have toilets, garbage cans, picnic tables and, occasionally, public telephones. Rest stops in areas of historic or geographical interest have explanatory signs or maps. Use caution when leaving your vehicle at night and carry a torch (flashlight).

Local roads can range from satin-smooth to pitted, depending on local spending. Unpaved roads indicated on maps or described in this text may be treacherous. Ask at a petrol station or a truck stop about local road and weather conditions before venturing on them. Car hire companies may prohibit driving on unpaved roads or hold drivers responsible for any damage regardless of insurance or CDW/LDW cover (see p. 56).

RULES OF THE ROAD

Lanes and Overtaking

Drive on the right. Vehicles are left-hand drive. The lane on the left, the *Number 1 Lane,* is the fastest; the right is slowest; and cars enter or leave traffic from the right (unless otherwise indicated by signs). Drive in the right lane unless overtaking another vehicle and always overtake on the left side.

A solid white line at least 1 m from the kerb marks a special lane for bicycles, usually labelled 'Bike Lane'.

Most drivers pass on the left, but *cars may and will pass you on both sides in a multi-lane road.* For many drivers from the UK, this is the most unexpected and most confusing feature of North American roads. Use direction indicators when changing lanes, but don't be surprised if other drivers don't bother. Never turn against a traffic signal red arrow.

Make right turns from the right-hand lane after stopping at stop signs or traffic lights. Turn left from the most left-hand lane of lanes going in your direction, unless the turn is prohibited by a no-turn sign. Do not drive in areas marked for public transportation, such as bus lanes or trolley tracks, or in pedestrian walkways.

If the centre line down the middle of a two-way road is a double solid line, overtaking is not allowed. Overtaking is permitted if the centre line is broken. Always overtake on the left. Highways in mountainous areas or along long narrow stretches have occasional passing (overtaking) lanes. Driving or parking on pavements is illegal.

Main road drivers have the right of way over cars on lesser roads, but at the junction of two minor roads, cars to your right have the right of way when arriving at the same time you do.

Freeway Driving

Lanes are numbered from left to right: number one is the extreme left-hand lane closest to the centre, number two is the next lane to the right, and so on. An 'exit' or 'off ramp' is the slip road leading off the freeway; an 'entrance' or 'on ramp' leads onto the freeway. 'Metering lights' are traffic signals controlling ramp access, found only in congested urban areas.

When freeway traffic does flow, it flows smoothly and quickly. The posted speed

Some Western Canada Driving Terms

Big rig A large lorry, usually a tractor pulling one or more trailers.

Boulevard stop Slowing at a stop sign, but not coming to a full stop.

Crosswalk A marked pedestrian crossing or zebra crossing.

Connector A minor road connecting two freeways.

Curve Bend.

Divided highway Dual carriageway.

Diversion A detour or temporary alternate route, usually to avoid construction.

DUI Driving Under the Influence, usually of alcohol.

Exit Slip road leading off a freeway, also called an *off ramp*.

Fender Bumper.

Freeway Motorway.

Garage or **parkade** Car park.

Gas(oline) Petrol.

Grade Gradient, hill.

Highway Trunk road.

Hood Bonnet.

Metering lights Traffic signals controlling access to freeways, bridges, etc.

Motor Home Motor caravan.

Off ramp Slip road leading off a freeway, also called an *exit*.

On ramp Slip road leading onto a freeway, also called an *entrance*.

Pavement The road surface. A UK 'pavement' is a *sidewalk*.

Ramp Slip road.

Rent Hire.

Rubberneck(er) One who impedes traffic by slowing down to peer while driving past the scene of an accident or some other unusual event.

RV (*recreational vehicle*) Motor caravan.

Shoulder Verge.

Sidewalk Pavement.

Shift(stick) Gear lever.

Switchback Serpentine road.

Tailgate Driving too closely to the vehicle immediately in front.

Tow truck Breakdown lorry.

Traffic Circle Roundabout.

Traffic cop Traffic warden.

Trailer Caravan.

Truck Lorry.

Trunk Boot.

Unpaved road Gravel or dirt road – check car hire restrictions and additional liabilities when driving unpaved roads.

Windshield Windscreen.

Yield Give way.

limit is generally 90 or 100 kph; 10 kph faster is common in the fast (left-most) lane. The safest speed is that which matches the general traffic flow in your lane regardless of the posted speed limit. If you are exceeding the posted speed limit, however, you may be ticketed even if other traffic is keeping to the same speed.

When entering a freeway, *don't stop* on the ramp unless access is controlled by a traffic signal. Accelerate on the ramp and merge into the freeway flow. Cars that stop on the ramp are likely to be hit from the rear.

Freeways and urban commuter arteries may have **car-pool** or **HOV** (high occupancy vehicle) lanes for vehicles carrying several passengers. Road signs will specify the number of passengers required to use those speedier lanes. Car-pool lanes are normally marked with a white diamond symbol painted on the road bed. Special bus lanes are also marked.

Horns

Horns should be sounded only as a safety warning, and never near a hospital.

Pedestrians

Pedestrians have the right of way at all

zebra crossings and at all intersections, whether or not a pedestrian crossing is marked, and they may point across the street to their destination. In other places, vehicles have the right of way. Visitors from California, where pedestrians have the right of way at all times, are a special hazard in Canada; they tend to step blithely off the kerb in mid-block expecting traffic to halt. Some towns and cities cite pedestrians for jaywalking, crossing in the wrong spot. If a vehicle is involved in an accident with a pedestrian in a zebra crossing, the presumption of error usually lies with the driver.

Seat Belts

Seat belts must be worn in Alberta and BC by the driver and all passengers. In addition, children under six years or 18 kg must ride in approved child safety seats. RV passengers outside the driving compartment must be safely seated while the vehicle is in motion; passengers in the driving area (as well as the driver) must use seat belts.

Vehicle Insurance

Alberta and BC require that all vehicles on the road be insured. Minimum required cover in Alberta is $200,000 for third party liability; in BC, No-Fault Accident benefits and $200,000 third party liability protection. Vehicles found to be without proper insurance cover may be (and are) impounded until insurance is obtained and penalties paid.

In practice, considerably more cover is desirable. Overseas visitors hiring a car are strongly advised to take out top-up liability cover such as the Topguard Insurance sold by Thomas Cook in the UK, which covers liability up to US$1 million. (This is not to be confused with travel insurance,

which provides cover for your own medical expenses – see p. 56.)

US citizens driving their own vehicles into Canada should secure a free *Canada Non-Resident Inter-Provincial Motor Vehicle Liability Insurance Card* from their insurance company before departure to verify cover.

Car hire agencies try to sell their own insurance to renters, called **collision damage waiver**, or **CDW**, and **loss damage waiver, LDW**. Refusing CDW makes the renter personally liable for any damage to the vehicle. US and Canadian drivers using their own or hired vehicles should ask their insurance company if their cover extends to Alberta and BC *and* meets the required minimum insurance cover. If not, arrange for insurance before departure. In addition, some credit cards provide insurance cover for car rentals; check with your credit card issuer for details.

CDW is strongly recommended for drivers from outside North America, and often required as part of a fly-drive package. Sometimes it is paid for when booking the hire abroad, sometimes it is payable locally on picking up or returning the car. Special hire rates occasionally include CDW.

Vehicle Security

Lock it when you leave, lock it when you're inside and don't forget the windows. Never leave keys, documents, maps, guidebooks and other tourist paraphernalia in sight. Be mindful of anyone lurking in the back seat or in the house part of an RV, especially at night. Watch other drivers for strange behaviour, especially if you're consistently being followed. Never leave the engine running when you're not in the vehicle. Keep car keys with you at all times and always park in well-lit areas.

RAIL ESSENTIALS

Railway links east were the economic bait to lure Alberta and British Columbia into Canada in the last century. Rail travel is a scenic alternative for those who want to see the splendours of Western Canada close-up without watching the road.

Rail possibilities range from quick steam train excursions to trans-continental journeys. Best known is **Rocky Mountaineer**, *1150 Station St, 1st Floor, Vancouver, BC V6A 2X7; tel: (800) 665-7245 or (604) 606-7245; fax: (604) 606-7250; web: http://www.rkymtnrail.com,* offering scenic rail tours May–mid Oct between Vancouver and Jasper or Banff, linked with coach tours along the Icefield Parkway between Jasper and Banff. The Mountaineer offers two classes: Signature (economy) and dome cars in Gold Leaf (first) class. All rail travel is during daylight, with overnights in Kamloops, Jasper and/or Banff. Mid-summer trips often sell out a year in advance.

Steam train buffs pack **Kettle Valley Railway (KVR)**, *Box 1288, Summerland, BC, V0H 1Z0; tel: (604) 494-8422; fax: (604) 494-8452,* May–Oct, for 45-min runs along a section of the historic Kettle Valley Railway in Southern BC's Okanagan Valley, behind a rare 1924 Shay Steam Locomotive engine.

BC Rail, *Box 8770, Vancouver, BC V6B 4X6; tel: (800) 663-8238 or (604) 984-5246; fax: (604) 984-5505; web: http://www.bcrail.com/bcr,* run the **Royal Hudson** steam train May–Sept, along the shores of Howe Sound from North Vancouver to Squamish. The route is part of BC Rail's all-year system from North Vancouver to Prince George, crossing alpine meadows, glacial lakes and arid canyons that are largely inaccessible by road. Year-round **Cariboo Prospector** makes the entire journey. The **Whistler Explorer** is a May–Sept day trip between Whistler (north of Squamish) and Kelly Lake (north of Lillooet), one of the route's most scenic stretches. All three trains are heavily booked in summer. BC Rail also combines routes with VIA Rail, coach and air sectors into circle or one-way tours covering much of Western Canada.

BC's dinner train, **Pacific Starlight**, May–Oct, is a five-star restaurant in 1940s-vintage art deco cars, making a 3½-hr nightly return trip between North Vancouver and Porteau Cove (Howe Sound).

VIA Rail Canada, *2 Place Ville Marie, Montreal, PQ, H3B 2C9; tel: (888) 842-7245; fax: (506) 859-9343; web: http://www.viarail.ca,* is Canada's national railway. VIA operate from Edmonton to Jasper in Alberta and north-west through the Rockies to Prince Rupert, or south-west to Vancouver. VIA trains in the West offer first-class (Silver & Blue) and economy seating, as well as sleeping accommodation and restaurant/lounge facilities. The art deco **Canadian**, which runs between Toronto and Vancouver by way of Edmonton, Jasper and Kamloops, and the **Skeena**, between Jasper and Prince Rupert via Prince George, pass through the most scenic countryside during daylight. The **E&N** (Esquimalt & Nanaimo) **Railway** is a daily sightseeing service along Vancouver Island's eastern side.

Book the Canadian and Skeena at least 4 months in advance for June–Aug travel. *Canrailpass* is valid for up to 12 days travel within a 30-day period on the VIA system.

57

CRUISE ESSENTIALS

Cruise business is booming in Western Canada, fuelled by a growing realisation that British Columbia has some of the world's finest scenery – much of it accessible only by water. The province's original 'cruise line' is **BC Ferries**; *tel: (888) 223-3779 or (250) 386-3431; fax: (250) 381-5452; web: http://bcferries.bc.ca/ferries*. Routes from mainland BC to the Gulf Islands and Vancouver Island are every bit as scenic as the longer and more expensive sightseeing cruises sold in Vancouver, Victoria and other coastal towns.

The longer ferry runs, **Port Hardy–Bella Coola** (see p.313), **Port Hardy–Prince Rupert** (see p.326) and **Prince Rupert–Skidmore** (Queen Charlotte Islands, see p.332), *are* cruises, complete with licensed lounges, restaurants, showers, entertainment and sleeping facilities for voyages that can take 30 hours. What they don't have is luxury cabins, elegant dining and fancy clothes. Informality is the rule: the only ties on board are likely to be those around the necks of the Captain and Chief Purser. Flat, practical shoes are for walking up and down stairways, over gangways and down long corridors or equally long outside decks.

Most ferries operate all year. Clothes are the same loose, casual shorts, jeans, parkas, sandals, hiking boots and runners you'll see at any highway rest stop. Rain falls all year along the coast and almost certainly Oct–June. Carry a jumper and a jacket with a hood, even when weather forecasts call for sunny skies and 30°C temperatures.

Enjoy the scenery and fresh air from ferry decks in summer or from comfortable inside seating during stormy, cold winter trips. Smoking is not allowed inside BC Ferries.

Meal service is regular, if not elegant, running more to cafeteria lines than white linen tablecloths. Many passengers bring food for picnics on board. Ferries between Port Hardy and Prince Rupert have cabins (at extra cost). Other ferries have sleeper seats or allow passengers to pitch tents inside.

Every coastal town has its own fleet of boats for local freight and ferry service, fishing, scuba diving and sightseeing. Best known are the **MV Lady Rose** (see p.341), *Box 188, Port Alberni, BC V9Y 7M7; tel: (250) 723-8313; fax: (250) 723-8314*, which runs from Port Alberni to Ucluelet and Bamfield on the western coast of Vancouver Island; the **MV Uchuck III** (see p. 332), *Box 57, Gold River, BC V0P 1G0; tel: (250) 283-2325; fax: (250) 283-7582*, which supplies isolated communities along the north-west shore of Vancouver Island; and the **MV Aurora Explorer**, *Box 451, Campbell River, BC V9W 5C1; tel: (250) 286-3347; fax: (250) 286-1149*, which services the Inside Passage out of Campbell River. All three carry essential cargo and supplies as well as passengers.

Vancouver, home port for the May–Sept Alaska cruise season, has Canada's largest cruise ship fleet. Ships sail to Vancouver's Canada Place cruise terminal or tie up east along the harbour about 0700 and leave the same day around 1700. A few call at Campbell River, Prince Rupert, or other ports along the Inside Passage, but most are headed for Alaska on 4–14 day itineraries.

TOURING ITINERARIES

Much of the pleasure of a driving holiday lies in tailoring your itinerary to match *your* interests. By dividing Western Canada into recommended routes, this book is intended to make it easy to plan your ideal tour. By linking several routes, you can create a trip to suit your tastes following a tried and tested path which introduces you to the best the tour has to offer. This chapter begins with practical advice on tour planning, followed by three ready-made itineraries designed to show you as much as possible of Western Canada's tremendous variety in a two- or a three-week trip and a six-week grand circuit. Feel free to vary our suggestions, using the full range of information contained in the route descriptions. The remaining pages suggest features you can use to create a variety of self-planned theme tours.

PRACTICAL HINTS

Here are a few tips to make practicable routes easier to plan and fun to follow:

1. Use the most detailed maps possible. The colour map section at the end of this book is useful for planning and following the basic routes, but a more detailed road map is indispensable, especially if you intend to wander from the outlined routes, a practice we highly encourage. Stop at the nearest CAA office as soon as possible after arriving in Canada and pick up maps for the areas you will be touring.
2. Don't schedule too much driving each

day. Allow a conservative 85 km per hour of freeway driving and 55 km each hour on secondary roads to allow for unplanned stops. It's better to have more time to explore along the way than to be pressed to arrive each evening. Driving on secondary roads in mountains can be surprisingly slow.
3. Check weather and road reports. Most paved roads are open all year, but some secondary highways are closed Oct–Nov until May–June, depending on the weather, including Hwy 40 into Kananaskis, portions of Hwy 1A west of Lake Louise, both in Alberta, and the road to the top of Mt Revelstoke, BC. Even major highways are occasionally closed for a few hours following major storms. Avalanche control can also close roads for several hours, particularly the Coquihalla Hwy (Hwy 5) between Hope and Kamloops and Rogers Pass (TransCanada Hwy 1), both in BC.
4. Unless accommodation is pre-booked, arrive each night with plenty of time to find a place to sleep. Advance bookings are essential for Banff and Jasper National Parks, Vancouver, Victoria, Whistler, Calgary around Stampede time (July) and the entire region in summer and at holiday weekends.
5. Allow time at the end of the trip to get back to the departure city the day before a scheduled flight home. Airlines don't hold planes for a single carload of late arrivals. Passengers travelling on cheap fares who miss a flight will have to buy new tickets home – at full price.
6. Give serendipity a chance by not planning in too much detail. Allow time to spend a few extra hours, or an extra day, in

some unexpected gem of a town or to turn down an interesting side road. If you want your days pre-planned in 15-min increments, you'll be happier on a fully escorted coach tour than on a self-drive holiday.

THE BEST OF THE CANADIAN ROCKIES

The following circular tours start and end in Calgary, but can be reversed or picked up in any convenient spot. Routes in BC can easily be combined with routes outlined in Thomas Cook's Touring Handbook *On The Road around the Pacific Northwest.*

These tours combine several recommended routes, with a few digressions and short-cuts added. Suggested overnight stops are in bold type. Adapt the tours freely or use the same cut-and-paste method to personalise your own tours.

14 Days

For those who want (or need) to 'do' Western Canada in one whirlwind bout of driving, it *can* be done. Just be sure to allow a few days at home to recover!

Day 1: **Calgary** (pp. 64–74).
Day 2: **Calgary** (pp. 64–74).
Day 3: Calgary to **Waterton Lakes National Park** (Calgary to Lethbridge, pp. 141–147, and Lethbridge to Cranbrook, pp. 157–164).
Day 4: Waterton to Head-Smashed-In Buffalo Jump and **Kananaskis** (Lethbridge to Cranbrook, pp. 157–164, and Lethbridge to Kananaskis, pp. 148–156).
Day 5: Kananaskis to **Banff/Canmore** (Calgary to Banff, pp. 78–86).
Day 6: Banff/Canmore to Kootenay National Park, Fort Steele and **Cranbrook** (Cranbrook to Banff, pp. 165–172).
Day 7: Cranbrook to **Osoyoos** (Cranbrook to Castlegar direct, pp. 173–180, Castlegar to Osoyoos, pp. 181–184).

Day 8: Osoyoos to **Vancouver** (Vancouver to Osoyoos, pp. 251–256).
Day 9: **Vancouver** (pp. 226–236).
Day 10: Vancouver via the Fraser Canyon to Kamloops, Salmon Arm and **Revelstoke** (Vancouver to Osoyoos, pp. 251-256, Hope to Kamloops scenic, pp. 257–268, Kamloops to Revelstoke, pp. 199–205).
Day 11: Revelstoke to Mt Revelstoke and Glacier National Parks and **Golden** (Revelstoke to Lake Louise, pp. 208–217).
Day 12: Golden to Yoho National Park, Jasper National Park and **Jasper** (Revelstoke to Lake Louise, pp. 208–217, Banff to Jasper, pp. 87–103).
Day 13: Jasper to **Edmonton** (pp. 104–107).
Day 14: Edmonton to **Calgary** (Edmonton to Red Deer, pp. 122–126, Red Deer to Calgary, pp. 127–133).

21 Days

Three weeks is a more realistic, though still rushed time to see Western Canada. Add another week or two to see the less travelled north-western reaches of the region.

Day 1: **Calgary** (pp. 64–74).
Day 2: **Calgary** (pp. 64–74).
Day 3: Calgary to **Drumheller** (Red Deer to Calgary, pp. 127–133).
Day 4: Drumheller to Dinosaur Provincial Park and **Lethbridge/Fort Macleod** (Red Deer to Calgary, pp. 127–133, Calgary to Lethbridge, pp. 141–147).
Day 5: Lethbridge/Fort Macleod to **Waterton Lakes National Park** (Lethbridge to Cranbrook, pp. 157–164).
Day 6: **Waterton Lakes National Park**.
Day 7: Waterton to Head-Smashed-In Buffalo Jump and **Kananaskis** (Lethbridge to Kananaskis, pp. 148–156).
Day 8: Kananaskis to **Banff/Canmore** (Calgary to Banff, pp. 78–86).

Day 9: Banff/Canmore to Lake Louise, Yoho National Park and **Golden** (Banff to Jasper, pp.87–103, Revelstoke to Lake Louise, pp. 208–217).
Day 10: Golden to **Glacier National Park**, **Mt Revelstoke National Park** and **Revelstoke** (Revelstoke to Lake Louise, pp. 208–217).
Day 11: Revelstoke to Sicamous, Salmon Arm and **Kamloops** (Kamloops to Revelstoke, pp. 199–205).
Day 12: Kamloops via Cache Creek and Fraser Canyon to **Vancouver** (Vancouver to Hope, pp. 251–256, Hope to Kamloops scenic, pp. 257–268).
Day 13: **Vancouver** (pp. 226–236).
Day 14: Vancouver by ferry to **Victoria** (Vancouver to Victoria, pp. 269–273).
Day 15: Victoria to **Nanaimo** (pp.294–298).
Day 16: Nanaimo (by ferry) to Horseshoe Bay and **Whistler** (Vancouver to Whistler, pp. 242–246).
Day 17: Whistler to **Cache Creek** (Whistler to Kamloops, pp. 247–250).
Day 18: Cache Creek to **Clearwater** and Wells Gray Provincial Park (Whistler to Kamloops, pp. 247–250, Valemount to Kamloops, pp. 221–225).
Day 19: Clearwater to **Valemount** (Valemount to Kamloops, pp. 221–225).
Day 20: Valemount to Mt Robson Provincial Park, Jasper National Park and **Jasper** (Jasper to Valemount, pp. 218–220).
Day 21: Jasper via the Icefields Parkway to Banff and **Calgary** (Banff to Jasper, pp. 87–103, and Calgary to Banff, pp. 78–86).

The Grand Tour
Six weeks allow enough time to enjoy the Rocky Mountains and the rest of Western Canada without total exhaustion. It's impossible to cover every route in this volume without several days of back-track-

ing, e.g. Port Hardy-Bella Coola *and* Port Hardy–Prince Rupert, so pick and choose the areas that seem the most interesting. If time allows, take a train between Vancouver and Calgary, hire a houseboat on Shuswap Lake or spend a few days helicopter hiking in the Cariboo, Bugaboo or Purcell Mountains.

Day 1: **Calgary** (pp. 64–74).
Day 2: **Calgary**.
Day 3: Calgary to **Drumheller** (Red Deer to Calgary, pp. 127–133).
Day 4: Drumheller to Dinosaur Provincial Park and **Lethbridge/Fort Macleod** (Red Deer to Calgary, pp. 127–133 and Calgary to Lethbridge, pp. 141–147).
Day 5: Lethbridge/Fort Macleod to **Waterton Lakes National Park** (Lethbridge to Cranbrook, pp. 157–164).
Day 6: **Waterton Lakes National Park**.
Day 7: Waterton to Head-Smashed-In Buffalo Jump and **Kananaskis** (Lethbridge to Kananaskis, pp. 148–156).
Day 8: Kananaskis to **Banff/Canmore** (Calgary to Banff).
Day 9: Banff/Canmore to Kootenay National Park, Radium Hot Springs and **Radium** (Cranbrook to Banff, see p.165–172).
Day 10: Radium to Fort Steele and **Cranbrook** (Cranbrook to Banff).
Day 11: Cranbrook to Creston, Kootenay Bay, ferry across Kootenay Lake to Balfour and **Nelson** (Cranbrook to Castlegar scenic, pp. 173–180).
Day 12: Nelson to Castlegar and **Grand Forks** (Cranbrook to Castlegar and Castlegar to Osoyoos, pp. 181–184).
Day 13: Grand Forks to Rock Creek and **Kelowna** (Castlegar to Osoyoos and Osoyoos to Kelowna, pp. 185–191).
Day 14: Kelowna to **Penticton** (Osoyoos to Kelowna).
Day 15: Penticton to Oliver, Osoyoos,

Manning Provincial Park and **Hope** (Osoyoos to Kelowna and Vancouver to Osoyoos, pp. 251–256).

Day 16: Hope via the Fraser Canyon to **Lillooet** (Hope to Kamloops scenic, pp. 257–268, and Whistler to Kamloops, pp. 247–250).

Day 17: Lillooet to **Whistler** (Whistler to Kamloops).

Day 18: Whistler to **Vancouver** (Vancouver to Whistler, pp. 242–246).

Day 19: **Vancouver** (pp. 226–236).

Day 20: Vancouver by ferry to **Victoria** (Vancouver to Victoria, pp. 269–273).

Day 21: **Victoria** (pp. 274–284).

Day 22: Victoria to **Nanaimo** (Victoria to Nanaimo, pp. 294–298).

Day 23: Nanaimo to **Campbell River** (Nanaimo to Campbell River, pp. 299–302).

Day 24: Campbell River to **Port Hardy** (Campbell River to Port Hardy, pp. 303–311).

Day 25: Port Hardy via BC Ferry Discovery Coast route to **Bella Coola**. (Ferry operates summer only. Port Hardy–Prince Rupert ferry routes operate all year, Port Hardy to Bella Coola, pp. 312–316).

Day 26: Bella Coola to **Nimpo Lake** (Bella Coola to Kamloops, pp. 317–324).

Day 27: Nimpo Lake to **Riske Creek** (Bella Coola to Kamloops).

Day 28: Riske Creek to **Wells** and Barkerville (Bella Coola to Kamloops).

Day 29: Wells to **100 Mile House** (Bella Coola to Kamloops).

Day 30: 100 Mile House to **Kamloops** (Bella Coola to Kamloops).

Day 31: Kamloops to **Sicamous** (Kamloops to Revelstoke, pp. 199–205).

Day 32: Sicamous to **Revelstoke** and Mt Revelstoke National Park (Kamloops to Revelstoke).

Day 33: Revelstoke to Glacier National Park and **Golden** (Revelstoke to Lake Louise, pp. 208–217).

Day 34: Golden to Yoho National Park and **Lake Louise** (Revelstoke to Lake Louise).

Day 35: Lake Louise via the Icefields Parkway to **Jasper** (Banff to Jasper, pp. 87–103).

Day 36: Day trip from **Jasper** to Mt Robson Provincial Park (Jasper to Valemount, pp. 218–220).

Day 37: Jasper to **Edmonton** (Jasper to Edmonton, pp. 104–107).

Day 38: **Edmonton** (pp. 108–118).

Day 39: Edmonton to **Elk Island National Park** (Edmonton Circuit, pp. 119–121).

Day 40: Edmonton to **Calgary** (Edmonton to Red Deer, pp. 122–126, and Red Deer to Calgary, pp. 127–133).

TOP PARKS

Banff National Park, *north-west of Calgary, AB*; is the best-known park in Canada. For millions of visitors, Banff *is* the Canadian Rockies, with its sculpted peaks surrounding the Bow River Valley crowned by the stately Banff Springs Hotel.

Barkerville Heritage Town, *Hwy 26, east of Barkerville and Wells, BC*, is the preserved and reconstructed capital of the Cariboo Gold Rush of the 1860s. Costumed interpreters bring the town to life in summer, although the site is open all year.

Dinosaur Provincial Park, *east of Calgary, AB off Hwys 1 and 551,* has yielded more individual dinosaur skeletons than any other spot on earth. The Royal Tyrrell Museum, in Drumheller, holds and displays hundreds of finds from the park.

Elk Island National Park, *east of Edmonton, AB on Hwy 16*, created in 1906, was Canada's first wildlife sanctuary for large mammals, including herds of both plains and woodland bison, elk, deer, moose and coyotes. The entire park is fenced, as much to keep humans out as to keep the animals away from surrounding agricultural lands.

Fort Rodd Hill/Fisgard Lighthouse National Historic Site, *14.5 km west of Victoria, BC, off Hwy 1A*, was a coastal artillery fortress until 1956. The 1860 Fisgard Lighthouse keeper's house is a museum.

Fort Steele Heritage Town, *Hwys 93/95 north of Cranbrook, BC*, is the preserved and reconstructed centre of the Kootenay Gold Rush of the 1880s and 1890s. The site is open all year, with costumed interpreters to bring the old buildings to life in summer.

Glacier National Park, *TransCanada Hwy 1 between Golden and Revelstoke, BC*, surrounds 1330 m Rogers Pass, encircled by icy spires and subject to more avalanches than any other paved highway in Canada.

Jasper National Park, *north of Banff National Park, AB, along the Icefields Parkway*, is the second crown jewel in Canada's National Park system. Jasper National Park offers even more vertical peaks, hanging glaciers and booming cataracts than its southerly neighbour, Banff National Park; major sights are accessible off the Icefields Parkway.

Kootenay National Park, *in BC, surrounding Hwy 93 west of Banff National Park*, is Canada's third most popular Rocky Mountain National Park. Kootenay has the greatest concentration of peaks in the Rocky Mountain park system, most of them 2800–3100 m. Don't miss the Paint Pots, source of yellow and ochre pigments used by First Nations throughout Western Canada.

Mt Revelstoke National Park, *Trans-Canada Hwy 1, just east of Revelstoke, BC*, is

BC's only drive-up mountain ascent. Wildflower displays are spectacular July–Aug.

Pacific Rim National Park, *west coast of Vancouver Island, BC*, protects some of the most unspoiled scenery on Vancouver Island. The Long Beach area, the most accessible of three units, stretches between Ucluelet and Tofino. Most of the park is accessible only by boat or on foot.

Manning Provincial Park, *between Hope and Penticton, BC, on Hwy 3*, protects 67,000 hectares of mountains, forest and alpine meadows for hiking, fishing, horse riding, cycling, camping and Nordic skiing.

Stanley Park, *downtown peninsula, Vancouver, BC*, is one of the world's finest urban parks with 80 km of roads and trails, gardens, an aquarium, restaurants and splendid views of Vancouver from all sides.

Waterton Lakes National Park, *Hwy 5 on the Montana border, south of Calgary, AB*, with its American twin Glacier National Park, forms one of the most diverse and scenic ecological regions in the entire Rocky Mountains. The park has more than 250 km of walking trails.

Wells Gray National Park, *north of Hwy 5 near Clearwater, BC*, is BC's largest provincial park and home to Canada's fourth tallest cataract, Helmcken Falls. A single road leads from Helmcken Falls to the foot of Clearwater Lake, with innumerable hiking trails leading into the wilderness.

Yoho National Park, *in BC, Trans-Canada Hwy 1 east of Banff National Park*, has more peaks over 3000m (twenty-eight), than any of the Rocky Mountain national or provincial parks. The name means 'awe' in the Cree language, appropriate for this land of steep, glacial valleys, pounding waterfalls, jade lakes, crystal caves, natural bridges, icy peaks, hoodoos and alpine meadows.

CALGARY

Calgary is a plains cow town-cum-oil town, an hour's drive east of the Canadian Rockies and the annual July host to one of the most renowned rodeos on earth – the Calgary Stampede. Farmers, ranchers, businesspeople, oil barons and bankers make Calgary Alberta's busiest city. Calgary's own museums and ambience are reason enough to spend several days exploring urban attractions before venturing off to Canada's Rocky Mountain National Parks.

TOURIST INFORMATION

Calgary Convention & Visitors Bureau, *237 8 Ave S.E., Calgary, AB T2G 0K8; tel: (800) 661-1678 or (403) 263-8510; fax: (403) 262-3809*, books some accommodation through the toll-free number. **Visitor Service Centres: Calgary Tower Centre**, *Centre St and 9 Ave S.E.,* open 0800–2000 (May–early Sept), 0830–1700 (Sept–May), and at **Calgary International Airport**, *Arrivals Level* in the covered wagon near baggage claim, open daily 1000–2200.

WEATHER

The dry warmth of the plains extends westward to Calgary, bringing cooler summer evenings June–Aug, with occasional thunderstorms. Winter, Dec–Feb and beyond, may be a blizzard one day or brilliant blue skies the next, with a disconcerting 20–25°C increase in temperature from warm **Chinook winds** blowing up to 100kph. Much like the south-moving *foehn*, which warms the northern side of Europe's Alps, the Chinook pushes warm Pacific air up the western slopes of the Rocky Mountains to meet a mass of Arctic air risen from the prairies to the Rockies' ridgeline, the Continental Divide. The warm air condenses into an arch which pushes the cold eastward, warming everything beneath it. Spring, Mar–May, predictably rainy, is an almost balmy average 9°C, while fall can last till Nov in warmer years.

Prepare for warm sunny days, the possibility of rain, cool evenings and, in winter, tote a warm coat, boots, gloves, hat and thermal underwear. Check Calgary temperature; *tel: (403) 263-3333,* or get a weather report with advisories from **Environment Canada**; *tel: (403) 299-7878.*

ARRIVING AND DEPARTING

By Air

Handling 7 million passengers annually, **Calgary International Airport (YYC)**, *2000 Airport Rd N.E.; tel: (403) 735-1372 or (403) 735-1200,* is 17 km north-east of downtown Calgary. The **Calgary Convention & Visitors Bureau Visitor Service Centre** is open daily 1000–2000 in a covered wagon on the Arrivals Level. Roving volunteer **White Hatters** in white cowboy hats, white shirts and red vests greet arrivals, answer questions and solve problems daily, 0800–2200.

Panoramic photographs splash the spectacular scenery of Alberta's parks and historic sites in the International Arrivals area. Baggage carousels have tableaux of pioneers, the Calgary Stampede, an *Albertosaurus* dinosaur, a Calgary Zoo gorilla and

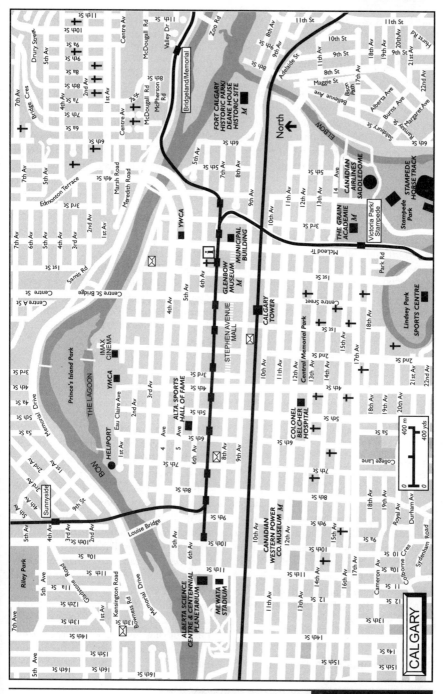

First Nations dancers. Luggage trolleys are free.

Departures Level facilities include lockers and **Kidsport Just Plane Fun**, with a gamesroom, a mock runway and switches and dials for a tyke-size jumbo jet. The airport has a picnic area – even a 7.5-km bike path for watching flight arrivals and departures at close range. Pick up a free *Discover Calgary* newspaper for seasonal information on local events and transportation.

The **Calgary Airporter**, *tel: (403) 531-3909,* provide YYC transport (Bay 3, Arrivals Level) from 0630–2330, between seven downtown hotels, single $8.50, return $15. **Calgary Transit**, *tel: (403) 262-1000,* run bus Route 57 (Bay 15, Arrivals Level) half-hourly 0540–1730, 2130, 2200 and 2230 from the Whitehorn C-Train station. The taxi queue ($20 to downtown) is outside Canada Customs, Arrivals Level. Many downtown hotels have courtesy shuttles.

Car hire is opposite baggage claim; exit the terminal, cross to the parkade to pick up cars. Follow City Centre signs south from the Airport Terminal, then turn right onto *McKnight Blvd* and go left on *Centre St* south to Downtown Calgary.

By Car

North of Bow River and Downtown Calgary, **Canada 1**, the TransCanada Highway, goes west to Banff and Vancouver and east over plains where dinosaurs once roamed. Hwy 2 runs north from Fort Macleod, jogs right at *Glenmore Trail,* then turns left, continuing north on the *Deerfoot Trail* to Red Deer and Edmonton. For downtown access, continue straight north of *Glenmore Trail* on *Macleod Trail,* Hwy 2A, to City Centre.

By Train

Rocky Mountaineer Railtours, *tel:* *(800) 665-7245,* offer two-day daylight rail excursions to or from Calgary to Vancouver, via Banff and Kamloops, May–mid Oct.

By Bus

Greyhound Lines, *877 Greyhound Way S.W.; tel: (800) 661-8747* or *(403) 260-0877,* and **Red Arrow**, *205 9 Ave S.E.; tel: (800) 232-1958* or *(403) 531-0350,* connect to Red Deer and Edmonton. **Brewster**, *tel: (800) 661-1152,* offer tours of the Rockies from Calgary via Banff.

GETTING AROUND

Public Transport
Calgary Transit, *240 7 Ave S.W.; tel: (403) 262-1000,* open Mon–Fri 0600–2300, Sat–Sun 0800–2130, has buses and light rail transit C-Trains, with stops every four to five blocks. Train platform ticket dispensers require exact change; adults $1.60, $5 for an all-day pass, with free transfers from bus drivers. A **Seventh Ave – Downtown free fare zone** extends between *City Hall* and *8 St S.W.*

Driving in Calgary
Centre St divides the city into east and west. The **Bow River** separates north and south on the quadrant, though the river turns abruptly south-east, east of the Calgary Zoo. The **Elbow River** snakes south-west of the Bow River around Stampede Park to the large Glenmore Reservoir and into Tsuu T'ina Nation Reserve.

Avenues are east–west; *streets* run north–south. The grid system allows for the same combination of avenue and street to intersect in the S.W., S.E., N.W. and N.E. directions, so verify addresses before setting off. Outlying housing estates road names begin with the same letter as the housing estate.

Major expressways, called *trails,* offer easiest traffic flow. The 40-km *Deerfoot Trail* is designed with 100kph speed limits for fastest north–south flow. Rush hour is 0715–0815 and 1645–1745. During the July Calgary Stampede, traffic is congested from mid-afternoon through early evening and on weekends near Stampede Park. **Calgary Herald Talkies**, *tel: (403) 243-7253, ext 4100,* has road information.

Downtown Calgary has one-way traffic, congested at rush hours. There are parkades every block or two in downtown, with cheapest parking from 1800–0600. Enquire at the Calgary CVB Visitor Service Centre for free summertime visitor 3-day meter parking passes. Some parkades and surface parking lots have discounted Sat prices, and on-street parking is free Mon–Sat from 1900 and all day on Sun.

Self-Transport
Stephen Ave, *8 Ave S.W./S.E.,* is pedestrian-only 0600–1800, offering a pleasant-weather walk from *Olympic Plaza* west to Eaton Centre (Devonian Gardens), then north on **Barclay Mall** to Eau Claire Market dining and recreation. The **Plus-15 skywalk** is a 16-km long elevated, enclosed walkway through downtown, interlaced with 55 bridges to connect government buildings, museums, attractions, oil company offices and department stores. Though designed for inclement weather, over 100,000 people access the skywalk daily, avoiding street-level traffic 15ft ('Plus-15') below.

Most of Calgary's 210 km of paved bike paths, also used by in-line skaters, follow the tree-lined Bow and Elbow Rivers. The Calgary CVB and equipment hire shops sell a trail map, $1. Per-day bike hire is $20, blades $10. The **University of Calgary**, *tel: (403) 220-5038,* hires sports equipment and camping gear.

STAYING IN CALGARY

Accommodation
Nearly half of Calgary's 8700 rooms are downtown. Other hotels are at or near the airport, while *Macleod Trail S.* and Hwy 1 west of town near the University of Calgary are good places to find cheaper as-you-go lodging. The **Calgary CVB** books some area accommodation; *tel: (800) 661-1678.*

Book well in advance for the first two weeks in July during the Calgary Stampede. At major downtown hotels, summer rates are higher than the rest of the year. The **Bed & Breakfast Association of Calgary**, *Box 1462, Station M, Calgary, AB T2P 2L6; tel: (403) 543-3900; fax: (403) 543-3901,* books 130 moderate rooms amongst 57 Bed and Breakfasts in the Greater Calgary area.

Chain hotels in Calgary include *BW, CI, CP, CS, DI, EL, Hd, HI, HJ, Ma, QI, Rm, Sh, S8, TL* and *Wt.*

CP Calgary Airport Hotel, *2001 Airport Rd N.E.; tel: (800) 441-1414 or (403) 291-2600; fax: (403) 250-8722,* expensive, is opposite the Arrivals Level. Most other airport area hotels are moderate; the **Pointe Inn**, *1808 19 St N.E.; tel: (800) 661-8164 or (403) 291-4681; fax: (403) 291-4576,* closer to downtown, is budget.

Adjacent to Calgary Tower, **The Palliser**, *133 9 Ave S.W.; tel: (800) 441-1414 or (403) 262-1234; fax: (403) 260-1207,* is CP's sophisticated, pricey, 1914 landmark. A moderate downtown choice, the **Prince Royal Suites Hotel**, *618 5 Ave S.W.; tel: (800) 661-1592 or (403) 263-0520; fax: (403) 262-9991,* has complete kitchens.

South of downtown, *Macleod Trail* has numerous motels, including the moderate, comfortable **Travelodge Macleod Trail**,

9206 Macleod Trail S.; tel: (403) 253-7070; fax: (403) 255-6740.

Eating and Drinking

Calgary, in the heart of Alberta Beefland, has several famed cowboy restaurants. **Ranchman's**, *9615 Macleod Trail S.; tel: (403) 253-1100*, open Mon–Sat, is a budget steakhouse, with walls chock-a-block with trophy saddles, gear and photos from past rodeo champions. Top Country & Western singers and honky-tonk bands play to a wooden dance floor crowned with a race-winning 1952 Stampede chuckwagon. Bobsleighs from the film *Cool Runnings* adorn the ceiling.

Cured ribs done to grandparents' recipes lure diners to budget–moderate **Billy MacIntyre's Cattle Company**, *#500 Brentwood Mall N.; tel: (403) 282-6614* or *7104 MacLeod Trail S.; tel: (403) 252-2260*. **Buzzards Cowboy Cuisine**, *140 10 Ave S.W.; tel: (403) 254-6959*, pushes beer with its budget barbecue and al fresco dining. **The Great Alberta Barbecue**, *west on Hwy 1; tel: (888) 533-3276* or *(403) 686-9443*, open 1130–1400 and 1700–2000 (May–Oct), offers a moderate steak, chicken and ribs buffet.

For lunch and afternoon tea, **Deane House Historic Site and Restaurant**, *806 9 Ave S.E.; tel: (403) 269-7747*, open Mon–Fri 1100–1700, Sat–Sun 1000–1700, is the former home of Fort Calgary's 1906–1914 Commanding Officer. **Naturbahn Teahouse**, *Canada Olympic Park; tel: (403) 247-5465*, is open mid June–Aug Mon–Sat 1100–1600, and year-round for Sun brunch 0930–1330.

Eau Claire Market has fish to Italian, a **Hard Rock Café**, pubs and coffeehouses. Try excellent vegetable appetisers and margaritas at **Joey Tomato's Kitchen**, *208 Barclay Parade S.W.; tel: (403) 263-6336*. North across the Lagoon in Prince's Island Park in a beautiful wooded glen, the **River Café**, *tel: (403) 261-7670*, open 1100–2200 (Mar–Dec), serves wood-fired Canadian Native candied salmon, sundried blueberries, goat cheese and fresh maple lemonade.

Try Canadian wine and appetisers at **Mescalero**, *1315 1 St S.W.; tel: (403) 266-3339*. The **Stephen Avenue Mall** has a variety of restaurants and coffee shops. **Uptown 17 Avenue SW**, from *4 St S.W.–14 St S.W.*, has restaurants, cafés, bistros and nightclubs, including **Koliba Moravian Restaurant**, *1112 17 Ave S.W.; tel: (403) 245-2827*, serving sauerkraut soup, smoked goose breast, veal in dill sauce and chicken paprikatch with Bohemian dumplings.

Muffin Break, *Southland Crossing Shopping Centre, 9737 Macleod Trail S.W.; tel: (403) 253-0255*, has excellent breakfast muffins. A Chinatown institution, **Golden Happiness® Bakery Ltd.**, *#101, 111 2nd Ave S.E.; tel: (403) 263-4882*, open daily 0730–2000, has scrumptious custard buns.

Communications

All hotels accept mail. Pick up General Delivery mail at **Calgary Central**, *207 9 Ave S.W., Calgary, AB T2P 2G8; tel: (403) 974-2078*. **Calgary South**, *6100 Macleod Trail S.E.; tel: (403) 974-2241*, is the other main Canada Post office. There is a post office at **Calgary International Airport**, Arrivals Level.

Money

There are **Thomas Cook bureaux de change** at *Calgary Airport* and at *3625 Shagnappi Trail NW, Market Mall*.

The *Calgary Herald*'s Fri *What's Up* section and the free review-filled Thur *FFWD>>* (*Fast Forward*) newspaper list culture and

68

nightlife offerings. *WHERE Calgary* monthly magazine has events throughout the region. For **First Nations** events; *tel: (403) 261-3022.*

Calgary Centre for Performing Arts, *205 8 Ave S.E.–220 9 Ave S.E.; tel: (403) 294-7455,* offers tours of its five theatres, $2. Within the complex, **Alberta Theatre Projects**' legitimate theatre and musicals perform Jan–July in Martha Cohen Theatre; *tel: (403) 294-7475,* with **Theatre Calgary**'s classic plays, comedies and large-scale musicals run Sept–May, in Max Bell Theatre; *tel: (403) 294-7440,* and the alternative **One Yellow Rabbit Performance Theatre**, *tel: (403) 244-9177,* is in the Big Secret Theatre.

Theatre Junction, Dr Betty Mitchell Theatre in Jubilee Auditorium, *1415 14 Ave N.W.; tel: (403) 205-2922,* presents well-known modern plays and Canadian playwrights, Wed–Sat Oct–May. The **Pleiades Theatre** at the Calgary Science Centre, *701 11 St S.W.; tel: (403) 221-3707,* presents Agatha Christie and local playwrights' murder mysteries.

Calgary Centre for Performing Arts Jack Singer Concert Hall is home to the **Calgary Philharmonic Orchestra**, *tel: (403) 571-0270.* **Calgary Opera**, *tel: (403) 262-7286* or *(403) 264-5614,* and **Alberta Ballet**, *tel: (403) 245-4222,* perform at Jubilee Auditorium, *1415 14 Ave N.W.; tel: (403) 297-8000* or *(403) 297-2249.*

Stage West Theatre Restaurants dinner shows, *727 42 Ave S.E.; tel: (403) 243-7077,* open nightly Tues–Sun with matinées Wed and Sun, offer Broadway headliners in musicals and farces, $27–$65. **Lunchbox Theatre**, *205 5 Ave S.W.; tel: (403) 265-4292* or *(403) 265-4297,* plays noontime comedies Mon–Sat, $9. Equally unserious are solo acts and competitive team improvisation Fri–Sun nights at **Loose Moose Theatre**, *2003 McKnight*

Blvd N.E.; tel: (403) 291-5682, $6–$8, less for students. **Yuk Yuk's Komedy Kabaret**, *5940 Blackfoot Trail S.E.; tel: (403) 258-2028,* and **Jester's Comedy Club**, *239 10 Ave S.E.; tel: (403) 269-6669,* cater to broad humour.

Calgarians particularly indulge an interest in Country & Western music at high volume during the Calgary Stampede, but **Ranchman's**, *9615 Macleod Trail S.; tel: (403) 253-1100;* **Rockin' Horse Saloon**, *7400 Macleod Trail S.; tel: (403) 255-4646;* and **Dusty's Saloon**, *1088 Olympic Way S.E.; tel: (403) 263-5343,* wail and stomp year-round.

Rock, folk and jazz clubs are clustered downtown along *17 Ave S.W.* The old-fashioned **King Edward Hotel**, *438 9 Ave S.E.; tel: (403) 262-1680,* is renowned as the 'Home of the Blues'.

Sports

Glacier-fed, robin's egg-blue Bow River, named for riverbank trees used by Aboriginal people for hunting bows, is famed for catch-and-release rainbow trout.

National Hockey League **Calgary Flames**, *tel: (403) 777-2177* or *(403) 777-4646,* play Oct–Apr in **Canadian Airlines Saddledome**, *Stampede Park.* The **Stamps**, the Canadian Football League **Calgary Stampeders**, *tel: (403) 289-0205* or *(403) 289-0258,* play American-style football late June–Oct at **McMahon Stadium**, *1817 Crowchild Trail N.W.* Minor league **Calgary Cannons**, *tel: (403) 284-1111,* play baseball Apr–Aug at **Burns Stadium**, *2255 Crowchild Trail N.W.*

Spruce Meadows, *178 Ave S.W., R.R. 9, Calgary, AB T2J 5G5; tel: (203) 974-4200,* is open daily for the public to enjoy its thoroughbred horse pastures and stables, a picnic, or winter pond ice-skating. Spruce Meadows hosts three prestigious equestrian show jumping tournaments: the

Oil in Alberta

First Nations used petroleum products in Alberta long before the internal combustion engine made oil a profitable commodity. In 1787, Alexander Mackenzie reported natives living near the Clearwater and Athabasca Rivers mixing natural bitumen with fir tree resin to make a caulking for canoes. More than a century later, JK 'Peace River Jim' Cornwall attempted to extract oil from the **Athabasca Oil Sands**, sometimes called **Athabasca Tar Sands** or **McMurray Oil Sands**, north of **Fort McMurray**. Vast deposits of oil sands at McMurray and **Cold Lake** have made Canada the world's leading producer of synthetic crude oil.

Even Cornwall's Athabasca Oil Sand project was a latecomer. About 1895, John George 'Kootenai' Brown, the first warden of what would become **Waterton Lakes National Park**, noticed oil on the surface of **Cameron Creek**. Brown and a partner skimmed the oil from the creek, bottled it, and sold it in **Fort Macleod**. When local entrepreneurs realised what Brown had discovered, they drilled Canada's first oil well in 1902 – Waterton's trees were protected by Forest Reserve status, but mining and oil drilling were allowed. When the **Rocky Mountain Development Company** struck oil at 311m, Oil City promptly sprang up on the shores of Cameron Creek, and died just as quickly when high transportation costs and low production closed the well.

Okotoks rancher William Herron fared better. In the early 1900s, he bought land along the Sheep River where natural gas had bubbled to the surface for centuries, formed **Calgary Petroleum Products**, and began drilling for oil. In 1914, he struck oil and sparked the Turner Valley oil boom. Alberta became the largest producer of oil and natural gas in the British Empire and Calgary the wealthiest city west of Toronto. Turner Valley oil was running out by the end of World War II, but natural gas production continued into the 1960s. Fortunately for Alberta industry, **Imperial Oil Ltd** struck the first of thousands of gushers near the small community of **Leduc**, 27 km south-west of Edmonton, in 1947. The Leduc Field catapulted Alberta into the top ranks of oil producers worldwide. The original oil derrick from Imperial Leduc #1 well is on display at the **Edmonton Tourism Visitor Information Centre**, 2404 *Calgary Trail Northbound, S.W.* Edmonton became the industry's new supply centre, while Calgary continued its traditional role as financier. Both cities reached for the skies with waves of new skyscrapers as oil prices skyrocketed in the 1970s.

Although falling oil prices brought economic depression in the 1980s, Alberta recovered in the 1990s. Oil still produces about 20% of revenues in the province. North Edmonton remains a petroleum processing and support centre. Oil refineries and subsidiary industries line Hwy16, the Yellowhead Highway, north and east from the city.

Some forecasts project depletion of Alberta's wells by 2006. Other forecasters are projecting new discoveries even larger than the existing fields. If new technology and rising prices allow economic production from the McMurray and Cold Lake Oil Sands, Alberta could remain a major oil producer well into the next generation.

70

National in early June; the North American, late June–early July; and the Masters in Sept, adults $5, children free, for each event. **Stampede Park**, *17 Ave S.E. and 2 St S.E.; tel: (403) 261-0214,* has thoroughbred horse racing Apr–June and harness racing late July–mid Oct, $2.25.

Race City Speedway Motorsport Park, *114 Ave and 68 St S.E.; tel: (403) 264-6515,* open May–Sept, has drag racing and other events. When snow disappears, golf becomes viable on numerous courses. Book 4 days in advance for 6 municipal golf course tee times; *tel: (403) 221-3510.*

Canada Olympic Park (COP), *88 Olympic Park Rd S.W.; tel: (403) 247-5452; fax: (403) 286-6608,* is a major sports facility. Using the 1988 Olympic Site, mid Nov–mid Mar, winter activities include alpine and Nordic skiing, snowboarding and a 1-min, 90-kph ride down the Olympic bobsleigh track (Oct–Feb, $39). Ride the 40-kph luge Nov–Feb, or June–Aug, $13. Mountain bikes race in summer. The **Olympic Hall of Fame and Museum**, *tel: (403) 247-5454,* open year-round, has 1924–1994 Winter Games exhibits and bobsleigh and ski jump simulators; admission can be combined with a COP tour which includes the view from the 90-m Ski Jump Tower.

Ice skate downtown in winter at **Olympic Plaza**, 1000–2100, or at the **University of Calgary's Olympic Oval**, *tel: (403) 220-7954.*

SHOPPING

Calgary wouldn't be 'Cowtown', without western wear *de rigueur* during the Calgary Stampede. White cowboy hats, modelled after Stetsons, have been an icon since Calgary Stampeder fans sported the white *chapeaux* when the team won the 1948 Grey Cup football championship from Ottawa in Toronto. During Stampede, stacks of white hats appear in most shops; **Smithbilt Hats Ltd.**, *1235 10 Ave S.W.; tel: (403) 244-9131* or *(800) 661-1354,* make some of the best.

Western gear shops sell cowboy hats, pearl-stud and plaid shirts, denim jeans, bandannas, belts, buckles and – crucial to cut the proper image – cowboy boots. **Alberta Boot Mfg. Co., Inc.**, *614 10 Ave S.W.; tel: (403) 263-4605,* sells 10,000 pairs of fancy boots, most about $250, bearing names like Burgundy Python, Cognac Ostrich and Brandy Kangaroo.

The Plus-15 skywalk system links several downtown shopping centres, including **Calgary Eaton Centre**, *Stephen Ave Mall (8 Ave S.W.) and 4 St S.W.; tel: (403) 298-4311,* open Mon–Wed, Sat 1000–1800, Thur–Fri 1000–2000, Sun 1200–1700, which connects to **Eaton's** department store, and via 4th-Level Devonian Gardens, to another shopping area, **TD Square**, *7 Ave S.W. and 2 St S.W.; tel: (403) 221-0600.* **The Bay**, *200 Ave S.W.; tel: (403) 262-0345,* is Canada's other venerable department store chain.

Find art, books and unique clothing on **Uptown 17**, *17 Ave S.W.* between *4 St S.W.–14 St S.W.,* and **Kensington Rd N.W.**, between *10 St N.W.–13 St N.W.*

Peruse First Nations art at the **Glenbow** (Museum) **Shop**, *130 9 Ave S.E. (Stephen Ave Mall); tel: (403) 268-4119;* **Bearclaw Gallery**, *1301 17 Ave S.W.; tel: (403) 228-6533;* **Galleria Arts & Crafts**, *1141 Kensington Rd N.W.; tel: (403) 270-3612;* and **Arctic Canada**, *1109A Kensington Rd N.W.; tel: (403) 270-3999.*

SIGHTSEEING

In 1875, scarlet-coated North West Mounted Police Troop 'F', built **Fort Calgary** at the confluence of the Bow and Elbow Rivers. During three years of service, constables received $0.75 per day, free clothing, kits, rations, transportation and lodging in barracks, with 160 acres of land at the end of the tour of duty.

Fort Calgary Historic Park, *750 9 Ave S.E.; tel: (403) 290-1875,* preserves the ruins of the 1875–1914 NWMP fort. Palisades and fort buildings are being reconstructed above the archaeological site. **Fort Calgary Interpretive Centre**, open May–mid Oct, adults $3, children 7–17 $1.50, covers early city history.

The NWMP, enlisting the aid of Catholic missionaries, participated in First Nations negotiations for Treaty Number

Cowboys and The Calgary Stampede

The cowboy is an icon of the Canadian West. Rugged, individualistic, strong, honest, taciturn, romantic and more at home on the open range than in a formal parlour, the cowboy has become a central figure in the myth of the Wild West.

The West was considerably less wild in Canada than it was below 'The Line', as the US-Canadian border was called in the late 19th century. The American West *was* a lawless place, opened for economic exploitation with little thought to law and order. Canada sent the North West Mounted Police west to tame the prairies before settlers were allowed in.

Cowboys were working American ranges as early as the 1830s, following the long-standing tradition of *vaqueros,* cattle drovers employed by colonial Spain in Texas, New Mexico, Arizona, California, Mexico and much of South America. The original 16th-century *vaqueros* set a style that endures today: wide-brimmed hats, fringed shirts, tall boots with spurs, leather or fur leggings called *chaps* (pronounced shaps), lariat ropes and handguns.

Ranches appeared in British Columbia as early as the 1860s, most often established by American cowboys who recognised prime grazing land as they drove herds north from Oregon and Washington States to feed miners in the Cariboo and later gold fields. Alberta's first cowboys appeared in the 1880s, lured by employment on immense ranches controlled from Eastern Canada and cheap land upon which they could hope to establish their own cattle empires. Many of Alberta's early cowboys were retired NWMP troopers loathe to leave the West.

American cowboys traditionally rode armed in a land that was without effective law enforcement. Cattle rustling and similar crimes were common. North of The Line, the NWMP were an effective deterrent to similar activities. While many Canadian cowboys carried handguns as well as rifles for hunting and protection against predators, their weapons were seldom carried openly. Disputes tended to be settled with fisticuffs, not bullets.

Most cowboys were young, single and ready to prove their mettle. The traditional cowboy contest was the **rodeo**, a test of riding, roping, wrestling and other skills needed on the open range. Canada's most famous rodeo, the annual **Calgary Exhibition and Stampede**, was launched in 1886. In 1912, an American trick roper named Guy Weadick came to Calgary and convinced Calgary's four leading ranchers that their local rodeo could become the greatest frontier show the world had ever seen. George Lane, AE Cross, AJ MacLean and Patrick Burns put up $100,000 and the Stampede was born. In 1912, 14,000 people paid to see a show that had been drawing a few hundred attendees. Interrupted by financial difficulties and World War I, Weadick was back in 1919 and the Stampede turned its first profit. In 1923, he added the first chuckwagon races. The Stampede has never looked back.

The 10-day affair in early July is Canada's richest rodeo, attracting professional cowboys and more than a million spectators from around the world. Quaint to outsiders, the **chuckwagon races**, or 'chucks', derived from settlers protecting food wagons. Four wooden wagons pulled by teams of horses, each with four outriders, do a figure-8 around barrels before racing 'like hell' for one-half mile.

The rodeo is grim, gruelling, the life-threatened quick reaction of a man or boy riding bareback, riding a bronc (unbroken horse), riding a bull, roping a calf, or wrestling a steer. Women compete in a race around three barrels in a cloverleaf pattern.

The Calgary Stampede is as much midway, eating, perusing exhibits and visiting the First Nations Village encampment as it is feats of riding and animal-taming skill. It's also a cowboy/cowgirl costume party which extends to Calgary's cowboy bars and main downtown plazas and free morning pancake feeds served from the back of competing chucks.

Seven, by which Sisika (Blackfoot), Kanai (Blood), Pikan (Peigan), Nakoda (Stoney) and Tsuu T'ina (Sarcee) agreed in 1877 to exchange central and southern Alberta land for small reserves, education, medical care, farm supplies, food, ammunition for hunting and annual payments of $5 per person. By 1879, buffalo had disappeared. Natives, particularly Sisika, were persuaded by missionaries that a railway was benign and beneficial. Instead, First Nations people starved.

By 1883, the CPR reached Calgary, a 75-soul hamlet of tents, wooden buildings, two stores, a Commanding Officer's house and the NWMP barracks. CPR publicity about 'Traversing the Great Wheat Region of the Pacific North West' drew farmers and businesses to 'the Rich Grazing Grounds and Cattle Ranches at the Eastern Base of the Rocky Mountains'.

Heritage Park, *1900 Heritage Dr. S.W.; tel: (403) 259-1910,* open daily 0900–1700 (mid May–early Sept) with free breakfast from 0900–1000 weekends (Sept–mid Oct), adults $10, children $6, steam train, wagon and Glenmore Reservoir sternwheeler rides each $2 extra, has 150 mostly original 1910-era buildings, with ladies baking, a blacksmith, a Mountie, a Main Street, a bakery and a popular restaurant in the Wainright Hotel.

Calgary Tower Visitor Service Centre has excellent self-guided heritage walking tour booklets of golden sandstone buildings along **Stephen Avenue**, the 1905–1914 **Connaught-Beltline District**, *12 Ave S.W.–17 Ave S.W. and 1 St S.W.–11 St S.W.,* and the **Mission District** near the Elbow River, a melting pot for French, First Nations, Métis, Chinese, Irish, Scots and English a century ago. Crime solving is revealed at the **Calgary Police Service Interpretive Centre**, *Police Administration Bldg, 316 7 Ave S.E., 2nd Level; tel: (403)*

268-4566, open Mon, Wed 0900–1600, Sat 1100–1600, Sun 1200–1600, adults $2.

The **Glenbow Museum**, *130 9 Ave S.E.; tel: (403) 268-4100,* open 0900–1700 (May–Oct), Tues–Sun 0900–1700 (Nov–Apr), adults $8, students $6, is Calgary's Cowboy Museum, though collections extend to First Nations artefacts, the 1885 Métis Riel Rebellion, Mounties, immigration, oil discovery, armour, West African and Asian exhibits and plains migration.

The 190.8-m needle that dominates downtown views is **Calgary Tower**, *101 9 Ave S.W. and Centre St S.; tel: (403) 266-7171.* Take a 62-second elevator to the **Observation Deck**, adults $5.50, children 13–18 $3.75, snack at **Tops Bar & Grill** or dine in the **Revolving Panorama Dining Room.**

Indoor 2½-acre **Devonian Gardens**, *317 7 Ave S.W., Level 4, TD Sq.; tel: (403) 268-3888,* open daily 0900–2100, is filled with local and tropical plants and flowers, perfect for strolling or joining downtown workers with a picnic lunch.

Outdoor Dorothy Harvie Gardens complement the **Calgary Zoo, Botanical Garden and Prehistoric Park**; *tel: (403) 232-9372,* open daily 0900–dusk (May–Sept): adults $9.50, children 2–17 $4.75; (Oct–Apr): adults $8, children 2–17 $4. Birds fly around the Tropic Garden, quail run around the Butterfly Garden, meerkats and leopard tortoises roam the Arid Garden, and ferns, bromeliads and epiphytes adorn the Rainforest. Zoo denizens include Dall and bighorn sheep, cougars, wolves, caribou, grizzly and black bears. Don't miss the Prehistoric Park walk through authentic-looking badlands 'peopled' with life-sized Mesozoic dinosaur models on the rampage with downtown Calgary's skyscrapers visible nearby. The zoo complex is bisected by the Bow River at St George's Island.

73

5555

Prince's Island, north across the Bow River from downtown and **Eau Claire Market**, is a grassy walking, biking and blading area, popular for concerts and picnics. **Fish Creek Provincial Park**, *Bow Bottom Trail; tel: (403) 297-5293*, is Canada's largest urban park, with walking and cycling, coyotes, badgers and deer, and numerous birds, including red-tailed hawks, great blue herons and bald eagles. The *Self-Guiding Bike Tour* park brochure covers forests, native prairie grasslands and original homesteads and ranches. Next to **Bow Valley Ranch**, *tel: (403) 297-5293*, a centre interprets the flora, fauna and history of the Bow River around Fish Creek. **Inglewood Bird Sanctuary**, *9 Ave S.E. and Sanctuary Rd; tel: (403) 269-6688*, favoured by wood ducks, has Bow River walking trails.

The **Calgary Science Centre**, *701 11 St S.W.; tel: (403) 221-3700*, open daily 1000–2000 (mid May–Labour Day), Tues–Sun 1000–1700 (mid Jan–mid May), adults $9, children 13-17 $7, under 13 $6, has interactive science exhibits, multi-media films and murder mysteries in the **Pleiades Theatre**, *tel: (403) 221-3797*. In summer, professional actors and razzle-dazzle special effects cleverly illustrate computer technology and other science.

Energeum, *650 5 Ave S.W.; tel: (403) 297-4293*, open Mon–Fri and (Aug only) Sun 1030–1630, shows off Alberta's energy industry – oil drilling, natural gas, coal and hydroelectricity. The **Grain Academy**, *Stampede Park Roundup Centre; tel: (403) 263-4594*, open Mon–Fri 1000–1600 (Apr–Sept) Sat 1200–1600, Alberta's agriculture museum, has an automated model train to demonstrate wheat processing and transport. Both museums are free.

The **University of Calgary**, *2500 University Dr. N.W.; tel: (430) 220-3147*, offers free campus tours Mon–Fri 1030 and 1330 (May–Aug). For campus events; *tel: (403) 220-3199*. Numismatic fans will find an ancient world coin collection on campus in the **Nickle Arts Museum**, *434 Collegiate Blvd N.W.; tel: (403) 220-7234*, open Tues–Fri 1000–1700, Sat-Sun 1300–1700, adults $2, children $1, free Tues.

Military buffs enjoy the Western Canadian perspective of the **Museum of the Regiments**, *4520 Crowchild Trail S.W.; tel: (403) 974-2850*, open Thur–Tues 1000–1600, with exhibits from Lord Strathcona's Horse (Royal Canadians), Princess Patricia's Canadian Light Infantry, The King's Own Calgary Regiment and the Calgary Highlanders. The **Naval Museum of Alberta**, *1820 24 St S.W.; tel: (403) 242-0002*, open Tues–Fri 1300–1700, Sat–Sun 1000–1800, features ship models, a submarine periscope and Royal Canadian Navy fighter planes. Restored aircraft are displayed at the **Aero Space Museum of Calgary**, *4629 McCall Way N.E.; tel: (403) 250-3752*, open daily 1000–1700, adults $6, students $3.50.

Tsuu T'ina Museum, *3700 Anderson Rd S.W., on the Sarcee First Nation Reserve; tel: (403) 238-2677*, open Mon–Fri 0800–1200 and 1300–1600, has tribal artefacts, including beadwork and clothing.

Chinese men from the Guangdong Province settled in Calgary after working on the CPR. **Calgary Chinese Cultural Centre**, *197 1 St S.W.; tel: (403) 262-6071*, is Chinatown's landmark, its dome a canny reproduction of Beijing's Temple of Heaven Hall of Prayers. The lower level history museum is open daily 1100–1700, adults $2, children $1.

Take a hot air balloon over Calgary year-round, weather permitting; **Balloon Dimensions; tel: (403) 254-5246; fax: (403) 254-8142**, and **Balloons over Calgary**, *7136 Fisher St S.E.; tel: (403) 259-3154; fax: (403) 255-3256*.

CALGARY CIRCUIT

Calgary is blessed with an interesting, compact downtown and main arteries, called trails, which help traffic flow to outlying attractions. Allow 1½ hours, longer during rush hour, to drive this 55-km circuit, which cannot be reversed due to downtown one-way traffic restrictions.

Consider parking at an inexpensive parkade

to explore small areas on foot, as this circuit does, by starting from Calgary Tower, a downtown landmark. The Plus-15 skywalk system permits winter visitors to stay warm while browsing the 600 shops, restaurants and museums along 16 km of downtown.

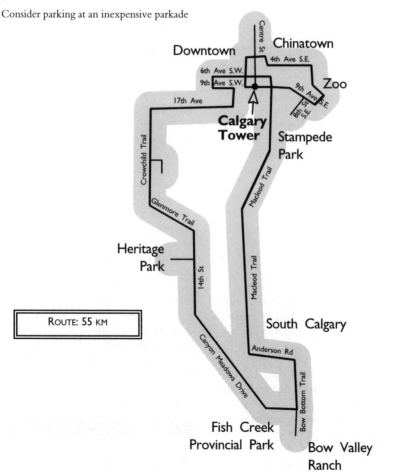

ROUTE: 55 KM

75

DOWNTOWN ON FOOT

Begin from the needle-shaped **Calgary Tower**, *101 9 Ave S.W.* and *Centre St S.*, with the Visitor Service Centre on the ground level. Stroll to several attractions before getting in the driver's seat.

Walk across the street to the **Calgary Marriott Hotel**, *110 9 Ave S.E.*, and the adjacent **Glenbow Museum** and **Calgary Centre for the Performing Arts**. Exit onto **Stephen Avenue Mall**, *8 Ave S.E.*, and **Olympic Plaza** (**Rope Square** during the Calgary Stampede), an outdoor event venue; the pond which becomes a winter ice-skating rink is to the right. On the north side of Olympic Plaza is the **Seventh Avenue Transit Mall**. The old and new city hall/municipal buildings are east.

Graceful sandstone buildings to the left, west along *Stephen Ave*'s daytime pedestrian-only mall, shelter small businesses and dozens of restaurants, pubs and coffee houses. The Plus-15 skywalk, 15 ft above street level, protects pedestrians and shoppers in a plastic-enclosed walkway over 16 km of the downtown area. Enter **TD Square** near *2 St S.W.*, and take the elevator to **Devonian Gardens** on the 4th Level. Exit into the Eaton Centre, then descend 5 m to ground level onto **Barclay Mall**, *3 St S.W.* Walk north seven blocks to **Eau Claire Market**'s dining and cinemas, or take a picnic lunch across a bridge over the Bow River to **Prince's Island Park**, for a fine view of downtown Calgary.

Return to Eau Claire Market, then walk left on tree-lined *Riverfront Ave*. **Calgary Chinese Cultural Centre** pagoda dome is right, near the massive lions guarding entry to **Centre Street Bridge**. Continue two blocks east on *Riverfront Ave,* then turn right onto *Macleod Trail*. The **City Hall** buildings are six short blocks south;

Olympic **Plaza** is right. Turn right on *9 Ave S.E.* to return to **Calgary Tower**. Take the elevator to the Observation Deck for views of downtown glass skyscrapers, the Canadian Airlines Saddledome, the prairies to the east and the Rockies to the west, before picking up your car from the parkade to begin the driving circuit.

DOWNTOWN

Exit Tower Centre Parkade onto *10 Ave S.W.* and go right for half a block. Turn right on *1 St S.W.* for one block and right again past **Calgary Tower** on *9 Ave S.W.* for three blocks.

Go left onto *Macleod Trail S.E.*, staying in the left lane. **Stephen Avenue Mall**, *8 Ave S.E.*, a pedestrian area, is left; to the right is the modern blue glass **City Hall** building flanked just north by the **Old City Hall** in golden sandstone. One block north, the **7 Ave Transit Mall** free zone and Calgary Transit C-Train platforms are to the left.

Turn left on *6 Ave S.E.* and go west thirteen blocks. Go left on *11 St S.W.* one block to *7 Ave S.W.* and the right-hand entrance to the **Calgary Science Centre**. Continue south on *11 St S.W.* Immediately right is the castle-like red brick 1916 **Merwata Armoury**, now a centre for military training and recreation.

Go left on *9th Ave S.W.* Skyscrapers with golden glass are left. Turn right on *5 St S.W.,* and go under an overpass. The **Alberta Boot Mfg. Co. Inc.**, is on the right. Turn right onto *17 Ave S.W.*, **Uptown 17 Avenue**, nine blocks of trendy eateries, coffee houses, galleries, bookstores and boutiques. Murals adorn sides of buildings.

SOUTH CALGARY

Turn left on *24 St S.W.* The **Naval Museum of Alberta** and the **H.M.C.S.**

Tecumseh are left. Two blocks beyond, *24 St S.W.* veers left into *Crowchild Trail,* south.

Take the *Flanders Ave* turn off to cross over *Crowchild Trail.* Go right on *Arras Dr.,* following signs to the **Museum of the Regiments**.

Return to *Crowchild Trail* and continue south. Follow signs to go left, south-east, on *Glenmore Trail,* crossing a short causeway over **Glenmore Park Reservoir**. Go right on *14 St S.W.* Look for the Canadian Pacific locomotive engine on the right at the entrance to **Heritage Park**.

Leave Heritage Park at *Heritage Dr.,* turning right to go 4 km south on *14 St S.W.* Turn left on *Canyon Meadows Dr.,* which winds 5 km around the northern side of **Fish Creek Provincial Park**, Canada's largest urban park. Turn right 2.5 km on *Bow Bottom Trail* to **Bow Valley Ranch**, with the provincial park's interpretive centre close by.

Return north 4 km on *Bow Bottom Trail* to go left 3 km on *Anderson Rd S.E.* Turn right onto *Macleod Trail S.* and go 7.5 km north to the main entrance of **Stampede Park**, on the right at *12 Ave S.E.*

EAST OF DOWNTOWN

Continue three blocks north on *Macleod Trail S.*, then turn right onto *9 Ave S.E.* 'King Eddy', the **King Edward Hotel** known as the 'House of Blues', is on the left at *4 St S.E.* **Fort Calgary** and its **Interpretive Centre** are three blocks east on *9 Ave S.E.*

Continue east, crossing the Elbow River via the 9th Avenue Bridge, otherwise known as the 'Duck' Inglewood Bridge. **Deane House Historic Site and Restaurant**, technically part of Fort Calgary, is on the immediate left. Go right onto *8 St S.E.* across the railway crossing, then turn right to go up *17 Ave S.E.* to (unsigned)

Scotman's Hill, in the Ramsay District. Turn left onto *Salisbury St* for a panoramic view of downtown highrise buildings, with the Elbow River below. On a clear day, the Rockies are visible far west of downtown Calgary. **Stampede Park** and the saddle-shaped **Canadian Airlines Saddledome** are below to the left.

Go around the block on *Ramsay Dr.* and return to *17 Ave S.E.* Go right, then turn left on *8 St S.E.* Go right on *9 Ave S.E.* to the shops and pleasant restaurants of the Inglewood District.

Turn left on *12 St S.E.*, crossing over two Bow River bridges to the **Calgary Zoo, Botanical Garden and Prehistoric Park**. There is a large parking area a few hundred metres left on *Memorial Dr.*

RETURN TO DOWNTOWN

Leave the zoo on *Memorial Dr. W.,* continuing 3.5 km towards downtown. Take the exit for *4 Ave S.E.* into **Chinatown**. **Dragon City** shopping mall is on the right. Go right on *Centre St.* Before reaching the imposing stone lions flanking the **Centre Street Bridge**, turn left onto *2 Ave S.W.,* with the flamingo pink **Calgary Chinese Cultural Centre** and its Temple of Heaven Dome ahead.

Go right on *1 St S.W.* for one block, then left onto *Riverfront Ave S.W.,* and left one block on *2 St S.W.* to **Eau Claire Market**, *2 Ave S.W.* and *2 St S.W.; tel: (403) 264-6460,* a Cineplex Odeon cinema and Calgary's **IMAX® Theatre**, *tel: (403) 974-4629.*

Turn right onto *2 Ave S.W.* for one block. Barclay Parkade is on the right. Go left on winding *3 St S.W.,* south along the **Barclay Mall**. Turn left on *9 Ave S.W.,* passing a regal Canadian Pacific locomotive engine and the **Palliser Hotel** on the right, to return to **Calgary Tower**.

CALGARY–BANFF

The craggy Rocky Mountains breach the horizon west of Calgary on a clear day, a breathtaking sheer rise of rock. Calgary is the gateway closest to the Rockies. Banff, at the southern end of the Banff and Jasper Rocky Mountain National Parks, is about 1½ hours drive, 125 km, from the city.

Leave Alberta's plains at Calgary, going west through ranchland, farmland and First Nations areas to the sheer grey foothills. Stay in Canmore, just outside Banff National Park, for less expensive lodging and access to the lakes and scenery on the western side of Kananaskis Country.

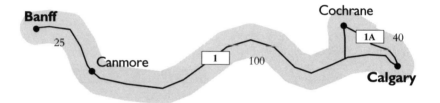

78

DIRECT ROUTE: 125 KM

ROUTE

From **Calgary Tower**, take *9 Ave S.W.* east for two blocks, go left for five blocks on *Macleod Trail,* then left on *4 Ave S.W.* for two blocks, and right onto *Centre St,* going north. Turn left onto *16 Ave N.W.,* which becomes TransCanada Hwy 1, and follow it for 101 km to Banff Townsite. **Cochrane** is 13 km north of TransCanada Hwy 1, on Hwy 22. Hwy 1A, the old highway, still runs from Calgary to Banff via Cochrane. Petrol is cheapest on Calgary's outskirts.

BUSES

Greyhound Lines of Canada operate four trips a day, taking 5¼ hrs. OTT table 120.

TOURIST INFORMATION

The **Travel Alberta Visitor Info-Centre**, *Canmore Service Rd, west end of Canmore near Banff National Park,* open year-round, has information on Alberta, BC and Montana, the national parks, the Icefields Parkway and weather.

CALGARY TO COCHRANE

Canada Olympic Park (COP), *88 Olympic Park Rd S.W.; tel: (403) 247-5452,* built for the 1988 Winter Olympic ski jump, luge and bobsled events, rises up the hill to the left, crowned by the 90 m ski jump. COP tours can be combined with the **Olympic Hall of Fame and Museum**. COP activities include winter skiing, snowboarding and bobsleigh, summer mountain biking and luge in both seasons (see Calgary, pp.64–74).

Barely a minute's drive west on the left at *101 St N.W.*, is **KOA Calgary West**, *Box 10, Site 12, Hwy 1, Calgary; tel: (800) 562-0842* or *(403) 288-0411,* open Apr 15–Oct 15, with 350 pitches and shuttle service to downtown Calgary. For an easy return to Calgary, turn left on Hwy 563, *Old Banff Coach Rd,* which *did* connect Calgary with Banff a century ago.

Ten km from Calgary on the left, **Calaway Park**, *tel: (403) 240-3822,* open late May–Thanksgiving, seniors $10, adults 7–49 $17.50, children 3–6 $12, has amusement rides and camping facilities. The Rockies appear as a solid barrier to the west. On private hilltops surrounding the highway are medicine wheels, numerous spokes radiating from a central rock pile, possibly used for solstice ceremonies, though First Nations groups no longer know the function of the 5-millennia-old sites. Take Hwy 22 north to Cochrane for ranching and rodeo history.

COCHRANE

Tourist Information: Cochrane & District Chamber of Commerce, *PO Box 1416, Cochrane, AB T0L 0W0; tel: (403) 932-6810,* operate **Westerton Cabin Visitor Information Centre**, open daily Victoria Day–Labour Day 0900–1800; the CC has information the rest of the year at **Cochrane Station**, *Bay # 6, 205 1st St E.* Cochrane has several in-town motels, with abundant area camping.

Western storefronts hint at ranching history. **Cochrane Ranche Provincial Historic Site**, *tel: (403) 932-2902,* open year-round, honours the first big leasehold ranch in Western Canada, an 1881 2-year attempt at raising cattle on a 189,000-acre spread, the launching of Alberta's beef industry. The Visitor Centre is open 1000–1800 June–Labour Day.

Under the watchful eye of the cowboy-on-his-horse 'Men of Vision' statue are many trails on the site's 150 acres. Cochrane Ranche is a popular picnic spot and includes **The Western Heritage Centre**, *tel: (403) 932-3514,* open 0900–2000 Victoria Day–Labour Day, 0900–1700 Sept–mid May, adults $7.50, children 12–17 $5.50, 7–11 $3.50, family $20. The **Canadian Rodeo Hall of Fame** covers rodeo history and cowboy livestock management, with visitors taking parts as rodeo clowns or bull riders.

Big Hill Springs Provincial Park, *tel: (403) 297-5293,* has picnic areas for day use amongst small waterfalls. **Heritage Canoe Adventurers Ltd**, *tel: (403) 932-3442,* offer Bow River *voyageur* paddling.

COCHRANE TO CANMORE

Jumping Pound Creek Bridge on Trans-Canada Hwy 1 was a First Nations buffalo jump. Buffalo were driven off a slope to their death, rendered into food, tools, skins and hide amidst much feasting.

The highway rises up 1440m Scott Lake Hill, then descends to the **Stoney Indian Reserve**. European explorers noted the Assiniboine method of preheating stones over a fire before dropping them into a watery stew mixture sitting in a hide bowl, and called the band 'Stoney'. The 3000-strong Stoney Nation, divided into Chiniki, Bearspaw and Wesley Bands, prefers Nakota or Nakoda ('the People') and centres around Morley, a few km north. Films like 'Little Big Man' have been shot on the reserve's rolling hills. The Stoney have prospered from oil and gas.

Nakoda Lodge, *Box 149, Morley, AB T0L 1N0; tel: (403) 881-3949; fax: (403) 881-3901,* on Chief Hector Lake a few km north of Hwy 1 on Hwy 1A, offers moderate rooms without air conditioning, a year-round budget–moderate restaurant, hiking trails, canoeing and fishing.

79

For good budget buffalo chili and Indian fry bread, reserve-grown produce, steak and chicken, **Chief Chiniki Restaurant**, *Hwy 1, Morley; tel: (403) 881-3748*, has a wooden-dome dining room with clear-day Rockies views. An **Arts & Craft Centre**, *tel: (403) 881-3960*, sells fine Stoney beadwork and jewellery.

Bicyclists have a designated path on the right (north) side of Hwy 1. For Kananaskis Country, turn left on Hwy 40 (pp.150–156). An alternative drive to Canmore on Hwy 1A has occasional summertime spotting of the Rocky Mountaineer wending its way towards the Rockies with grey granite crags as a backdrop. Ten km north is **Stoney Indian Park**, *tel: (403) 881-3939*, with hiking, fishing, camping and tepee hire; the Chief Chiniki Restaurant buffalo herd is visible from an overlook.

TransCanada Hwy 1 traverses **Bow Valley Provincial Park**, *tel: (403) 673-3663*. Enjoy riverside camping; *tel: (403) 673-2163*, picnicking, trails, mountain biking, fishing for trout and whitefish, elk and bear, lakeside bird-watching, carpets of wildflowers and winter Nordic skiing. At the northernmost tip of Kananaskis Country, the park's aspen parkland backs up against the massif of Mt Yamnuska.

Rafter Six Ranch Resort, *PO Box 6, Seebe, AB T0L 1X0; tel: (888) 267-2624* or *(403) 673-3622* or *(403) 264-1251*, south of the TransCanada, has moderate rooms all year in the huge log main building, with cabins and chalets on offer May–mid Oct. In season, the resort has a range of activities, including horse riding, a swimming pool, breakfast and sunset supper wagon rides, a country chapel, white water rafting, *voyageur* canoeing, location filming (Marilyn Monroe in 'River of No Return', 'Grizzly Adams') and the summer-only **Passing of the Legends Museum**, with local cowboy and First Nations artefacts.

Just north of the TransCanada on the Bow River, reach **Brewster Kananaskis Guest Ranch**, *PO Box 964, Banff, AB T0L 0C0; tel: (800) 691-5085* or *(403) 673-2100*, via Hwy 1X, with cabins, chalets, rafting, trail riding and barbecues, May–Oct.

The hamlet of **Seebe** owes its existence to hydroelectric power production. At **Exshaw**, a smoke plume of a large limestone cement plant breaks into the clear sky over **Lac des Arcs** which mirrors **Grotto Mountain**.

Grotto Mountain and other foothills give way to the Rockies' Front Range at the beginning of **Bow Valley Corridor**. There are several motels with services at **Deadman's Flats**, named after an insane French miner who killed his brother with an axe. On the left is a magnificent grouping of peaks, **Three Sisters**, serving as a wild backdrop to Canmore which mined the anthracite coal from the mountains' base for almost a century.

Tourist Information: Town of Canmore, *700 9 St; tel: (403) 678-1500*, and **Canmore Chamber of Commerce**, *801 Main St, No. 10; tel: (403) 678-4094*. **Travel Alberta**, *tel: (800) 661-8888*, and the **Travel Alberta Visitor Information Centre**, *Canmore Service Rd*, open year-round, have information on the area, the Rockies, Alberta, BC and Montana.

ACCOMMODATION

Most years, Banff Townsite lodging is full-up from Victoria Day to Labour Day. Popular campsites and lodging in Kananaskis Country just east, Calgarians' getaway area, is often full. Canmore, 20 km east of Banff, appears a *faux-chalet* town sprung up to service park visitors. Most lodging is along *Bow Valley Trail*; book early.

One of the finest is moderate–pricey **Canmore Regency Suites**, *1206 Bow Valley Trail (Hwy 1A); tel: (800) 386-7248* or *(403) 678-3799; fax: (403) 678-3413,* 2- or 3-bedroom units with fireplaces and cheerful innkeepers. Convenient for Brewster Tour connections, is expensive **Greenwood Inn Hotel & Conference Centre**, *511 Bow Valley Trail; tel: (800) 263-3625* or *(403) 678-3625.* **McNeill Heritage Inn**, *500 Three Sisters Dr.; tel: (403) 678-4884,* is a moderate–expensive six-room Bed and Breakfast in the old 1907 Canmore Mine manager's home.

EATING AND DRINKING

Pizza, beer, bakeries and fast food are easy to find. The **Bread Basket Bakery**, *Main St; tel: (403) 678-4355,* is a friendly spot for bagels, juice and coffee. **Sherwood House**, *8 (Main) St and 8 Ave; tel: (403) 678-5211,* is a budget pizzeria with burgers, steaks and vegetarian dishes. **Canmore Rose & Crown**, *749 Railway Ave; tel: (403) 678-5168,* has budget British–style pub food in a popular Alberta chain restaurant. **IGA**, *Railway Ave,* has a good selection for picnickers and day hikers.

SIGHTSEEING

An *Historic Walking Tour of Canmore* brochure is widely available in shops and hotels in town. The booming town on the boundary of Banff National Park, rapidly expanding to provide overflow lodging and dining for park visitors, is among Canada's fastest growing areas. As modern as most of Canmore appears, it began as a Canadian Pacific Railway divisional point in 1883, becoming a centre for anthracite (hard) coal mining within the decade, rating its own NWMP barrack by 1893.

From 1902–1929, Canmore, named after 11th-century Scotland's King Malcolm of Canmore, was part of Banff National Park. Policy on resource extraction changed, and Canmore was removed from the park. Anthracite mining continued until 1979 when natural gas supplies made coal economically uncompetitive.

Canmore Centennial Museum, *907 7 Ave; tel: (403) 678-2462,* open daily 1200–1600, with longer summer hours, has an excellent display of miners' equipment, artefacts and photos. The free museum also has 1988 (Calgary) Olympics mascot costumes and the Three Sisters Doll Museum collection of more than 700 dolls in period dress.

The **North West Mounted Police Barracks**, *8 St and 5 Ave; tel: (403) 678-1955,* open Wed–Sun 1200–1900 summer, shorter hours in winter, is the original and only remaining log barracks built as an outpost. In 1893, two NWMP officers and horses took up residence, deemed a necessity to keep the peace amongst rowdy miners during prohibition. NWMP artefacts are displayed amid 1920s furnishings. There is a small tea room (call for hours) and **Sgt Preston's Outpost Gift Shop**.

Canmore Summer Nights, *St Michael's Hall, 709 7 St; tel: (403) 678-1878,* present naturalist talks on birds, bears, wolves, flora and hiking, Tues–Sat, mid June–mid Sept, $6 or $15 for a family, with Sun music concerts, $10, $25 per family.

Canmore is an outdoor centre. Mountain climbing is popular, while Nordic skiing is best on the 56-km **Canmore Nordic Centre**, *Box 1979, tel: (403) 678-2400,* trail system designed for the 1988 Olympics. Trails are used for hiking, cycling, jogging, roller blading – even roller skiing on a dedicated 2½-km loop, to polish Nordic skiing technique during off season. Walk the 1½-km **Larch Islands Interpretive Trail** on Canmore's southwest side through lush wetlands of black-birch and balsam poplar stands, to see

81

wildflowers, especially Franklin's lady-slipper June–early July.

Canmore provides the 'back road to Kananaskis Country', a dusty, somewhat rough drive by emerald-water lakes, sheer cliffs and marshes rich with fish and water-fowl. (See Lethbridge–Kananaskis, pp. 148–156.) To access the 'back road' from *8 (Main) St* in downtown Canmore, turn left onto *8 Ave,* which turns into *Bridge Rd* as it crosses the Bow River, and becomes *Rundle Dr.* as it veers left. Go left on *Three Sisters Dr.* for 1½ km, then take the Nordic Centre turn-off right onto Hwy 242 toward Spray Lakes.

CANMORE TO BANFF

Pay the daily park fee, adults $5, over 64 $4, children 6–16 $2.50, at the Banff National Park Gate or, if you have a pass, drive through the right-hand non-stop lane. Although the TransCanada widens to three lanes in each direction, the speed limit slows to 90 kph; RVs may slow traffic further in summer. Most of the 10 km from the park gate to the two Banff exits have wire fence along both sides of the highway to protect animals from vehicles.

BANFF TOWNSITE

Tourist Information: Banff/Lake Louise Tourism Bureau, *PO Box 1298, Banff, AB T0L 0C0; tel: (403) 762-8421; fax: (403) 762-8163;* **Banff National Park**, *PO Box 900, Banff, AB T0L 0C0; tel: (403) 762-1550; fax: (403) 762-3229; http://www.worldweb.com/parkscanada-banff/* have local information. **Parks Canada Building**, *223 Banff Ave,* houses the Banff National Park information desk, back-country hiking/camping registration and the **Banff Visitor Centre**, *tel: (403) 762-1550,* open 0800–2000 (late June–Labour Day), 0800–1800 (rest of Sept), 0900–1700 (Oct–May). (See Banff National Park,

pp. 89–91, for park attractions and activities outside the townsite.)

Environment Canada, *tel: (403) 762-2088,* has information on Banff weather.

ACCOMMODATION

Banff has all levels of lodging, from an attractive youth hostel and a *BW,* to Bed and Breakfasts and the Banff Springs Hotel. With millions of visitors overnighting or spending several days using Banff Townsite as a base, all 5500 rooms in Banff and Lake Louise book months in advance. May–Sept tends to be sold out; winter holidays and weekends are equally crowded, and both seasons command premium rates. Visitors who wait may end up in Canmore or in Golden, a long drive over the western side of the Rockies. **Banff/Lake Louise Central Reservations**, *PO Box 1628, Banff, AB T0L 0C0, tel: (800) 661-1676 or (403) 762-5561; fax: (403) 762-8795,* makes bookings or check with **Travel Alberta**, *tel: (800) 661-8888.*

The **Banff Hostel**, *Tunnel Mountain Rd, Box 1358, Banff, AB T0L 0C0; tel: (403) 762-4122; fax: (403) 762-3441,* is sleek and modern above the townsite.

The **Banff Springs Hotel**, *405 Spray Ave, PO Box 960; tel: (800) 441-1414 or (403) 762-2211;* is the monumental château in the forest in most Rockies pictures. Purpose-built in 1888 by the Canadian Pacific Railway Company for tourists the rails brought to the Rockies, the resort hotel took its final multi-tower form in 1928. Extensive public areas offer dining, imbibing, gifts, clothing and souvenir shops, and may be self-toured with a *Banff Springs Hotel Walking Tour* brochure. **Solace**, *tel: (403) 762-1772,* is the hotel's luxury spa arranged around a skylit pool. The 27-hole **Banff Springs Golf Course**, *tel: (403) 762-6801,* has premier views of the Bow Valley.

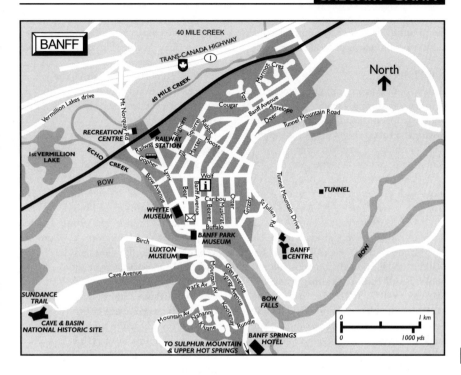

The **Mount Royal Hotel**, *138 Banff Ave; tel: (800) 267-3035 or (403) 762-3331,* has moderate–expensive rooms in downtown Banff; photographs in the lobby document the Brewster family's franchise in Rockies Parks transportation over the decades.

EATING AND DRINKING

Call in advance to ensure a table, and avoid the busiest hour, 1900–2000. The Banff Springs Hotel hosts the most formal dining in town, the moderate–pricey **Alberta Room** and the **Rob Roy Room**, *tel: (403) 762-6860.* The hotel's tiny moderate **Grapes Wine Bar**, *tel: (403) 762-6860,* serves a perfect fondue in a *weinstube* décor in the original hotel writing room.

Take the Sulphur Mountain Gondola to the casual, budget–moderate self-serve **Summit Restaurant**, *tel: (403) 762-5438*

or *(403) 762-2523,* Canada's highest panoramic-vista dining at 2285 m.

Banff Townsite is well-supplied with Japanese and Korean restaurants. **St James's Gate Olde Irish Pub**, *207 Wolf St; tel: (403) 762-9355,* budget–moderate, has huge club sandwiches with French fries for about the same as a nearby McDonalds meal.

Athena Pizza, *112 Banff Ave; tel: (403) 762-4022,* is good for budget–moderate steak and pizza. **Melissa's**, *218 Lynx St; tel: (403) 762-5511,* gets rave reviews, especially for breakfast.

ENTERTAINMENT

There is a lounge and bar scene, from Banff Springs Hotel saloons to downtown Banff beer bars. Afternoon–evening happy hour prices make social drinking less dear. Bands play jazz and folk music in summer; the

CALGARY—BANFF

free monthly *Wild Life* lists current entertainers and showtime at local cinemas.

SHOPPING

Banff is not a bargain shopping experience. Canadian clothing, from woollens to boots, is of outstanding quality. **Banff Springs Hotel** shops are well-supplied with clothing, Canadiana (maple syrup, Mounties paraphernalia) and gifts.

A *Banff Ave* stroll offers a huge variety of shops with souvenirs. Don't miss the **Banff Book & Art Den**, *110 Banff Ave; tel: (403) 762-3919*, with an extensive stock of Rockies and Western Canada guidebooks, field guides, maps, Canadian and First Nations novels, non-fiction and children's books. **Banff Indian Trading Post**, *Cave Ave; tel: (403) 762-2456*, has a huge selection of First Nations and Native American artefacts, jewellery and handmade moccasins.

SIGHTSEEING

Banff's attractions include several museums, breathtaking views of mountains, a resident elk population, hot springs, golfing, biking and fly-fishing in summer and winter skiing and ice-skating. Wapiti (elk), deer, wolves, coyotes, bear, beaver and Canada geese roam the townsite area.

Towering, side-leaning **Mt Rundle** dominates the approach from Canmore. Banff Townsite is marked by the sheer rise of **Cascade Mountain** at the far end of *Banff Ave*. The **Bow River**, with **Bow Falls** below the Banff Springs Hotel, meanders through town. The **Vermilion Lakes Scenic Drive** stretches parallel to TransCanada Hwy 1; take the first right turn off the Mt Norquay/Banff exit interchange and watch for bald eagles in an area used by aboriginal peoples 10,500 years ago.

Of the two Banff exits off TransCanada

Hwy 1, the more westerly, opposite the Mt Norquay Scenic Drive, is the most direct to downtown Banff. To access the length of *Banff Ave*, or to drive the scenic **Tunnel Mountain Road** (most closed in winter), take the first exit off TransCanada Hwy 1.

In any season, follow *Buffalo St* east of downtown to its junction with *Tunnel Mountain Rd* for the beautiful classic view of the Banff Springs Hotel. In summer, drive the length of *Tunnel Mountain Rd* starting from TransCanada Hwy 1, past elk and hoodoos. Stop across from Tunnel Mountain (RV) Campground, where an overlook dramatically illustrates the 'Giant Sandwich' geological formation of Mt Rundle, estimated to be over 300 million years old. Massive grey limestone cliffs delineate the base Palliser Formation; easily eroded brown limestone shale creates the centre Banff Formation; at the top, grey limestone marks the Rundle Formation. Continue through forest on *Tunnel Mountain Rd*, with views of the townsite, to the Banff Springs Hotel overlook.

Eight minutes pass quickly on the **Sulphur Mountain Gondola** *(entrance on Mountain Ave); tel: (403) 762-5438 or (403) 762-2523*, open Christmas–late Nov. Fares: mid May–mid Oct, adults $12, children 5–11 $6; mid Oct–mid May, adults $10, children 5–11 $5. Mountain peaks are visible all around 2285-m Sulphur Mountain on a clear day; the Banff Springs Hotel and townsite appear miniaturised below. Dine with a view at the **Summit Restaurant**, or walk the **Vista Trail Walkway** to the Observatory on Sanson's Peak.

Seven km from downtown Banff, 5.6 km from the TransCanada Hwy 1 exit, is the summit of 2252-m **Mt Norquay**. The switchback route up **Mt Norquay Scenic Drive** has several pullouts for panoramic views of the townsite, Mt Rundle and

84

Canadian Pacific Hotels and Rocky Mountain Tourism

The Canadian Rockies have been open for visitors since the end of the last Ice Age about 8000 years ago, but it took the Canadian Pacific Railway to turn one of nature's wonders into one of the world's most popular tourist attractions. The credit goes to CPR General Manager and builder Cornelius Van Horne.

Even before Canada's first transcontinental railway was completed in 1885, Van Horne recognised that financial success depended on a steady stream of paying passengers. CPR trains headed west were jammed with immigrants, most of them riding on highly discounted single tickets. The railway needed income.

Van Horne picked tourism. 'Since we can't export the scenery, we'll have to import the tourists.' It was a highly profitable model that the CPR followed for decades.

The new line reached Calgary early in 1883 and pushed on to **Lake Lousie** that autumn. On Nov 8, 1883, three railway workers who were prospecting for gold on their day off came across a warm stream flowing into the Bow River. They traced the sulphurous stream to a hole in the ground. When one of the trio lowered himself into the hole, he found an aquamarine pool of warm water, better known today as Cave and Basin. Once word of the discovery got out, government and CPR began encouraging visitors to the hot springs as a source of revenue.

In 1885, 25 square km around the spring was established as a reserve. A number of small hotels sprang up near Siding 29, now **Banff**. The next year, Van Horne began pushing government officials to expand the reserve and rename it **Rocky Mountains Park**, a change that occurred in 1887. He also commissioned the most spectacular mountain hotel in the world.

Just a short carriage ride from both railway station and hot springs, the building guaranteed magnificent views of the surrounding mountains. No expense was spared. Van Horne had a valley viewing terrace added and the **Banff Springs Hotel** opened on schedule on June 1, 1888.

85

It was the largest hotel in the world, 250 rooms and prices starting at $3.50 per night, meals included. A massive publicity campaign in the US, Eastern Canada and Europe turned the quiet town into a destination resort for the rich and famous. Promoted as North America's alpine wonderland, climbers, sightseers, hunters, fishers and the merely curious made Banff a most popular holiday spot.

When amateur alpinist Philip Stanley Abbott fell to his death in 1896, many called for the new-to-Canada sport of mountain climbing to be banned. Instead, Canadian Pacific Hotels imported teams of Swiss mountain guides to ensure that guests suffered nothing worse than sore muscles and the occasional sprained ankle.

The Swiss guides were an instant hit. So were other CP hotels in the Rockies, all of them set in National Parks created at the behest of CPR: **Chateau Lake Louise (Banff National Park); Glacier House (Glacier National Park)** and **Mount Stephen House (Yoho National Park)**.

The Canadian Northern Railway followed the same formula, building the original **Jasper Park Lodge** in **Jasper National Park**. CPR built luxury railway and steamship hotels from Victoria (The Empress Hotel) and Vancouver (Hotel Vancouver) to eastern hubs in Toronto and Montreal. CP Hotels has long since become independent of Canada's railways, but it remains the country's largest chain of luxury hotels.

Sulphur Mountain; Rocky Mountain bighorn sheep and wildlife graze in forest near the roadway in winter. Hike to Mystic Lake and Elk Lake from the trailhead across the road from the ski area.

Banff Mt Norquay ski area, tel: (403)

762-4421; fax: (403) 762-8133, open early Dec–mid Apr, offers alpine skiing and snowboarding, with access to Nordic terrain and touts night skiing between starlit mountain peaks. The Cascade Lodge has a ski school and dining facilities, but no accommodation.

As the Canadian Pacific Railway pushed across Western Canada, the magnificent Rockies scenery was seen as ideal for tourism and company profits. In 1883, three railway workers came across a cave with hot springs, run-off from Sulphur Mountain into the Bow River, gravity-pulled 3 km into the earth, where it boils from earth core heat. Disputes over ownership rights to the 29°–32°C springs led the Government of Canada to declare it federal property in 1885 and to include it in the country's first national park, Rocky Mountains Park, in 1887.

Cave & Basin National Historic Site, *311 Cave Ave; tel: (403) 762-1557,* open 0900–1800 (June–Labour Day); 0930–1700 early Sept–May; adults $2.25, children $1.25, families $5 (discount available for multiple park museum sites), is the original discovery site, no longer used for bathing, though the sulphur-scented cave, a grotto filled with mineral-rich tufa formations, is accessible. Several exhibits and a film explain the area's history. Elk are often spotted in the parking area. The 0.6-km **Marsh Trail Loop** has a bird-watching blind and plants, including orchids.

For immersion in 40°C mineralised waters, the **Upper Hot Springs**, *Mountain Ave en route to the Sulphur Mountain Gondola entrance; tel: (403) 762-1515,* mid May–Oct adults $7, children 3–15 $6, mid Oct–mid May adults $5, children $4, offers an all-year outdoor pool and spa.

Banff National Park Administration Building, *across the Bow River from downtown at the foot of Banff Ave,* is

surrounded by **Cascade Gardens.** Late spring–fall, walk up the slope behind the building for a flower-bedecked view across downtown Banff to Cascade Mountain.

Banff Park Museum National Historic Site, *91 Banff Ave; tel: (403) 762-1558,* open 1000–1800 (June–Aug); 1000–1500 (Sept–May); adults $2.25, children 6–18 $1.25 (discount available for multiple park museum sites), was built in 1903 in crossed-log style. Inside, roof skylights bathe three floors in natural light. Wood-panelled walls, wooden floors and cases hold taxidermy specimens of animals and birds, collections of birds' eggs, mounted animal heads and the old director's office, all deliberately maintained in 1914 park interpretation style. Dress warmly in winter, lightly in summer, as there is no heat or air conditioning.

Luxton Museum of the Plains Indian, *1 Birch Ave; tel: (403) 762-2388,* open 0900–2100 (mid May–mid Oct); adults $5, children 13–18 $3.75, 6–12 $2, is run by the Buffalo Nations Cultural Society in a building resembling a stockade. Porcupine quill and beadwork artefacts and clothes are exquisite; unlike often-hokey Western films, the dignified peace pipes are elegant. A separate room contains dioramas of Plains Native family groups and tepee (Sioux for 'dwelling place') construction.

Whyte Museum of the Canadian Rockies, *111 Bear St; tel: (403) 762-2291,* open daily 1000–1800 (mid May–mid Oct); Tues–Sat 1000–2100 (July–Aug); Tues–Wed, Fri–Sun 1300–1700, Thur 1300–2100 (mid Oct–mid May), adults $3, children 12–18 $2, is Banff's tribute to its explorers, mountaineers, missionaries and artists who made the area famous. The museum complex includes pioneer homes and log cabins; Plains Native beadwork in the log Moore House is outstanding.

BANFF–JASPER

Azure-blue lakes, sheer jagged peaks, herds of deer and elk, tawny bears, mountain sheep clinging to crags, glaciers and ice-milk rivers, pink alpenglow, wildflower meadows and waterfalls etching the land, Rocky Mountains vistas are startlingly varied. The 230-km Icefields Parkway, Hwy 93 from Lake Louise to Jasper, is named for the glaciers that loom from the Columbia Icefield to form the edges of mountains.

Traffic, long grades and road repair/construction delays make travelling the 285 km from Banff to Jasper a gruelling all-day proposition. Three to seven hours allows time to explore, spot wildlife, picnic, hike and see the most famous natural sights.

87

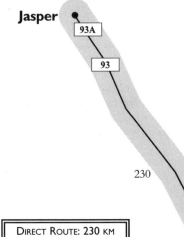

Jasper
93A
93
230

DIRECT ROUTE: 230 KM

93

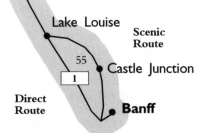

Lake Louise
Scenic Route
55
Castle Junction
1
Direct Route
Banff

ROUTES

DIRECT ROUTE

Take TransCanada Hwy 1 from Banff to Lake Louise Village. Veer right, following signs onto Hwy 93, the Icefields Parkway, 202 km, then follow Hwy 93A for 23 km to rejoin Hwy 93 for the last 5 km to Jasper Townsite.

SCENIC ROUTE

The **Bow Valley Parkway**, the Hwy 1A alternative to TransCanada Hwy 1 between Banff and Lake Louise, is a slow, narrow roadway with lay-bys, picnicking, wildlife, birds, views of Castle Mountain and access to Johnston Canyon. Watch for cyclists along this scenic 55-km route which begins 5 km west of Banff, from TransCanada Hwy 1. Or, follow the Bow Valley Parkway halfway to Castle Junction, then follow signs towards Trans-

GETTING TO THE ROCKIES

Highways stay open year-round. **Brewster Airport Express Service**, *tel: (800) 661-1152 or (403) 762-6767* (Banff), provide transportation from Calgary International Airport to Banff, $34 single, Nov–Mar. The **Calgary Ski Bus**, *tel: (403) 250-7677*, return $42, adults $55–$60 including lift tickets, offer mid Dec–Apr transport to Lake Louise.

Rocky Mountain Railtours, *tel: (800) 665-7425*, offer May–mid Oct two-day daylight rail excursions to or from Calgary to Banff, Kamloops and Vancouver, or Vancouver, Kamloops and Jasper. **VIA Rail**, *tel: (888) 842-7245*, connect Vancouver and Edmonton to Jasper. **Brewster**, *tel: (800) 661-1152*, operate Gray Line Tours between Banff, Lake Louise and Jasper, including Snocoach tours of the Columbia Icefield and connections to Calgary; book bus tours with train reservations or independently.

TOURIST INFORMATION

Information on the mountain parks: **Parks Canada**, *220 4 Ave S.E., Room 552K, Calgary, AB TG2 4X3; tel: (800) 748-7275;* **Banff National Park**, *PO Box 900, Banff, AB T0L 0C0; tel: (403) 762-1550; fax: (403) 762-3229; web: http://www.worldweb.com/parkscanada-banff/;* **Jasper National Park**, *PO Box 10, Jasper, AB T0E 1E0; tel: (403) 852-6161; fax: (403) 852-5601; web: http://www.worldweb.com/parkscanada-jasper/;* **Travel Alberta**, *tel: (800) 661-8888;* **Banff/Lake Louise Tourism Bureau**, *PO Box 1298, Banff, AB T0L 0C0; tel: (403) 762-8421; fax: (403) 762-8545;* **Jasper Tourism & Commerce**, *PO Box 98, Jasper, AB T0E 1E0; tel: (403) 852-3858; fax: (403) 852-4932.*

The Rockies Parks have an annual tabloid-size *Banff, Jasper, Kootenay, Yoho National Parks Official Visitors Guide*, with maps, activities and descriptions of each park's main attractions. Individual parks also have free seasonal newspapers or map/information sheets at park entrances and visitor centres.

National park camping is on a first come, first served basis, with pitch tickets available from campsite kiosks; be prepared for July–Aug crowds and arrive early. Tunnel Mountain Village II, Lake Louise Trailer and Mosquito Creek in Banff National Park, and Wapiti Campground in Jasper National Park are open year-round. **Backcountry campers** appear in person to purchase a mandatory **Wilderness Pass** ($6 per night to $30 maximum) from Park Information Centres, to discuss routes with rangers, receive a *Backcountry Users Guide*, and should consider a $10 non-refundable advance booking in popular backcountry camp areas.

WEATHER

A lovely blue-sky day in the Canadian Rockies may seem balmy, even when the actual temperature is rather cool. Late July–Aug and mid Sept–Oct are historically best-weather months, though rain and snow can fall. Coats, gloves, hats and scarves hedge against the changeable weather. Sunscreen creme, a hat and sunglasses are vital in any season.

The Rockies have the driest snow powder of any Canadian mountain range, delightful for alpine and Nordic skiing, but subject to avalanches. For **avalanche warnings**, check with the parks Nov–Apr, or *tel: (800) 667-1105*. The dry snow means bitter cold snowstorms, though Chinook winds may warm the area near Banff before surging east towards Calgary. By Oct, snow provides a thin blanket. By Christmas, the snow is usually fine. Best

Rocky Mountain Parks

Five million annual visitors each seek a unique thrill, filling adjoining Banff and Jasper National Parks with vehicles in summer, overflowing accommodation and adding a human dimension to the geography, flora and fauna. Despite the crowds, it's not hard to find solitude. Park trails are easy to follow; off the main highways and parkway, side roads lead to peaceful meadows.

Animals often graze near the highways, causing what park rangers call 'bear jams', as vehicles pull over to spot wildlife and take photographs. Roads clog and humans risk danger or death by encroaching on animal territory. Snow may fall in summer. Weather fronts can change the sky from blue to grey to white to slate in less than an hour with temperatures shifting to match. The parks remain open year-round. Winter snow garbs the land and mountains in sheer white, wind carving ice crystals off peaks, fog rising from half-frozen rivers, lakes an icy white expanse. Fewer visitors venture to the Rocky Mountain Parks in winter, though animals are no less visible and skiing, snowboarding and ice skating are enticing.

Banff, Lake Louise Village and Jasper have most park accommodation, providing lodging and a base from the southern, middle or north ends of the national parks. Castle Mountain Junction, Saskatchewan (River) Crossing and other lodges and hostels offer rooms or cabins in less built-up areas.

Most visitors drive from Calgary to Banff, then proceed northward towards Jasper, though this driving route may be taken from either direction. Connections with other parks en route provide sightseeing flexibility and a larger range of accommodation. To access other parks from the main Banff–Jasper National Parks corridor, turn onto Hwy 93 north-west of Banff to go south through Kootenay National Park (see p. 169); from Lake Louise, follow TransCanada Hwy 1 west and south-west through Yoho National Park (see p. 212); or take Hwy 11 east from Saskatchewan River Crossing through the little-known White Goat Wilderness to Rocky Mountain House and Red Deer (see p. 135). West of Jasper Townsite, Hwy 16 leads to BC's Mt Robson Provincial Park (see p. 219).

89

skiing is Feb–Mar with a good snowpack and generally warmer weather. Park Information Centres have current weather reports, or *tel: (403) 762-2088* for Banff, *(403) 862-3185* for Jasper.

DRIVING

Speed limits within the parks are generally 90kph, 60kph on the Bow Valley Parkway between Banff and Lake Louise Village. Fill up with petrol frequently; there are no services for 155 km on the Icefields Parkway between Saskatchewan River Crossing and Jasper.

Watch for cyclists, animals and the illegal knot of cars and RVs wherever wildlife presents a photo opportunity. **Alberta**

Motor Association watches **road conditions**; *tel: (403) 240-5300,* or phone the national parks; *tel: (403) 762-1450.* Use winter tyres in snow.

BANFF NATIONAL PARK

Hot springs running from Sulphur Mountain to the Bow River, discovered by Canadian Pacific Railway workers in 1885, were a draw for tourists being lured west into the mountains by the CPR. The railway company lost no time in establishing palace hotels with exquisite views, where the well-heeled could stroll, hike or canoe to natural wonders while pampering and groaning meals waited within.

Banff National Park, established as

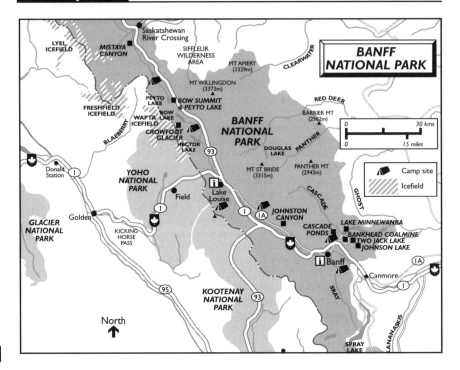

Rocky Mountains Park in 1887, includes Banff Townsite's 7500 souls (see pp. 78–86, for **Banff Townsite**), Canadian Pacific's Banff Springs Hotel, Lake Louise's small purpose-built village and CP's Chateau Lake Louise resort on the lake.

A buffalo paddock herd has been moved elsewhere in the Parks Canada system, following a decision to restore wildlife and vegetation in the Bow River Valley and limit townsite growth before park natural resources are irreversibly depleted.

Lake Minnewanka Scenic Drive, good for spotting bighorn sheep, loops 21 km, starting from opposite the *Banff Ave/Tunnel Mountain Road* interchange on TransCanada Hwy 1. **Lower Bankhead**, explored via a 1-km trail, was a CPR locomotive engine supply coal mining area from 1904–1922.

Wide **Lake Minnewanka**, Banff National Park's largest lake, is flanked like bookends by solid masses of mountains. **Lake Minnewanka Boat Tours**, *PO Box 2189, Banff AB T0L 0C0; tel: (403) 762-3473,* offer 1½-hr lake cruises mid May–Sept, adults $22, children 5–11 $11. **Stewart Canyon Trail** starts from the summer season snack bar, skirting the north shore of Lake Minnewanka's manmade reservoir. In winter, **Sunfish Scuba**, *4630 16 Ave N.W., Calgary; tel: (403) 288-7427,* offer ice diving to Minnewanka Landing Resort Community, inundated during construction of the 1941 hydroelectric dam.

In summer, picnic around **Lake Minnewanka**, or on its arm, **Two Jack Lake**. Two Jack Lake has 80 pitches for lakeside camping and 381 at the Two Jack Main Campground nearby, both open mid May–early Sept. Picnic, bird-watch, hike a

2.8-km trail and swim in the cool waters of tree-lined **Johnson Lake**, accessible from the scenic drive.

BANFF TO LAKE LOUISE (TRANSCANADA HWY 1)

Though animal protection fencing continues about 10 km north-west of Banff, wildlife still crosses this major throughway. Elk wander in any season. While the Bow Valley Parkway is considered one of the most scenic drives in North America, the TransCanada on the west side of the Bow River Valley is only minimally less breathtaking and, construction traffic and animal jams willing, is a swift way to see Lake Louise and its nearby summer-accessible sister, Lake Moraine.

Ten km west of Banff, turn left on *Sunshine Rd* for 8 km to **Sunshine Village Ski Resort**, *Box 1510, Banff, AB T0L 0C0; tel: (403) 762-6500; fax: (403) 762-6513, web:http://www.skibanf.com,* open mid Nov–May. **Sunshine Inn**, *tel: (403) 762-6555* or *(800) 661-1676,* expensive, is the only on-mountain lodging in the park. The resort is spread over three mountains, including **Goat's Eye Mountain**. Sunshine claims all natural snow; for 24-hr Snowphone; *tel: (403) 762-6543.* Lookout Mountain's Continental Divide High Speed Quad offers single-run, two province skiing in Alberta and BC. A hot outdoor pool, a snowboard park and a 1070-m vertical drop are enticements. **Mt Assiniboine**, a magnificent 3618-m pyramid-shaped peak, is close by.

North of the *Sunshine Rd* exit, the divided highway ends. **Castle Mountain Viewpoint**, 21 km from Banff, was named by 1858 Palliser Expedition geologist Sir James Hector for its towering coloured layers of stone. Nine km north is **Castle Junction**, connecting to Hwy 93 south, the Banff–Windemere Parkway to Koote-

nay National Park. Lake Louise Village is 28 km north on TransCanada Hwy 1.

BANFF TO LAKE LOUISE (BOW VALLEY PARKWAY)

The Bow Valley Parkway was the only route from Banff to Lake Louise when built in 1920. Choose the 55-km parkway in summer if there's time. The 60 kph speed limit and heavy traffic makes this pleasant route on narrow-lane stretches through forests below cliffs a slow endeavour. Here is wildlife without the fences, underpasses or bear, wolf and cougar wildlife overpasses found on TransCanada Hwy 1 north of Banff. Parkway lay-bys are frequent enough to enjoy views and picnic.

The craggy, grey **Sawback Range** is east. The tree spikes of **Sawback's** prescribed burn area, deliberately fired to produce new vegetation 15 km north-west of Banff, cut a dramatic swath.

Johnston Canyon, 23 km and a half-hour drive from Banff, is among the most popular park attractions. Walk the suspension walkway early and late in the summer to avoid catwalk congestion; photography is best in the afternoon when sunlight reaches canyon walls. Wear sturdy shoes to tackle the uneven pathway, and excellent snow boots in winter.

The walkway leads 1.1 km along the misty, narrow limestone canyon to the **Lower Falls**, plunging into a clear blue pool. To see all seven waterfalls in the canyon, hike 1.6 km further to the **Upper Falls**, where water cascades down 30m.

Johnston Canyon Resort, *PO Box 875, Banff, AB T0L 0C0; tel/fax: (403) 762-2971,* open mid May–Sept, has moderate cabins, grocery and souvenir stores, petrol, a tennis court and informal dining. **Johnston Canyon**, *PO Box 900; tel: (403) 762-1581,* open mid May–mid Sept, has 140 camp pitches.

91

Rocky Mountain Animals

Canadian Rockies highways are studded with signs warning of wild animals. The Rockies provide one of the richest wildlife habitats in North America. Deer, elk, mountain goats, bighorn sheep and other large animals are daily visitors along many mountain roads, especially in winter, when they frequent the asphalt to lick salt off the roadway.

Bear jams, traffic jams caused by vehicles stopping so the occupants can watch animals, have become common hazards, especially in summer. The most frequent cause of premature death for large animals in the mountains is the front end of an automobile or truck.

Feeding wild animals makes them demanding, aggressive and dangerous, especially once the food supply is cut off. Even small creatures such as ground squirrels can deliver painful bites if the biscuits run out before they're ready to stop eating. And deer don't cope with sandwiches any better than human stomachs would cope with their diet of grasses, young tree shoots and sedges. Don't feed the animals!

Beaver were why Whites came to the Rockies two centuries ago. The 20-kg rodents were hunted nearly to extinction for their dense undercoat of ruddy brown fur, used to make stylish felt hats in Europe. Beavers dam small streams with logs, sticks, roots, stones and mud to create ponds up to 3m deep. The resulting ponds occasionally flood roads, campsites and basements, but the animals themselves are extremely shy. See them at dawn or dusk along the shores of Lake Louise. When alarmed, beaver use their broad, flat tail to slap the water in warning to other beavers nearby.

Rocky Mountain **bears** come in two varieties, **Black** and **Grizzly**. Both species can be almost any colour from golden to jet black, although cinnamon brown to black are most common. Black bears are often seen foraging for insects, plants and berries along roads spring–autumn. Grizzlies are less tolerant of humans, though both species avoid confrontation whenever possible (see pp. 35 for tips on dealing with bears).

Bighorn Sheep are common on grassy slopes throughout the mountains. Both sexes are dirty grey to brown and have horns, which can curl backwards a full 360° on males. Males are a little less than a metre tall and weigh up to 125 kg. Females are about 20% smaller and have straight, goat-like horns. Hunting has made bighorns shy in most areas, but they are common along roadways in national parks where hunting is not allowed. They frequent highways in winter to lick road salt. Best place to see bighorns is along Hwy 16 in Jasper National Park.

Bison are the largest native land animals in North America, 170cm tall, average weight over 700 kg. Millions of bison once roamed the prairies and the west slope of the Rockies as far north as Golden, but were hunted to extinction in the 19th century. Present-day herds are descended from survivors imported from the United States. Elk Island National Park, Rocky Mountain House National Historic Site and Waterton Lakes National Park have the largest herds in Southern Alberta.

92

Castle Mountain, 2766m, is easy to spot 5 km north as **Castle Cliffs** begin to dominate the parkway eastern side. Sawback Range is replaced by a fortress-like notched pink, gold and orange mountain mass. A favourite with rock climbers, Castle Mountain adds horizontal layers of lacy snow in winter.

Open year-round at the mountain's base, **Castle Mountain Village**, *Box 178, Lake Louise, AB T0L 1E0; tel: (403) 522-2783 or (403) 762-3868; fax: (403) 762-8629,* has moderate–expensive cottages and chalets, a grocery store and petrol. **Castle Mountain Campground**, *tel: (403) 762-1581,* open late June–Labour Day, has 44

Coyotes have survived persistent attempts at extermination. Their yips and howls can be heard near towns, though coyotes prefer open forest and meadows. The size of a small German shepherd with similar colouration, coyotes are common around towns, picnic sites and campsites.

Most **deer** in the Rockies are either **white-tailed** or **mule** deer. Both are generally light brown in summer and dirty grey in winter. The mule deer, named for its ears, has a white rump and tail and favours open forests bordering prairie. White-tailed deer have a dark tail–until they run, holding the tail erect to reveal its white underside. White-tails prefer thickets along rivers and lakes. Both species are about 100cm at the shoulder and weigh 80–120 kg. They are common around campsites, highways and Jasper townsite.

Elk, or **wapiti**, stand about 150cm tall and weigh 250–400 kg. The males grow impressive racks of antlers, which they shed each spring. They live on prairies to alpine habitats, congregating at lower elevations in winter. The easiest place to see elk is near the railway station in Jasper and in Banff near Cave-and-Basin.

Moose, known as elk in Europe, are the giants of the deer family. Standing 1.8m at the shoulder and weighing more than 450 kg, moose look like a caricature, complete with oversized nose, spindly legs, tiny eyes, big ears and enormous spreading flat antlers (on males). Look for moose in marshy areas from the Rockies to the Pacific Ocean, where long legs allow them to graze in deep water. Drive cautiously. Moose often kneel on highways to lick road salt; their dark colour makes them hard to see at dusk.

Mountain goats live on steep, almost vertical slopes where they are safe from less surefooted predators. Both sexes are white with black horns, about one metre tall and weigh up to 130 kg. Goats are shy on the slopes, but put up with humans a few dozen metres away at salt and sulphur licks. Jasper National Park has two licks just off the highway, both with parking: the Goats-and-Glaciers Viewpoint, 38 km south of Jasper on the Icefields Parkway, and Disaster Point, 29 km east of Jasper on Hwy 16.

There are three types of **wild cats** in Western Canada: **lynx**, **bobcat** and **cougar/puma/ mountain lion/panther**. All three are extremely shy and seldom seen. Lynx are widespread in remote forested regions, looking like oversized housecats with tufted ears and oversized paws that let them walk easily in deep, soft snow. Bobcats are a little smaller than lynx and prefer more open habitat, such as the badlands near Dinosaur Provincial Park. Both eat small mammals, especially snowshoe hares. Cougars live in mountain and foothill regions where they hunt deer and grow up to 75 kg.

Wolves are considerably shyer than coyotes and about a third larger. Once ranging from the prairies to the mountain treeline, relentless hunting and loss of habitat has driven wolves into more remote mountains and forests from Jasper north. They tend to be secretive and range over hundreds of kilometres. Seldom seen, wolf packs are often heard howling in mountain valleys. Howl back and the pack will likely start up a duet.

93

pitches. **HI Castle Mountain Hostel**, *c/o Box 1358, Banff AB T0L 0C0; tel: (403) 762-4122,* is open all year. TransCanada Hwy 1, 0.25 km west at **Castle Junction**, connects with Hwy 93 to Kootenay National Park.

Picnic 30 km from Banff at **Storm Mountain Viewpoint**, with a nice view over the river valley. Three km north, the **Castle Mountain Internment Camp Monument** is marked by a statue of a man asking 'Why?', a memorial to citizens of the Austro–Hungarian Empire and Ukrainians interned between 1914–1920 in harsh conditions in fierce Rockies weather. Moderate log chalets and rooms

12 km south of Lake Louise Village at **Baker Creek Chalet, Guest Lodge and Bistro**, *PO Box 68, Lake Louise, AB T0L 1E0; tel: (403) 522-3761; fax: (403) 522-2270*, offer Nordic and alpine skiing.

LAKE LOUISE

Tourist Information: Lake Louise Visitor Centre, *Samson Mall Area, Lake Louise Village; tel: (403) 522-3833*, open daily 0800–2000 (mid June–Labour Day), 0800–1800 (early June and Sept), 0900–1700 (Oct–May). Lake Louise Village, with petrol, dining and accommodation is 4.5 km downhill from the lake. Ask for the *Lake Louise Drives & Walks* brochure.

ACCOMMODATION

Lake Louise lodging is limited, commanding premium prices in summer, on holiday weekends and during the Christmas season. Book well in advance and enquire about inclusive meals or ski packages.

The *grande dame*, **Chateau Lake Louise**, *Lake Louise, AB T0L 1E; tel: (800) 441-1414 or (403) 522-3511; fax: (403) 522-3834*, expensive–pricey, is Canadian Pacific's cream-coloured highrise castle on the lake, with lakeside view rooms facing west to Victoria Glacier. **Deer Lodge**, *PO Box 100; tel: (800) 661-1595 or (403) 522-3747; fax: (403) 522-3883*, and **Paradise Lodge and Bungalows**, *PO Box 7; tel: (403) 522-3595; fax: (403) 522-3987*, open mid May–mid Oct, both expensive with mountain cabin décor, are a short way down from the lake on *Chateau Hill Rd*.

Amongst several choices in Lake Louise Village just off TransCanada Hwy 1, the **Post Hotel**, *Village Rd, PO Box 69; tel: (800) 661-1586 or (403) 522-3989; fax: (403) 522-3966*, expensive–pricey, has Swiss owners and European style in a posh lodge of pine and river stone. **Lake Louise Inn**, *210 Village Rd, PO Box 209; tel: (800)*

661-9237 or (403) 522-3791; fax: (403) 522-2018, is a large complex with 222 moderate–expensive rooms.

HI Canadian Alpine Centre & International Hostel, *Village Rd, Box 115, Lake Louise, AB T0L 1E0; tel: (403) 522-2200; fax: 522-2253*, offers ski instruction.

EATING AND DRINKING

The **Chateau Deli**, *Chateau Lake Louise Glacier Wing*, has generous prepared-to-order sandwiches, cakes, desserts, tasty coffee and hot chocolate for top-quality, filling cheap–budget meals perfect for picnics and knapsacks. Chateau Lake Louise has fine dining with live entertainment in the **Edelweiss Dining Room**, cheerful painted furniture and an excellent breakfast buffet in the **Poppy Room** and Old English High Tea daily 1200–1600 in summer in the Lakeview Lounge.

The **Post Hotel**, *tel: (403) 522-3989*, elegantly serves a budget–moderate range from duck sausage omelettes to fish, grilled lamb or veal *bratwurst* with *rosti*. **Lake Louise Station**, *200 Sentinel; tel: (403) 522-2600*, in the 1910 log CPR railway depot and the 1925 CPR *Delamere* dining car, has a large menu from 1130–2400. **Bill Peyto's Café**, *Village Rd at International Hostel; tel: (403) 522-2200*, is open 0700–2100, with hearty food in the cheap–budget range. There is a grocery store and liquor store in Samson Mall.

SIGHTSEEING

What Stoney Natives called 'Lake of Little Fishes' was sighted in 1882 by a CPR crew supplier, Tom Wilson, who was intrigued by avalanche sounds booming near a Stoney camp. Awestruck, Wilson named it Emerald Lake. Lake Louise was rechristened in 1884 in honour of Princess Louise Caroline Alberta, fourth daughter of

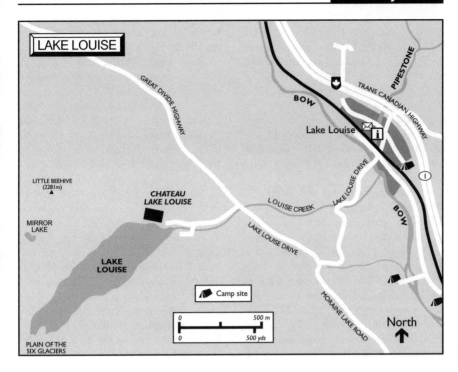

Queen Victoria and wife of Canada's Governor General.

June–Oct, the teal-aqua blue waters of Lake Louise stretch to the **Plain of the Six Glaciers** and mile-high **Victoria Glacier**. The sheer rise of Fairview cools the south side, while a path skirts the lake's north shore. From Nov–May, the frozen lake is covered with snow, drawing mid-season walkers in snow boots well onto the blinding white expanse for picture-taking or a straight-line trek to the Plain of the Six Glaciers. Chateau Lake Louise on the east end swarms with tourists from around the globe, taking snapshots, bird-watching, shopping in the hotel's arcades, dining, or gazing awestruck at the view. Summer visitors can hire a canoe, ride a horse, bicycle, or swim in the water no warmer than 8°C in August.

Friendly Giant Lake Louise Sight-

seeing Gondola, tel: (403) 522-3555, June–mid Sept, to Whitehorn Lodge at the Ski Louise winter area east of TransCanada Hwy 1, provides panoramic views towards the lake 6 km west.

In summer, intrepid walkers head out pre-dawn to catch pink reflecting on the snowy tip of Victoria Glacier, named after Britain's Queen Victoria. **Lake Louise Shoreline Trail** runs for 2 km; continue a more difficult 3.3 km on the **Plain of the Six Glaciers Trail** to a rubble expanse at the foot of Mt Victoria, with views of Upper and Lower Victoria Glaciers. Snacks are available at the Teahouse.

There is also a Teahouse at the end of the challenging 3.5-km hike on the **Lake Agnes Trail** north-west of Lake Louise.

The narrow 11-km drive south from *Chateau Hill Rd* to **Moraine Lake**, with a sheer drop to the valley on the east side, is closed to vehicles in winter, but accessible for Nordic skiing. Viewed from the top of the **Rockpile**, Moraine Lake is framed by ten sawtooth peaks ending in moraines at the robin's-egg blue water's edge. The **Rockpile** just east of the parking area requires a 300-m ascent over an uneven path and huge boulders. A flatter path follows the lake's west shore to the south end, with views of canoeists paddling toward glaciers.

Moraine Lake Lodge & Cabins, *PO Box 70; tel: (403) 522-3733; fax: (403) 522-3719,* open June–Sept, has pricey accommodation for age 16 up, a budget–pricey dining room, gift shop and canoe ($22 per hour) and rowboat hire.

In winter, Chateau Lake Louise has an ice skating rink on the edge of the lake, horse-drawn sleigh rides (adults $12, children under 8 $10), tobogganing, dog sled rides, snowshoeing and Nordic skiing (ask for the *Lake Louise Area Cross-Country Ski Trails Map*).

Lake Louise Ski Area, *PO Box 5, Lake Louise, AB T0L 1E0; tel: (800) 258-7669, (403) 522-3555 or (403) 256-8473; web: http://www.skilouise.com,* east of Trans-Canada Hwy 1, spread across four mountains, operates early Nov–May. There is no lodging, but three day lodges have restaurants and cafeterias. Volunteers act as Ski Friends, leaving several times daily from the north end of Whiskeyjack Lodge to guide skiers to the best snow.

LAKE LOUISE TO JASPER (ICEFIELDS PARKWAY)

Driving it, the twists, turns, glacier vistas, blue lakes and waterfalls along the sleek, well-paved Icefields Parkway seem natural, not man-made. A 1930s Depression make-work project turned a rough wagon road into a one-lane throughway, later widened. Even in poor weather, a moun-

tain peak comes out or a lake miraculously appears through a drizzle.

Bow Pass, 2069m, is less than an hour's drive from Lake Louise, a must for seeing Peyto Lake, the blue jewel at the top of a path to the summit. **Sunwapta Pass**, 2035m, creates the boundary between Banff and Jasper National Parks just south of the Columbia Icefield, reached from the south via the steeply-graded Icefields Parkway.

North-east of Lake Louise Village, veer right onto Hwy 93. Viewpoints are frequent – pull completely off the highway for best views. **Herbert Lake** has picnicking and is a good place to observe birds and butterflies. **HI-Mosquito Creek Hostel**, *tel: (403) 762-4122; fax: (403) 762-3441,* has cabins and outdoor toilets, 24 km from Lake Louise across from the **Mosquito Creek Campsite**. Both, aptly named for biting insects that swarm near the Bow River in summer, are open year-round.

On the left below sheer grey cliffs is **Crowfoot Glacier**, close enough to appear to hang on the shelf above another layer of cliffs. Two of three talons of ice remain – the third has disappeared in the 20th century from glacial retreat. Below, 36 km north of Lake Louise, is one side of **Bow Lake**, a frigid flatness fed by the Wapta Icefield's Bow Glacier, visible to the west. The Bow River begins here, flowing south to Banff and east to Calgary. **Num-Ti-Jah Lodge**, *Box 39, Lake Louise, AB T0L 1E0; tel: (403) 522-2167; fax: (403) 522-2425,* moderate–expensive at Bow Lake's north end, is noted for its striking red roof on a lodge expanded from hunter-trapper Jimmy Simpson's modest 1920's-era log cabin. A 400-m loop trail goes from the parking area to the lodge; a longer trail follows Bow Lake's north shore to a terminal moraine looking west to Bow Glacier and a falls.

Three km north of Bow Lake, turn left, west, at **Bow Summit** to the **Peyto Lake** parking area. The chilly 350-m uphill climb through fir and subalpine spruce is lush with anemone, glacier lilies, mountain heather and other wildflowers, but mosquitoes are vicious. Every tour group stops for photos with much jockeying for a spot. The 3-km long lake spreads along the Mistaya River Valley below the viewpoint, a startling opaque teal blue from glacial silt particles reflecting light.

Wild Bill Peyto, after whom Peyto Lake is named, is another Rockies icon. Postcards show the 1890s piercing gaze, thick moustache, pipe, felt hat and buckskins befitting an English immigrant who had learned trapping, mining and trail guiding. Peyto found the lake when off for a rest after finishing camp tasks during an 1896 exploratory expedition.

North along Hwy 93, **Waterfowl Lakes** have bird-watching, fishing, canoeing, 116 camp pitches and occasional moose. *Mistaya* is grizzly bear in the Stoney First Nations language. Stop at the **Mistaya Canyon** lay-by to follow a 450-m path to a bridge over the Mistaya River for waterfalls in a narrow sandstone cleft.

Six km north, the North Saskatchewan River braids whitish pale green on the left and purer green on the south (right) side. In 1807, explorer-cartographer David Thompson traversed this wild, rushing section of the river and Howse Pass, due west. Two km north, the David Thompson Hwy, Hwy 11, runs east along his exploration route to **Rocky Mountain House** and **Red Deer**. (See Red Deer–Saskatchewan River Crossing, pp. 134–137.)

Saskatchewan River Crossing: The Crossing, *Hwy 93 at Hwy 11, Lake Louise, AB T0L 1E0; tel: (403) 761-7000; fax: (403) 761-7006,* has moderate–expensive simple rooms and a lounge, but is best

known for a coach rest stop restaurant, snack bar and well-stocked gift shop.

Eleven km north at Rampart Creek is a well-known rock and ice-climbing area. **Rampart Creek Campground**, with 50 pitches, is open mid June–Labour Day. **HI-Rampart Creek Hostel**, *tel: (403) 762-4122; fax: (403) 762-3441,* is open May–mid Oct, 26 Dec–1 Jan, Jan–Apr weekends. Twenty km further north, on the right, is the **Weeping Wall** with a veil of water or winter-frozen ice hanging like smooth silk over grey stone. Look for ice climbers braving the limestone base of **Cirrus Mountain**.

Hwy 93 literally makes the **Big Bend**, a steep switchback that feels like driving on the edge of the world. At the top is the **Parker Ridge Trailhead**, a chilly 7-km return hike south onto the southern tip of the Columbia Icefield with a vista to Saskatchewan Glacier. Tundra wildflowers carpet the route, which can have up to 6 m of snow in winter for Nordic skiers. Shaggy white-coated mountain goats with pointed black horns cling to the bare rocks near the alpine treeline. Just north of the trailhead under looming Mt Athabasca, **HI-Hilda Creek Hostel**, *tel: (403) 762-4122; fax: (403) 762-3441,* is open May–mid Oct, Dec 26–Jan 1 and Jan–Apr weekends.

97

JASPER NATIONAL PARK

The park begins at 2035-m Sunwapta Pass as Hwy 93 follows the Sunwapta River north. Two campsites, **Wilcox Creek** and **Columbia Icefield** (tent pitches) are north of the pass.

The Columbia Icefield

Star of the southern end of the park, the **Columbia Icefield** offers a chance to walk on a glacier. The Icefield straddles the Continental Divide, spreads across

325 square km, may be 365 m deep and is the world's other hydrological apex after Siberia, draining into the Pacific, Arctic and Atlantic Oceans. Vastness aside, walking on slippery ice near ever-shifting treacherous blue crevasses in constantly-changing weather and temperatures is a thrill. Melt from the toe of receding **Athabasca Glacier** is pure water which snowed onto the surrounding peaks hundreds to thousands of years ago, compacting into ice under the pressure of repeated, non-melting snowfall. The downhill flow which created the 6-km long, mile-wide glacier is not static but constantly advances or retreats, causing the unstable top layers to creak and groan into crevasses.

Columbia Icefield Centre, *tel: (403) 852-6550,* open 0900–1700 (May–Sept), 1000–1600 (1–15 Oct), has a **Parks Canada Information Centre**, exhibits on the glacier, an ice cave mock-up, a restaurant, cafeteria, gift shop and an expensive 32-room **hotel**; *tel: (403) 762-6735; fax: (403) 762-6765,* open 15 May–early Oct, with third floor glacier views.

The Icefield Centre is also the base for Brewster Snocoach and icewalks out onto the Athabasca Glacier just east. **Brewster Athabasca Glacier Snocoach Tours**, adults $22.50, children 6–16 $5, use purpose-built buses with jumbo snow tyres to haul up a gravel road (rock and debris shoved and ground by the moving glacier create *moraines)* onto the ice. Dress warmly to exit onto the glacier for 20 mins to see the blue crevasses, sample trickling glacier water (have a bottle handy) and take photographs. Bookings aren't required for the 1½-hr tours which depart every 15 mins, but crowds swarm from 1030–1500.

From mid June–mid Sept, **Athabasca Glacier IceWalks**, *Icefield Centre Hotel front desk; tel: (800) 565-7547,* offer 3-hr walks 1130 Mon–Wed, Fri–Sat, adults $28,

children 7–17 $12, or strenuous 6-hr hikes, adults $32.

Watch for bighorn sheep as Hwy 93 descends north of the Icefield. There are several viewpoints along the Icefields Parkway along the 50 km to Sunwapta Falls, including spreading **Tangle Falls** 7 km north of the Icefield Centre. **HI-Beauty Creek Hostel**; *c/o Box 387, Jasper, AB T0E 1E0; tel: (403) 852-3215; fax: (403) 852-5560,* open May–Sept, on Sunwapta River, is 17 km from the Centre, and **Jonas Creek Campground**, open May–Oct, is 14 km further north.

Sunwapta Falls

Sunwapta Falls Resort, *PO Box 97, Jasper, AB T0E 1E0; tel: (403) 852-4852; fax: (403) 852-5353,* open May–Oct, offers expensive accommodation, dining and a good selection of gems amongst gift shop souvenirs. This stop, about halfway between the Columbia Icefield Centre and Jasper, has a 2-km trail to **Sunwapta Falls**, a lovely several-part plunge of water over and through limestone, best photographed in the afternoon. June–Oct, camp beside **Honeymoon Lake**, a few km north of the resort.

The route continues north following the **Athabasca River**. Mountain goats descend from precarious rock perches for the mineral licks close to **Mount Kerkeslin Campground**, open May–Sept.

Veer left onto Hwy 93A. **Athabasca Falls** is a short walk from the parking area, and a 2-min misty walk along a fenced path bridges the gorge through which the Athabasca River flows fiercely, plunging 23 m into and around quartzite. In winter, the flow is stilled as an ice wall frozen beneath the walkway. Athabasca Falls is a favourite with Nordic skiers who can glide virtually to the falls overlook. **Mt Kerkeslin**, 2984 m, dominates the view to the east.

98

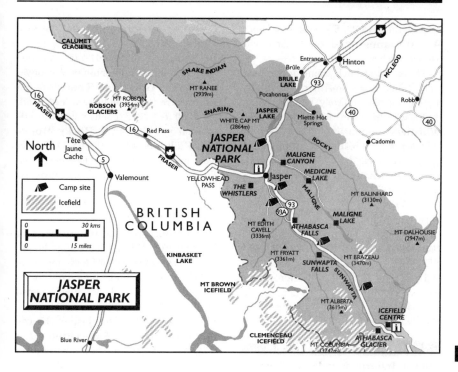

HI-Athabasca Falls Hostel, *c/o Box 387, Jasper, AB T0E 1E0; tel: (403) 852-3215; fax: (403) 852-5560,* open daily May–Sept, Wed–Mon Oct–Apr, is east of the falls and highway. Thirteen km north, 238-pitch **Wabasso Campground** can accommodate both tents and RVs from mid June–Sept.

Like Mt Rundle near Banff, **Mt Edith Cavell** stands like a 3363m sentinel in the Jasper area. A World War I British nurse serving in Belgium, Cavell was executed for alleged aid to prisoners; the peak was named to honour her bravery. Turn left onto *Mt Edith Cavell Rd;* RVs are unable to handle the twisting road. Expect delays and traffic control when the road is open, June–Oct. The 15-km drive towards Cavell Lake is worth the time – and the reflection of the mountain. There are several hiking trails, including an easy 1.5-km

loop trail with views of **Cavell** and **Angel Glaciers**, and a challenging 4-km hike through Cavell Meadows' wildflower carpet and more vistas of Angel Glacier. **HI-Mt Edith Cavell Hostel**, *c/o Box 387, Jasper, AB T0E 1E0; tel: (403) 852-3215; fax: (403) 852-5560,* open mid June–Oct, is well-located for hikers. Nordic skiers use the road in winter.

North on Hwy 93A, turn left onto a winding road to **Ski Marmot Basin**, *Box 1300, Jasper, AB T0E 1E0; tel: (403) 852-3816; fax: (403) 426-852-3533; snowphone tel: (403) 488-5909,* favoured by local skiers and snowboarders who like accessing the slopes from the car park during the Dec–Apr season. Facilities include three day lodges, restaurants, lounges, equipment hire and a gift shop. A daily shuttle service from main Jasper hotels avoids a drive from the townsite.

Back on Hwy 93, 5 km south of Jasper, **Wapiti Campground**, open year-round, has 366 pitches.

Think woodchuck, think groundhog, well, think hoary marmot, the black-footed, vaguely squirrely resident whose shrill 'whistle' gives its name to **The Whistlers** (mountain). Turn left on *Whistlers Rd*. **Whistlers Campground**, open May–Oct, has 781 pitches. **HI-Jasper International Hostel**, *Whistlers Rd, Box 387, Jasper, AB T0E 1E0; tel: (403) 852-3215; fax: (403) 852-5560,* open year-round, is en route to the lower terminal **Jasper Tramway** entrance, *PO Box 418, Jasper, AB T0E 1E0; tel: (403) 852-3093,* open late Mar–Oct, adults $16, children 5–14 $8.50. Canada's longest and highest (2500m) tramway has dining at the top, with views of Jasper Townsite and the Athabasca and Miette Rivers.

JASPER TOWNSITE

100

Tourist Information: Jasper Tourism & Commerce, *632 Connaught Dr., PO Box 98, Jasper, AB T0E 1E0; tel: (800) 473-8135* or *(403) 852-3858; fax: (403) 852-4932,* has information on the townsite and Jasper National Park. **Parks Canada Jasper Information Centre**, *500 Connaught Dr.; tel: (403) 852-6176; http://www.worldweb.com/parkscanada-jasper,* open 0800–1700 (mid May–mid June), 0800–1900 (mid June–Labour Day), Mon–Fri 0900–1700 Sat–Sun 0800–1700 (Sept–mid May), has park and area information, cross-country (Nordic) skiing and bicycling brochures and issues backcountry permits for Jasper National Park.

Environment Canada, *tel: (403) 852-3185,* has information on Jasper weather.

GETTING TO JASPER

Most of Jasper's 3 million annual visitors arrive by car; some hire a car in Jasper. The closest air service is into the **Jasper/Hinton Airport**, 64 km east of Jasper. **Brewster**, *tel: (800) 661-1152,* provide bus services from Edmonton or Vancouver and operate **Gray Line Tours** between Jasper, Lake Louise and Banff. **VIA Rail**, *tel: (888) 842-7245,* connect Jasper to Edmonton and Vancouver. **Rocky Mountain Railtours**, *tel: (800) 665-7425,* offer May–mid Oct two-day daylight rail excursions to or from Jasper and Vancouver via Kamloops.

ACCOMMODATION

Jasper Tourism & Commerce has a list of accommodation, including hotels, motels and lodges, but does not make bookings. Year-round, about 1700 rooms are available close to Jasper, supplemented by about 350 more in summer. There are no chain hotels. The **Jasper Home Accommodation Association**, *Box 758, AB T0E 1E0,* provides a list of Parks Canada-inspected-and-approved private homes – some Bed and Breakfasts, which are a cosy alternative in Jasper's very walkable townsite.

Jasper Park Lodge, *south-east of Jasper Townsite, the Railway Tracks, Hwy 16 and the Athabasca River, PO Box 40, Jasper, AB T0E 1E0; tel: (800) 441-1414* or *(403) 852-3301; fax: (403) 852-5107,* is the expensive–pricey Canadian Pacific Hotels entry with 442 rooms, famed for room service delivery by bicycle. No château here, the lodge, nestled near green **Lac Beauvert**, was rebuilt cabin-style after a fire in 1952. Framed by grey stone, the huge windows of the Great Hall and Emerald Lounge in the Main Lodge lobby overlook the lake and outdoor swimming pool. Shops, a health club and the superb Edith Cavell Dining Room are on the lower level. The 18-hole golf course tees were designed to line up with mountain

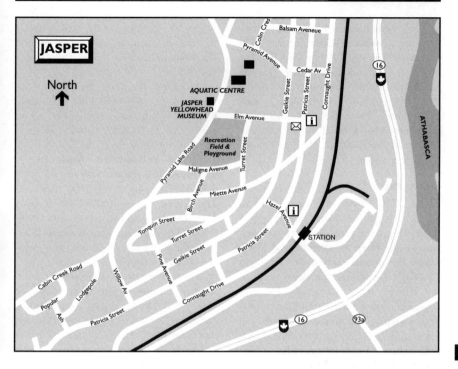

views late Apr–Oct, and wapiti – elk – wander everywhere in all seasons.

Glassy **Lac Beauvert** has canoe hire with trails around the lake. Frozen in winter, the lake, and Lake Mildred along the lodge exit road, have ice skating in winter. The lodge's location near the Athabasca River permits ski-in/ski-out to most rooms. **Tekarra Lodge**, *PO Box 669; tel: (800) 661-6562 or (403) 852-3058,* open May–mid Oct, moderate–expensive, has cabins with porch views of river rafters braving the confluence of the Miette and Athabasca Rivers. **The Glass House**, *715 Miette Ave, Box 2163; tel: (403) 852-3861,* has cosy moderate rooms in a skylit private home and mouth-watering home-made breads as a breakfast add-on.

EATING AND DRINKING

The only fast food is **A&W**, though there are several coffee shops and grocery stores for provisioning for a day's activities as well as Korean and Japanese restaurants. Several eateries along *Patricia St* have upstairs mountain view dining.

Jasper Park Lodge has several outstanding dining options: try the wild mushroom soup in the much-acclaimed posh **Edith Cavell D Room** with a view onto Lac Beauvert, and the excellent budget granola and bagel Jogger's Breakfast at **Meadows Café**. The **Beauvert Dining Room** is spacious with a lake view. Dine in summer at **La Terrasse** above the pool. There's pan-Canadian cuisine from caribou to braised buffalo at the moderate **Moose's Nook**.

Watch the mountain sunset from **Miss Italia Ristorante**, *upstairs, 610 Patricia St; tel: (403) 852-4002,* which serves home-made pasta, pizza, BC salmon in season and heavenly bruschetta, a fresh tomato dipping sauce. **Fiddle River**, *upstairs, 620 Connaught Dr.; tel: (403) 852-3032,* has moderate seafood for dinner. **Jasper Marketplace**, *627 Patricia St; tel: (403) 852-3152,* opens early for breakfast or picnic makings. There are 11 lounges and nightclubs. The '**Athy B**', *in the Athabasca Hotel, 510 Patricia St; tel: (403) 852-3386,* is a local hangout.

SIGHTSEEING

Today, Jasper Townsite houses 5000 in an orderly street plan resembling a boomerang on a map. The railway track and parallel Hwy 16, Yellowhead Hwy, follow the outside curve south of town. *Connaught Dr.* follows the curve north of the railway track. *Connaught Dr.* and *Patricia St* create a commercial T-shirt, souvenir shopping and dining zone, between *Hazel* and *Cedar Aves. Miette Ave* diagonally bisects the commercial area, running east to the Railway Station. The pink building near the station has clean public toilets.

European presence began in 1811 when explorer and North West Company trader David Thompson left William Henry in the Jasper area to set up a trading post while Thompson's party searched for a mountain pass along the Athabasca River route. The location of Henry's House is lost, but the trading post and rest stop thrived for several decades, alongside clerk Jasper Hawes' namesake, Jasper House. In 1862, gold-seeking Overlanders from Britain walked through on a 5600-km trek towards the Cariboo gold fields.

Jasper National Park was established in 1907, followed by the arrival of the Grand Trunk Pacific Railway and settlement of Jasper in 1911. The trains still dominate much of downtown, plaintive whistles carrying through the night. In winter, the wapiti (elk) stay close to the railway tracks; in summer, wapiti are everywhere around the townsite and the Jasper Park Lodge lawns.

The Den, *105 Miette Ave, Whistlers Inn downstairs; tel: (403) 852-3361,* open daily 0900–2200, admission (June–Sept) adults $2.95, children 6–16 $2.50, has a collection of Alberta wildlife specimens.

Jasper–Yellowhead Museum & Archives, *400 Pyramid Lake Rd; tel: (403) 852-3013,* open 1000–2100 (Victoria Day–Labour Day), 1000–1700 (Labour Day–Thanksgiving Day), Thur–Sun 1000–1700 (Thanksgiving Day–Victoria Day), $2, is the local history museum, with early-day park photographs and artefacts.

The outdoors is Jasper's real draw. Winter activities include alpine (Marmot Basin) and Nordic skiing, snowboarding (Marmot Basin), ice skating (Lac Beauvert and Mildred Lake), hockey (Lake Mildred), dogsledding, horsedrawn sleigh rides; *tel: (403) 852-4215,* Jasper Park Lodge golf course, adults $13, children 6–12 $6.50, ice climbing, snowshoeing, tobogganing and ice crawling.

Boots and crampons equip hikers to walk along the side, then on the Maligne River Canyon floor. In summer, the water roars through the canyon; in winter, all is frozen, creating great sheaths of mounded ice feathering into icicles over hidden outcroppings which create mini-caves, challenging for ice-climbers. The narrow canyon walls cast an eerie and beautiful twilight even at midday. **Jasper Adventure Centre Ltd.**, *604 Connaught Dr., Box 1064; tel: (800) 565-7547 or (403) 852-5595,* offer a 3-hr guided walk, adults $25, children $13.

SIDE TRACKS FROM JASPER TOWNSITE
To reach **Maligne Canyon**, take

Connaught Dr. north-east from the railway station, crossing the tracks, to Hwy 16. Turn left onto the Yellowhead Hwy for 1.5 km, then turn right across the Athabasca River. Go left on *Maligne Lake Rd* 2.5 km, then right, following signs to the third left-hand turn, to Maligne Canyon car park.

Maligne Canyon Cafeteria, *tel: (403) 852-3583*, serves delicious light meals Apr–Oct; listen for woodland birdsong on the fenced 3.7-km walk along the canyon's edge. *Under* the Maligne River is another river of water, flowing with such force underground that it fills Medicine Lake to the south. As runoff diminishes during the summer, Medicine Lake shrinks while draining below, rather than into a visible waterway.

HI-Maligne Canyon Hostel, *c/o Box 387; tel: (403) 852-3215; fax: (403) 852-5560*, is open daily, except Wed (Oct–Apr).

Roche Bonhomme, sometimes called 'the Old Man', is the rock formation to the north-east that looks like a man, perhaps a Native chief, lying down.

Maligne Lake Rd roughly follows the course of the **Maligne River**. The unhappy name, *la traverse maligne,* was given in 1846 by Jesuit missionary Fr Pierre de Smet who lost his belongings and horses to the 'wicked' river. The river has whitewater for rafters. Conical mountains near **Medicine Lake** is a prime spot for wildlife: wapiti, mountain goats, black bears and occasional deer create animal jams.

Jasper National Park's largest lake, 48 km from Jasper, is a day resort. **Maligne Lake** facilities May–early Oct include a cafeteria, a gift shop and canoe, rowboat, kayak and fishing boat hire at the

Maligne Lake Boathouse, *tel: (403) 852-3370*. Fishers cast for stocked rainbow and Eastern brook trout. **Maligne Tours**, *626 Connaught Dr.; tel: (403) 852-3770; fax: (403) 852-3405*, offer 90-min narrated boat tours to **Spirit Island** in the lake, adults $31, children 6–12 $15.50. Horse riding and walking the 3-km loop around the lake or long, strenuous hikes up to a vista of the lake and ring of mountain peaks are other options.

The road to the lake is open in winter for Nordic skiing and snowshoeing in the Maligne Lake area.

Rafting on the Maligne and Athabasca Rivers includes traversing whitewater rapids. A number of companies offer rafting mid May–mid Sept, including **Jasper Raft Tours Ltd**; *tel: (403) 852-2665*; raft trips are $30–$70, depending on length, scenery and class of rapids. **Rocky Mountain Voyageurs**; *tel: (800) 565-7547 or tel/fax: (403) 852-3343*, 2-hr canoe trip paddles a calm section of the Athabasca River, adults $41, children 6–12 $24. Ask for rain gear as freezing rain can fall without preamble.

North of the townsite, follow *Pyramid Lake Rd* 7 km to **Pyramid Lake**, perfectly reflecting a triangular mountain. **Patricia Lake**, with expensive May–mid Oct **Paticia Lake Bungalows**, *Box 657; tel: (403) 852-3560*, is on the way. **Pyramid Lake Resort**, *Box 388; tel: (403) 852-4900; fax: (403) 852-7007*, has expensive chalets with great lake views and sunny al fresco summer dining. Hire motor boats, canoes, kayaks and other watercraft, or fish, hike or picnic. **Pyramid Stables**, *PO Box 787; tel: (403) 852-3562*, offer horseriding. Winter brings Nordic skiing and skating. ⬛

103

JASPER–EDMONTON

A stunning series of lakes and wetlands favoured by elk, Rocky Mountain sheep and goats lines Hwy 16, the Yellowhead Hwy, for 50 km east of Jasper Townsite to the Jasper National Park boundary. Miette Hot Springs wait 17 km up a road built on rock formed hundreds of millions of years ago. Once outside the park, where lodging and dining are less dear, the next 315 km of this 365-km route to Edmonton become flatter and less interesting by the minute, though there are well-marked turn-offs to winter ski areas and pleasant lakes along most of the route. Plan on driving five hours from the townsite to the province's capital city or drive the route in reverse for thrilling views of the sheer Rocky Mountains on the approach to Jasper.

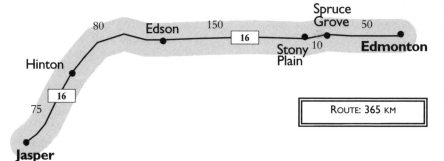

ROUTE: 365 KM

ROUTE

Take *Connaught Dr.* north from the Jasper train station and turn north onto Hwy 16, continuing 363 km north and east to Edmonton.

BUSES AND TRAINS

Greyhound Lines of Canada operate four trips a day, taking 2 hrs. OTT table 120.

The Canadian train runs three times a week. Journey: 5¼ hrs. OTT table 4.

JASPER TO MIETTE HOT SPRINGS

In any season, groups of elk (wapiti) are likely to be standing, lounging or sleeping on the right side of the road or near the railway tracks as you drive north on *Connaught Dr.* The road curves right; veer left, north, onto the Yellowhead Hwy, Hwy 16.

Many Jasper-area attractions are east of town. One-and-a-half km north on Hwy 16, turn right and cross the Athabasca River to go south to Jasper Park Lodge and Lac Beauvert; follow signs to Lakes Annette and Edith; or, go north on *Maligne Lake Rd* to Maligne Canyon and the lake.

North on Hwy 16, cross the Snaring and Athabasca Rivers while watching for ubiquitous elk. In summer and fall, male elk have multiple-point antlers which appear top-heavy as they move slowly in and out of lakes and ponds. Fall is the rutting season when male elk clash and crash their heads to determine breeding dominance – observe the battle from afar. Beautiful mountains are reflected in Jasper Lake and Lake Talbot. Thirty-six km from Jasper is a 5-km long, 70 kph speed limit elk protection zone, where curly-horned bighorn sheep *(mouflon d'Amerique)* and mountain goats enjoy roadside salt licks. Watch the fearless animals from your vehicle at the lay-by on the right side of the road; feeding wildlife rates a heavy fine.

MIETTE HOT SPRINGS

Seven km north, turn right onto *Fiddle Valley Rd* at **Pocohontas Bungalows**, *PO Box 820, Jasper, AB T0E 1EO; tel: (800) 843-3372* or *(403) 866-3955; fax: (403) 866-3777*, with a restaurant, 41 moderate cabins, 15 motel rooms and suites. RVs and trailers are not recommended beyond the **Pocohontas Campground**, *tel: (403) 866-3783*, 2 km along *Fiddle Valley Rd*. A short loop trail reaches nearby ruins and coal mine tailings left from 1912–1921 Jasper Park Collieries operations. Walk a little further along a creek to **Punchbowl Falls**.

Golden-pink **Roche Miette** is the peak west of Hwy 16. Most of the winding 17-km road to **Miette Hot Springs** is closed mid Oct–mid May. Park at the **Fiddle River** lay-by 9 km up the road to stand on 140–150 million-year-old rock while admiring the 360 million-year-old **Ashlar Ridge** across the canyon.

Pocohontas miners constructed the first buildings at **Miette Hot Springs**, *PO Box 2579, Jasper; tel: (403) 866-3939; fax: (403) 866-2112*, open mid May–mid Oct. At 53.9°C, these are the hottest thermal springs in the Rocky Mountains. Luckily,

the sulphur-scented pools; *tel: (403) 866-2233*, adults $4–$5, children $3.50–$4.50, family $11.50–$14.50, are cooled to a mere 39°C! **Miette Hot Springs Resort Bungalows & Motel**, *PO Box 907, Jasper; tel: (403) 866-3750; fax: (403) 866-2214*, offer moderate–expensive lodging. There's picnicking and a small café, a restaurant at the Bungalows and a short path up a lawn to the ruined 1937–1984 hot springs building, with a boardwalk continuation to the springs.

MIETTE HOT SPRINGS TO HINTON

Return to the Yellowhead Highway, cross the Fiddle River and exit Jasper National Park at the East Gate. **Overlander Mountain Lodge**, *Box 6118, Hinton, AB T7V 1N2; tel: (403) 866-2330; fax: (403) 866-2332*, just outside the park has moderate–expensive rooms and a restaurant with Alberta meat specialities. Just after a right-hand lay-by, **Folding Mountain Resort**, *PO Box 6085, Hinton, AB T7V 1X5; tel: (403) 866-3737; fax: (403) 866-2164*; open May–mid Oct, is an RV park with a moderate motel and services. For tent campers, there's 23-pitch **Wildhorse/Kinky Lakes Campground**, open May–Sept.

The Hwy 16 speed limit increases to 100 kph. Turn left, north, onto Hwy 40 for 19 km to locally-popular **William A Switzer Provincial Park**, *PO Box 6178, Hinton; tel: (403) 865-5600; fax: (403) 865-1282*, for year-round camping at several spots, including a few lakeside pitches at **Gregg Lake Campground**.

Black Cat Guest Ranch, *north-west from Hwy 40, Box 6267, Hinton, AB T7V 1X6; tel: (800) 859-6840* or *(403) 865-3084; fax: (403) 865-1924*, has moderate–expensive Rockies-view rooms with meals, hiking, horses for hire ($16 per hour), hot tubs and nearby rafting.

MIETTE HOT SPRINGS • MIETTE HOT SPRINGS TO HINTON

The landscape flattens abruptly and the sawmill plume is visible as Hwy 16 approaches **Hinton**.

HINTON

Tourist Information: Hinton & District Chamber of Commerce, *308 Gregg Ave, Hinton, AB T7V 1X3; tel: (403) 865-2777; fax: (403) 865-1062,* or the **Town of Hinton**, *813 Switzer Dr., Hinton, AB T7V 1V1; tel: (403) 865-6004; fax: (403) 865-5706,* have information on Hinton's non-chain accommodation, dining, an 18-hole golf course and industrial tours to a sawmill or coal mines.

Hinton's 10,000 residents have Hi-Atha Sawmill and Weldwood Pulpmill to divide the half-century-old town south of the Athabasca River into **The Hill** and **The Valley**. The **Alberta Forest Service Museum**, along the Forestry School Interpretive Trail at the Forest Technology School, *1176 Switzer Dr.; tel: (403) 865-8211,* open Mon–Fri in summer, has artefacts from forest management and fire-fighting, with fine views of the Rockies.

HINTON TO EDSON

Contact the Chamber of Commerce for July–Aug tours of **Obed Mountain Coal** (20 km east) or **Cardinal River Coals** (40 km south), the latter mining coal up to the boundary of Jasper National Park, amidst protests from environmentalists.

The highest point on the Yellowhead Hwy, 1164-m **Obed Summit**, is the area past **Obed Mountain Coal** where Hwy 16 turns east. Tiny **Obed Lake Campground**, with 7 pitches, opens May–Sept.

The highway opens out fully onto tree-dottted plains into petroleum country.

EDSON

Tourist Information: Edson & District Chamber of Commerce, *5433 3 Ave, Edson, AB T7E 1L5; tel: (403) 723-4918; fax: (403) 723-5545,* has information on accommodation, camping and local attractions.

The highway divides through town, with *2 Ave* going east and *4 Ave* going west, both lined with the town's motels. Edson bills itself as the Slo-Pitch Capital of Canada, with 21 baseball diamonds in **Vision Park**.

The 1910 Grand Trunk Railway **Galloway Station Museum**, *in Centennial Park, 5433 3 Ave; tel: (403) 723-5696,* open 0930–1630 (July–Aug), next to the Chamber of Commerce visitor centre, covers Edson origins as a railway hub for settlers moving north via Edson to the remote Peace River Valley. **Red Brick Arts Centre & Museum**, *4818 7 Ave; tel: (403) 723-3582,* has local objects in a gracious 1914 red brick school building.

Edson Native Interpretive Trail, *5919 2 Ave (Hwy 16 W.), Box 6508, Edson, AB T7E 1T9; tel: (403) 723-6221* or *(403) 723-5494,* open 1000–1900, offers First Nations history and cultural demonstrations on the *Trail of Legends,* pow-wows and dances, a café with bannock, frybread, buffalo burgers, smoked fish and dried meats, Aboriginal art from Cree, Blackfoot, Saulteaux (Chippawa) and Métis, and teepee hire.

While Edson currently relies upon oil and some timber processing, it's still possible to find a **Farmer's Market**, Fri 1100–1400.

EDSON TO STONEY PLAIN

Soon after leaving Edson, a sign warns of smoke and limited visibility for the next 80 km. **Nilton Junction**, 40 km east, has services. Pause briefly at **Nojack**, where a tiny motel and petrol station grace a stretch of the road that sounds as if it's named for astonishment or a losing hand of cards.

Hike, swim, fish or camp at **Pembina River Provincial Park**, *tel: (403) 727-3643*.

Approaching Stoney Plain, Edmonton's lights appear on the horizon.

STONEY PLAIN

Tourist Information: Stoney Plain & District Chamber of Commerce, *5010 51 Ave, Box 2300, Stoney Plain, AB T7Z 1X7; tel: (403) 963-4545*, has local information and a mural heritage walk brochure.

Dogrump Creek or Dog Creek wasn't elegant enough for a region trying to attract German and Austrian farmers to settle west of Edmonton in the 1890s. An early settler applying for a post office name may or may not have named it for the native Stoney people who lived in the area. Stoney may have been an unappealing image to potential settlers; though stories vary, the name and town became Stoney Plain.

The **Murals Heritage Walk**, *Heart of Town Association, 4905 51 Ave; tel: (403) 963-2151*, is a 16-painting depiction of town history and founders; most murals are along *50 St.*

Multicultural Heritage Centre, *5411 51 St; tel: (403) 963-2777*, open daily Mon–Sat 1000–1600, Sun 1000–1830, has a free museum in a high school with a settler's cabin, **Oppertshauser Gallery** showing local art, a craft and gift shop and pioneer-style lunches at **Homesteader's Kitchen Restaurant**.

Andrew Wolf Wine Cellars, *Hwy 16, Box 628; tel: (403) 963-7717*, open Mon–Fri 1100–1930, Sat 1100–1800, offer free tours of the castle-style winery, wine tasting, a gift shop, picnicking and a small zoo. Napa Valley, California vinifera and century-old French oak casks used in California are used to produce the unusual range of wines from varietals to spiced peach and apple wine. **Alberta Fairytale Grounds**, *7 km north-west on Hwy 779; tel: (403) 963-8161*, open 1000–1800 May–Sept, adults $4.50, children 3–12 $3.25, has clockwork characters in tiny houses appropriate to each story.

SPRUCE GROVE

Tourist Information: Spruce Grove & District Chamber of Commerce, *Hwy 16 at 99 Campsite Rd; tel: (403) 962-2561*, share space with **Edmonton Tourism/ Spruce Grove Visitor Information Centre**. Both provide information for the entire area around Edmonton.

Spruce Grove is east of Stoney Plain and 15 mins west of Edmonton. Spruce Grove is the Honey Processing Centre of Canada. **Beemaid Honey**, *70 Alberta Ave; tel: (403) 962-5573*, offer free Mon–Fri tours of the local co-operative honey processing plant and demonstrate beeswax candle making.

SPRUCE GROVE TO EDMONTON

Ten km west of downtown Edmonton, go 14 km south on Hwy 60 to **Devonian Botanic Garden**, *tel: (403) 987-3054; fax: (403) 987-4141*, open 1000–1900 (mid May–Labour Day), 1000–1600 (Sept–mid Oct) and Sat–Sun 1100–1600 winter, adults $5, children 4–12 $3. Alberta Plant Garden and a Native People's Garden grow local flora; the authentic Kurimoto Japanese Garden is a woodland jewel. A butterfly house shows tropical species. Peonies, primula and iris fill other gardens, with a 110-acre natural area for wandering.

Hwy 16 forks as it approaches the town of Edmonton. Hwy 16 continues as *Stoney Plain Rd* to the heart of downtown; Hwy 16X, the *Yellowhead Trail*, skirts petroleum producers in the industrial district of north Edmonton.

107

EDMONTON

Canada's Oil Capital is also Alberta's provincial capital, a prairie centre for petroleum and coal processing, railways and agriculture. Edmonton, nestled firmly on the winding North Saskatchewan River, four hours drive east of Jasper, is a fine base for exploration.

Old Strathcona's gracious red-brick buildings survive in an historic district filled with restaurants, shops and counter-culture fillips. Trade traditions continue at the huge West Edmonton Mall, living history portrays immigrant farm life at the Ukrainian Cultural Heritage Village, and buffalo still roam at Elk Island National Park. Downtown Edmonton boasts a glass pyramid conservatory, a compact Chinatown, innovative public architecture and magnificent river vistas.

TOURIST INFORMATION

Edmonton Tourism Visitor Information Centre, Shaw Conference Centre, *9797 Jasper Ave N.W., No. 104, Edmonton, AB T5J 1N9; tel: (800) 463-4667* or *(403) 496-8400*, open Mon–Fri 0800–1700, and **Gateway Park**, *2404 Calgary Trail (Hwy 2), 10 km south of downtown Edmonton*, open 0800–2100 (Victoria Day–pre-Labour Day) and Mon–Fri 0830–1630, Sat–Sun 0900–1700 (Labour Day–pre-Victoria Day), have information on the area, Elk Island National Park, national heritage sites and the Reynolds-Alberta Museum in Wetaskiwin (see p.123). For **Edmonton Tourism Spruce Grove**

VIC, see p.107. **Edmonton City Hall**, *99 St* and *102A Ave;* **West Edmonton Mall**, *8770 110 St, Upper Level across from World Waterpark;* and **Edmonton International Airport**, *25 km south of downtown via Hwy 2*, have information kiosks.

WEATHER

Environment Canada, *tel: (403) 468-4940*, has local weather forecasts. Summer temperatures average 17°C in June, with frequent thunderstorms. Expect freezing nights in spring and fall, with daytime temperatures rising to 10°C. Edmonton is open to winds blowing across the plains. Wind chill lowers winter temperatures to -19°C or below. Snowfall averages 132cm, and, while roads are kept clear, the flat landscape is subject to white-out with landmarks becoming invisible behind snow drifts and equally white sky. For **local road conditions**; *tel: (403) 471-6056.*

ARRIVING AND DEPARTING

By Air
Twenty-five km south of downtown Edmonton off Hwy 2, **Edmonton International Airport (YEG)**, *tel: (800) 268-7134* or *(403) 890-8382*, is modern and spacious. Chairs, phones and a colourful candy vending machine wait in the enclosed, heated Meeting Point/Rendezvous Point building just off the economical outdoor parking area.

The **Airport Information Booth**, *Arrivals Level, right of the entry across from the Meeting Point*, is open daily 0730–2330. Luggage trolleys are free. There is baggage storage and foreign exchange.

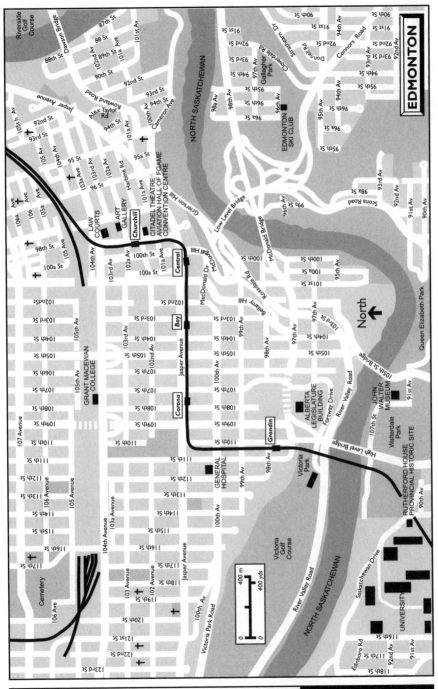

North

109

Car hire agencies are across from the baggage carousels on the Arrivals Level. Two red automatic stations accept advance parking payments (first 15 mins free), $1 per half-hour. YEG's long-stay parking lot offers free vehicle-to-terminal transport, winter plug-ins, dead battery boosts and a snow-free auto upon your return.

Sky Shuttle, *tel: (888) 438-2342* or *(403) 465-8515*, runs from the airport to downtown Edmonton every 20 mins, adults $11, $18 return, children 3–12 $5.50. Other routes run at 45-min intervals to the West End, including the West Edmonton Mall, and hourly to the University of Alberta, south-east of downtown. **Taxis** to downtown are $30 and there is also **limousine** service.

By Car

Edmonton lies on the axis of two major highways. The *Calgary Trail*, **Hwy 2**, extends 294 km south to Calgary, continuing on to Fort Macleod, Cardston and the US border. Hwy 2 curves north-west to Slave Lake and Peace River, then south to Grand Prairie and west to the BC border. **Yellowhead Hwy 16**, the *Yellowhead Trail*, turns south on *170 St*, then turns right onto *Stony Plain Rd* to run west 362 km to Jasper, continuing to Prince George and Prince Rupert. Hwy 16 east runs to Saskatoon and Winnepeg.

By Train

VIA Rail's trans-Canada route, the *Canadian*, thrice-weekly year-round, connects Edmonton, *10004 104 Ave; tel: (888) 842-7245* or *(403) 422-6032*, with Vancouver and Jasper and runs east to Toronto via Saskatoon and Winnepeg.

By Bus

Greyhound Lines, *10324 103 St; tel: (800) 661-8747* or *(403) 421-4211*, connect with major Canadian and US cities. **Red Arrow**, *10014 104 St; tel: (800) 232-1958* or *(403) 424-3339*, offer a more posh service to Red Deer and Calgary.

GETTING AROUND

Public Transport

Edmonton Transit System (ETS), *Downtown Information Centre, Central LRT Station, street level, 100 A St and Jasper Ave; tel: (403) 496-1600*, open Mon–Fri 0930–1700, sell tickets and passes and have route maps. ETS route information; *tel: (403) 496-1611*, is available Mon–Fri 0630–2230, Sat 0700–1800, Sun 0900–1730. **LRT** (light rail transit), trolleys and buses cover Edmonton, but not the airport. Service, generally 0500–0200, is more frequent in summer; the LRT runs every 5–15 mins, depending on demand.

Fares, with one transfer, are paid with exact change, adults $1.60, children 6–15 $1; daily passes, adults $4.75, children $3.75; or a 10-ride ticket book, adults $16, children $10. Children under 5 ride free. The LRT is free Mon–Fri 0900–1500, Sat 0900–1800 between Churchill Station *(City Hall/Sir Winston Churchill Sq.)* and Grandin Station *(Government Centre)*.

Driving in Edmonton

Named roads, drives, trails, avenues and streets mix it up a bit, but Edmonton's grid system, with street numbers starting from the city's south-east corner, is easy to navigate: *streets* are north–south, *avenues* are east–west. Before setting out, verify which area or neighbourhood the street or avenue is in — otherwise you'll end up across town!

Traffic circles (roundabouts) have rules: when approaching, stay in the right lane if taking the first or second exit; stay left if taking the second or third exit. Within the circle, the outside vehicle gives way to the inside vehicle. Exit the circle from the lane you've travelled on within the circle.

Traffic congests during rush hours, 0700–0900 and 1500–1800, near the West Edmonton Mall *(170 St* and *90 Ave)*, *Stony Plain Rd/102 Ave* and its downtown extension, *Jasper Ave*, and on *Whitemud Dr.* (Hwy 2); snow slows the flow.

Bridges cross the North Saskatchewan River from the south side to the higher north bank. The Hotel Macdonald surmounts downtown access via the **Low Level Bridge**. The **J D McDonald Bridge** goes downtown on *97 Ave*. The **105 St Bridge**, one-way north, passes a large water filtration plant. The **High Level Bridge**, noted for an occasional man-made waterfall bigger than the flow of Niagara Falls, goes one-way south from the Alberta Legislature Building to the University of Alberta. **Groat Bridge** flows into *Groat Rd* corridor, completely bypassing the Provincial Museum of Alberta.

Heated downtown **underground parkades**, *tel: (403) 496-6569,* $0.50–$3 per hour, connect business, government and arts venues via **pedways**, which offer protection from winter weather. **Park in the Heart parkades**, *tel: (403) 424-4085,* charge $2 1800–0100 and $1 for the first 3 hrs before 1800 on weekends. Some businesses and hotels offer **Downtown Dollars**, useful for parkades, meters, ETS buses and LRT. Parking meters are $1.25 per hour; most are free after 1800, Sundays and holidays.

STAYING IN EDMONTON

Accommodation

Downtown Edmonton is the most expensive; consider the West End along *Stony Plain Rd* or the South Side along *Calgary Trail* for cheaper accommodation. Edmonton Tourism has an accommodation list

which includes Bed and Breakfasts, or book through the **Bed & Breakfast Association of Greater Edmonton**, *tel: (800) 884-8803* or *(403) 465-3838.*

Downtown chain hotels include *BW, CP, DI, EL, HJ, Rn, Sh,* and *Wt.* **Hotel Macdonald**, *10065 100 St; tel: (800) 441-1414* or *(403) 424-5181,* is the elegant, pricey, CP château flanking downtown on a rise above the river. Built in 1915 by Grand Trunk Railway, the 'Mac' has an elegant lobby giving onto landscaped gardens, fine dining in the Harvest Room and a Wedgwood Room faithfully rendered in the famed blue and white china pattern. **Union Bank Inn**, *10053 Jasper Ave; tel: (403) 423-3600,* uses a former financial building as an expensive 14–room Bed and Breakfast. **HI Edmonton Youth Hostel**, *10422 91 St; tel: (403) 429-0140,* is northeast of Downtown and Chinatown.

The **West End** is closer to the West Edmonton Mall, fast food and other dining, with chain hotels like *BW, CI and TL.* The moderate **West Harvest Inn**, *17803 Stony Plain Rd (Hwy 16 W.); tel: (800) 661-6993* or *(403) 484-8000,* is well-located. The expensive 352-room **Fantasyland Hotel**, *West Edmonton Mall, 17700 87 Ave; tel: (800) 661-6454* or *(403) 444-3000,* has theme rooms like Igloo, Canadian Rail, Arabian, African, Roman, Polynesian, Victorian Coach and the Truck Room, complete with a bed in the rear of a yellow pick-up truck and a traffic policeman looming over the Jacuzzi.

Other possibilities include **South Side** accommodation near *Calgary Trail*, with chains *BW, CS, Hd* and *Rm,* and **Convention Inn**, *4404 Calgary Trail; tel: (800) 661-1122* or *(403) 434-6415.*

Eating and Drinking
The Hotel Macdonald **Harvest Room**, *10065 100 St; tel: (403) 424-5181,* has fine

dining under high ceilings with the coats of arms of BC, Alberta and Saskatchewan on stained-glass windows; a terrace overlooks the gardens. High tea is served Fri–Sun 1500–1600. For a glimpse of ethnic food variety, visit **Downtown City Farmer's Market**, *10165 97 St; tel: (403) 496-6298*, Sat 0800–1400. **Chateau Louis**, *11727 Kingsway; tel: (403) 452-7770*, has a budget Ukrainian buffet Sun 1630–2030.

Old Strathcona is thick with restaurants like cheerful **Julio's Barrio**, *10450 82 Ave; tel: (403) 431-0774*, with huge portions of Mexican food, and Greek **Yianni's Taverna**, *10444 82 Ave; tel: (403) 433-6768*. Close by is **Da De O**, *10548 82 Ave; tel: (403) 433-0930*, moderate Cajun food in an old diner. The **Old Strathcona Farmer's Market**, *103 St at 83 Ave; tel: (403) 439-1844*, open Sat 0800–1500, has Saskatoon berry pie in summer, braided Ukrainian Easter bread and painted eggs in spring and fine goose down duvets made by Hutterite farm wives wearing bright floral dresses and scarves.

West Edmonton Mall has a **Planet Hollywood**, **Hard Rock Café**, **Tony Roma**'s ribs, an art gallery, pizza and steak at **Café Modern Art**, several pubs and outstanding Chinese food at bright, cheerful, budget **Chili Hot Hot (West)**, *tel: (403) 413-4892*.

Communications and Money

Edmonton General Delivery, *Edmonton Main Wicket, 9828 104 Ave, Edmonton, AB T2P 2G8* receives mail, as will any hotel.

There are **Thomas Cook bureaux de change** at *8770 170th St, West Edmonton Mall* and downtown at *102 2nd St.*

ENTERTAINMENT

On Fri, both daily papers publish entertainment sections: the *Edmonton Journal*'s *What's On* and the *Edmonton Sun*'s *Weekend Express*. Free on Thur, *Vue Weekly* and *See Magazine* review the area's nightlife, events and entertainment. The *WHERE Edmonton* monthly magazine has events throughout the region.

Most nightclubs charge a cover. **Old Strathcona** has plenty of nightlife, pubs and live music, including blues at the **Commercial Hotel**, *10329 82 Ave; tel: (403) 439-3981*. Jazz is it on Tues, Fri, Sat at **Yardbird Suite**, *10203 86 Ave; tel: (403) 432-0428*. **The Sidetrack Café**, *10333 112 St; tel: (403) 421-1326*, has daily live music. Check the **West Edmonton Mall**, *(800) 661-8890* or *(403) 444-5200*, for current entertainment around **Bourbon St**.

Country & Western music and dancing is on at **Cook County Saloon**, *8010 103 St; tel: (403) 432-2665*, Tues–Sat 1900–0200; **Cowboy's Country Saloon**, *10102 180 St; tel: (403) 481-8739*, 1800–0200; **Wild West Saloon**, *12912 50 St; tel: (403) 476-3388*, open Mon–Thur 1900–0300, Fri–Sat 1500–0300.

Yuk Yuk's, *Bourbon St Entrance 6, West Edmonton Mall; tel: (403) 481-9857*, is the hot comedy spot. Edmonton has four casinos and many more legitimate theatre companies. **Mayfield Dinner Theatre**, *Mayfield Inn, 16615 109 Ave; tel: (403) 483-4051*; **Celebrations Dinner Theatre**, *13103 Fort Rd; tel: (403) 448-9339*, and **Jubilations Dinner Theatre**, *West Edmonton Mall; tel: (403) 484-2424*, offer dining and dramatic entertainment.

Citadel Theatre, *9828 101 A Ave (at 99 St); tel: (403) 426-4811* or *(403) 425-1820*, has year-round presentations with a Sept–May Main Season, tickets $20–$45. Adjacent **Winspear Centre for Music**, *4 Sir Winston Churchill Sq.; tel: (403) 429-1992* or *(403) 428-1414*, seats 1900 for concerts.

From Dec–early May, the **Edmonton Opera**, *10232 112 St, Suite 320; tel: (403) 429-1000*, sings classics from Verdi to Gilbert & Sullivan. The **Edmonton Symphony Orchestra**, *10160 103 St; tel: (403) 428-1108* or *(403) 428-1414*, and the **Alberta Ballet Company**, *tel: (403) 424-3136*, share performing venues with the Opera, *Northern Alberta Jubilee Auditorium, University of Alberta, 87 Ave* and *114 St; tel: (403) 427-9622*.

Klondike Days, *tel: (403) 479-3500*, ten days in mid July, celebrate 19th-century pioneers. Local people dress in period finery and have a parade, with other entertainment centred around *Sir Winston Churchill Sq.* and **Northlands Park**.

Sports

Northlands Park, *7300 116 Ave; tel: (403) 471-7379*, has harness racing early Mar–mid May and mid Sept–mid Dec (the latter is thoroughbred racing season). Motorsports include tractor pulling and mud bogs at **Capital Raceway**, *3123 92 St; tel: (403) 462-8725*.

NHL **Edmonton Oilers Hockey Club**, *11230 110 St; tel: (403) 474-8561*, play Oct–Apr in **Edmonton Coliseum**, *7424 118 Ave*. CFL **Edmonton Eskimos**, *9023 111 Ave; tel: (403) 448-1525*, play in the **Commonwealth Stadium**, *11000 Stadium Rd*, June–Nov. **Edmonton Trappers**, *tel: (403) 429-2934*, play Triple A baseball Apr–Sept at **Telus Field**, *10233 96 Ave*.

The **Riverside** and **Highlands Golf Courses** blend with parks along the North Saskatchewan River to create a green belt from spring–early winter for jogging, strolling and bicycling. **Winter Wonderland Walks** are led by **River Valley Parks**, *tel: (403) 496-7275*. Riverfront parks are popular with Nordic skiers, snowshoers and ice skaters.

Downhill skiing, sledding and tobogganing take advantage of slopes near Muttart Conservatory's pyramids run by the **Edmonton Ski Club**, *tel: (403) 465-0852*. Take horse-drawn sledge and wagon rides, or watch the Edmonton Oilers practice at the West Edmonton Mall's indoor **Ice Palace**, *tel: (403) 444-5200*, or venture outdoors to ice-skating rinks by City Hall or the Alberta Legislature Building.

SHOPPING

The **West Edmonton Mall**, *8770 170 St; tel: (800) 661-8890* or *(403) 444-5200*, shops open Mon–Fri 1000–2100, Sat 1000–1800, Sun 1200–1700, is one of Canada's most varied and entertaining shopping, dining and recreation areas. About 800 stores stock everything from designer wear to pragmatic boots, furnishings to sports souvenirs.

Eaton's and **The Bay** are among large **Civic Centre** department stores. Art galleries line *124 St*, 3 km west of downtown. **Old Strathcona** shops range from **Sanctuary Curio Shoppe**, *10310 81 Ave; tel: (403) 944-2654*, combining conjuring paraphernalia with leather gear, to hand-made soap at **Virginia's Soap Deli**, *8218 104 St; tel: (403) 430-1466*.

SIGHTSEEING

Edmonton has been a trading hub since the establishment of rival trading posts by the North West Company and Hudson's Bay Company at nearby Fort Saskatchewan in 1795 to trade with the Cree for beaver, otter, marten and fox pelts, and with the Blackfoot for muskrat furs, buffalo meat, bear and fish. Europeans, particularly Ukrainians, homesteaded the plains east and north-east of Edmonton, farming wheat for Canada's Eastern markets.

Local entrepreneurs fictitiously touted Edmonton to 1500 gullible gold-seekers as

113

The Hudson's Bay Company

Canada owes its existence to the commercial drive of the Hudson's Bay Company. Chartered by King Charles II of England in 1670, the company received the rights to trade in and colonise all of North America drained by rivers flowing into the Hudson Strait. In modern terms, the 'Company of Adventurers' gained northern Quebec and Ontario, Manitoba, Saskatchewan, southern Alberta and a portion of the Northwest Territories. Later discoveries gave the HBC Oregon and Washington in the United States as well as British Columbia. Although the HBC had to cede its US holdings when the border between America and British America was settled in the 1840s, the company retained an economic and psychological monopoly that spanned the continent.

The impetus for the HBC's great grab was not land, but furs. Beaver hats were all the rage in Europe, driving the price of prime pelts to astronomical levels. Beaver had been all but exterminated in Europe by the 17th century, but were plentiful across North America. So were fox, martin, lynx, wolf and other luxurious furs. Pacific sea otters were worth far more than their weight in gold in the China trade.

The endless drive for more furs led the HBC to explore every river and stream that flowed into Hudson's Bay. In 1754, Anthony Henday paddled up the North Saskatchewan River to become the first White to enter Alberta. Other traders soon followed, including the Montreal-based North West Company, which sent its own traders westward in 1787.

The two companies were locked in fierce competition, often building trading posts, or forts, side by side. Explorers from both companies searched frantically for routes over the Rockies to the Columbia River, gateway to the Pacific Northwest.

NWC partners Alexander Mackenzie, Simon Fraser and David Thompson pioneered northern routes over the Rockies to the Pacific Coast from the 1790s. Mackenzie reached the mouth of the Bella Coola River in 1793, the first non-Native to cross the continent north of Mexico. Fraser fought through treacherous rapids to present-day Vancouver in 1808, realising that he, too, was too far north and that the Fraser River was too perilous to become a major trade route. In 1811, Thompson finally paddled the length of the Columbia, only to discover American traders already ensconced at Fort Astoria on the Pacific Ocean.

The NWC took over Astoria during the American-British War of 1812, then began building its own string of outposts up the mighty river. The 49th Parallel divided American and British territory east of the Rockies; the two powers jointly occupied the West. When the HBC absorbed the NWC in 1821, England gained an economic monopoly spanning the continent. It was the HBC's economic preoccupation, more than any other single factor, that differentiated American and Canadian settlement in the West. America believed it had a manifest destiny to rule from sea to sea, a destiny forged in rebellion against Britain and tempered by steady expansion by pioneers who moved west in advance of law, order and government.

The HBC, and their counterparts in colonial government, preferred profits to destiny. Since law, order and stability were seen as more profitable than American-style anarchy, Canada made a concerted effort to establish control over the West *before* settlers arrived by establishing the North West Mounted Police in Alberta and hard-nosed magistrates throughout British Columbia. The HBC exists today as The Bay chain of department stores.

the all-Canadian 'gateway' to Yukon Territory gold fields in 1897, though no overland route existed. Would-be prospectors stayed, and within less than a decade, Edmonton, soon to amalgamate with Strathcona south of the river, became the new province's capital. Alberta's Legislature met on the site of the fifth Fort Edmonton. In 1947, 40 km south-west of Edmonton, Leduc #1 Well gushed black gold (crude oil), adding petrochemicals to the economy.

Stroll the 30-min red brick **Heritage Trail** from the **Alberta Legislature Grounds** at *108 St*, turning right on *99 Ave*, left on *104 St*, then right on *Mac-Donald Dr.*, with the North Saskatchewan River and the château-style Hotel Macdonald on the right. Tree-lined streets give way to the glass and metal Shaw Conference Centre and pink-glass Canada Place, where Old Town Edmonton once thrived. **City of Edmonton**, *Planning and Development, Exchange Tower, 10250 101 St, 2nd Floor; tel: (403) 496-6160*, open Mon–Fri 0800–1630, has a **Downtown Edmonton Walking Tour** flyer.

The **124th Street and Area Business Association**, *10350 124 St, Suite 204; tel: (403) 482-5552*, has a 1-hr, self-guided **Original West End Tour** brochure covering the area near the Provincial Museum of Alberta. Eight galleries showcase Canadian artists in the **124 Street Area**, *Jasper Ave to 111 Ave.*

Old Strathcona Foundation, *10324 82 Ave, Suite 401; tel: (403) 433-5866*, has an excellent **Walk Through Old Strathcona** brochure and map. Drive, don't walk, through **Refinery Row**, *101 Ave corridor east of 50 St*, for a distinctly odiferous and uncharming impression of the post-1947 petrochemical industry.

Long before oil, Fort Edmonton was a profitable trading post in the wilderness. **Fort Edmonton Park**, *Fox Dr.* and *Whitemud Dr.; tel: (403) 496-8787*, open mid May–Sept, adults $6.75, children 13–17 $5, 3–12 $3.25, is a reconstruction based on four periods of city history. The 1846 HBC fur trading fort's four-storey

Rowand House log exterior and furnishings evoke the chief factor's daily life. The 1885 Settlement Era, the 1905 Provincial Capital and a small 1920 section have living history interpretation. A 1919 Baldwin Steam Train, a streetcar, stagecoach ($1) or wagon ($1) are park transport.

Next to Fort Edmonton Park, **John Janzen Nature Centre**, *tel: (403) 496-2939*, has nature displays for children; take the 4-km self-guided nature trail along the North Saskatchewan River Valley.

The 1912 **Alberta Legislature Building**, *Interpretive Centre, 10800 97 Ave N.W.; tel: (403) 427-7362* or *(403) 427-2826*, open Mon–Fri 0830–1700, Sat–Sun 0900–1700 (Victoria Day–Labour Day); Mon–Fri 0900–1630 Sat–Sun 1200–1700 (Sept–Oct and Mar–Victoria Day); Mon–Fri 1200-1630, Sun 1200–1700 (Nov–Feb), offers free guided tours. The building, on the fifth Fort Edmonton site, is surrounded by a beautiful 57-acre park, a long series of (wading) pools and a north side fountain/winter ice rink.

The 1913 sandstone residence of Alberta's Lieutenant Governors, **Government House**, *adjacent to the Provincial Museum of Alberta, 12845 102 Ave; tel: (403) 488-5900*, has free tours Sun 1300–1700 Feb–Nov. The **Provincial Museum of Alberta**, *12845 102 Ave; tel: (403) 453-9100*, open Tues–Sun 0900–1700, with longer hours in spring, adults $5.50, children 7–17 $3, has an outstanding Aboriginal People's Gallery and rock and mineral collections.

City Hall, *1 Sir Winston Churchill Sq.; tel: (403) 496-8200* or *(403) 496-8256 (free tours)*, open Mon–Fri 0700–1000, Sat–Sun 1100–1700, is a modern glass pyramid, spacious and bright inside, giving way to a fountain/ice rink and 23-bell carillon tower outdoors. Across *99 St* is **Edmonton Art Gallery**, *2 Sir Winston Churchill*

115

Sq.; tel: (403) 422-6223, open Mon–Wed 1030–1700, Thur–Fri 1030–2000, Sat–Sun 1100–1700, adults $3, children 13–17 $1.50, with historical and contemporary Canadian and international art collections. **Citadel Theatre** and **Winspear Centre** are a block south. **China Gate**, *97 St* and *Harbin Rd,* across from the Winspear Centre, marks the entrance to Chinatown's small businesses, restaurants and skid row residents, all within a few blocks of the government centre at **Canada Place** and the **Hotel Macdonald**.

The free **Edmonton Police Museum**, *9620 103A Ave; tel: (403) 421-2274,* open Mon–Fri 0900–1500, in the force's downtown headquarters, is filled with artefacts and cold-weather uniforms worn by the city's late 19th-century law enforcers. Across the river at the University of Alberta, costumed interpreters give tours of **Rutherford House Provincial House**, *11153 Saskatchewan St.; tel: (403) 427-3995* or *(403) 427-2022,* open 1000–1800 (May 15–Labour Day), 1200–1700 (Labour Day–May 14), adults $2, children $1.50, the 1915 home of Alberta's first premier, Alexander Rutherford. Its **Arbour Restaurant**, *tel: (403) 422-2697,* open Tues–Sun 1130–1600, serves light lunch and tea.

Old Strathcona's, *Old Strathcona Business Association, 10324 Whyte Ave (82 Ave), Suite 401; tel: (403) 437-4182; fax: (403) 433-4657,* hippie-punk atmosphere creates the trendy dining, shopping and theatre area south of the North Saskatchewan River. In Aug, Old Strathcona's lovely sandstone buildings, vibrant Farmer's Market and interesting museums host the **Fringe Festival**, *tel: (403) 448-9000,* 1200 performances on 17 stages.

Model and Toy Museum, *8603 104 St; tel: (403) 433-4512,* open Wed–Sat 1200–1700, Sun 1300–1700 year-round, longer hours July–Aug, donation, is a couple's collections of paper toys and models of historic buildings, birds, ships, aircraft as well as paper dolls. The gift shop sells paper craft kits and models. The **Telephone Historical Centre**, *10437 83 Ave; tel: (403) 441-2077,* open Mon–Fri 1000–1600, Sat 1200–1600, adults $2, children $1, is an unabashed pitch for the telephone company, but antique telephones and a talking robot set it apart. **C & E Railway Museum**, *10447 86 Ave; tel: (403) 433-9739,* open Wed–Sun 1000–1600 June–Aug, in a replica 1891 Calgary-Edmonton Railway station, has historic photographs and costumes.

A real steam or diesel train operates holiday weekends at the **Alberta Railway Museum**, *24215 34 St N.W.; tel: (403) 472-6229,* open 1000–1800 (Victoria Day–Labour Day), adults $3, children 13–18 $2, 3–12 $1, train rides $1. The **Edmonton Society of Model Railroad Engineers** have modular model train layouts covering historic Canadian rails at *Londonderry Mall, 137 Ave and 66 St,* open Sat–Sun 1200–1700, Tues 1900–2100.

Bush pilot history is told through restored aircraft at the **Alberta Aviation Museum**, *11410 Kingsway Ave; tel: (403) 453-1078,* open Mon–Sat 1000–1700, Sun 1100–1700, adults $4, children 6–12 $2. **Edmonton Space & Science Centre**, *11211 142 St; tel: (403) 452-9100,* open 1000–2000, has interactive science exhibits and a video display of Edmonton's horrific July 31, 1987 tornado. Skip the linty IMAX® film. Adults $7 or $12 (admission plus one show), children 13–17 $6–$11, 3–12 $5–$8. A free **Observatory**, *southeast of the Centre,* is open 1300–1700, 2000–2400, weather permitting.

Glass pyramids serve as a unique city landmark at the **Muttart Conservatory**, *9626 96A St; tel: (403) 496-8755,* open

Sun–Wed 1100–2100, Thur–Sat 1100–1800, adults $4.25, children 12–18 $3.25, 2–11 $2. Outdoor trial gardens encourage Edmontonians to see which annuals will grow locally, while the pyramids house four plant groupings: 'Show', with monthly changes of splashy plantings; 'Temperate'; 'Tropical' and 'Arid'.

Much of Edmonton seems to spend free time along the river, **River Valley Parks**, *tel: (403) 496-7275.* The **High Level Bridge** *(109 St)* is occasionally transformed by water pumped into the **Great Divide Waterfall**, with fine viewing from **Kinsmen Park** or from the **105 Street Bridge**. **John Walter Museum**, *10627 93 Ave, Kinsman Park; tel: (403) 496-7275,* open Sun afternoons year-round, shows a businessman's three progressively grander homes. The paddlesteamer **Edmonton Queen**, *9734 98 Ave (Rafter's Landing); tel: (403) 424-2628,* offers summer lunch, happy hour, dinner or weekend brunch cruises, with or without meals, on the North Saskatchewan River, adults $5.95–$39.95, children 3–10 $9.95–$24.95.

West Edmonton Mall, *8770 170 St; tel: (800) 661-8890 or (403) 444-5200,* shops are open Mon–Fri 1000–2100, Sat 1000–1800, Sun 1200–1700. Amusements include bungy jumping, an artificial beach, **Ice Palace** skating rink, **Palace Casino**, dolphins, **Galaxyland Amusement Park**'s roller coasters and rides, **Deep Sea Adventure** submarines, a 16-slide **World Waterpark**, laser tag, virtual reality games, a replica of Columbus' *Santa Maria*, a miniature golf course, cinemas, **Jubilations Dinner Theatre**, **Yuk Yuk's Komedy Kabaret** and **Red's**, *tel: (403) 481-6420,* a combination nightclub, pub, billiards parlour and bowling alley, complete with lasers, fog machines and glow-in-the-dark pins and balls for Cosmic Bowling™.

SIDE TRACKS FROM EDMONTON

Drive 45 km east of Edmonton on Hwy 16, the Yellowhead Hwy, to **Elk Island National Park**. Cement factories and oil refineries yield to hay bales and yellow canola 10 km east of town.

To visit Fort Saskatchewan where Edmonton's original trading rivals, the HBC and North West Company, established forts in 1795, turn right after 18 km onto Hwy 21. **Fort Saskatchewan Visitor Information Centre**, *10030 99 Ave (Old CN Station); tel: (403) 998-4355,* is open year-round Mon–Fri 1000–1700, Sat–Sun 1200–1700 (July–Aug). The **City of Fort Saskatchewan Economic Tourism and Development**, *10005 102 St; tel: (403) 992-6231,* has a self-guiding tour brochure to historic attractions, most of which have disappeared. This was the site of the NWMP's second Northwest Territories fort (after Fort Macleod). **Fort Saskatchewan Museum**, *10104 101 St; tel: (403) 998-1750,* 1000–1800 (July–Aug), 1100–1500 (Sept–June), $1, covers Mountie history. Sheep graze in town Thur–Sun in summer.

Thirty-five km from Edmonton, go right 3 km to **Strathcona Wilderness Centre**, *Baseline Rd and Range Rd 212; tel: (403) 922-3939.* Rent canoes to paddle on Bennett Lake, home to ducks, grebes and Canada geese, and search 12 km of trails for beaver and moose. A boardwalk accesses a black spruce bog in the 500-acre park. In winter, try Nordic skiing.

Elk Island National Park, *RR # 1, Site 4, Fort Saskatchewan, AB T8L 2N7; tel: (403) 992-2950; fax: (403) 992-2951,* adults $4, children 6–16 $2 per day, is the prairies before settlement and homesteading. Technically an aspen

117

parkland, the flora are a transition between southern prairie grasslands and northern arboreal forests.

Turn left onto the 60 kph, 20-mile long Elk Island Parkway, and stop at the **South Gate Visitor Centre**, *tel: (403) 922-5833*, open daily May–Oct, fewer days in winter, for maps, a hiking trail brochure and information on wildlife, camping and recreation. Established in 1906, the park protected the world's only herd of prairie elk on Island Lake.

1100 bison are a huge attraction. Drive the short *Bison Loop Rd* north of the Hwy 16 park entrance where plains bison wander. *Stay in your vehicle.* These behemoths, and the larger **wood bison** subspecies, pastured just south of Hwy 16, are skittish. Mid July–mid Aug is bison rutting season – aggression is king.

White-tail and mule deer, moose, coyote, beaver, bear, muskrat and trumpeter swans reside in the 195 square km park. Tawayik Lake picnic area has an observation platform for bird-watching and bison spotting. Summer brings carpets of clover and prairie sunsets; winter is for Nordic skiing and snowshoeing.

Astotin Recreation Area on the park's north end has the **Park Information Centre**, *tel: (403) 922-5790*, 1030–1800 daily (May–Sept), Sat–Sun 1030–1800 (Oct–Apr), an **Interpretive Centre**, *tel: (403) 992-6392*, Thur–Mon 1200–1800 (July–Aug), Sat–Sun 1200–1800 (May–June, Sept–Oct), and trails along the shores of **Lake Astotin**. After swimming, rinse off and immediately towel vigorously to discourage swimmer's itch, a disease caused by tiny flatworm which burrow into the skin. Calamine lotion, histocaine or lanocaine may help. Astotin also has boating, picnicking, Sandy Beach campsite and a 9-hole golf course; *tel: (403) 998-3161*.

The **Ukrainian Pioneer Home**, closed to the public, is a replica of a 19th-century settler home. **Ukrainian Cultural Heritage Village**, *3 km east of Elk Island National Park on Hwy 16; tel: (403) 662-3640*, open 1000–1800 (mid May–Aug), 1000–1600 (Sept–mid Oct), adults $6.50, children 7–17 $3, is an open-air museum with role-playing by living history actors. The village 'women' cook real chicken soup, feed chickens, bake bread in clay ovens and readily answer questions about their homes, built from 1892–1930. Original houses, businesses and several still-used churches evoke the isolation of original plains settlers, many of whom started life in Canada in underground dirt dwellings. Ukrainians arrived to homesteads 20 km north of the village in 1891, hoping to escape from inherited division of land into small parcels, inflated land prices, crippling interest and unprofitable crops. Ukrainian men, who customarily left home to work on large farms, in oil fields or in mines, were easily persuaded to move their families to a parkland where wood and land were both plentiful.

Ukrainians settled in Manitoba, Saskatchewan and Eastern Alberta. **Vegreville**, *further east on Hwy 16*, is famed for a huge patterned Easter Egg. More than 12% of Edmonton's population is of Ukrainian descent, and the **Ukrainian Museum of Canada (Alberta)**, *10611 110 Ave; tel: (403) 483-5932*, open May–Aug; **Ukrainian Canadian Archives and Museum of Alberta**, *9543 110 Ave; tel: (403) 424-7580*, open Tues–Fri 1000–1700, Sat 1200–1700; and **Fort Edmonton Park's Ukrainian Bookstore**, display artefacts, clothing, woven textile panels and kaleidoscope-pattern eggs. ▨

EDMONTON CIRCUIT

As a provincial capital city, Edmonton is blessed with attractive government buildings and interesting museums. This 53-km driving circuit should take 1½ hours unless downtown *Jasper Ave, Stony Plain Rd,* or the area around the West Edmonton Mall is in the throes of rush hour or a snowstorm. If driving in winter, check in advance for attraction hours and plan to stop several times en route to get your bearings. Fort Edmonton is only open mid May–Sept except for special holiday events.

Some Edmonton bridges and downtown streets are one-way, limiting this circuit to the direction indicated. Several bridges bypass downtown sights, so some backtracking is obligatory. Use this circuit as an introduction to the city, then return later to visit museums, enjoy outside activities and explore historic neighbourhoods. If time permits, take a day or two to add a side track to Elk Island National Park and the Ukrainian Cultural Heritage Village, about 45 km north-east of Downtown Edmonton (see pp. 117–118).

ROUTE: 53 KM

119

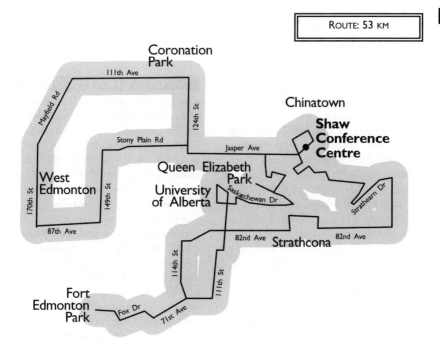

DOWNTOWN

Begin at the **Shaw Conference Centre**, *9797 Jasper Ave N.W.* (Edmonton Tourism Visitor Information Centre is downstairs). Across the street is a landscaped park, perfect for picnicking, in front of the pink-glass **Canada Place** government building. Drive east one block, turning left on *97 St.* **Chinatown**, marked by red English–Chinese street signs, extends right beyond the dragons dancing on **China Gate** at *Harbin Rd.* **Winspear Centre** concert hall is on the left.

Turn left on *102 A Ave,* heading west. **Edmonton Art Gallery**, *99 St* and *102A Ave,* is on the right. To the left on *99 St,* also called *Rue Hull,* is **Citadel Theatre**. **Edmonton City Hall**'s fountain/winter ice rink, pyramid and carillon are right; *Sir Winston Churchill Sq.,* downtown Edmonton's main gathering place, is left across from City Hall. Turn left onto *100 St* by *Sir Winston Churchill Sq.;* **The Bay** department store is to the right, with the **Eaton Centre** and **Eaton's** one block west. There is a good espresso snack bar and Internet access across from the square in the **Stanley A. Milner Main Library**, joined by a pedway with a convenient underground parkade.

Sir Winston Churchill Square is the centre for summer outdoor festivals, including July **Klondike Days**. Some Edmontonians dress in 19th-century period costumes, recalling a soda-fountain and country-fair atmosphere that is fiction and wishful thinking. Street performers walk on stilts, eat fire and do magic tricks for crowds of happy children. A statue of the British Prime Minister presides over it all.

Klondike Days are pure boosterism – mostly reflecting a long rivalry with Calgary, Cowtown home of the Stampede (see p.72), which finishes just as Klondike

Days begin. Edmontonians sport black instead of white hats and have concerts in lieu of chuckwagon races.

Continue south on *100 St* and cross *Jasper Ave;* the **Hotel Macdonald** château is on the left, overlooking the North Saskatchewan River. Continue straight down *McDougall Hill* over the **Low Level Bridge**, following signs for **Muttart Conservatory** via *E. 98 Ave* through a circular spaghetti maze of roads, then turn right on *96 A St* to the Conservatory pyramids and spring–fall trial gardens. The **Edmonton Ski Club** operates the ski slope just south, a fine spot from which to view downtown in any season.

Go east on *97 Ave* from the Conservatory parking lot. Turn right onto *Cloverdale Rd;* the ski hill is on the right. At the top, turn left onto *Connors Rd* for one tiny block, making a U-turn onto *Strathearn Dr.,* for a panoramic cityscape of the river's north side. Go right on *85 St* for 2 km through residential districts, passing **Bonnie Doon Shopping Centre** on the left.

OLD STRATHCONA

Gracious tree-lined streets shelter 19th-century red-brick homes in an area known for its modern-day hippies, punks, hip shops and throbbing club scene. Turn right onto *82 Ave/Whyte Ave to* **Old Strathcona**. Go right on *99 St* for five blocks, left on *87 Ave* for three blocks, then veer left onto *102 St/86 Ave* for another two blocks. Go left on *104 St* to the **Old Strathcona Model and Toy Museum**. The **C & E Railway Museum**, *10447 86 Ave,* is close by. To see the heart of Edmonton's alternative neighbourhood, go right on *82 Ave/Whyte Ave* for eight blocks, past punks, tourists, shopkeepers, restaurateurs, entrepreneurs and artists, most al fresco, weather permitting.

FORT EDMONTON PARK

82 Ave/Whyte Ave jogs left at *112 St.* Enter the traffic circle (roundabout) and follow the sign for the *114 St* exit. Continue for seven blocks on *114 St* to a second traffic circle. Exit the circle at *71 Ave/Belgravia Rd*, going south-west. Veer right onto *Fox Dr.*; the **Whitemud Equine Centre**, in **Whitemud Park**, is on the right. Turn right onto *Fort Edmonton Park Rd* to the **John Janzen Nature Centre** and, mid May–Sept, **Fort Edmonton Park**. Though 'Fort Edmonton' was built several km from this site, the modern reconstruction accurately reflects the founding and eras of Edmonton's development.

UNIVERSITY OF ALBERTA

Leave Fort Edmonton Park and retrace the route to *71 Ave/Belgravia Rd* by taking *Fort Edmonton Park Rd* to *Fox Dr.*, turning left, then left again onto *71 Ave/Belgravia Rd.* Half-way around the traffic circle, continue straight east on *72 Ave.* Turn left on *111 St*, go right one-half block on *University Ave*, then left on *110 St.* Turn left onto *Saskatchewan Dr.*, which skirts the bluffs above the North Saskatchewan River, and park at meters or in the pay parking lot. **Rutherford House Provincial House** is on the left, with the **University of Alberta Campus** ahead. Go left onto *111 St* for four blocks, left two blocks on *87 Ave*, then left one block on *109 St* while immediately moving to the right lane.

RIVER VALLEY PARKS

Take a sharp right onto *Saskatchewan Dr. E.*; below on the left are **Walterdale Park** and **Queen Elizabeth Park**. The yellow-orange **Strathcona Information Caboose** is on the right at *102 St.* Just beyond, make a sharp left turn onto *Queen Elizabeth Park Dr.*, staying in the left lane to enter

Queen Elizabeth Park. Cross *Walterdale Hill* near the **105 Street Bridge** approach to enter **Walterdale Park**, with the **John Walter Museum**, views of the **High Level Bridge**, and jogging, biking, blading and winter Nordic skiing.

Return to *Walterdale Hill* and turn left onto the short **105 Street Bridge**. Immediately veer right onto *103 St.* Go left on *97 Ave*, left again on *106 St*, then right on *96 Ave*, and right on *Fort Way Dr.* to the **Alberta Legislature Building**, where parking space is limited.

Take *Fort Way Dr.* east around the legislature grounds through a gracious park. *Fort Way Dr.* becomes *107 St* as it turns north. The striking pillars and modern architecture of **Grant MacEwan Community College** are straight ahead. Drive 2.2 km left on *Jasper Ave* to **124 Street**, turning right to peruse nine blocks of art galleries. Go left on *111 Ave* for 2 km to *142 St* and the **Edmonton Space and Science Centre** on the edge of **Coronation Park**.

WEST EDMONTON

Continue west on *111 Ave*, following it left as it becomes *Mayfield Rd.* Go south for 2 km at *170 St* to the **West Edmonton Mall (WEM)** complex *(90 Ave to 87 Ave)*.

Exit **WEM** and go 2½ km east on *87 Ave.* Go left on *149 St* for another 2½ km, then turn right onto *Stony Plain Rd*, which turns into *102 Ave* after 1.8 km. The **Provincial Museum of Alberta** and **Government House** are on the right. The **Glenora District**, north, west and south-west of the museum, has lovely tree-shaded mansions with beautiful gardens. Continue on *102 Ave*, crossing over *Groat Rd*, then turn right for one block at *124 St* to follow *Jasper Ave* left to Downtown Edmonton and Shaw Conference Centre.

EDMONTON–RED DEER

The 155-km drive south on Hwy 2 to Red Deer is an efficient 1½-hour drive to the halfway point between Alberta's main cities, Edmonton and Calgary. Vary this route with visits to attractions along side roads. Red Deer is also the beginning of the back road to the Canadian Rockies on the David Thompson Hwy, via Rocky Mountain House and Saskatchewan River Crossing in Jasper National Park.

Edmonton
20
Devon
33
19
Leduc
2 57
13 Wetaskiwin
2
2A
35
Ponoka
2
30
2A
Lacombe
20
Red Deer

| DIRECT ROUTE: 155 KM |

ROUTES

DIRECT ROUTE

Hwy 2 through Edmonton is *White-mud Dr.;* follow signs for Hwy 2 South onto the *Calgary Trail.* Or from downtown Edmonton, begin at the Shaw Conference Centre, *9797 Jasper Ave N.W.* (Edmonton Tourism Visitor Centre is downstairs), going west on *Jasper Ave.* Turn left on *109 St* and cross the High Level Bridge over North Saskatchewan River. Immediately after the bridge, turn left onto *Saskatchewan Dr.* Go right on *104 St,* which becomes *Calgary Trail Southbound,* Hwy 2. Continue on Hwy 2 to Red Deer.

SCENIC ROUTE

Take Hwy 2 from Edmonton, following it until you reach the Hwy 13 exit. Head east along Hwy 13 for 19 km to **Wetaskiwin**. From Wetaskiwin, take Hwy 2A south-west to **Ponoka**. From here, follow Hwy 2A to **Lacombe**. Rejoin Hwy 2 just outside Red Deer.

BUSES

Greyhound Lines of Canada and Red Arrow operate 14 trips a day. Journey time: 2–2½ hrs. See OTT table 106.

EDMONTON TO LEDUC

Gateway Park Edmonton Tourism Visitor Information Centre, *2404 Calgary Trail Northbound (Hwy 2),* open 0800–2100 (Victoria Day–pre-Labour Day) and Mon–Fri 0830–1630, Sat–Sun 0900–1700

(Labour Day–pre-Victoria Day), 10 km south of downtown Edmonton, is on the left, marked with Imperial Leduc #1 Oil Derrick out front. Inside the InfoCentre is the **Imperial Leduc #1 Oil Derrick Interpretive Centre**, with some photos and exhibits partially blocked by T-shirt stands. Black gold changed Alberta's post-World War II history when oil was discovered west of Hwy 2 near Devon, in 1947.

◤ SIDE TRACK TO DEVON

Go west off Hwy 2 onto Hwy 19 for about 12 km to Devon.

DEVON

Devon's flat countryside well away from oceans belies reef-building 410–360 million years ago by corals and stalkless sponges called *stromatoporoids*. The Pacific Ocean repeatedly flooded and retreated over Alberta; some of the piled, fossilised sealife created major cliffs, like those near Banff (Mts Rundle and Norquay and Cascade Mountain), and along Crowsnest Pass (Hwy 3), Yellowhead Hwy (Hwy 16) near Jasper and David Thompson Hwy (Hwy 11) west of Rocky Mountain House to Saskatchewan River Crossing. Devonian reef life was periodically covered by marine plankton which decayed and packed onto the corals. Bacteria got rid of oxygen and nitrogen, leaving hydrogen and carbon to heat up, forming underground hydrocarbon pools.

Alberta, the Energy Province, has 60% of Canada's conventional crude oil reserves, 85% of its natural gas and most of the heavy oil and oil sands reserves, placing it amongst the world's top ten natural gas and crude oil producers. The industry began at Leduc # 1 only after Imperial Oil had drilled 133 dry holes!

One km south of Devon on the east side of Hwy 60 is the site of the **'Discovery' well**, now marked by a 54-m tall duplicate of Leduc #1 derrick, which gushed the Devonian period's hidden treasure from 1540m underground in Feb 1947. Devon town sprang up to service an immediate Leduc-Woodbend oilfield boom; Leduc # 1 alone produced 72 million barrels of oil. An interpretive information centre; *tel: (403) 987-4323*, is open 1000–1800 (July–Aug), at the **Leduc #1** site with an **Oil Industry Hall of Fame**. The University of Alberta Devonian Botanic Garden is 5 km north. ◪

LEDUC

The food processing town of Leduc is east of Hwy 2. *BW* and *TL* motels reflect its proximity to the airport. **Lions Campground**, *east side of South Park*, offers RV and tent pitches. Leduc has 27 parks, including **William F Lede Park**'s 25-km paved pathway, fishing at **Fred John's Park**, and canoeing, Nordic skiing and ice-racing on **Telford Lake**. **Dr. Woods House–Museum**, *4801 49 Ave, Leduc, AB T9E 7G6; tel: (403) 986-1517*, Tues–Sun 1100–1700 (June–Aug); Tues, Thur, Sun, 1300–1600 (Sept–May), living quarters and doctor's surgery in a 1927 Craftsman bungalow has a self-guided audio tour.

WETASKIWIN

Tourist Information: Wetaskiwin Chamber of Economic Development & Tourism, *4910-55A St, Wetaskiwin, AB T9A 2R9; tel: (800) 989-6899 or (403) 352-4636; fax: (403) 352-4640.* Breakfast and afternoon tea are served at 1912 **MacEachern Tea House**, *4719 50 Ave; tel: (403) 352-8308*, open Mon–Sat 0930–1630, Sun (July–Aug), known for delicious cheesecake.

123

Blackfoot and Cree war party leaders fought on a local hill to exhaustion, pausing only for each chief to smoke his pipe. Noting the Cree's broken pipe, the Blackfoot lent him his own; they recognised that they had honoured tradition with a peace pipe, and made peace. *Wetaskiwin-Spatinow* is the **Place Where Peace Was Made**.

Wetaskiwin is Canada's **Motor City** – more automobiles are sold here – a tribute to Stan Reynolds who sold inexpensive transportation to returning World War II veterans. His collections of cars, machines and aircraft grace several museums.

Reynolds-Alberta Museum, *Hwy 13; tel: (800) 661-4726 or (403) 352-5855,* open daily 0900–1700 (Sept June), 0900–1900 (end of June–Labour Day), adults $6.50, children 7–17 $3, is a provincial heritage museum with hands-on exploration of 1890s–1950s machinery and transportation-related gadgets. Watch experts rebuild a vehicle, from restoration of an original engine to painting and detailing a machine's exterior, or attend a Jan–Feb one-day 'Learn from the Experts' workshop ($75 & GST per course).

Wander by more than 100 automobiles, trucks (lorries), motorcycles, bicycles, ploughs, threshers and steam and internal combustion tractors on display inside. A warehouse has 1200 more artefacts; museum exhibits explain how mechanical parts work and where and how the cars and farm equipment were utilised. From May–Sept, ride in a chauffeur-driven 1937 Packard, a 1927 Ford Model T Touring Car, or another of five posh classics; play on 1930s midway rides; or fly in a 1943 Boeing Stearman open cockpit bi-plane or a 1946 Cub Super Cruiser. The museum farms 28 hectares using restored machines.

Canada's Aviation Hall of Fame, part of the Reynolds-Alberta Museum, is across the runway at the Wetaskiwin Municipal Airport Hangar. More than 145 Canadians who contributed to flight development and technology have been inducted into the Hall of Fame. Seventeen vintage aircraft hang over exhibits.

Reynolds Museum/Reynolds Aviation Museum, *4110 57 St; tel: (403) 352-6201,* is open daily 1000–1700 (mid May–Labour Day), call for hours other times of year, adults $3.50, children 6–12 $2.50. Stan Reynolds' private museum displays cars, fire engines, finely-restored aircraft and an assortment of military vehicles.

Ask about downtown walking tours of 11 historic *50 Ave* area buildings at the **Wetaskiwin & District Museum**, *5010 53 Ave; tel: (403) 352-0227,* open Tues–Fri 1300–1600 year-round, longer hours weekends (summer). First Nations and settlement history is displayed in a pioneer schoolroom, hotel room, general store, kitchen and garage. South of Wetaskiwin is the Louis Bull Tribe reserve and summer-only **Alberta Central Railway Museum**, *RR #2; tel: (403) 352-2257,* in a replica CPR station with rolling stock.

PONOKA

Ponoka is the site of the five-day **Ponoka Stampede and Exhibition** (first weekend July). **Town of Ponoka**, *5102-48 Ave, Ponoka, AB T4J 1P7; tel: (403) 783-6363.*

LACOMBE

Tourist Information: Town of Lacombe, *5034 52 St, Lacombe, AB T4L 1A1; tel: (403) 782-6666.*

Lacombe is named after Roman Catholic missionary priest Fr. Albert Lacombe, who proselytised among the Blackfoot, Cree and Métis from Red Deer to St Albert north of present-day Edmonton. Lacombe has Alberta's best collection of Edwardian-era buildings.

Agriculture dominates, though the town has the **Michener House Museum**, *5036 51 St; tel: (403) 782-3933*, birthplace of Canada's 1967–74 Governor-General, Roland Michener. **Ellis Bird Farm**, *8 km south-east of Lacombe; tel: (403) 346-2211 or (403) 885-4477*, open in summer, is a working farm where crops and flowers are planted and wetlands created to encourage native Alberta bluebirds and other wildlife.

RED DEER

Tourist Information: Red Deer Visitor and Convention Bureau, *PO Box 5008, Red Deer, AB T4N 3T4; tel: (800) 215-8946 or (403) 346-0180; fax: (403) 346-5081; web: http://www.visitor.red-deer.ab.ca*, and its **Heritage Ranch Visitor Information Centre**, *west on 43 St to 25 Riverview Park*, open Mon–Fri 0900–1700, Sat–Sun 1000–1700, extended summer hours, has a mini-map with lists of attractions and restaurants and information on lodging, dining, historic attractions, agriculture, flower displays and the 75 km of walking, biking, Nordic skiing and equestrian trails in Waskasoo Park.

Bright green **U-bikes** are free for use in Red Deer from well-marked racks, ideal for sightseeing or biking through the parks.

ACCOMMODATION AND FOOD

Book in advance. Red Deer's midpoint location between Edmonton and Calgary makes it a convention/conference centre. Most of Red Deer's 16 motels, all moderate, are on Hwy 2 or along *Gaetz Ave (50 Ave)*, the divided extension of Hwy 2A. Chains: *Hd*, *S8* and *TL*. **Black Knight Inn**, *2929 50 Ave, Red Deer, AB T4R 1H1; tel: (403) 343-6666*, has large rooms. **Central Alberta (dinner) Theatre**, *tel: (403) 343-6666*, opens mid Nov–Apr. **Red Deer Lodge**, *4311 49 Ave; tel: (800) 661-1657 or (403) 346-8841*, is the largest

motel. **Red Deer Lions Municipal Campground**, *4723 Riverside Dr.; tel: (403) 342-8183*, offers 126 pitches near the Red Deer River.

McIntosh Tea House Bed & Breakfast, *5631 50 St; tel: (403) 346-1622*, with three rooms, is open for lunch Mon–Sat 1100–1600. Spanish-style pottery livens up budget–moderate **Wildflower Bistro**, *1927 Gaetz Ave; tel: (403) 341-5400*, closed Sun. Chinese, Italian and Greek restaurants join fast-food joints.

SIGHTSEEING

Scottish settlers, possibly suffering from a bout of nostalgia, called the large herds of elk (wapiti) red deer after their homeland species. Waskasoo Seepee, 'Elk River', was the Plains Cree name for the Red Deer River. Aboriginal peoples had used the calm Red Deer River as a safe crossing point for centuries. In 1882, the area was a halfway stop between Edmonton and Calgary for traders, missionaries and settlers.

By 1885, Red Deer had **Fort Normandeau**, one of three forts in the area built in reaction to the North West (Riel) Rebellion. Métis claims to land and declining buffalo hunting upon which they depended had led to armed opposition to the Ottawa government's plans for plains settlement. In 1870, under the flamboyant leadership of Louis Riel, Métis and their allies forced the establishment of a tiny Province of Manitoba. Riel, exiled to the US, returned to the Saskatchewan area in 1884 when the newly-finished CPR railway's transport of settlers and the law and order enforced by NWMP presence changed the lives of Métis, other mixed-heritage peoples and First Nations tribes.

Riel's inspirational rabble-rousing led to the seizure of a church and his 1885 declaration of a provisional Saskatchewan government. His troops were out of control.

To defend neighbouring Alberta Territory, stockade forts were constructed at **Battle River Crossing** (Fort Ostell at Ponoka), on a Wetaskiwin farm and in a rebuilt hotel at **Red Deer Crossing** (Fort Normandeau). A murder was followed by the shooting of an Indian agent, priests and six others at Frog Lake by a band of Cree led by a shouting Riel brandishing a cross. Riel was determined by experts of the day to be sane, a jury recommended mercy, but he was hanged and the rebellion was smashed.

Waskasoo Park

Waskasoo Park, *tel: (403) 342-8159,* or the VCB *(403) 346-0180,* includes a replica of **Fort Normandeau**, *west of the railway tracks via 32 St; tel: (403) 347-7550,* with fort and interpretive centre open 1200–1700 (mid May–late June), 1200–2000 (late June–Labour Day), Sun cultural demonstrations and May holiday weekend 1885 military re-enactments.

Summer–fall, stop at the **Red Deer Direct Seeding Demo Farm**, *south side of 32 St,* for self-guided auto or foot touring on dirt paths through a wildfowl wetland preserve and cereals test garden dedicated to using less fertilisers.

Heritage Ranch is Waskasoo Park's western gate, with trails linking all of the park's attractions except Fort Normandeau. **The Red Deer CVB InfoCentre**, *tel: (403) 346-0180,* is open year-round. **Heritage Ranch Equestrian Centre**; *tel: (4303) 347-4977,* offers rides on ponies, hay wagons, carriages, sleigh rides in winter and guided trail excursions. Spot muskrat and goslings along the Red River or hire a canoe. Hiking trails are groomed Nordic ski trails in winter.

Watch baseball or play horseshoe toss at **Great Chief Park**, *4707 Fountain Dr.; tel: (403) 342-8255,* open mid May–Oct. **Bower Ponds**, *tel: (403) 347-9777,* have

bicycle, paddleboat, canoe, rollerblade and ice-skate hire with trout-stocked ponds for fishing. In summer, look at ethnic arts and take afternoon tea at 1911 **Cronquist House**, *tel: (403) 346-0055.*

Lions Campground and a children's play area are north-west. On the river's east bank are **Three Mile Bend** dog-walking area and **River Bend Golf Course**, also a Nordic skiing area. **Discovery Canyon** has a water slide and a shallow pond for children and tubes for hire ($3).

Kerry Wood Nature Centre, *entrance via 55 St and 45 Ave; tel: (9403) 346-2010,* open daily 1000–1700, 1000–2000 (late May–Labour Day), has natural history exhibits; **Gaetz Lakes Sanctuary** for migratory birds has trails to a bird blind and viewing decks. Walk in **McKenzie Trail Recreation Area** spruce forest.

Downtown Red Deer

Alberta's fourth largest city, with 60,000 citizens, survives on agriculture, the petroleum industry, manufacturing of fertiliser and upholstered furniture and government. Red Deer's picnic favourites include the **City Hall** lawn, *49 Ave* and *Ross St,* across from the Old Court House, with 45,000 plants in summer. **Red Deer and District Museum**, *4525 47A Ave; tel: (403) 343-6844,* $2 donation, has some aboriginal and farmstead artefacts. The museum has self-guiding brochures for three walking tours, including the Parkvale tour which begins with the pioneer buildings in **Heritage Square**, *45 St* and *47A Ave.* The odd-looking **Norwegian Aspelund Laft House**, made of tightly fitted logs, is capped with a sod roof sprouting summer wildflowers. The modern spiral architecture of **St Mary's Church**, *30 Ave* and *Ross St,* is Blackfoot architect Douglas Cardinal's interpretation of Battle River geography and aboriginal sensibilities.

RED DEER–CALGARY

This 145-km route through Central Alberta's plains is a quick, straight jaunt. Plan two hours to drive from Red Deer's parks (at the eastern gateway to the David Thompson Hwy into the mid-Rockies) to Calgary, hub for southern Rockies activity and jumping-off point for explorations of the province's south end. Hwy 2 can be driven in either direction, connecting with the Edmonton–Red Deer route (see pp. 122–126). A long side track to Drumheller, with a connection to Dinosaur Provincial Park World Heritage Site, is a Jurassic throwback to the Age of Dinosaurs in the badlands of Southern Alberta.

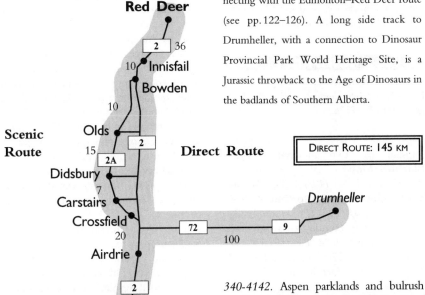

Scenic Route

Direct Route

DIRECT ROUTE: 145 KM

127

ROUTE

DIRECT ROUTE

Take Hwy 2 south for the 145-km journey from Red Deer to Calgary. Three km south of the crossing of Hwys 2 and 2A is **Slack Slough**, *Alberta Fish and Wildlife Division Red Deer Office; tel: (403)* *340-4142*. Aspen parklands and bulrush marshes provide excellent cover for Canada geese, mallards and migrating tundra swans. View spring–summer wildflowers from the north side viewing platform.

SCENIC ROUTE

Follow Hwy 2 through **Innisfail** as far as **Bowden**, where Hwy 2A crosses Hwy 2. Join Hwy 2A, which runs west of the main highway, stopping at prairie towns, **Olds**, **Didsbury** and **Carstairs** along the way to explore museums. Find a town park, usually near the centre, for a picnic, or dine in a coffee shop elbow-to-shoulder with farmers and local businesspeople. After Crossfield, rejoin Hwy 2 just north of **Airdrie**.

BUSES

There are 13 trips a day from Red Deer to Calgary with Greyhound Lines of Canada and Red Arrow, 3 of which follow the scenic route. Journey: 2–3 hrs. OTT table 106. There is also a service between Drumheller and Calgary with Greyhound Lines of Canada (twice daily; OTT table 131) and Ferguson Bus Lines (four times a week; OTT table 127). Journey: 2 hrs.

INNISFAIL

Tourist Information: Town of Innisfail, *4943 53 St, Innisfail, AB T4G 1A1; tel: (403) 227-3376.*

ACCOMMODATION

Innisfail has two moderate motels: **Bluebird Motel**, *4001 48 Ave, Innisfail, AB T4G 1J6; tel: (403) 227-3334*, and **The Highwayman Motor Inn**, *4704 42 Ave, Innisfail, AB T4G 1P6; tel: (403) 227-6001*. **Anthony Henday Campground**, *4943 53 St at Hwy 54, Innisfail, AB T4G 1A1; tel: (403) 227-3376; fax: (403) 227-4045*, open May–Oct, has 40 pitches.

SIGHTSEEING

In 1754, Hudson's Bay Company scout Anthony Henday, with Cree guides, spotted the Rockies from Mud Creek. The 1886 **'Spruces'** log building, the only extant stage Stopping House between Edmonton and Calgary, is now one of 13 historic buildings encompassed by the **Innisfail Historical Village Museum**, *52 Ave and 42 St, Box 6042, Innisfail, AB T4G 1S7; tel: (403) 227-2906*, open Tues–Thur and Sat–Sun 1100–1730, Fri 1100–1730 and 1900–2100, and holiday Mon (mid May–Labour Day), adults $2, children $1. The **Bowden Train Station**,

used by the CPR from 1904–1968, due south of Innisfail, is a fine example of the first building settlers saw when they arrived on the plains. A (farm) threshing bunkhouse, a hired man's cabin, country store, school, blacksmithy and garage are other pre-1940s buildings in the village, with a picnic area and tea room.

The 1893 **Dr George House Provincial Historical Site**, *5713 51 Ave; tel: (403) 227-1920*, combines a natural history museum and offices in the brick house built by Innisfail's original physician, Dr Henry George. Though George and his wife, an artist who designed the Province of Alberta's crest, later moved to Red Deer, the doctor was a collector and had established the first museum in the Northwest Territories in his house. Have a summer snack at the museum's **Katy Jane's Tea Room**, *tel: (403) 227-4881*.

Markerville, *16 km west of Innisfail on Hwy 54, then 3 km north*, settled in 1888–1889 by Icelanders from the Dakotas, became the centre for Icelandic-Canadian culture. A homesteader, Stephan G. Stephansson, wrote fiery poetry in Icelandic and became Iceland's most famous poet since the 13th century. Swedes and Danes settled surrounding villages. **Stephansson House Provincial Historic Site**, *7 km north of Markerville; tel: (403) 728-3929*, open 1000–1800 (mid May–Labour Day), is the poet's hand-built home displaying his prolific works.

Colour section (i): Banff National Park (pp.89–91): Moraine Lake and Lake Louise.
(ii): Jasper National Park (pp.97–100): Mt Edith Cavell and Jasper Park Lodge Pool.
(iii): Edmonton (pp.108–118): Sir Winston Churchill Square and Muttart Conservatory.
(iv): Ochre Beds and Paint Pots, Kootenay National Park (p.169–172); Drumheller Hoodoo (p.131).

The C & E Trail

As straight and straightforward as Hwy 2 appears, the trail connecting Edmonton and Calgary did not become truly important to explorers, missionary priests and early plains homesteaders until the Canadian Pacific Railway arrived in Calgary in 1883. Before the 1880s, few people lived along the route that came to be called the C&E Trail. A 'commute' from the NWMP post at Calgary to the trading centre in Edmonton took several weeks by ox cart or wagon through muskeg, swamp and forest. Fording creeks and the Red Deer River was a wet and sometimes harrowing experience.

With CPR access to Calgary and the West, trade arrived, and Fort Calgary became an important link in the traditional routes between Edmonton, Rocky Mountain House and Fort Macleod. Several entrepreneurs tried to set up a stagecoach service to deliver Royal Mail between Edmonton and Calgary, with staging stops en route. To their distress, the government elected to continue Edmonton mail delivery by cart and to route Calgary's post through Medicine Hat and Fort Macleod. One stagecoach operator finally succeeded in servicing the route, a 5-day, 4-night journey costing $25, with a 45 kg baggage allowance. The trip was dangerous, subject to wheels stuck in mud, snow or ice, or sleighing precariously on specially-fitted runners. Highwaymen preyed on the stages. Some stage Stopping Houses survived, forming the basis for towns like Innisfail and Airdrie.

The 1885 Riel Rebellion in Saskatchewan spurred the need to have transportation and communications ready in case of turmoil. General Thomas Bland Strange, commanding the Alberta Defence Force charged with defending settlements against the perceived threat of allied Métis and First Nations Cree and Blackfoot, travelled between Calgary and Edmonton to reassure farmers and merchants. His impressive convoy included 800 men and 175 wagons.

The Edmonton to Calgary route had been proved viable, despite the mud and muck. By 1891, the CPR had seen the potential market and inaugurated a two-day service on the Calgary & Edmonton Railway (C&E) between the cities. Towns along today's Hwy 2, including Olds, Didsbury, Carstairs and Crossfield, sprang to life with the arrival of the rails and telegraph. Grain elevators stand tall near the railway tracks, their cached cereals the modern-day 'freight' being hauled to markets in Eastern Canada or the Far East via Calgary or Edmonton.

129

From Hwy 2, drive 56 km east of Innisfail on Hwy 590, turn right onto Hwy 21, then take the rough winding road (unsuitable for RVs) 19 km east of Huxley across the prairies to **Dry Island Buffalo Jump Provincial Park**, *tel: (403) 442-4211* (summer), *(403) 823-1749* (winter). This is rock etched in layers of coloured sandstone cliffs, badlands from where, two millennia ago, First Nations people drove bison to their deaths 50 m below in Red Deer River Valley. Prairie falcons are among 150 bird species. When mayflies hatch at dusk in late July–early Aug, take a torch to the river to watch goldeneye ducks gorging.

Canada's only **RCMP Police Dog Service Training Centre**, *Hwy 2, 4 km south of Innisfail; tel: (403) 227-3346,* is open year-round. Book in advance to see dogs demonstrate law-enforcement techniques and obedience, Wed at 1400 (Victoria Day–Thanksgiving); the rest of the year, kennel tours and a video are presented Mon–Fri 1300–1500.

BOWDEN

Tourist Information: Town of Bowden, *Box 338, Bowden, AB T0M 0K0; tel: (403) 224-3395.*

Bowden Motor Inn, *Hwy 2 S., Box*

519; tel: (403) 224-3404, and **Westwind Antiques & Motel**, Hwy 2 S. Service Rd; tel: (403) 224-3332, are both moderate. **Bowden Heritage Rest Area**, Hwy 2. S. Service Rd, Box 338; tel: (403) 224-3395, open May–Oct, has 22 pitches.

Bowden farms hay, oats, wheat and barley. Nurseries cultivate reforestation seedlings near hills covered by aspen.

Red Lodge Provincial Park, 15 km west of Bowden on Rd 587, PO Box 130, Bowden, AB T0M 0K0; tel: (403) 224-3216 or (403) 887-5575 (winter), or (403) 224-2547 (camping reservations), is open May–Thanksgiving for forest camping and hiking, with fishing, swimming and canoeing on the Little Red Deer River.

OLDS

Tourist Information: Town of Olds, 4911 51 Ave, Olds, AB T4H 1R5; tel: (403) 556-6981; fax: (403) 556-6537.

ACCOMMODATION

Olds has four moderate motels, including BW. Closer to budget are **Circle Five Motel**, #17 4513 52 Ave; tel: (403) 556-7755, **Sportsman's Inn Motel**, 5622 46 St; tel: (403) 556-3315, and **Siesta Motel**, 5218 46 St; tel: (888) 774-7727 or (403) 556-3376. **O.R. Hedges Park**, 4911 51 Ave; tel: (403) 556-6981, is open May–Sept with 43 pitches.

SIGHTSEEING

Olds was founded in 1891 by CPR traffic manager George Olds. **Olds Agriculture College**, tel: (403) 556-8330, is known for innovative agricultural development. Despite the farmland surrounding Olds, the campus' 486 hectares have beautiful gardens with specimens of all trees grown in Alberta. Walk through the horticulture department building for indoor cultivars and see the small dairy herd and pig farm.

Mountain View Museum, 5038 50 St, Olds, AB T0M 1P0; tel: (403) 556-8464, has exhibits of settler and farm life, including a kitchen with a wood-burning stove, in an old telephone exchange building. Open Mon–Fri 0900–1700 (July–Aug), Tues–Thur 1300–1700 (Sept–June)

DIDSBURY

Tourist Information: Town of Didsbury, PO Box 790, Didsbury, AB T0M 0W0; tel: (403) 335-3391; fax: (403) 335-9794.

Didsbury boasts two moderate motels, an S8, a Bed and Breakfast and a campsite. **Grimmon House Bed and Breakfast**, 1610 15 Ave, PO Box 1268; tel: (403) 335-8353; fax: (403) 335-3640, has a backyard gazebo. **Rosebud Valley Campground**, PO Box 790, tel: (403) 335-8578, open mid May–Oct, has 28 pitches in town.

Mennonites from Ontario homesteaded Didsbury in 1893. **Didsbury & District Museum**, 2118 21 Ave; tel: (403) 335-9295, is open Wed–Fri 1300–1700 year-round, Sat 1300–1700 summer. The 1906 schoolhouse has toys, washing machines, military memorabilia and elevators (lifts), with rooms set up as a general store, doctor's office, chapel – even a schoolroom.

CARSTAIRS

Tourist Information: Town of Carstairs, 1119 Osler St, Carstairs, AB T0M 0N0; tel: (403) 337-3341.

ACCOMMODATION

Moderate **Golden West Motor Inn**, PO Box 1060, Carstairs; tel: (403) 337-3333, is supplemented by the 28-pitch **Carstairs Municipal Campground**, Hwy 2A; tel: (403) 337-3341, open May–Oct, next to an 18-hole golf course. **Gray Fox Ranch Bed & Breakfast**, RR 2, Hwy 580; tel: (403) 337-3192, a Victorian farmhouse on a working ranch, and **Temarest**, *RR 1; tel: (403) 337-3069,* in an English Tudor-style home, are moderate.

SIGHTSEEING

Carstairs was founded by Scots, who named it for a town in Lanarkshire, Scotland. Carstairs lives on agriculture and the petroleum industry. **Carstairs Roulston Museum**, *1138 Nanton St; tel: (403) 337-3710,* in the former Knox Presbyterian Church, has homestead-era artefacts.

PaSu Farms, *Hwy 580, 9 km west of Carstairs; tel: (403) 337-2800,* open Tues–Sat 1000–1700, Sun 1200–1700, sells Alberta-made woollens, sheepskin and African hangings. The farm's **Devonshire Tea Room** is a fully-licensed restaurant, open Tues–Sun 1000–1700, with classic English tea at 1400, a Carvery Brunch on Sun, and fine dining Thur–Sat evenings. **Custom Woolen Mills Ltd.**; *tel: (403) 337-2221,* open Mon–Fri 0900–1700, is 20 km north-east of town via Hwy 581 to Hwy 791. The Wool Shoppe sells finished yarns, knitting and wool craft supplies, but the enticement is a chance to see wool processing as it was done for several hundred years. Carding machinery in use was made 1860–1910, the spinning mule dates from 1910 and the knotting machine is c.1917.

⬛ SIDE TRACK
TO DRUMHELLER

Watch for brown *Royal Tyrrell Museum of Palaeontology* signs.

For the most direct route, turn left (east) from Hwy 2 south of **Crossfield** (10 km north of Airdrie) onto Hwy 72. Continue 34 km to **Beiseker** to join Hwy 9 to Drumheller.

From Calgary, take TransCanada Hwy 1 *(16 Ave N.W.)* east for 30 km, then turn left on Hwy 9 and follow its zigzag route by fields, farms and grain

elevators for 110 km to Drumheller. The plains are flat, filled with green hay, yellow canola, and occasional red barns and red-wing blackbirds against a blue sky. In winter, it's a bleak, surreal unbroken white expanse to the east.

North-west of **Irricana**, **Pioneer Acres**, *tel: (403) 935-4357,* open 0900–1700 May–Sept, has working antique farm equipment, a blacksmithy and a 1929 house on 20 hectares.

The highway gradually descends across the plains; 100 km from Calgary, depressions appearing in the landscape continue until the Badlands dramatically appear 22 km on at **Horseshoe Canyon Provincial Recreation Area**, south-west of Drumheller. First Nations people believed it to be haunted.

DRUMHELLER

Tourist Information: Big Country Tourist Association, *170 Centre St, PO Box 2308, Drumheller, AB, T0J 0Y0; tel: (403) 823-5885; fax: (403) 823-7942,* has maps, a Visitor Guide and information on accommodation, dining, museums, activities, the 48-km Dinosaur Loop Trail, recreation, hoodoos, mines and winter skiing and snowboarding on the badlands. Two **Visitor InfoCentres** open year-round: **Drumheller Regional Chamber of Development & Tourism**, *60 1 Ave W. (near Dinny Statue), Box 999, Drumheller, AB T0J 0Y0; tel: (403) 823-1331 or (403) 823-8100; fax: (403) 823-4469,* and **Sun City Market**, *Hwy 9 S.; tel: (403) 823-8746.*

ACCOMMODATION AND FOOD

Though Drumheller has 10 moderate motels, 11 Bed and Breakfasts and four campsites, the popularity of multiple-day stays in Dinosaur central, especially in summer, necessitates booking well in advance. The chain motels, **BW Jurassic Inn**, *1103 Hwy 9 S.; tel: (800) 528-1234* or *(403) 823-7700,* and **Super 8 Motel**, *680 2 St S.E.; tel: (403) 823-8887,* are among the newest and best.

There's an assortment of fast food in Drumheller and a wide range of Greek, Italian and Canadian fare at **Stavros Family Restaurant**, *190 Railway Ave W.; tel: (403) 823-6362.* For dessert, indulge in a $1.25 cheesecake-flavoured ice-cream from **Tastee Delite**, *202 2 St W.; tel: (403) 823-7363.*

SIGHTSEEING

As humorous as all the dinosaur images and statues around Drumheller may seem, this spot in south-central Alberta is on one of the world's largest Cretaceous Period (140–65 million years old) dinosaur boneyards. Geologist Joseph Burr Tyrrell was paddling down the Red Deer River in 1884 when he looked up a cliff at the large toothy skull of an unknown dinosaur species – later named *Albertasaurus.*

Bone excavations began and continue in Alberta, directed by the **Royal Tyrrell Museum of Palaeontology**, *Hwy 838, Box 7500, in Midland Provincial Park, Drumheller, AB T0J 0Y0; tel: (403) 823-7707 or (888) 440-4240; fax: (403) 823-7131, http://www.tyrrellmuseum.com/tour,* one of the world's outstanding fossil museums. The museum is open daily 0900–2100 (Victoria Day–Labour Day), 1000–1700 (Labour Day–Thanksgiving), Tues–Sun 1000–1700 (mid Oct–mid May); adults $6.50, children $3, families $15.

Set in the badlands, the museum presents 35 complete dinosaur specimens (dinosaur fossils too delicate to be displayed have been cleverly cast to seem as old the originals) in Dinosaur Hall, including a menacing *Tyrannosaurus rex.* Plan at least a half-day to follow a dinosaur print path through more than 3 billion years of life on earth. Exhibit after exhibit has rare fossils of simple life forms, ancient insects, plants, fish, birds, mammals – even some where characteristics are combined, or defy classification. In winter, pick up the Bone Line phone receiver for details of what preparators working behind the Preparation Lab window a few metres away are doing to gently free fossils from rock.

The Royal Tyrrell Museum is a prime attraction on the **Dinosaur Trail**, a 48-km driving loop through the badlands. From downtown Drumheller, go north on Hwy 838, the **North Dinosaur Trail**. **Homestead Antique Museum**, *901 N. Dinosaur Trail; tel: (403) 823-2600,* open mid May–mid Oct, adults $3, hides in a huge round building with collections from dolls and a complete barber shop to cases of trinkets. **Midland Provincial Park**, *tel: (403) 823-1749,* ranger post signs interpret early coal mining. Hike Royal Tyrrell Museum badlands trails.

The white **Little Church** on the left holds six people. The road rises into benchland beyond the **Drumheller Golf & Country Club**. Oil pumps are scenic, but hazardous, pumping away on the plains. Pull into the parking area of **Horsethief Canyon** for a spectacular view over the striated badlands. It's a free 5-min ride crossing the Red Deer River with a vehicle on the cable-operated **Bleriot Ferry**, summer only 0800–2245. In winter, the ferry doesn't operate; driving the Dinosaur Trail requires backtracking on both sides of the river. From the west bank, drive south on Hwy 837, the **South Dinosaur Trail**, stopping at **Orkney Viewpoint** for another appreciation of the badlands from atop a scenic bluff. **Canadian Hovertours**, *tel: (403) 823-5100*, conduct 45-min May–Sept hovercraft tours along the Red Deer River Valley, adults $19.95, children under 12 $9.95. Walk over **Rosedale Suspension Bridge**, replacement for a 1931 bridge that took over from cable transport of men and coal from mines on the Red Deer River's east bank. **Drumheller Dinosaur and Fossil Museum**, *335 1st St E.; tel: (403) 823-2593*, May–mid Oct, adults $2, a pale contender to the Royal Tyrrell Museum, has a few dinosaur fossils, including an *Albertasaurus* head. Avoid overcrowded amphibians and snakes at **Reptile World**, *Hwy 9; tel: (403) 823-8623*.

Take Hwy 10 south-east from Drumheller to **Hoodoos Recreation Area**, a wild grouping of white caprocks topping eroding golden-brown pillars of rock, where films like *Superman* and *Running Brave* were made.

Six km east of the hoodoos, **East Coulee School Museum**, *tel: (403) 822-3970*, evokes a former coal mining town. Close by, the **Atlas Coal Mine Museum**; *tel: (403) 822-2220 or (403) 342-6889*, open 1000–1800 (mid May–mid Oct), offers hard-hat tours of the 8-storey tipple. Demonstrations include tours of a simulated mine tunnel on the site of the last of 138 coal mines registered in the Drumheller Valley.

The Royal Tyrrell Museum supervises fossil collecting at a UNESCO World Heritage Site, worth 2-days excursion from the Drumheller side track or a drive east from Calgary. **Dinosaur Provincial Park**, *PO Box 60, Patricia, AB T0J 2K0; tel: (403) 378-4342; web: http://www.gov.ab.ca/~env/nrs/dinosaur*, adults $2, children $1.50, is preserved for rich beds of late Cretaceous fossils, its spreading badlands and the rich riparian habitat along Red Deer River. **Camping reservations**, *tel: (403) 378-3700*, $5.35 reservation fee.

Check interpretive exhibits and pick up brochures at the park **Field Station**, open daily 0815–2100 (mid May–Sept), shorter hours the rest of the year. A public loop road permits vehicle access on a restricted route through lunar badlands scenery. Walking trails explore badlands, a fossil hunter's trail, cottonwood flats and the prairie. Rangers lead *centrosaurus* bone-bed hikes and fossil safaris and offer a badlands bus tour, adults $4.50, children 6–15 $2.25 per tour, purchased at the Field Station information counter on the day of the tour (book bus tours in advance; *tel: (403) 378-4344*). Inquire about free tickets to behind-the-scenes tours of fossil lab activities.

133

Tourist Information: City of Airdrie; *tel: (403) 948-8800*, or contact **Calgary Convention & Visitors Bureau**, *tel: (800) 661-1678 or (403) 263-8510*.

Airdrie's proximity to Calgary and the international airport (10 km) rates a moderate *BW*.

Booming Airdrie began as a railway station with a Stopping House and is now a Calgary dormitory community. **Nose Creek Valley Museum**, *1701 Main St S.; tel: (403) 948-6685*, open Mon–Fri 1000–1700 (June–Aug), Mon–Fri 1300–1700 (Sept–May), Sat–Sun 1300–1700 year-round, has Stone Age, Blackfoot and Shoshone artefacts and covers the petroleum and agricultural industries.

RED DEER–SASKATCHEWAN RIVER CROSSING

The David Thompson Hwy, the least-known route into the Canadian Rocky Mountain Parks, is steeped in Canada's revered exploration history. Lakes, hiking, bison and stunning mountain wilderness are equal to any in the more famous parks. Rocky Mountain House National Historic Site, open spring–fall, is roughly a third of the way along this 4-hour, 260-km drive west to Banff National Park.

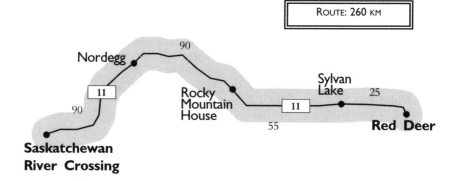

ROUTE: 260 KM

Nordegg 90

11

90 Rocky Mountain House 11 Sylvan Lake 25

55 Red Deer

134

Saskatchewan River Crossing

ROUTE

Go west on *67 St* in Red Deer, on Hwy 11, the David Thompson Hwy, crossing Hwy 2, to **Saskatchewan River Crossing**, a journey of 245 km.

Tourist Information: David Thompson Country Tourist Council, *4836 Ross St, Red Deer, AB T4N 5E8; tel: (403) 342-2032.* Wilderness information: **Alberta Provincial Parks Service**, *Rimbey; tel: (403) 843-2545*, and **Alberta Fish and Wildlife Division**, *Rocky Mountain House; tel: (403) 845-8230.*

West of downtown Red Deer malls yield to green fields. Sat only **Calida Greyhound Track**, *tel: (403) 887-5782*, is just before the right turn onto Hwy 20 to **Sylvan Lake**.

BUSES

Prairie Bus Lines operate a service from Red Deer to Rocky Mountain House. Journey time: 1½ hrs. See OTT table 99.

SYLVAN LAKE

Tourist Information: Town of Sylvan Lake, *4926 50 Ave, Sylvan Lake, AB T4S 1A1; tel: (403) 887-2141*, and **Sylvan**

Lake Chamber of Commerce Tourist InfoCentre, *50 Ave, near the grain elevators;* *tel: (403) 887-5050.* For information on day use only **Sylvan Lake Provincial Park**, *tel: (403) 887-5575.*

ACCOMMODATION AND FOOD

Bed and Breakfasts, seven campsites and moderate motels are on *Lakeshore Dr.* **Jarvis Bay Provincial Park**, *tel: (403) 887-5522,* has 171 pitches. Book early.

Fast food and ice-cream shops are numerous. **Sandals Family Restaurant**, *5220 Lakeshore Dr.; tel: (403) 887-2788,* known for ribs, has a patio lakeview and Sun Brunch.

SIGHTSEEING

Long sandy strands have attracted families of sunbathers since 1901. There's a loop from Hwy 11: turn right at Hwy 20, continue 5 km to *Lakeshore Dr.,* then return to Hwy 11 by *50 St.* **Sylvan Lake Marina** lighthouse is modern.

There's beach volleyball or jet skis and boats from **Sylvan Marina**, *tel: (403) 887-2950.* **Miss Mermaid Cruise**, *tel: (403) 887-2950,* offer May–Oct lunch and dinner cruises; **Zoo Cruise**, *tel: (403) 887-3000,* have family cruises and night-time circuits for adults. **Wild Rapids Water Slide Park**, *Lakeshore Dr.; tel: (403) 887-3636,* is open mid June–Labour Day, adults $18, those shorter than 1.2m $14.

Miniature golf courses and three full-scale golf courses lure duffers. **Royal Standard Paintball**, *tel: (403) 748-3198,* joins **Parasailing**; *tel: (403) 887-5644,* and **Railside Bowl**; *tel: (403) 887-5303,* as novel activities. Fishing for walleye is prohibited, but Sylvan Lake's pier and **Jarvis Bay cliffs** are good spots for northern pike (jackfish), whitefish, perch and ling. In winter, ice-skate on the lake.

Sylvan Flower Farm, *Kuusamo Rd;* *tel/fax: (403) 887-2808,* opens 1200–2100 (June–Aug), 0900–1700 (Sept–May). A gift shop sells 30 varieties of dried flowers from a 30,000-bundle drying barn.

West of the Sylvan Lake area, Hwy 11 rolls through farmland dotted with occasional windmills to Rocky Mountain House.

ROCKY MOUNTAIN HOUSE

Tourist Information: Rocky Mountain House Tourist Information Centre, *Hwy 11 and 54 Ave, Rocky Mountain House, AB T0M 1T0;* open mid May–mid Oct, or **Town of Rocky Mountain House**, *tel: (403) 845-2866.*

ACCOMMODATION AND FOOD

Rocky Mountain House has six moderate motels and **Riverside Bed & Breakfast**, *Box 643; tel/fax: (403) 845-5901.* Open May–mid Sept are **Aspen Campground**, with 48 pitches, and **Centennial Park**, *54 St;* both *PO Box 1509, tel: (403) 845-3720.*

Food is mostly on Hwy 11; **Burger Baron**, *tel: (403) 845-6009,* has fine pizza.

SIGHTSEEING

Closed in winter, **Rocky Mountain House National Historic Site**, *5 km west of town on 52 A (Hwy 11A); tel: (403) 845-2412; web: http://www.worldweb.com/Parks Canada-Rocky,* is open 0900–1700 (mid Apr–early May), 1000–1800 (May–Labour Day), Mon–Fri 1000–1700, Sat–Sun 1030–1800 (Sept–Thanksgiving), adults $2.25, children 6–16 $1.25.

Beaver instigated the 1799 founding of rival forts by the North West Company and the Hudson's Bay Company. Rocky Mountain House on the North Saskatchewan River was in a tempting location – close enough to the Rockies and the trading Kootenai (Ktunaxa) First Nation to make a trading post desirable. During its

135

Explorers and Traders

Blame the whims of fashion for the exploration of the Canadian Rockies. Europe's insatiable demand for beaver hats from the mid 1600s into the 1830s fuelled the commercial exploitation of Western Canada by the Hudson's Bay Company and the North West Company. Locked in intense, bloody rivalry for four decades, Canada's fur trading empires battled to open new trading areas along supply lines that spanned North America.

Britain granted Rupert's Land, the territory from Hudson's Bay west to the Rocky Mountains, to the HBC in 1670. From their base at York Factory on the shores of Hudson's Bay, HBC traders explored westward by canoe, establishing a network of forts where local Indians traded furs for firearms, clothing, blankets, knives and cooking pots.

Nearly a century passed before Anthony Henday spent the winter of 1754–1755 near today's Innisfail, the first White to see the Rocky Mountains. It wasn't until 1792 that Peter Fiddler became the first White to enter the Rockies.

Each spring, traders loaded their canoes to the gunwales with bales of furs and paddled downstream to York Factory, from where the furs were shipped to Europe. In summer, they paddled back to their forts, loaded with supplies and trade goods for the coming season. Freight canoes carried about 1350 kg and a crew of six to eight. Between the 1740s–1790s, canoes were largely replaced by York boats, wooden boats modelled on traditional craft from the Orkney Islands that could carry 2700 kg with the same crew.

In 1787, serious competition appeared. Independent traders in Montreal formed the North West Company and a new business plan. Where the HBC relied on Natives to *bring* furs to their posts, Norwesters went *to* the Natives. **Voyageurs**, largely French-speaking traders from Quebec, explored westward settling in First Nations villages to collect furs. Each company hoped for a stranglehold with strategic posts on every major river. The dream was a route through the Rockies to the Columbia River, the Pacific Ocean and on to China.

In 1789, Norwester **Alexander Mackenzie** followed what became the Mackenzie River north from Lake Athabasca, in Northern Alberta, to the Arctic Ocean. In 1792, he followed the Fraser River and walked overland to Bella Coola, the first known non-Native to cross the continent north of Mexico.

Simon Fraser followed the Rocky Mountain Trench and the Fraser River to found Fort George (now Prince George) in 1807. The next year, he continued down the Fraser River to the Pacific, finding that it was too rough for reliable navigation. Fellow Norwester **David Thompson** had named the Fraser for its explorer, who had named the Thompson River after friend David, who had never seen his namesake.

Thompson is Canada's most important and least-remembered explorer. In more than 20 years of travel, Thompson travelled more than 90,000 km by canoe, horse and afoot to map nearly 4 million square km of Western Canada, as well as major portions of Idaho, Montana, Oregon and Washington in the US.

In the process, he discovered the source of the Columbia River at Columbia Lake (1807) and found Athabasca Pass (1811), which became Canada's main route over the Rocky Mountains until the Canadian Pacific Railway crossed the Kicking Horse Pass in 1884. Thompson was the first White to travel the length of the Columbia River (1811) – arriving at the Pacific Ocean four months after American fur traders had built Fort Astoria and established land claims that resulted in the division of Western America between Britain and the United States at the 49th Parallel. Thompson's uncommonly precise maps were used into the 20th century, but he died in poverty and virtual obscurity near Montreal in 1857.

75-year off-and-on-again use, Rocky Mountain House separated First Nations Cree and Assiniboine from the Blackfoot pushing north, while providing explorers like David Thompson a spot from which to explore passes via the Saskatchewan and Athabasca Rivers.

By 1875, five forts had occupied the site. Interpretive trails follow the river. Audio narratives recount 1835–1861 and 1864–1875 period forts' activity along a 0.9-km prairie path, which passes a Red River cart, burial ground and two extant chimneys. A longer 3.2-km trail by wildflowers winds through forest near tepees and a York boat. Costumed interpreters fry bannock (bread), dry buffalo meat, dip candles and brew Labrador tea. Sites of the 1799–1835 HBC fort and the 1799–1821 NWC fort are separated by a superb viewing platform above the Buffalo Paddock.

Rocky Mountain House Museum, *4604 49 Ave; tel: (403) 845-2332,* open Mon–Fri and summer weekends, adults $2, has a 1915 rope-making machine.

Winter activities include Nordic skiing, sleddog mushing and curling. The **Kurt Browning Arena,** *tel: (403) 722-3022,* open 0800–1600 (summer), houses the local champion figure skater's medals and memorabilia.

The **Crimson Lake Provincial Park,** *16 km north-west, tel: (403) 845-2340,* (162-pitch campsite; *tel: (403) 845-2330),* has windsurfing and trails through black spruce bogs, sand dunes and tamarack swamps to find 13 elusive species of orchids and carnivorous sundew plants.

NORDEGG

Tourist Information: Nordegg Heritage Centre, open daily 0900–1700 (late June–early Sept), Sat–Sun (mid May–early Oct).

Nordegg has cafés and moderate **Nordegg Resort Lodge,** *General Delivery, Nordegg, AB T0M 2H0; tel: (800) 408-3294* or *(403) 721-3757.* **HI-Shunda Creek Hostel,** *Shunda Creek Recreation Area Rd, General Delivery, Nordegg AB T0M 2H0; tel/fax: (403) 721-2140,* opens daily.

Ninety-six km west of Rocky Mountain House, the Brazeau Collieries mined semi-bituminous coal to fire up steam locomotive engines from 1911–1955. **Nordegg Historical Society,** *tel: (403) 845-4444,* offers late June–Labour Day guided tours of colliery ruins and townsite.

NORDEGG TO SASKATCHEWAN RIVER CROSSING

Hwy 11 turns south-west from Nordegg. Cattle wander the **Big Horn Stoney Reserve. Crescent Falls** and llama trekking are 6 km to the right soon after the reserve's Native gift shop and services.

Cross the **Bighorn River. Bighorn Damsite InfoCentre,** open 0830–1630 (Victoria Day–Labour Day), left, explains the creation of **Lake Abraham,** Alberta's largest man-made lake.

Bighorn Wildland Recreation Area is noted for 700 km of trails and the **Kentucky Plains Wildlife Sanctuary.**

Craggy, pale mountains rise high. Moderate **David Thompson Resort,** *Box 1929, Rocky Mountain House, AB T0M 1T0; tel: (403) 721-2103,* has petrol, a swimming pool, windsurfing, volleyball, horseshoes, fishing, hiking and nearby trail rides.

Cross the Cline River and drop quickly to **Kootenay Plains Ecological Reserve. Siffleur Falls,** at the southern end of Abraham Lake, is 4 km left. Expect black bears, wolves, wapiti and deer near **Banff National Park. Saskatchewan River Crossing** (see Banff–Jasper, pp. 87–103) is 5 km west.

137

WEST CANADIAN TRAINS

The train is the inside way to see the best of BC and Alberta's interior scenery without having to clutch a steering wheel, read a route map, fight traffic or worry about finding meals.

RAILING THE ROCKIES

Step into Canadian history, a tradition of Western Canadian settlement, resource exploitation and commercial success. Rails take goods to market, provide transportation between towns and cities and bring people from somewhere else to see natural wonders. The drill has not changed since Canadian Pacific Railway President William Van Horne, his eyes on the Rocky Mountains, pronounced over a hundred years ago, 'If we can't export the scenery, we'll import the tourists'. Tourists who photograph, eat, drink, enjoy outdoor recreation and mountain châteaux luxuries are astonished by scenery so dramatic that four Canadian National Parks – **Banff**, **Jasper**, **Yoho** and **Kootenay** – are a UNESCO World Heritage Site.

VIA Rail Canada trans-Canadian routes cross the Rockies from Edmonton to Jasper and on to Vancouver and run from Jasper to Prince Rupert via Prince George. The **Rocky Mountaineer**, which runs May–mid Oct from Vancouver via Kamloops to Jasper or Banff, is a 100% tourist train, delivering history and facts about the scenery, trees, wildflowers, wildlife, birds, engineering feats, tunnels, explorers, local industries and place names – even about the railways which built and use(d) the tracks.

CPR surveyors and engineers designed routes to follow the natural course of rivers, where canyon walls provided support for track and provided riders with a view. The Rocky Mountaineer follows seven historic subdivisions along its two routes. Each is about 200 km long, used historically by the CPR and CN (Canadian National) for crewing and administration. Each mile in each subdivision is signposted, white mileposts with numbers beginning at '0' from the east and south.

Both Rocky Mountaineer itineraries depart from Vancouver's **Pacific Central Station** to **Kamloops**, skirting the Fraser River's treacherously narrow Hells Gate and traversing the Thompson River's Jaws of Death Gorge. Rolling stock rushes by arid hills, patches of cultivated ginseng under plastic tarps and modest farm houses.

The **Coast Mountains** appear within 45 mins of leaving Vancouver, though the **Rockies** aren't visible until the second day, east of Kamloops. The two-day route crosses an impressive set of ranges: Coast, Northern Cascades, Monashee (Jasper Route), Selkirk, Purcell, Columbia and the West, Main and Front Ranges of the Rockies, each successively higher and sharper looking than the one just traversed.

After overnighting at a Kamloops motel, passengers reboard the Rocky Mountaineer. The land is wilder along the Jasper route, less populated as the train goes north along the North Thompson River. Little Hell's Gate is almost as harrowing as its larger namesake – in 1862, the Overlanders spent three days portaging 13½ km around the rapids. Watery geometry, 92-m high Pyramid Falls cascades to the base of the railway.

Mt Albreda Glacier is followed by 30

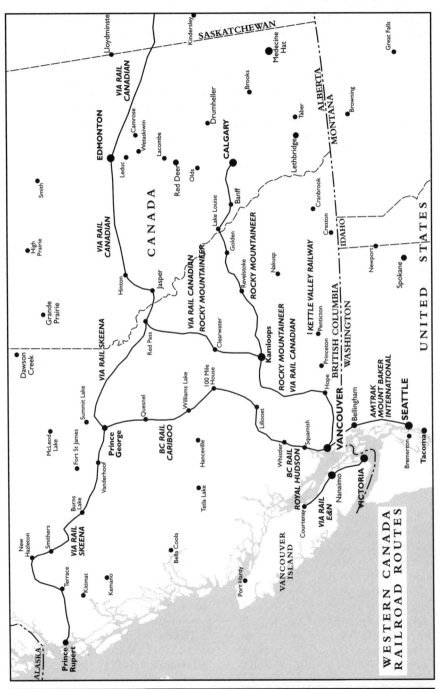

139

WESTERN CANADA RAILROAD ROUTES

km of glaciers atop the **Premier Range Peaks**, named after early Canadian Prime Ministers. Mt Robson, a dominant 3991-m high mass iced with rivulets of snow, is the Canadian Rockies highest peak. Rainbow Falls plunges into aquamarine Moose Lake. The line crosses 1144-m Yellowhead Pass, then quickly drops past Mt Edith Cavell to **Jasper Townsite**.

The Rocky Mountaineer southern Rockies route goes east from Kamloops to Banff. It parallels busy TransCanada Hwy 1, playing nip and tuck with canyon walls and the highway, depending on where surveying engineers could find stable surface for track. Past hoodoos, sandstone pillars eroding into columns below plate-shaped capstones, the shorebirds and houseboats of Shuswap Lake appear. At Notch Hill near Sorrento, the train curves dramatically as if reversing direction, creating a perfect view of its full length. A cairn marks Craigellachie, where Donald Smith, an original CPR syndicate member, drove the last ordinary iron spike of the continent-connecting Canadian Pacific Railway in 1885. After Revelstoke, named after the English lord whose bank underwrote CPR funding in the late 1880s, the train passes Mt Revelstoke National Park. The railway criss-crosses the swift Illecillewaet River ten times, plunging into tunnels and sheltering beneath avalanche-deflecting snow sheds.

Every mountain in the **Selkirk Range** dwarfs the one before. In Glacier National Park, 8-km long Connaught Tunnel rises up through Mt Macdonald on the way underneath Rogers Pass. The graceful, delicate-looking arch of Stoney Creek Bridge, 150m long and 100m above the creek, belies the weight of railway traffic. Because avalanches were so destructive around Rogers Pass, CPR built the Connaught Tunnel in 1916 and abandoned the surface route through the pass. In 1988, CP Rail used laser and satellite surveys to design the 14.4-km Mt Macdonald Tunnel, North America's longest. The Rocky Mountaineer uses the quainter 1916 Connaught Tunnel.

From Golden in the Columbia River Valley, the train winds above wildly rushing Kicking Horse River, changing sides seven times as it enters Yoho National Park. After stopping at Field, the train snakes up the Big Hill through the figure eight of the Lower and Upper Spiral Tunnels, constructed at great cost to reduce the hazardous grade to an acceptable 2.2%.

The Rocky Mountaineer earns its name crossing the **Continental Divide** at 1640-m high Mt. Stephen, where run-off from snow, rain and glaciers separates to flow north into the Arctic Ocean, east into watersheds draining into the Atlantic or west to the Pacific. In Banff National Park, glimpse 3496-m Victoria Glacier above the hidden Lake Louise. Castle Mountain's golden turrets rise across the Bow Valley as the train follows the Bow River towards **Banff Townsite**, the activity centre of Banff National Park.

The southern itinerary continues through Bow Valley, leaving the foothills of the Rockies Front Range for **Calgary**.

Plan on two days travel to/from Vancouver on either route, or five days for the complete loop. For highlights of Banff and Jasper National Parks, including the Bow Valley Parkway, Johnston Canyon (walk), Lake Louise, Moraine Lake, Peyto Lake, the Icefields Parkway, Athabasca Glacier on the Columbia Icefield, Athabasca Falls, and Maligne Lake near Jasper, hire a car or take a Brewster coach tour of the most famous sights.

Tickets for the Rocky Mountaineer and VIA Rail Services are sold in the UK by **Leisurail**; *tel: 01733 335599.*

CALGARY–LETHBRIDGE

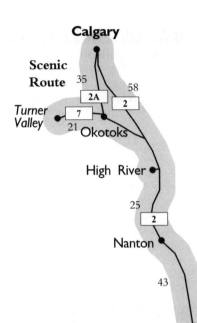

Calgary

Scenic Route 35

58

2A

2

Turner Valley 7

21 **Okotoks**

High River

25

2

Nanton

43

Claresholm

Direct Route

2

42

3

Fort Macleod 52

Lethbridge

DIRECT ROUTE: 220 KM

The prairies open up into rangeland south of Calgary. To the west are the grey peaks of Kananaskis Country, the Rocky Mountain Foothills. Most of this 220-km route follows the Macleod Trail south along the original road between North West Mounted Police outposts in Calgary and Fort Macleod. To the side of the highway, century-old wagon wheel tracks may still occasionally be seen. Lethbridge, Alberta's third largest city, is a convenient base for area touring. Plan on about three hours to drive from Calgary to Lethbridge, longer for stops at Head-Smashed-In Buffalo Jump and Fort Macleod.

141

ROUTES

DIRECT ROUTE

→ Begin from downtown Calgary at Calgary Tower, *101 9 Ave S.W.* and *Centre St S.* Drive one block east. Turn right onto *1 St S.E.* seven blocks south until it veers left at Lindsay Park to merge with the *Macleod Trail*. *Macleod Trail* becomes Hwy 2 when it crosses *Marquis of Lorne Trail* and *178 Ave*. Follow Hwy 2 south to Hwy 3, the Crowsnest Hwy, and turn left to Lethbridge.

SCENIC ROUTE

▶ Leave Calgary on Hwy 2A and continue 35 km to **Okotoks**. From here, follow Hwy 2A to rejoin Hwy 2. Follow Hwy 2 through the towns of **High River**, **Nanton** and **Claresholm**. At Hwy 3, turn left to **Fort Macleod** and Lethbridge.

Tourist Information: Alberta South Tourism Development Region, *2805*

Scenic Dr., Lethbridge, AB T1K 5B7; tel: (800) 661-1222, have information on towns, museums and historic sites along this route, and book some accommodation. Most towns on and near Hwy 2 have at least one moderate motel and a campsite.

BUSES

Greyhound Lines of Canada operate four trips a day, taking 3¼ hrs. See OTT table 137.

OKOTOKS

Tourist Information: Okotoks Economic Development Officer, *Town Hall, 14 McRae St, Okotoks, AB T0l 1T0; tel: (403) 938-8907.* In summer, **The Station Visitor Information Centre,** *55 N. Railway St; tel/fax: (403) 938-3204.*

VIC self-guided walking tour maps of 21 historic buildings include early 20th-century spots converted to restaurants. **Foothills Cattle Company,** *35 Riverside Dr.; tel: (403) 938-2901,* open Mon–Sun 1100–2300, serves steaks in a barn which once was the town creamery. Victorian-era **Ginger Tea Room and Gift Shop,** *43 Riverside Dr.; tel: (403) 938-2907,* is crammed with antiques.

Blackfoot told tales of a rock, *Okatok,* chasing the band's legendary creator and trickster, Napi. **Big Rock,** 10 km west of Okotoks, is a 9-m high, 16,500-tonne quartzite erratic (boulder) thrown up on an advancing glacier near present-day Jasper 15,000 years ago. The Macleod Trail linked Forts Macleod and Calgary and travellers soon began stopping en route to admire the world's largest glacial erratic.

On the east side of town, **Okotoks Bird Sanctuary** provides an elevated observation deck for waterfowl spotting. West of Okotoks is **Black Diamond,** once a coal mining centre, and **Turner Valley.**

SIDE TRACK FROM OKOTOKS

From Okotoks, go west on Hwy 7 for about 21 km.

TURNER VALLEY

Tourist Information: Town of Turner Valley Visitor Information Centre, *223 Main St N.E. at the replica oil derrick, Turner Valley, AB T0L 2A0; tel: (403) 933-4944; fax: (403) 933-5377.*

In 1914, long before the 1947 Leduc #1 strike near Devon, A.W. Dingman struck gas in Turner Valley. **Turner Valley Gas Plant National Historic Site,** site of Dingman #1 discovery well, tanks, pipelines and scrubbing equipment, offers tours 1000–1800 (May–Sept); arrange Oct–Apr tours with the Town. Dingman #2's seeping gas at the **Burning Ground** flares from a fissure.

HIGH RIVER

Tourist Information: High River Chamber of Commerce, *406 1 St, PO Box 5244, High River, AB T1Y 1M4; tel: (403) 652-3443.*

High River, Canada's Beef Capital, rolls out the cowboys for nine days in mid June for the **North American Chuckwagon Championships,** *tel: (403) 652-7349,* a miniature version of the Calgary Stampede (see p.72). **Museum of the Highwood,** *4 Ave at 1 St W. in a former CPR station; tel: (403) 652-7156,* open Mon–Sat 1000–1700, Sun 1300–1700 (Victoria Day–Labour Day), explains the chuckwagon races featured in local wagon-team riding competitions and the Calgary Stampede. Rolling stock used on railway routes across the prairies from 1941–1960 are in a separate Railway Museum section, with light meals at the **Whistle Stop Café.** For

North West Mounted Police

In the mid 1860s, White hunters were wiping out the plains Indians' source for food, clothing and shelter – the buffalo. After the American Civil War, US Army troops were deployed to America's West to secure homesteaders' land against Indians. Many Native Americans fled north. Whisky traders, stymied by US laws forbidding transport of whisky across Indian reservations, and outlaws pushed north into a sparsely-settled region of the new Canadian Confederation where it appeared no law could reach them. Alcohol was a poisonous weapon used by whisky traders to seduce Natives dependent on trading posts for staples.

Seeing the unbridled settlement of the Western USA by outcasts characterised as desperados, degenerates and expungers of the law, spurred on by reports of rampant whisky trading north from Montana and outraged by a massacre of Assiniboine Aboriginals by Whites, the Ottawa Government decided to act before opening up Western Canada to mass settlement.

The 1873 answer was a troop of mounted soldiers sworn to eliminate whisky trading, crime and abuse of citizenry – the North West Mounted Police. After a trek west along the Canada-US border to the Belly and Bow Rivers' junction, horses and men were ragged.

NWMP officers went south to Fort Benton, Montana for supplies, picking up scout Jerry Potts. The troop spilt, with assistant commissioner Col. James F. Macleod left in charge of pursuing the whisky traders. Potts guided Macleod's troops north to an infamous den of traders at Fort Whoop-Up (north-west of modern-day Lethbridge), but the traders had fled.

In Oct 1874, Macleod's men began to build Fort Macleod on the banks of the Old Man River. As construction continued in -30°C cold and snow, Macleod personally tried and sentenced whisky traders and assured First Nations Chiefs that the law applied equally.

143

Western togs and boots, shop at **Bradley's Western Wear & Saddlery**, *123 3 Ave W.; tel: (403) 652-2504.*

Turn right going west on Hwy 540 for 34 km to the **Bar U Ranch National Historic Site** (see Lethbridge–Kananaskis, pp. 148–156). **Cayley**, 10 km west of Hwy 2 and 10 km north of Nanton, is a Hutterite farming community.

NANTON

Tourist Information: Town of Nanton, *Box 609, Nanton, AB T0L 1R0; tel: (403) 646-2029; fax: (403) 646-2653,* has summertime Visitor Information Centres at **MacEwan School Tourist Information Centre**, *20 Ave (Hwy 2 N.),* and at the **Nanton Lancaster Society Air Museum**, *21 Ave (Hwy 2 S.).*

Divided Hwy 2 runs through Nanton.

Sample **Nanton Spring Water** at the red sign **'The Tap'**, by the cenotaph just south of MacEwan School InfoCentre, from May–Oct. Between Hwy 2 N. *(20 Ave)* and Hwy 2 S. *(19 Ave),* and *19* and *20 (Main) Sts,* are antique stores and galleries in elegant wooden-front buildings. For an overnight in downtown Nanton, there's the 1918 **Ferris House Bed and Breakfast**, *2420 20 St; tel: (403) 646-5692,* or **McKeage Tea House**, *2022 21 St (Hwy 2 S.); tel: (403) 646-5724;* the tea room serves light lunch and desserts 0900–1700.

Air buffs stop at **Nanton Lancaster Society Air Museum**, *21 Ave (Hwy 2 S.) at 18 St; tel: (403) 646-2270,* open daily Sat–Sun (May–Oct, Nov–Apr), which displays the Canadian-built four-engine Avro Lancaster Bomber used as the workhorse by the combined RCAF and RAF (British

Commonwealth Air Training Plan – BCATP) Bomber Command during World War II.

NANTON TO CLARESHOLM

Vehicles parked in neutral gear and Nanton Spring Water appear to roll up a hill in an optical illusion at **Magnetic Hill**, 23 km south-west of Nanton on Hwy 533.

The **Town of Stavely**, *PO Box 249, Stavely, AB T0L 1Z0; tel: (403) 549-3761*, put on the first *indoor* rodeo in 1929, a professional rodeo still held in early May.

CLARESHOLM

Tourist Information: Town of Claresholm, *Box 1000, Claresholm, AB T0L 0T0; tel: (403) 625-3381*.

The 1910 sandstone CPR station is now **Claresholm Museum**, *5126 1 St W., Claresholm, AB T0L 0T0; tel: (403) 625-3131*, open 0930–1730 (Victoria Day–Thanksgiving). A one-room schoolhouse is part of the museum which serves as the **Claresholm InfoCentre**. A BCATP base in World War II, the wheat production centre later became a NATO training base. **Appaloosa Horse Club of Canada Museum**, *4189 3 St E.; tel: (403) 625-3326*, open Mon–Fri 0830–1630, devoted to the spotted horses bred by Nez Perce, has saddles, plates and an Appaloosa-shaped whisky bottle.

HEAD-SMASHED-IN BUFFALO JUMP

Tourist Information: *west from Hwy 2 on Hwy 785, Box 1977, Fort Macleod, AB T0L 0Z0; tel: (403) 553-2731; fax: (403) 553-3141; web:http://www.head-smashed-in.com,* open daily 0900–1700 (0900–1900 June–Sept), adults $6.50, children $3, families $15. To book Blackfoot tepee camping, *tel: (403) 553-2731*, $40 per night. The **Interpretive Centre** includes a gift shop with

First Nations handicrafts and Native-subject books, a cafeteria specialising in buffalo meat dishes, a film theatre and Blackfoot-guided walks along the cliffs.

Fierce winds blow up to 150 kph half the time; in winter, warm Chinook winds melt the snow, exposing animal-attracting grasses. The ridge over the fescue and mixed grass prairie, where buffalo once leapt to their deaths, seems an empty place. So many buffalo were stampeded to doom that bone deposits are 10m deep.

This UNESCO World Heritage Site is the planet's best-preserved buffalo jump, where Blackfoot drove life-sustaining buffalo to their deaths by stampeding them over a cliff for 5500 years. The **Head-Smashed-In Interpretive Centre** is built in several levels directly into the cliff-face.

A legendary brave was stationed at the base of the cliff as the bison leaped from above. The warrior's face was smashed by the crush of buffalo carcasses which had fallen on him, the result of bad positioning and a better-than-average hunt.

Exhibits flow *down* through display levels covering Blackfoot mythology and the Creator Napi, buffalo, Blackfoot seasonal activities, the buffalo jump hunt and Blackfoot-White contact.

In summer, Blackfoot bands warred or joined forces to feast, gossip and mount trading expeditions, while keeping a close watch on the buffalo cows, winter-born calves, young bulls and bulls in rut grazing the prairies in late summer. By autumn, the buffalo were rich in fat from summer grazing, hides long and thick for frigid winter. Males had mated and wandered off, leaving calmer cows and calves. The onset of cooler weather retarded meat spoilage.

Only in years when buffalo were numerous and grazing and climatic conditions favourable did tribal elders authorise a hunt. The Blackfoot organised provisions

144

Bison, not Buffalo

The North American buffalo is a myth. Early White settlers thought the immense plains creatures to be relatives of African and Asian buffaloes, but bison are more closely related to domestic cattle than to buffalo. They're the largest land animals in North America: the average bull is 350 cm long, stands 170 cm tall and weighs in at 730 kg.

Sixty million of these shaggy brown giants once roamed the Great Plains, providing food, tools, clothing, shelter, art and even religion for First Nations on both sides of the 49th Parallel. Archaeological evidence suggests that the bison population remained remarkably stable over some 10,000 years of aboriginal hunting with bow and arrow, spear and club. Skilful hunters could kill single bison by stalking. Mounted hunters could bring down a few dozen animals before the herd stampeded out of danger at up to 50 kph. Large scale hunts could drive several hundred bison over cliffs, such as at **Head-Smashed-In Buffalo Jump**.

White and Métis hunters arrived with firearms in the early 19th century. By the 1880s, over-hunting had reduced the bison population to about 1000; decades of careful husbandry have rebuilt North American herds to perhaps 100,000. The swift destruction of the bison population and resulting mass starvation led to the demise of Native tribes on the prairies and the opening of Alberta to White control and eventual settlement.

Modern bison are divided into two subspecies. *Woodland bison*, generally found in colder wooded areas, are larger and shaggier than their *plains bison* cousins. The largest population of wood bison lives in **Wood Buffalo National Park**, on the northern border between Alberta and the Northwest Territories. **Elk Island National Park**, east of Edmonton, is one of the few places to see both subspecies. **Waterton National Park** has a herd of plains bison in the Bison Paddock, off Hwy 6 near the north entrance to the park. **Rocky Mountain House National Historic Site** maintains a small herd of plains bison in its Buffalo Paddock.

145

and water on the Olsen Creek Basin. Wood or buffalo chips were gathered for fuel to stoke fires for heating stones to be placed in water. The stone-boiled water was poured into buffalo skin-lined pits where rendered buffalo meat was boiled. Butchering tools were sharpened. Drive lanes hundreds of metres long were built perpendicular to the cliff edge. Buffalo chips, sod and branches supplemented the 8 km of stone cairns built as lane markers.

Tradition held that buffalo survivors could tell their kind how to avoid hunters. Buffalo runners, young men disguised in wolf and buffalo-calf skins, wandered for days near the herds to scare and alarm the lead females amongst the almost-blind animals into leading a stampede toward the apparent safety of the sheltered lanes channelling animals 100 m along the cliff.

The animals fell 12 m. Hunters stationed at the bottom of the cliff finished the buffalo off with spears, stone-tipped arrows and clubs. Meat was boiled, hides were prepared, dried meat was mixed with berries or chokecherries for nourishing pemmican, and horns were fashioned into spoons. The buffalo tongues were given to medicine men and women. At the end of the hunt, the Blackfoot celebrated with a huge feast on the prairie near the jump.

FORT MACLEOD

Tourism Information: Town of Fort Macleod, *258 Main St, Box 1959, Fort Macleod, AB T0L 0Z0; tel: (403) 553-4425.* **Fort Macleod & District Chamber of Commerce Visitor Information Centre**, *Hwys 3/2 junction, east end of Main St; tel: (403) 553-4955.*

ACCOMMODATION AND FOOD

Fort Macleod has seven moderate motels, three Bed and Breakfasts and **Daisy May Campground**, *Lyndon Rd, PO Box 805; tel: (403) 553-2455*, open May–Oct.

Restaurants offer standard Canadian and Chinese cuisine.

SIGHTSEEING

The NWMP's first 1874 fort on an island in the Old Man (Oldman) River flooded frequently. The **Fort Museum** is located on the south riverbank site of the second fort, from 1883–1904. The **Fort Museum of the North West Mounted Police**, *219 25 St, PO Box 776; tel: (403) 553-4703*, is open daily 0900–1700 (May–June, Sept–mid Oct), 0900–2030 (July–Labour Day), Mon–Fri 1000–1600 (mid Oct–23 Dec and Mar–Apr), adults $4, children 12–18 $2, 6–11 $1.25, families $14. Exhibits show the NWMP kept active on snowshoes while spending leisure time ice-skating, curling with rocks, fencing, playing lacrosse, bowling and playing polo. Plains Indian beadwork in the reconstructed fort has been gathered from throughout Alberta. The 40-min **Fort Museum Mounted Patrol Musical Ride** at the museum, 1000, 1130, 1400 and 1530 (July–Aug), is precision riding at its best, swirling horses under eight red-coat uniformed riders crisply executing parade ground routines.

Follow *26 St* east, then turn left to the NWMP burial ground with the grave of Jerry Potts, the half-Native guide who helped The Force for twenty years after leading Col. James Macleod to Fort Whoop-Up (see p. 157).

Fort Macleod's short business district is on a well-preserved 1890s–1930s **Historic Main Street**. Ask the Chamber of Commerce for a keyed map to the brick and stone buildings, built after a fire wiped out

most of the wooden downtown. The 1912 **Empress Theatre**, *Main St; tel: (800) 540-9229* or *(403) 553-4404*, presents first-run films all year and **Great West Theatre**'s plays about Canadian history July–Aug, adults $10, children 12–18 $5, under 12 $5.

Peruse the huge mural of copied photographs painted on the east wall of the Curling Rink, *3 Ave* and *21 St*. **Macleod Livery Ltd.**, *211 25 St, next to the Fort Museum; tel: (403) 553-4868* or *(403) 553-2026*, open Victoria Day–Labour Day, still works on wagons, wagon wheels and farriering (horseshoeing), while running downtown tours in restored horse-drawn wagons and carriages and trail rides along the Old Man River.

LETHBRIDGE

Tourism Information: Alberta South Tourism Development Region Scenic Drive Information Centre, *2805 Scenic Dr. at Hwys 4/5 junction, Lethbridge, AB T1K 5B7; tel: (800) 661-1222*, open 0900–2000 (mid May–Labour Day), 0900–1700 (Labour Day–mid May), and **Brewery Hill Information Centre**, *1 Ave S., Lethbridge west entrance off Hwy 3*, open 0900–2000 (mid May–Labour Day), 0900–1700 (Sept–Oct and Mar–mid May).

ACCOMMODATION AND FOOD

Alberta South TDR, *tel: (800) 661-1222*, book some lodging. Lethbridge chains include *BW, DI, QI, S8* and *TL*. **Sandman Hotel**, *421 Mayor Magrath Dr.; tel: (800) 726-3626* or *(403) 328-1111; fax: (403) 328-9488*, is a comfortable choice convenient to Hwy 3. Lodging, including Bed and Breakfasts, is moderate.

Fast food, motel coffee shop, Canadian, Chinese, Italian and Japanese are the main dining choices. **The Penny Coffee House**, *331 5 St S., Lethbridge, AB T1J 2B4; tel: (403) 320-5282*, open daily, budget, has delicious split pea soup, salads and sandwiches amidst posters and news clippings. It connects to well-stocked **B Macabee's Booksellers**, *tel: (888) 511-2665* or *(403) 329-0771*. Tea cakes are wonderful at the Lethbridge bakery location of **Luigi's Pizza + Steak House** chain, *306 13 St N.; tel: (403) 327-2766, Mon–Sat 0700–2100, Sun 1200–1800*.

SIGHTSEEING

Lethbridge's 65,000 people are supported by grain, sugar beet and cattle production, tourism and petroleum. Prosperous Hutterite ladies wearing patterned skirts and head scarves meet downtown to chat and do business. Cowboys pile out of pick-up trucks, First Nations people shop, Japanese-Canadian heritage is recognised in a city garden and a small Chinatown thrives.

Under pressure in the USA in the 1850s–1860s, whisky traders seeking new customers without regulation moved north into the Blackfoot-controlled Old Man River area. Fort Hamilton, nicknamed Fort Whoop-Up for the raucous activities instigated by the traders, was notorious for abuse of First Nations people.

Cree, traditional Blackfoot enemies, drifted north from the USA, fleeing White settlement, US Army-Indian Wars and smallpox. In 1870, a battle commenced when Cree attacked two groups of Blackfoot by Old Man River, and suffered 300 casualties at today's **Indian Battle Park**.

The 1874 arrival of NWMP Col. Macleod's troop and scout Jerry Potts at Fort Whoop-Up stopped the whisky trade. The NWMP permitted other trade, subject to the law, and were stationed at the fort until 1892. **Fort Whoop-Up Interpretive Centre**, *Indian Battle Park; tel: (403) 329-0444,* open Mon–Sat 1000–1800, Sun 1200–1700 (May–Sept), Tues–Fri 1000–1600, Sun 1300–1600 (Oct–Apr), is a

replica of the 1869 fort (7 km from its original location), with original cannon and summertime costumed interpreters and dramas. First Nations people arriving to trade pelts and hides were permitted inside a few at a time to quell any protest at their treatment. 'Whoop-Up Wallop' and 'Whoop-Up Bug Juice' left out whisky in favour of pure alcohol spirits well-diluted with river water and flavouring – lye, chewing tobacco, ginger, molasses, Castile soap and ink. A cup of 'whisky', less potent for less sober Native negotiators, bought traders a buffalo robe worth $6 in the Eastern USA.

Pick up self-guiding brochures to three nature trails at the **Helen Schuler Coulee Centre**, *Indian Battle Park; tel: (403) 320-3064*. The paved **Nature Quest Trail** introduces the cottonwood forests of the 81-hectare **Lethbridge Nature Reserve**. **Oxbow Loop Trail** approaches the Oldman River along its floodplain and the **Coulee Climb Trail** explores its water-carved canyon. The world's longest (1.6 km) and tallest (100m) trestle bridge, CPR **High Level Bridge** spans the coulee not far from **Coalbanks Interpretive Site**, Lethbridge's first permanent settlement.

View Indian Battle Park from the free **Sir Alexander Galt Museum** viewing gallery, *5 Ave S. and Scenic Dr.; tel: (403) 320-3898,* 1000–1800. Galleries cover coal history, dry-farming irrigation in Lethbridge's semi-arid climate and immigration.

Elizabeth Hall Wetlands and **Alexander Wilderness Park** are other parks. **Nikka Yuko Japanese Garden**, *Henderson Lake Park; tel: (403) 328-3511,* open 0900–2000 (mid May–Sept), adults $3, children 12–17 $2, opens on a Japanese house and tea ceremony room. Paths meander to bridges over a stream through a flower-free garden filled with trees, shrubs, a pagoda and giant bell.

147

LETHBRIDGE–
KANANASKIS

Although Kananaskis Country is a 45-min drive from Calgary, this 335-km route offers a mid June–Nov alternative to driving into the Rocky Mountains on major highways. Duplicating part of a Crowsnest Hwy route, this itinerary veers north from farmland into

the heart of Alberta's ranchland. Kananaskis' grey peaks, rolling mountains and pristine blue lakes are west. Kananaskis Country, less-known than its north-west neighbour, Banff National Park, offers spectacular hiking and alpine and Nordic skiing in an area chosen for the 1988 Olympic Winter Games alpine events.

Starting from Lethbridge, allot 4½ hours to drive through Kananaskis Country to Trans-Canada Hwy 1. The Kananaskis back road from Fortress Junction to Canmore offers more splendid scenery, a 2-hour drive ending a few kilometres from Banff National Park.

Kananaskis

148

40   103

Longview

22

DIRECT ROUTE: 335 KM

232

Lethbridge–
Cranbrook
p. 157 ◁

3

Lethbridge

ROUTE

From Lethbridge, take Hwy 3, the Crowsnest Hwy, west to Lundbreck (see

Lethbridge–Cranbrook, pp. 157–164). Turn right, going north on Hwy 22, left to beyond Longview on Hwy 541, then north on Hwy 40. Hwy 40 from Highwood House to Highwood Pass south of the Peter Lougheed Provincial Park Visitor Information Centre is closed from Dec–mid June to protect wildlife.

TOURIST INFORMATION

Travel Alberta, *tel: (800) 661-8888*, and **Alberta South Tourism Development Region**, *2805 Scenic Dr., Lethbridge, AB T1K 5B7; tel: (800) 661-1222*, have information for areas south of Calgary. For **Kananaskis Country**, *tel: (403) 673-3985*, or **Alberta Environmental Protection Natural Resources Service**, *800 Railway Ave, Suite 201-Provincial Bldg, Canmore, AB T1W 1P1; tel: (403) 678-5508; fax: (403) 678-5505; web: http:// www.gov.ab.ca/~env/nrs/kananaskis.*

LETHBRIDGE TO LONGVIEW

Take Hwy 3, the Crowsnest Hwy, west from Lethbridge past Fort Macleod, Brocket, Pincher and Cowley's line of wind machines to **Lundbreck** (see p. 161). Just west of Lundbreck, turn right, going north on Hwy 22. Fill up with petrol in Fort Macleod or Pincher Creek, as there are no services on Hwy 22 for 135 km.

Fields of hay and grazing cattle fill the landscape. Hwy 22's lack of tourist facilities, its direct route and smooth roadway through to Calgary make it convenient for fast-paced lorries.

Twenty-five km north of Hwy 3 on the left is a rest stop with picnic tables, toilets and camping for $2 per night. **Chain Lakes Provincial Park**, *tel: (403) 646-5887*, 53 km further north, has a phone, camping, fishing for stocked rainbow trout and winter ice fishing on a reservoir created from dammed springs. Bird-watching is good around the marshy shoreline.

One hundred km north of Hwy 3, **Bar**

U Ranch National Historic Site, *PO Box 168, Longview, AB T0L 1H0; tel: (800) 568-4996 or (403) 395-2212; fax: (403) 395-2331; web: http://www.worldweb.parks canada-BarU*, open mid May–Oct, adults $3.75, children 6–17 $1.75, is an excellent introduction to the open range style of ranching common from the 1880s.

The ranch was named for its cattle brand by the North West Cattle Company syndicate. Cowboys came from Montana and beyond, including Harry Longbaugh, later infamous as the 'Sundance Kid' of outlaw and Hollywood fame. Another American who crossed the border was George Lane, advancing from foreman to majority owner between 1884–1927. Lane was one of the 'Big Four' ranchers who in 1912 underwrote the Calgary Stampede.

The Land Act changed in 1896, dismantling leased ranchland to encourage homesteading in the West. The Bar U persisted, known for its fine management and for raising champion Percheron draft horses. The ranch was sold to meatpacking millionaire Pat Burns, another of the Stampede 'Big Four', who operated the ranch until 1950. The Bar U's buildings and range sprawl near Pekisco Creek, a riparian area favoured by wapiti, moose and beavers. The Rocky Mountains provide a dramatic backdrop due west.

The **Visitor Orientation Centre** has ranching exhibits and a video of Bar U history. Costumed interpreters lead guided tours of the 35 ranch buildings. The **Roadhouse Restaurant**, open Mon–Fri 0800–1800, Sat–Sun 0800–2000, serves ranch-style food, while **Pekisko Creek General Store**, open 1000–1800, sells local arts and crafts. Drive west along the road beyond the entrance to the Bar U for a fine overview of ranch and range.

Watch for deer on Hwy 22 approaching **Longview**, the southern edge of **Turner**

149

Valley oil country (see p.142). To the east, near Hwy 2, is **High River**, nominal Beef Capital of Canada (see p. 142).

LONGVIEW

Longview has several budget–moderate restaurants and moderate **Blue Sky Motel**, *Box 286, Longview, AB T0L 1H0 tel: (403) 558-3655*, open year-round. **Tales & Trails**, *Box 142; tel: (403) 558-2390*, open late May–Sept, has 34 pitches. **Highwood River Bed & Breakfast**, *PO Box 239; tel: (403) 558-2456; fax: (403) 558-2297*, moderate, has river and mountain views.

Longview, most recently a film location for *Legends of the Fall* and Clint Eastwood's 1992 western, *Unforgiven*, began as a Stoney First Nations camping area along the Highwood River. In 1884, White settlers from Montana started a ranching community a little east of modern Longview. The oil and gas boom in the Turner Valley in 1914 transformed Little New York, as Longview was known, into a town of 2500 (Little Chicago and Little Philadelphia were other hamlets). The Leduc oil strike in 1947 shifted petroleum exploration north and knocked the population back to 300, a convenient petrol stop. Look for local **Longview Beef Jerky**.

Go left on Hwy 541. Fifteen km west is the fenced grave of Longview's original settler, John Sullivan, who was dragged and killed by a runaway horse in 1900. Three of his four children, also buried here, died of diphtheria 9 years earlier. Enter **Kananaskis Country** 35 km west of Longview.

KANANASKIS COUNTRY

Tourist Information: Kananaskis Country, *tel: (403) 673-3985*, or **Alberta Environmental Protection Natural Resources Service**, *800 Railway Ave, Suite 201-Provincial Bldg, Canmore, AB T1W 1P1; tel: (403) 678-5508; fax: (403)*

678-5505; web: http://www.gov.ab.ca/~env/ nrs/kananaskis, have K-Country information. There are several Visitor Centres along Hwy 40, including **Highwood House**, **Peter Loughheed Provincial Park**, **Kananaskis Village** and **Barrier Lake**. Ask for the free *Kananaskis Country at a Glance* map.

For political and economic reasons, Kananaskis never made it into the Rocky Mountain Parks crown jewels, though a combination of wilderness areas, provincial parks and recreation-dedicated areas make the eight sections of Kananaskis Country appealing – and less crowded than Banff and Jasper National Parks despite K-Country's proximity to Calgary.

Kananaskis, 'the Meeting of the Waters', is a Bow River tributary named by Capt. John Palliser, whose 1857–1860 scientific expedition journal records a Native legend of a man named Kananaskis who survived a stunning axe blow to the head.

ACCOMMODATION

Kananaskis Village was purpose-built for the Olympics with most of the lodging in K-Country, 420 rooms spread between three hotels: pricey **CP The Lodge at Kananaskis** and **Hotel Kananaskis**, *PO Box 249, Kananaskis Village, AB T0L 2H0, tel: (800) 441-1414 or (403) 591-7711; fax: (403) 591-7700*, and expensive **Best Western Kananaskis Inn**, *PO Box 10; tel: (800) 528-1234 or (403) 591-7500; fax: (403) 591-7633*.

Book well in advance for **William Watson Lodge**, *Peter Lougheed Provincial Park, PO Box 130, Kananaskis Village; tel: (403) 591-6350; fax: (403) 591-7372*, universal access cabins near Lower Kananaskis Lake, with apartments for those with physical, mental and sensory limitations. Facilities include a day lodge, six RV pitches and a campsite.

Ranching

C anada's ranching felt a strong British influence. The Canadian cowboy took tea-breaks, played polo and used both Western and British-style tack. The **EP Ranch**, *near the junction of Hwys 22 and 540*, owned from 1920–1962 by Edward, Duke of Windsor, took its initials from Edward, Prince (of Wales). The vastness of the prairies and warm Chinook winds melting winter snow provided both space to raise cattle and grass for winter grazing.

Buffalo once roamed the land in great herds, taking advantage of a food supply of fescue and other grass available year-round. Hunting quickly diminished the herds, herds which the Blackfoot and other First Nations people depended upon for food, clothing, shelter and ritual objects.

The first ranchers were NWMP men, who finished their 3-year postings in the mid 1870s and claimed their promised land allotment. Retired NWMP guessed that if the land could sustain thousands of bison, it could equally sustain cattle. Chinooks, however, are undependable, and would-be ranchers quickly learned from occasional years of unrelenting snow that hay and feed needed to be set out to ensure winter fodder.

By the 1880s, the CPR was pushing west towards BC and the 1877 Treaty 7 had moved First Nations groups south onto reserves. The federal Land Act of 1881, with amendments favourable to ranchers, permitted leasing of 100,000 acres (40,470 hectares) of land for 21 years at a penny an acre. Many ranch owners remained in Eastern Canada, forming investment syndicates where members acted as stockholders and directed business from afar.

Rangelands were open and the syndicates bought in. Cattle were exported to the USA and Great Britain. Corporate ranching became the norm at such spots as **Cochrane Ranche** (Provincial Historic Site, see Calgary–Banff, pp.78–86), **Waldrond** (ranch house in Pincher Creek's Kootenai Brown Historic Park, see Lethbridge–Cranbrook, pp.157–164), **Oxley Ranching Company**, **Quorn Ranch** and the **Bar U**.

Mt Kidd RV Park, *Hwy 40, PO Box 1000, Kananaskis Village; tel: (403) 591-7700,* open year-round, has 229 pitches, a laundry and bicycle hire. Sleep in a teepee or a trapper tent at budget **Sundance Lodges (Tipis) & RV Park**, *Hwy 40, Box 190, Kananaskis Village; tel: (403) 591-7122; fax: (403) 591-7440,* open mid May–Sept.

Rafter Six Ranch Resort, *near TransCanada Hwy 1, PO Box 6, Seebe, AB T0L 1X0; tel: (888) 267-2624, (403) 673-3622 or (403) 264-1252,* has moderate lodge rooms, and open cabins and chalets May–mid Oct (see Calgary–Banff, pp.78–86).

The **Brewster Kananaskis Guest Ranch**, *Bow River, north of TransCanada Hwy 1 via Hwy 1X, PO Box 964, Banff, AB T0L 0C0; tel: (800) 691-5085 or (403)* 673-2100; fax: (403) 673-2100, offers moderate cabins and chalets May–mid Oct.

HI-Ribbon Creek Hostel, *off Hwy 40 near Nakiska Ski Hill, Box 1358, Banff, AB T0L 0C0; tel: (403) 591-7333 or (403) 762-4122; fax: (403) 762-3441,* is a 20-min walk from Kananaskis Village with a shuttle connection to other Alberta Hostels June–Sept.

Mt Engadine Lodge, *Smith-Dorrien/ Spray Lake Rd, PO Box 8239, Canmore, T1W 2T9; tel: (403) 678-4080; fax: (403) 678-2109,* has moderate rooms in the backcountry between Kananaskis and Canmore.

There are 31 drive-in **campsites** with 2300 pitches and 15 backcountry campsites; *tel: (403) 297-3362,* Mon–Fri, for bookings at popular spots.

EATING AND DRINKING

Kananaskis Village is the centre for restaurant and deli dining. **The Lodge at Kananaskis** and **Hotel Kananaskis** share 3 restaurants, 2 lounges and a combination deli-chocolatier, all open at least May–Sept. Accompanied by a pianist, pricey **L'Escapade Dining Room** serves delicately-seasoned Canadian specialities, such as Arctic caribou, Alberta beef, BC salmon, Northwest Territories muskox and Yukon Arctic char. The moderate **Best Western** restaurant is less formal, with a popular lounge.

Boulton Creek Trading Post, Fortress Mountain, Kananaskis Country Golf Course, Nakiska Ski Area and **Mt Engadine Lodge** have moderate dining. **Highwood House, Boulton Creek** and **Kananaskis Village** have grocery stores, though it is cheaper to buy foodstuffs in Calgary or Canmore if starting out from the north end of this route.

152

SIGHTSEEING

Highwood

Hwy 541 follows the Highwood River past Highwood House, where the route turns north to become Hwy 40. This is a section of the **Trail of the Great Bear**, a grizzly bear terrain extending from Yellowstone National Park to the Yukon, a mostly-preserved zone where wildlife ranges over traditional habitat. **Highwood House** has a ranger station/Visitor Centre, *tel: (403) 933-7172* or *(403) 558-2151,* a grocery store, phone and petrol.

The section of road north along Hwy 40, **Highwood House** to **Highwood Pass**, is closed Dec–14 June to protect and manage animal species in the 44½-km long **Highwood Road Corridor Wildlife Sanctuary**. The speed limit slows to 90 kph along a road laced with picnic areas:

Fitzsimmon's Creek, Cat Creek, Lineham Creek, Lantern Creek, Trout Ponds, Mist Creek, Picklejar and **Mt Lipsett**. Cows wander on the road and coyotes roam Kananaskis' Highwood section. Rocky Mountains rise in grey wedges to the west, flanked by spruce and lodgepole pine.

Look for the **Lost Lemon Mine** sign, telling a tale of Montana miners Jack Lemon and Black Jack who found gold near the Highwood River headwaters. They couldn't agree whether to prospect then or to stake it and return to mine the claim later. Taking an axe, Lemon chopped up a sleeping Black Jack, regretted it and confessed to a priest, including directions to the erstwhile mine. The priest delegated someone to find the spot and mine the gold; two Stoney braves had witnessed the atrocity, knew the effect mining would have, and, it is said, wiped out all traces of the claim.

Peter Lougheed Provincial Park

Enter the provincial park 2 km north of the Lost Lemon Mine sign. The park is named for Alberta's 1971–1975 premier, who was responsible for organising Kananaskis Country. Further north on Hwy 40, **Peter Lougheed Provincial Park Visitor Information Centre,** *tel: (403) 591-6344; fax: (403) 591-7583,* sells hiking trail brochures.

Highwood Pass, 2209m, is a wild, empty area surrounded by glacial rubble. The **Rock Glacier Trail** on the right is a short 140-m hike up through the alpine threshold, complete with tiny greyish pikas, 'rock rabbits', squeaking from haystack-type stores of food cached amidst the rocks. Pikas seldom move more than 10m from their stacks and tend to blend in with the rocks, but their holes are quite visible.

Turn left 15 km north to the VIC and other facilities. The 16-km *Kananaskis Lakes Trail* (road) goes south from the VIC around the east side of Lower Kananaskis Lake, and curves to the right. The road is crowded in summer with cars, RVs, bicyclists, mountain bikers and hikers. A parking area between Lower and Upper Kananaskis Lakes offers access to fishing for cutthroat and rainbow trout, hiking and other activities. The views of Mt Indefatiguable and its fellow mountains are stunning. For superb Kananaskis Lakes views, depart from North Interlakes picnic area 2.3 km up **Mt Indefatigable**, but be prepared for the strenuous 460m gain in elevation which defies the peak's name!

Back Road From Kananaskis to Canmore

Exit Hwy 40 to the left, but take the *Smith-Dorrien/Spray Trail* to the right before the main road leads to the Peter Lougheed Provincial Park Visitor Information Centre. This mostly gravel road, rough and dusty in spots, begins an ultra-scenic 65-km drive through the backcountry at the base of the Rockies Front Ranges. The first section follows **Smith-Dorrien Creek** north, then picks up along **Smuts Creek**, which flows into the pristine blue waters of **Spray Lakes Reservoir**. The last section breeches the mountains above **Canmore** (see Calgary–Banff, pp. 78–86).

After leaving Peter Lougheed Provincial Park's western massifs, pause at Smuts Creek to look at magnificent vistas from both sides of the bridge, which resemble the stark bare areas of the Graubunden area of the Swiss Alps. **Mt Engadine Lodge** overlooks water threading through brush in a vibrant green wetland. Follow signs west along a 5-km scenic drive to **Mt Shark** trailhead.

Rocky Mountain sheep roam the roads near Spray Lake Reservoir. Mountains thrust sideways, a backdrop for a placid, man-made lake fringed by a sandy beach. On the east side of the road, rock faces are grey, white, golden, a jumble of jagged ridges. **Spray Lake Ranger Station**, *tel: (403) 591-6344*, is at the north end.

The dams on this route form lakes. Trans Alta Utilities release water for hydropower. Beyond the **Bow-Crow Forest**, a clear emerald green lake abuts a striking peak in the shape of a sideways pyramid. Prepare for a steep descent to Canmore without lay-bys.

Canmore Nordic Centre, *tel: (403) 678-2400; fax: (403) 678-5696*, caters to Nordic skiers and hosts the North American Biathlon Championships and International Dog Sled Races in winter.

Barrier Lake/Ribbon Creek

Continue north on Hwy 40 from the *Kananaskis Lakes Trail* exit. Kananaskis Country's **Barrier Lake/Ribbon Creek** section has most of the recreational area's lodging and services. **Fortress Junction Service Centre** has groceries and petrol.

Exit left for **Fortress Mountain**, favoured by powder skiers and snowboarders for its long Nov–Apr season. Fortress Mountain's base is the highest in Alberta's Rockies, 2040m. **Ski Kananaskis**, *1550 8 St S.W., Suite 505, Calgary, AB T2R 1K1; tel: (800) 258-7669 or (403) 229-3537; fax: (403) 244-3774*, have information and book both **Fortress Mountain** and **Nakiska Ski Resort**. **Fortress Mountain Snow Phone**, *tel: (403) 244-6665*, gives current weather conditions.

Mt Kidd RV Park, *tel: (403) 591-7700*, open year-round, is left just before the turn to **Kananaskis Country Golf Course**, *PO Box 1710, Kananaskis Village; tel: (403) 591-7070 or (403) 591-7272; fax: (403) 591-7072*, a 36-hole public

153

First Nations and Aboriginal Peoples

Few peoples in history or in myth have captured the popular imagination as fully as the First Nations of the North American plains. The common word for North America's indigenous peoples, 'Indian', conjures up images of fierce hunters riding barebacked through herds of thundering bison and equally fierce warriors decorated in flowing feather bonnets and fringed buckskin riding into battle without regard to personal safety or survival. Even Aboriginals elsewhere in Canada and America feel compelled to don plains-like costumes and head-dresses in order to be recognised as 'real' Indians.

There's a kernel of truth to the image, but the stereotype is more myth than reality. The pride, courage and prowess were real enough, though the flowing head-dresses were worn by late 19th-century Dakotas fleeing the United States Army. The mounted hunter and warrior were also real, but only for a few decades before White incursions destroyed traditional ways of life. For most of their existence, the plains First Nations hunted, warred and travelled on foot, their largest beasts of burden dogs who carried 35 kg at most.

The plains tribes were only a handful among hundreds of Aboriginal groups living across North America. There are six distinct native cultural areas in Canada, all of them spilling into neighbouring countries. After four centuries of continual outside influences, there remain eleven distinct language groups among Canadian First Nations (six of them found only in British Columbia) and more than fifty distinct languages.

Algonkian is the most widespread language group, including Cree, spoken from Northern Quebec to the Rockies. **Athapaskan** languages are spoken from interior Alaska to Hudson's Bay, including Gwich'in, Beaver, Carrier (Dene), Chilcotin and Sarcee in Alberta and BC. **Haida** is found only in the Queen Charlotte Islands. **Kutenai** is spoken only in South-eastern BC. **Salishan** groups have spread from Vancouver Island into BC's vast interior plateau, including the Nuxalk, Comox and Squamish on the coast, and Lillooet, Thompson, Shuswap and Okanagan inland. **Siouan** is spoken by Dakota in the prairie provinces. **Tlingit** speakers range from North-western BC and the Southern Yukon into Alaska. **Tsimshian** languages are found primarily on the north coast of BC, including Nisga'a and Gitksan. **Wakashan** peoples occupy the central mainland coast of BC and northern Vancouver Island, including the Kwakiutl, Kwagiulth and Nuu-chah-hulth (Nootka).

Only two language groups are not found in Western Canada, **Iriquoian**, used from Ontario and Quebec south into New York, and **Eskimo-Aleut**, spoken in Arctic regions from Siberia to Canada and Greenland.

Genetic and archaeological evidence suggest that the First Nations came to North America from Asia. When is less certain. There were several waves of migration during the last Ice Age, 10,000 to perhaps 40,000 years ago, when so much water was locked into glaciers that the sea level was up to 100m lower than at present. Nomadic groups probably followed game across a broad neck of land that is now the Bering Sea, following ice-free corridors south along the coast and down the eastern front of the Rocky Mountains. By the time the first Europeans reached North America, the Vikings around 1000 AD and the Spanish in 1492, First Nations groups had long since established themselves from the Arctic to Cape Horn.

The Vikings abandoned their toehold in today's Newfoundland in the face of resistance from local First Nations and worsening weather in the 13th century. The Spanish stayed. And while the *conquistadors* never reached Canada, their diseases did. Smallpox, measles and other diseases imported by Europeans spread along native trade routes that spanned North America. When British and Canadian explorers reached the prairies and BC in the 18th century, they encountered tribes that had already been decimated by smallpox.

English and French fur traders in Eastern Canada had a more immediate impact. They

154

introduced metal tools, cooking pots, firearms, manufactured clothing, spirits and other Western items as trade goods, as well as new diseases. Geography favoured the Cree and Assiniboine (or Stoney), who set themselves up as middlemen between fur traders to the east and more remote tribes to the west. As trapping depleted beaver in Eastern Canada, the Cree began moving north and west, displacing existing tribes.

At the same time, the horse was moving north. Introduced into North America by the Spanish in the 16th century, horses reached the southern plains as early as 1640. The Assiniboine were using horses as pack animals by the 1730s and riding them into war by the 1770s. Blackfoot (called Blackfeet in the US), who lived to the west, obtained horses slightly earlier, but the more northerly Cree were horse-poor into the 19th century.

The horse dramatically altered life on the prairies. For millennia, First Nations had followed seasonal bison migrations on foot, hunting individual animals and small groups. With the horse, they could chase huge herds and hunt more efficiently, significantly increasing the food supply.

Horses allowed bands to travel further, faster, and with more possessions, bringing them into even greater conflict with widening circles of neighbours. Warfare, a traditional, if sporadic part of prairie life, became almost continuous. Horse raiding was not theft, but an act of courage to be celebrated and encouraged. Battle skills honed against other tribes kept the far larger and better-armed US Army busy for more than twenty years, a conflict Canada avoided by sending the North West Mounted Police west in advance of settlers.

As the Cree and Assiniboine moved west from their traditional lands on the eastern edge of the prairies, they invaded the Blackfoot Nation. The Siksika, the Blood (or Kainai) and the Peigan (or Piikani) had roamed Alberta for generations, the Siksika near the North Saskatchewan River, the Blood along the Red Deer and the Peigan on the Bow. The Cree pushed the Blackfoot, and their allies the Sarcee, south. The last major Blackfoot-Cree battle was fought near Fort Whoop-Up in 1870.

155

Displaced Blackfoot, in turn, pushed the Kutenai, who once ranged into Southern Alberta from BC, west across the Rockies. Other tribes, including the Dakota who destroyed the US Seventh Cavalry at Little Big Horn under the leadership of Sitting Bull, fled north into Canada. The massive displacements finally ended as Métis and White hunters destroyed the bison herds. Faced with starvation, the prairie tribes ceded their traditional lands to Canada by treaty between 1871 and 1877 in return for reserves and promises of assistance – promises that were routinely broken. BC tribes fared even worse. Entire villages were abandoned due to disease. A single smallpox epidemic in 1862–1863 killed at least one-third of BC's Native population. The Lakes Okanagan fled to the United States, joining relatives on a reservation near Colville, Washington. The Nicola disappeared entirely, their lands taken over by Thompson and Okanagan bands. The Carrier pushed south into Chilcotin country, abandoned as the Chilcotin moved eastward into former Shuswap lands along the Fraser River that became vacant as the Shuswap population collapsed.

With the exception of a few early treaties on Vancouver Island, most First Nations lands were simply appropriated as miners, timbermen, ranchers and farmers moved into BC. Natives who survived the onslaught were banished to reserves. Potlatches and other traditional practices were prohibited as wasteful and unproductive. Children were removed from their families and sent to boarding schools where Native languages were forbidden in an attempt to anglicise the indigenous population.

Generations of protest and legal action are having an effect. The current Canadian Constitution grants special status to Indians, Inuit and Métis. Courts across Canada are beginning to order the return of vast tracts of appropriated lands and compensation for what are now seen as past injustices. And in 1998, the Canadian government officially apologised for past actions against its Native population.

course designed by Robert Trent Jones, open May–mid Oct, weather permitting. Green fees are $40 to play a course surrounded by solid peaks with mist rising pink from water traps at dawn. **Boundary Ranch**, *Box 44, Kananaskis Village; tel: (403) 591-7171; fax: (403) 591-7326*, offers trail rides, hay rides, back country horse packing trips from late June–early Sept and a Surf and Saddle trail ride with white water rafting through Class I–III rapids on the Kananaskis River.

Kananaskis Village, with the impressive mass of Mt Kidd looming to the west, is 5 mins north. Turn left to access **The Lodge at Kananaskis**, **Hotel Kananaskis** and **Best Western Kananaskis Inn**. All have restaurants and lounges.

Village services include a **post office**, *tel: (403) 591-7555*, hot tubs, steam room and showers, $2; coin-operated **tennis courts**, **Ribbon Creek Grocery Store**, **Peregrine Sports and Rentals**, *tel: (403) 591-7453*, with mountain bikes, canoes, hiking boots, tennis equipment, roller blades and motor scooters amongst equipment for hire. **Village Trading Post**, *tel: (403) 591-7979*, has Canadian crafts at **Mountain Gallery** and Canadian Western wear from **Jackalope Lodge**.

Near **HI-Ribbon Creek Hostel** is **Nakiska Ski Resort**, *tel: (800) 258-7669*, **Snow Phone**, *tel: (403) 591-7777*, which hosted the 1988 Calgary Winter Olympics alpine events. Terrain is rated 70% intermediate and 14% expert. Lift tickets are interchangeable with Fortress Mountain for the Dec–mid Apr ski/snowboard season. **Nordic skiing**; *tel: (403) 591-6344*, with both groomed and set track, is ubiquitous throughout K-Country.

The Kananaskis Valley was flooded behind **Barrier Dam** to create **Barrier Lake**, the long waterway on the left of Hwy 40. The **Forest Management**

Interpretive Trail, *Alberta Forest Service, 8660 Bearspaw Dam Rd N.W., PO Box 3310, Station B, Calgary, AB T2M 4L8; tel: (403) 239-0004*, is across from the dam on the lake's north end. The trail's two loops cover watershed yield, flora and forest fires. What began in the 1930s as a way to show the public how logging of forests affected mountain drainage was used for relief and youth training camps and later as World War II enemy alien and prisoner of war camps. The prisoner of war-era 'Colonel's Cabin' is a Provincial Historic Resource, open summer weekends. The University of Calgary also operates an Environmental Science Centre.

Alberta Forest Service maintains **Barrier Lake Forestry Trails**. Turn right, east onto Hwy 68 near **Lusk Creek** picnic area. Four eco-regions are presented: **montane**, with aspen and fescue grasslands giving way to lodgepole pine and Douglas fir; **sub-alpine**, with lodgepole pine yielding to Englemann spruce and subalpine fir with lush stream vegetation; Rocky Mountain foothill lower boreal **cordilleran**, with balsam poplar and aspen forming a drier landscape; and the **alpine** eco-region, with needle leaf trees and plants acclimatised to year-round cool weather.

Hwy 68 passes several picnic areas on the way to **Sibbald Viewpoint** at the entrance to **Sibbald Reforestation Exhibit** and a trail to **Sibbald Lake**. **Jumpingpound Demonstration Forest Interpretive Centre**, open May–Oct, offers walking and driving tours through a managed forest.

Stop at **Barrier Lake Visitor Information Centre**, *Hwy 40; tel: (403) 673-3985; fax: (403) 673-3684*, and **Bow Valley Provincial Park**, *TransCanada Hwy 1; tel: (403) 673-3663*, (see Calgary–Banff, pp.78–86), for information.

LETHBRIDGE– CRANBROOK

Travel on the Crowsnest Hwy from Southern Alberta's prairies through lower Rocky Mountain coal mining country to Cranbrook, a Rocky Mountain Trench city born when the railway arrived in Southern BC. This 310-km route can be driven in under five hours, but Hwy 3 scenery is best enjoyed in a full day. Add two days to explore Waterton Lakes National Park, a side track from this route, and take in Cardston's magnificent carriage museum.

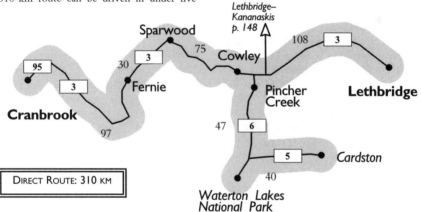

DIRECT ROUTE: 310 KM

157

Lethbridge–Kananaskis p. 148

ROUTE

Follow Hwy 3, the Crowsnest Hwy, from Lethbridge to Pincher, then turn left onto Hwy 6 for 3 or 4 km to **Pincher Creek**. From here you can side-track 44 km to **Waterton Lakes National Park**. To visit **Cardston** and the **Remington-Alberta Carriage Centre**, turn left off Hwy 6 onto Hwy 5.

Return to Hwy 3 and head west through **Cowley, Sparwood** and **Fernie** beyond Elko, BC. Continue 58 km northwest on Hwy 3/93, then turn left on Hwy 93/95 to Cranbrook.

BUSES

There are two trips a day, changing at Fort Macleod. Journey time: 8½ hrs. See OTT tables 128 and 137.

TOURIST INFORMATION

Tourist Information: Travel Alberta, *tel: (800) 661-8888,* with an InfoCentre at Crowsnest Pass, and **Tourism BC,** *tel: (800) 663-6000,* have information and make accommodation bookings for their respective provinces. **Alberta South Tourism Development Region,** *2805 Scenic Dr., Lethbridge, AB T1K 5B7; tel:*

(800) 661-1222, covers Alberta south of Calgary.

LETHBRIDGE TO PINCHER CREEK

The Crowsnest Hwy over the Crowsnest Pass at today's Alberta/BC border was favoured by Kootenay (Ktunaxa) joining buffalo hunts on the plains. The black crow on highway signs recalls horse-stealing Crow braves camped in Blackfoot territory who were massacred in their 'nest'.

Left of Hwy 3, south-west of Lethbridge to Cardston, is the large Kainai (Blood First Nation) Reserve, a flat expanse broken by farms and windmills. The Blood, with the Sisiska east of Calgary and the Peigan further west on Hwy 3, formed three tribes within the Blackfoot Confederacy.

Fort Macleod is the site of the first North West Mounted Police fort which established the rule of Canadian law against whisky traders and criminals in 1874 (see Calgary–Lethbridge, pp. 141–147). Just north-west off Hwy 2 on Hwy 785 is **Head-Smashed-In Buffalo Jump Interpretive Centre** (see Calgary–Lethbridge, p. 144), depicting Blackfoot reliance upon once-numerous bison.

Brocket is the Piikani tribal centre for **Peigan First Nation Reserve**, *Box 70, Brocket, AB T0K 0H0; tel: (403) 965-3940, fax: (403) 965-2030.* The smallest tribe to sign Treaty 7 in 1877, the Peigan tried farming after the buffalo disappeared. Agriculture failed in the arid climate but the Peigan became successful cattle ranchers. **Oldman River Cultural Centre,** *tel: (403) 965-3939,* has Peigan beadwork and artefacts. **Tipi Village** shows teepee construction, with dancing and drumming. **Peigan Crafts Ltd.** factory, *tel: (403) 965-3755; fax: (403) 965-3970,* sells fleece-lined moccasins with Peigan designs.

Pincher is the tiny town on Hwy 3

158

known for **Crystal Village**, several hundred thousand glass insulators formed into a miniature hamlet. **Pincher Creek** is south.

PINCHER CREEK

Tourist Information: Town of Pincher Creek, *Box 159, Pincher Creek, AB T0K 1W0; tel: (403) 627-3156,* and **Pincher Creek Chamber of Commerce and Information Centre,** *PO Box 2287; tel: (403) 627-5199.*

ACCOMMODATION

Pincher Creek has eight motels, including *S8,* cabins, camping, teepees and 16 Bed and Breakfasts within 20 km of town.

SIGHTSEEING

Pincher Creek was named for the farrier (horseshoer) hoof-trimming tool that prospectors dropped in the creek in 1868. In 1877, the Peigan and other First Nations signed Treaty 7, and by 1878, the NWMP had built an outpost to combat lawlessness and to care for The Force's horses. Farming (Hutterites, Doukhobors and others) and ranching (large corporate-run ranches and Peigan) flourished along with a later petroleum and sulphur plant south of town.

Pincher Creek & District Museum and Kootenai Brown Historic Park, *1069 James Ave; tel: (403) 627-3684,* open 1000–2000 (mid May–early Sept), Wed, Sun 1300–1700 (early Sept–mid May), adults $4, children 10–17 $2, has 1880s–1950s household artefacts. The historic park preserves 11 buildings, among them an NWMP post, an 1894 one-room schoolhouse, George 'Kootenai' Brown's Waterton Lake log cabin, a pioneer cabin, the Waldrond Ranch House from an early 20th-century corporate cattle ranch, a blacksmithy and a Doukhobour log barn and bathhouse.

The 1910 **Lebel Mansion Historic**

Site, *692 Kettles St; tel: (403) 627-5272,* open daily 1300–1700, with an art gallery, was the town hospital for 60 years. **Napi Friendship Centre**, *622 Charlotte St; tel: (403) 627-4224,* open Mon–Fri 0800–1700, sell First Nations artwork.

Heritage Acres Museum, *Oldman River Antique Equipment and Threshing Club; tel: (403) 627-2082,* north-east of Oldman River Dam, open May–Sept, has a large collection of farm equipment and a Doukhobour barn. Book in advance to visit the working **Pincher Creek Hutterite Colony**, *3 km west of town on Hwy 507; tel: (403) 627-4021.* Though from an Anabaptist religious tradition, unlike the Doukhobor religious dissidents who fled Russia several decades later (see Cranbrook–Castlegar, pp.173–180), Hutterites left Russia in the 1870s as religious pacifists living in a rural communal society. From 1942–1972, legislation limited the proximity of Hutterite communities, contributing to widespread distribution of ultra-prosperous, mechanised farming communities in Alberta and BC. Hutterite women dress in long, colourful patterned skirts, aprons and scarves; men wear hats and denims.

Thirteen km north of Pincher Creek, the **Oldman River Dam Recreation Area**, *tel: (403) 627-3765,* has fishing, windsurfing, kayaking, canoeing, boating and camping around the reservoir.

SIDE TRACK
FROM PINCHER CREEK
Take Hwy 6 south 44 km from Pincher Creek to **Waterton Lakes National Park**. Turn right onto Hwy 5 to reach **Waterton Townsite**.

Call in advance for Glacier National Park, MT, USA. The only road connection between the parks, Chief Mountain International Hwy (and the Chief Mountain Border Crossing) is

closed mid Sept–late May. Outside the parks, Carway, AB/Peigan, MT and Roosville, Hwy 93, BC (south of Elko) are open year-round.

Approach the park over shimmering golden farmland or snowy flatness in winter. Where are the Rockies, of which Waterton Lakes National Park and a string of parks to the south in the USA are a part? The mountains rise unheralded from the plains, without foothills. When tectonic plates collided millions of years ago, PreCambrian bedrock slid along a thrust fault *over* Cretaceous rock that had formed much later. Instead of buckling and shoving up great masses of rock like the area on the east (front) ranges of the Rockies in Banff and Jasper National Parks, the old rock pushing the Lewis Overthrust shoved down and then displaced material before it, creating flat prairies.

159

WATERTON LAKES NATIONAL PARK

Tourist Information: *Waterton Park, AB T0K 2M0; tel: (403) 859-2224; fax: (403) 859-2650; web: http://www.worldweb.com/parkscanada-waterton,* or **Glacier National Park**, *Montana, USA; tel: (406) 888-7800; web: http://www.gps.gov/glac,* have information on the joint Waterton/Glacier International Peace Park and World Heritage Site. Waterton's daily fee is $4 for adults, $2 for children 6–16.

Waterton is fully open mid May–Labour Day. **Park Headquarters**, *Mt View Rd, Waterton Townsite; tel: (403) 859-2224,* has information Mon–Fri 0800–1600 year-round. The **Visitor Reception Centre**, *Hwy 5 opposite the Prince of Wales Hotel, Waterton Townsite; tel: (403) 859-5133,* is open 0800–1800 (mid May–mid June), 0800–2000 (mid

June–Labour Day), some hours (Sept–mid Oct). **Heritage Centre**, *Waterton Ave, Waterton Townsite; tel: (403) 859-2267*, open daily in summer, and **Waterton Townsite Chamber of Commerce**, *Box 55, tel: (403) 859-2203*, offer information.

Waterton-Glacier Guide newspaper, Canadian/US Park Services *Waterton Lakes/Glacier International Peace Park* map; and *Glacier National Park including Waterton Lakes National Park American Parks Network* booklet, which explains the flora, fauna and geology of the region, are free.

ACCOMMODATION AND FOOD

Central Reservation Service, *tel: (800) 215-2395*, books Waterton Lakes and Glacier National Parks. All Waterton lodging except camping is in Waterton Townsite.

The pricey **Prince of Wales Hotel**, *tel: (403) 236-3400 or (602) 207-6000 (USA)*, open mid May–late Sept, the Great Northern Railway's lure for the well-heeled in 1927, is the châlet-style lodge with steep green roofs over a butter-yellow façade which dominates the townsite and its lake vista.

Elegant log cabin atmosphere and open all year, the moderate–expensive **Kilmorey Lodge**, *PO Box 100, tel: (888) 859-8669 or (403) 859-2334; fax: (403) 859-2342*, the moderate lakefront **Bayshore Inn**, *PO Box 38; tel: (403) 859-2211 or (403) 238-4847; fax: (403) 859-2291*, open mid Apr–mid Oct, and **HI Waterton International Hostel**, *Cameron Falls Dr. and Windflower Ave, PO Box 4, Waterton Lakes National Park, AB T0K 2M0; tel: (403) 859-2150; fax: (403) 859-2229*, are other choices. The **Townsite Campground**, open mid Apr–mid Oct, has 238 pitches, and two

other campsites in the park open mid May–mid Sept.

The **Prince of Wales Hotel** has a breakfast buffet, English and Continental cuisine for lunch and dinner and serves afternoon tea in **Valerie's Tea Room** 1400–1700. The Bayshore Inn's cheap Kootenai Burger and breads at **Country Bakery**, *303 Wildflower Ave*, rate a stop.

SIGHTSEEING

Waterton Lakes and Glacier National Parks are congested July–Aug. Glacier National Park is best known for the 83-km **Going-To-The-Sun Road**, with peaks to the west and Montana's plains to the east, open to vehicles mid June–mid Oct. A pleasant way to sense both parks is mid May–Sept **Waterton Inter-Nation Shoreline Cruises**, *Waterton Marina; tel: (403) 859-2362*, along the Canadian Rockies' deepest lake, with eagle spotting.

An extensive system of trails twines through both parks; backcountry overnight camping permits from park rangers cost $6 per night. Trails cross the Yellowstone–Yukon **Trail of The Great Bear**, a corridor where grizzly bears are active day and night.

Cameron Falls, on the west side of **Waterton Townsite**, has 1.6-billion-year-old limestone, the oldest exposed rock in the Canadian Rockies. A 3.2-km loop trail skirts the Townsite. It's a steep 1.2-km hike to windy **Bear's Hump** for a spectacular view of Waterton Lake. **Alpine Stables**, *tel: (403) 859-2462*, offer horseback rides May–Sept. Duffers can tee off on 18 holes at **Waterton Lakes National Park Golf Course**, *PO Box 2000; tel: (403) 859-2114*. Fishing, boating and biking are popular, and **Pat's Fishing, Camping**

& RV, *tel: (403) 859-2266*, is outfitter central for bicycles, scooter hire, or fishing equipment and licences.

Hwy 5 is ploughed in winter. The 16-km **Akamina Parkway** from the Townsite to **Cameron Lake**, lined with wildflowers in summer, is usually accessible in winter. Nordic skiers and snowshoers favour skiing around the lake, which gets Alberta's heaviest snowfall and looks south to Montana.

Turn west from Hwy 5 to drive through the rolling prairies of **Blakiston Valley**. The golf course sits incongruously in the landscape just south. At the end of the 14½-km **Red Rock Canyon Parkway** is **Red Rock Canyon** with a 700-m loop trail around the rust, moss green and chalk-white rocks of the 1.5-billion-year-old Grinnell Formation. Another 1-km trail leads to **Blakiston Falls**. Just before the Hwy 6 park entrance, turn west for a short loop drive around the **Bison Paddock** exhibition herd. 🔼

🔽 **SIDE TRACK
TO CARDSTON**

Just after entering the Waterton Lakes National Park on Hwy 6, veer left onto Hwy 5, going 40 km east across the prairies to **Cardston**. If going directly from Lethbridge, take Hwy 509 south through the Kainai (Blood) First Nation Reserve. Go south on Hwy 2 following signs to **Remington-Alberta Carriage Centre**.

CARDSTON

Tourist Information: Town of Cardston Tourism & Economic Development Office, *PO Box 280, Cardston, AB T0K 0K0; tel: (403) 653-3366; fax: (403) 653-2499*, has Tourist InfoCentres at **Remington-Alberta**

Carriage Centre, *tel: (403) 653-1993, fax: (403) 653-5160; web: http://www.remingtoncentre.com*, open 0900–2000 (June–Labour Day), 0900–1700 (Labour Day–May), and at *490 Main St (at Bridge); tel: (403) 653-3787*, open mid May–Labour Day.

Just north of the Canadian-US border entry at Carway, AB/Peigan, MT, Cardston is known as Alberta's Temple City for the Jesus Christ of Latter Day Saints (Mormon) **Alberta Temple**, *343 3 St W.; tel: (403) 653-1696*.

Cardston bustles with business, but the **Remington-Alberta Carriage Centre**, *PO Box 1649* (see above for details); adults $6.50, children 7–17 $3, family $15, has 217 splendidly-restored horse-drawn carriages, wagons and sleighs. Exhibits explain every mode of transport used, from hearse to farm wagon, offering a few driver's-eye views of passing scenery on video. Vehicles not on full display are visible in a 2-storey Vehicle Storage area. Yellowstone carriage rides run in summer and bob-sleighs in winter. 🔼

PINCHER CREEK TO SPARWOOD

Back on Hwy 3, at **Cowley**, on the ridge to the left are Waterton Hydroelectric Project's 52 electricity-generating **wind turbines**, which take advantage of winds that have been measured at 160 kph. Many Alberta buildings were once built of native sandstone. **Windmill Quarry**, *Box 130, Cowley; tel: (403) 628-3912 or (403) 628-2221*, offers tours. Several hundred Doukhobors from BC settled this area in 1915.

Turn left 4 km beyond **Lundbreck** to drive 3 km south to **Lundbreck Falls Provincial Recreation Area**, where the Crowsnest River falls 12m. Hwy 22 heads north towards Calgary, and is a back route to Kananaskis Country (see Lethbridge–Kananaskis, pp. 148–156).

Though the Rockies appear to have plenty of forests, plains and flatland, settlers needed a more reliable all-year source of fuel. The railways which brought settlers to Alberta and BC also needed fuel for steam locomotives. Southern Alberta, from Drumheller west to the border at Crowsnest Pass, had a rich seam of coal, exploited in the early 20th century by some of the most profitable mines in North America, until oil and gas-based fuels became more economical. The **Crowsnest Pass Ecomuseum Trust**, *PO Box 1440, Blairmore, AB T0K 0E0; tel: (403) 562-8831*, has coal mine history information. Five communities, Hillcrest, Bellevue, Frank, Blairmore and Coleman, form the **Municipality of Crowsnest Pass**, *Box 600, Blairmore, AB T0K 0E0; tel: (403) 562-8833; fax: (403) 562-0000*.

Ten km west of Lundbreck on the right is **Leitch Collieries Historic Site**, adults $2, children 7–17 $1.50, 1907–1915 ruins of one of Canada's largest coal mines. Signs explain the mining process. Go 5 km west on Hwy 3 to **Hillcrest**.

In 1914, **Hillcrest Mine** was the site of Canada's worst mine disaster, 189 men killed in explosions which ripped through the mineshafts or from inhaling the 'afterdamp' of carbon monoxide and carbon dioxide generated when explosions consumed oxygen. Mass graves were dug at the **Hillcrest Cemetery**, *8th Ave, Hillcrest*, for victims who could not be identified. Coal mining continued at Hillcrest Mine until 1939.

The next town west is small **Bellevue**, where the French-owned West Canadian Collieries Ltd operated the **Bellevue Mine** from 1903–1962. In Dec 1910, an explosion and afterdamp inhalation killed 30 of 42 nightshift miners. **Crowsnest**

Pass Ecomuseum Trust; *tel: (403) 562-8831*, conduct realistic dark and damp mine tours in summer.

The Crowsnest Hwy runs through **Frank Slide**, where on 29 Apr, 1903 at 0410, Turtle Mountain's summit tossed 30 million cubic metres of limestone down on the Frank townsite, killing about 70 of 600 residents. The sheer force of 3 square km of soil displacement is credited to unstable geology, coal mining techniques employed by the Canadian-American Coal and Coke Company, water seepage into cracks near the summit and bad weather, but the sheer horror of the moment remains in a landscape of lunar starkness.

Frank Slide Interpretive Centre, *PO Box 959, Blairmore, AB, T0K 0E0; tel: (403) 562-7388; fax: (403) 562-8635*, open 0900–2000 (15 May–Labour Day), 1000–1600 (Sept–14 May), adults $4, children 7–17 $2, explains the slide, mining conditions, labour strikes and living conditions in the mine's heyday. Outside is a huge sweep of rubble around the 1500-m walking trail which begins just outside the centre. Ask at the centre for a *Ride Through the Slide* self-guided auto tour brochure.

Frank survives, with extensive seismic monitoring of Turtle Mountain, called 'The Mountain that Walks' by First Nations. Rocky Mountain sheep wander.

Blairmore, with three exits, is Crowsnest Pass' main population centre. The 1912 **Cosmopolitan Hotel**, *13001 20 Ave; tel: (403) 562-7321*, moderate, offers a base for exploring the mining areas. Play golf at the **Crowsnest Pass Golf & Country Club**, or, in winter, alpine ski in town at **Pass Powderkeg Ski Hill**; *tel: (403) 562-8334*, closed Mon. Both activities belie a violent 1920s mining labour history and the 1932 election of Communist Party of Canada supporters to town council positions.

Coleman has rallied from mine closure and has one motel, the **Stop Inn**, *tel: (403) 562-7381*. The **Crowsnest Museum**, *7701 18 Ave; tel: (403) 563-5434*, open daily 1000–1200, 1300–1600 (summer), Mon–Fri 1000–1200, 1300–1600 (winter), a former high school, has pioneer and coal mining era artefacts.

The **Crowsnest Volcanics** near Coleman display volcanic activity 93 million years ago. **Crowsnest Pass Travel Alberta InfoCentre** is 12 km west in an airy blue-roofed wooden building with a fine view of Crowsnest Mountain. Opposite, on the north side of Hwy 3, is Crowsnest Lake, favoured by windsurfers and rainbow and cutthroat trout fishers. Moderate **Kosy Knest Kabins Triple K Hotel**, *tel: (403) 563-5155; fax: (403) 563-3325*, open May–Nov is lakeside.

At the Alberta-BC border, look at 1357-m **Crowsnest Pass**, one of the lowest Rockies passes. The CPR put a railway line through to Cranbrook (bypassing Fort Steele) in 1898, and settlers followed. Just over the BC border is day-use rest area **Crowsnest Provincial Park**, *tel: (250) 422-3212*. **Inn on the Border**, *Hwy 3, Crowsnest; tel: (250) 425-0153*, is a moderate Bed and Breakfast in a scenic spot.

Unused mineshafts are visible in the hills lining Hwy 3 as the Crowsnest Hwy enters the **Elk Valley**. Mining is still viable 16 km west of the border at the Westar Mines, Canada's largest surface mine. Mining towns **Michel** and **Natal** were bulldozed by the BC government in the 1960s for redevelopment. The **Michel Country Inn**, *Michel; tel: (250) 425-0110*, still operates as a hotel, pub and restaurant.

SPARWOOD

Tourist Information: Sparwood and District Visitor InfoCentre, *Hwy 3 and Aspen Dr., Box 1448, Sparwood, BC V0B 2G0; tel: (250) 425-2423; fax: (250) 425-7130*, has information on the two motels and two Bed and Breakfasts, dining, the Titan truck and books coal mine tours.

Sparwood, the town that replaced Natal and Michel, claims the world's largest dump truck, a 9-m high green Terex Titan lorry with 3-m high wheels and a 317.5-tonne capacity stationed next to the InfoCentre. The prototype was built for Canada's largest open-pit coal mine operated by Elkview Coal Corporation. Book July–Aug tours at the InfoCentre. Downtown murals cover Michel and Natal history.

Go 29 km south on Hwy 3 from Sparwood to **Fernie**. The **Olsen Rest Area**, 13 km from Sparwood, has breathtaking views of the Rockies. **Hosmer**, 4 km south, is popular with fishers and rafters who take on Class I and II rapids from Hosmer to Elko, south of **Fernie**.

FERNIE

Tourist Information: Fernie InfoCentre, *Hwy 3 and Dicken Rd, Fernie, BC V0B 1M0; tel: (250) 423-6868; fax: (250) 423-3811*, is open year-round.

Fernie has nearly a dozen motels, including *S8*, and eight Bed and Breakfasts, some bookable through **Fernie Destinations**, *tel: (888) 754-7325 or (250) 423-9284*. **HI-Fernie Hostel**, *892 6 Ave, Box 580; tel: (250) 423-6811; fax: (250) 423-6812*, is next to a motel. **Mt Fernie Provincial Park**, *Hwy 3; tel: (250) 422-3212*, open May–Oct, has 38 camp pitches west of town. Fernie is well-endowed with fast food and restaurants offering beef to borscht, Italian to Chinese.

Coal and lumber have been Fernie's economy, though there is a tourist-oriented strip of fast-food joints, restaurants and petrol stations on Hwy 3. The InfoCentre has an excellent 2-km *Heritage Walking Tour* brochure covering wide streets laced with brick and stone buildings constructed after successive fires nearly wiped out the town.

The 1911 château-style red brick **Provincial Court House**, *401 4 Ave*, is stunning against a mountain backdrop. **Fernie Arts Station**, *601 1 Ave; tel: (250) 423-4842*, built in 1908 as the CPR station, now houses artists studios, a gallery, Whistle Stop Restaurant and a theatre. A 1905 Roman Catholic rectory/convent is the **Fernie and District Historical Museum**, *502 5 Ave; tel: (250) 423-7016*, open Mon–Fri 1300–1700 July–Aug.

Fernie is known for mountains like the Three Sisters, named for three Indian maidens turned into mountains to match the gods' punishment for an indecisive suitor, Mt Proctor. Legend tells of the Ghostrider, the Indian maiden spurned by town founder William Fernie, who saw her wearing a necklace of coal and enticed the band to show him the black gold's origins, subsequently abandoning the young woman. The Ghostrider appears before sunset across the face of Mt Hosmer, maiden and mother pursuing Fernie.

Fernie Snow Valley Resort, *tel: (250) 423-4655; fax: (250) 423-6644*, advertises natural snow and has accommodation. Alpine and Nordic skiers, snowboarders and snowmobilers enjoy the powder 5 km south-west of Fernie off Hwy 3. In summer, the area offers chairlift rides, hiking and mountain biking. A late Nov–mid Apr ski season shuttle transports skiers from Fernie to the slopes, $2.

Thirteen km south, the terrain shifts from the Rockies to flatter woodland. Tiny **Elko** is 25 km south of Fernie. Veer north-west and descend via Hwy 3/93 to **Jaffray** and **Wardner**, continuing to the Hwy 93/95 junction. Turn right to **Fort Steele** (see Cranbrook–Banff, pp. 165–172), or left 6 km to Cranbrook.

CRANBROOK

Tourist Information: Cranbrook Visitor InfoCentre, *2279 Cranbrook St N., Box 84, Cranbrook, BC V1C 4H6; tel: (800) 222-6174 or (250) 426-5914; fax: (250) 426-3873*, open daily 0900–2000 in summer, Mon–Fri 0830–1630 in winter.

ACCOMMODATION AND FOOD

A regional shopping and commercial hub, Cranbrook has two dozen hotels, motels, Bed and Breakfasts and campsites. Most are located along Hwy 3, *Cranbrook St*, including budget **Inn of the South**, *803 Cranbrook St; tel: (800) 663-2708 or (250) 489-4301; fax: (250) 489-5758*. Chains include *BW* and *S8*.

Cranbrook St is also home for many of the town's 50-odd fast-food outlets and restaurants. One of the most popular spots is the moderate **Kootenay Cattle Co**, *40 Van Home St N.; tel: (250) 489-5811*.

SIGHTSEEING

The VIC has a free self-guided **Cranbrook Heritage Tour** of buildings in the old section of town, near the railway station, including the old brick clock tower at *Baker* and *Cranbrook Sts*.

Follow *Baker St* one block west to the **Canadian Museum of Rail Travel**, *1 Van Home St N., Hwy 3 at Baker St; tel: (250) 489-3918*, open 0800–2000 (July–Aug), 1000–1800 (fall and spring), Tues–Sat 1200–1700 (winter), adults $6.75, children $3.25, family $16.50. The museum centres on nine original carriages of CPR's 1929 TransCanada Limited, the only surviving set of integrated carriages originally designed as a rolling hotel. The carriages, the epitome of pre-Depression luxury and the last of their kind built in Canada, are arranged along an interior viewing corridor. The dining car *Argyle* is open for light meals and tea.

CRANBROOK–BANFF

The 280 km between Cranbrook and Banff span one of the greatest concentrations of breathtaking scenery in Canada. The highway follows the Rocky Mountain Trench from the Kootenay River to the Columbia River, then climbs into Kootenay National Park and down into Banff National Park and Banff. It's an easy one-day drive, but try to allow half a day at Fort Steele, near Cranbrook, and a full day for the drive from Radium Hot Springs over Vermilion Pass to Banff. Best overnights are Fairmont Hot Springs, Radium Hot Springs or Kootenay Park Lodge.

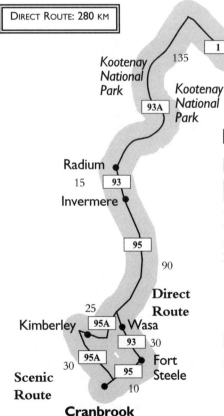

DIRECT ROUTE: 280 KM

Kootenay National Park

135

1

Banff

Kootenay National Park

93A

Radium

15 | 93

Invermere

95

90

Direct Route

25

Kimberley | 95A | Wasa

93 | 30

30 | 95A

Scenic Route

95 | Fort Steele

10

Cranbrook

165

ROUTES

DIRECT ROUTE

Take Hwy 3 north-east from Cranbrook to the junction with Hwy 93/95, then continue 7 km north on Hwy 93/95 to Fort Steele. Turn north via Wasa to follow Hwy 93/95 through **Invermere** to **Radium Hot Springs**, then take Hwy 93, the Banff-Windermere Parkway, east through Kootenay National Park to Banff National Park and TransCanada Hwy 1. Turn south to Banff.

SCENIC ROUTE

A 55 km north-west loop from Cranbrook accesses the Bavarian Alps atmosphere of Kimberley, the area's ski resort, but by-passes Fort Steele.

Take Hwy 95A north of Cranbrook. Stop just before the Marysville Bridge over Mark Creek for a short walk south to

Marysville Falls. The Kimberley Travel Info Centre has a self-guided **Nature Walk** brochure with a map of flora and fauna to watch for along a 6-km path which continues to downtown Kimberley. Rejoin Hwy 95 just north of Wasa, then follow the Direct Route to Banff.

BUSES

Greyhound Lines of Canada operate one daily service, taking 6½ hrs. Dewdney Coach Lines operate a service Mon–Fri to Radium. See OTT table 112.

FORT STEELE

Tourist Information: Fort Steele Heritage Town, *Fort Steele, BC V0B 1N0; tel: (250) 426-7352 or (250) 489-3351; fax: (250) 489-2624,* town open daily, facilities open mid June–Sept, adults $5.50, children 13–18 $3.25, 6–12 $1, family $10.75.

ACCOMMODATION AND FOOD

The ground floor of the **Wasa Hotel** is a museum with East Kootenay mining, farming and Ktunaxa displays. In summer, actors recreate daily street life – visitors are encouraged to heckle politicians. Bright red horse-drawn wagons provide town tours in summer, $1.

Just north of Fort Steele at the 400-pitch **Fort Steele Resort & RV Park**, *tel: (250) 489-4268 or (250) 489-0953,* is the terminus of the **Dewdney Trail**, a 1.2-m wide mule trail hacked through the wilderness from Hope in 1865 to assert British authority over the flood of American miners. Fort Steele Heritage Town ticket office has maps to the gravel roads and trails along **Wild Horse Creek** mining sites and ruins; gold panning is popular.

Businesses include the **International Hotel Restaurant**, *tel: (250) 426-6719,* for lunch and dinner; the self-serve **Tea Room Restaurant** with balcony views of the Rockies' Steeples Range; wood-fired oven-baked goods at the **City Bakery**; **Mrs Sprague's Confectionery, Kershaw's General Store**, the **Wild Horse Theatre** and the **Fort Steele Steam Railway**.

SIGHTSEEING

The 1864 discovery of gold on **Wildhorse Creek** brought a flood of miners north from the United States. John Galbraith realised it would be more profitable to mine the miners than the gold fields and built a cable ferry across the Kootenay River, quickly followed by a store, saloon and brothel. Galbraith's Ferry thrived while the gold lasted. By the 1880s, most miners had departed. The few who remained turned to farming and fencing the rich plains and meadows that had been traditional grazing lands of the Ktunaxa (Kootenai) First Nation.

Mounting tensions peaked with the murder of two Whites in 1884. Two Ktunaxa men were jailed on flimsy evidence and promptly rescued by a Ktunaxa chief. In the summer of 1887, settlers called in the North West Mounted Police. NWMP Inspector Sam Steele and 75 men built winter quarters and persuaded the Ktunaxa to return the two accused. Steele tried the pair, acquitted them and returned to Alberta, having established the primacy of Colonial law. Grateful settlers renamed their town Fort Steele.

Boom times returned as silver, lead and zinc began flowing from nearby mines in 1893. Expectations that the railway would cross the Crowsnest Pass to Fort Steele fuelled land speculation. Cranbrook got the railway and Fort Steele collapsed.

The population dropped from 4000 in 1897 to 150 in 1902, but the town survived into the 1960s when BC resurrected

166

CRANBROOK–BANFF

what remained as a heritage town. Some of the 60-odd buildings are originals, some were moved to the site and some are reconstructions. Most are fully furnished. The look is 1890s, with costumed staff and volunteers making wagon wheels and ice-cream, shoeing horses and performing tasks with period tools in summer.

Bummers Flats, 9 km north, is a bird nesting area with waterfowl, bluebirds, pileated woodpeckers, meadowlarks and turkey vultures. The larger **Wasa Slough Wildlife Sanctuary** is 5 km north.

WASA

Wasa Lake vies with **Osoyoos** and **Christina Lakes** as BC's warmest for summer swimming. **Wasa Lake Provincial Park**, *tel: (250) 422-4200*, with 104 pitches, is popular for swimming and water sports. **Wild Rose Ranch & Resort**, *8 km north of Wasa Lake on Wolf Creek Rd, Box 181, Kimberley, BC V1A 2Y6; tel: (800) 324-6188 or (250) 422-3403; fax: (250) 422-3149*, is a lovely moderate lodge nestled between the Rockies and the Purcell Range, with horse riding, fly-fishing or winter ice fishing for trout: native cutthroat, rainbow, brook (char) and bull (Dolly Varden), with moose, elk, deer and bighorn sheep nearby.

KIMBERLEY

Tourist Information: Kimberley Travel Info Centre, *350 Ross St, Kimberley, BC V1A 2Z9; tel: (250) 427-3666; fax: (250) 427-5378*, marked with an oversized mascot called Happy Hans, has maps, a dining list and information on the Kimberley Ski Hill and other 'Bavarian City of the Rockies' amenities. Chalet motels and several Bed and Breakfasts line the streets.

Kimberley's Bavarian kitsch dates from the 1970s. East Kootenays miners named

the town after the South African diamond mine in 1896. Cominco's Sullivan Mine, opened in 1917, claims to be the world's largest lead and zinc mine – at least until its scheduled closure about 2000. **Bavarian City Mining Railway**, *c/o Kimberley Bavarian Society, Chamber of Commerce at the InfoCentre; tel: (250) 427-3666*, runs late June–Labour Day from downtown past old mine sites to Happy Hans Campground, adults $5 return, children 13–18 $4, 6–12 $2.

Cominco Gardens, *tel: (250) 427-5160*, well known for Rose and Prairie Gardens, display 48,000 blooms June–Oct. Don't miss doughy *bretzels*, served piping hot at **Kimberley City Bakery Ltd.**, *287 Spokane St; tel: (250) 427-2131*, on the **Platzl**. Restaurants and shops adorned with flower baskets and hand-painted fire hydrants line the red brick *Platzl*, a pedestrian mall graced by **Happy Hans'** hourly emergence (summer season) from the world's largest **Cuckoo Clock**, when he yodels for $0.25. Behind the clock, the **Kimberley Heritage Museum**, *105 Spokane St; tel: (250) 427-7510*, open Mon–Sat, features the history of local mining and sports.

The **Kimberley Ski and Summer Resort**, *Box 40; tel: (250) 427-4881; fax: (250) 427-3927*, offers downhill and Nordic skiing from early Dec–mid Apr, and tennis, bumper cars and a chair lift ride in summer. **Trickle Creek Golf Resort**, *tel: (250) 427-5171*, has mountain vistas and challenging altitude changes. Hwy 95A rejoins Hwy 93/95.

KIMBERLEY TO INVERMERE

Hwy 93/95 follows **Kootenay River** to **Canal Flats**, named for a failed canal linking the Kootenay with **Columbia Lake**, headwaters of the **Columbia River**. The 2-km canal was completed in 1889, but

167

used only twice, and was abandoned in 1902. The town of Canal Flats is just east of the highway, on the way to **Canal Flats Provincial Park**, *on Columbia Lake*, and the canal site.

The highway skirts the west side of Columbia Lake, crossing Columbia River at the north end. Just north of **Dutch Creek** on the left are magnificent golden hoodoos said by the Ktunaxa to be decomposed ribs of a fish wounded by Coyote.

Four km north-eastward lies **Fairmont Hot Springs**, *Box 10, Fairmont Hot Springs, BC V0B 1L0; tel: (800) 663-4979 or (250) 345-6311; fax: (250) 345-6616,* a resort, spa, ski hill, Nordic ski track, an RV park, moderate–expensive accommodation and high-mineral, no-sulphur hot springs. The Ktunaxa recognised the restorative powers of the 35–45°C springs long ago. The hillside springs have been a resort since the early 1900s. Activities include swimming and diving pools, skiing (304m vertical), two golf courses, trail riding, hiking and flightseeing.

Windermere Lake is just north, a popular summer home and recreation lake. The town of **Windermere**, *east side of the lake,* has the take from BC's biggest robbery, **St Peter's Anglican Church**, *Kootenay St; tel: (250) 342-6644.* The church was built in **Donald**, 209 km away, in 1887. When the Canadian Pacific Railway moved its operations to **Revelstoke** (see p.203), most of Donald moved, too. Two residents went east to Windermere, taking the church with them. At the north end of Windermere Lake is the road west to **James Chabot Beach Provincial Park** and the town of **Invermere**.

Tourist Information: Columbia Valley Chamber of Commerce, *Box*

1099, Invermere, BC V0A 1K0; tel: (250) 342-2844; **InfoCentre**, *630 3rd St; tel: (250) 342-6316,* open May–Sept.

The **Windermere Valley Museum**, *622 3rd St, Invermere, BC V0A 1K0; tel: (250) 342-9769,* open daily July–Aug, weekends May and Sept, by appointment in winter, displays railway and mining history in heritage buildings. A cairn marks the site of **Kootenae House**, *right off Wilmer–Panorama Rd onto Westside Rd,* David Thompson's 1807 trading post. **Panorama Resort**, *17½ km west on Toby Creek Rd, Panorama, BC V0A 1T0; tel: (800) 663-2929 or (250) 342-6941; fax: (250) 342-3395,* is an all-season alpine resort with hiking, mountain biking, trail riding, golf, tennis, whitewater rafting, helicopter skiing and alpine skiing (1158m vertical).

The highway climbs through Shuswap Indian Reserve to a lay-by 1½ km north of the Invermere junction with panoramic views of **Columbia Valley**, the local name for the Rocky Mountain Trench. Watch for Rocky Mountain bighorn sheep on approaching **Radium**.

Tourist Information: Radium Hot Springs Chamber of Commerce, *Box 225, 7585 Main St W., Radium Hot Springs, BC V0A 1M0; tel: (800) 347-9704 or (250) 347-9331; fax: (250) 347-9736.*

ACCOMMODATION

Radium Hot Springs Resort, *8100 Golf Course Rd, Box 310, Radium Hot Springs, BC V0A 1M0; tel: (800) 667-6444 or (250) 347-9311; fax: (250) 347-6299,* expensive, is the top resort in the valley with two of the best golf courses in the BC interior. Motels line Hwy 93/95 and Hwy 93 to the gates of Kootenay National Park.

Named for slightly radioactive and extremely popular hot springs 3 km east,

Radium provides services for visitors to Kootenay National Park, where the springs are located. Turn west to the centre of town. Turn right from Hwy 93/95 onto *Redstreak Rd* to 242-pitch **Redstreak Campground**, open early May–late Sept, in Kootenay National Park. Hiking trails from the campsite access the townsite with views over the Columbia Valley and Radium Hot Springs pools.

Fill up with petrol for the upward haul on the Banff–Windermere Hwy through the park over Vermilion Pass at the Continental Divide.

KOOTENAY NATIONAL PARK

Tourist Information: Kootenay National Park, *PO Box 220, Radium Hot Springs, BC V0A 1M0; tel: (250) 347-9615; fax: (250) 347-9980; web: http://www.worldweb.com/ParksCanada-Kootenay/*. **Kootenay National Park West Gate Information Centre**, *Radium Hot Springs Pools; tel: (250) 347-9505*, open 0900–1900 (late June–Labour Day), 0900–1700 (May–June, Sept–Oct), shorter winter hours, is the main info centre, with park information, maps and backcountry permits. **Vermilion Crossing Park Information Centre**, *Kootenay Park Lodge*, provides information but no telephone, and is open summer with limited winter hours. There are *no public telephones* between Radium Hot Springs and Storm Mountain Lodge in Banff National Park! Fill up with petrol in Radium, as Vermilion Crossing's petrol station, the only possibility before Banff National Park, may be closed. Be prepared for freezing weather any time when travelling above 1500m.

Most of today's 1.2 million annual visitors drive through quickly, perhaps picnicking, soaking in Radium Hot Springs, stopping at viewpoints, hiking to see

coloured mud historically used by First Nations people, or following paths up Marble Canyon. Two companies, **Kootenay River Runners**, *tel: (800) 599-4399* or *(403) 762-5385* or *(250) 347-9210*, and **Western Canadian River Adventures**, *tel: (403) 470-0072*, offer Kootenay River rafting. The lack of visitor facilities beyond Radium Hot Springs and Vermilion Crossing, wild mountain peaks, rushing rivers, numerous animals and birds and few signs, creates a wilderness feeling unmatched along other Rocky Mountain routes.

Enter Kootenay National Park 1½ km east on Hwy 93. Just inside the West Gate is a short, narrow defile, brilliant red **Sinclair Canyon**. **Radium Hot Springs** is 1 km beyond.

Don't be confused by the name – the town on Hwy 93/95 is called both Radium and Radium Hot Springs. The actual hot springs are just within the park boundary. First Nations peoples used the waters therapeutically. In 1914, McGill University scientists found the springs' radium and radon to be radioactive but not dangerously so – less than emissions from a watch.

Unlike the other parks' sulphur-scented springs, Radium's are odourless. The mineral content has been compared to Bath, England. Dual outdoor pools offer a temperature choice: a cool 27°C pool for swimming and a hot 40°C pool for soaking; *tel: (800) 767-1611* or *(250) 347-9485*, open year-round, adults $4.50–5, children $4–4.50, family $13.50–15. Other facilities include massage, Park InfoCentre, a bookstore and a restaurant-gift shop open May–Oct.

Radium Hot Springs Lodge, *Box 70, Radium Hot Springs, BC V0A 1M0; tel: (250) 347-9341*, has 66 expensive rooms across the highway from the pools. Other accommodation near the pools include: **Addison's Bungalows**, *Box 56; tel: (250)*

169

KOOTENAY
NATIONAL PARK

YOHO
NATIONAL
PARK

ALBERTA

Castle Junction

TOKUMM CREEK

VERMILLION
PASS

THE CONTINENTAL
DIVIDE & FIREWEED TRAIL

93

BOW

ICE

MARBLE
CANYON

PAINT
POTS

REDEARTH

BANFF
NATIONAL
PARK

MT BALL
(3312m)

VERMILLION

SUNSHINE VILLAGE
SKI AREA

KOOTENAY
NATIONAL
PARK

MT VERENDRYE
(3086m)

VERMILLION CROSSING
VISITORS CENTRE

KOOTENAY

Harrogate

BRITISH
COLUMBIA

MT WARDLE
(2810m)

SIMPSON

93

95

Spillimacheen

COLUMBIA

SPLIT PEAK
(2929m)

North

KOOTENAY CROSSING
WARDEN STATION

DOLLY VARDEN

Brisco

MT HARTKIN
(2981m)

93

FRANCES CREEK

95

MT KINDERSLEY
(2691m)

KOOTENAY

Edgewater

Camp site

Icefield

KOOTENAY
OLIVE VALLEY VIEWPOINT
LAKE

FORSTER CREEK

RADIUM HOT
SPRINGS POOLS

SINCLAIR CANYON

Radium
Junction

Radium Hot Springs
VALLEY VIEW TRAIL

Settlers Road

0   10 kms

0   5 miles

93

95

DRY GULCH
PROV. PARK

170

347-9545, and **Blakley's Bungalows**, *Box 190; tel: (250) 347-9918*, both moderate, and **Mt Farnham Bungalows**, *Box 160; tel: (250) 347-9515*, moderate–expensive.

Flaming red cliffs along Redwall Fault are a good place to spot bighorn sheep. **Olive Lake** picnic area, 10 km north-east at 1486-m **Sinclair Pass**, has a fine 0.5-km return boardwalk trail to the olive-green lakeshore, with bronze-cast interpretive details like a bear paw, a fish and tree bark.

Four km further is the stunning **Kootenay Valley Viewpoint**, a 1370-m high panorama of rushing threads of Kootenay River backed by the solid grey wall of the Mitchell Range. Hwy 93 turns right to follow the river.

Ten km north, 98-pitch **McLeod Meadows Campground** is open mid May–mid Sept. A 2½-km hike through pine and Douglas-fir to **Dog Lake** is a good leg stretch; there's a good view east to **Mt Harkin** from the highway. Seven km beyond is **Dolly Varden Campground**, a picnic area in summer which becomes the park's only winter campsite in Sept.

With mountains spiking on both sides, watch for elk (wapiti), white-tailed and mule deer, moose, black bears and other wildlife near the road. Lack of human facilities encourages animals to forage. Stop at the **Kootenay River Crossing** viewpoint to admire Hector Gorge and wildlife.

Hwy 93 travels north-east from the Kootenay River and begins to parallel the Vermilion River near **Hector Gorge**. A picnic area at the viewpoint is a good place to spot Kootenay National Park's symbol, mountain goats, gathering to devour salt and minerals from natural licks.

Another lick near **Wardle Creek Picnic Area** is favoured by moose. The **Sir George Simpson Historic Site Monument** recalls the hard-driving HBC

governor's 1841 passage during a round-the-world trip. Hike east along one of the **Simpson River Trail's** two forks into *roadless* **Mt Assinboine Provincial Park**, named after the 3561-m peak rising sheer above surrounding ridgelines. There is rustic camping and cabins at **Mt Assiniboine Lodge**, *Mt Assiniboine Provincial Park, c/o Box 1829, Golden, BC V0A 1H0; tel: (250) 344-2639; fax: (250) 344-5520*, open Feb–Apr, late June–mid Oct, with twelve expensive American Plan cabins overlooking **Magog Lake**, favoured by fishers, climbers, hikers and Nordic skiers.

Hwy 93 turns left to reach **Vermilion Crossing** a few km north. **Mt Verendrye**, 3086m, is west. **Kootenay Park Lodge**, *Box 1390, Banff, AB T0L 0C0; tel: (403) 762-9196; fax: (403) 262-5028*, open May–Sept, has moderate cosy cabins with fireplaces. There is a restaurant, store, a petrol station and the **Vermilion Crossing Park Information Centre**. Park wardens supply trail information.

Eight km north-west is the **Floe Lake Trail**, an 11-km trek to icebergs drifting on Floe Lake. Stop at **Numa Falls**, viewed from a bridge over Numa Creek. The **Numa Creek Trail** goes south-west 4 km before branching to several mountain passes and a lake, glacier or rockwall.

Take the easy 1-km hike to the **Paint Pots**, beginning in verdant forest, crossing a suspension bridge over the Vermilion River, passing through bird-beloved wetlands, skirting rust-coloured ochre beds, and giving onto a series of holes in the clay filled with water and natural pigments. The striking red which gave the Vermilion River its name and contrasting yellow and green hues are eerie.

Ktunaxa gathered the oxidised pigments and baked the clay with animal grease for body paint. Early 20th-century commercial exploitation, seen in equipment

171

Kootenay National Park

Kootenay (pron. coot-in-knee), First Nations 'people from beyond the hills', gave their name, Ktunaxa, Kootenai, Kootenae or Kootenay to the river and, in 1920, to the national park. Ochre mud just west of the Continental Divide lured the Ktunaxa, who probably traded the 'paint' with other Aboriginal peoples. Hot springs at the end of valleys stretching south-westward were used medicinally.

HBC Governor George Simpson travelled through the present-day park in 1841, followed within a few weeks by James Sinclair, another HBC man leading a party of settlers and Métis to the Columbia River and Oregon Territory. Doctor-geologist James Hector, who explored the Kicking Horse Pass and River (see pp.213, 217) in 1858, explored and recommended Vermilion Pass as the best CPR route through the Rockies. Kicking Horse Pass was chosen instead for reasons never clarified.

Of the four central Canadian Rockies Parks, Banff, Jasper, Yoho and Kootenay, only the latter was developed out of a need for an all-weather road, rather than for CPR profit and public pleasure.

Road construction began in 1912, predicated on funding from the Dominion Government and BC and Alberta Provinces. Alberta completed the roadway from Calgary to Vermilion Pass before World War I. Lack of funding from BC led to a 1920 agreement that the Dominion Government would finish the road if BC ceded five miles on either side of the highway for a national park. The Banff–Windermere Highway (Parkway), finished in 1923, opened both sides of the Rockies to motorised touring.

corroding in the stream, failed, leaving the delicate landscape littered with debris.

Wear warm clothing and stout walking shoes for the rocky 0.8-km path along Tokumm Creek through 600-m long **Marble Canyon**. The glacial creek flows into the Vermilion River. Seven stout bridges offer stomach-flopping views of the roaring blue-green water foaming on huge rocks in the impossibly narrow gorge below; the magnificent waterfall at the end is wide and sprawling. **Marble Canyon Campground**, open mid June–Labour Day, has 61 pitches; there may be a summer Park InfoCentre at the parking area.

The bare trees of the 1968 Vermilion Pass Burn (forest fire) become obvious as Hwy 93 rises towards 1651-m **Vermilion Pass**. **Stanley Glacier Trail**, a difficult 5-km hike beginning 4 km north-east of the canyon, is one spot where the forest fire shows, along with wildflowers in summer and a perfect U-shaped glacial valley vista.

Vermilion Pass at the **Continental Divide**, is the provincial border and the boundary between Kootenay and Banff National Parks. The 1-km **Fireweed Trail** loop offers a quick introduction to the burn, triggered by lightning. Periodic fires have initiated new growth, including the bright pink fireweed which appears soon after a burn.

Enter **Banff National Park**. Three miles east of Vermilion Pass, CPR's 1922 **Storm Mountain Lodge**, *Box 670, Banff, AB TEL 0C0; tel/fax: (403) 762-4155,* open late May–Sept, offers twelve expensive cabins, a restaurant and public telephone. There are several trails in the area.

The Hwy 1 junction is 5 km east; go left, 27 km north to Lake Louise or 27 km south to Banff. For a scenic alternative, continue straight across the TransCanada Hwy to Castle Mountain at Hwy 1A, the Bow Valley Parkway (see Banff–Jasper, pp. 87–103).

CRANBROOK–CASTLEGAR

This route across the south-east corner of BC is for mountain lovers. The Crowsnest Hwy runs west from Cranbrook, nestled between the Rockies and the Purcells, over the highest paved pass in Canada and down to the Kootenays. The direct 270-km route can be covered in a day. Allow three to five days by way of the 290-km scenic route to explore BC's highland heart.

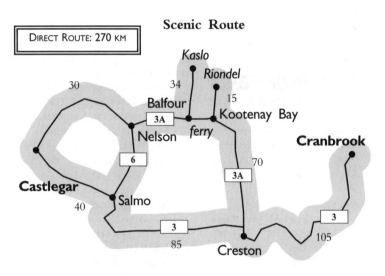

Scenic Route

DIRECT ROUTE: 270 KM

Kaslo
Riondel
30   34   15
Balfour
3A   Kootenay Bay
Nelson   ferry
                              Cranbrook
6   70
                 3A
Castlegar
40   Salmo
                              3
              3
              85   105
                    Creston

Direct Route

173

ROUTES

DIRECT ROUTE

Follow Hwy 3, the Crowsnest Hwy, west from Cranbrook past Moyie. The time zone changes to Pacific Time near Yahk. Continue to **Creston**, across the marshy expanses of the Kootenay River and into the Kootenay Mountains to **Kootenay Pass**, the highest paved pass in Canada. Twist down the western slopes to

Burnt Flat and **Salmo**. Continue north and west past the confluence of the Columbia and Kootenay Rivers at Castlegar. Allow a full day, or, better yet, two to three days with an overnight in Creston.

SCENIC ROUTE

Follow Hwy 3 west from Cranbrook to **Creston**. Turn north on Hwy 3A to follow the eastern shore of Kootenay Lake to the end of the road at Kootenay Bay. Take the **ferry** across the lake to

Balfour. A side-track leads 34 km north to **Ainsworth Hot Springs** and **Kaslo**. Return to Balfour and follow Hwy 3A to **Nelson**, then follow the Kootenay River south-west to **Castlegar**. Allow one *very* long day, or, preferably, spend at least one night in Creston and two or more nights in Nelson. The ferry runs all year, but the back-up can stretch most of the day in summer.

BUSES

Greyhound Lines of Canada operate two trips a day from Cranbrook to Castlegar via Creston, Salmo and Nelson. Journey time: 4 hrs. OTT table 128.

CRANBROOK TO CRESTON

Take Hwy 3 west past the **Elizabeth Lake Sanctuary**, on the south side of the highway, and the **Summer Infocentre**. The turnoff for **Jim Smith Lake Provincial Park**, *tel: (250) 422-4200*, is 2 km west; the lake and park are 4 km north from the turn-off.

174

Hwy 3 curves into the vast forests of the Purcell Mountains past **Moyie Lake Provincial Park**, *tel: (250) 422-4200*, with 104 camping pitches, and a viewpoint over **Moyie Lake**. A sign commemorates the passage of David Thompson in 1808 while searching for a route between the Rocky Mountains and the Columbia River. His party nearly perished in spring floods. The town of **Moyie** and its turn-of-the-century firehall are 1 km beyond the sign.

Look for the information sign near **St Eugene Mine**, once the richest silver/lead mine in Canada. The ore body was discovered by a Kootenay Indian named Pierre from the St Eugene Mission near Fort Steele (see p.166). Pierre and mission superior Fr. Coccola sold their claim to miner James Cronin. The miner opened what

became a fabulously profitable mine. Pierre and the priest built churches for Moyie and the Mission; both are still in use. All that remains of the mine are slag heaps, overgrown stone and cement foundations and a cemetery half-obscured by trees. A road sign 16 km west marks the time zone change from Mountain Time to Pacific Time.

Yahk was once a major producer of railway ties but never recovered from the Great Depression, often called the 'Dirty Thirties' for the tonnes of topsoil blown off the central plains and prairies of North America. The biggest modern export is 'Yahk and Back' T-shirts. **Yahk Provincial Park**, just south, has good fishing for rainbow and cutthroat trout. Four km west is the junction with Hwy 95, which leads 12 km south to Kingsgate, a 24-hour US border crossing into Idaho.

Hwy 3 swings north toward **Kitchener**, a small settlement on the boundary between BC's Rocky Mountain and Kootenay regions. Continue west over Goat Creek through **Erickson**, a farming community dotted with orchards and fruit stands at the junction with Hwy 21 south to the US border at **Rykerts**. The customs post is open daily 0800–2300.

CRESTON

Tourist Information: Creston & District Chamber of Commerce, *Box 268, Creston, BC V0B 1G0; tel: (250) 428-4342; fax: (250) 428-9411*; **Visitor Information Centre**, *log Building, 1711 Canyon St (Hwy 3)*, at the east end of town.

ACCOMMODATION AND FOOD

Downtowner Motor Inn, *1218 Canyon St, Creston, BC V0B 1G0; tel: (800) 665-9904 or (250) 428-2238; fax: (250) 428-9974*, is extremely convenient and good value.

The best choice for carnivores is the **Rendezvous Restaurant**, *1230 Canyon St; tel: (250) 428-9554*, budget–moderate. Best vegetarian restaurant in the region is the **Kootenay Rose Coffeehouse**, *129 N. 10th Ave; tel: (250) 428-7252*, cheap–budget. **Uptown Café**, *1417 Canyon St; tel: (250) 428-3565*, is popular for cheap breakfasts and huge portions with all meals.

SIGHTSEEING

Creston is perched above a broad plain where the Kootenay River once wandered between the Purcell and Selkirk Mountains before entering Kootenay Lake. Most of the marshy valley has been diked, drained and levelled into rich farmland, including some of BC's most productive wheat fields.

About 7000 hectares of original marshland has been preserved in the **Creston Valley Wildlife Management Area**, *Box 640, Creston, BC V0B 1G0; tel: (250) 428-3260; fax: (250) 428-3276*. The wetlands are home to 265 species of migrating waterfowl, as well as moose, deer, elk, otters and other permanent residents. The **Creston Valley Wildlife Centre**, *10 km west on Hwy 3; tel: (250) 428-3259*, operates a museum, guided canoe trips, hikes, meadow and marsh walks and lectures. The best months to visit are Mar, for the spring bird migration, and Oct for the fall flocks winging south.

Creston developed as the Kootenay's major agricultural town rather than a mining boom town. During the 1860s, Creston was a transportation and supply hub for the **Dewdney Trail** from Hope to Fort Steele. Hwy 3, the Crowsnest Hwy, follows most of the original trail route to the Kootenay gold fields.

Creston's claim to artistic fame is a series of nine murals, starting with **McDowell's Department Store** on *Canyon St*. Local history is on display at **Creston Valley**

Museum and Archives, *219 Devon Rd; tel: (250) 428-9262*, open daily May–Oct, by appointment the rest of the year. The museum occupies an impressive stone house overlooking the valley and has a rare 'sturgeon-nosed' Kutenai canoe. The only other canoe builders who pointed the ends of their craft down into the water were the Goldi peoples of the Amur River Basin in Siberia.

Take Hwy 3 across the Creston Valley. The road climbs into the **Selkirk Mountains** immediately beyond the Creston Valley Wildlife Management Area. **Blazed Creek Rest Area**, 17 km west, is a convenient stop. The highway immediately climbs 18 km to **Kootenay Pass**, often called **The Skyway**, at 1774 m the highest paved pass in Canada. The highway is open all winter, but may be closed temporarily (a few minutes to a few days) by adverse weather or avalanche conditions. If the pass is closed, detour along the scenic route, Hwy 3A north along Kootenay Lake, by ferry across the lake to Balfour, then south-east to Nelson and Castlegar.

The Skyway is surrounded by **Stagleap Provincial Park**, 1130 hectares designated to protect rare woodland caribou that migrate through the region. There are pleasant picnic sites beside the highway at **Bridal Lake**. A portion of the original Dewdney Trail runs along the north shore of the lake.

The west side of Kootenay Pass is a rollercoaster that twists and turns across five canyons and several avalanche chutes. The best – and only – stopping spot is **Lost Creek Rest Area**, 13 km from the summit. Two km west is **Burnt Flat Junction** and Hwy 31, which runs 10 km south to the US border at Nelway, open 0800–2400. Hwys 3 and 6 run together for 14 km to Salmo.

175

SALMO

Tourist Information: Infocentre, *Hwy 3, marked with three flagpoles;* open summer only.

In the 1850s, Salmo was called Salmon River after the abundant runs of salmon that migrated up the Columbia and Salmon Rivers. Dozens of dams on the Columbia River in the US and Canada destroyed the salmon runs, but fishing for Dolly Varden and other non-migratory trout is fabulous. Don't miss the stone murals depicting local history on the outside of several downtown buildings. New murals are added each year by students at **Kootenay Stone Masonry Training Institution and Kootenay Stone Centre,** *Box 486; tel: (250) 357-9515.* The local golf course (nine holes) is also the runway of the regional airport, usually called the Golfport. Pilots buzz the greens before landing.

Hwy 3 swings sharply north at **Beaver Creek Bridge** and climbs 12 km to 1214-m **Bombi Summit**. RVers should use the brake check area at the top of the summit before the sharp descent to Castlegar and the Columbia River. The best view of the Columbia Valley and the confluence of the Columbia and Kootenay Rivers is from the **Ootischenia Lookout Rest Area,** 8 km below the summit on the west side of Hwy 3.

The junction with Hwy 3A to Nelson is 4 km below the rest area. Or continue on Hwy 3 for Castlegar.

CRESTON TO KASLO

Just north of the junction with Hwy 3 is **Bo-Fjords,** one of Canada's leading breeders of Norwegian fjord horses, the world's largest draft horses. For tours; *tel: (250) 428-2181.* Just beyond is a large picnic area overlooking the valley with a sign describing reclamation efforts in the 1880s.

The road drops down toward the valley floor and the town of **Wynndel,** dominated by a grain elevator.

Sirdar, 10 km north, was once the site of an important BC Southern Railway roundhouse and turntable. Store, post office and pub were named for Field Marshall Lord Kitchner, who was Sirdar, or Commander, of the Egyptian Army in 1892. The south end of **Kootenay Lake** is 6 km north.

Several resorts and small towns line the lakeshore, including **Kuskanook, Twin Bays** and **Sanca.** Just north of Sanca is the **Glass House,** *tel: (250) 223-8372,* $5 entry fee, a lakeside home built of 500,000 empty embalming fluid flasks. Mortician David Brown built the home 'to indulge a whim of a peculiar nature' according to his wife. House, landscaped grounds and stunning lake vistas are open for tours daily May–Oct and by appointment the rest of the year. The lakeside resort town of **Boswell** is 2½ km north.

Lockhart Beach Provincial Park, *tel: (250) 825-3500,* is nestled in a forest of Douglas-fir, ponderosa pine and western red cedar. The beach park abuts **Lockhart Creek Provincial Park,** an undeveloped swath of forest protecting the headwaters of Lockhart Creek. **Gray Creek** is a thriving service and recreation centre that bills itself as 'metric free', still selling gas in gallons and recording temperatures in degrees Fahrenheit.

The real population centre is over the hill in **Crawford Bay,** the largest community on the eastern side of Kootenay Lake. The town boasts a championship 18-hole golf course, **Kokanee Springs Golf Course,** *tel: (800) 979-7999* or *(250) 227-9226,* and a number of cottage industries, including **North Woven Broom,** *tel: (250) 227-9245,* selling handmade brooms; **Kootenay Forge,** *tel: (250) 227-9466,* an artisan blacksmithy; and **Weavers' Corner**, *tel: (250) 227-9655,* a handweaving studio. All are open daily in summer, weekdays in winter.

⮕ SIDE TRACK TO RIONDEL

Turn right on a secondary road 6½ km west of Crawford Bay to tiny **Riondel** and the once-thriving **Bluebell Mine**, which produced silver and lead. The abandoned mine site is just behind the recreation field in this neat retirement town. ⬥

Return to Hwy 3A and **Kootenay Bay**, a small settlement at the ferry landing. The free 45-min ferry across Kootenay Lake is billed as the world's longest free ride, but the line-up can stretch all day. There are 18 daily sailings in each direction in summer, a dozen daily departures in winter. Timetables are posted at the beginning of Hwy 3A in Creston, at the ferry landing, and in tourist publications throughout the region. The ferry lands in the small resort community of **Balfour**, on the west arm of Kootenay Lake.

⮕ SIDE TRACK TO KASLO

From Balfour, follow Hwy 31 north for 36 km to **Ainsworth Hot Springs**, **Kaslo** and the *ss Moyie*, the last steamboat to sail Kootenay Lake. Much of the highway along the west side of Kootenay Lake is little more than a ledge blasted into the cliffs. The views across the lake along the shoreline are spectacular, but lay-bys are few and far between. Access to the east side of wilderness **Kokanee Glacier Provincial Park**, *RR 3, Nelson, BC V1L 5P6; tel: (250) 825-3500; fax: (250) 825-9509,* is via a gravel road 10 km

north of Balfour. The road follows **Coffee Creek**, a narrow waterway that boils down a small gorge, forcing the road into a sharp hairpin turn.

Ainsworth Hot Springs, *Box 1333, Ainsworth Hot Springs, BC V0G 1A0; tel: (800) 668-1171 or (250) 229-4969,* has the highest mineral content of any hot springs in Canada, discovered when miners drilled into hot water instead of galena (silver and lead) ore. The baths are 45°C and the views stunning. A 20-m lighted cave leads to the source, a natural steam bath with stalactites. At the turn of the century, Ainsworth supported five hotels. One remains open and is usually full in summer and at weekends or holidays.

The turn-off for **Cody Caves Provincial Park**, *tel: (250) 353-7425,* open June–Oct, is north of Ainsworth. The rough gravel track is passable only by high-clearance vehicles. Access is by guided tour only, but except for a few modern ladders, the cave remains much as Henry Cody first saw it a century ago. About 1 km of passages snake through forests of stalagmites, stalactites and soda straws. Don't even think about walking inside without ropes, hard hats, spare torches, waterproof boots and an experienced guide.

Mirror Lake, *Box 540, Kaslo, BC V0G 1M0; tel: (250) 353-7102,* now a private campsite, was an important shipbuilding yard during the Kootenay mining boom earlier in the century.

KASLO

Tourist Information: Kaslo & District Chamber of Commerce, *Box 329, Kaslo, BC V0G 1M0; tel: (250) 353-7323;* **Visitor Centre**, *324 Front St,* open daily (mid May–mid Sept).

177

Kaslo was born as a lumber town, but silver and lead discoveries brought a flood of miners in the 1890s. As mining and forestry declined, Kaslo's physical setting on the shores of Kootenay Lake made tourism an important force.

The town of fewer than 1000 inhabitants has more than 60 heritage buildings, crowned by the *ss Moyie*, a sternwheel steamboat that sailed the lake for half a century. The boat has been dry-docked on the lakefront and restored as the **ss Moyie National Historic Site**, *Box 537, Kaslo, BC V0G 1M0; tel/fax: (250) 353-2525*, open daily mid May–mid Sept or by appointment. Built in 1898 for the Canadian Pacific Railway, the *Moyie* sailed Kootenay Lake until 1957. She was the last passenger-carrying sternwheeler in regular service in Canada and is the oldest vessel of her type in the world. Machinery, cargo decks, public areas, staterooms and wheelhouse have been restored to their appearance in the late 1920s, complete with gleaming brass and gold leaf.

178

KASLO TO NELSON

Hwy 3A follows the north shore of the west arm of Kootenay Lake. Most of the undeveloped south shore is inaccessible except by boat. The lake between holds record-sized trout and **kokanee**, or landlocked salmon. **Kokanee Creek Provincial Park**, 12 km west of Balfour, includes **Redfish Creek Spawning Channel**, an artificial spawning channel filled with bright red kokanee mid Aug–mid Sept. The lakeside park also has one of the largest osprey populations in North America. Nests look like heaps of sticks atop abandoned lake pilings. A rough gravel road leads north into **Kokanee Glacier Provincial Park**.

Continue west along the lakeshore. What looks like a steamboat cabin perched beside the highway 14 km west of Kokanee Creek is the restored upper saloon and wheelhouse of the *mv Nasookin*, once the largest steamboat on the lake. Cross the bright orange bridge into Nelson.

NELSON

Tourist Information: Nelson and District Chamber of Commerce, *225 Hall St, Nelson, BC V1L 5X4; tel: (250) 352-3433; fax: (250) 352-6355.*

ACCOMMODATION

There are few motels in Nelson, but the town is well-supplied with Bed and Breakfasts, most in heritage buildings. Centrally-located **Garden Inn**, *408 Victoria St, Nelson, BC V1L 4K5; tel: (250) 352-3226; fax: (250) 352-3284*, moderate, is one of the most pleasant choices.

EATING AND DRINKING

A steady influx of professionals fleeing the urban life of Calgary, Toronto and Vancouver keeps Nelson's restaurant standards high.

Top choice is the **All Seasons Cafe**, *620 Herridge Lane; tel: (250) 352-0101*, with moderate Northwest dishes and an outstanding wine list. **Kootenay Baker**, *295 Baker St; tel: (250) 352-2274*, is the best bakery in town. **Max & Irma's Kitchen**, *515A Kootenay St; tel: (250) 352-2332*, has the best pizza. **Main Street Diner**, *616 Baker St; tel: (250) 254-4848*, offers solid Greek fare. **Library Lounge** in the **Heritage Inn**, *422 Vernon St; tel: (250) 352-5331*, is an elegant green lampshade, dark leather lounge.

SIGHTSEEING

Nelson looks familiar even if you've never been there. A sparkling Victorian town of brick and gingerbread beside an alpine lake, Nelson was the set for Steve Martin's 1986 film *Roxanne*, a modern remake of *Cyrano de Bergerac*. Local artists enshrined Martin on a mural at the end of *Vernon St* next to historical scenes of trains, streetcars and steamboats.

The town began as a mining camp in the 1880s, then diversified into lumber. Faced with declining population in the 1970s, Nelson obtained a Provincial grant to refurbish its historical core to attract new residents and the beginnings of a tourist industry. The town blossomed into a rural refuge for artists and urban professionals who expect live theatre and perfect *cappuccino* after a hard day at the computer or the mountain bike.

The Chamber of Commerce offers walking and driving tours of Nelson's 350 heritage buildings, led by costumed guides in summer or self-guided in any season. Highlights are the **courthouse** and **city hall**, *Vernon and Ward Sts*, designed by F.M. Rattenbury, the architect responsible for the Parliament Buildings and Empress Hotel in Victoria (see p.281). **Artwalk** is a dozen rotating gallery spaces featuring works by 75 local artists; ask for a map at the Chamber. Next door, the **Chamber of Mines Eastern BC Museum**, *215 Hall St; tel: (250) 352-5242*, has one of BC's largest rock and mineral collections.

The **Nelson Museum**, *402 Anderson St; tel: (250) 352-9813*, open afternoons, recalls local mining and steamboat history. **Streetcar No. 23**, $2, which runs from downtown along the lake to **Lakeside Park** at the foot of the Nelson Bridge, is Canada's only working heritage streetcar. The park, with a sandy beach, boats for hire, shady trees and expansive lawns, is Nelson's favourite outdoor gathering spot. The **Nelson Brewing Company**, *512 Latimer St, Nelson, BC V1L 4T9; tel: (250)*

352-3582; fax: (250) 352-3466, offers daily tours and tasting.

In winter, skiers head for **Morning Mountain**, *tel: (250) 352-9969*, the local ski hill 8 km west on Hwy 3A. The more adventurous prefer **Whitewater Ski Area**, *Box 60, Nelson, BC V1L 5P7; tel: (800) 666-9420 or (250) 354-4944; fax: (250) 354-4988*, considered to have some of the best lift-accessible powder skiing in the Pacific Northwest.

NELSON TO CASTLEGAR

Take Hwy 3A west from Nelson. The **Grohman Narrows Provincial Park** offers pleasant picnicking overlooking the narrows where Kootenay Lake empties into the Kootenay River. The highway crosses the Kootenay River 2½ km beyond.

Four West Kootenay Power dams, **Corra-Linn**, **Upper Bonnington**, **Lower Bonnington** and **South Slocan**, plus the **Kootenay Canal**, exploit the 200m drop between Kootenay Lake and the Columbia River to generate hydro-electricity. Just downstream from Corra-Linn Dam is **Bonnington Falls**, a series of low falls that blocked navigation between the Columbia and Kootenay River systems. Bonnington was an important fishing site for the Lake's Kootenay, or Krunaxa, First Nations, for at least 4000 years before Columbia River dams destroyed the salmon runs. A sign at the falls describes West Kootenay Power and its generating system. The **Kootenay Canal Generating Station** is open for tours Mon–Fri (May–Aug); *tel: (250) 359-7287*.

Continue 13½ km west of the junction with Hwy 6 (north into the Slocan Valley) for a lay-by with a good view of Lower Bonnington Dam. A second lay-by 1500m west offers a good view of **Brilliant Dam** and, just downstream, the **Brilliant**

179

Suspension Bridge dwarfed by the modern highway bridge over the Kootenay River and Castlegar.

CASTLEGAR

Tourist Information: Castlegar and District Chamber of Commerce, *1995 6th Ave, Castlegar, BC V1N 4B7; tel: (250) 365-6313; fax: (250) 365-5778.*

ACCOMMODATION

Sandman Hotel Castlegar, *1944 Columbia Ave, Castlegar, BC V1N 2W7; tel: (800) 726-3626* or *(250) 365-8444; fax: (250) 365-8423,* is good value and convenient.

SIGHTSEEING

Castlegar is perched on the benchlands just west of the Columbia River, opposite the confluence with the Kootenay River. The town began as a railway and timber community and is still home to an odoriferous pulp mill just below **Hugh Keenlyside Dam**, *tel: (250) 365-5299,* 8 km upstream on the Columbia River. The dam, which backs water into **Arrow Lakes** stretching 230 km north to Revelstoke (see p.203), is open daily for self-guided tours in summer.

Castlegar is also home to a large Doukhobor community, a Russian pacifist group who settled the flat farmland on the east side of the Columbia in 1908. The group built one of the first bridges across the Kootenay River, the steel-and-concrete **Brilliant Suspension Bridge**, at the bottom of *Airport Hill*. It is briefly visible driving across the new span on Hwy 3A. To walk *to* the old bridge, park at the south end of the new bridge and follow the abandoned highway about 100m downhill; the bridge is closed to all traffic, including pedestrians.

The **Doukhobor Historical Village**, *across from Castlegar Airport; tel: (250) 365-6622,* open daily May–Sept, by appointment other times, highlights the life and times of this communal group which lived by the motto 'Toil and a Peaceful Life'. Communities occupied distinctive villages made up of one or two great houses and one or more rows of smaller dwellings and outbuildings.

Spiritual leader Peter Verigin, who led the group from Russia to Canada, was killed by a bomb planted on his train carriage in 1924. He is buried on a hillside overlooking the Brilliant Suspension Bridge. About 5000 Doukhobors still live in the Kootenay-Boundary area from Castlegar west to Grand Forks. Nearly all have become integrated into the mainstream community, but many of their distinctive farm buildings can be seen from highways and country roads.

Castlegar's other repository of history is the **Castlegar Museum**, *400 13th Ave, Castlegar, BC V1N 1G2; tel: (250) 365-6440,* in the former CPR station, open Mon–Sat all year.

Zuckerberg Island Heritage Park, *9th St and 7th Ave; tel: (250) 365-5511,* open daily, was once home to First Nations families who left the 2-hectare island peppered with pit dwellings. In 1931, Alexander Feodorovitch Zuckerberg arrived in Castlegar to teach Doukhobor children and settled on the island. He built a home in the form of an onion-domed Russian Orthodox chapel. His house has been fully restored and the island has become a popular park for family fishing and picnics. Access is by a pedestrian suspension bridge.

CASTLEGAR–OSOYOOS

This 220-km section of the Crowsnest Hwy runs from dense cedar and hemlock forests in the heart of the Kootenay Mountains to Canada's only true desert. Like the rest of the Crowsnest, it follows the Dewdney Trail, a 4-foot wide track scraped, hacked and blasted from what had been nearly impenetrable mountains between Hope and Fort Steele,

near Cranbrook, as 19th-century mining discoveries pushed settlement from the Fraser Valley toward the Rocky Mountains. The mule trek that once took weeks can be accomplished in a comfortable day's drive, but try to allow at least one overnight in Grand Forks to explore off the highway.

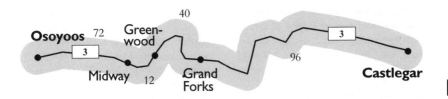

```
                           40
Osoyoos  72    Green-                           3
         3     wood                    96
    Midway  12      Grand                    Castlegar
                    Forks
```

ROUTE: 220 KM

ROUTE

Take Hwy 3, the Crowsnest Hwy, west from Castlegar over Bonanza Pass and on to **Grand Forks**. Cross Phoenix Mountain Summit to **Greenwood**, the Kettle Valley Railway terminus at **Midway, Rock Creek**, and over Anarchist Summit to the Okanagan Valley desert and Osoyoos.

CASTLEGAR TO GRAND FORKS

Hwy 3 climbs south from Castlegar but soon turns west 27 km to **Nancy Greene Lake** and Hwy 3B leading south to the US border. **Nancy Greene Provincial Park**, *tel: (250) 825-3500,* is just beyond the junction. For excellent Nordic skiing in winter, turn left at the 'Ski Trails' sign

4½ km beyond the park entrance. Continue another 6 km to 1535-m **Bonanza Pass**, known locally as Blueberry Paulson Summit, for Blueberry Creek to the east and the tiny town of Paulson to the west. The Paulson Bridge, 10 km west of the pass, spans a dramatic canyon 90m above **McRae Creek**.

The north end of **Christina Lake** is surrounded by **Gladstone Provincial Park**, *tel: (250) 825-3500,* 39,322 hectares of largely undeveloped wilderness. The dry cedar and hemlock forest is an important winter range for deer and elk. There are three dozen informal pitches on the east side of the lake, 6 km north of Hwy 3.

The **Christina Lake Chamber of**

Commerce, *Hwy 3, Christina Lake, BC V0H 1E2; tel: (250) 447-6161*, touts the lake as the warmest in BC (average July water temperature 23°C), a temperature claim shared by Osoyoos (see p.255) and Wasa (see p.167).

Hwy 395 turns south 3 km from Christina Lake, leading to the US border at **Cascade** and on to Spokane, Washington, 144 km beyond (see Thomas Cook's *On the Road around the Pacific Northwest*). Hwy 3 continues west into Boundary Country, the transition zone between the high Kootenay peaks and the fertile Okanagan-Similkameen River Valleys further west.

GRAND FORKS

Tourist Information: Chamber of Commerce of Grand Forks, *Box 1086, 7362 5th St (next to the Boundary Museum), Grand Forks, BC V0H 1H0; tel: (250) 442-2833; fax: (250) 442-5688.*

ACCOMMODATION AND FOOD

Motels cluster along Hwy 3. Budget–moderate **Grand Forks Motor Inn**, *2729 Hwy 3, Grand Forks, BC V0H 1H0; tel: (250) 442-2127; fax: 250-442-2844*, is excellent value.

Grand Forks has BC's best selection of Doukhobor restaurants. Top choice for Russian dishes is **The Chef's Garden Restaurant**, *4415 Hwy 3* (5 km south of the city centre); *tel: (250) 442-0257*. The **Grand Forks Hotel Pub & Restaurant**, downtown at *7382 2nd St; tel: (250) 442-5944*, runs a close second. Both are cheap–moderate. **Aromas Espresso Cafe & Bakery**, *7229 5th St; tel: (250) 442-0119*, is a good budget breakfast or lunch stop.

SIGHTSEEING

Named for its location at the confluence of the Kettle Valley and Granby Rivers, Grand Forks was an agricultural town. The region boomed with the 1900 opening of the **Granby Smelter**, built to process ores from nearby Phoenix mines, and once the largest copper smelter in the British Empire. It closed in 1919; the glistening heaps of ebony slag near *Granby Rd* just north of town are now mined to make industrial abrasives. The **Phoenix Forest and History Tour** follows 22 km of paved and gravel roads to Phoenix Mines site and on to Greenwood. Self-guiding brochures are available at the Grand Forks Chamber of Commerce and the Greenwood Museum.

Boundary-area mines and smelters lured both Canadian and American railway builders anxious to tap the region's mineral wealth. The early success of America's Great Northern line in drawing traffic south to Spokane, WA ensured provincial and federal support for the all-Canadian Kettle Valley Railway. Railway service was curtailed sharply when the falling price of copper, zinc and other metals precipitated widespread mine closures following World War I. The last local rail line was abandoned in 1990.

Grand Forks has more than 300 heritage buildings from the mining and railway era. The **Boundary Museum**, *7370 5th St* (next to the Chamber of Commerce); *tel: (250) 442-3737*, publishes an excellent self-guided walking tour brochure. The museum houses artefacts from First Nations settlement through the Doukhobors, miners, railway builders and later arrivals. **Mountain View Doukhobor Museum**, *Hardy Mountain Rd, Grand Forks, BC V0H 1H0; tel: (250) 442-8855*, open daily June–Oct, is in an original Doukhobor communal house built in 1912. Many other Doukhobor buildings can be seen from *Hardy Mountain Rd* as it winds back to Hwy 3 near The Chef's Garden Restaurant. **Grand Forks Milling Co-operative**,

182

Mill Rd; tel: (250) 442-8252 (call in advance for tours), was built in 1915 to supply flour to the flourishing Doukhobor community: Pride of the Valley flour is still milled from local grain without additives.

The best highway overview of the Boundary region is the 30-km **North Fork Scenic Drive** which follows the Granby River north past the Granby Smelter slag heaps before looping back to Hwy 3 via *Hardy Mountain Dr.* **Thimble Mountain** offers the best off-road routes for walking or cycling, including a half-day mountain bike run along the **Boundary Subdivision Rail Trail**, an abandoned railway right-of-way with tunnels and heritage buildings. The Chamber of Commerce has free detailed area maps.

GRAND FORKS TO GREENWOOD

Hwy 3 drops to the US border before turning north into the relatively low **Monashee Mountains**. The Phoenix Forest and History tour begins at the junction of Hwy 3 and *Phoenix Rd*, 19 km west of Grand Forks. The same road leads to the **Phoenix Alpine Ski Hill**, *tel: (250) 442-2813*, with runs named for local copper mine claims.

Follow the Phoenix Forest and History Tour. Fifteen roadside markers explain local railways, mine tailings, logging operations, mine sites, town sites and history. Gravel roads are well-maintained and passable by passenger vehicles and RVs all year. Allow at least 2 hrs for the drive, which ends at Greenwood Museum.

Alternatively, continue on Hwy 3 over 1105-m **Eholt Summit**, named after the abandoned mining town of Eholt. Drive past **Wilgress Lake** 16 km to Greenwood.

GREENWOOD

Tourist Information: Greenwood Museum and Tourist Info Centre, *Box 399, 214 S, Copper St (Hwy 3), Greenwood, BC V0H 1J0; tel: (250) 445-6355.*

Today the smallest city in BC, Greenwood was a boomtown in north-western North America at the turn of the century. As the service centre for dozens of Boundary mines, Greenwood grew from a pair of cabins in 1897 to more than 7000 residents in 1907, with three banks, sixteen hotels, fifteen general stores, and the busiest red light district between Calgary and Victoria.

When the mining boom collapsed after World War I, Greenwood became a virtual ghost town. It took a second World War and Canada's decision to follow the USA in imprisoning citizens of Japanese ancestry to revive the town. More than 1000 Canadians of Japanese descent were interned in Greenwood's empty buildings. When many BC city councils advocated deportation of Japanese-Canadians in 1945, Greenwood invited its one-time prisoners to stay. Many did. The **Greenwood Museum**, *214 S. Copper St (Hwy 3); tel: (250) 445-6355,* open mid June–mid Sept, recounts both the mining boom and the Japanese internment in sometimes painful detail. The Phoenix Forest and History Tour ends (or begins) at the museum.

Just south of the museum is **Lotzkar Park**, site of the BC Copper Company smelter, the largest of three smelters that once made Greenwood and Grand Forks rivals for the title of top copper producer. The park is one of the best preserved smelter ruins in North America, with a 55-m brick smoke stack and a massive ridge of black smelter slag that once glowed dull red in the bright sunlight of high noon. Locals call it a corner of hell gone cold.

The slag is composed of shiny glass-like impurities that floated to the top as copper ore was smelted in immense electric-fired furnaces. Molten copper was poured into ingots; white hot slag was hauled away in

183

huge bell-shaped carts and dumped below the smelter. Most of the slag was compacted into a solid mass, but the final few **hell's bells** remain where they were dumped, mute testimony to the industrial might that once made the Boundary one of the wealthiest, and most polluted, corners of British Columbia.

Continue west on Hwy 3 to **Boundary Creek Provincial Park**, *tel: (250) 825-3500*, the remains of ore stacks and slag heaps from what was once the largest copper processor in North America. The park, just north of the US border, also has pleasant camping pitches beneath the cottonwood trees along Boundary Creek. **Boundary Falls Park**, 1 km west, was a liquor smuggling depot during America's Prohibition years following World War I.

MIDWAY

Tourist Information: Kettle River Museum, *Box 149, Midway, BC V0H 1M0; tel: (250) 449-2222.*

Midway lives up to its name, halfway between the Rockies and the Pacific Ocean, halfway along the Dewdney Trail from Hope to Fort Steele and halfway on the freight wagon road from Marcus, WA to Oliver, BC. Planned as a smelter town, Midway instead became a railway centre, a major station for the Vancouver, Victoria and Eastern Railway, controlled by American transportation giant Great Northern Railway, and the western terminus for Canada's Kettle Valley Railway, connecting Hope with Canadian Pacific Railway lines running eastward.

The **Kettle River Museum**, *Box 149; tel: (250) 449-2222 or (250) 449-2229*, open daily (May–Sept), tours by prior arrangement the rest of the year, is next to the old CPR station, which has been restored as a railway museum. The main building concentrates on area history. The

Kettle River Railway bed extends north to Penticton, much of it accessible on foot or by mountain bike. **Great Northern Railway bed** is accessible 2 km down *Dump Rd.* The museum has directions.

Midway's other claim to fame is a pair of **entwined trees**, next to the Medical Clinic. The nearby USA-Canada boundary, established in 1846, separated Okanagan First Nations bands that once gathered nearby to fish and pick berries. Band elders supposedly entwined two pine saplings to symbolise their continuing unity despite the newly-created international frontier.

MIDWAY TO OSOYOOS

Continue west on Hwy 3 to Kettle Valley, home to one of the oldest golf courses in BC, built before World War I. Just west of town, Hwy 33 leads north to the **Kettle River Provincial Recreation Area**, *tel: (250) 825-3500*, a pleasant riverside park favoured by local residents. Children of all ages leap from an abandoned Kettle Valley Railway bridge into the Kettle River while their more sedate relatives walk or cycle along the abandoned railbed. The park is equally popular for winter Nordic skiing.

Hwy 3 goes through **Rock Creek**, a copper boomtown that has almost disappeared, and over 1233-m **Anarchist Summit**. The summit was named for settler Richard Sidley, regarded locally as an anarchist. A rest area near the top offers good views westward toward the green oasis of Osoyoos set amidst the surrounding desert. Allow extra time for the hairpin turns on the western side of the grade. The best view of Osoyoos, **Osoyoos Lake** and the spit that nearly splits the lake in half is from the top of the valley rim, 21 km west of Anarchist Summit. Follow signs for scenic viewpoints from westbound or eastbound lanes and continue down the steep grade into Osoyoos (see p. 255).

OSOYOOS–KELOWNA

This 100 km route traces the heart of the Okanagan Valley, from the desert near Osoyoos to the dry slopes surrounding Kelowna. The valley follows a string of lakes connected by the Okanagan River, remnants of the immense glaciers that carved this cleft in the mountains. Benches and rolling slopes lining the valley are cloaked with BC's richest orchards and vineyards. The drive can be accomplished in an easy morning, or stretch it to several days visiting wineries, wildlife refuges and museums.

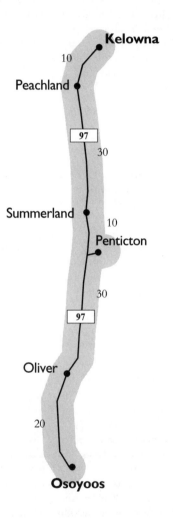

Kelowna
10
Peachland
97
30
Summerland
10
Penticton
30
97
Oliver
20
Osoyoos

185

ROUTE: 100 KM

ROUTE

Follow Hwy 97 north from Osoyoos to **Oliver, Okanagan Falls, Penticton, Summerland, Peachland** and **Kelowna**.

BUSES

Greyhound Lines of Canada operate one direct journey a day (3½ hrs) and one with a change at Penticton (5 hrs). There are also three daily services from Penticton to Kelowna. See OTT table 110.

OSOYOOS TO OLIVER

The southern end of the Okanagan Valley is planted to soft fruit. Growers sell seasonal apples, plums, peaches, cherries, pears, apricots and more at roadside stands. **Touch of Sun Dried Fruit**, *31416 123rd St, Rd 16, RR2, Osoyoos, BC V0H 1V0; tel: (250) 498-4284; fax: (250) 498-2361,* offer free tours and samples 0800–1700 daily; book in advance.

Orchards extend from the shores of Osoyoos Lake up the valley slopes to **The Ditch**, a concrete-lined irrigation canal built as a provincial works project after World War I. Later projects channelised the Okanagan River. Irrigation and reclamation succeeded so well that Canada's only desert has been reduced to a few endangered pockets.

The **Osoyoos Oxbows Fish and Wildlife Management Reserve**, *east of Hwy 97 on Road 22, 7½ km north of Osoyoos,* protects most of the valley's surviving pre-irrigation habitat, including river marshes, meadows and desert. Look for burrowing owls, orioles, woodpeckers, chukar partridge, turkey vultures, northern Pacific rattlesnakes, lizards and prickly pear cactus. An 18-km walking and cycling path follows the Okanagan River from the head of Osoyoos Lake to the McAlpine Bridge, north of Oliver.

Most south valley vineyards are planted uphill of The Ditch. Many vineyards east of Hwy 97 are on the **Inkaneep First Nation (Osoyoos Indian Band) Reserve**; *tel: (250) 498-3444.*

Inkaneep grapes become wine at **Inniskillin Okanagan Vineyards**, *Road 11, Oliver, BC V0H 1T0; tel: (250) 498-6663; fax: (250) 498-4566,* one of five wineries on the 'Golden Mile', named after awards won by **Inniskillin, Domaine Combret**, *Road 13, Oliver, BC V0H 1T0; tel: (250) 498-8878; fax: (250) 498-8879,* **Divino Estate**, *Road 8; tel: (250) 498-2784; fax: (250) 498-6518,* **Gehringer Brothers**, *Road 8; tel: (250) 498-3537,* and

Tinhorn Creek, *Road 7; tel: (250) 498-3743.*

Inniskillin also has wineries in Ontario and California. Domaine Combret emphasises French-style whites. Divino shows strong Italian influences while Gehringer produces German styles with intense fruit flavour. Tinhorn shines with reds, especially Merlot and Pinot Noir.

Tourist Information: Oliver & District Chamber of Commerce, *36205 93rd St (the former Canadian Pacific Railway station), Oliver, BC V0H 1T0; tel: (250) 498-6321; fax: (250) 498-3156.*

Budget–moderate motels line Hwy 97. Top choice is moderate **Southwind Inn Motor Hotel**, *34017 Hwy 97 S., Oliver, BC V0H 1T0; tel: (800) 661-9922; fax: (250) 498-3938.*

The **Okanagan-Similkameen Co-operative Growers' Association**, *9315 348th Ave; tel: (250) 498-3491,* offer summer tours of the 1923 packing house. **Oliver Heritage Society Museum**, *9728 356 Ave; tel: (250) 498-4027,* in the former Provincial Police Headquarters, displays artefacts from Fairview, the area's original gold mining settlement.

Picnic and recreation areas line the shores of **Tuc-el-Nuit Lake**, just east off *Tuc-el-Nuit Dr.* **Mt Baldy**, *Box 1528, Oliver, BC V0H 1T0; tel: (250) 498-7719; fax: (250) 498-6300; snowphone tel: (250) 498-2262,* is a popular local ski area 35 mins east on *362 Ave.*

The valley narrows toward **Vaseux Lake**, 14 km north of Oliver, a spring and autumn Migratory Bird Sanctuary and resting point for hundreds of species. **Vaseux Lake Provincial Park**; *tel: (250) 494-6500,* has a dozen pitches along the shallow lake. The cliffs to the east are home to Canada's largest colony of white-throated swifts. Mountain goats and the world's largest herd of California bighorn sheep, about 850 head, are sometimes seen descending McIntyre Bluff to drink mornings and evenings.

Okanagan Falls once thundered from the south end of **Skaha Lake**. River reclamation has turned the torrent into minor rapids, usually called 'OK Falls'. The best valley views (and some of the best wine) are from **Hawthorne Mountain Vineyards**, *Box 498 Green Lake Rd; tel: (250) 497-8267; fax: (250) 497-8073*, 5 km south of OK Falls bridge.

Deep blue Skaha Lake was once called Dog Lake, but early tourist promoters preferred the more mysterious Shuswap word for dog. The lake stretches 20 km from OK Falls (once Dog Town) north to Penticton. Hwy 97 climbs past the tiny town of Kaleden to **Okanagan Game Farm**, *9 km north of OK Falls; tel: (250) 497-5405,* open 0800–dusk daily, adults $10, children $7, with 120 species from ankoli to zebras.

The highway drops to the head of Skaha Lake and the Channel Parkway Bypass, which follows the channelised Okanagan River 8 km north to Okanagan Lake, bypassing Penticton.

PENTICTON

Tourist Information: Penticton Chamber of Commerce, *185 Lakeshore Dr., Penticton, BC V2A 1B7; tel: (800) 663-5052* or *(250) 493-4055; fax: (250) 492-6119.*

ACCOMMODATION

Budget–moderate motels face Skaha Lake and line *Lakeshore Dr.* and *Riverside Dr.* near Okanagan Lake. Chains include *BW, HI* and *TL.* Top waterfront choice is the

187

Okanagan Wine

Okanagan Valley farmers have been growing wine grapes for decades, but there were few high-quality *vinifera* varieties in the valley until the 1990s. The change was sparked by a 1988 provincial pull-out programme that encouraged growers to replace old vineyards in anticipation of the North American Free Trade Agreement that would eventually open BC to cheaper, higher quality wines from the USA. Designed to catapult BC onto the world wine scene, the programme worked. The province also revised antiquated winery licensing laws which traditionally favoured mass production over high quality. **Farm Wineries** may produce up to 45,000 litres of wine annually. At least 75% of the wine must be made from grapes grown on the farm, which must include at least 0.8 hectares of vineyards. **Estate Wineries**, which generally produce the best wines, must have at least 80 hectares of vineyards and may produce up to 180,000 litres of wine yearly. At least half of the grapes that go into an estate wine must come from the winery's own vineyards and all of the grapes must be grown in BC. Major wineries operate with few restrictions on capacity or source of grapes.

All three types of wineries may conduct tastings and sell their own product. Tasting is generally free, though some wineries charge a small fee (usually $2) for ice wine or other special products. Many wineries have outdoor picnic areas where visitors can enjoy the view (and a bottle of wine). Winery restaurants serve their own wines, competing products and beer. Wine prices are virtually identical at the winery, a winery restaurant and BC Liquor Stores. Expect to pay a little more in a privately owned Beer and Wine Store and about 50% above the BC Liquor price in restaurants.

Most BC wines carry a **VQA** (Vintners Quality Alliance) seal, Canada's answer to the French AOC or the Italian DOC wine appellation system. Although a VQA seal doesn't guarantee that the wine will be to every taste, it does mean that the wine meets specific growing

Clarion Lakeside Resort, *21 Lakeside Dr. W., Penticton, BC V2A 7M5; tel: (800) 663-9400 or (250) 493-8221; fax: (250) 493-0607*, on Okanagan Lake.

More spectacular is **God's Mountain Crest Chalet**, *RR2, S15, Comp 41, Penticton, BC V2A 6J7; tel: (250) 492-8252; fax: (250) 490-4800*, a whitewashed mountain villa perched above Skaha Lake. Both are moderate–expensive.

EATING AND DRINKING

The best (and most expensive) choices are **God's Mountain Crest Chalet** (reservation required) and **1912**, *Kaleden; tel: (250) 497-6868*. **Granny Bognars'**, *302 W. Eckhardt; tel: (250) 493-2711*, moderate–pricey, has an excellent local wine list and Northwest cuisine. **Theo's**, *687 Main St; tel: (250) 492-4019*, is a Greek winner.

Villa Rosa, *795 Westminster Ave W.; tel: (250) 490-9595*, pricey, and **Front Street Pasta Factory**, *75 Front St; tel: (250) 493-5666*, moderate, are the top Italian choices.

SIGHTSEEING

Long known for peaches and beaches, Penticton is capitalising on the Okanagan wine boom. The **British Columbia Wine Information Centre**, *888 Westminster Ave W.; tel: (250) 490-2006; fax: (250) 490-2003*, has one of the valley's best retail selections of BC wines. Equally popular is the **Tin Whistle Brewery**, *954 Eckhardt Ave W.; tel: (250) 770-1122*.

The grandest attraction is the **s.s. Sicamous**, *1099 Lakeshore Dr. W.; tel: (250) 492-0403*, open daily (mid June–mid Sept), Mon–Fri the rest of the year, a restored 72-m sternwheeler steamboat that

and production quality standards. VQA wines have also been vetted by a tasting panel from the British Columbia Wine Institute. But the lack of a VQA seal doesn't necessarily indicate lack of quality. Some very highly-regarded estate wineries don't submit their wines for VQA designation.

Most BC wine is produced by four dozen wineries in the Okanagan Valley. The south end of the valley, near Osoyoos, is a desert which gets less than 15cm of rain annually. The cooler and higher north end of the Valley, Kelowna and beyond, gets about 40cm each year. And while wineries are located throughout the Okanagan Valley, most of the vineyards are concentrated in the southern end between **Osoyoos** and **Okanagan Falls**.

Classic red grapes do best on the warmer south-facing slopes of the south valley. White wines are more common than reds because white grapes ripen more predictably in BC's cooler northern summers. Red grapes need more hot days to fully develop their natural sugars. The Okanagan's most prominent winery product is **ice wine**, made from grapes that have been picked and pressed while frozen. Freezing concentrates the grape sugars and flavours, producing wines that are extremely rich: without the honeyed sweetness common in late harvest wines. Because freezing also greatly reduces the amount of juice that can be pressed, ice wine is usually sold in half-bottles that cost several times more than ordinary wine.

The easiest introduction to BC wine is a visit to the **British Columbia Wine Information Centre**, *888 Westminster Ave W., Penticton, BC V2A 7K9; tel: (250) 490-2006; fax: (250) 490-2003,* or **The Wine Museum**, *1304 Ellis St, Kelowna, BC V1Y 1Z8; tel: (250) 868-0441; fax: (250) 868-9272.* Both offer easy explanations of how wine is made (though neither has a winery on premises), good suggestions for nearby wineries to visit and a better wine selection than local BC Liquor Stores. The **British Columbia Wine Institute**, *Suite 5, 1864 Spall Rd, Kelowna, BC V1Y 4R1; tel: (800) 661-2294 or (250) 762-4887; fax: (250) 862-8870,* has general information on BC wine and wine touring brochures covering the entire province.

189

once plied Lake Okanagan. **Penticton R.N. Atkinson Museum and Archives**, *785 Main St; tel: (250) 490-2451; fax: (250) 492-0440,* open Mon–Sat 1000–1700, has an excellent collection of First Nations and pioneer artefacts.

Penticton is also an outdoor activity centre, spurred by the **Ironman Canada Triathlon**, the last Sun in Aug. The Chamber of Commerce publishes an excellent map of area walking, cycling and skiing trails for the other 51 weeks. The **Skaha Bluffs**, east of Skaha Lake, offer excellent rock climbing. Skaha and Okanagan Lakes are busy water sport centres. A summer favourite is rafting the placid Okanagan River channel to Skaha Lake. Several operators set up temporary shop on Okanagan Lake; prices include ground transport back.

Apex Mountain Resort, *Box 1060, Penticton, BC V2A 7N7; tel: (250) 492-2880; fax: (250) 292-8622,* Nov–Mar, is 32 km southwest on *Green Mountain Rd.*

Hwy 97 follows the west side of Okanagan Lake northward from Penticton. The benches above are planted in vineyards. Much of the lakeshore is parkland with picnicking, fishing and boating, but no overnight accommodation.

SUMMERLAND

Tourist Information: Summerland Chamber of Commerce, *15600 Hwy 97 (at Thompson Rd), Summerland, BC V0H 1Z0; tel: (250) 494-2686; fax: (250) 494-4039.*

Summerland has been fruit country since the turn of the century. Alberta newspaperman John Moore Robinson subdivided Summerland (named after a hymn) in 1902, built an irrigation system and advertised heavily. Prairie farmers were only too happy to desert Alberta, Saskatchewan and Manitoba for lakeside orchards.

More than 100 fruit and vegetable varieties have been created at **Summerland Research Station Ornamental Gardens and Interpretive Centre**, *4200 Hwy 97 S., Box 1363, Summerland, BC V0H 1Z0; tel: (250) 494-7711*. Ornamental gardens open 0800–2230 daily; the interpretive centre opens afternoons Mon, Fri July–Aug. **Summerland Sweets**, *RR2, S69 (Canyon Rd); tel: (250) 494-0377*, open daily (July–Aug), Mon–Sat (Sept–June), is one of BC's largest producers of fruit syrups, jams and other sweets.

The Chamber of Commerce publishes a self-guided Summerland walking tour booklet featuring heritage buildings. More local history is preserved at **Summerland Museum**, *9521 Wharton St; tel: (250) 494-9395*, open daily 1300–1600 (June–Aug), Tues–Sat (Sept–May). The museum also publishes an excellent self-guided walking guide covering 4½ km of lakeshore.

Summerland's main attraction is **Kettle Valley Steam Railway**, *Box 1288; tel: (250) 494-8422; fax: (250) 494-8452*, open May–Oct, adults $9.75, youth $8.75, children $6.50, family $35. The KVSR runs on 16 km of the original Kettle Valley Railway (see pp. 57, 190). The train, powered by a 1924 Shay Steam Locomotive, offers stunning clifftop views of Okanagan Valley.

Okanagan Lake Provincial Park, *16 km north of Summerland; tel: (250) 494-6500*, has the largest campsite on the lake, 168 pitches. A lay-by 6 km north overlooks **Rattlesnake Island** and **Squally Point**. An underwater cave off the point is home to **Ogopogo**, a friendly prehistoric creature described in great detail by First Nations and early settlers, as well as current

residents. Real or not, Ogopogo is protected under the BC Wildlife Act.

PEACHLAND

Tourist Information: Peachland Museum, *5890 Beach Ave, Peachland, BC V0H 1X0; tel: (250) 767-3441*, open daily (July–Aug).

Gasthaus on the Lake, *5740 Beach Ave; tel: (250) 767-6625*, is a popular German restaurant.

KELOWNA

Tourist Information: Westbank & District Chamber of Commerce, *2375 Pamela Rd, Westbank, BC V4T 2H9; tel: (250) 768-3378; fax: (250) 768-3465*, and **Kelowna Visitors and Convention Bureau**, *544 Harvey Ave, Kelowna, BC V1Y 6C9; tel: (800) 663-4345 or (250) 861-1515; fax: (250) 861-3624*.

ACCOMMODATION

Kelowna is the largest population centre in the Okanagan with the largest supply of accommodation. Chains include BW, CS, CI, DI, Hd, SM and S8. Prices are lower in **Westbank**, south of the floating bridge across Okanagan Lake.

The most scenic choice is moderate **Wicklow Bed & Breakfast**, *1454 Green Bay Rd, Westbank, BC V4T 2B8; tel: (250) 768-1330; fax: (250) 768-1335*, overlooking Okanagan Lake. The **Okanagan Bed & Breakfast Association**, *Box 5135, Kelowna, BC V1Y 8T9; tel: (250) 764-2124; fax: (250) 764-2892*, has two dozen members.

EATING AND DRINKING

Best Westbank choices are **Cafe Soleil**, *2424 Main St; tel: (250) 768-1030*, continental, and **Ripples**, *2437A Main St; tel: (250) 768-9961*, Italian, both moderate. Good Kelowna choices include **Divinos**,

190

594 Bernard Ave; tel: (250) 860-8477, moderate continental, **Oodles Pasta House**, *538 Leon Ave; tel: (250) 862-8655,* budget–moderate Italian, and the **Woodfire Bakery**, *2041 Harvey; tel: (250) 762-2626,* cheap–budget breakfast and lunch.

SIGHTSEEING

Kelowna (pronounced *kah-loan-ah*) began as **Father Pandosy's Mission**, *Benvoulin and Casorso Rds,* open daily (Apr–Oct), founded in 1859 by an Oblate missionary. Restored log buildings provide a vivid example of early Okanagan life. The townsite was shifted to Okanagan Lake in 1892, the better to move supplies and people by steamboat.

The town grew comfortably with logging, fruit orchards and holiday homes along sparkling lakeshore beaches that always seemed to bask in summer-like sunshine. In 1990, Hwy 97C, the Okanagan Connector from the Coquihalla Highway, put Kelowna just 4 driving hours from Vancouver. The population exploded, as did restaurants, sports and cultural activities. **City Park**, stretching 1 km from the floating bridge to the large white sculpture, *The Sail,* at the foot of *Bernard St,* is a pleasant introduction to the deep blue lake and comfortable brick buildings beneath gracefully spreading trees.

BC Orchard Industry and Wine Museum, *1304 Ellis St; tel: (250) 763-*

0433, details Kelowna's two leading industries. **Kelowna Centennial Museum**, *470 Queensway; tel: (250) 763-2417,* includes an 1861 trading post, an Interior Salish pit house and Kelowna's first radio station. **Okanagan Orchards**, *2755 KLO Rd; tel: (250) 762-8092,* Canada's largest, is open for tours July–Sept.

Top winery tours: **Mission Hill Winery**, *1730 Mission Hill Rd; tel: (250) 768-7611; fax: (250) 768-2044,* with award-winning wines and spectacular views across Okanagan Lake; **Quail's Gate Vineyard Estate Winery**, *3303 Boucherie Rd; tel: (250) 769-4451; fax: (250) 769-3451,* for stunning ice wines; and **Summerhill Estate Winery**, *4870 Chute Lake Rd; tel: (250) 764-8000; fax: (250) 764-2598,* BC's largest sparkling wine producer.

Check at the Kelowna VCB for a map and directions to the KVR railbed through **Myra Canyon**. The rough road is *usually* passable by passenger cars. The rails are long gone, but the gently sloping railbed (2% maximum grade) and trestles are well maintained for walkers and cyclists. **Big White Ski Resort**, *Box 2039, Stn R, Kelowna, BC V1X 4K5; tel: (250) 765-3101; fax: (250) 765-8200,* 24 km east on Hwy 33, at 2319m, is BC's highest ski resort. The skiing is fabulous in good weather, but frequent poor visibility earns the nickname 'Big White Out'.

KELOWNA–KAMLOOPS

It takes less than half a day to drive the 200 km from the rolling vineyards and fruit orchards around Kelowna to the green forests of the northern Okanagan and the dry uplands of the Thompson River Valley at Kamloops. From Kelowna to Vernon, the highway runs between the long expanse of Okanagan Lake and a chain of smaller glacial lakes. Cattle ranches dominate from Vernon eastward to Kamloops, a region of tiny towns sandwiched between enormous cattle ranches and dense forests. For a more leisurely look at the north end of the Okanagan Valley, overnight in Vernon.

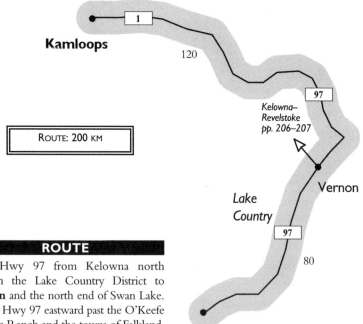

Kamloops

1

120

97

Kelowna–
Revelstoke
pp. 206–207

ROUTE: 200 KM

Vernon

Lake
Country

97

80

Kelowna

ROUTE

Take Hwy 97 from Kelowna north through the Lake Country District to **Vernon** and the north end of Swan Lake. Follow Hwy 97 eastward past the O'Keefe Historic Ranch and the towns of Falkland, Westworld, Monte Lake and Monte Creek to TransCanada Hwy 1. Take Hwy 1 east to Kamloops.

BUSES

There are two bus journeys a day from Kelowna to Kamloops at 0900 and 1400, taking 2¾ hrs. See OTT table 110.

LAKE COUNTRY DISTRICT

Hwy 97 leaves Kelowna through a spreading strip of shopping malls. **Far West Factory Outlet**, *2469 Hwy 98 N., Kelowna, BC V1X 4J2; tel: (250) 860-9010; fax: (250) 860-0145,* has the best buys on outdoor gear in the Okanagan Valley. To tour the commercial forests that cover most of the region above the lower valley slopes, contact the **Interior Lumber Manufacturers' Association**, *#360-1855 Kirschner Rd, Kelowna, BC V1Y 4N7; tel: (250) 860-9663; fax: (250) 860-0009.*

The first community north is **Winfield**, slowly being engulfed by Kelowna's sprawl. The **Lake Country Heritage and Cultural Society**, *Okanagan Centre Rd W., Box 25, Winfield, BC V0H 2C0,* open Tues–Sat 0900–1630 (May–Sept), offers memorabilia from the Lake Country District. **Gray Monk Estate Winery**, *1055 Camp Rd, Box 63, Okanagan Centre, BC V0H 1P0; tel: (800) 663-4205 or (250) 766-3168; fax: (250) 766-3390,* open daily 1000–1700 (May–Oct), Mon–Sat 1100–1700 (Nov–Apr), is one of BC's oldest and best-known wineries. Excellent free tours are conducted hourly 1100–1600 (mid May–Oct). The tiny town of **Okanagan Centre** offers magnificent hillside views westward over Okanagan Lake.

Lake Country takes its name from the chain of three lakes, **Ellison**, **Wood** and **Kalmalka**, that lie just east of Hwy 97. Like Okanagan Lake, the trio were carved by glaciers that retreated from the area about 10,000 years ago. Nearly rectangular Wood Lake and much larger Kalmalka Lake offer good fishing for Kokanee and rainbow trout.

A narrow land bridge separates Wood and Kalmalka Lakes. The highway climbs into the hills overlooking Kalmalka Lake to the **Kalmalka Lake Viewpoint**, a large lay-by 8 km north of the land bridge. Tourist brochures call Kalmalka the 'Lake of a Thousand Colours' for its ever-changing hues. The sparkling pools of emerald green are said to be the work of elusive (and illusive) Kalooey bears swishing their tails in the normally blue waters.

The lake was actually named for an amorous Okanagan First Nations leader, Kalmalka, who lived at the head of the lake during the early days of White settlement. The lay-by offers panoramic views north to the Coldstream Valley and eastward into the Monashee Mountains.

One km north is **College Way**, the turn-off for **Kalmalka Lake Provincial Park**, *tel: (250) 494-6500.* There is no camping at the park, but the surrounding area is prime nesting and feeding habitat for a wide variety of waterfowl. Wildflowers fill the hillsides above the car park with colour in May. The open hillsides are also known for rattlesnakes. The shy snakes would rather flee than bite, but will strike if cornered. **Kekuli Bay Provincial Park**, *off Kalmalka Lakeview Dr.; tel: (250) 494-6500,* is also day-use only, but has excellent boat-launching facilities. The park is extremely busy at mid-summer weekends. Continue 10 km north to Vernon.

193

VERNON

Tourist Information: Vernon Tourism, *6326 Hwy 97 N., Box 520, Vernon, BC V1T 6M4; tel: (250) 542-1415; fax: (250) 542-3256.* To book hotels and golf, ski or cycling packages, *tel: (800) 665-0795.*

ACCOMMODATION

Vernon is the hub of the North Okanagan. Chains include *BW* and *TL*. Most motels are clustered at the south and north end of town along Hwy 97. Older and less expensive choices are at the south end, newer and chain choices are at the north end.

EATING AND DRINKING

Though less urbanised than Kelowna, Vernon has a wide variety of restaurants. **The Italian Kitchen Company**, *2916*

30th Ave; tel: (250) 558-7899, moderate, is the best Italian choice. **Café Asiago's**, *3202 31st Ave; tel: (250) 542-3970,* moderate, combines Italian with Northwest touches. The **Mongolian Barbecue**, *4300 27th St; tel: (250) 558-3558,* serves budget–moderate Mongolian-inspired stir fries.

SIGHTSEEING

Vernon sits at the confluence of four valleys at the head of Kalmalka Lake. Pleasant Valley, the largest, stretches north to **Sicamous** (see p. 201). The town began as *Listip Moschin,* 'jumping over place', a meeting and trading point along an aboriginal route between the Shuswap Lakes to the north and the Columbia River to the south-east. The site became a transportation hub for Hudson's Bay Company fur traders and all who followed.

The first successful White settler was Cornelius O'Keefe. He found natural meadows at the north end of Okanagan Lake filled with bunch grass 'higher than a horse's belly' while driving cattle from Oregon north to Cariboo gold fields in the 1860s. Seven years later, O'Keefe had pre-empted land, imported breeding stock and set about becoming the interior's first cattle baron. His restored ranch complex, 12 km north-east of Vernon, has become a popular cowboy-era museum (see p. 195).

The city that grew to service the O'Keefe and other ranches was named for early settler George Forbes Vernon, the chief commissioner of Lands and Works. In 1891, Vernon sold 5376 hectares to Lord Aberdeen, Scottish émigré and future Governor-General of Canada. Aberdeen renamed the ranch Coldstream and allowed his somewhat eccentric wife to persuade him of the value of orchards over cattle. Their Coldstream Ranch grew to become one of the largest fruit producers

in the British Empire. When large-scale irrigation was introduced in 1908, orchards quickly supplanted cattle as the primary crop. By 1917, Vernon was shipping more than 1000 boxcars of apples and miscellaneous fruit yearly despite World War I labour shortages. **Dawson Orchards**, *3097 Davison Rd, S-2, C-10, RR#4 ; tel: (250) 549-3266; fax: (250) 549-2440,* open mid July–Dec, offer free orchard and garden tours daily.

Much of Vernon's original town centre remains, its brick buildings renovated for more modern use. Vernon Tourism has free self-guided walking tour maps. Shopping malls and other newer buildings are concentrated in the north end of town.

The **Greater Vernon Museum and Archives**, *Civic Centre Complex, 3009 32nd Ave; tel: (250) 542-3142,* displays local artefacts. **Sen'klip Cultural Interpretive Centre and Theatre Company**, *west side of Okanagan Lake on Westside Rd, 2902 29th Ave; tel: (250) 549-2921; fax: (250) 542-3707,* concentrates on Okanagan First Nations history and culture. The **Vernon Art Gallery**, *3228 31st Ave; tel: (250) 545-3173; fax: (250) 545-9096,* focuses on local and BC artists. **Okanagan Opal**, *junction of Hwys 97 and 97A, Box 298; tel: (250) 542-5173; fax: (250) 542-1103,* offer weekend opal-digging tours June–Sept, $30 per person per day, and free opal cutting and polishing demonstrations all year.

Vernon is also becoming an outdoor activities centre. **Silver Star Mountain**, *20 km north-east on Silver Star Rd (48th Ave), Box 3002, Silver Star Mountain, BC V1B 3M1; tel: (800) 663-4431 or (250) 542-0224; fax: (250) 542-1236,* is a Victorian Village ski area turned four-season resort. In winter, Silver Star has 84 runs down 760 vertical metres covered by an average of 570 cm of snow. Nordic skiers have 37 km of groomed trails linked with another 50 km of track at the adjacent **Sovereign Lake Cross Country Ski Area**, *Box 1231, Vernon, BC V1T 6N6; tel: (250) 558-3036.*

In summer, most ski runs are open for mountain biking. There is also an extensive system of walking paths leading down from the top of the chair-lift. Accommodation, restaurants and all other facilities are open year-round.

There are hundreds of kilometres of cycling and mountain biking routes in the valley and up into surrounding mountains. For less vigorous sightseeing, **Skywalker Balloons**, *16709 Maki Rd, Winfield, BC V0H 2C0; tel: (250) 766-2804 or (250) 766-3744,* offer hot air balloon trips year-round. Top golf course in the valley is the 27-hole **Spallumcheen Golf & Country Club**, *9401 Hwy 97 N., Vernon, BC V1T 6M8; tel: (250) 545-5811; fax: (250) 549-7476.*

VERNON TO KAMLOOPS

Hwy 97 continues 5 km north along the shores of **Swan Lake** to **Swan Lake Junction**, the junction with Hwy 97A to Sicamous (see p.201). Hwy 97 continues west past the **Swan Lake Bird Sanctuary**, *north end of Swan Lake,* home to white geese, swans and herons, to the historic **O'Keefe Ranch**, *Box 955, Vernon, BC V1T 6M8; tel/fax: (250) 542-7868,* open daily 0900–1700 (mid May–Thanksgiving). Founded in 1867 by one-time cattle drovers Cornelius O'Keefe and Thomas Greenhow, the O'Keefe Ranch grew to more than 8000 hectares before being sold off for orchards in 1907. What remained of O'Keefe's cattle empire was run by Cornelius' son Tierney O'Keefe into the late 1960s.

Among the restored buildings are O'Keefe's first log house (1876), opulent Victorian-inspired O'Keefe mansion (1886, still a private residence), St Anne's Roman Catholic church (1889) and a general store with the Okanagan Valley's first post office (1872). Other buildings moved to the ranch or rebuilt from period materials house a cowboy and ranching museum, working blacksmithy, early school, antique farm equipment and other exhibits. The ranch also raises four-horned goats and other antique farm animals that are no longer raised commercially and are on the verge of extinction.

Westside Rd turns south 1 km beyond the ranch to follow the western shore of Okanagan Lake. Hwy 97 climbs through increasingly green hills toward the **Salmon River**. The highway runs through a patchwork of small farms, cattle ranches and dense forests separating the isolated towns of **Falkland** and **Westwold** to **Monte Lake** and a village of the same name, then follows **Monte Creek** downhill through increasingly arid country toward Hwy 1 and the **Thompson River**. The last major patch of green is **Duck Meadow**, a 90-hectare wetland that was drained for hayfields in the 1870s and reclaimed in the 1990s. The restored marsh is an important stop on the Pacific Flyway and an excellent spot for birding in all seasons.

The town of **Monte Creek** marks the junction of Hwys 97 and 1. Turn west toward Kamloops 7 km to a lay-by and Stop of Interest near the former Monte Creek railway station. 'Gentleman Bandit' Bill Miner robbed a Canadian Pacific train in 1906, one of Canada's most famous train robberies. Miner, an American, picked the wrong train and netted just $15. He was caught after an 80-km horseback chase, tried in Kamloops and sentenced to life in the BC Penitentiary. Miner escaped to the US in 1907; his story resurfaced in a 1980's Hollywood epic, *The Grey Fox.*

TransCanada Hwy 1 follows the **South Thompson River** westward through a narrow, desert-like valley. Irrigation has turned much of the valley floor and surrounding hillsides green, but falling elevation brings lower rainfall and higher summer temperatures. The low black tents covering roadside fields shade ginseng, one of BC's newest and most lucrative crops. Fields are closed to the public, but **Sunmore**, *925 McGill Pl., Kamloops, BC V2C 6N9; tel: (250) 374-3017; fax: (250) 374-3011*, offer free tours Mon–Fri.

The north side of the Thompson River is largely agricultural. The more accessible south bank is a series of hamlets, housing estates and shopping malls that blend imperceptibly into Greater Kamloops. **Kamloops Wildlife Park**, *Box 698, Kamloops, BC V2C 5L7; tel: (250) 573-3262; fax: (250) 573-2406*, open 0800 daily, adults $6.50, youth $4.50, children $3.50, has 65 species of local and endangered animal species on display, from black and grizzly bears to zebras.

KAMLOOPS

Tourist Information: Tourism Kamloops, *1290 W. TransCanada Hwy (exit 368), Kamloops, BC V2C 6R3; tel: (800) 662-1994 or (250) 374-3377; fax: (250) 828-9500*, open daily, and **High Country Tourism**, *#2 1490 Pearson Pl., Kamloops, BC V1S 1J9; tel: (250) 372-7770; fax: (250) 828-4656*.

ACCOMMODATION

Kamloops is BC's principal interior city. Chains include *BW, CS, DI, Hd, HI, Rm, S8* and *TL*. Less expensive motels are concentrated along Hwy 1 between exits 366 and 369 and along Hwy 5. Moderate–expensive choices line *Columbia St* (exit 369) as it twists downhill from Hwy 1 into the city centre. Moderate **Ramada Inn**,

555 W. Columbia St, Kamloops, BC V2C 1K7; tel: (800) 663-2832 or (250) 374-0358; fax: (250) 374-0691, is good value in a convenient location. **South Thompson Inn & Guest Ranch**, *15 mins east of town off Hwy 1, RR2 Site 12, Comp 25, Kamloops, BC V2C 2J3; tel: (800) 797-7713 or (250) 573-3777; fax: (250) 573-2853*, expensive, is a Kentucky-styled resort set on a 26-hectare horse ranch next to **Rivershore Golf & Country Club**. Somewhat further removed is **Sun Peaks Resort**, *45 mins north off Hwy 5, 3180 Creekside Way, Sun Peaks, BC V0E 1Z1; tel: (800) 333-9112 or (250) 578-7878; fax: (250) 578-7865*, expensive–pricey, with skiing, golf, walking and mountain biking.

EATING AND DRINKING

Kamloops has dozens of choices, from familiar fast-food chains to pricey dinner houses. The best selection is in the city centre on *Victoria, Seymour* and *Paul Sts*. **Stockmen's Restaurant**, *540 Victoria St; tel: (250) 372-2281*, is a moderate mainstay for steaks in BC's biggest cowboy town. **Apollon**, *369 Victoria St; tel: (250) 372-5852*, is a good choice for moderate Greek fare. **Bagel Street Café**, *428 Victoria St; tel: (250) 372-9322*, has cheap–budget breakfast and lunch choices. **Two River Junction**, *625 Pleasant St; tel: (250) 314-3939*, pricey, offers an 1880s musical revue with dinner. Advance booking required.

SIGHTSEEING

Kamloops is BC's fifth largest city in population and number one in area, spreading over 31,000 hectares of the Thompson River Valley. The city sprawls across the convergence of the South Thompson and North Thompson Rivers, which flow westward as the Thompson River to meet the Fraser River at Lytton (see p.266).

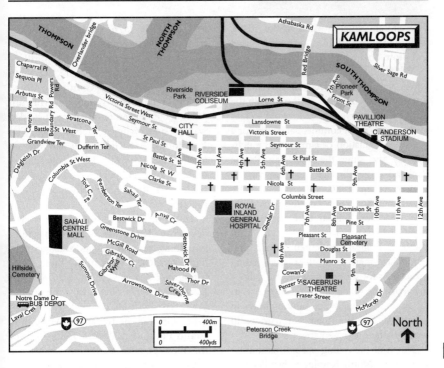

Geography gives Kamloops its name – *kamloopa* is a Secwepemc (Shuswap) native word that means 'where the rivers meet'. The old town centre on the low southern banks of the South Thompson looks across to what has been a major Secwepemc settlement for 5000 years and is now the **Kamloops Indian Reserve**, *315 Yellowhead Hwy; tel: (250) 828-9700; fax: (250) 372-8833.*

Secwepemc Museum & Heritage Park, *355 Yellowhead Hwy, Kamloops, BC V2H 1H1; tel: (250) 828-9801; fax: (250) 372-1127,* is a combination museum, university, cultural and public education centre designed to bring Secwepemc culture to the world. The museum offers a distinctly First Nations' spin on local history, with excellent displays depicting the Secwepemc Nation and its territory that once stretched north to Soda Creek (se p.

321), east to the Rockies and west to the Fraser River. The Kamloops Band is one of 17 contemporary Secwepemc bands, and one of the most prosperous thanks to agricultural and industrial holdings. The Heritage Park covers a riverside archaeological site that has been occupied since about 3000 BC. Seasonal programmes include native food plants, a salmon-fishing station, song, dance, storytelling and theatre, and reconstructions of several different types of dwellings for summer and winter use. A small restored marsh attracts waterfowl spring–autumn.

St Joseph's Church, *Kamloops Band Reserve, Chilcotin Rd west of Hwy 5; tel: (250) 374-7323,* is an Oblate mission church first built in 1846. The present church was completed in 1900 and restored in 1985, complete with interior decorations in sparkling primary colours.

The church cemetery dates to the 1840s, with gravestone displays growing larger and more ornate into the 1990s.

White history first touched Kamloops when the HBC arrived in 1812. Fort Kamloops was an oasis for fur traders in the early 19th century, a depot for gold seekers in the 1860, and a commercial centre for a growing population of farmers and ranchers. By the time the Canadian Pacific Railway came through on the way to Vancouver in 1886, government were already building a new courthouse and citizens were launching an unsuccessful bid to wrest the provincial capital away from Victoria. English gentlemen farmers and remittance men spent their days raising gamecocks for shooting parties and galloping across the rolling hills in scarlet coats to the sounds of hounds and hunting horns in search of foxes – their compatriots in nearby Ashcroft chased coyotes.

Much of the rolling upland foxhunting country of North Kamloops has become housing estates, but 15,000 hectares have been preserved as **Lac du Bois Grasslands Provincial Park**, *BC Parks Thompson River District, 1210 McGill Rd; tel: (250) 851-3000,* a visually stunning area with no facilities and no paved roads. The **Eastern Section**, *off Westsyde Rd on the western side of the North Thompson River,* is largely untouched grasslands dotted with lakes and occasional stands of trees. The **Western Section**, *off Tranquille Rd beyond Tranquille,* is a series of rugged mountain canyons overlooking the Thompson River and Kamloop Lake. Wildflower displays are spectacular May–July, depending on elevation and exposure, and easily accessible on excellent gravel roads.

Kamloops Museum and Archives, *207 Seymour St, Kamloops, BC V2C 2E7;* *tel: (250) 828-3576,* depict local history from the Secwepemc through the early 20th century. Dozens of graceful turn-of-the-century structures dot the old town centre, including a 1909 courthouse turned youth hostel. The Kamloops Museum publishes excellent (and free) self-guided walking and cycling tour brochures. The **Kamloops Art Gallery**, *in the Museum building; tel: (250) 828-3543,* concentrates on local artists and publishes a free walking guide to half a dozen local commercial galleries.

Much of the south bank of the river is devoted to **Riverside Park**, with tennis, swimming, rose gardens and walking trails. The sternwheeler **Wanda Sue**, *2472 Thompson Dr., Kamloops, BC V2C 4L1; tel: (250) 374-7447,* offers daily Thompson River cruises from the park mid May–Sept. On the north shore, **McArthur Island Park**, *tel: (250) 828-3580,* is one of the most popular recreation sites in the city, with swimming, tennis, playgrounds, walking and cycling paths, baseball, golf, and more.

Recreation is big business in Kamloops: the city has 84 baseball diamonds, 73 football pitches, 5 ice arenas, 40 gymnasiums, 7 golf courses, 53 tennis courts and a 5000-seat coliseum. That's in addition to the 300-some lakes within an hour's drive, skiing at **Sun Peaks**, *3180 Creekside Way, Sun Peaks, BC V0E 121; tel: (800) 333-9112 or (250) 578-7878; fax: (250) 578-7865,* and more family-orientated **Harper Mountain**, *2042 Valleyview Dr., Kamloops, BC V2C 4C5; tel: (250) 372-2119; snowphone (250) 828-0336.* Both resorts offer alpine and Nordic skiing; Sun Peaks also has an extensive schedule of golf and other summer activities.

KAMLOOPS–REVELSTOKE

This 215-km run along TransCanada Hwy 1 can be finished in an easy morning, climbing from the Fraser River watershed over the Monashee Mountains and into the Columbia River Basin at Revelstoke. Schedule at least one overnight in Sorrento or Sicamous to explore side roads along the lakes. Or, follow thousands of Canadians who hire houseboats by the day or the week to explore shorelines that no road is ever likely to touch.

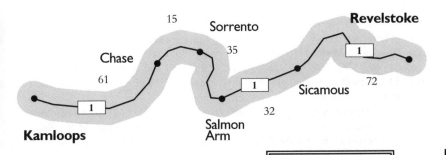

ROUTE: 215 KM

ROUTE

Follow TransCanada Hwy 1 from Kamloops to Revelstoke. Take the Kelowna–Kamloops route (see pp.192–198) in reverse to **Monte Creek** and continue east along the South Thompson River. The high cliffs on the north side of the river are the remains of ancient glacial lakeshores that have been eroded into columns called **hoodoos**. The oldest human remains in BC, a man trapped in a mud flow about 8500 years ago, were found at **Gore Creek**, near the north end of the bridge at Pritchard.

BUSES

Greyhound Lines of Canada operate 3 trips a day, taking 3½–4 hrs. OTT table 118.

CHASE

Tourist Information: Chase and

District Chamber of Commerce, *400 Shuswap Ave, Chase, BC V0E 1M0; tel: (250) 679-8432; fax: (250) 649-3120.*

ACCOMMODATION

Moderate–expensive **Quaaout Lodge**, *Box 1215, Chase, BC V0E 1M0; tel: (800) 663-4303 or (250) 679-3090; fax: (250) 679-3039,* is a lakeside resort near Chase. Budget–moderate motels include **Chase Country Inn and RV Park**, *807 Cedar Ave, Chase, BC V0E 1M0; tel: (800) 921-9311 or (250) 679-3323,* and **Overlander Motel**, *181 Shuswap Ave, Chase; tel: (250) 649-8633.*

SIGHTSEEING

Chase began in 1865 as a ranching and lumber town on the shores of Little

Shuswap Lake. **Chase Museum & Archives**, *1042 Shuswap Ave; tel: (250) 679-8847,* open daily June–Labour Day in the former Blessed Sacrament Church, is overflowing with early memorabilia, from the office of Chase's first physician to the mahogany bar from an early hotel. The town is better known as the western terminus of the Shuswap Lake system. Canoeists put into the South Thompson River at Chase for the easy 58-km trip downstream to Kamloops. The municipal beach is busy; local Nordic ski trails are nearly as popular in winter. The **Chase Bridge** crosses the South Thompson River to **Niskonlith Lake Provincial Park**, *1210 McGill Rd, Kamloops, BC V2C 6N6; tel: (250) 851-3000,* 14 km north on a good gravel road, with 30 pitches and good rainbow trout fishing. Wildflower displays around the lake are spectacular May–June.

Just east of town is the **Chase Falls** lay-by with a short path leading to the scenic falls. A herd of Rocky Mountain bighorn sheep from **Squilax Mountain** is often seen on the bluffs south of the highway. View Little Shuswap Lake from the **Jade Mountain Lookout**, 2 km east. The **North Shuswap Bridge** crosses the **Little River** between Little Shuswap Lake and far larger **Shuswap Lake**. The 4-km long river is renowned for trout fishing in Feb, Mar and Oct and was once a major fishing and trading spot for Secwepemc (Shuswap) First Nations.

CHASE TO SORRENTO

Squilax-Anglemont Rd runs north from the bridge to **Roderick Haig-Brown Provincial Park**, *1265 Dalhousie Dr., Kamloops, BC V2C 5Z5; tel: (250) 828-4494,* on the 11-km long **Adams River**, flowing from **Adams Lake** into Shuswap Lake. More than a million sockeye migrate from the Pacific Ocean up the Fraser,

Thompson, South Thompson and Little Rivers in Oct every 4 years (1998, 2002, etc.). Smaller numbers swim the 485-km in intervening years. By the time the fish reach the Adams River, their silvery bodies have turned bright red with olive green heads. The males develop a marked hump behind the head, prompting the common names *humpback salmon* or *humpies*.

The park protects habitat and spawning beds along the Adams River, also used by Chinook, coho and pink salmon. Observation decks provide a clear view of spawning; naturalists are on duty during major sockeye runs. The run attracts feasting crowds of bears, eagles and gulls. Whitetail and mule deer, beavers, otters, mink and squirrels are permanent park residents.

One km beyond the North Shuswap Bridge is the tiny town of **Squilax** (the Secwepemc word for bear), noted for a budget hostel housed in three 1940s Canadian National Railway cabooses and an old general store that is home to one of two local colonies of rare Yuma bats. About 600 of the minuscule (6g) bats migrate to the store's attic each spring to bear their young, then leave in autumn to hibernate in an unknown location.

SORRENTO

Tourist Information: Sorrento District Chamber of Commerce, *TransCanada Hwy, Box 7, Sorrento BC V0E 2W0; tel: (250) 675-3515; fax: (250) 675-3516,* **Visitor InfoCentre** open July–Aug.

Sorrento is a well-established resort community with summer homes, motels and family resorts spread along several kilometres of highway.

SORRENTO TO SALMON ARM

Hwy 1 climbs south from Sorrento through the hamlet of **Balmoral** to

Canoe Point Rd, leading down to lakeside **Sunnybrae Provincial Park** and **Herald Provincial Park**; *tel: (250) 851-3000*. Sunnybrae has picnicking, swimming, beaches and fishing, Herald has it all plus camping and a boat ramp. A short trail from Herald Park leads to **Margaret Falls** on **Reinecker Creek**. The circular depressions west of the creek are the remains of *kekuli*, circular pit houses used by the Secwepemc in winter. The ruins of the pioneer Herald family farm buildings are also in the park. **Paradise Point**, 2 km beyond Herald Park, is part of **Shuswap Lake Provincial Marine Park**. Most park units are accessible only by water.

The highway emerges high above Shuswap Lake with broad views of the lake and rich agricultural land surrounding **Salmon Arm**. On the way into town, detour to **Gort's Gouda Cheese Farm**, *1470 50th St S.W., Salmon Arm, BC; tel: (250) 832-4274*, tours Mon and Fri 1400, producers of fine Gouda, feta, quark and yogurt cheeses.

SALMON ARM

Tourist Information: Salmon Arm & District Chamber of Commerce, *751 Marine Park Dr. N.E., Box 999, Salmon Arm, BC V1E 4P2; tel: (250) 832-2230; fax: (250) 832-8382*, open daily; **Shuswap Lakes Tourism Association**, *Box 1670, Salmon Arm, BC V1E 4P7; tel: (250) 832-5200; fax: (250) 832-8382*; and **Shuswap Lake Houseboat Association**, *Box 318, Sicamous V1E 2V0; tel: (250) 836-2450; fax: (250) 836-4824*.

ACCOMMODATION

Chains include *BW, CS, S8* and *TL*. **Salmon Arm Bay Houseboats**, *Box 1480, Salmon Arm, BC V1E 4P6; tel: (800) 665-7782* or *(250) 832-2745; fax: (250) 836-4824*, hire houseboats.

SIGHTSEEING

White settlers arrived with the Canadian Pacific Railway in 1885. The town was named for the immense salmon runs which once made their way into the lake arm from the Pacific Ocean, but the salmon disappeared when the Fraser River was blocked by railway construction at Hells Gate in 1913 (see p.265). **R. J. Haney Heritage Park & Museum**, *Hwy 97B, 4 km south, Box 1642; tel: (250) 832-5243*, open Wed–Sun 1000–1600 (May–Aug), includes the local museum, heritage buildings and a creekside walking path.

Salmon Arm is a prosperous fruit and dairy centre with a burgeoning outdoor recreation sector. At least 150 bird species nest around the mouth of **Salmon River**. Watch Clark's and western grebe breeding displays Apr–June. Best birding is from the **Salmon Arm Bay Wharf**, curving out from **Rotary Peace Park**, lakeside across from the Chamber of Commerce.

SALMON ARM TO SICAMOUS

Hwy 1 follows Shuswap Lake eastward. The Hwy 97B junction is 4 km east, with access to **Haney Heritage House, Larch Hills Cross Country Ski Area** (150 km of groomed Nordic ski track and summer walking paths), **Enderby, Vernon** and the **Okanagan Valley** (see pp.185–191). **Canoe** is the dormitory town for Salmon Arm. Credit the local wood mill for the smoky haze that sometimes obscures lake vistas. Shuswap Lake's expanse is best seen from **Shuswap Rest Area**, a picnic area 15 km east of Canoe.

SICAMOUS

Travel Information: Sicamous and District Chamber of Commerce, *1138 Riverside Ave (at Main St), Box 346, Sicamous, BC V0E 2V0; tel: (250) 836-3313; fax: (250) 836-4368*.

ACCOMMODATION

Motels and resorts line Hwy 1 and Hwy 97A from Vernon (see p. 193). Best value is the **Sicamous Inn**, *east of Hwy 97A junction, Box 910, Sicamous, BC V0E 2V0; tel: (800) 485-7698 or (250) 836-4117; fax: (250) 836-3116.*

Sicamous calls itself Canada's houseboat capital for the 300-plus houseboats available for hire Mar–Oct. Houseboats, essentially RVs on pontoons, sleep 4–12 with complete kitchen and ensuite facilities. Neither experience nor licence is required to hire a houseboat, and it is difficult to lose one's way on the narrow Shuswap Lake complex. **Shuswap Lake Houseboat Association**, *Box 318, Sicamous V1E 2V0; tel: (250) 836-2450; fax. (250) 836-4824,* has hire and holiday information.

SIGHTSEEING

Originally a railway construction camp, Sicamous, *narrow* or *squeezed in the middle* in Secwepemc, has become a resort community along the **Shuswap Narrows** between **Mara Lake** and **Shuswap Lake**. The four arms of the Shuswap Lake complex resemble a rather ragged *H*, hemmed in by the 2200-m Monashee Mountains. More than 1000 km of shoreline ranges from sheer cliffs and treacherous rock slides to golden sandy beaches such as **Finlayson Park**, north of the Hwy 1 bridge.

Short of hiring a houseboat, the best way to see Shuswap Lake is with **Shuswap Lake Ferry Service**, *Box 370; tel: (250) 836-2200,* adults $16–25, children $8–$16. The sternwheeler *m.v. Phoebe Ann* carries 40 passengers, the barge *m.v. Stephanie* hauls cars and freight as well as passengers. Both vessels sail year-round to **Seymour Arm**, the north-eastern extension of the lake. The *Phoebe Ann* cruises to **Cinnemousin Narrows**, the crossbar in Shuswap's *H*-shape, July–Aug. With caution

and advance booking, it is possible to drive the gravel roads from Squilax to Seymour Arm and take the barge to Sicamous.

SICAMOUS TO REVELSTOKE

Hwy 1 follows the **Eagle River** east from Sicamous. Local travellers and tour coaches alike stop at **'d' Dutchmen Dairy**, *1 km east of Sicamous; tel: (250) 836-4304,* with 50 flavours of what may be BC's finest commercial ice-cream. **Eagle River Nature Park**, *10 km east,* is popular for walking and Nordic skiing through an ancient cedar grove. **Yard Creek Provincial Park**, *tel: (250) 851-2000,* is one of the most popular stopping points on the Trans-Canada Highway, with 90 pitches and pleasant trails through old-growth rain forest. One km east is **Eagle River Trout & Char**, *Box 97, Malakwa, BC V0E 2J0; tel: (250) 836-4245; fax: (250) 836-4797,* a trout and arctic char fish farm. The fish market sells outstanding smoked trout and char, tasty additions to standard picnic fare.

A stone cairn at the large lay-by at **Craigellachie**, 11 km east, celebrates the driving of the last spike in the Canadian Pacific Railway in 1885. An information display and railway souvenir gift shop are open in summer, railway traffic passes all year. The **Eagle River Fish Hatchery**, 4 km east, offers daily self-guided tours of Chinook and coho ponds. Just beyond is **Beardale Castle Miniatureland**; *tel: (250) 836-2268,* open 0900–dusk (May–Sept), adults $5, children $2.75, miniature German, Swiss and Canadian villages and a railway. **Enchanted Forest**, *Box 2938, Revelstoke, BC V0e 2S0; tel: (250) 837-9477,* open 0800–dusk (mid May–mid Sept), adults $5, children $3, has fairy-tale figurines and ruins arranged along a forest walking trail. The Forest is opposite **Griffin Lake**, the first in a string of five glacial lakes that drain into the Eagle River.

Next in line is **Three Valley Lake**. At the eastern end is **Three Valley Gap**, *Box 860, Revelstoke, BC V0E 2S0; tel: (250) 837-2109; fax: (250) 837-5220*, a moderate motel with a 'ghost town' of BC historic buildings. **Victor Lake**, 4 km east, has a pleasant picnic area and information sign describing railway surveyor Walter Moberly's discovery of Eagle Pass by tracking eagles in flight. Moberly's discovery opened the way to Vancouver for the CPR. The highway climbs another 2 km to **Summit Lake**, the divide between the Fraser and Columbia River watersheds with a good view of railway tunnels. The steep drop down the eastern side of the Monashees ends at Hwy 23, which runs south along **Upper Arrow Lake**. Just east of the Columbia River, Hwy 23 runs north to **Revelstoke Dam**, which forms **Lake Revelstoke**, and **Mica Dam**, which creates **Kinabasket Lake**.

REVELSTOKE

Tourist Information: Revelstoke Chamber of Commerce, *204 Campbell Ave, Revelstoke, BC V0E 2S0; tel: (250) 837-5345; fax: (250) 837-4223*, open Mon–Fri; **Visitor InfoCentre**, *Hwy 1 at Hwy 23 north*, open summer only.

ACCOMMODATION AND FOOD

Chains include *BW* and *TL*. This popular holiday spot has modern motels and heritage Bed and Breakfasts. Moderate **Piano Keep**, *815 Mackenzie Ave, Revelstoke, BC V0E 2S0; tel/fax: (250) 837-2120*, is favoured by visiting artists and musicians.

Top restaurants are **The One Twelve**, *The Regent Inn, 112 E. First St; tel: (250) 837-2107*, continental; **Black Forest**, *TransCanada Hwy; tel: (250) 837-3495*, German; and **Peaks Lodge**, *TransCanada Hwy; tel: (250) 837-2178*, Asian fusion; all are moderate–pricey. **Tony's Roma**, *306 Mackenzie Ave; tel: (250) 837-4106*, is a popular budget–moderate Italian spot; **Mt Begbie Brewing Company**, *201 C Victoria Rd E.; tel: (250) 837-2756*, offers tours and tastings year-round.

SIGHTSEEING

Surrounded by Monashee and Selkirk peaks, glaciers and hundreds of kilometres of walking and Nordic ski trails, at the head of Upper Arrow Lake, the foot of Lake Revelstoke and the doorstep of Mount Revelstoke National Park, Revelstoke is cashing in on outdoor tourism. Established as a railway hotel stop, the town has **Revelstoke Railway Museum**, *719 Track St W., Revelstoke, BC V0E 2S0; tel: (250) 837-6060; fax: (250) 837-3732*, open daily 0900–2000 (July–Aug), 0900–1700 (spring and autumn), by appointment in winter, adults $5, children $2, family $10. 1940s and 1950s glamorous steam trains are its speciality. The town was named after Lord Revelstoke, the London banker who rescued the CPR from looming bankruptcy to finish its transcontinental railway line. Get the museum's free *Railway Heritage Driving Tour* brochure tracking Hwy 1 from Craigellachie into the Rocky Mountains.

Early area history is displayed at **Revelstoke Museum**, *315 W. First St; tel: (250) 837-3067*, open daily. **Revelstoke Art Gallery**, *upstairs; tel: (250) 837-3067*, displays paintings by local artists. The early 20th-century **Revelstoke Courthouse**, *1100 Second St W.; tel: (250) 837-7636*, has been elegantly restored around the original stained glass, marble panelling and furniture. Both buildings are included in the museum's free *Heritage Walking & Driving Tour* brochure. **Piano Keep Gallery**, *117 Campbell Ave; tel: (250) 837-6554*, adults $5, children $2.50, family $20, is a delightful piano museum with dozens of restored instruments.

203

The Royal Canadian Mounted Police

N o Canadian symbol is more instantly recognisable than the scarlet serge tunic of the Royal Canadian Mounted Police. The Mounties, as the RCMP is popularly called, have become the most easily recognised law enforcement agency in the world – and one of the most respected. 'The Mounties always get their man' may have been penned in Hollywood, but The Force has kept Canada one of the safest countries in the world.

Before the Mounties, the Canadian West was as wild as any American frontier. Present-day Alberta and Saskatchewan were nominally controlled by the Hudson's Bay Company until 1870, when the area fell under federal jurisdiction as the Northwest Territories. The only human inhabitants were First Nations with a scattering of Whites and Métis. Most of the non-Indians were American whisky traders, driven north by US Army troops trying to rid their own territory of undesirables.

Trading raw spirits for buffalo and other pelts was hardly new, but American recipes combined water, chewing tobacco, red peppers and red ink with cheap whisky to create 'fire water' that was short on alcohol, high in profit and too often lethal. Forts along the Whiskey Trail from Fort Benton, Montana, to Fort Whoop-Up, near today's Lethbridge, and along branch trails east and west, amounted to an invasion from the south.

In 1873, Prime Minister Sir John Macdonald proposed to establish the North-West Mounted Rifles, modelled on the US Army's mounted troops and the Irish Constabulary. The name was changed to the North West Mounted Police to assuage American fears of a rival military force in the far west, but the task was unchanged: bring law and order to the North-West and defeat the whisky trade before settlers arrived.

Macdonald assembled 300 men and officers 'of good character, capable of riding', under Commissioner George Arthur French, a former British lieutenant colonel, and Assistant Commissioner James Macleod. The NWMP began their March West on July 8, 1874. It should have been a straightforward march, even with horses, wagons, carts, oxen, cattle, field guns, forges and hay mowing machines. The 3-km train followed a track laid out by the joint US-Canadian boundary survey team. Instead, the 94-day, 1450-km ride westward across the Prairies from Fort Dufferin, Manitoba became the crucible that forged the legend of the RCMP.

The new Mounties were Easterners, unused to the rigours of travel and weather in the West. Their elegant, oversized horses lacked the stamina and endurance of Western ponies. And the massive company started its journey late in the year, after much of the water and grazing had dried up. Horses and pack animals began dying within days, men not long after.

After 16 days, one of six divisions detoured north to the HBC post at Fort Edmonton. The remainder plodded westward. When they met their first band of Sioux, fleeing from US troops, Commissioner French held a parlay to distribute food, gifts and Canada's vision of the West, where Indian and White would be equal, held accountable to the same law and given equal punishments for equal offences. The food was welcomed, but the explanation of Canadian intent was met with outright laughter after Sioux experience with American law.

By Sept, 8–10 horses were dying daily. When the troop finally reached the confluence of

Grizzly Plaza, *Mackenzie Ave* and *Victoria Rd*, is guarded by a pair of larger-than-life bronze bears. The pedestrian plaza, with a pleasant gazebo and benches for free summer evening entertainment, opens on streets lined with restored turn-of-the-century buildings. **Revelstoke Dam**, *3 km north on Hwy 23; tel: (250) 837-6211,* open May–mid Oct for self-guided tours, forms Lake Revelstoke,

the Bow and Belly Rivers, the supposed location of Fort Whoop-Up, there was no fort to be seen. With no feed for horses or men and short on supplies, French and Macleod rode south to Fort Benton, where they picked up supplies and a new scout, Jerry Potts.

French took 98 men to Swan River, near the Manitoba–Saskatchewan border, to establish a headquarters detachment. Potts led Macleod and the rest of the Force straight to Fort Whoop-Up, near the Oldman and St Marys Rivers. By the time the NWMP arrived, the whisky traders had fled, a scene repeated at nearly every other whisky fort the Mounties visited. The few whisky sellers who didn't leave were promptly arrested by NWMP constables, tried and sentenced by NWMP officers and imprisoned in NWMP guardhouses. Even before Fort Mcleod was completed on the Oldman River in late 1874, the whisky trade had been destroyed.

The legend of the unstoppable NWMP continued to build as the Mounties negotiated treaty after treaty with First Nations which had caused the US Army nothing but grief. By and large, the Mounties *did* enforce Canadian law with an even hand, though the treaties were no more fair or generous than those imposed by force below the 49th Parallel.

When the Canadian Pacific Railway arrived in the early 1880s, settlements grew up around Calgary, Lethbridge, Macleod and other NWMP posts. As settlement spread, Force patrols called at every homestead and farm en route. The Mounties enforced the law, carried mail and gossip and hauled relief supplies. Not surprisingly, they were soon seen as a bulwark against the expansionist Americans to the south. Buoyed by success, The Force entered The Yukon in 1895, sailing north from Seattle, WA to Skagway, Alaska, then walking over the 1067-m Chilkoot Pass as thousands of miners would do in the years to follow. When the Klondike Gold Rush broke in 1898, scarlet-uniformed NWMP waited at the top of every pass into Canada to remind the largely-American flood of miners that they had not passed beyond the rule of law.

With just 285 men to police a territory larger than most European countries, the NWMP became legend. The Yukon Force logged more than 150,000 km on patrol annually, most of it by dog-sled. Robert Service and Jack London extolled the virtues of the incorruptible men in red. So did England's King Edward VII, who granted the accolade *Royal* in 1904. *Sgt Preston of the Yukon* became a top radio, then television drama into the 1950s. In 1936, cinema sweethearts Nelson Eddy and Jeanette MacDonald brought tears to eyes world-wide in *Rose Marie*, the story of a Yukon Mountie who gives up the love of his life to get his man.

In 1920, the RNWMP absorbed Canada's Dominion Police to become the Royal Canadian Mounted Police. The Force established posts from the Arctic Yukon to Baffin Island. In 1942, the RCMP schooner *St Roch* completed the first Pacific–Atlantic crossing of the Northwest Passage, then went home again in 1944 to become the first vessel to sail the ice-choked waterway in both directions. The ship is on display at the Vancouver Maritime Museum.

By the 1950s, the RCMP had taken over policing duties in all of the provinces except Ontario and Quebec and was signing contracts for municipal policing across Canada. In 1966, the Force dropped its equitation requirement, recognising that few of its officers ever saw a horse – except volunteers mounting the famed Musical Ride. The Ride, based on British Army cavalry drill movements from the 1870s and 1880s, is staged four times daily July–Aug at Fort Macleod and has become a mainstay at local and provincial fairs across Canada.

205

extending 120 km north to Mica Dam. **Arrow Lakes** thrust 220 km south to Hugh Keenleyside Dam near Castlegar (see p. 180). The Chamber of Commerce publishes free walking maps of four dozen trails around Revelstoke as well as guides to cycling, Nordic skiing and snowmobiling. **Mount Revelstoke National Park**'s drive-up summit is 17 km east on Hwy 1 (see p. 208).

KELOWNA–REVELSTOKE

The route from Kelowna to Revelstoke traces the Okanagan Valley from vineyards into colder apple and cattle country, then follows rich agricultural valleys between the rolling hills of the Thompson Plateau (west) and the Monashee Mountains (east). From Enderby, the highway parallels the Shuswap River to Mara Lake and Sicamous. The 220 km drive takes less than half a day, or overnight in Vernon to explore Okanagan north.

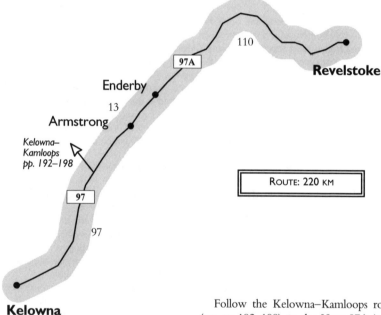

ROUTE: 220 KM

ROUTE

Take Hwy 97 north from Kelowna to Vernon and the Hwy 97A junction. Continue north on Hwy 97A (Hwy 97 turns east to O'Keefe Ranch and Monte Creek – see p. 195) to Armstrong, Enderby and Sicamous.

Follow the Kelowna–Kamloops route (see pp. 192–198) to the Hwy 97A junction at **Swan Lake**. **Spallumcheen** is 4 km north, a small farming community set amidst 26,000 hectares of prime agricultural land.

BUSES

There is no direct link between Kelowna and Revelstoke, but a service via Salmon Arm leaves four times a day. Journey time: 3½ hrs. See OTT tables 110 and 118.

ARMSTRONG

Tourist Information: Armstrong-Spallumcheen Chamber of Commerce, *3550 Bridge St, Box 118, Armstrong, BC V0E 1B0; tel: (250) 546-8155; fax: (250) 546-8868;* summer **Visitor Info-Centre**, *in the caboose, 3201 Smith Dr.; tel: (250) 546-8616.*

Armstrong is the commercial centre of the Spallumcheen Valley, best known for the **Armstrong Cheese Factory**, *3155 Pleasant Valley Rd, Box 519; fax: (250) 546-3120.* Cheese-making depends on the milk supply, but large windows afford good views of the factory floor. The factory sells cold drinks and ice-cream as well as a wide selection of house cheeses. The **Caravan Farm Theatre**, *4886 Salmon River Rd; tel: (250) 546-8533,* is a settled version of what was once BC's only theatre company touring by horse-drawn wagon.

Armstrong–Spallumcheen Museum, Archives and Art Gallery, *Railway Ave and Bridge St, Armstrong, BC V0E 1B0; tel: (250) 546-8318,* open Fri–Sun (June–Sept), features local history (including that of E.C. Heaton Armstrong, head of the London bank that funded the 1892 Shuswap and Okanagan Railway through town) and turn-of-the-century livestock.

Buy local farm products at the **Armstrong Farmer's Market**, *IPE Grounds,* Sat 0800–1200 (Apr–Oct). **The Olde Schoolhouse**, *Pleasant Valley Rd; tel: (250) 546-8488,* mainland BC's oldest surviving schoolhouse, now serves budget lunches and afternoon teas.

The 13 km north to **Enderby** are dominated by the **Enderby Cliffs** looming 600 m above the east shore of the **Shuswap River**. The shallow river, running north into **Mara Lake**, is popular with houseboaters, canoeists, kayakers and spawning salmon.

ENDERBY

Tourist Information: Enderby & District Chamber of Commerce, *700 Railway Ave, Box 100, Enderby, BC V0E 1V0; tel: (250) 838-6727; fax: (250) 838-0123,* open Mon–Sat.

Enderby is a placid farming town with a Main Street that looks little changed in half a century. **Enderby and District Museum**, *City Hall Complex, 901 George St (Hwy 97A), Enderby, BC V0E 1V0; tel: (250) 838-7099,* open Mon–Sat, collects local history and art. The museum also publishes free self-guided walking maps to Enderby's several dozen historical buildings and Enderby Cliffs hiking trails.

RiversBend Fallow Deer Farm, *40 Mathews Rd, RR2, S-5, C-15, Enderby, BC V0E 1V0; tel: (250) 838-7980,* offer farm tours by advance booking. **Kingfisher Environmental Interpretive Centre**, *25 km east of Enderby,* 2550 *Mabel Lake Rd, RR#2, Site 14A, Comp 6, Enderby, BC V0E 1V0; tel: (250) 838-0004,* is one of Canada's most successful salmon hatcheries, and features a half-size *kekuli*, the traditional Shuswap Indian winter pit house, plus forest and riverside interpretive trails.

ENDERBY TO REVELSTOKE

The highway forks 6 km north of Enderby: Hwy 97B goes north-west to Trans-Canada Hwy 1 and Salmon Arm (p. 201); Hwy 97A continues north. **Grindrod**, 4 km beyond the fork, was named after the Canadian Pacific Railway's first BC telegraph inspector.

Mara Provincial Park is a day-use area on the east side of **Mara Lake**, 13 km north of Grindrod. Best lake view is from the **Mara Lake Rest Area**, 7 km north. The lake is popular with houseboaters from **Sicamous**, 15 km beyond.

Follow the Kamloops–Revelstoke route (see pp. 199–205) to Revelstoke.

REVELSTOKE–
LAKE LOUISE

The 230 km from Revelstoke to Lake Louise includes some of the most stunning scenery in either British Columbia or Alberta. Hwy 1 climbs past Mt Revelstoke, the provinces' only drive-up summit ascent, to Rogers Pass and Glacier National Park before dropping to the Rocky Mountain Trench and Golden. The highway rises into the heart of the Rocky Mountains in Yoho National Park, over Kicking Horse Pass and down into Banff National Park and the splendours of Lake Louise. The route can be accomplished in half a day, but overnights in Golden and Field, or camping in Glacier and Yoho National Parks, allow time to explore one of Canada's most scenic driving routes.

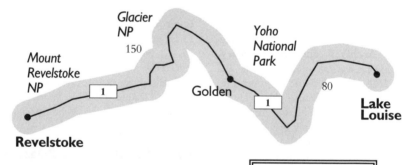

ROUTE: 230 KM

ROUTE

Follow TransCanada Hwy 1 from Revelstoke to Golden; cross the Rocky Mountains to Lake Louise.

BUSES

Greyhound Lines of Canada operate four trips a day, taking 4½ hrs. OTT table 118.

REVELSTOKE TO GOLDEN

The entrance to **Mount Revelstoke National Park**, *Third St at Campbell Ave, Box 350, Revelstoke, BC V0E 2S0; tel:*

(250) 837-7500; fax: (250) 837-7536, is on *Summit Rd*, 1 km east of Revelstoke. Mount Revelstoke is open all year for Nordic skiing and other winter activities. The highway to the summit closes as the snow level falls from Sept onward. A single admission is valid for Mount Revelstoke and **Glacier National Park**, an hour's drive east.

Summit Rd winds 26 km to the top of 1830-m Mt Revelstoke. Don't miss scenic lay-bys on the way up with views across the town of Revelstoke, Arrow Lakes and the Monashee Mountains. Allow about 45 mins to drive up or down, longer if traffic is heavy. The road is steep, but passable by trailers and RVs. Access to the most popular part of the summit, **Meadows in the Sky**, a series of rolling alpine meadows carpeted in wildflowers July–Aug, is via a 1-km walking path or a shuttle from car parks at the **Balsam Lake** picnic area below the peak. Disabled persons apply for special permission to take their own vehicles to the summit.

Period 1914 photographs show entire families hiking the **Meadows in the Sky Trail**, gaping at **The Icebox**, a shaded rock cleft where snow persists into late summer, and admiring views stretching over 100 km in every direction. Many meadow trails have been paved for disabled access. Sweeping views now include massive clearcuts scarring nearby mountainsides. **Summit Cycle Tours**, *Box 2647, Revelstoke, BC V0E 2S0; tel/fax: (250) 837-3734,* coast downhill from the summit, although gentle pedalling *is* required for about 200m. A 10-km walking trail links the summit and central Revelstoke.

Hwy 1 follows the Illecillewaet River eastward to the **Illecillewaet Glacier**, best seen from **Illecillewaet Campground** on the west side of Rogers Pass. The first 30 km of highway skirts Mount Revelstoke National Park. Eastbound lanes open onto the **Illecillewaet Rest Area**, a layby with a cairn commemorating the 1962 opening of the Rogers Pass highway, pioneered by the Canadian Pacific Railway in 1885. Ten km east is **Skunk Cabbage** picnic area with a short self-guided walk along the Illecillewaet River. Birding is good spring–autumn. An 800-year-old grove at **Giant Cedars**, 3 km beyond, features a boardwalk trail through a typical Columbia Mountain rain forest.

Rangers check vehicles for park passes, which can be obtained at the *Summit Rd* entrance, from machines at Skunk Cabbage and Giant Cedars, or from the Rogers Pass visitor centre in Glacier National Park. **Woolsey Creek**, 1 km east, is the eastern boundary of Mount Revelstoke National Park. Three km beyond is the turn-off to summer-only **Albert Canyon Hot Springs**, discovered by CPR workers early in the century, with a campsite, mineral pool, swimming pool, store and coffee shop. Unrestored ruins of the original CPR settlement are a short walk away, with wild strawberries and forget-me-nots slowly growing over the collapsing cabins and schoolhouse.

The first of three major **snowsheds** begins 10 km east of Albert Canyon. Heavy snowfall and near-vertical terrain make this one of the most active avalanche areas in the world. Use headlights in the sheds, reinforced concrete tunnels that protect the highway from cascading snow, ice, rock and trees. Avalanches, 'white death', eventually forced the CPR to abandon its tracks over Rogers Pass and tunnel beneath the mountain to escape annual fatalities. Hwy 1 follows the CPR's old route, but more effective snowsheds and avalanche controls keep the highway open all year.

Bostock Creek Bridge, 4 km east, is the western edge of **Glacier National Park**, *Third St at Campbell Ave, Box 350, Revelstoke, BC V0E 2S0; tel: (250) 837-7500; fax: (250) 837-7536.* There are picnic tables on the north side of the highway. Heavy snowfall feeds more than 400 active glaciers and icefields in the park, covering nearly 12% of its total area. The **Selkirk Mountains**, the westernmost range of the Columbia Mountains covering central BC, have been scraped and eroded into a series of fishbone spines and jagged peaks cut by narrow valleys as spectacular as any in the

209

Rocky Mountains. Mountain goats are the most commonly-seen large animals. Hwy 1 follows the original CPR route over Rogers Pass, abandoned in 1916 because of annual avalanche damage. The park has 140 km of trails with Nordic skiing in winter and guided hikes in summer; check park bulletin boards or the visitor centre at Rogers Pass for timetables.

The next major lay-by is 7 km east on the south side of the road, overlooking the west portal of 14.7 km-long **Mount MacDonald Tunnel**, the longest railway tunnel in North America 394 m beneath Rogers Pass. Best visibility is from the eastbound direction; the wide lay-by is excellent for spotting and photographing trains. The MacDonald Tunnel opened in 1986, replacing the **Connaught Tunnel** which had taken CPR's tracks underground in 1916.

Best view of **Mt Sir Donald**, at 3297 m the park's highest peak, is from the picnic area at the **Illecillewaet River bridge** 3 km east. Continue 1.5 km to **Loop Brook Campground**, open mid July–mid Sept, with 20 pitches. Another 1.5 km east, CPR's original tracks made several loops over and around **Loop Brook**, seven complete circles that tamed the uphill grade to a manageable 2.5%. The 20-m stone pillars that once supported Loop Brook Bridge are intact, circled by a 30-min loop trail offering striking views of **Bonney Glacier**.

The **Illecillewaet Campground**, the park's largest with 59 pitches, is 1.5 km east of Loop Brook. **Illecillewaet Glacier** can be seen from the highway, but the view is better from the campsite entrance or the easy trail leading to the site of CPR's renowned **Glacier House**, built in 1886 to avoid hauling heavy dining cars over Rogers Pass. The hotel, closed in 1916 when the Connaught Tunnel replaced the pass route, burned in 1929. A Parks Canada interpretive trail explores what was once among the most famous hotels in North America. The **Great Glacier Trail** is the best route to the glacier, which seems to flow from the skies above. Illecillewaet (like most North American glaciers) has been retreating since the late 1880s.

Rogers Pass, 1325 m, is 3 km east. There are lay-bys with picnic tables on both sides of the highway and a marker arch on the north side. Views of **Mt Sir Donald** and **Mt Rogers** are excellent on clear days. Walk the 1.2-km **Abandoned Rails Trail** eastward along the right-of-way to view the ruins of snowsheds with timbers 60 cm in diameter lying snapped like so many bits of straw to appreciate CPR's problems.

The path leads to the pass service area with petrol, a store and the **Rogers Pass Interpretation Centre**; *tel: (250) 837-6274,* open daily, modelled after CPR's great snowsheds, but built of stronger materials. Displays chronicle the natural and railway history of the pass, found in 1882 by railway engineer Maj A.B. Rogers. The terrain is so rugged that Rogers attacked the pass from both sides before realising that he was following the same route. A model railroad recreates the pass in the 1890s, when intrepid passengers paid extra to ride the 'hot seat', a single chair bolted to the front of the locomotive directly above the cowcatcher. Once tied firmly into the chair on the east side of the pass, there was no getting out until Glacier House, well below the summit. The Centre bookstore has the region's best stock of books, maps and other information about Glacier and Mount Revelstoke National Parks.

The east entrance to Rogers Pass is 9 km downhill. A lay-by offers good views over **Beaver Valley**, as does a second

210

lay-by 2 km beyond. The park's entrance is 4 km east as Hwy 1 follows the **Beaver River** down toward **Columbia Reach** on **Kinabasket Lake**, created by the **Mica Dam** on the **Columbia River** north of Revelstoke (see p.203). The park boundary, and the Mountain Time Zone, are another 4 km east. Eastbound travellers should reset their watches one hour ahead, westbound travellers one hour back.

The highway leaves the Beaver River to cross the **Columbia River** at **Donald Station**, a former CPR repair and control centre, and runs south along the bottom of **Rocky Mountain Trench**. The Trench is a rift valley dividing the relatively young Rocky Mountains from the much older Columbia Mountains. The earth's crust stretched, then collapsed to form the valley, which is slowly filling with debris washing down from the mountain ranges on each side. The trench runs from central USA, through Canada and north into Alaska, one of the earth's most striking geographic features visible from the moon.

The trench forms a narrow valley, gradually widening to the south, which contains the Columbia River. The valley floor is largely waterfowl wetlands. Vast herds of elk and deer migrated up and down the valley until White settlement increased hunting pressure and habitat destruction. The slopes above the Trench are drier and warmer than the rest of the Rockies or the Columbia Mountains, making them an important winter range for bighorn sheep, deer, cougars and coyotes. Golden, Radium Hot Springs and Invermere are popular winter escapes for Rocky Mountaineers seeking respite from colder winds, greyer skies and deeper snow at home.

Burges and James Gadsden Provincial Park protects most of the **Moberly Marsh**, 15 km from the Columbia River, an important stopping point for migratory waterfowl. Look for muskrat lodges, osprey and bald eagles on the 3.5-km riverbank **Dyke Trail**. At Golden, TransCanada Hwy 1 climbs toward **Yoho National Park** and **Kicking Horse Pass**; Hwy 95 follows the Columbia River south.

GOLDEN

Tourist Information: Golden & District Chamber of Commerce, *500 10 Ave N., Box 1320, Golden, BC V0A 1H0; tel: (800) 622-4653 or (250) 344-7125; fax: (250) 344-6688, open daily in summer, Mon–Fri in winter.*

ACCOMMODATION

Golden has about three dozen motels, including *BW* and *S8*, as well as numerous Bed and Breakfasts. Most motels are along Hwy 95; the expensive **Prestige Inn**, *1049 TransCanada Hwy, Golden, BC V0A 1H0; tel: (250) 344-7990; fax: 250-344-7902*, is among the largest and best-located for Hwy 1 travellers.

EATING AND DRINKING

Katerina's Steak House, *825 S. 10th Ave; tel: (250) 344-5695,* has Golden's best moderate steaks. **La Cabina**, *1105 9th St; tel: (250) 344-2330,* is a budget–moderate Italian favourite. **Jenny's Java Express & Internet Café**, *505 9th Ave N.; tel: (250) 344-5057,* has cheap coffee, date squares and e-mail.

SIGHTSEEING

Golden is a trainspotter's dream, wide vistas along the railway in both directions, massive train yards, and history that began with the arrival of the Canadian Pacific Railway in 1884–1885. Once the transcontinental railway was completed, Golden became the junction between train traffic and steamboats along the Columbia. When the CPR began touting the alpine

211

charms of Glacier House and Glacier National Park, Swiss guides were brought in to lead trainloads of tourists into the nearby Rocky and Columbia Mountains.

Mountain hiking is popular. Heli-hiking from **Purcell Lodge**, *Box 1829, Golden, BC V0A 1H0; tel: (250) 344-2639; fax: (250) 344-5520,* on the edge of Glacier National Park, is accessible only by helicopter or a strenuous trek into the Purcell Mountains. River rafting on the Kicking Horse and Blaeberry Rivers is thrilling. Try winter activities, from alpine and Nordic skiing at **Whitetooth Ski Area**, *13 km west off 7 St N., Box 1925; tel: (250) 344-6114,* to snowboarding, snowshoeing and heli-skiing untracked slopes. **Golden Mountain Adventures**, *Box 248, Golden, BC V0A 1H0; tel: (250) 344-2499,* co-ordinate mountain activities from three dozen local companies.

Golden Golf and Country Club, *Box 1615, Golden, BC V0A 1H0; tel: (250) 344-2700,* has 18 holes surrounded by mountain peaks and roaming deer. The **Golden and District Museum**, *1302 11th Ave, Golden, BC V0A 1H0; tel: (250) 344-5169,* open daily (July–Aug), weekdays (May, June and Sept), has a log schoolhouse and blacksmithy.

Hwy 1 rises east of Golden. Stop 1 km from town at a lay-by on the right for an overview of Golden and its rails, before continuing to follow the Kicking Horse River 25 km to **Yoho National Park**.

YOHO NATIONAL PARK

Tourist Information: Yoho National Park, *PO Box 99, Field, BC V0A 1G0; tel: (250) 343-6324; fax: (250) 343-6630; web: http://www.worldweb.com/ParksCanada-Yoho/.* **Yoho Park Information Centre**, *south side of TransCanada Hwy 1; tel: (250) 343-6783,* open 0900–1900 (late June–Aug), 0900–1700 (mid May–late June and

Sept), reduced winter hours, in Field, offers park, BC and Alberta information, park passes, three-month-in-advance camping bookings, backcountry permits, a gift shop and a Burgess Shale Fossil Exhibit (comparable to the one in the Lake Louise Information Centre, see p.94).

Yoho National Park, west of Banff National Park, claims 700,000 annual visitors. The 82 km on TransCanada Hwy 1 from Columbia Valley-bound Golden over Kicking Horse Pass at the Continental Divide to Lake Louise rates at least a full day to explore Yoho's lakes and waterfalls and spot mountain goats, with time to puzzle through the railway engineering feat of the **Upper and Lower Spiral Tunnels**.

Yoho's summer is mid June to sometime in September, though snow flurries fall above 1500m year-round, which prevents camping during the 8-month-long winter. The park has several lodges; **Field** has approved accommodation.

Cree First Nation people were struck by the area's beauty; 'yoho' means awe and wonder. Turn right 5 km east of the park entrance going south 2.5 km on a dirt road. Conditioned hikers walk 2.4 km to **Wapta Falls,** where the Kicking Horse River plunges 30m, tossing down 255 cubic metres of water per second. The falls can be viewed from above, middle, or, from the bottom with a backdrop of 3000m mountains. Nordic skiers access frozen falls.

One km north of *Wapta Falls Rd*, turn left to reach 58-pitch **Chancellor Peak Campground**, open May–Sept, with lovely mountain vistas from the riverbank. **Hoodoo Creek Campground**, with 106 pitches and interpretive programmes, is open late June–Labour Day, 1 km further east. The campsite is named after the **Leanchoil Hoodoos**, eroded glacier debris topped with capstones thrusting from the side of Mt Vaux. Plan on carrying water and steep going for a 450-m rise during the 1.5-km hike to the upper viewpoint to look down on the capstones, or, veer off to a lower viewpoint. Continue 13 km north to **Ottertail Viewpoint**, an excellent north side view of the Kicking Horse River Valley.

Nineteen km east on Hwy 1, turn left onto *Emerald Lake Rd.* One km up the road is a parking area adjacent to **Natural Bridge**, where the Kicking Horse River crashes green and misty. Photography is best in the afternoon.

Emerald Lake

Ten km north of the TransCanada Hwy, Emerald Lake is green even on an overcast May–Nov day when it isn't frozen over. Yoho National Park's largest lake, 28 m deep, is prized by canoeists and hikers.

Named by Lake Louise's discoverer, guide Tom Wilson, during preparations for CPR construction, the railway company built a lakeside lodge 20 years later. The **Emerald Lake Lodge and Conference Centre**, *PO Box 10, Field, BC V0A 1G0; tel: (800) 663-6336 or (250) 343-6321; fax: (250) 343-6724,* is open year-round, 85 pricey rooms in rustic cabin-style buildings around the renovated stone-fireplace and hewn timber lodge.

Lodge dining includes the pricey **Mt Burgess Dining Room** with air-dried buffalo, caribou medallions, venison, ham and buffalo barley soup, and summertime afternoon tea on the veranda. **Cilantro on the Lake**, less formal, has good service and fine lakeside views. The **Kicking Horse Bar** has a 1890s oak bar from the Yukon.

Start at the south end of the parking area for an easy 0.7-km walk up to **Hamilton Falls**, or continue a day-long 10-km round trip on the **Hamilton Lake Trail** in July to search for glacier lilies and anemones.

The Naming of Kicking Horse

In 1858, 23-year-old James Hector, a Scots geologist with the Palliser Expedition, ventured into the Yoho Valley searching for a route to the Columbia River. It was an area avoided by native peoples, though intrepid Hector followed local guides away from an easier route via the Kootenay and Vermilion Rivers to the confluence of the Beaverfoot and Wapta Rivers above Wapta Falls, near the present-day western park entrance. An agitated horse in the river took direct aim for Hector's chest, knocking him out so deeply that his men believed him dead. To everyone's shock, Hector revived, and the troop named the river and the pass after the thrashing equine.

The **Emerald Sports & Gift Store**, *tel: (250) 343-6000; fax: (250) 343-6377,* at the south-west end of Emerald Lake, has fine quality, expensive Canadian handicrafts and hires canoes ($18.24 per hour), fishing gear and horses in summer and Nordic ski gear and snowshoes in winter. A rustic bridge crosses a short appendage of the lake to Cilantro on the Lake and the lodge complex. Hikers begin the 5-km **Emerald Lake Loop Trail** from the parking lot side of the bridge, going clockwise for best views. Spot moose, jays, Clark's nutcrackers, and search for yellow lady's slipper orchid amongst summer wildflowers; in winter, Nordic skiers and snowshoers enjoy the loop. Vegetation varies widely depending on runoff into the glacier-formed lake, and protection afforded by surrounding mountains. Look east for a left-to-right panorama of **Mts Wapta**, **Field** and **Burgess**. **Burgess Pass**, directly in front of the peaks, is

213

YOHO
NATIONAL PARK

North

BOW
LAKE
93

CROWFOOT
GLACIER

BANFF
NATIONAL
PARK

WAPTA
ICEFIELD

YOHO
GLACIER

HECTOR
LAKE

YOHO

WAPUTIK
ICEFIELD

ALBERTA

93

BOW

THE PRESIDENT

YOHO
NATIONAL
PARK

TAKAKKAW
FALLS

SHERBROOK
LAKE

HERBERT
LAKE

EMERALD
LAKE

LOWER SPIRAL
TUNNEL
VIEWPOINT

WAPTA
LAKE

AMISKWI

KICKING
HORSE
PASS &THE
GREAT DIVIDE

1A

Lake
Louise

LAKE
LOUISE

OTTERHEAD

NATURAL
BRIDGE

Field
FIELD
VISITOR
CENTRE

CATHEDRAL
MOUNTAIN

214

1

MT TEMPLE
(3542)

LAKE
O'HARA

MORAINE
LAKE

KICKING HORSE

OTTERTAIL

MT OWEN

KICKING HORSE PASS

HANBURY
GLACIER

TOKUMM

1

KOOTENAY
NATIONAL
PARK

BRITISH
COLUMBIA

WAPTA FALLS

ICE

MT GOODSIR
(3563)

Camp site

Icefield

BEAVERFOOT

COLUMBIA

95

0   10 kms

0   5 miles

Parson

where a wealth of fossils was discovered 515 million years after being encased in mud near their Cambrian-era shallow sea home.

The Burgess Shale

A CPR engineer found 'stone bugs', flat, disc-shaped trilobite fossils, arthropods most resembling modern-day horseshoe crabs, on Mt Stephen, due east of present-day Field.

By 1909, palaeontologist Charles Walcott, secretary of the Smithsonian Institution, was conducting digs in the Rockies. An expert on the Palaeozoic Cambrian Period (590–500 million years ago), Walcott recognised trilobites in shale he uncovered while removing an obstruction for a horse path through the Burgess Pass area.

Sixty-five thousand fossil specimens were excavated by Walcott's teams in later years; fully 170 species have been identified, though some specimens defy classification. Scientists continue to study the Burgess Shale, a World Heritage Site fossil bed so well preserved that soft body tissues and digested matter are perfectly etched.

To protect the fossil sites, public access is severely restricted. It is illegal to displace or remove fossils. **Monarch Campground**, Yoho National Park Information Centre in Field and the **Lake Louise Information Centre** have Burgess Shale exhibits. The Royal Tyrrell Museum of Palaeontology (Drumheller, p.131) has excellent examples of trilobites and other Burgess Shale fossils.

Yoho–Burgess Shale Foundation, *tel: (800) 343-3006,* offer strenuous guided 15-person hikes (weather-permitting July–Sept). The 20-km return hike to Walcott's Quarry, $46, is moderate but long; the difficult 6-km return to the Mt Stephen Trilobite Beds is short, but steep, $29.

Field

Tourist information at the Yoho Park Information Centre. Field has 17 moderate rooms in eight guesthouses scattered over two blocks and the expensive 14-unit **Kicking Horse Lodge**, *Box 174, Field, BC V0A 1G0; tel: (800) 659-4944* or *tel/fax: (250) 343-6303.*

Field is an original 1884 CPR railway town three blocks long and equally wide. In 1886, the CPR built its first de luxe Rockies hotel, **Mount Stephen House**, under the looming mass of 3199-m **Mt Stephen**. The *de rigueur* Swiss-guide-equipped stop on the CPR Rockies circuit is long gone, though the rails continue to dominate the town.

Tourism, including winter ice climbing, draws most visitors who stop at the Info-centre for park, local and information on both provinces. Across from the Info-centre, **Yoho Bros. Trading Company**, *TransCanada Hwy 1,* has a tea-house and gift shop, and is a meeting point for some mountain activities. **The Siding General Store**, *Stephen Ave; tel: (250) 343-6462,* has a small café for breakfast and sandwiches, and sells snack food and drinks.

Glance up from the flat riverbed of the Kicking Horse Valley to regal Mt Stephen, a major depository of trilobite fossils in lower-level shale. Shale tops quartzite, covered in turn by colourful sculpted layers of limestone. South-east of Mt Stephen is Mt Dennis, a darker, flatter, comparatively negligible peak of shale layering. Field's mountains are a textbook illustration of the Western Rockies Ranges (Mt Dennis), and the Eastern Rockies Ranges on the Continental Divide (Mt Stephen).

Continue north-east 4 km on Hwy 1. Turn left onto *Yoho Valley Rd,* to **Takak-kaw Falls**. The narrow, winding 15-km road is impossible for RVs anytime and closed to vehicles in winter when Nordic skiers take on the challenge of switchbacks en route.

Cathedral Mountain Lodge & Chalets, *PO Box 40, Field, BC V0A 1G0; tel/fax: (250) 343-6442 or (403) 762-0514*, open mid May–mid Oct, expensive–pricey, has a tea room, grocery store and gift shop. Late June–early Sept, 36-pitch **Monarch Campground** is open at the beginning of *Yoho Valley Rd*. Look for the Burgess Shale Exhibit. Just beyond is the 86-pitch **Kicking Horse Campground**, open mid May–mid Oct. Two trails begin near the campsite: the 2.5-km **Centennial Loop Trail** is good for admiring Mt Stephen and other peaks, mountain goat spotting and wildflower identification; the interpretive 1.2-km **Walk in the Past Trail** is a hike up a section of the Big Hill to the CPR's original railway grade, used before 1909 Spiral Tunnels completion.

Spiral Tunnels on the Big Hill

Engineering feat. Supreme arrogance. Stubbornness. One of Canadian rail history's most ingenious solutions to steeply-graded Rockies geology, the Spiral Tunnels remain a visual puzzle to observers stopping at the **Upper and Lower Spiral Tunnel Viewpoints**. For more than 20 years, prior to the 1909 lessening of the grade on the Big Hill, the slope running roughly west from Kicking Horse Pass, runaway trains were frequent when equipment or signalmen failed to co-ordinate to divert locomotive engines onto spurs.

The solution? Picture a figure eight on a slope with the endpoint loops separated by a stretch of generally straight track. The 7 km addition to CPR track reduced the previous straight track's grade from an accident-prone 4.5% to the 2.2% required by CPR charter. Two locomotive engines, travelling up the 6.6-km Big Hill five times faster than before the Spiral Tunnels were

in place, pulled loads previously hauled by four engines.

Why was the original track used from 1886–1909 so steep? The 1881–1886 CPR construction-era general manager (later president), William Cornelius Van Horne, was determined to build the transcontinental railway cost-efficiently and quickly, to create profits for shareholders and overcome (accurate) public impressions of scandal, corruption and mismanagement of an enterprise pitched as continent and Dominion uniting. Though extensive surveying had indicated other possibilities, Van Horne and others chose the little-known Kicking Horse Pass route. A 'temporary' variance for the 4.5% grade, granted to the CPR until the 2.2 grade requirement could be met, stretched more than two decades.

Following engineering concepts used in Switzerland's St. Gotthard Railway Baischina Gorge Tunnels, CPR came up with the spiral, joining looping tunnels on a slope, roughly positioned one above the other. The $1.5-million-dollar tunnels were completed in May 1905, on time, within budget, with tunnel shafts varying by no more than 5 cm from each direction when construction crews met.

Whether standing at one of the viewpoints or travelling on a train, the tunnels, one straight and two spiral shafts, 992-m Upper Spiral Tunnel and 891-m Lower Spiral Tunnel, make no directional sense. It suffices that the curves and rise (or fall, going west) are gradual, and that scenery from any tunnel entrance/exit is stunning.

One km from TransCanada Hwy 1, the interpretive **Upper Spiral Tunnel Viewpoint** offers views to Cathedral Mountain and Mt Stephen, and occasional train-spotting. Freight has priority on Canadian rails, so the more scenic passenger trains schedules vary – be prepared to wait, camera set, for a brief glimpse.

The green Kicking Horse River left its glacial silt, or milk, in upstream lakes. The milky white Yoho River joins the surprisingly clear Kicking Horse River at **Meeting of the Waters** viewpoint. Three sharp switchbacks just beyond cause vehicles to creep up *Yoho Valley Rd.*

Twelve km on, an old hotel's staff lodge serves as the *HI*-**Whiskey Jack Hostel**, *c/o PO Box 1358, Banff, AB T0L 0C0; tel: (403) 762-4122; fax: (403) 762-3441,* open mid June–mid Sept, with a front-porch view of Takakkaw Falls. **Takakkaw Falls Campground**, open mid June–mid Sept, 300m from the falls parking area, has 35 pitches. Use carts provided to haul luggage and provisions to pitches.

Toward the end of *Yoho Valley Rd,* the 254-m free-fall of **Takakkaw Falls** plays hide-and-seek. Van Horne used the Cree First Nation expression for 'magnificent' in naming another of CPR's tourist attractions. It's 600m on a paved path from the parking area to the falls. The roar of water, especially July–Aug during maximum flow from **Waputik Icefield**, is deafening, augmented by huge boulders tumbling at random. Rain gear may be helpful with heavy mist; watch for rainbows.

Back on Hwy 1, 7 km east of Field, stop at the **Lower Spiral Tunnel Viewpoint**. Trains appear to exit the tunnel vertically, go right (east) at mid-view, then go left (west) as train track approaches closer.

Sherbrooke Falls are on the left of Hwy 1. **Wapta Lake**, source of Kicking Horse River, is next on the right. **West Louise Lodge**, *Box 9, Lake Louise, AB T0L 1E0; tel: (250) 343-6311; fax: (250) 343-6786,* has moderate rooms across from Wapta Lake.

Lake O'Hara

Thirteen km south of the TransCanada Hwy 1 is a recreational lake. To protect fragile species and scenery, access to pricey (American Plan) **Lake O'Hara Lodge**, *PO Box 55, Lake Louise, AB T0L 1E0; tel: (250) 343-6418* (mid June–Sept) or *(403) 678-4110* (Oct–early June), a 30-pitch rustic tent campsite, and the lake is by bus (June 19–Oct 1, adults $12 return, children 6–16 $5, with a day-trip/camping $10 reservation fee); *tel: (250) 343-6433.* Park on the south side of the highway; it is well-marked.

An alternative is to hike to **Lake O'Hara**, either on the 12-km **Cataract Brook Trail** or on the 11-km **Lake O'Hara Fire Road** – a Nordic ski trail to the lake in winter. The châlet-style wooden lodge and its cabins, another CPR alpine spot from the 1920s, is a base for an extensive 80-km system of hiking trails to a number of alpine blue lakes. Glaciers and waterfalls enhance the vistas – Lake Louise, in Banff National Park, is due east across the Continental Divide.

TransCanada Hwy 1 continues east to 1650-m **Kicking Horse Pass**, the boundary between BC and Alberta Provinces and Yoho and Banff National Parks. This is the spine of a continent; provincial flags whip jauntily in the wind above the **Great Divide Interpretive Exhibit**.

Hwy 1A divides off the TransCanada at the Lake O'Hara Parking area and continues to Kicking Horse Pass where the road is marked with a wooden arch as the *Great Divide Highway*. This less-travelled scenic back road, which parallels the TransCanada to Lake Louise, becomes a Nordic ski track in winter.

217

JASPER-VALEMOUNT

This 125-km route crosses Yellowhead Pass, the lowest, the most scenic and the least-travelled route through the central Rockies. The highway follows gentle river canyon grades between peaks soaring 3000m above a broad mosaic of valley wetlands and forests filled with moose, deer and birds. The entire trip takes less than two hours, or it could stretch to days exploring the trails criss-crossing Mount Robson Provincial Park on the western side of the Pass. Drive with the sun at your back, westbound in morning or eastbound in the afternoon, for the best views.

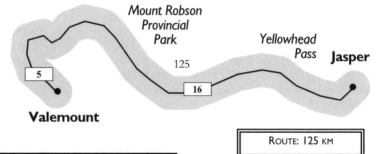

ROUTE: 125 KM

ROUTE

Follow Hwy 16, the Yellowhead Hwy, from Jasper over Yellowhead Pass into BC and **Mount Robson Provincial Park** to Hwy 5. Take Hwy 5 south to Valemount.

BUSES AND TRAINS

Greyhound Lines of Canada operate four trips a day, taking 30 mins. OTT table 120.

Trains on the Canadian route make the journey three times a week, taking 1 hr.

THE YELLOWHEAD PASS

Yellowhead Hwy follows **Miette River** up toward the **Continental Divide**. Rivers on the east side drain north into the Arctic Ocean; rivers on the west side flow into the Pacific Ocean. The Divide is the Alberta and BC boundary and separates Mountain and Pacific Time Zones. Both highway and pass are named after an early blond-headed trapper who worked near **Tête Jaune Cache** (Yellowhead's cache), at Hwys 16/5 junction (see p.338).

Trappers liked the Yellowhead, which they called Leather Pass for the skins they shipped eastward each year, because it is the lowest (1146m) and easiest pass in the central Rockies. Early travellers preferred the more rugged **Athabasca Pass** to the south which leads to the Columbia River, providing much easier access to interior BC as well as Washington and Oregon in the United States and the Pacific Ocean.

The foaming Fraser River, west of the Yellowhead Pass, didn't deter the **Over-landers**, a group of 1862 immigrants who faced swindlers, ignorance and nature on their way to the BC gold fields. The first

tourists arrived the next year, a sickly viscount and his physician. Poor planning and
bad guides nearly killed them.

The next celebrated visitors were
Canadian Pacific Railway Engineer-in-
Chief Sandford Fleming and Rev George
Munro Grant. The pair were considerably
better prepared than either of their predecessors, including a weekly plum pudding
with sufficient brandy to set the pudding
alight, wash it down and provide nightly
toasts to the Queen and to everyone's
health. Even allowing for the Rev Grant's
insistence that Sunday be a day of rest, the
trip west took just two months.

Fleming's experience convinced him
that the Yellowhead Pass was CPR's best
route over the Rockies. After Fleming left
the CPR in 1880, the Canadian government opted for a southerly route through
Kicking Horse Pass and the Selkirk Range
in order to discourage encroachment by
American railway builders.

The Yellowhead Pass was largely
ignored until the Grand Trunk Pacific and
Canadian Northern Railway revived
Fleming's plans. The companies built parallel routes through the pass in the early
20th century and went separate ways from
Tête Jaune Cache. When the absurdity of
two railway lines running within metres of
each other became apparent, the competitors consolidated a single route through the
pass. Both companies were eventually
absorbed into the Canadian National
Railway system.

Auto enthusiasts were driving the abandoned rights of way as early as 1922, often
building makeshift bridges as they went.
During the Great Depression, between
1929 and World War II, unemployed men
from the cities were sent to build roads
throughout the Rocky Mountains, including the Yellowhead Pass. When World
War II broke out, Japanese-Canadians

from the BC coast were sent to the same
forced labour camps. The **TransMoun-
tain Oil Pipeline**, completed in 1952,
gave the Yellowhead Pass its first all-season
road, but it took roadbuilders until 1968 to
seal the surface between Jasper and Hwy 5.

The west entrance to **Jasper National
Park** is 20 km west of Jasper. All travellers
using park facilities must pay the entrance
fee. Jasper National Park, the province of
Alberta and the Mountain Time Zone all
end at the **Continental Divide**, 4 km
west. Westbound travellers should set their
watches back one hour, eastbound travellers ahead an hour.

MOUNT ROBSON PROVINCIAL PARK

The BC side of Yellowhead Pass lies
within **Mount Robson Provincial
Park**, *Box 579, Valemount, BC V0E 2Z0;
tel: (250) 566-4325; fax: (250) 566-9777.*
Yellowhead Lake is noted for fishing and
boating. The relatively shallow lake is
warm enough for swimming in late summer. A boat ramp and picnic area are
located at the east end of the lake, which
drains into **Robson River** and joins **Fraser River**, running 1368 km to the Pacific
Ocean at Vancouver. The Robson snakes
through the broad glacial valley between
Rainbow Range (north) and the **Selwyn
Range** (south) of the Rocky Mountains.
Most of the surrounding peaks are 2800 m
or higher, but the valley floor is just over
900 m. The difference in altitude creates an
impression of much higher and vaster massifs hovering over the verdant valley below.

Moose Marsh, 20 km west, is prime
habitat for moose, beaver, osprey and
waterfowl. The best way to explore the
marsh is by canoe. Just downstream is
Moose Lake, with a boat launch and picnic facilities at the east end. Marsh and lake
are favourites with wildlife enthusiasts in all

219

seasons. **Red Pass**, at the west end of Moose Lake, is named for the red rock of surrounding hillsides, and opens onto **Shale Hill**, a steep shale slope that plummets into the river below.

Overlander Falls is one of the most popular stops in the park. An easy forest trail leads down to the river at the base of the falls from a car park on the south side of the highway.

The park was created to preserve 3945-m **Mt Robson**, the highest peak in the Canadian Rockies. **Park Headquarters** and **Visitor Centre** are 1.5 km west of Overlander Falls on the north side of the highway. The Visitor Centre has a small natural history museum and park displays. Nearby are restaurants, a gas station and 2 campsites: **Robson Meadows Campground**, with 125 pitches, and **Robson River Campground**, with 19 pitches. **Mount Robson Adventure Holidays**, *Box 687 MA, Valemount, BC V0E 2Z0; tel: (800) 882-9921 or (250) 566-4386; fax: (250) 566-4351,* just west of the gas station, has an outstanding programme of gentle river rafting, canoeing and hiking. Rafting the Fraser River or canoeing Moose Marsh, are excellent introductions to area flora and fauna, from moose, bear and wolves to beaver, muskrats and waterfowl. Best time to view spawning Chinook salmon and the eagles and bears that congregate to feed on them is Aug–Sept.

The *real* reason to stop at the Visitor Centre is **Mt Robson**, rising 3945 almost-sheer-metres above the valley floor and 550m above neighbouring peaks. It takes a degree of luck to see the entire mountain, 6.5 km from the Visitor Centre. As the day progresses and temperatures rise, warm air often rushes up the mountain, condensing as dense clouds that obscure the peak.

The Overlanders called it **Cloud-Cap Mountain**. Resident Shuswap Indians knew it as *Yuh-hai-has-hun,* Mountain of the Spiral Road, for immense ledges that seem to angle upward like a spiral from today's Visitor Centre. Unfortunately, the ledges are stacked like the layers of a cake, not a smooth road to the summit.

Mt Robson may have been named after Colin Robertson, a Hudson's Bay Company factor who sent Iroquois fur trappers into the region in the 1820s. Maps from 1863 show it as 'Robson's Peak'. By any name, the mountain and park are a hiker's paradise. Park wardens maintain an extensive network of trails, from the half-hour return stroll to Overlander Falls to multi-day treks to circumnavigate Mt Robson. One of the most popular is an easy 9-km return walk through shady forest up **Berg Trail** to **Kinney Lake**, famous for mirror-like morning reflections of Mt Robson. The north side of Mt Robson carries one of the most spectacular glacier systems in the Rockies, accessible via a 20-km hike up Berg Trail. A rigorous route around the mountain emerges east of Moose Lake.

MOUNT ROBSON PROVINCIAL PARK TO VALEMOUNT

Hwy 16 continues west to **Mt Terry Fox Rest Area**, 6.5 km beyond the park entrance. The large lay-by has picnic tables and a lawn play area with **Mt Terry Fox**, 2650m, looming behind. The mountain is named after Terry Fox, who electrified Canada in 1980 by starting to run across the country after losing a leg to cancer.

Rearguard Falls, 3.5 km west of the rest area, is the limit of migration for Fraser River salmon, blocked by the 10-m cascade. Three km west is the **Tête Jaune Cache Rest Area**, overlooking **Fraser River**, and the junction with Hwy 5.

Follow the Prince Rupert–Valemount route (pp.329–338) south to Valemount.

VALEMOUNT–KAMLOOPS

The Yellowhead Highway South is made for mountain lovers. Hwy 5 leaves the Rocky Mountain Trench to follow the swirling green waters of the North Thompson River from the Cariboo Mountains through the heart of BC's wet interior forest belt to the rolling grasslands and cattle country of Kamloops. There are few civilised attractions along this 325-km route, just mountains, ice-fields and one of BC's grandest rivers, with an occasional small town carved out of the forest. The entire drive can be done in one long day, but allow at least one overnight, preferably two, near Clearwater to visit Wells Gray Provincial Park along the only good road into this vast mountain wilderness.

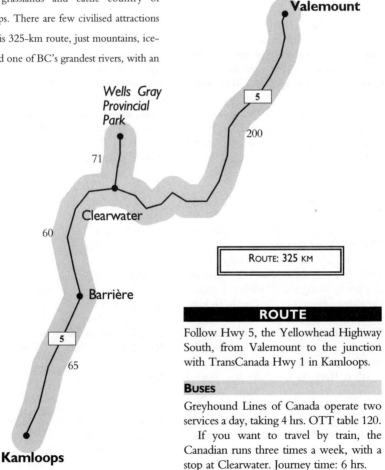

221

ROUTE: 325 KM

ROUTE

Follow Hwy 5, the Yellowhead Highway South, from Valemount to the junction with TransCanada Hwy 1 in Kamloops.

BUSES

Greyhound Lines of Canada operate two services a day, taking 4 hrs. OTT table 120.

If you want to travel by train, the Canadian runs three times a week, with a stop at Clearwater. Journey time: 6 hrs.

VALEMOUNT TO CLEARWATER

Hwy 5 leaves Valemount in the **Rocky Mountain Trench**, the geological boundary between the Rocky Mountains and the **Cariboo** and **Monashee** ranges. **Cranberry Marsh**, 2 km south of Valemount, lies within the **Robert W Starratt Wildlife Sanctuary**, a reserve with nesting islands for migratory birds and walking paths for birders. The 200-hectare marsh is prime habitat for waterfowl, beaver, muskrat, moose, walkers and (in winter) Nordic skiers.

Explorer David Thompson, after whom the Thompson River is named, built canoes at the confluence of the Columbia and the **Canoe River** near the **Canoe River Bridge**. **Camp Creek Rest Area**, 4 km south of the bridge, has an information sign about the North Thompson's first tourists, Viscount Milton and Dr Walter Cheadle. The pair passed in 1863, just a year after the **Overlanders** (see p.218) and had an equally horrific trip down the North Thompson River.

The highway climbs out of the Rocky Mountain Trench to the **Albreda River**, which flows down from the **Albreda Glacier**, almost directly ahead, and on to the North Thompson River bridge, 11km south. Best stop for a picnic is 29 km south at a lay-by along the **Thunder River**, a clamorous tributary of the North Thompson. The rugged countryside south to **Avola** could be a remote park except for the clear-cuts that pockmark nearby mountainsides.

Blue River is a railway and logging town turning to tourism. **Mike Wiegele Resort**, *Hwy 5, Box 159, Blue River, BC V0E 1J0; tel: (800) 661-9170 or (250) 673-8381; fax: (250) 673-8464*, is an expensive lakeside lodge specialising in winter heli-skiing and summer heli-hiking, heli-fishing

and heli-sightseeing in the nearby Monashee and Cariboo Mountains. Blue River's other draw is **Wells Gray Provincial Park**, *Box 4516, RR2, Clearwater, BC V0E 1N0; tel: (250) 587-6150*. The park is 24 km west on a rough gravel road (not recommended vehicles) and another 2.5 km on foot to the wilderness **Myrtle Lake Nature Conservancy Area** for hiking and canoeing (no boat motors or other mechanised equipment allowed). For easier access, drive 107 km south to Clearwater.

The highway climbs to **Messiter Summit**, 735m, 19 km south of Blue River. The summit has a good view of the U-shaped North Thompson River Valley stretching south, with the Monashee Mountains on the east and the Cariboo Mountains to the west. Near the bottom of the hill, look for the gravel access road to **Little Hell's Gate Regional Park**, open May–Oct and *not* accessible to trailers or large RVs. The 3-km road winds down to **Porte d'Enfer,** Hell's Gate, named by French-speaking trappers. The North Thompson makes an abrupt turn through a 4.5-m gorge and erupts into a series of boiling whirlpools. The Overlanders spent 3 days walking 14 km around the maelstrom.

The river spreads into a series of marshy lakes near **Tum Tum Creek**, 12 km downstream. Several beaver lodges are visible from the highway south of the creek. The photogenic village of **Avola**, 5 km south, spills down the hill to the riverside. A log building in the centre of town is now **The Log Inn Pub**; *tel: (250) 678-2337*, which bills itself as the 'Largest and Friendliest Pub in Avola'. It's the *only* pub in Avola, a good place to chat with local loggers, railway workers and farmers. The library occupies another log building a few metres away, once the Avola schoolhouse.

Wire Cache Rest Area, a large lay-by 14 km south, was named for telegraph wire left when a telegraph line between Edmonton and Cache Creek was abandoned. Sawmill tours are sometimes available in the hamlet of **Vavenby**: **Slocan Forest Products Ltd**; *tel: (250) 676-9518; fax: (250) 676-9494,* or **Weyerhaeuser Canada Ltd**; *tel: (250) 676-9521.* **Birch Island**, 14 km south, was once the largest settlement on the North Thompson. Today, it's a hamlet and a pleasant lay-by named after a river island.

CLEARWATER

Tourist Information: Clearwater & District Chamber of Commerce, *Box 1988, RR1, Clearwater, BC V0E 1N0; tel: (250) 674-2646; fax: (250) 674-3693;* **Visitor InfoCentre**, *425 E. Yellowhead Hwy (at Clearwater Valley Rd),* open daily (May–Oct), Mon–Sat (Oct–Apr).

ACCOMMODATION

Clearwater is the commercial centre of the North Thompson region and offers the only accommodation for **Wells Gray Provincial Park**. Top choice near the park is moderate–pricey **Nakiska Ranch**, *Trout Creek Rd, Box 1763, RR1, Clearwater, BC V0E 1N0; tel: (250) 674-3655; fax: (250) 674-3387,* a working cattle ranch with a Swiss-run Bed and Breakfast in elegantly restored ranch buildings surrounded by parkland. Best choice in town is **Wells Gray Inn**, *Clearwater Village Rd and Hwy 5, Box 280, Clearwater, BC V0E 1N0; tel: (800) 567-4088* or *(250) 674-2214; fax: (250) 674-3018,* moderate, or **Clearwater Adventures Resort**, *373 Clearwater Valley Rd (at Hwy 5), Box 1813, Clearwater, BC V0E 1N0; tel: (250) 674-3909; fax: (250) 674-3916,* moderate–pricey.

SIGHTSEEING

Clearwater is named after the Clearwater River, which joins the North Thompson

just south of town. Most services are east of the highway, in the old town. A newer section spreads west from the highway toward **Dutch Lake**, with swimming, canoeing and fishing.

Tourism takes many forms in Clearwater. **Wells Gray Backcountry Chalets**, *Box 188B, Clearwater, BC V0E 1N0; tel: (888) 754-8735* or *(250) 587-6444; fax: (250) 587-6446,* have mountain chalets for hut-to-hut hiking and Nordic skiing. **Interior Whitewater Expeditions**, *Box 393, Clearwater, BC V0E 1N0; tel: (800) 661-7238* or *(250) 674-3727; fax: (250) 674-3701,* provide whitewater rafting and kayaking. **Crazy Moon**; *tel: (250) 674-3657,* offer guided mountain bike tours. **Stillwater Horseback Adventures**, *Box 98, Heffley Creek, BC V0E 1Z0; tel: (250) 674-2997,* have guided half-day and overnight trail rides in the park. **Wells Gray Air Services**, *Aspen Hill, Clearwater, BC V0E 1N0; tel/fax: (250) 674-3115,* provide flightseeing over Wells Gray, the Cariboo Mountains and the Gold Rush country around **Barkerville** (see p.323).

Best source for local activities is the **InfoCentre**, *Hwy 5 and Clearwater Valley Rd,* which leads to Wells Gray Provincial Park. Look for the oversized Jerry the Moose statue. Displays explain local history, the Overlanders' trip down the North Thompson, the Secwepemc Nation and the park. The centre bookstore has BC's best selection of Wells Gray information, including *Exploring Wells Gray Park,* by Roland Neave, and the 1:125,000 *Topographic Map of Wells Gray Provincial Park* (PS-WG3), essential for hikers, boaters and Nordic skiers.

SIDE TRACK TO WELLS GRAY PROVINCIAL PARK

Follow *Clearwater Valley Rd* 71 km north from the InfoCentre past Spahats

223

Creek Park, Dawson Falls and the turnoff for Helmcken Falls to Clearwater Lake. The road is partially paved. Gravel sections are well-maintained and passable by autos, RVs and trailers.

Most of this 520,000-hectare park is inaccessible except by canoe, horse or on foot. Bordered on the east and north by mountains and by upland plateau on the west, the scenery rises from alpine meadows to unclimbed and unnamed mountain peaks and glaciers. The park has five major lakes, two large river systems, numerous small lakes, waterfalls, cataracts, extinct volcanoes, lava beds and mineral springs.

Black and grizzly bears are common throughout the park, including along *Clearwater Valley Rd*. Mule deer, caribou, moose and mountain goats are frequently seen, as are smaller animals such as coyotes, wolves, beaver, squirrels, wolverines, minks, martins, golden eagles and rufous hummingbirds.

There are 122 pitches in four campsites as well as 25 wilderness camping areas. Park wardens answer questions at **Dawson Falls**, **Helmcken Falls** and **Clearwater Lake**, July–Aug. Check park signboards for scheduled walks, talks and other programmes.

The road climbs sharply from Clearwater onto the **Spahats Plateau**, created by a series of volcanic eruptions. **Spahats Creek Provincial Park**, *tel: (250) 851-3000*, has 20 pitches and a 10-min walk to 61-m **Spahats Falls**. The creek has carved its canyon more than 120m deep through successive layers of lava. Enter **Wells Gray** at **Hemp Creek**, 17km north of the falls.

Dawson Falls is 5 km north. The **Myrtle River**, 91m wide, drops 18m to form a miniature version of Niagara Falls. Just beyond is the far more

interesting **Mushbowl**, sometimes called the **Devil's Punch Bowl**, huge holes gouged into the lava by the rushing river. The road forks just beyond the car park. Follow signs 4 km west to **Helmcken Falls**, 137m, the fourth largest waterfall in Canada after Hunlen in Tweedsmuir Park (404m), Takakkaw in Yoho Park (310m) and Della on Vancouver Island (185m). The falls were named for Vancouver pioneer and politician John Helmcken. Best time to visit is late afternoon when the setting sun sets the billowing spray ablaze with a smouldering red-orange corona.

Return to the main road and continue 14 km north to the **Ray Farm and Mineral Spring Trail**. The 1.2-km trail leads to the Ray Farm, homesteaded in 1911 by John Ray. Ray and family abandoned the farm in 1947 for civilisation and schools in **Blackpool**, south of Clearwater. Decaying barns and the partially stabilised main house remain beside a pleasant meadow that is one of the best places in the park for birding. Mineral springs in the meadow attract bear, mule deer, moose and coyotes, among other animals. The trail continues another 30 mins to the **Ray Mineral Spring**, bubbling slowly from the top of a mineral dome deposited from the orange-coloured water. Return to the Ray Farm car park, or continue 1.1 km to

---

Colour section (i): A garden in Nelson (p.178); St Joseph's Church, Kamloops (pp.196–198); inset, Summerland fruit (p.190).

(ii): Dining on Emerald Lake, Yoho National Park (pp.212–217); Mt Robson (p.220).

(iii): Vancouver City Library (see pp.226–236).

(iv): Taking the Seabus to Vancouver; Hells Gate (p.265): Airtram over Fraser River.

VALEMOUNT-KAMLOOPS

the **Ray Mineral Spring car park**, about 2 km north of Ray Farm parking. Between the two car parks, the road descends to **Alice Lake**, named after John's wife Alice. The broad, treeless shoreline appeared when a beaver dam burst in 1977 and dropped the water level in the frigid lake by 2m.

Bailey's Chute, just north, is the upper limit of the Clearwater River salmon run. Best time to watch the leaping Chinook is late Aug–Sept. **Clearwater Lake**, 23 km long and a favourite put-in point for boaters and canoeists, is 11 km north. Return to Clearwater. ⬛

CLEARWATER TO BARRIÈRE

Hwy 5 continues south past **North Thompson River Provincial Park**; *tel: (250) 851-3000*, at the confluence of the Clearwater and North Thompson Rivers. The site was once a Secwepemc winter village. Round depressions are the remains of *kekuli*, or pit houses. There are several lay-bys amongst the cottonwoods downstream; fishing for rainbow and Dolly Varden trout and whitefish is excellent. **Little Fort** is named after the Hudson's Bay Company fur trading post located here, 1850–1852. Hwy 24 leads west to Hwy 97 near **100 Mile House** (see p. 323). The free reaction ferry across the North Thompson is on call daily 0700–1845, but does not operate in high water (usually June), when the river is frozen or when ice is flowing. An aerial tramway carries foot passengers when the ferry is closed; vehicles must cross at Clearwater or Barrière.

Hwy 5 passes the small communities of **Darfield** and **Chinook Cove** before reaching *Dunn Lake Rd*, a scenic gravel alternative along the opposite shore of the North Thompson River between Clearwater and Barrière. The community of

Chu Chua is headquarters for the **Simpcw North Thompson Indian Band**, *Box 220, Barrière, BC V0E 1E0; tel: (250) 672-9995; fax: (250) 672-5858*, the local band of the Secwepemc Nation.

BARRIÈRE

Tourist Information: The Barrière and District Chamber of Commerce, *Box 1190, Barrière, BC V0E 1E0; tel: (250) 672-9221.*

The site was named in the 1820s for rocks in the river which formed a barrier to navigation. The **North Thompson Museum**, *352 Lilley Rd;* open mid May–Sept, is a 1930s-era forestry warehouse.

BARRIÈRE TO KAMLOOPS

The lay-by, 24 km south of **Louis Creek**, is a popular spot to watch the annual raft race from Clearwater to Kamloops, the calmer (though far from placid) section of the river. **Fish Trap Rapids**, 3 km downstream, was a traditional Secwepemc fish trapping site during the salmon run. The **McClure Ferry**, 4 km south of the town of **McClure**, is another free reaction ferry across the North Thompson. *Westside Rd,* a mostly-gravel track on the west bank, runs south to Kamloops and north to Barrière.

Heffley–Louis Creek Rd, 20 km south, leads east through scenic cattle and farming country to **Sun Peaks Resort**, *3180 Creekside Way, Sun Peaks, BC V0E 1Z1; tel: (800) 333-9112 or (250) 578-7878; fax: (250) 578-7865*, with skiing, golf, walking, mountain biking and a selection of expensive–pricey accommodation. The turnoff to Kamloops' family ski hill, **Harper Mountain Ski Area**, *2042 Valleyview Dr., Kamloops, BC V2C 4C5; tel: (250) 372-2119; snowphone (250) 828-0336*, is 20 km south. Continue south to TransCanada Hwy 1 and Kamloops.

225

VANCOUVER

Big-city Vancouver carries the trappings of a small town. Immigration from around the world has given it more foreign-born citizens than any other city in Canada, yet it remains essentially Canadian, a polite, tidy place where everyone seems to know everyone else and quite likes it that way. Canada's third largest city is an overgrown village sitting on the edge of a rain forest with some very serious mountains rising almost within walking distance from City Hall.

TOURIST INFORMATION

The **Greater Vancouver Convention and Visitors Bureau** and **Tourism Vancouver**, *Suite 210 Waterfront Centre, 200 Burrard St, Vancouver, BC V6C 3L6; tel: (604) 682-2222; fax: (604) 682-1717.*

Visitor Information Centres are located at *Vancouver International Airport arrivals terminals* and *200 Burrard St*, open daily, and at *Pacific Centre*, open daily in summer.

Downtown Ambassadors; *tel: (604) 685-7811*, wearing blue walking shorts, crested white shirts and Downtown Ambassadors logo, proffer help on city centre streets 1000–1800 in summer from *Canada Place* south to *Robson St* and along *Robson* from the West End to BC Place Stadium. The *Georgia Strait, 1770 Burrard; tel: (604) 730-7000*, a free weekly newspaper, has the most complete listing of local events, cultural attractions, performances, cinemas and other happenings, with reviews and opinion from a decidedly independent perspective.

WEATHER

The Pacific Ocean buffers the extremes of winter and summer. Daytime temperatures occasionally hit 33°C, but 20–25°C is more common. Summer is usually sunny, with the most reliable sunshine in May and mid Sept–early Oct.

While the rest of Canada shivers beneath winter white, Vancouver temperatures can hit 15°C. Snow is heavy on the ski slopes of Grouse Mountain just across the harbour but rare in the city centre.

Downtown Vancouver receives more than 1400mm of rain yearly, most of it in winter. It rained for a memorable 40 days and 40 nights in 1966. More often, rain falls from skies the colour of wet wool blankets for 2–3 days, then clears temporarily to reveal crystal clear vistas of snow-capped peaks before clouds, fog and rain return.

ARRIVING AND DEPARTING

By Air

Vancouver International Airport, (YVR), *Box 23750, Airport Postal Outlet, Richmond, BC V7B 1Y7; tel: (604) 276-6101; fax: (604) 276-6516*, is 30 mins south of the city centre by car. Airport-area hotels have free shuttles.

YVR Airporter; *tel: (604) 244-9888 or (800) 668-3141*, travel between the airport and major city hotels, $9 single, $15 return. A taxi is about $15. **BC Transit** *tel: (604) 521-0400*, stops at the domestic terminal. Car access is via BC 99. Use Exit 39 if travelling northbound, Exit 39A if southbound, and follow the airport signs. International flights arrive and depart

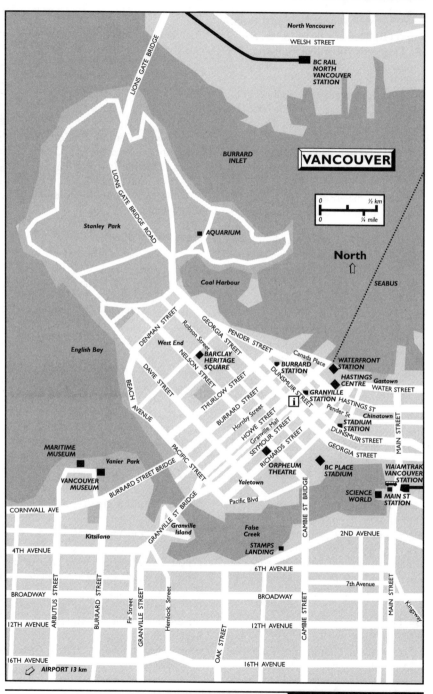

from the **International Terminal Building (ITB)**. Domestic flights use the adjoining **Domestic Terminal Building**. The complex surrounds a central parkade and hire car pick-up area.

Free luggage trolleys are available in the baggage claim areas. Car hire check-in counters are immediately outside the customs area. Follow the walkway through the parkade and down luggage trolley ramps leading to the hire car park.

Coaches load and unload at kerbside bays outside the arrivals level. Taxis, hotel courtesy shuttles and other transport services alight at marked stops on the centre roadway. There are shops and food outlets in the gate areas, but the selection is far better in the central hall, tastiest at the ITB Food Court.

Once checked in, international passengers clear Canadian Immigration and Security on the way to duty-free shopping and boarding gates. US-bound passengers clear US Customs and Immigration in Vancouver.

By Car

Primary access from the US is **BC 99**, from the border at the Peace Arch past White Rock, Delta, Richmond (and YVR) into the city centre. From Vancouver Island, **BC Ferries**; *tel: (604) 277-0277,* dock in Tsawwassen, south of the city centre, and Horseshoe Bay, on the north shore of Burrard Inlet. From the north, the *Sea to Sky Highway,* BC 99, follows Howe Sound past Horseshoe Bay to the Lions Gate Bridge and into the city centre. From the east, **Canada 1**, the TransCanada Hwy, runs into the city centre.

By Train

AMTRAK; *tel: (800) 872-7245,* has daily service between Seattle and Vancouver. **VIA Rail**; *tel: (800) 561-8630,* serves

Canadian points east. Both routes use **Pacific Central Station**, *Main & Terminal Sts, Vancouver, BC V6A 2X7.* **BC Rail**; *tel: (604) 631-3500,* has daily services between Prince George and the **BC Rail Station**, *1311 W. 1st St, N. Vancouver.*

By Bus

The **Pacific Central Station**, *Main & Terminal Sts,* is also the long distance bus terminal. **Pacific Coach Lines**; *tel: (604) 662-8074,* **Maverick Coach Lines**; *tel: (604) 662-8051,* and **Greyhound Lines**; *tel: (604) 662-3222,* provide services.

GETTING AROUND

Greater Vancouver spreads from the US border north to Horseshoe Bay and east into the Fraser Valley. The compact central city is well served by public transport, but driving to the University of British Columbia, the North Shore, Capilano and Grouse Mountain will save time. Parking is often scarce, particularly in Yaletown, Gastown and Chinatown. Try to avoid commuter routes at rush hours, 0730–0900 and 1600–1800, especially roads leading to *Lions Gate Bridge* and *Granville St.* Bicycling is a popular alternative to driving in all but the wettest winter weather.

Visiting Americans breathe a sigh of relief in Vancouver, which is quite safe compared to cities on the US side of the border. Canadians generally take law and order much more seriously than Americans, who sometimes exalt violence to a degree that is not accepted in Canada. Canada's tight restrictions on firearms also contribute greatly to lower crime rates.

Vancouver is not, however, immune to drug-related crimes. It's not wise to wander east beyond the crowds of Gastown at night without company, or to explore the narrow alleys around *E. Hastings, Granville* or *Seymour Sts.*

Public Transport

Vancouver has the most extensive public transport system in Canada. **BC Transit**, *13401-108th Ave, Surrey (Gateway Sky-Train Station, Lower Plaza level), BC V3T 5T4; tel: (604) 521-0400 or (604) 985-7777*, schedules are timed for quick connections. A free brochure, *Discover Vancouver on Transit*, available at most tourist information centres and brochure racks, gives detailed route information for most popular destinations. A full-colour *Transit Guide* showing complete routes for all three systems costs $1.50.

Fares are exact change only, based on three zones and time of day. Maximum fare, crossing three zones during rush hours (Mon–Fri before 0930 and 1500–1830) is $3 adults, $1.50 for children and seniors. Off peak fares are $1.50 and $0.75. Day passes, valid outside rush hours, are $4.50 and $2.25. One fare covers bus, trolley, rail and SeaBus (ferry). Transfers are valid for 90 mins. **Waterfront Station** is the nexus for all three systems.

Bus and **trolley** routes serve every major visitor attraction. Buses run daily but frequency varies.

The **SkyTrain** light rail system covers the 28 km between Burnaby, New Westminster and Surrey in 39 mins. Four downtown stations are underground and clearly marked at street level, 16 others are elevated. Trains run every 2–5 mins daily.

SeaBus harbour ferries cross between Vancouver and the North Shore in 12 mins. Service operates daily every 15–30 mins. Main transfer points to ground transport are Waterfront Station in Vancouver and Lonsdale Quay in North Vancouver.

False Creek Ferries

Aquabus; *tel: (604) 689-5858*, is a fleet of small boats serving False Creek from Science World to Concord Presentation Centre, Stamps Landing, Granville Island and the Hornby Street Dock. Competing **False Creek Ferries**; *tel: (604) 684-7781*, runs from Science World to Stamps Landing, Granville Island, the Aquatic Centre and the Maritime Museum. Fares are $1.75 to $5 depending on distance.

Driving in Vancouver

Traffic flows smoothly outside commuting hours, but roadways are narrow. Residential streets are often choked to a single lane by parked vehicles while larger multilane thoroughfares can suddenly shrink to a single line of traffic. Left-turn lanes and left-turn traffic signals are rare. *Granville St*, the main north–south artery, is a particular problem. With few left-turn signals, traffic can back up in seconds when a single car attempts to turn left.

Parking meters are common except in residential districts. Car parks cost $1.25 per hour to $15 per day. Parking regulations are strictly enforced. Parked cars which impede traffic flow are quickly towed away.

STAYING IN VANCOUVER

Accommodation

Tourism BC; *tel: (800) 663-6000*, can book most Vancouver-area accommodation, but advance booking is essential Apr–Oct and wise the rest of the year. A steady stream of Alaska cruise ship passengers, Vancouver-bound tourists, conventions and business travellers keeps hotels busy all year. Chains include *BW, CI, CP, CS, FS, Hd, HI, Hy, PP, Rn, Sh, TL* and *Wt*. Best sources for Bed and Breakfasts are the **Tourism BC** booking service and **British Columbia Bed and Breakfast Directory**, *1609 Blanshard St, Victoria, BC V8W 2J5; tel: (604) 382-6188 or (800) 661-6188; fax: (604) 382-9172*.

229

There are more than 16,000 rooms in Greater Vancouver, 10,000 of them in the downtown core. The average room rate is just over $100 per night, dipping mid Oct–end May and soaring summer–autumn. Highest rates are in the city centre. Least expensive are the airport area and outlying towns such as Richmond, Burnaby and Langley. Best balance of price and convenience is south of False Creek from *Main St* west to UBC.

Grande Dame of Vancouver hotels is CP's **Hotel Vancouver**, *900 W. Georgia St, Vancouver, BC V6C 2W6; tel: (604) 684-3131 or (800) 441-1414; fax: (604) 662-1929.* Next door is the somewhat stuffy **Hotel Georgia**, *801 W. Georgia St., Vancouver, BC V6C 2W6; tel: (604)682-5566 or (800) 663-1111; fax: (604) 682-8192.* **Wedgewood Hotel**, *845 Hornby St, Vancouver, BC V6Z 1V1; tel: (604) 689-7777 or (800) 663-0666; fax: (604) 688-3074,* is a modern version of the same luxury with better food than its two competitors. Other top choices include the **Metropolitan Hotel Vancouver**, *645 Howe St, Vancouver, BC V6C 2Y9; tel: (800) 667-2300 or (604) 687-1122; fax: (604) 689-7044,* with its trendy and busy **Diva at the Met** restaurant, and the more subdued, European-styled **Sutton Place Hotel**, *845 Burrard St, Vancouver, BC V6Z 2K6; tel: (604) 682-5511; fax: (604) 682-2926.* All are expensive–pricey.

The most convenient hotels for cruise ship passengers are the **Pan Pacific Hotel Vancouver**, *#300-999 Canada Place, Vancouver, BC V6C 3B5; tel: (800) 663-1515 or (604) 662-8111; fax: (604) 685-8690,* and, across the street, **Canadian Pacific's Waterfront Centre Hotel**, *900 Canada Place Wy, Vancouver, BC V6C 3L5; tel: (604) 691-1991; fax: (604) 691-1838,* both expensive–pricey.

Best budget–moderate rooms are the

Hostelling International Vancouver Jericho Beach, *1515 Discovery St, Vancouver, BC V6R 4K5; tel: (604) 224-3208; fax: (604) 224-4852;* **Hostelling International Vancouver Downtown**, *1114 Burnaby St, Vancouver, BC V6E 1P1; tel: (604) 684-4565; fax: (604) 684-4540;* the **University of British Columbia Conference Centre**, *5961 Student Union Blvd, Vancouver, BC V6T 2C9; tel: (604) 822-1010; fax: (604) 822-1001;* and the **YMCA Hotel/Residence**, *733 Beatty St, Vancouver, BC V6B 2M4; tel: (604) 895-5830; fax: (604) 681-2550.*

Not long ago, Bed and Breakfast meant a spartan spare room, but luxury has become the norm. **Heather Cottage**, *5425 Trafalgar St, Vancouver, BC V6N 1C1; tel/fax: (604) 261-1442,* is a prime example. Heritage homes are also emerging as guesthouses. **The Manor**, *345 W. 13th Ave, Vancouver, BC V5Y 1W2; tel: (604) 876-8494; fax: (604) 876-5763,* is among the best. Both are moderate–expensive.

Eating and Drinking

Vancouver is becoming one of North America's hottest food cities. Credit the lucky confluence of rising incomes, a steady tide of immigration, demands by a growing cinema and television industry and a young population. Trendy Vancouver restaurants are more international than their counterparts in Seattle, San Francisco or Los Angeles, a bit less expensive and far friendlier. Wine lists are extensive, if somewhat expensive, thanks to provincial taxes and liquor controls. Vancouver claims the highest per capita wine consumption in North America.

Northwest or **West Coast Cuisine** implies fresh local ingredients (especially seafood) with varying combinations of Asian and Mediterranean flavours and cooking methods. **Canadian cuisine**

typically brings 1950s fare: fried steaks drowned in sauce; mystery-meat scaloppini or egg foo yung. The *Georgia Strait* (see p.232) has the most straightforward food reviews and reliable restaurant descriptions.

Bishop's, *2182 4th Ave; tel: (604) 738-2025*, is reputedly the most polished West Coast restaurant in Vancouver. **Bacchus Ristorante**, *Wedgewood Hotel, 845 Hornby St; tel: (604) 689-7777*, has the best blend of Northern Italian and Northwest cuisine. **900 West**, *Hotel Vancouver, 900 W. Georgia St; tel; (604) 684-3131*, is an unabashed knockoff of San Francisco megachef Jeremiah Tower by Tower himself. **Diva at the Met**, *Metropolitan Hotel, 645 Howe St; tel: (604) 602-7788*, is less pretentious and at least as good. All are pricey. **Liliget Feast House**, *1724 Davie St; tel: 681-7044*, is Vancouver's top First Nations eatery, moderate–pricey.

Stanley Park has food to match its views. The pricey **Fish House**, *8901 Stanley Park Dr.; tel: (604) 681-7275*, is the best fish restaurant in the city. **The Teahouse Restaurant**, *7501 Stanley Park Dr. (at Ferguson Pt); tel: (604) 669-3281*, moderate–pricey, specialises in Northwest cuisine. **Prospect Point Café**, *Prospect Point, Stanley Park; tel: (604) 669-2737*, budget–moderate, is a casual version of The Teahouse.

Star Anise, *1485 W. 12 St; tel: (604) 737-1485*, moderate, is a fine Asian-Northwest fusion. **Tang's Noodle House**, *2807 W. Broadway; tel: (604) 737-1278*, cheap–budget, is one of the city's favourite Chinese restaurants. Best bet for dim sum, Chinese dumplings, is **Pink Pearl**, *1132 E. Hastings; tel: (604) 253-4316*, in Chinatown. The best sushi bargain is the **Japanese Deli House**, *381 Powell St; tel: (604) 681-6484*, for budget all-you-can-eat sushi or tempura at lunch. **Thai House**, *1116 Robson St; tel: (604)*

683-3383, budget–moderate, is crowded at lunch and nearly as popular for dinner at locations in Kitsilano, Richmond and Metrotown as well as downtown.

Buddhist Vegetarian Restaurant, *137 East Pender St; tel: (604) 683-8816*, budget–moderate, is an excellent vegetarian choice. **The Jewel of India**, *52 Alexander St; tel: (604) 681-3678*, moderate, has a fine selection of meat and fish as well as outstanding veg. **Steamworks Brewing Company**, *375 Water St; tel: (604) 689-2739*, budget–moderate, has Vancouver's best beer and a solid restaurant. **Newsbreak Deli**, *Suite 32-200 Granville St; tel: (604) 669-0667*, is popular for cheap lunch and breakfast with Canada Place-area office workers

Any of Vancouver's ethnic enclaves, Chinatown, Japantown, Little India, Little Italy or Greektown, are good choices for cheap–moderate ethnic restaurants, or sample them all at **Granville Island Public Market**, *Granville Island; tel: (604) 666-6477*. Dozens of stalls sell everything from local breads and goat cheese to imports from around the globe. Harbour-side tables inside and out offer pleasant views in any weather. **Granville Island Brewery**, *Granville Island; tel: (694) 687-2739*, has daily tours at 1500 with free samples. Best place to drink in peace, if not quiet, is **Mulvaney's Restaurant**, *Granville Isl; tel: (604) 685-6571*, cheap–moderate, with great beer, good food and loud music.

Coffee has become as much an institution in Vancouver as it has in Seattle. With 170 officially rainy days each year, frequent doses of caffeine help keep grey-sky depression at bay. Starbucks is Canada's reigning coffee chain, but Vancouver has no lack of independent coffee roasteries and coffee bars. **Murchie's Tea & Coffee**, *970 Robson St; tel: (604) 662-3776, and branch locations*, has roasted and served

231

coffee since 1908. The Yaletown branch has an interesting coffee museum. **Ciao Espresso Bar**, *1074 Denman St; tel: (604) 682-0112*, is a prized hangout for writers who thrive on steady diets of caffeine and tobacco. Singles mingle on comfortable sofas at **Dakoda's**, *1602 Yew St; tel: (604) 730-9266*, then stop next door for designer condoms at Willi Wear before retiring to more private pursuits. **Joe's Cafe**, *1150 Commercial Dr.*, is a vigorous mix of poolhall hustlers, bohemian philosophers, poets, feminists, political agitators and the occasional politician.

Communications

There are dozens of post offices in Vancouver. Mail can be addressed to hotels.

Money

Thomas Cook Foreign Exchange branches: *Eaton's Dept Store, 701 Granville St; tel: (604) 687-6111; Pan Pacific Hotel, 999 Canada Place; tel: (604) 641-1229; Eaton Centre, 2139A 4700 Kingsway, Burnaby; tel: (604) 430-3990; Marlin Travel, Park Royal Shopping Centre, 2009 Park Royal South; tel: (604) 922-9301*, and *Guildford Town Centre, 1111 Guildford Town Centre, Surrey; tel: (604) 584-3338.* All offer assistance with lost or stolen Thomas Cook Traveller's Cheques.

Forget the days when Vancouver rolled up the sidewalks at 2200. The city has 32 professional theatre groups and two dozen performance venues, plus 18 professional dance companies and music venues specialising in *taiko* (Japanese drumming), jazz, blues, rock, classical, opera and more. Best information: *The Georgia Strait*; the Thur *Vancouver Sun* or the Fri *Province* newspapers. **Arts Hotline**; *tel: (604) 684-ARTS (2787)*, has pre-recorded information.

Granville Mall, *Granville St, Hastings–Georgia Sts*, a slightly seedy section of town, is **Theatre Row** with the cheapest cinemas in Vancouver. All films are half-price on Tuesdays. Nearby is the **Orpheum Theatre**; *tel: (604) 280-4444*, home of the **Vancouver Symphony**. Vancouver's other top concert venue, the **Yale Hotel**, *1300 Granville St; tel: (604)681-9253*, is the pre-eminent blues house; safest parking is at the hotel or the equally raucous strip club next door.

Yaletown is the current night-time hotspot. Even the **Yaletown Brewing Co**, *1111 Mainland St; tel: (604) 688-0064*, is likely to have a queue Fri–Sat nights. **Bar None**, *1222 Hamilton St; tel: (604) 689-7000*, has queues most nights for live blues, rock and soul. Hotter still are pool halls, starting with the original **Soho Cafe**, *1144 Homer St; tel: (604) 688-1180*, and **Automotive Club**, *1095 Homer St; tel: (604) 682-0040*, a former auto dealership.

Acts as diverse as the Three Tenors and Aerosmith play **BC Place**, *777 Pacific Blvd S.; tel: (604) 661-7373.* The **Ford Centre for the Performing Arts**, *777 Homer St; tel: (604) 606-0616*, hosts touring Broadway and other stage shows. **Vancouver Opera**, *845 Cambie St; tel: (604) 682-2871; fax: (604) 682-3981*, plays Oct–May.

The major department stores are **Eaton's**, *701 Granville St; tel: (604) 685-7112*, plus other locations, and **The Bay**, *674 Granville; tel: (604) 681-6211*. BC's largest shopping centre is **Metrotown Centre**, *4800 Kingsway, Burnaby; tel: (604) 438-2444*, 15 mins by SkyTrain from the city centre. **Pacific Centre**, *Georgia & Howe Sts; tel: (604) 688-7236*, is the leading inner city mall. Other major shopping areas include **Granville Island**, *W. 4th Ave*,

Kitsilano, and *Robson St,* Vancouver's less-studied answer to Beverly Hills' *Rodeo Dr.*

Top shops for First Nations items are **Hill's Indian Crafts**, *165 Water St; tel: (604) 685-4249; fax: (604) 682-4197,* and **Inuit Gallery of Vancouver**, *345 Water St; tel: (604) 688-7323,* both in Gastown. Best source for books is **Duthie Books**, *919 Robson St; tel: (604) 684-4496,* and other locations. For guidebooks and travel-related items, try **The Travel Bug**, *2667 W. Broadway; tel: (604) 737-1122,* in Kitsilano.

SIGHTSEEING

Vancouver got its start in 1791 when Spanish Captain Jose Maria Narvaez anchored west of **Point Grey**, now home to the **University of British Columbia**. Capt George Vancouver anchored nearby the next year and rowed into Burrard Inlet. The UBC **Museum of Anthropology** (MOA), *6393 N.W. Marine Dr.; tel: (604) 822-5087; fax: (604) 822-2974,* has one of the world's finest collections of First Nations art with modern and antique totems, feast dishes and carvings in gold, stone and wood. Tens of thousands of additional artefacts are visible in storage cases. Don't miss outdoor totems behind the museum building. The **Nitobe Memorial Garden**, *200m north on S.W. Marine Dr.,* a Japanese Garden, and UBC's **Botanical Garden**, *6804 N.W. Marine Dr.; tel: (604) 822-9666,* are among BC's finest.

The city of Vancouver began in 1862 when 'three greenhorns' decided to make bricks on the wild shore of Coal Harbour instead of scrabbling for gold in nearby mountains. John Morton, Samuel Brighouse and William Hailstone paid $550.75 for what would become the **West End**, stretching from sea to sea, Coal Harbour to English Bay. Home to the rich and powerful during the Edwardian era, the West

End has become a mix of tree-lined streets, modern flats, mansions and trendy restaurants sandwiched between Stanley Park and downtown. **Denman St** is the West End's high street, a 7-block strip of restaurants and coffee bars.

Roedde House Museum, *1415 Barclay St; tel: (604) 684-7040,* open weekends, one of the few surviving Victorian buildings in the West End, is part of **Barclay Heritage Square**, *Barclay, Nicola, Haro and Broughton Sts,* a collection of nine period homes in their original settings.

Stanley Park*; tel: (604) 257-8400,* is one of North America's finest urban parks, 400 hectares of forest laced with 80 km of walking and cycling paths. The most popular path is a 10-km shoreline loop around the peninsula. Highlights include totem poles, sweeping vistas across Vancouver and the North Shore, three restaurants (p.231), picnic grounds, a rose garden, beaches and the **Vancouver Aquarium**, *Stanley Park; tel: (604) 268-9900; fax: (604) 631-2529,* which specialises in the Pacific Northwest, one of the best aquaria in the region.

Yaletown is a former warehouse district on the north shore of **False Creek**, a shallow inlet stretching east from English Bay. Architects, designers, TV producers and filmmakers are cheek-to-jowl with trendy restaurants, nightspots and pool halls. Parking is at a premium, especially as development burgeons on the 83 hectares along False Creek that was the site of EXPO 86. **BC Sports Hall of Fame**, *777 Pacific Blvd, Gate A, BC Place Stadium; tel: (604) 687-5520,* showcases the history of sports in the province. **Science World**, *1455 Quebec St; tel: (604) 268-6363,* has hands-on exhibits. An OMNIMAX theatre beneath the silver geodesic dome has one of the world's largest screens.

One million cubic metres of mud dredged from False Creek early this century

233

First Arts

After decades of suppression by Christian missionaries and federal Indian Reserve agents, Western Canada's aboriginal arts, crafts and culture are being revitalised and brought back into daily life. First Nations' events such as annual pow-wows in Kamloops, BC and Head-Smashed-In Buffalo Jump, AB, and Native events at the Calgary Stampede lure thousands of participants from tribes across North America as well as tens of thousands of onlookers.

The First Nations of Western Canada are often divided into four groups based on the resources they relied upon for survival: the coastal **People of the Salmon**, the interior BC plateau **Traders**, the **People of the** (Rocky) **Mountains** and the plains **People of the Buffalo**. The coastal and plains peoples are the social and artistic extremes. A mild climate and easy access to rich salmon and forest resources gave **coastal nations** ample leisure time to develop a rich artistic tradition centred on large, semi-permanent villages of wooden long-houses. Totem poles, elaborate dance costumes and carved masks, woven blankets, basketry and immense giveaways of wealth called *potlatch* were essential elements. Animals were favourite artistic themes, especially the bear, beaver, killer whale, raven and other clan spirits. The **plains nations**, faced with harsher conditions and fewer resources, lived in portable teepees in smaller, nomadic groups that valued hunting and military prowess above all else. Artistry was expressed in practical items such as bead, quill and painted decorations on buck-skin clothing and teepees, decorated moccasins, feathered headdresses, painted animal skulls, peace pipes, rawhide carrying bags called *parfleches* and intricate basketry. Artistic elements tended toward geometric patterns, floral designs and representations of the sun, sky and plains animals, especially the buffalo upon which their way of life depended.

234

Trading and mountain nations combined coastal and plains traditions, depending on their own resources and locations. Groups that could depend on annual salmon runs for a rich diet, for example, were closer in art and spirit to the coastal nations. Groups that depended on the luck of the hunt adopted more of the art and culture of the plains tribes.

Vancouver has long been a cultural centre for Canada's First Nations. Spurred by academic interest at the University of British Columbia, totem pole carving was revived in 1949 after gen-erations of laws forbidding many traditional practices. The new totems helped fuel a nation-wide cultural renaissance and a resurgence of aboriginal artistic forms which had all but disappeared except in museum collections. By the 1990s, modern interpretations of the bold, stylised images of coastal First Nation themes had become as much a part of Western Canada as European, Chinese and East Indian motifs.

Vancouver International Airport has one of Canada's finest public collections of First Nations' art. Gitksan carvers created the three totems rising outside the international terminal. Banners, prints, thunderbirds, model totem poles and traditional welcoming figures are displayed throughout the arrival and departure areas. The artistic focus is *The Spirit of Haida Gwaii, the Jade Canoe,* a 6-m bronze by Bill Reid incorporating traditional Haida themes. Reid is also well-represented at UBC's **Museum of Anthropology (MOA)**, which has a display of

transformed a sandbar into a metal bashing haven called Industrial Island. Island facto-ries produced 50 years of rivets, chain, nails, cement and industrial pollutants. When the public revolted in the 1960s, industry was eased out and the site cleaned up. The run-down eyesore has become **Granville Island**, one of North America's most suc-cessful urban makeovers and a refuge for artists, casual shoppers and entertainers.

jewellery and other small works as well as larger wood sculptures. He helped create the Haida houses and totem poles standing behind the MOA overlooking the Georgia Strait. A larger collection of modern poles by other carvers is on display in Stanley Park.

The commercial and artistic success of Reid, Mungo Martin and others has helped create a worldwide market in First Nations arts and crafts. The MOA gift shop has an excellent collection of affordable prints and copies of display pieces. Commercial gallery prices are higher, but so are selection and quality. Vancouver Island gallery prices, particularly in Campbell River, Port Hardy, Tofino and Ucluelet, are slightly lower than in Vancouver.

The plains nations, the Slavey (Dene-thah), Cree, Stoney (Nakoda), Sarcee (Tsuu T'ina) and Blackfoot (Siksika), haven't produced the kind of name artists the coastal traditions have nurtured. The lack of individual name recognition has kept gallery prices in Calgary and Edmonton below Vancouver levels. Best places to view both traditional and modern plains art are the **Glenbow Museum** in Calgary, the **Moore House** at the **Whyte Museum** complex and the **Luxton Museum**, both in Banff, the **Provincial Museum of Alberta** in Edmonton and **Head-Smashed-In Buffalo Jump** near Fort Macleod.

There are ample opportunities to buy, as well. As with other artwork, look for the artist's signature on each piece and ask for a certificate of authentication. Paintings, sculptures and other large pieces are usually signed, but it is not always practicable to sign jewellery, moccasins, headdresses and other pieces. With or without signature, 'Indian-style', 'in the tradition of', 'Indian heritage' and similar phrases are usually attempts to circumvent laws prohibiting the promotion and sale of art made by non-Natives as Native-made pieces.

Several Vancouver galleries are owned by First Nations artists. **Potlatch Arts Ltd**, *8161 Main St, Suite 100; tel: (604) 321-5888,* is a collector's gallery that sells wood carvings, glass sculptures and other art. Totem pole carver and jeweller Norman Tait has his own gallery, **Wilp's Ts Ak Gallery, 'The House of the Mischievous Man'**, *2426 Marine Dr.; tel: (604) 925-5771,* where visitors can watch carvers working wood, gold and silver. **Wickaninnish Gallery**, *The Net Loft, Granville Island,* is one of Vancouver's best sources for traditional and contemporary BC Native jewellery. **The Cedar Root Gallery**, *1607 E. Hastings St; tel: (604) 251-6244,* is a small, community-based gallery specialises in new artists and experimental works.

235

In the Calgary area, try the **Glenbow Museum Gift Shop**; *130 9 Ave S.E.; tel: (403) 268-4100,* **Cottage Fine Arts**, *6503 Elbow Dr. S.W.; tel: (403) 252-3797,* and **Sarcee Arts and Crafts**, *3700 Anderson Rd S.W.; tel: (403) 238-2677.* Best sources in the Edmonton area include **Bearclaw Gallery**, *10403 124 St; tel: (403) 482-1204,* **Fort Door Indian Crafts**, *10308 81 Ave; tel: (403) 432-7535,* the **Great Canadian Aboriginal Trading Co**, *10590 109 St; tel: (403) 423-1744,* and **Indian Trader**, *West Edmonton Mall; tel: (403) 444-1165.*

Traditional ceremonies, such as potlatches and pow-wows, are also being revived. Potlatches are generally private affairs, but non-Natives are usually welcome at pow-wows, gatherings that focus on dances and other public events, including art sales. Check with the CVB and local newspapers for dates, time and locations. The **Aboriginal Tourism Authority**, *Box 1240, Station M, Calgary, AB T2P 2L2; tel: (403) 261-3022; fax: (403) 261-5676; web: http:// www.aboriginalnet.com/tourism,* has lists of Native events throughout Western Canada.

Gastown, *Water St between Alexander and Richards Sts,* was settled in 1870 by a saloon-keeper called Gassy Jack for his ability to maintain a running conversation with no help. Once a rowdy red light district handy to the docklands, Gastown has become a tamer, if no less popular, entertainment venue. Hanging flower baskets adorn lamp standards spring–autumn.

Chinatown, *E. Pender and Keefer Sts,*

Carrall–Gore Sts, began as a ghetto for Chinese immigrants. Reviled for their race and despised for their willingness to accept low wages, thousands of Chinese labourers were imported in the 1880s to build Canada's railroads. Most eventually drifted into Vancouver and other major cities, settling in Chinatowns for mutual protection against periodic rampages by Whites.

Anti-Chinese violence has disappeared, but the sentiment remains. Thousands of well-to-do Hong Kong Chinese moved to Vancouver during the run-up to the June, 1997 handover of the British colony to China. There is occasional talk of Vancouver's transformation into 'Hongcouver', though most new arrivals settled in Richmond, near the airport.

Parking is a challenge in Chinatown. Best bet is near **Dr Sun Yat-Sen Classical Garden**, *578 Carrall St; tel: (604) 689-7133,* calling itself the first authentic classical Chinese garden to be built outside China. **Sam Kee Building**, *8 W. Pender St,* is the narrowest commercial building in the world, less than 2m wide after the city expropriated most of the building to widen *Pender St.*

Kitsilano, *Burrard to Alma Sts, English Bay south to 16th Ave,* is one of Vancouver's liveliest neighbourhoods, a mix of left-over hippies, young families and UBC students. Classic views of Vancouver, the city centre and Stanley Park, are everyday sights from popular **Vanier Park** and **Kitsilano Park**, on English Bay. **Fourth Ave** is one of the city's premier shopping districts, known more for individual shops than chain outlets. **Broadway**, sometimes called **Greektown**, is a secondary shopping area.

The **Vancouver Maritime Museum**, *1905 Ogden Ave; tel: (604) 257-8300,* has model ships, naval uniforms and other maritime artefacts. Highlight is **St Roch**

National Historic Site, a 1928 ship built for arctic patrol by the Royal Canadian Mounted Police and now open for exploration inside the museum. St Roch was the first vessel to sail the Northwest Passage from Pacific to Atlantic Oceans, the first to make the return voyage and, after sailing through the Panama Canal, the first to circumnavigate North America.

Vancouver Museum, *1100 Chestnut St; tel: (604) 736-4431; fax: (604) 736-5417,* has an extensive collection of BC First Nations art, relics and costumes as well as city history exhibits. In the same building, the **Pacific Space Centre**; *tel: (604) 738-7827,* offers planetarium and laser-light shows.

Gordon Southam Observatory; *tel: (604) 738-2855,* is open Fri–Sun 1900–2300, weather permitting, for viewing through a 500mm Cassegrain telescope.

The best overall view of Vancouver is from 167-m **The Lookout!**, *atop Harbour Centre, 555 W. Hastings St; tel: (604) 689-0421; fax: (604) 685-7329.* The white sails to the west are the roof of **Canada Place**, Vancouver's cruise ship terminal, and **IMAX Theatre**; *tel: (604) 682-4629.* Directly across Burrard Inlet is **Capilano Suspension Bridge**, *3735 Capilano Rd; tel: (604) 985-7474,* a scenic pedestrian bridge over Capilano Canyon. Rising in the background, 4100-ft **Grouse Mountain**, *6400 Nancy Greene Wy; tel: (604) 984-0661; fax: (604) 984-6360,* is a winter ski area and a summer walking retreat. Access is by aerial tramway.

Van Dusen Botanical Garden, *5251 Oak St; tel: (604) 266-7194,* is one of Canada's most comprehensive collections of ornamental plants. The **Bloedel Floral Conservatory**, *Queen Elizabeth Park, 33rd and Cambie Sts; tel: (604) 872-5513,* is a tropical garden within a triodetic dome, surrounded by 53 hectares of arboretum.

VANCOUVER CIRCUIT

The route begins and ends at *W. 4th Ave* and *Burrard St* for convenience, but you can pick it up at any point. The circuit can be taken in either direction (except for the Stanley Park and Gastown sections, which are one-way), but the directions given reduce left turns and take advantage of one-way streets. Avoid the downtown and Lions Gate Bridge sections during commuting hours, 0730–0900 and 1600–1800.

Allow at least half a day for this 100-km driving circuit. Visiting all of the museums and attractions could stretch to the better part of a week.

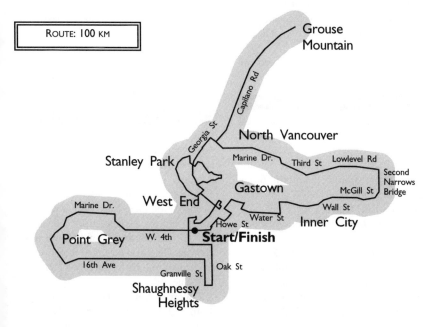

ROUTE: 100 KM

Grouse Mountain

Capilano Rd

Georgia St.

North Vancouver

Stanley Park

Marine Dr.   Third St   Lowlevel Rd

Second Narrows Bridge

McGill St

Gastown

Marine Dr.   West End

Wall St

Water St   Inner City

Howe St

Point Grey   W. 4th   **Start/Finish**

16th Ave   Oak St

Granville St

Shaughnessy Heights

KITSILANO

The *4th Ave* shopping district begins at *Burrard St,* but shops are busier, trendier and more expensive west of *Maple St.*

During the 1970s, Kitsilano was Canada's hippie haven, a past that is fondly remembered but almost invisible beneath a veneer of 1990s prosperity. Shopping ends abruptly at *Balsam St,* where *4th Ave* becomes a residential street. The next major shopping area is *MacDonald–Alma Sts.* One block west of *Alma* on the left is the Jericho Barracks, Vancouver Detachment, Canadian Forces Base Chilliwack. **Jericho Beach Park** is on the right.

Watch for cyclists as the road veers to the right and becomes *N.W. Marine Dr.* toward **Locarno Park, Locarno Beach** and **Spanish Banks Beach**, all fronting on **English Bay**. The three parks merge imperceptibly, with expansive vistas across English Bay to North Vancouver and east to the inner city and Stanley Park. The beachfront walkway is extremely popular with walkers, runners, cyclists and dog walkers – watch where you step. There is ample parking, particularly near Locarno Park, as well as picnic and recreational facilities.

238

POINT GREY

Captain George Vancouver anchored just off Point Grey in 1792, only to find that two Spanish ships had preceded him. Vancouver led the way north up the Georgia Strait, around the north tip of Vancouver Island and south to Nootka Sound, the first step in a successful campaign to convince Spain of British superiority in the region.

Pacific Spirit Regional Park begins at the city limits just west of Spanish Banks. The 770-hectare park surrounds the **University of British Columbia** campus on **Point Grey**, providing a buffer against urban expansion as well as one of Vancouver's most expansive parks. Wild parklands lie between road and ocean. The expensive, well-protected homes on the other side of the road are built on UBC Endowment Lands.

UBC is constructed in grey concrete

and red brick. At the first stop sign, the junction with *Chancellor Dr.,* turn right. Just after the turn is the entrance to the parking lot for the UBC **Museum of Anthropology** (MOA), on the right. The main UBC parkade is to the left, but the museum lot is more convenient. Parking regulations are strictly enforced on the campus. Parking is by permit only except in scattered locations, including MOA. Buy parking tickets from the yellow boxes in the MOA lot, which accept both coins and credit cards. MOA's main entrance is at the far end of the parking lot. The outdoor totem exhibition area is over a small rise behind the lot and to the far left behind the museum building. Walk the 200m west along *Marine Dr.* to **Nitobe Japanese Tea Gardens**, on the left.

Marine Dr. curves south around Point Grey. The **Botanical Garden** spreads right across the hillside, 2 km beyond the MOA parking lot.

SHAUGHNESSY HEIGHTS

When leaving the Botanical Garden, turn right onto *Marine Dr.* and immediately move to the left-hand lane. At the first traffic signal, turn left onto *16th Ave.* Follow *16th Ave* east through the campus and Pacific Spirit Park back into Vancouver proper and the pleasant, tree-shaded residential neighbourhoods of **Shaughnessy Heights**. The road is a broad parkway, but residential parking frequently blocks the kerb lane.

Follow *16th Ave* to *Granville St* and turn south (right), toward the airport. The street is lined with grand houses, most of them well-screened by tall hedges and trees. Rather than trying to turn left across heavy traffic, continue to *34th Ave,* turn west (right) and right again (north) onto *Connaught Dr.,* then right (west) again onto *33rd Ave.*

Follow *33rd Ave* across Granville to the next traffic signal and turn south (right) onto *Oak St,* following signs for **Van Dusen Botanical Gardens**. Take *Oak* to *37th Ave* and turn west (right) at the large sign for Sprinklers Restaurant and turn into the first drive for the Van Dusen Botanical Gardens parking lot.

MARITIME MUSEUM AND VANIER PARK

After leaving Van Dusen, turn north (left) onto *Oak St* 1 km to *W. 12th Ave,* at Vancouver Hospital. Turn west (left) onto *W. 12th* at the left turn lane. The imposing red brick building at *Hemlock St* was originally a Presbyterian church, now Holy Trinity Anglican Church. Continue west across *Granville St* through more shady residential areas to *Arbutus St* and turn north (right) into a light industrial area that is quickly being overrun by private homes. Several blocks north of *W. 4th Ave* are still paved with brick and become slippery in rain. Continue downhill toward **Kitsilano Pool**, **Hutton Park** and **Vanier Park**, with English Bay in the distance.

Follow signs for the **Maritime Museum** and **Vancouver Museum**, skirting the edge of Vanier Park. The entrance for the Maritime Museum is to the north (left), just beyond the tall totem pole, also on the left. Parking is extremely limited near Vanier Park; the Maritime Museum is handy for Vancouver Museum parking as well as for the heritage ships moored just behind and Vanier Park itself. Parking regulations are strictly enforced.

WEST END

After leaving the Maritime Museum, go straight on *Chestnut St* to *Whyte Ave* and turn east (left) for the **Vancouver Museum** and observatory. From the museum, turn south (left) onto *Chestnut* for one block, then go west (right) on *Greer Ave,* following signs for the bicycle route to the Burrard Bridge. Turn south (left) onto *Cypress Ave,* then east (left) onto *Cornwall Ave.* Keep in the left-hand lanes and veer left onto the **Burrard Bridge** at the Molson Brewery (not open to the public). There is a good view south-east to Granville Island from mid-span, but no place to stop on the bridge.

After crossing the bridge, continue straight on *Burrard St* for ten blocks to *Georgia St.* Turn east (right) for one block to *Hornby St* and turn south (right). The **Vancouver Art Gallery**, *750 Hornby St; tel: (604) 682-668,* is on the left. To the right is the **BC Provincial Courts** building, with an urban park and waterfalls rising above street level. Turn south (right) onto *Howe St* at **Eaton's** department store and west (right) onto *Smythe St.* Follow *Smythe* across *Burrard* to *Thurlow* and turn south (left) for two blocks to *Nelson St.* Turn west (right) onto *Nelson* for four blocks to *Nicola St,* then turn north (right) one block to *Barclay.* Turn east (right) on Barclay to the restored mansions of **Barclay Heritage Square** and the **Roedde House Museum**.

239

STANLEY PARK

Take the first left turn after the museum. Continue north to *Robson St* and turn west (left), passing the **Robson Public Market** on the south (left) side of the street on the way to *Denman St.* Turn north (right) on *Denman,* following signs for ferries to Nanaimo and the Sunshine Coast. Stay in the right-hand lane to avoid delays caused by cars turning left. At *Georgia St,* turn north (left) toward **Stanley Park**. Stay in the right-hand lanes and curve right into the park.

Park roads are one-way in an anti-clockwise direction. Parking regulations are enforced all year; buy parking coupons at the yellow dispensers, which accept coins and credit cards. Parking tickets are valid throughout the park. Best bet is to buy all-day parking at the first convenient stop and concentrate on enjoying the park. The first parking lot on the left is convenient for visits to the **Aquarium** and **horse tram tours** of the park. One kilometre beyond is the main parking area and **totem pole** display. Just ahead and on the right are broad views back to the inner city and the sail-like roofline of **Canada Place**, Vancouver's cruise ship terminal and convention centre. Expect to see cruise ships docked at Canada Place during the day May–Oct. Ships returning from Alaska dock around 0800 and depart about 1800 the same day. The **Nine O'clock Gun**, on the waterfront just past a bronze statue of a runner, is fired at 2100 each evening. The cannon was originally sounded at 1800 to signal the close of commercial fishing each day. A flashing light warns passersby that the gun is about to fire.

A convenient lay-by is 1 km ahead, with good views across to docks on the North Shore. The bright yellow piles are sulphur waiting to be loaded aboard ships; the tan-coloured piles are wood pulp, also waiting to be loaded. The suspension bridge to the left is **Lions Gate Bridge**, the main artery to the North Shore. Just beyond **Brockton Point** is Vancouver's answer to Copenhagen's Little Mermaid, **Girl in a Wetsuit**, a bronze statue of a woman diver in a wet suit. A left-hand exit 1 km ahead leads out of the park and back to *Georgia St.* Continue straight to continue the park tour. The entrance to Lions Gate Bridge, 1 km ahead, is closed 1530–1830 to minimise traffic in the park.

Prospect Point is the best view down on Lions Gate. The informal restaurant has good views of harbour traffic; garbage bins

are popular with raccoons and other park residents. Continue around the point past parking areas for **Third Beach** and the **Teahouse Restaurant** at **Ferguson Point**, **Second Beach** and the start of two-way traffic near the **Fish House Restaurant**. Watch for geese and small children on the road. The **Seawall Promenade**, leading south to the Burrard Bridge, is an extremely popular beach and walkway.

NORTH VAN(COUVER)

Just after leaving the park, *Beach Ave* curves to the right, following the Seawall Promenade. Instead, go straight one short block to *Denman St* and turn north (left) back to *Georgia St.* Turn left onto *Georgia*, this time staying in the left-hand lanes to pass **Lost Lagoon** and join BC 99 through the park to Lions Gate Bridge.

Cross the bridge and then turn east (right) onto *Marine Dr.*, following signs for North Vancouver, Capilano Canyon and Grouse Mountain. Move to the left-hand lane and turn north (left) at the first traffic signal, *Capilano Rd.* Petrol is slightly cheaper in North Van than across the harbour in Vancouver.

Capilano Rd climbs through 3 km of housing estates to **Capilano Suspension Bridge**. The bridge is on the left, parking is on the right. The swaying pedestrian bridge, built a century ago for fishing and logging access, was Vancouver's first tourist attraction. Continue 4 km north on *Capilano Rd,* which becomes *Nancy Greene Way,* to **Grouse Mountain** and the tramway, open all year.

Return to *Marine Dr.* and turn east (left) through North Vancouver. Veer right onto *Third St,* following the Scenic Drive signs, to *Forbes Ave* and right again to *Esplanade,* past **Lonsdale Quay and Public Market**, just to the right at the end of *Lonsdale Rd.* Continue east along Esplanade and veer right onto *Low level Rd* to follow the railway tracks east. There are excellent views south (right) to Vancouver unless trains are parked on the sidings.

INNER CITY

Road signs for Vancouver begin appearing about 3 km east. Move into the right-hand lane and cross Burrard Inlet on the **Second Narrows Bridge**, often called **Iron-workers Memorial Bridge**, on *Canada 1*. The right-hand lanes offer good views west over the Vancouver docklands. Take the first exit after the bridge, following signs for the bicycle route onto *McGill St.* Follow *McGill* past **Exposition Park** and along the waterfront for 3 km. Turn north (right) onto *Wall St* and continue through residential areas above the docks for another 2 km, then go north (right) again onto *Dundas St.* Pass the **BC Sugar Museum**, *at the foot of Roger St; tel: (604) 253-1131,* with photos, videos and artefacts of sugar production in BC, to *Heatley St.*

Turn south (left) onto *Heatley* and cross *E. Cordova St* one block to *Hastings.* Go east (left) on *Hastings* to *Hawks St* and turn north (left)·to *Powell St.* Turn west (left) to pass **Oppenheimer Park** and **Japantown**, which never recovered from the forced relocation of Japanese-Canadians to the interior of BC during World War II.

Continue two blocks to *Gore St* and turn south (left) along the edge of **Chinatown** to *E. Pender.* Turn west (right) through the heart of Chinatown, past the Chinese Cultural Centre behind the large gate on the south (left) side of the street with the **Dr Sun-Yat Sen Chinese Gardens** behind.

GASTOWN

Turn north (right) onto *Abbott St* to *E.*

Cordova St and turn east (right) along the edge of **Gastown** two blocks to *Columbia St.* Go two blocks north (left) on *Columbia* to the dead-end and turn west (left) onto *Alexander St.* At the first stop sign, where the brick pavement begins, turn north (right) onto *Water St.* A flamboyant statue of **Gassy Jack**, who built the first bar in Gastown, is on the left. The Gastown **steam clock** is on the north (right) at *Cambie St.* Traffic slows to a crawl through Gastown with pedestrians wandering the streets as though it is a pedestrian mall.

At the end of *Water St*, turn south (left) into *Richards St,* immediately west (right) onto *W. Hastings St,* then south (left) onto *Howe St.* The **Four Seasons Hotel** is on the east (left) and the **Hotel Georgia** on the west (right) at *Georgia St.* Cross *Georgia.* West (right) is the **Vancouver Art Gallery**, on the east (left) is **Eaton's**. Turn (left) onto *Robson St.* **Cinema Row** and *Granville St* are to the south (left) one block ahead.

Continue on *Robson* across *Howe St,* with the new **Vancouver Public Library** on the north (left), looking like a modernistic Roman Coliseum. Go south (right) onto *Hamilton,* which jogs right and left to become *Maitland St* and run through the narrow streets of warehouses-become-trendy **Yaletown** to a dead end at *Davie St.* Turn north (right) for five blocks to *Granville St* and turn south (left). The **Yale Hotel** is on the left just before the **Granville Bridge**.

Stay in the right-hand lane and follow signs for *4th Ave W.,* turning onto *Pine St,* then north (right) following signs for Granville Island. Turn east (right) onto *W. 3rd Ave* to drive beneath the bridge and onto **Granville Island**. When leaving Granville Island, follow signs for *4th Ave W.* Follow *4th Ave* one block back to *Burrard St.*

241

VANCOUVER–WHISTLER

The Sea to Sky Highway is aptly named, snaking from West Vancouver along the cliffs lining Howe Sound as far as Squamish, then twisting up mountain canyons to the resort development of Whistler. The 120-km drive can zip past in two hours if traffic co-operates, but allow three hours midweek and closer to four hours at the weekend. In winter, the return trip to Vancouver can take most of the day if snow snarls going home traffic on Sunday. No matter how good the weather, drive cautiously. The roadway can be narrow and steep, the scenery spectacular and the verges absent.

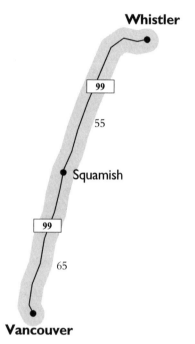

242

```
ROUTE: 120 KM
```

ROUTE

From the *Burrard St Bridge,* turn onto *Pacific St* and immediately go left onto *Howe St.* Follow *Howe* to *Georgia St* and turn left into the middle lanes. At the edge of **Stanley Park**, follow the overhead signs for *Lions Gate Bridge. Georgia* becomes BC 1A and 99 in the park. At the north end of Lions Gate Bridge, stay in the middle lane, following traffic signs for **West Vancouver** and **Squamish** to veer right, pass beneath the bridge and immediately cross the **Capilano River** headed west.

One km beyond Lions Gate Bridge,

turn right at the first traffic signal onto *Taylor Way* and drive uphill in the middle lane. Follow signs for BC 99 north onto the expressway toward **Horseshoe Bay**, **Squamish** and **Whistler**. The expressway has good views north to the mountains and south across Vancouver Harbour. Follow the expressway 11 km to Exit 1 for Squamish and Whistler. (The expressway continues to the BC Ferries dock at Horseshoe Bay.) Take Exit 1 onto BC 99, the *Sea to Sky Highway.* The road follows the edge of Howe Sound past **Porteau**

Cove and the abandoned copper mine at Britannia Beach to **Shannon Falls Provincial Park** and **Squamish**. Occasional views up the Sound reveal the pulp mills belching the blue-grey haze that obscures mountain views and the queasy chemical stench that sometimes fouls the air.

From Squamish, the highway turns into the mountains and narrows. A marked scenic viewpoint to the right, 15 km beyond Squamish, has the best view back to Howe Sound. There are occasional overtaking lanes, but expect slow going behind motorcoaches and lorries as far as **Brandywine Falls Provincial Park**. On the return trip, lumber trucks speed down the highway loaded with logs for the Squamish mills. Whistler development begins 12 km north of **Brandywine**; Whistler Village is 4 km beyond the travel infocentre at Whistler Creekside.

Maverick Coach Lines operate seven trips a day, taking 2½ hrs. See OTT table 72.

BC Rail have a daily service leaving at 0700. Journey time: 2½ hrs. OTT table 6.

SIDE TRACK FROM VANCOUVER

The Royal Hudson, *1782 W. Georgia St, Vancouver, BC V6G 2V7; tel: (800) 663-1500 or (604) 688-7246,* a beautifully restored steam locomotive engine, provides daily rail service in summer between **North Vancouver** and **Squamish** along the edge of **Howe Sound**. The day tour includes boat passage in one direction.

VANCOUVER TO SQUAMISH

The Sea to Sky Highway, BC 99, was carved into the cliffs forming the eastern side of Howe Sound, the most southerly fjord in North America. The 1958 highway follows the route of the Pacific Great Eastern Railway, completed to Squamish in 1956. Before the rail line and highway, the only transport along Howe Sound was a daily steamer between Vancouver and Squamish. The frequent lay-bys have stunning views across the water, but nearly all are on the Sound side of the road. Left turns are generally prohibited on the Sea to Sky, so northbound traffic misses the best views.

One of the first good northbound views is at **Porteau Cove Provincial Park**; *tel: (205) 898-3678,* 25 km north of Exit 1. The cove served as a sand and gravel quarry early in the century. The pits and surrounding community became a regular stop for the Howe Sound Steamer, but the community evaporated after the pits and nearby Britannia Mine were closed. Beachcombers haunt the rocky beach while scuba divers explore four ships that were sunk just off shore. Everyone tries to ignore the pulp mill visible across the Sound, difficult when southerly winds blow the haze and stench down the Sound. A second mill at the head of the Sound also contributes to the pollution.

It's impossible to miss **Britannia Beach**, 8 km north of Porteau Cove. On the Sound side sits the rusting hulk of the *SS Prince George,* once the largest ship on Howe Sound. The ship, which had been slated to become a floating museum, burned at dock in 1994 and remains the centre of continuing litigation.

Almost directly across the highway is **Britannia Mine**, once the largest copper mine in the British Empire. The abandoned mine climbs the mountainside east of the road, its broken windows glinting in the setting sun. Mine and site have become the **B.C. Museum of Mining**, *PO Box 188, Britannia Beach, BC VON 1J0; tel: (604) 688-8735,* open May–Oct.

244

Copper was discovered at Britannia Beach in 1888. Oliver Furry, a trapper who gave his name to a creek and a golf course just south of Britannia Beach, staked the first claims in 1897. The mine ran continuously from 1899 until rising costs and falling copper prices forced it to close in 1974. The surviving mine buildings are being converted to museum use. The interpretative centre, in what was once the Engineering Building, traces local mining history. A mine tour includes a train ride 400 m into the old shafts for a look at the early days of hard rock mining, complete with hard hats. The mine site is a National Historic Site as well as a popular cinema and TV set. **Murrin Provincial Park**, 5 km north of Britannia Beach, offers spectacular views of the nearly vertical mountains surrounding Howe Sound. The horizontal scratches in the rock faces are evidence of the immense glaciers, which carved an ordinary river valley into today's granite-lined fjord.

Howe Sound also claims the third highest waterfall in BC in **Shannon Falls Provincial Park**. The 335-m cascade is an easy 5-min walk through a dense patch of forest from the parking area. The park is also popular for a strenuous climb up 652-m **Stawmus Chief**, the massive peak north of the falls overlooking the Sound. The trail up the second largest granite monolith in the world (after Gibraltar) gains 550 m in just 2.5 km. The rock is a favourite with technical climbers from around the world. Best spot to watch climbers worming their way skyward is a lay-by on the eastern side of the road 1 km north of the park entrance. Almost directly across from the park is the dock for BC Ferries' route across Howe Sound to the **Western Pulp Squamish Operation**, *PO Box 5000, Squamish, BC V0N 3G0; tel: (604) 892-6644*, the largest pulp mill

on the Sound. Tours of the mill, Thur 1000–1400 (May–Sept), can be booked in advance. Western Pulp maintains an extensive network of walking trails around the mill. Walkers must obtain permission in advance; *tel: (604) 892-6611*, and sign in at the first aid station at the mill before setting out. Squamish is 3 km north.

SQUAMISH

Tourist Information: Squamish & Howe Sound Chamber of Commerce, *PO Box 1009, Squamish, BC V0N 3G0; tel: 604-892-9244; fax: (604) 892-2034*, at the west end of *Cleveland Ave*, open Mon–Fri 0900–1700.

Squamish is schizophrenic. A pair of massive pulp mills, out of sight if seldom out of smell, make Squamish the largest deep sea wood pulp port on the west coast of North America and a hotbed of forest industry partisans. But the number of recreational outfitters, companies selling sea kayaking, fishing, rock climbing, scuba diving and walking trips, is growing yearly.

The entrepreneurs who depend on uncut forests, clean air and healthy waters are only too happy to point out the environmental havoc wreaked on Howe Sound by the timber industry. The **Soo Coalition for Sustainable Forests**, *PO Box 1759, Squamish, BC V0N 3G0; tel: (604) 892-9766*, promotes the timber side with the kind of smooth arguments and colourful literature North Americans have come to expect from well-financed political campaigns. The **Coalition Visitor Centre**, *Cleveland Ave and Victoria St*, also arranges tours of nearby dryland sort and sawmill operations Mon–Fri at 1300.

Despite decades of intensive logging and pollution, Squamish remains the winter home for about 3000 bald eagles, possibly the largest concentration of bald eagles in North America south of Alaska. The town is also the gateway to recreational activities on Howe Sound and throughout **Garibaldi Provincial Park**, which covers much of the mountainous area northeast of town. Squamish also offers the only fast food fix between Vancouver and Whistler. Rail buffs from around the world make pilgrimage to the **West Coast Railway Heritage Park**, *Box 2790 Stn Terminal, Vancouver, BC V6B 3X2; tel: (604) 898-9336, 3 km north of McDonald's on BC 99 in Squamish, then west 1 km on Centennial Way.* The park has more than 50 vintage railway carriages and locomotive engines, including a superb 1890 Executive Business Carriage finished in hand-rubbed teak, a restored colonist car that once carried settlers across Canada on hard benches, Pacific Great Eastern's only surviving steam locomotive engine and an enormous orange snowplough.

SQUAMISH TO WHISTLER

Brohm Lake and **Brohm Lake Interpretative Forest** are 13 km beyond the Railway Park. The shallow lake offers fishing and, for those immune to icy temperatures, swimming. The 400-hectare forest area has 11 km of connecting trails with spectacular views of the **Tantalus Mountain Range** and one of the largest icefields in North America.

The best view back to Howe Sound is 3 km beyond Brohm Lake. Follow the scenic view signs onto a short section of the old highway. The southbound lanes have a similar scenic lay-by, but the view is better from the northbound side. The road narrows and winds another 27 km to the **Brandywine Falls Provincial Park**, *on the east side of the highway,* named for an early bet on the height of the falls by railroad surveyors who were short of cash but well-stocked with brandy and wine. In early summer, when snow melt is at its

peak, 600 cubic metres of water shoot over the edge of the cliff each minute, but the 66-m falls are worth the 10-min walk through the forest in any season.

The first evidence of Whistler appears 9 km later. **Whistler Interpretative Forest**, *Municipal Hall, 4325 Blackcomb Wy, Whistler, BC V0N 1B4; tel: (604) 932-5535; fax: (604) 932-6636,* extends to the right with an extensive network of walking and mountain biking trails. All of the trails are open for walkers but some are closed to mountain bikers. To the left is **Function Junction**, a cluster of businesses that supply Whistler with beer, bread, masseuses and other essentials. Whistler's ever-expanding condominium complexes have spread to within 3 km of Function Junction. The first Travel InfoCentre is the **Whistler Chamber of Commerce**, *Box 181, Whistler, BC V0N 1B0; tel: (604) 932-5528, east on Lake Placid Rd in Whistler Creekside,* open daily 0900–1700. **Whistler Village**, one of the world's most popular mountain resorts, is 4 km north.

WHISTLER

Tourist Information: Whistler Chamber of Commerce, *Box 181, Whistler, BC V0N 1B0; tel: (604) 932-5528, at the Whistler Gondola base;* **Whistler Resort Association**, *4010 Whistler Wy, Whistler, BC V0N 1B0; tel: (800) 944-7853 or (604) 664-5625; fax: (604) 938-5758.*

ACCOMMODATION

Chains include *CP, HI, PP, Rd* and *RI*. **Whistler Resort Association**, *4010 Whistler Wy, Whistler, BC V0N 1B0; tel: (604) 932-4222 or (800) 944-7853; fax: (604) 932-7231,* co-ordinate lodging for the entire resort. **Whistler Bed & Breakfast Inns**; *tel: (604) 932-3282 or (800) 665-1892,* book local Bed and Breakfasts. **The Fireplace Inns**, *4250 Village Stroll,*

245

Whistler, BC V0N 1B4; tel: (604) 932-3200 or (800) 663-6416; fax: (604) 932-2566, is solid value in Whistler Village, with fireplaces in all rooms. Top choice is CP Hotels' pricey **Chateau Whistler**, 4599 Chateau Blvd, Whistler, BC V0N 1B0; tel: (604) 938-8000 or (800) 268-9411 (Canada), (800) 828-7447 (USA); fax: (604) 938-2020, at the foot of Blackcomb Mountain. **Residence Inn**, 4899 Painted Cliff Rd, Whistler, BC V0N 1B4; tel: (604) 905-3400; fax: (604) 905-3432, moderate–expensive, has a prime ski-in, ski-out location partway up Blackcomb Mountain.

EATING AND DRINKING

Whistler has all the usual chains as well as sidewalk cafés, snack shops and elegance. **Caramba!**, 12-43 14 Main St Town Plaza; tel: (604) 938-1879, is a lively, moderate choice for Italian. Pricey **Ristorante Araxi**, 4222 Village Sq.; tel: (604) 932-4540, is more staid. **Zeuski's Taverna**, Town Plaza; tel: (604) 932-6009, is moderate, lively and Greek. **Cows**, Whistler Village Centre; tel: (604) 938-9822, budget, has Whistler's best ice-cream. **Ingrid's Village Café**, 4305 Skiers Approach; tel: (604) 932-7000, has out-the-door lines for budget vegetarian fare. **Whistler Cookie Co.**, 7-4433 Sundial Pl.; tel: (604) 932-2962, is a local budget favourite for breakfast.

ENTERTAINMENT

Whistler exists to entertain, and entertain it does, with the emphasis on skiing, mountain biking, walking and other outdoor activities. The resort also offers just about every form of aprés-sport activity imagination can create, from a **Hard Rock Café** to hot tubs and hotel discos. The hotel front desk can point out the current hot spots.

SIGHTSEEING

Whistler was envisaged as a site for the Winter Olympic Games, but the International Olympic Committee's lack of co-operation hasn't slowed what has become one of North America's most successful resort developments. What began as a ski resort has become equally busy in summer. The European-style village (nearly all a pedestrian zone) is a mountain theme park for adults, its steep roof lines and pastel colours an alluring contrast against the snow-capped mountains and deep blue sky. Lifts whisk skiers, snowboarders, mountain bikers and the merely curious up the resort's two mountains, Whistler (2287m) and Blackcomb (2182m) from the village centre. Five lakes loop through the valley like blue-green beads on a necklace, set off against forests, championship golf courses and an extensive network of walking and biking routes that become cross-country skiing trails in winter.

Style is posh, prices are expensive. A resort that began as a garbage dump for an unruly collection of weekend cabins in the 1970s is short on history, but the **Whistler Museum and Archives**; tel: (604) 932-2019, open daily, does what it can with logging, early fishing resorts and archaic skiing gear. In winter, downhill skiing and snowboarding on more than 200 named runs is exceptional with the continent's longest fall line drops. In summer, the mountains offer spectacular walking, with trails circling upper slopes, alpine lakes and flower-filled meadows as well as the valley below. Most mountain skiing trails are opened to mountain biking, which has become the dominant summer sport. **Whistler Back Roads**, Box 643, Whistler, BC V0N 1B0; tel: (604) 932-3111; fax: (604) 932-1204, has the best selection of bikes for hire as well as guided mountain rides.

WHISTLER–KAMLOOPS

Most travellers follow Hwy 99 as far as Whistler, then return to Vancouver. It's their loss. The Sea to Sky Highway runs another 185 km through stunning mountains and marble canyons to the dry, rolling hills of the Southern Cariboo near Hat Creek Ranch and Hwy 97. The entire 300-km drive to Kamloops takes a longish day, or overnight in Lillooet or Cache Creek for more time to enjoy the wrenching transition from Coastal Mountains to rolling ranching country.

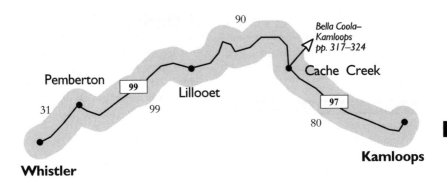

```
ROUTE: 300 KM
```

ROUTE

Take Hwy 99 north from **Whistler** to **Pemberton** and Mt Currie, then climb into the mountains to **Lillooet**. From Lillooet, the highway follows the original Cariboo Road as far as **Pavilion**, then turns toward Hat Creek Ranch and Hwy 99. Turn south on Hwy 99 to follow the route to **Cache Creek**, then east above North Thompson River to **Kamloops**. The entire route is paved, but there are sections of hairpin turns and steep grades.

The highway curves out of **Whistler Village** past **Green Lake** and climbs 28 km into the Coastal Mountains to **Nairn Falls Provincial Park**, *Box 220, Brackendale, BC V0N 1H0; tel: (604) 898-3678.* An easy return walk to the 60-m falls takes about 40 mins.

PEMBERTON

Tourist Information: Pemberton Chamber of Commerce, *Box 370, Pemberton, BC V0N 2L0; tel: (604) 894-6175;* **InfoCentre**, *Hwy 99 at Portage Rd*, open June–Aug.

Once a quiet farming town, Pemberton is growing as employees and holidaymakers retreat north from the crowds of Whistler.

Hiking, fishing, river rafting, glider tours, horse and llama trekking, Nordic skiing, mountain biking and horseback riding are just a few of the local recreational activities. Several hot springs are hidden along back roads; ask for directions and road conditions at the InfoCentre. The **Pemberton Museum**, *7424 Prospects St,* open daily (July–Aug), documents the Fraser River Gold Rush in a settler's house and covers the Lil'wat Band of the Stl'atl'imx Nation in two other buildings. The Band has its headquarters 6 km east in **Mt Currie**, named for a Scots settler who began ranching the valley with his Lil'wat wife in 1885. The **Spirit Circle Art, Craft and Tea Company**; *tel: (604) 894-6336,* a blond-coloured wooden building covered in First Nations designs, has the tastiest restaurant in the area.

PEMBERTON TO LILLOOET

Until recent years, the pavement ended 9 km north of Mt Currie where the Birkenhead River empties into a vast delta and Lillooet Lake. Rotting pilings at the end of the lake mark a former steamboat landing. What was once a rugged 4x4 route to Duffey Lake and Lillooet is now paved and open all year, but the initial climb into the **Cayoosh Range** of the **Coastal Mountains** is steep and filled with hairpin turns. A wide lay-by at the top of the hill offers splendid views back down the valley.

Joffre Lakes Provincial Recreation Area protects a trio of turquoise lakes connected by a tough trail that climbs more than 500m in 5 km. **Duffey Lake**, just north of the highway beyond the Recreation Area, is much more accessible. The north end of Duffey Lake is the halfway point to Lillooet. Grand mountains in the distance and thimbleberry bushes along the verge make for a scenic road, but lay-bys are few and rocks numerous after every

rainstorm. Sections of road have 13%–14% grades between awesome hairpin turns.

The climate dries quickly as the highway drops into the rain shadow of the Coastal Mountains. **Seaton Lake**, first visible from a lay-by high above the green waters, is surrounded by sagebrush. BC Rail's **Cariboo Prospector** line (see p. 57) emerges from the roadless mountains just above the lake and snakes into Lillooet. The highway drops steeply past a BC Hydro dam to the **Seaton Creek Spawning Channel**, west of the highway. Pink salmon return to spawn in Oct.

LILLOOET

Tourist Information: Lillooet and District Chamber of Commerce, *Box 650, Lillooet, BC V0K 1V0; tel: (250) 256-4364; fax: (250) 256-0043;* **Travel InfoCentre**, *790 Main St; tel: (250) 256-4308,* open daily (May–Oct).

ACCOMMODATION

The **Mile-0-Motel**, *616 Main St, Lillooet, BC V0K 1V0; tel: (888) 766-4530* or *(250) 256-7511; fax: (250) 256-4124,* and **4 Pines Motel**, *108 8th Ave, Lillooet, BC V0K 1V0; tel: (250) 256-4247; fax: (250) 256-4120,* both budget–moderate, are central, clean and good value. There are no chain motels.

SIGHTSEEING

Lillooet, at the junction of the Fraser River and Cayoosh Creek, has long been home to First Nations who came for the rich salmon fishing along the Fraser River and its tributaries each year. White settlers arrived with the Fraser River and Cariboo Gold Rushes in the 1850s. Would-be miners travelled north from Port Douglas, on the lower Fraser River, through Harrison and Anderson Lakes to Lillooet and the rugged Cariboo Wagon Road that eventually reached Barkerville. The **Mile Zero Cairn**, opposite the Tourist Info-Centre, marks the beginning of the **Wagon Road** and the numbered Mile Houses established as roadhouses and supply points on the way north.

Oxen pulled most of the freight wagons; because ox teams can't back up, *Main St* was built wide enough to turn the double wagons and twenty pair of oxen it took to haul 20-tonne loads over 2000-m Pavilion Summit to Clinton. Stagecoach passengers on the same route had to get out to help push coaches uphill.

Lillooet Museum, *Box 441, Lillooet, BC V0K 1V0; tel: (250) 256-4308,* open May–Oct, shares the former St Mary's Anglican church with the Travel Info-Centre. The one-time church is filled with mining and pioneering artefacts. The nearby **Miyazaki Heritage House**, *6th Ave off Main St,* was occupied by Dr Masajiro Miyazaki and his family during their World War II internment in the then-isolated community. The **Hangman's Tree** on the benchland above *Main St* was supposedly used by Judge Matthew Baillie Begbie on his gold field rounds in the 1860s.

With an elevation of 250m, Lillooet boasts of mild, almost snowless winters. The town also holds the record for Canada's highest temperature, 44.4°C, recorded in July, 1941. The arid heat prompted freight haulers to import Bactrian camels as pack animals in 1862. The experiment failed miserably. Not only were the soft-footed camels ill-suited to the Cariboo's rocky trails, but the camels spooked other animals on the trail, kicked and spat at anything that moved, ate laundry and smelled foul. Surviving camels were abandoned when the Dromedary Express was disbanded in 1864 and subsequently died of exposure.

LILLOOET TO CACHE CREEK

Hwy 99 crosses the Fraser River on the **Bridge of 23 Camels**, which opened in 1981. The old bridge, a suspension span at the east end of Lillooet, can still be used by foot traffic. Once beyond the junction with Hwy 12, which follows the Fraser River south to Lytton (see p.266), Hwy 99 follows the original Wagon Road, corkscrewing up to the rolling benchlands high above the river. Many of the hillsides and natural terraces are irrigated for fields or grazing, others are covered with low black tents that shade fields of ginseng.

Highlight of the tiny town of **Pavilion**, 34 km from Lillooet, is the **Pavilion General Store**, one of the oldest buildings in BC still on its original site. The view across the mountains is stunning, but cold drinks and ice-cream make the store a summertime oasis in this mountain desert. The original Wagon Road, now *Pavilion Mountain Rd*, turns north to Kelley Lake and Clinton just beyond the General Store. The steep gravel road is passable in good weather, but becomes extremely slippery after rain.

Hwy 99 continues east into **Marble Canyon**, named for 1000-m cliffs of red and yellow limestone, to **Pavilion Lake** and **Marble Canyon Provincial Park**; *tel: (250) 851-3000,* with camping, hiking and fishing on **Crown** and **Turquoise Lakes**.

Hat Creek Ranch, *Box 878, Cache Creek, BC V0K 1H0; tel: (800) 782-0922* or *(250) 457-9722,* adults $5, children $2, family $10, open daily (mid May–mid Oct), fills the valley floor near the junction of Hwys 99 and 97. The 1861 ranch was one of the largest roadhouses on the Cariboo Wagon Road. Buildings and grounds have been restored to their 1901 appearance. Costumed interpreters lead wagon and stagecoach rides on one of the

249

few extant sections of original Wagon Road as well as trail rides from well-watered valley pastures into the sage and cactus filled hills. A fully-furnished farmhouse, barns, working blacksmithy, gardens, collections of antique farm machinery and a Native village are also open.

Hwy 99 ends at Hwy 97 just east of the ranch. Turn north (left) for Clinton, 100 Mile House and Williams Lake, south (right) for Cache Creek, Savona and Kamloops.

CACHE CREEK

Tourist Information: Cache Creek Chamber of Commerce, *Box 460, Cache Creek, BC V0K 1H0; tel: (250) 457-9566; fax: (250) 457-9669.*

Desert Motel, *1069 S. TransCanada Hwy 1, Cache Creek, BC V0K 1H0; tel: (800) 663-0212 or (250) 457-6226,* and **Tumbleweed Motel**, *1221 Quartz Rd, Cache Creek, BC V0K 1H0; tel: (800) 667-1501 or (250) 457-6522; fax: (250) 457-9233,* are good budget–moderate choices.

Sometimes called 'Canada's Arizona' for its desert climate, Cache Creek is the halfway point between the lower Fraser River and the Cariboo. Still a region of vast ranchlands and working cowboys, the town is also a growing centre for outdoor recreation and jade (nephrite) hunters. **Cariboo Jade**, *1093 Todd Rd; tel: (250) 457-9566; fax: (250) 457-9669,* offers jade-cutting and polishing displays as well as finished jewellery. The town has adopted a 1950s theme to boost bi-weekly drag races at **Nl'ak'apxm Eagle Motorplex**; *tel: (250) 453-9131,* 6 km south on Hwy 1.

CACHE CREEK TO KAMLOOPS

Hwy 1, the TransCanada Highway, joins Hwy 97 eastbound at Cache Creek. As the highway approaches the fast-flowing

Thompson River east of Cache Creek, look for the remains of orchards on the hillsides below and abandoned wooden aqueducts on the slopes above. A lay-by on the south side of the highway shows the location of **Walhachin**, once a flourishing town. English settlers transformed the desert into rich orchards, watered by carefully-tended flume systems. A storm demolished the flume after farmers returned to England to fight World War I; the unwatered orchards withered in the fierce summer heat.

Juniper Beach Provincial Park; *tel: (250) 851-3000,* lies along the Thompson 3 km east of the ghost town of Walhachin. The park is popular with Kamloopians for swimming and walking, but keep an eye out for prickly pear cacti along the paths. **Steelhead Provincial Park**, 16 km east of Juniper Beach at the east end of **Kamloops Lake**, is a favourite for fishing, boating and swimming.

Midway along the lake is the town of **Savona**, named for François Saveneaux (Savona), who established the first regular ferry service across the Thompson River where it flows out of Kamloops Lake. Best view of the lake is from a lay-by 4 km east of *Savona Rd* (leading to **Savona Provincial Park**), with a clear view across the lake to the reddish **Painted Bluffs**. Railway lines follow the shoreline on both sides of the lake, which was once a highway for steamboats.

Hwy 97 continues through rolling desert country, passing the black shade of more ginseng fields, green hayfields and bristling blocks of sagebrush. Twenty-six km from the Kamloops Lake lay-by, Hwy 5, the **Coquihalla Hwy** (see p.258), joins Hwy 97. The first exit for Kamloops is *Columbia St,* just over 1 km east of the Hwy 5A junction. For details, see Kelowna to Kamloops (pp.192–198).

VANCOUVER–OSOYOOS

It's possible to drive the 370 km between Vancouver and Osoyoos in one long day, but only if you're willing to miss some of the most pleasant sights in southern BC. Manicured formal gardens, rustic hot springs, majestic mountains and splendid walking trails are only a few of the reasons to linger along the route. If time allows, take two days, with an overnight in Hope. Better still, take three to four days, stopping in Hope, Manning Provincial Park and Princeton, plus two or three days in the Okanagan Valley.

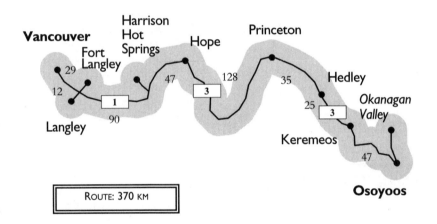

251

ROUTE

From Central Vancouver, take *W. 12th Ave* eastbound and merge into *Grandview Ave* near *Slocun St* on the east side of the city. Follow traffic signs for Canada 1 eastbound and enter the expressway just east of *Boundary Rd* in the Municipality of Burnaby. Follow Canada 1 over the Fraser River on the Port Mann Bridge and continue eastward past a succession of Fraser Valley towns to **Hope**, at the head of the valley. Continue east 7 km to Exit 177, Hwy 3, the Crowsnest Highway, heading south-east into the Cascade Mountains to Manning Provincial Park, north to **Princeton** and south-east again into the desert of the **Okanagan Valley** and Osoyoos. The Okanagan's vineyards, BC's wine country, stretch north along both sides of the Okanagan River toward Kelowna, 123 km north (see p.190).

The Fraser Valley is one of BC's

richest agricultural areas. Immense fields of grain, raspberries, strawberries and other crops compete with dairy herds for space along the flat plain that stretches from both sides of the Fraser River to lap at the base of the Cascades. Views across the valley to the jagged Cascade peaks are likely to remain relatively unspoiled: most of the valley east of the town of **Langley** has been put into an agricultural preserve that offers landowners tax incentives to keep their property in agriculture rather than selling out to developers and contributing to the sprawl of **Greater Vancouver**. For a guide to the agricultural area, pick up *Farm Fresh Guide*, which covers Langley, and *The Harvest Guide*, encompassing the rest of the central Valley from Abbotsford to Sardi.

BUSES

Greyhound Lines of Canda operate one trip a day from Vancouver to Osoyoos, taking 9 hrs. OTT table 110. There is also a service every day exept Sat to Keremeos. Journey time: 6½ hrs. OTT table 110.

LANGLEY AND FORT LANGLEY

Tourist Information: Fort Langley and District Chamber of Commerce, *23245 Mavis St (in the historic railway station), Box 75, Fort Langley, BC V1M 2R5; tel: (604) 888-1477; fax: (604) 888-2657.*

ACOMMODATION

The best lodging choice in town is the budget–moderate **West Country Hotel**, *20222 56th Ave, Langley, BC V3A 3Y5; tel: (604) 530-5121; fax: (604) 530-9763.*

SIGHTSEEING

Langley, south of the expressway, is a thriving farming community on the edge of Greater Vancouver. **Fort Langley**, north of the expressway, is a smaller town of antique stores, small restaurants and a largely reconstructed **Fort Langley National Historic Park**, *23433 Mavis St, Fort Langley, BC V1M 2R5; tel: (604) 888-4424,* open daily, adults $4, children $2, the birthplace of modern British Columbia. The Hudson's Bay Company built a fort at Langley in 1824 to serve as a secondary depot for inland fur trading operations. The riverside site was already a traditional meeting and trading place for First Nations from the Pacific Coast to the Rockies. The Fraser Valley was poor in furs, but the broad Langley Prairie soon became a highly profitable farming operation, with exports going as far as Hawaii.

Company farming came to an abrupt end with the Fraser River Gold Rush in 1858. Gold fever drove farmers up the Fraser River. When news of the gold strike reached San Francisco, tens of thousands of American miners headed north, most passing through Fort Langley on their way upstream. The Fort became a profitable commercial centre, but the influx from south of the border worried the HBC. Company officials lobbied for the creation of a crown colony to prevent annexation by an expansionist America that had taken California from Mexico a decade before. British Columbia was proclaimed on 19 Nov 1858 in the fort's **Big House** (the Manager's residence), a ceremony that is re-enacted every year by BC's current Prime Minister and cabinet.

Royal Engineers pointed out that the Fort, on the south bank of the river and almost within view of the US border, was vulnerable to American attack. The capital was moved to New Westminster in 1859 and Fort Langley returned to farming. HBC finally closed the post in 1886.

The Fort, with its original storehouse and reconstructed Big House, servants' quarters, workshops, log palisade and bastions, is a living history museum. It doesn't smell as the original HBC trading post must have, but costumed interpreters convey a sense of what life was like when BC was the edge of the world, right down to the daily challenges of forging tools in the heat of summer or baking bread in the damp and dank of winter.

The **Langley Centennial Museum and National Exhibition Centre**, *9131 King St; tel: (604) 888-3922,* and the adjoining **BC Farm Machinery and Agricultural Museum**; *tel: (604) 888-2272,* explore other eras. The Centennial Museum houses an extensive collection of First Nation artefacts as well as recreations of farm and small town life in the late 19th–early 20th century. The Farm Museum has one of BC's largest collections of vintage agricultural equipment, from steam stump pullers to a Tiger Moth aeroplane.

Langley is also home to one of BC's most decorated wineries, **Domaine de Chaberton Estates**, *1064 216 St; tel: (604) 530-1736,* 12 km east of town. Chamberton, the only Estate Winery in the Fraser Valley, specialises in French and German white varieties. The winery is open for tasting daily and for tours at weekends.

LANGLEY TO HARRISON HOT SPRINGS

The expressway bypasses most towns east of Langley. **Abbotsford**, the largest town in the central Fraser Valley, hosts a major airshow in August. The other eleven months, it's the self-proclaimed Raspberry Capital of the World.

Recreational farmers are more interested in **Chilliwack**, 83 km east of Langley, and **Minter Gardens**, *north on BC 9 from Exit 135, 52892 Bunker Rd, Rosedale, Box 40, Chilliwack, BC V2P 4V4;*

tel: (604) 794-7191 (Apr–Oct), (604) 792-3799 (Nov–Mar) or *(888) 646-8377,* where a full-colour seed catalogue come to life. Minter isn't ready to challenge Victoria's Butchart Gardens, but it follows the same tradition of generous planting and meticulous maintenance. And Butchart can't begin to match Minter's backdrop of Cascade mountain peaks dominated by 2334-m Mt Cheam. The Gardens are open Apr–Oct.

For a closer look at commercial agriculture, turn north (left) onto BC 9, 1 km after leaving Minter to return to Canada 1. **Agassiz** calls itself 'The Corn Capital of BC' for the fields of maize surrounding the community. Turn left at the town hall, drive one long block and turn right at the traffic signal. Cross the railroad tracks and immediately turn left onto BC 7 to the **Agassiz Harrison Museum**, *6947 #7 Hwy, Agassiz, BC V0M 1A0; tel: (604) 796-3545,* open 1000–1600 (May–Sept). The museum, in the restored 1893 train depot, focuses on agricultural development. After leaving the museum, continue 1 km east on BC 7 and turn right onto BC 9, passing farms and hazelnut orchards on the way to **Harrison Hot Springs**.

HARRISON HOT SPRINGS

Tourist Information: Harrison Hot Springs Chamber of Commerce, *499 Hot Springs Rd, Harrison Hot Springs, BC V0M 1K0; tel: (604) 796-3425; fax: (604) 796-3188.* Harrison Hot Springs is a spa, the largest lake in south-western BC and a popular recreation area. It's also one of BC's most active areas for current reports of Sasquatch, a shy, hairy, oversized humanoid that figures in First Nations lore from California to Alaska. Claimed sightings have continued into the 1990s, but, like Scotland's Loch Ness Monster, evidence remains scanty.

253

Hot springs facilities include a Public Pool, where mineral water from the springs has been cooled to 39°C from its initial 71°C, and full spa facilities at moderate–expensive **Harrison Hot Springs Hotel**, *Harrison Hot Springs, BC V0M 1K0; tel: (604) 796-2244 or (800) 663-2266; fax: (604) 796-3682,* but most visitors spend more time camping, boating, fishing and walking the forest than soaking. There are also about two dozen smaller motels, Bed and Breakfasts, campsites and RV parks nearby.

Return to Canada 1 eastbound or follow BC 7 east 37 km to **Hope**.

HOPE

Tourist Information: Hope & District Chamber of Commerce, *919 Water Ave, Hope, BC V0X 1L0; tel: (604) 869-2021; fax: (604) 869-2160.*

ACCOMMODATION AND FOOD

Hope has the largest selection of food and lodging in the area. **Quality Inn**, *350 Hope Princeton Hwy, Hope, BC, V0X 1L0; tel: (604) 869-9951; fax: (604) 869-9421,* moderate, is the only chain in town. The budget **Skagit Motel**, *655 3rd Ave; tel: (604) 869-5220 or (800) 667-5567,* is a good town centre choice.

SIGHTSEEING

Established as an HBC trading post at the head of the Fraser Valley, Hope became a commercial centre during the 1858 Gold Rush and the subsequent opening of eastern BC. **The Hope Museum**, *919 Water Ave; tel: (604) 869-7322,* traces local history from First Nations days through gold mining, railroads and World War II, when more than 2300 Japanese-Canadians were imprisoned at **Tashame**, 14 km east. Part of the $12 million Federal restitution fund established in 1988 built a Japanese garden

in **Memorial Park**, across the street from the Skagit Motel. The park also has a collection of oversized chain saw carvings of salmon, eagles and other local creatures. Hope has appeared in a number of films, including Sylvester Stallone's *Rambo: First Blood*.

The **Othello Tunnels**, part of the **Coquihalla Canyon Recreation Area**, *Tunnels Rd, 8 km east of town,* are popular with walkers and mountain bikers. The tunnels were cut in the 1910s for the Kettle Valley Railway, built to block northward expansion by US railroads. The KVR was abandoned after washouts in 1959. Allow an hour to walk through the five tunnels along the rushing Coquihalla River.

HOPE TO PRINCETON

Take Canada 1 east from Hope and exit onto BC 3, the **Crowsnest Highway**, which becomes a dual track road. Ten km beyond is a raw scar where 46 million cubic metres of rock and mud fell down the north side of the valley in 1965. The Hope Slide raised the valley floor by 70 m and killed four people.

The most scenic and slowest section of the Crowsnest Hwy is **Manning Provincial Park**, *Box 3, Manning Park, BC V0X 1R0; tel: (250) 840-8836; fax: (250) 840-8700,* 71,000 hectares of rugged mountains, deep valleys, subalpine meadows and whitewater rapids. Two major rivers flow out of the park, the **Skagit**, which turns south into Washington and the Pacific Ocean, and the **Similkameen**, which runs east to the Okanagan and then into the Columbia River.

Visitor facilities are concentrated around the **Park Visitor Centre**, just east of the moderate–expensive **Manning Park Resort**, *Manning Park, BC V0X 1R0; tel: (250) 840-8822; fax: (250) 840-8848.* The Visitor Centre introduces park plants, wildlife trails, campsites and recreational activities; the Resort has the only restaurant and non-camping lodging within the park.

PRINCETON

Tourist Information: Princeton and District Chamber of Commerce, *Box 540, Princeton, BC V0X 1W0; tel: (250) 295-3103; fax: (250) 295-3255.* Princeton is the first town east of Manning Park, a gold rush settlement that has combined farming and outdoor activities to become a regional commercial centre. **Princeton and District Pioneer Museum**, *167 Vermilion; tel: (250) 295-7588,* the largest local museum in the Valley, concentrates on mining and ranching.

HEDLEY

Hedley sprang to life as a gold mining town in the late 19th century, but would-be miners started every day by climbing **Nickel Plate**, the mountain east of town, to the diggings. By 1909, the town had six hotels, a bank, a school and its own newspaper. An aerial tramway hauled miners up to the shafts each day and ore back down to stamp mills near town until the mine closed in 1956. Much of the town burned in 1956 and 1957, but the mountainside buildings are still visible hundreds of metres above. The cliffs are dauntingly honeycombed with abandoned mine shafts, making both hiking and climbing extremely dangerous.

KEREMEOS

Tourist Information: Keremeos & District Chamber of Commerce, *415 7th Ave, Keremeos, BC V0X 1N0; tel: (250) 499-5225; fax: (250) 499-2252.*

Opened during the BC gold rushes of the 1850s and 1860s, Keremeos quickly turned to the relative security of agriculture. **The Grist Mill and Gardens**, *Upper Bench Rd; tel: (250) 499-2888,* is BC's only water powered mill with its original machinery intact. The restored mill, operated by the British Columbia Heritage Trust, opens May–Oct. Heritage orchards, gardens and fields grow antique flowers, fruits, vegetables, and grains that have long since disappeared from commercial cultivation. Flour ground at the mill is sold on site and used in the **Tea Room** bakery. The Red Bridge just west of town was originally a railway bridge, then converted for road traffic. It is the last surviving covered bridge in Western Canada.

Keremeos also has two wineries, **St. Laszlo Estate Winery**, *Site 95, Comp 8, Keremeos, BC V0X 1N0; tel: (250) 499-2856,* 1 km east of town, and **Crows Nest Vineyards**, *Box 501, Keremeos, BC V0X 1N0; tel: (250) 499-5129,* just east of Cawston.

OSOYOOS

Tourist Information: Osoyoos Chamber of Commerce, *Box 227, Osoyoos, BC V0H 1V0; tel: (250) 495-7142; fax: (250) 495-6161.*

ACCOMMODATION

Osoyoos is the commercial hub of the agricultural **Okanagan Valley**. There are a dozen or so motels in town, including the moderate **Desert Motor Inn**, *7702 62nd Ave, Osoyoos, BC V0H 1V0; tel: (250) 495-6525.* **Motel Row** is the stretch of *Main St* (BC 3) just east of the bridge across Osoyoos Lake. **The Southwind Inn**, *Box 1500, Oliver, BC V0H 1T0 tel: (250) 498-3442,* 50 km north in Oliver, is far more convenient for winery touring. For Bed and Breakfast accommodation, contact **Okanagan Bed & Breakfast Association**, *Box 5135, Kelowna, BC V1Y 8T9; tel: (250) 764-2124; fax: (250) 494-1821;* or **Okanagan Similkameen Tourism**

Association, *1332 Water St, Kelowna, BC V1Y 9P4; tel: (250) 860-5999.*

SIGHTSEEING

The Okanagan Valley, spreading east and west of the Okanagan River, is the final extension of the Mojave Desert that stretches northward from Mexico along the basin between the Rocky Mountains and the Sierra Nevada/Cascade Mountains. Originally covered with cactus and prickly brush, the Okanagan began to bloom with massive irrigation projects that put former soldiers to work after World War I. **The Osoyoos Museum**, *Osoyoos Lake in Gyro Park; tel: (250) 495-5215,* open June–Sept, depicts the early history of Canada's only desert.

Osoyoos Lake is Canada's answer to Southern California, a balmy recreation area famed for swimming and water skiing. For the best view of the lake and valley, take BC 3 west to lay-bys at the top of the ridge.

SIDE TRACK
FROM OSOYOOS

OKANAGAN VALLEY

To cruise the Okanagan present, future and past, follow BC 97 north through Valley orchards and vineyards to the **Dominion Radio Astrophysical Observatory**, *PO Box 248, Penticton, BC V2A 6K3; tel: (250) 493-7505; fax: (250) 493-7767.* The highway north from Osoyoos passes a steady succession of apple, pear, cherry, peach and other orchards interspersed with expanding vineyards. Fruit stands open with cherry season in June; most of the wineries are open for tasting and tours all year. The spreading green of agricultural irrigation has turned once-ubiquitous cacti into endangered species.

Turn west (left) onto *386 Ave (Seacrest Rd)*, 6 km north of **Oliver** and begin climbing through stands of Ponderosa pines. Take *Fairview-Whitelake Rd* north (right) 4 km later through a broad agricultural valley. **Spotted Lake**, laden with minerals that deposit a mottled white layer on the surface, is on the right. The first sign of the Observatory is a thick cross of telephone poles, the remains of an early radio telescope. White dish-shaped antennas come into view just beyond. The entrance is 13 km from the *386 Ave* turnoff. Look for the array of seven white dishes and a single enormous dish pointing skyward from a futuristic pylon.

The Observatory was built in the Whitelake Basin because surrounding mountains shelter the isolated valley from the radio frequency pollution created by modern life. The Observatory is open daylight hours all year, with guided tours Sun 1400–1700 (July–Aug). Visitor parking is about half a kilometre from the main antenna to minimise electrical interference – staff vehicles are fitted with special electronic dampers on the ignition and other electrical systems.

Return 20 km along the *Fairview-Whitelake Rd* to a T junction at the *Oliver–Cawston Road*. Turn left (downhill) 2 km to a marker on the right for **Fairview**, the centre of population in the Okanagan a century ago.

The rowdy mining town declined as the mines played out, but permanent settlers began moving into the area to take advantage of cattle ranching and farming opportunities nearer the Okanagan River. Today, nothing remains of Fairview but a few foundations overgrown with sagebrush and an historical marker. ◣

HOPE–KAMLOOPS

Few short routes are as varied as this journey between the wet forests of the lower Mainland and the dry cattle country of interior BC. The 200-km direct route, along the Coquihalla Highway, and the scenic alternative, up the Fraser River Canyon, are both engineering marvels. If time permits, drive both routes to enjoy not only the sweeping mountain vistas of the Coquihalla but also the twisting, stomach-clenching views down to the churning waters of the Fraser River.

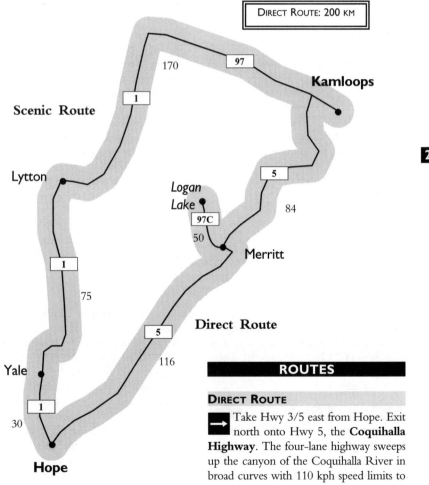

DIRECT ROUTE: 200 KM

170

97

Kamloops

1

Scenic Route

257

5

Lytton

Logan
Lake

84

97C

50

Merritt

1

75

5

Direct Route

Yale

116

ROUTES

1

30

DIRECT ROUTE

➡ Take Hwy 3/5 east from Hope. Exit north onto Hwy 5, the **Coquihalla Highway**. The four-lane highway sweeps up the canyon of the Coquihalla River in broad curves with 110 kph speed limits to

Hope

a toll plaza near the summit. The entire route is controlled-access freeway with few entrances or exits and no place to get lost. Continue down into the **Nicola Valley**, past the town of **Merritt** and up again onto the **Nicola Plateau**. Hwy 5 drops into the Thompson River Valley to join Trans-Canada Hwy 1 just west of Kamloops. Follow Hwy 1 east to Kamloops. The entire 200-km route takes 2½ hrs, or allow an overnight in Nicola Valley to explore.

SCENIC ROUTE

Follow TransCanada Hwy 1 north from the centre of Hope along the banks of the Fraser River. The highway crosses the Fraser just north of town and twists north along the west side of the Fraser River Canyon past **Yale** to Spuzzum, where it crosses back to the west side of the canyon. Continue to the aerial tramway at **Hells Gate**, then on to Boston Bar and **Lytton**, the junction of the Fraser and Thompson Rivers. Hwy 1 follows the Thompson River north to Spences Bridge and Ashcroft to Cache Creek and the junction with Hwy 97. Take Hwy 1/97 east to Savona and Kamloops. The entire 275-km journey takes half a day, or overnight in Lytton and Cache Creek (see p.250) to better explore the area.

BUSES

Greyhound Lines of Canada operate two daily services via Lytton, changing at Cache Creek. The journey takes 3¾ hrs in total. See OTT tables 100 and 110. There are also two services via Merritt, taking 3 hrs. OTT table 118.

HOPE TO MERRITT

The high-speed **Coquihalla Highway** was rushed to completion in 1986, just in time to give Expo 86 crowds a new, five-hour route from Vancouver to the Interior.

The Coquihalla is BC's only **toll road**, with a single toll plaza near the summit. Travel from both ends of the highway to the scenic mountain playgrounds on each side of the summit is free. A final phase, the **Okanagan Connector** between **Merritt** and **Peachland** (in the Okanagan Valley), opened in 1990.

Occasional stretches of the Coquihalla follow the line of the **Kettle Valley Railway**, opened between Hope and the West Kootenay Mountains (see p.254) in 1916. Many stations were named for Shakespearean characters – Othello, Romeo, Juliet, Iago and so on – but the line was plagued by bad weather and marginal engineering. After decades of runaway trains, derailments, avalanches and slowly declining traffic, the KVR was closed in 1959. Tracks were ripped out, tunnels filled and trestles blasted away to keep the public out of the mountains and out of trouble. Remnants of the line can be seen near Hope (the Othello Tunnels, see p.254), Kelowna (rebuilt as a walking and mountain biking path, see p.191) and Summerland (summer steam train service, pp.57, 190).

There are no gas stations or other services on the highway, but there are plenty of parks, lay-bys and walking trails on both sides of the summit. Merritt is the major stop for food, petrol or supplies.

The Coquihalla is open all year, but a number of **avalanche chutes**, or avalanche paths, cross the roadway. Occasional barrages of high explosive howitzer shells from roadside gun emplacements are used to trigger small avalanches before the snow pack builds to dangerous depths. Expect occasional and very temporary road closures in winter when avalanches are being set off. In summer, hikers occasionally find unexploded shells in the hills. Like all unexploded military ordinance, the unfired shells may be highly unstable and could explode if moved. Leave the shells where they are, mark the location and report them to the nearest police, parks office or InfoCentre.

Some slopes are too exposed for artificial avalanche controls. Instead, the highway was built beneath **snow sheds**, heavily reinforced concrete tunnels that allow the avalanche to thunder overhead unimpeded. Sheds are open along one side for light and ventilation, which can create an unforgettable impression when an avalanche comes thundering down the mountain to slide past the open side of the shed in a cascade of snow, ice, rock and splintered tree trunks.

In summer, beware of overheating your engine on the long uphill grades, especially if pulling a trailer or driving an RV. If overheating is a concern, it is minimally easier to drive southbound than northbound: the steepest grade is a long 8% climb northbound that begins north of the toll booth. Driving southbound has more downhill grades than uphill pulls.

Hwy 5 turns north across the Nicola River 7 km after leaving Hwy 3. To visit the **Othello Tunnels**, take the Othello Road exit to Kawkawa Lake and the **Coquihalla Canyon Provincial Recreation Area**. The main attractions are KVR tunnels that have been refurbished as a riverside walking and mountain bike path. Much of the Rambo film *First Blood* was filmed in the canyon and nearby Hope, sparking a string of Hollywood hits that used the sheer canyon walls and rushing river to good effect.

Construction on the KVR began in 1910 after chief engineer Andrew McCulloch surveyed the canyon from a basket hanging over the gorge, 91 m above the rushing river. The birdseye view convinced him that it was possible to tunnel through awkward spots in the Coquihalla

Canyon rather than seeking another route. Work crews blasted five short tunnels through solid granite to link up with track being laid further north. Three of the five have been reopened. The tunnels are short, but torches (flashlights) are useful for the uneven and unlit path.

Seven km north is a large gravel lay-by on the east side of the highway, favoured by fishers in search of Dolly Varden trout in spring and autumn, coho salmon in autumn, and steelhead trout in summer and winter. The river is open for fly-fishing only, with strict closures, bait and catch restrictions posted at the lay-by. Serious fishers with 4x4s follow the old Coquihalla Road to less accessible riffles and pools. There are a number of lay-bys to the north, most of them reachable only from the northbound traffic lanes.

The closest U-turn point is 6 km north at **Dewdney Creek** via *Carolin Mines Rd,* which leads to a working gold mine that does not welcome visitors. In winter, watch for road closure barriers that block traffic while road crews clear avalanches and rock falls above. The weather can change suddenly in any season.

Ladner Creek Bridge, 2 km north, gently curves 40m above the creek. The old KVR right-of-way loops around to cross the creek higher upstream. The exit for *Shylock Rd,* 1.5 km north of Ladner Creek, is a popular U-turn spot. The Stop of Interest marker, located near the former KVR Portia Station, details the engineering and weather problems that plagued the railway.

The highway veers north-west from *Shylock Rd* to follow Boston Bar Creek uphill toward **Needle Peak**. The topography changes dramatically, with rock faces west of the highway sprouting strings of waterfalls. The chain-up area for northbound traffic is 3 km beyond *Shylock Rd.*

259

Expect to see snow in protected areas along the road into June and July.

The first avalanche gun emplacement is just north of the **Portia Bridge** over **Boston Bar Creek**. Artillery is removed once avalanche danger has passed for the year, leaving concrete pads and space to pull off the highway to enjoy the scenery. The box canyon 2.5 km north of the Portia Bridge holds the record for the deepest snowfall on the Coquihalla, 4.6 m in 1976. The canyon is a textbook example of glacial scouring and erosion.

Eleven major avalanche chutes cross the highway between the box canyon and the summit, 10 km north. The **Great Bear Snowshed**, nearly 30 m long and one of the world's longest highway snowsheds, begins 1.5 km north of the canyon. The snowshed is named for the oversized images of bears carved into its lintels. The highway veers back to the east to rejoin the Coquihalla River Canyon north of the snowshed. Best vantage point is from the avalanche gun emplacement about 1 km uphill from the snowshed.

The official viewpoint is just beyond, a rest area beneath the towering slab of **Zopkios Ridge**. The three peaks, **Yak**, **Nak** and **Thar**, are named after ruminants from the high Himalayas. Facilities are on the west side of the highway, including a heated waiting room for winter emergencies. Northbound travellers can access the rest area by way of a culvert beneath the highway.

Another rest area is 2.5 km uphill near the summit of Boston Bar Creek and the site of the former Romeo Station on the KVR. The 1244-m **Coquihalla Highway Summit**, is 2.5 km north from the rest area. There are excellent views to the east across the upper canyon of Coquihalla River. The pass isn't especially high by Western Canada standards, but seems more

remote because the surrounding peaks are great granite slabs rising naked from lower forested slopes. The area surrounding the summit is part of **Coquihalla Summit Provincial Recreation Area**, extending north beyond the toll plaza.

Falls Lake picnic area, 1.5 km north of the summit, has a pleasant picnic area and hiking up old logging roads along Falls Lake Creek to the lake itself. **Bridal Veil Falls** are downstream, behind the last original trestle from the KVR. To reach the falls and trestle, follow the old pipeline road downstream from Coquihalla Lakes (see below), rough in spots but passable by passenger vehicles in good weather. RVs and trailers should stick to the main highway. The picnic area is also the final U-turn before the **toll plaza**, 4 km north. The toll is $5 for motorcycles and $10 for cars, light trucks with trailer or camper and all RVs, payable by cash, Visa or MasterCard.

Britton Creek Rest Area is 2.2 km north of the toll plaza, with heated waiting rooms and picnic tables. The rest area is north of **Coquihalla Lakes**, headwaters for the Coquihalla River. *Coldwater Rd* provides access to the lakes and continues south to Bridal Veil Falls and the KVR trestle. *Coldwater Rd* north continues to Merritt.

Just north of the rest area is the **Coldwater River**, which runs from Zopkios Ridge to the Nicola River. The highway crosses the Coldwater repeatedly over the next 16 km. High fences along the road are designed to keep cattle and deer out of the traffic lanes.

The land quickly becomes dry north of the Coquihalla Summit. By **Juliet Creek**, 10 km north of the first Coldwater River bridge, the forest has turned almost completely to lodgepole pine, which is the most common conifer in the Interior dry belt. The **Coldwater River Provincial**

Recreation Area, just north of the Juliet Creek bridge, has pleasant picnicking beside the river. Best fishing is July–Nov for rainbow and Dolly Varden trout. The long 6% grade beginning 13 km north of the Recreation Area runs to Merritt, the largest town in the very rural and quiet Nicola Valley.

MERRITT

Tourist Information: Merritt and District Chamber of Commerce, *Box 1649, Merritt, BC V0K 2B0; tel: (250) 378-5634; fax: (250) 378-6561*; InfoCentre, *log building at the intersection of Hwy 5 and 5A; tel: (250) 378-2281,* open daily 0900–1700 (May–Sept), 1000–1600 (Sept–May).

ACCOMMODATION

The centre of a booming tourism, fishing and outdoor recreation area, Merritt has more motel rooms and campsites than most Interior cities. Local landmark is the **Coldwater Hotel**, *1901 Voght St; tel: (250) 378-2821; fax: (250) 378-3570,* moderate, topped by a gleaming copper turret. The hotel was the finest in the Interior when it opened in 1908, complete with en suite facilities and steam heat. Guest rooms and other facilities were modernised in the late 1980s. Chains include *BW, TL.*

SIGHTSEEING

Merritt was born as a collection of sawmills and coal mines in the 1870s. Fame and fortune arrived when the Canadian Pacific Railway choose to bring its line to the confluence of the Nicola and Coldwater Rivers, bypassing what had been the busy ranching town of Nicola. Merritt boomed, fuelled by railway traffic, nearby coal mines and a growing population of ranch and farm families. The last of Merritt's coal mines closed in 1945, although underground fires continue to consume one

seam; ask if smoke is visible when visiting the Travel InfoCentre.

Tourism has overshadowed ranching, thanks to more than 150 fishing lakes scattered about the Nicola Valley as well as hiking paths, Nordic skiing in winter and stunning scenery in any season. The **Nicola Valley Museum and Archives**, *2202 Jackson Ave; tel: (250) 378-4145,* traces local history from the days of the Nlaka'pamux First Nations to ranching, lumbering and mining. The museum is best known for displays on James Teit (1864–1922), one of the most detailed early chroniclers of the history, culture and religion of BC's Interior First Nations.

Merritt is also home to three of BC's most historic cattle ranches, the Nicola Ranch, Quilchena Cattle Co and Douglas Lake Cattle Co. The **Nicola Ranch***; tel: (250) 378-6499; fax: (250) 378-2727,* surrounds what remains of the town of **Nicola**, just east of Merritt on Hwy 5A. Most of the town, buildings included, moved to Merritt when the railway arrived in 1906. The **Murray United Church**, built in 1876, is surrounded by gravestones dating to 1873. Across the highway, the 1913 **Nicola Courthouse** has become a pricey Bed and Breakfast. The 113,000-hectare ranch has about 5000 head of cattle and Canada's largest herd of fallow deer. Tours of the fallow deer farm and townsite are available; *tel: (250) 378-6499,* at least 24 hours in advance.

Century-old **Quilchena Cattle Co** is one of BC's largest working cattle ranches, but is better known as the home of the moderate **Quilchena Hotel**, *Box 1, Quilchena, BC V0E 2R0; tel: (250) 378-2611; fax: (250) 378-6091,* built in 1908 in anticipation of a railway line that never arrived. Its 16 elegant rooms are furnished in period antiques; the moderate–pricey restaurant is one of the most popular in the

261

region. The Quilchena's most famous guest was Bill Miner, better known as the Grey Fox, an American who became BC's most successful train robber. Bullet holes in the bar date from Miner's unintended stay not long after the hotel opened.

The **Douglas Lake Ranch**; *tel: (800) 663-4838,* claims to be the largest working cattle ranch in Canada, with 202,000 hectares and more than 18,000 head of cattle. The ranch offers guided tours, horsepacking, excellent fly fishing on private streams and accommodation ranging from campsites to a full-service lodge. All tours and accommodation must be reserved in advance.

The best view of Merritt and the Coldwater Valley are from the **Merritt City View Point**, *Juniper Dr. and follow the signs.* The **Godey Creek Trail**, *behind the Travel InfoCentre,* climbs a short hill for a slightly different view of town and valley. The broad trails leading out of Merritt are the old KVR railbed, now a popular walking, cycling and skiing route. The right-of-way leads west to Spences Bridge and east into the mountains of the Coquihalla. Ask about trail conditions at the InfoCentre.

⟐ SIDE TRACK FROM MERRITT

Valley mining history remains alive at **Highland Valley Copper**; *tel: (250) 523-2443, local 307 (ask for the tour guide),* 50 km north-west on Hwy 97C in **Logan Lake**. The open pit mine, one of North America's largest, is open for daily tours May 1–Sept 1 (advance reservation). Visitors must wear long trousers and closed shoes. Children under 12 are not allowed in the mill area. ⬛

MERRITT TO KAMLOOPS

A long grade up to the high forest of the Nicola Plateau begins 5 km north of Nicola. The chain-up area offers fine views north-east toward Nicola Lake and hillsides covered with the black tents of ginseng fields. The tunnel beneath the road is for cattle and wildlife. The 1445-m summit is 13 km north. Hwy 5 crosses 20 km of plateau and begins a 4.5-km downgrade toward *Meadow Creek Rd.* Westbound, *Meadow Creek Rd* leads to **Logan Lake**, a service town for Highland Valley Copper, and on to Ashcroft (see opposite). East of Hwy 5 is a string of fishing lakes, including **Walloper**, **Lac Le Jeune**, **Stake** and **McConnell**. All four feature excellent rainbow trout fishing, hiking, mountain biking and Nordic skiing.

If freeway driving has lost its allure, follow *Le Jeune Rd* north to Kamloops, where it meets Hwy 1 just east of the Hwy 5 junction.

Hwy 5 begins its final descent into the Thompson River Valley 8.5 km north of *Meadow Creek Rd,* dropping down increasingly parched slopes toward Kamloops. The highway meets Hwy 97/1 just inside Kamloops. Continue east to Kamloops and the Thompson River (see p.195).

FRASER RIVER CANYON

The scenic route north from Hope along the Fraser River canyon was pioneered by First Nations traders who used ropes and logs to make their way along the oftensheer walls. Simon Fraser paddled and walked down the canyon in 1806, complaining that 'We had to pass where no human being should venture. Yet in those places there is a regular footpath impressed, or rather indented, by frequent travelling upon the very rocks.'

Fifty years later, word of gold discoveries on the Fraser River spurred tens of thousands of miners to scramble north from Hope. The mad rush soon passed, but gold discoveries in the Cariboo in 1860

Northwest Gold Rushes

Dozens of Hollywood epics have cast fur trappers, farmers and timbermen as the romantic heroes of Western Canada. It was gold miners, many of them failed prospectors from California's famous 1848 Gold Rush, who did more than any other group to transform the region from a trackless frontier into a tempting land ripe for settlement.

Fur trappers followed long-established First Nations' trails west across the Rocky Mountains, but few ventured off well-worn tracks until California gold strikes fired their own dreams of mineral wealth. It was gold prospectors, blazing new trails through scorching deserts and virgin forests, who laid the economic and political foundations of Western Canada.

American prospectors struck gold in the Queen Charlotte Islands in 1851 and the Hudson's Bay Company may have traded for gold from Central BC as early as 1852, but neither discovery sparked much interest. An 1856–1857 find on the Fraser River led to the creation of British Columbia.

News of the Fraser River strike spread widely after the HBC shipped 800 ounces of raw gold to the nearest mint, San Francisco, in Feb, 1858. Every craft that could float left San Francisco jammed with miners bound for Canada. Shipping on Puget Sound was paralysed as ships, rowboats and rafts made their way to Victoria, the sole source for mining licenses, then up the Fraser River to Hope, Yale, Boston Bar and beyond.

More than 30,000 gold seekers converged on Victoria between May and July of 1858 alone, almost all of them Americans. The business community prospered, but government were worried. British authority was little more than a string of Hudson's Bay Company trading posts. Unruly Americans could annex HBC territory as boldly as they had taken California from Mexico and forced Britain northward out of Oregon and Washington.

Britain replaced HBC commercial control with direct rule. The move consolidated political control but hastened the decline of the HBC. James Douglas, governor of Vancouver Island, became the first governor of the new colony of British Columbia in Nov, 1858. He promptly requested British troops and British justices to enforce British law, measures that kept BC British through waves of immigrant miners rushing to gold strikes on the Boundary, Similkameen and Thompson Rivers, the Okanagan Valley, the Cariboo Mountains, The Yukon Territory and the Kootenay Mountains.

Even Alberta, far from the gold strikes, boomed. When news of the 1897 Yukon Territory gold strike spread, Edmonton, a town of 1000 souls at the end of the rails, quickly mushroomed as the mining supply hub closest to Dawson City and the Klondike River gold fields.

263

renewed calls for a road, or at least a dependable track, through the Fraser River canyon. By 1864, the **Cariboo Wagon Road** had been completed to Lytton, opening the Interior to miners, loggers and settlers. The modern highway follows the same general route, and often the same roadbed, as the original.

The railway soon followed. The Canadian Pacific Railway set off the first of thousands of Fraser Canyon dynamite charges in 1880, blasting ledges and tunnels

where only sheer rock had existed before. Four tunnels were cut within 1.5 km of Yale, six more in the next 0.5 km. Canyon track was completed in 1885, following the less precipitous west side of the canyon. The Canadian National Railway later built its track on the east side of the river.

Lake of the Woods, more formally known as **Shkam Lake**, is 5 km north of Hope. This small jewel of a lake is popular for swimming (summer) and fishing (winter and summer) both for its beauty and a strict prohibition against boats with motors. Twelve km north is the turnoff for **Emory Creek Provincial Park**; *tel: (604) 824-2300.* The park covers the site of Emory City, an 1858 gold rush town. Emory boasted the first newspaper to be published on the BC mainland, but the town was abandoned after the gravel bars yielded their gold. After White miners gave up, they allowed Chinese miners to pan the tailings, the scrap heaps of already-mined rock, gravel and sand. The Chinese reportedly extracted more than twice as much gold from tailings as their White predecessors had found in the first place by working more diligently. A roadside plaque explains the vital role Chinese immigrants played in building the CPR.

YALE

Tourist Information: Visitor Information Booth, *31187 Douglas St, Box 74, Yale, BC V0K 2S0; tel: (604) 863-2324,* open June–Sept.

Yale began life as a pair of Sto:lo First Nations villages on each side of the Fraser River. The site was the head of navigation for canoes from as far away as Vancouver Island headed for fishing sites on the rapids just upstream. The HBC opened a fur post called 'The Falls', after the rapids; it was renamed Yale after James Murray Yale, the HBC officer in charge at Fort Langley.

The town erupted in the Gold Rush. As the head of navigation for steamboats as well as canoes, Yale boomed with a steady influx of miners, merchants, gamblers, prostitutes, preachers and saloon keepers. The boom continued with Cariboo gold discoveries, when Yale became the main transfer point between steamboats and freight wagons travelling the Cariboo Wagon Road. Yale boomed again with the coming of the CPR, then settled into quiet relative obscurity.

Yale Museum, *31179 Douglas St; tel: (604) 863-2324 or (604) 863-2428,* open daily (June–Sept), weekends and holidays (Apr–June and Sept–Oct), explores local First Nations history as well as the Gold Rush, Wagon Road and CPR in a restored 1868 house. **St. John the Divine Church**, part of the museum heritage site, is the oldest church in BC still on its original foundation. The church was built in 1859 by Royal Engineers. Gravestones in the cemetery date back to 1850. Recreational gold panning is permitted at **Foreshore Park**, ask for details at the museum. Walking tours of the museum, church and town can be booked in advance for any time of the year.

Yale is also home to **Fraser River Raft Expeditions**, *Box 10, Yale, BC V0K 2S0; tel: (800) 363-7238 or (604) 863-2336; fax: (604) 863-2355,* which offer one- to eight-day rafting or paddling expeditions on the Fraser. The most thrilling trip is a one-day paddle from Spences Bridge to Yale. For the less adventurous, the company also runs motorised rafts from Boston Bar to Yale. Both trips blast through the rapids at Hells Gate.

One km south of Yale is the **Spirit Cave Trail**, a one-hour climb to spectacular views of the Cascade Mountains from the cave mouth. The trailhead is on the east side of the highway.

North of Yale is the **Yale Tunnel**, the first of seven tunnels between Yale and Hells Gate.

Just north of the tunnel is **Lady Franklin Rock**, the final barrier to navigation upstream. The rock, still an important Native fishery, is named after the wife of explorer Sir John Franklin who disappeared in 1845. Lady Franklin staged her own wilderness search for Sir John, following the Fraser north as far the black boulder that bears her name.

YALE TO HELLS GATE

Spuzzum is a tiny village with gas and food, the site of a Nlaka'pamux village, an HBC depot and a toll post on the Cariboo Wagon Road. A ferry hauled freight and passengers across the Fraser River before the Alexandra Bridge opened in 1863.

The international orange **Alexandra Bridge**, 4 km north of Spuzzum, was built in 1962. Two km north is **Alexandra Bridge Provincial Park** surrounding the original suspension bridge. An easy walking path from the car park on the west side of Hwy 1 crosses the railway tracks to the old highway over the 1926 bridge. The Fraser River roars beneath the open grating of the bridge deck, used only by pedestrians. The bridge replaced an 1863 structure that used the same concrete abutments. **Alexandra Lodge**, just north of the park, was built as a Wagon Road roadhouse and may be open in summer. Lodge and bridges were named in 1863 for Alexandra, Princess of Wales.

HELLS GATE

Hells Gate, *tel: (604) 867-9277; fax: (604) 867-9279*, 10.5 km north of Alexandra Bridge Provincial Park, is the narrowest spot in an already-narrow canyon. First Nations used a network of logs pegged to the rock walls to traverse this choke point. An average of 850,000 cubic metres of water blasts through a space about the width of a city street every minute. Although river rafters and kayakers shoot the Gate daily, only one riverboat, the *Skuzzy*, was ever able to navigate the fierce rapids. The boat winched itself upstream on anchor bolts driven into the canyon walls.

The rapids are even more fearsome now than when the *Skuzzy* passed this way in 1882. In 1913, careless CNR construction workers touched off a rockslide that nearly filled the riverbed and blocked the annual salmon run. For years, First Nations fishers carefully netted salmon below the landslide and carried them around the blockage by hand, trying to maintain the runs upon which their lives depended.

For the most part, they failed. Fish ladders built in 1945–1946 helped, but Salmon Arm (see p. 201) and dozens of other upstream communities lost their salmon runs forever in one of the worst environmental disasters in modern North America. In the best of years, today's salmon runs are less than one-third the pre-1913 volume.

The best way to see the rapids is the **Airtram** which descends 153 m to a museum, viewing point and restaurant on the opposite shore. If time permits, walk across the suspension bridge just downstream of the Airtram landing. The museum has excellent displays on the life-cycle of the salmon. Trains pass on both sides of the canyon about every 30 mins. **Rainbow Heli-Tours**, *tel: (888) 997-9792*, offer helicopter tours from a landing pad just south of the upper Airtram station on the west side of the highway.

HELLS GATE TO LYTTON

Boston Bar, 11 km north of Hells Gate, is one of the few Fraser River Gold Rush towns to survive. Named by First Nations after the Americans, or 'Boston Men', who swarmed over the rich gravel bar, the town switched economic gears from gold to lumber. Much of the haze that sometimes blankets the canyon comes from Boston Bar mills.

The highway snakes above the foaming Fraser, eventually climbing to a lay-by at the top of **Jackass Mountain**, 25 km north of Boston Bar. This grade was the steepest on the Cariboo Wagon Road. The summit is named for the many mules, or jackasses, that stumbled and plunged into the river far below. Three km north is **Kanaka Bar**, named after the Hawaiians who panned for gold here. Nearby fields grew BC's first recorded crop of alfalfa in the 1860s, used as fodder for Wagon Road draft animals.

Siska, 5 km north of Kanaka Bar, is one of eleven Nlaka'pamux Nation communities in the Fraser Canyon. Several Siska artists are building worldwide reputations, primarily for carvings made of soapstone taken from quarries hidden on traditional lands. Some of the best are on display (and sale) at the **Siska Art Gallery and Band Museum**, *Box 519, Lytton, BC V0K 1Z0; tel: (250) 455-2219; fax: (250) 455-2539.* Siska has also produced a renowned dance troupe, the **Coyote Dancers**, as well as **Siska Halaw Singers and Drummers**. Just north of town is a lay-by with a view down to the two **Siska (Cisco) Bridges**. The CPR, which built the first, crosses from the east bank of the Fraser to the west side, while latecomer CNR crosses from west to east – neither side of the canyon is wide enough for both railways to run side-by-side. Both tracks are in active use.

LYTTON

Tourist Information: Lytton and District Chamber of Commerce *Box 460, Lytton, BC V0K 1Z0;* the **Visitor InfoCentre**, *400 Fraser St; tel: (250) 455-2523; fax: (250) 455-6669,* is open year-round.

Lytton, at the junction of the coffee-coloured Fraser and the ice-blue Thompson, has long been a First Nations capitol. HBC explorers called it 'The Forks' and established Fort Dallas. The fort was renamed in 1858 after Sir Edward Bulwer-Lytton, then Secretary of State for the British Colonies.

The Fraser, the third longest river in Canada, flows 1368 km from the Rocky

Mountains near Mt Robson (see p.220) to the Pacific at Vancouver, 180 km downstream from Lytton. The river was named after Simon Fraser, who descended from Prince George to the sea 1806–1808, by fellow explorer, David Thompson, who travelled the Columbia River from its Canadian headwaters to the Pacific Ocean between Washington and Oregon in the United States.

Fraser, in turn, named the Thompson River after Thompson, who never travelled or even saw the broad stream that bears his name. The Thompson runs from the Columbia Mountains in Wells Gray Park (see p.223) as the North Thompson River, joined in Kamloops by the South Thompson River, flowing from Little Shuswap Lake (p. 201), to join the Fraser at Lytton.

The one-time Gold Rush town survives on logging and river rafting. The **Lytton Museum**, next to the InfoCentre, highlights Gold Rush and Cariboo Wagon Road history. Five km of riverfront has been set aside as a **Gold Panning Recreational Reserve** with hand panning only. Ask about restrictions and gold pans at the Museum or InfoCentre.

Just north of Lytton is the **Lytton Ferry**, a reaction ferry powered only by the current of the Fraser River. On the far bank is the Stein Valley, an undeveloped area sacred to the Nlaka'pamux. The Nation rallied the St'at'imc People at the south end of the watershed, near Mt Currie, and lower mainland BC environmental groups to keep loggers out of the area in the 1980s and early 1990s.

Now the **Stein Valley Nlaka'pamux Heritage Park**; *tel: (250) 455-2304,* the area is the only unlogged watershed within a reasonable drive of Vancouver. A road leads from the ferry 4.5 km to a parking lot and trail. The Stein River and ancient pictographs are about 2 km up the easy trail.

The park and trail follow the Stein river 75 km upstream into the Coastal Mountains to the headwaters at 2400 m. Allow nine days for the rugged return trek, or opt for easier walking in the lower valley.

Hwy 12 crosses the Thompson River to follow the Fraser upstream to Lillooet (see p. 248). Hwy 1 continues 8 km north along the Thompson to **Skihist Provincial Park**; *tel: (250) 851-3000*, with fine views of the nearly-vertical walls of the Thompson Canyon and passing trains. **Little Hells Gate** rapids, 5 km north, are a favourite spot to watch migrating salmon in autumn and river rafters in summer. The highway north runs between steel retaining walls. Verges are occasionally wide enough to pull off the highway and watch river rafters descending the river. Most are coming from a lunch or rest stop just upstream at **Goldpan Provincial Park**; *tel: (250) 851-3000*. As the name suggests, gold can still be panned from river gravel.

The Great Landslide occurred 11 km north, on the outskirts of **Spences Bridge**. Look for the small Anglican church and graveyard on the east side of Hwy 1 and continue just north to the Point of Interest sign. The lower side of the mountain across the river collapsed on 13 Aug, 1905, burying a small Nlaka'pamux village and damming the Thompson River for 5 hours. The waterfall just upstream, **Murray Creek Falls**, tumbles over the lip of a reddish cliff into a pool that has become a favourite stop for river rafters and photographers.

The Nlaka'pamux had an important community at the confluence of the Thompson and Nicola Rivers. Later European arrivals called the place Cook's Ferry, after the ferry which carried passengers across the river until Thomas Spence

built a toll bridge in 1865 and renamed the town for his livelihood. Both rivers have good fishing and wildlife viewing. Keep an eye out for osprey nesting in tall trees along the water and bighorn sheep on surrounding cliffs. In winter, watch for sheep on the highway descending from the cliffs to feed on roadside grasses and lick salt from the pavement. There are several seasonal fruit and ice-cream stands along Hwy 1 north of town.

Hwy 8 runs south-east from Spences Bridge to Merritt (see p. 261), a pleasant backcountry drive. The last spike of the Canadian Northern Pacific Railway (now part of the Canadian National Railway) was driven about 20 km north of Spences Bridge in 1915. The natural benches, or terraces, in the canyon were created when the Thompson was dammed into broad lakes at different periods during recent Ice Ages.

The **Red Hill Rest Area**, 8 km further north, is a pleasant stopping point. The red hills stand out against the more familiar browns and greens of the valley. **Ashcroft Manor**, *404 Brink St, Box 127, Cache Creek, BC V0K 1H0; tel: (250) 453-9983; fax: (250) 453-9600*, is on the east side of the highway 4.5 km north. The manor, built in 1862, was part of a roadhouse, grist mill, sawmill and farm complex that supplied the Cariboo Wagon Road. The manor served as one of BC's first courthouses. Much of the complex burned in 1943, but the roadhouse and log church survived. The roadhouse has become a museum, gallery and gift shop. The tea house, with a broad deck beneath spreading shade trees, is especially popular in summer.

Continue 7 km north to the junction with Hwy 97 at **Cache Creek** (see p. 250) and follow Hwys 97/1 84 km east to Kamloops (see pp. 196–198).

VANCOUVER–VICTORIA

The ferry ride between Vancouver and Victoria takes ninety spectacular minutes, threading between the rugged, tree-lined shores of Gulf Islands that sometimes seem almost close enough to touch. Only five of the two hundred or so islands lying between Vancouver and Victoria are inhabited, but stopping at all can easily stretch the journey to anything from five days to a lifetime.

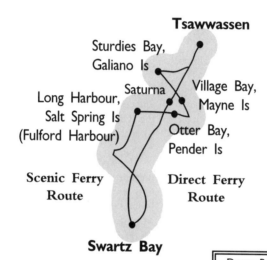

Tsawwassen

Sturdies Bay, Galiano Is

Saturna

Long Harbour, Salt Spring Is (Fulford Harbour)

Village Bay, Mayne Is

Otter Bay, Pender Is

Scenic Ferry Route

Direct Ferry Route

Swartz Bay

DIRECT ROUTE: 90 MINS

ROUTES

DIRECT ROUTE

The direct ferry route runs from **Tsawwassen**, south of Vancouver, to **Swartz Bay**, north of Victoria.

SCENIC ROUTE

The island-hopping route combines several services to stop at **Sturdies Bay** on **Galiano Island**, **Village Bay** on **Mayne Island**, **Otter Bay** on **Pender Island**, **Long Harbour** on **Salt Spring Island** and on to Swartz Bay.

BC Ferries, *1112 Fort St, Victoria, BC V8V 4V2; tel: (888) 223-3779 (inside BC) or (250) 386-3431 (outside BC); fax: (250) 381-5452; web: http://www.bcferries.bc.ca/ferries*. Ferries from Vancouver leave the terminal at **Tsawwassen**, 45 mins south of Vancouver off BC 99. Southbound from Vancouver, take Exit 28 to BC 17, which leads directly to the ferry dock. Northbound, take Exit 20 to BC 10 westbound, then turn south (left) onto BC 17 to the ferry dock. BC 17 lanes lead directly to

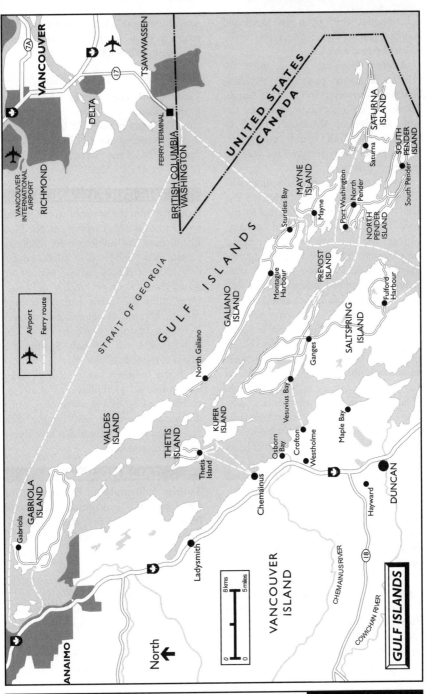

ticket booths, which open onto numbered boarding lanes. Ticket takers and traffic wardens direct vehicles.

Advance bookings are required for vehicles (but not passengers) travelling between Tsawwassen and the Gulf Islands. There are no reservations between the Gulf Islands and Vancouver Island or between the Gulf Islands themselves. Bookings are never required for walk-on or bicycle passengers.

Bookings may be made in writing or by telephone with Visa or MasterCard and may be changed or cancelled up to five days before sailing without penalty. Changes less than five days before sailing are subject to a $10 fee for each segment changed. Vehicle check-in is 40 mins before the scheduled sailing time at Tsawwassen and 30 mins before sailing at Gulf Island ports. Vehicles that arrive between check-in and sailing time revert to stand-by status and may not be allowed to board. Since there are only two daily departures on some routes, missing a sailing could mean spending an extra night in the islands.

Schedules and fares change seasonally. There are at least two return sailings daily from Vancouver to the Gulf Islands with additional departures at weekends, holidays and during the summer. There are at least six daily return trips between the Gulf Islands and Vancouver Island (Swartz Bay). Pay peak fares at weekends, mid June–mid Sept.

BC Ferries Gulf Island ships have self-service cafeterias, indoor seating and a better selection of tourist literature than you're likely to find outside the main tourist information centres in Vancouver and Victoria.

Ferries from the Gulf Islands and from Tsawwassen dock at Swartz Bay, at the northern tip of the Saanich Peninsula, 30 mins north of Victoria by car. From the ferry dock, follow the signs for BC 17

southbound into Victoria or pick up the return portion of the Victoria Circular Tour (see pp.285–288).

BUSES

Pacific Coach Lines operate a bus service from Vancouver to Victoria twelve times a day. The journey takes 3½ hrs, including the ferry crossing. See OTT table 71. For details of BC Ferry Services in the Gulf Islands, see OTT tables 27–34.

THE GULF ISLANDS

Protected from the worst of winter storms by Vancouver Island mountains, the Gulf Islands have the mildest, most moderate climate in BC and less than half the rainfall of Vancouver. Rocky and low, none of the islands have adequate supplies of water. Open fires are often banned spring–autumn because of the wildfire danger. Accommodation is scarce on all of the islands, but less so on **Salt Spring**, the largest of the Gulf Islands. Advance accommodation bookings are needed all year. The principal activities are walking, cycling, birding, fishing, swimming, scuba diving, sea kayaking and boating. Salt Spring and Mayne Islands also have thriving arts communities.

GALIANO ISLAND

Tourist Information: Galiano Island Chamber of Commerce and Travel Infocentre, *Sturdies Bay, Box 73, Galiano Island, BC V0N 1P0; tel: (888) 223-3779 or (250) 386-3431.*

ACCOMMODATION

Galiano Getaways!; *tel: (250) 539-5551,* provide bookings for most of the inns, cottages and Bed and Breakfasts on the island. Most are moderate–expensive. Camping is available at **Montague Harbour Provincial Marine Park**, 40

The Pig War

A merica was a 150-year headache for Britain. Matters went from war with the French to skirmishes with colonists, revolution in 1776 and yet another war in 1812. It took the death of a pig to bring hostilities to a close.

The first European who might have seen the San Juan Archipelago was a Greek explorer sailing for Spain under the name Juan de Fuca in 1592. By the time Spain got around to exploring in greater detail in 1790, the British had arrived in force. It took Capt George Vancouver four years to talk the Spanish into relinquishing their claims to the Pacific Northwest, but convince them he did. The United States was more obdurate.

American explorers Lewis and Clark paddled down the Columbia River in 1805, followed by Capt Charles Wilkes who charted much of Puget Sound in 1841. Reinforced by growing emigration from eastern America, the US claimed the entire Pacific Northwest from California north to Alaska. '54°40' or Fight!' was the rallying cry in the US presidential election of 1844.

Both countries breathed a sigh of relief when diplomats set the US-Canada border at the 49th Parallel in 1846. England got Vancouver Island, with the sea boundary running along the main channel between the islands and the mainland. Unfortunately, there are two main channels, Haro Strait, west of the San Juan Islands, and Rosario Strait, to the east.

The ambiguity could have been an oversight. It may also have been a strategic move. James Douglas, governor of Vancouver Island and former head of the Hudson's Bay Company in the North West, knew the strategic importance of San Juan Island, which controlled the Haro Strait and the approaches to Victoria. America had already won the Columbia River and forced him to move HBC operations from Vancouver, Washington to Victoria. He was determined to hold the new border.

Once the border treaty was signed, Douglas moved a small garrison force to a pretty cove midway down the west coast of San Juan Island. The Americans built their own fort at the barren southern end of the island. A few dozen settlers from both nations trickled in.

An amiable stand-off ensued until June, 1859. A prickly American, Lyman Cutlar, planted potatoes in the middle of an HBC sheep pasture. Cutlar's potato patch was visited repeatedly by a British hog, so the American shot the trespasser.

The HBC demanded damages and, when Cutlar refused, demanded trial in Victoria. American officials insisted that US courts had jurisdiction.

Douglas dispatched warships to enforce British sovereignty. The American commander dispatched his own ship, ostensibly to defend against 'Indian attack'. The British flotilla could easily have flattened the feeble American defences, but Americans vastly outnumbered the British throughout the North West. The battle might have spread to Vancouver Island itself, which counted four Americans for every British subject.

Cooler heads decided on a joint occupation by one hundred men from each nation until the matter could be settled. Both governments immediately turned their attentions to domestic matters and ignored the Pig War. So did the soldiers, who replaced the earthworks and tents of English Camp and American Camp with comfortable wooden buildings, parade grounds and formal gardens. The two commanders took turns hosting monthly balls while other ranks openly traded beer, spirits and other supplies across what was supposed to be a line of hostilities.

Britain and America eventually submitted the matter to Germany's Kaiser Wilhelm I for arbitration. By the time Wilhelm decided for America in 1872, San Juan Island had become an extremely comfortable, if somewhat boring, posting. British Marines lowered their colours for the last time on 25 Nov, 1872, finally ending more than a century of colonial hostilities in North America.

271

pitches, and **Dionisio Point Provincial Park**, 15 pitches; information for both available at *2930 Trans Canada Highway, RR 6, Victoria, BC V9B 5T9; tel: (250) 391-2300.*

SIGHTSEEING

Galiano is the most northerly of the Gulf Islands, named after Spanish explorer Dionisio Alcala Galiano, who charted the area in 1792. The main commercial centre is **Sturdies Bay**, at the south end of the long, narrow and flat island. There are also settlements at **Montague Harbour** and **Spotlight Cove**, at the north end. More than 130 species of birds, as well as a number of endangered plant and animal species, make the island popular with birders, walkers and cyclists. Protected waters also make swimming, scuba diving, sea kayaking and boating popular year-round. The 57-square-km island has a permanent population of about 900.

MAYNE ISLAND

Tourist Information: Mayne Island Community Chamber of Commerce, *Box 160, Mayne Island, BC V0N 2J0; tel: (250) 539-5311.*

ACCOMMODATION

Oceanwood Country Inn, *C-2 Leighton Lane, RR #1, Mayne Island, BC V0N 2J0; tel: (250) 539-5074; fax: (250) 539-3002,* expensive, is the finest inn and gourmet restaurant on the island with expansive vistas across Navy Channel to North Pender Island.

SIGHTSEEING

BC Ferries dock at **Village Bay**, which has a bay but no village. For ferry information; *tel: (888) 223-3779 or (250) 386-3431.* The crossing from Galiano Island takes 25 mins.

Mayne was once a major staging area for gold miners on the way from the mining permit office in Victoria to the Cariboo Gold Rush on the mainland. **Miners Bay** remains the main town on the island. Farmers followed the miners, turning Mayne into a major vegetable and fruit supplier for Vancouver until Japanese-Canadian farmers were interned inland during World War II. Today, Mayne is a popular second-home and retirement island, with many private residences. The original 1896 gaol, Plumper Pass Lockup, is now **Mayne Museum**; *tel: (250) 539-5286.* **Active Pass Lighthouse** opens daily 1300–1500. The hilly island is popular with cyclists. Permanent population is about 800 scattered across 21 square km.

PENDER ISLANDS

Tourist Information: Pender Island Lions Club, *Box 75, Pender Island, BC V0N 2M0; tel: (250) 629-3072; fax: (250) 629-3085;* **Pender Island Visitor Information Booth**, *2332 Otter Bay Rd,* open daily (June–Sept).

ACCOMMODATION

Bed and Breakfasts of North & South Pender Islands, *RR #1, Pender Island, BC V0N 2M0;* make bookings for the dozen or so Bed and Breakfasts on the two islands.

SIGHTSEEING

BC Ferries dock at **Otter Bay**. For local ferry information; *tel: (888) 223-3779 or (250) 386-3431.* The crossing from Mayne Island takes 20 mins.

North and South Pender Island are joined by a narrow wooden bridge over an artificial canal. Much of the population lives on North Pender, the larger of the two. **Driftwood Centre**, mid-island, is the major commercial hub. **Port Washington**, north of the ferry terminal at

Otter Bay, also has several artist-owned galleries and studios. Public recreation areas include an archaeological dig at a traditional Salish site on the north side of the canal open for tours in summer. An annual summer tournament at the Frisbee® disk park at Magic Lake draws contestants from around the world. The 24–square-km island has a permanent population of about 2000.

SATURNA ISLAND

BC Ferries dock is at Lyall Harbour; tel: (888) 223-3779 or (250) 386-3431. Crossing time to Mayne and Pender Island is 35–40 mins.

Most services and most of the half-dozen Bed and Breakfasts are within a few kilometres of the ferry landing. With fewer than 300 permanent residents scattered across 31 square km, the most startling sight is likely to be the splash of an eagle fishing or a deer walking through an open meadow. The island is quite hilly, unlike Pender, creating challenges for cyclists and blind corners for motorists. Best views are from the peak of 490-m Mt Warburton Pike and East Point Lighthouse, atop a barren plateau surrounded by wave-sculpted sandstone formations. The US Coast Guard station on Patos Island and Mt Constitution on Orcas Island, both in the San Juan Islands, are clearly visible.

SALT SPRING ISLAND

Tourist Information: Salt Spring Island Chamber of Commerce, 121 Lower Ganges Rd, Ganges, BC V8K 2T1; tel: (250) 537-5252; fax: (250) 537-4276.

ACCOMMODATION

Canadian Gulf Islands B&B Reservation Service, 637 Southwind Rd, Galiano Island, BC V0N 1P0; tel: (250) 539-2930; fax: (250) 539-5390, book

more than a hundred inns, cottages, houses and Bed and Breakfasts in the Gulf Islands, most of them on Salt Spring. A Salt Spring Chamber of Commerce booklet lists accommodations, including Salt Spring Island Hostel, 640 Cusheon Lake Rd, Salt Spring Island, BC V8K 2C2; tel: (250) 537-4149, the only Gulf Islands hostel.

SIGHTSEEING

BC Ferries has three docks: Vesuvius Bay, with service to Crofton; Fulford Harbour, with service to Swartz Bay; and Long Harbour, with service to Tsawwassen and Swartz Bay plus Galiano, Mayne and Pender Islands; tel: (888) 223-3779 or (250) 386-3431. Crossings range from 10–90 mins.

Named after the salt water springs on the north end of the island, SSI (as it is usually abbreviated) is the largest (180 square km) and most populous of the Gulf Islands (about 9500 permanent residents). It also claims more artists per capita than anywhere else in Canada. More than 75 studios produce everything from practical pottery to whimsical macramé. The greatest concentrations of studios are near Ganges, Fulford and Vesuvius Bay, the major population centres.

SSI is also the most-visited of the Gulf Islands, which gives it the worst traffic problems. Hire cars are available in Ganges, but bicycles and mopeds are more popular than autos. Salt Spring Marina at Harbour's End, 120 Upper Ganges; tel: (250) 537-5810, has a good selection of bicycles and scooters. Favourite destinations include Ruckle Provincial Park, south-west end of SSI, the largest park in the Islands and one of SSI's most scenic spots, Mount Maxwell Provincial Park, central island, and the Apr–Oct Saturday Market, Centennial Park, Ganges, the most popular open market in the islands.

273

VICTORIA

Victoria is BC's capital and oldest city. Once an industrial centre, Victoria has traded the clamour and the pollution of metal-bashing for environmental activism, tourism and, of course, government. A mild climate, attractive urban setting and easy access to some of the most spectacular outdoor scenery in the Pacific Northwest has created a bubbling mixture of artists, big-city refugees, green activists and mostly-young entrepreneurs straining to turn environmental concern into long-term business opportunity.

Victoria is unfairly known as the stuffiest, most backward looking city in Canada. 'More English than the English,' is how favourite daughter Emily Carr characterised her own father, a 19th-century immigrant, and the city itself. It may have been true once, but modern Victoria is eagerly combining one of Canada's greatest concentrations of heritage buildings with an aggressive turn toward the future. Restored brick storefronts and century-old mansions shelter the kind of social concerns that would have moved the original occupants to call for police protection.

TOURIST INFORMATION

Tourism Victoria Visitor InfoCentre, *812 Wharf St, Victoria, BC V8W 1T3; tel: (250) 953-2033; fax: (250) 382-6539,* open daily. *Monday Magazine, 1069*

Blanshard St, Victoria, BC V8W 2J5; tel: (250) 382-6188, available free each Friday in shops and newspaper boxes, has the most complete listing of current events and reviews in Victoria.

WEATHER

Sheltered from storms by mountains on all sides and warmed by the Pacific Ocean, Victoria has the sunniest and mildest urban climate in Canada. Summer temperatures average 17°C and seldom hit 30°C. Rain is infrequent May–Sept. Winter averages 7°C. Annual rainfall is 690mm, less than half of what Vancouver endures each year.

ARRIVING AND DEPARTING

By Air
Victoria International Airport; *tel: (250) 953-7500,* is 20 km and 30 mins north of the city centre, $30 by taxi. **Airporter**, *767 Audley St, Victoria, BC V8X 2V4; tel: (250) 386-2525; fax: (250) 386-2526,* has a coach service between the airport and sixty hotels every 30 mins, $17 single, children under 5 free, advance booking required. **BC Transit**, *Box 610, Victoria, BC V8W 2P3; tel: (250) 382-6161; fax: (250) 995-5639,* $2.25, exact fare only.

The **Inner Harbour** has seaplane and helicopter service to Seattle, Vancouver, the San Juan Islands, the Gulf Islands and other destinations.

By Sea
Most of Victoria's three million annual visitors arrive by water. Advance booking is required for all ferries except **BC Ferries**,

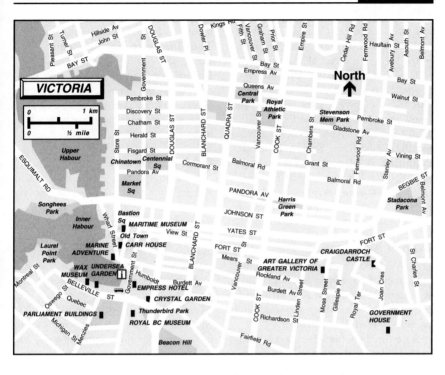

Map of Victoria showing Inner Harbour, Old Town, Chinatown, and major landmarks including Parliament Buildings, Royal BC Museum, Empress Hotel, Art Gallery of Greater Victoria, Craigdarroch Castle, and Government House.

1112 Fort St, Victoria, BC V8W 4V2; tel: (250) 386-3431; fax: (250) 381-5452, which serve Swartz Bay, at the north end of the Saanich Peninsula, 45 mins by car from the city centre, from Vancouver (Tsawwassen) and the Gulf Islands. Ferry services connect with BC Transit in both Victoria and Vancouver.

Black Ball Transport (MV Coho), 430 Belleville St, Victoria, BC V8V 1W9; tel: (250) 386-2202; fax: (250) 386-2207, has car and passenger service between Victoria's Inner Harbour and Port Angeles, WA. **Victoria Rapid Transit**; tel: (250) 361-9144, offer passenger and bicycle service on the same route May–Oct.

Washington State Ferries, 2499 Ocean Ave, Sidney, BC V8L 1Tl; tel: (250) 656-1831; fax: (250) 656-3760, has vehicle and passenger service to Anacortes, WA. Credit cards are not accepted, but fares may be paid in either US or Canadian currency.

Victoria San Juan Cruises; tel: (800) 443-4552, has passenger service between Bellingham, WA and the Inner Harbour via Roche Harbor (San Juan Island, WA), May–Oct.

Victoria Clipper, 254 Belleville, Victoria, BC V8V 1W9; tel: (250) 382-8100 or (800) 888-2535; fax: (206) 443-2583, have daily passenger catamaran service between the Inner Harbour and Seattle, the fastest ships on the route. Clipper also operate a car ferry mid May–mid Sept.

By Land

All land transport between Victoria and the mainland requires a ferry connection through Swartz Bay, or Sidney, or the Inner Harbour. **Pacific Coach Lines**,

210-1150 Station St, Vancouver, BC V6A 4C7; tel: (250) 385-4411, run between central Victoria and central Vancouver.

The **Victoria Coach Station**, 700 Douglas St, is behind the Empress Hotel. The main highways into Victoria are TransCanada Highway from the north, BC 14 from Port Renfrew and the west and BC 17 from the Saanich Peninsula. **Esquimalt & Nanaimo (E&N) Railway**, 450 Pandora Ave, Victoria, BC V8W 1N6; tel: (800) 561-8630 or (250) 383-4324, has a daily return service between Victoria and **Courtenay** via Nanaimo.

GETTING AROUND

Greater Victoria covers much of the southeast corner of Vancouver Island, but most of touristic Victoria is within a 10-block easily walkable area along the south and east sides of the **Inner Harbour**.

Streets are busy until the last restaurants and pubs close in the early morning hours. Sex has been big business in Victoria since the boom days of the last century, though today's trade is conducted largely through escort ads in the telephone book Yellow Pages. As in most cities, it's best not to walk empty streets alone at night, but there are no dangerous neighbourhoods to avoid. Since Victoria is on an island with limited and easily controlled access, criminals prefer the mainland where escape is easier.

Public Transport

It is entirely practicable to explore Victoria by public transport, **BC Transit**, Box 610, Victoria, BC V8W 2P3; tel: (250) 382-6161; fax: (250) 995-5639. The fare within the city centre and the southern Saanich Peninsula is $1.75 for adults, $1.10 for seniors, secondary school students and children. Sheets of 10 discount tickets are $13.50. **Super PASS** is $5.50 daily or $50

monthly; $4 and $32 concession. The **Tourism Victoria Infocentre**, 812 Wharf St, sells day passes. The Victoria Regional Transit System Rider's Guide, available from BC Transit, lists all routes. Service on main lines runs 0600–2400, but some rural routes have as few as two daily buses.

Driving in Victoria

Narrow streets, busy traffic and limited parking make it difficult to explore the city centre by car. There is ample parking off the west side of Wharf St along the Inner Harbour as well as parkades east of Government St. Street parking is regulated by meters, with time limits strictly enforced.

Traffic is heavy in the city centre and major commuter arteries, particularly BC 17 and BC 1A, 0730–0900 and 1600–1800 Mon–Fri. Left turns are extremely difficult in the city centre due to heavy traffic and the near-total absence of left turn signals or left turn lanes.

STAYING IN VICTORIA

Accommodation

There are more than 6500 rooms in Greater Victoria, ranging from elegant hotels to modest Bed and Breakfasts. There are also three million visitors each year, which makes advance bookings a necessity.

Most rooms at all price levels can be booked by credit card through **Tourism Victoria**; tel: (800) 663-3883. Chains include BW, CP, CS, DI, HI, QI, Rm and TL. Inexpensive motels are clustered along BC 1A eastbound and BC 17 southbound. **Best Canadian Bed & Breakfast Network**, 1090 W. King Edward Ave, Vancouver, BC V6H 1Z4; tel: (604) 738-7207; fax: (604) 732-4998, and **Canada-West Victoria Reservation Service**, 6203 Central Saanich Rd, Victoria, BC V8Z 5T7;

tel: (250) 652-8685; fax: (250) 652-8679, book area Bed and Breakfasts. Tourism Victoria has **hostel** information.

Victoria's most prestigious address is Canadian Pacific's château-like **Empress Hotel**, 721 Government St, Victoria, BC V8W 1W5; tel: (250) 384-8111 or (800) 441-1414; fax: (250) 381-5959, the most imposing building on the Inner Harbour. Opened in 1908, the ivy-covered Empress sits surrounded by gardens on what was once a malodorous tidal flat. Although swamped by tourists in summer, the elegant Edwardian décor of the original lobby is worth a visit. Top underground level corridors are lined with photographs showing the upper crust from around the world at play during the first half of the century. The hotel is best known for its overpriced **Afternoon Tea**, but **The Empress Dining Room** is one of the better Northwest restaurants in town. Moderate–expensive **Executive House Hotel**, 777 Douglas St, Victoria, BC V8W 2B5; tel: (800) 663-7001 or (250) 388-5111; fax: (250) 385-1323, rises directly behind the Empress. Upper floors have sweeping views across the Inner Harbour.

Laurel Point Inn, 680 Montreal St, Victoria, BC V8V 1Z8; tel: (250) 386-8721 or (800) 663-7667; fax: (250) 386-9547, overlooking the Inner Harbour entrance, and **Ocean Pointe Resort**, 45 Songhess Rd, Victoria, BC V9A 6T3; tel: (800) 667-4677 or (250) 360-2999; fax: (250) 360-1041, on the west side of the Inner Harbour, offer pricey modern luxury.

Days Inn on the Harbour, 427 Belleville St, Victoria, BC V8V 1X3; tel: (800) 329-7466 or (250) 386-3451; fax: (250) 386-6999, and **Quality Inn Harbourview**, 455 Belleville St; tel: (800) 424-6423 or (250) 386-2421; fax: (250) 386-8779, both moderate–expensive, are directly across the street from the US ferry docks

and a pleasant 10-min walk along the Inner Harbour from The Empress.

There are dozens of Bed and Breakfasts in and near the tourist core. Among the best is the expensive **Inn on St Andrews**, 231 St Andrews St, Victoria, BC V8V 2N1; tel: (250) 384-8613, a wonderfully restored mansion in a quiet residential area.

Eating and Drinking

Victoria's most famous repast is **Afternoon Tea**, epitomised by the 100,000-plus mid-afternoon meals served in the main lobby of **The Empress Hotel** each year. Look for finger sandwiches, crumpets, scones, pots of whipped cream and jam, paté and, of course, tea. Advance booking required.

Credit an early 19th-century Duchess of Bedford with the idea. Praying that a light snack would counteract 'that sinking feeling around five o'clock', she tried snacking on tea and small sandwiches. The custom caught on, evolving into the formal Afternoon Tea and the more serious meal called High Tea.

Many restaurants in Victoria offer Afternoon Tea as a light repast. Prices are budget–moderate, depending on location and quantity. Victorians avoid summer crowds at The Empress but return during the slower winter months. Local year-round favourites include **James Bay Tea Room and Restaurant**, 332 Menzies St (behind Parliament Buildings); tel: (250) 382-8282, **Tudor Rose Restaurant and Tea Room**, 253 Cook St (near Beacon Hill Park); tel: (250) 382-4616, **Blethering Place Tea Room and Restaurant**, 206-2250 Oak Bay Ave (Oak Bay Village); tel: (250) 598-1413, **Oak Bay Beach Hotel**, 1175 Beach Dr.; tel: (250) 598-4556, and **The Olde England Inn**, 429 Lampson St, Esquimalt; tel: (250) 388-4353.

Best choice for a quick meal is the top-level food fair at **Victoria Eaton Centre**,

277

Government St, Fort–View Sts; tel: (250) 389-2228. Most Inner Harbour restaurants cater to tourist tastes for pizza, pasta and ice-cream.

Wharfside, 1208 Wharf St; tel: (250) 360-1808, is a moderate tourist restaurant with excellent harbour views serving respectable fish and pizza. **Chandlers Seafood Restaurant**, 1250 Wharf St; tel: (250) 385-3474, and **Herald Street Café**, 546 Herald St; tel: (250) 381-1441, are the best seafood restaurants, moderate–pricey. **Deep Cove Chalet**, 11190 Chalet Rd; tel: (250) 656-3541, pricey, gets the nod as the best (and most expensive) French-inspired restaurant in Victoria.

The Olde England Inn, 429 Lampson St, Esquimalt; tel: (250) 388-4353, has the best traditional roast beef and Yorkshire pudding on Vancouver Island. **Siam**, 512 Fort St; tel: (250) 383-9911, budget–moderate, has outstanding Thai dishes. **Green Cuisine**, 560 Johnson St, Market Sq., Courtyard Level; tel: (250) 385-1809, has shockingly good budget veggie choices.

Top breakfast or lunch choice is **Sally Café**, 714 Cormorant St; tel: (250) 381-1431, with fine budget omelettes, sandwiches, soups and pastries. Try **Topo's Ristorante**, 2950 Douglas; tel: (250) 383-1212, for Northern Italian, or **San Remo**, 2709 Quadra St; tel: (250) 384-5255, for Greek. **India Curry House**, 506 Fort St; tel: (250) 384-5622, and **Taj Mahal**, 679 Herald St; tel: (250) 383-4662, are two solid Indian possibilities. All are budget–moderate.

Pubs are the most popular spots for eating, drinking and evening entertainment. The **Elephant & Castle**, 100 Victoria Eaton Centre, Government and View Sts; tel: (250) 383-5858, cheap–budget, is the most 'English' of the city's many pubs and extremely popular with tourists. **The**

Charles Dickens Pub, 633 Humboldt St (ground floor, Empress Hotel); tel: (250) 361-2600, budget, is a quieter alternative. **Swans Hotel**, 506 Pandora Ave; tel: (250) 361-3310, has one of BC's best breweries, **Buckerfield's Brewery**, on the premises, as well as a fine budget–moderate Northwest restaurant.

Communications
There are dozens of post offices in Victoria. Mail can be addressed to hotels.

Money
Thomas Cook Foreign Exchange is located at Sussex Pl., G3-1001 Douglas St, Victoria, BC V8W 2C5; tel: (250) 385-0088; fax: (604) 383-6169.

ENTERTAINMENT
Victoria is a fertile incubator for local bands which graduate to wider fame on the mainland. Local venues and performers change frequently, but Monday Magazine stays abreast of who's hot.

McPherson Playhouse, 3 Centennial Sq.; tel: (250) 386-6121, is the centre of professional theatre with a regular summer schedule of noon concerts and evening musical comedy. The McPherson is also the venue for **The Pacific Opera**, 1316 B Government St, Victoria, BC V8W 1Y8; tel: (250) 385-0222; fax: (250) 382-4944, which performs Sept–May.

Victoria Symphony, 846 Broughton St, Victoria, BC V8W 1E4; tel: (250) 386-6515, performs a pop and masterworks series Sept–Apr at the **Royal Theatre**. The **Victoria Conservatory of Music**; tel: (250) 386-5311, also performs at the Royal. **Beacon Hill Park** and **Centennial Square** host outdoor concerts and events May–Sept. Rock concerts and other major events play **Memorial Arena**, 1925 Blanschard; tel: (250) 361-0506.

The **Netherlands Centennial Carillon**, *Government and Belleville Sts; tel: (250) 387-1616*, the largest carillon in Canada, plays in recital every Sun at 1500 (Apr–Dec) and Fri at 1900 (July–Aug). The bells sound on the quarter hour 0700–2200 daily.

SHOPPING

Victoria provides ample opportunities to spend. **Victoria Eaton Centre**, *Government St, Fort–View Sts; tel: (250) 389-2228*, has more than a hundred shops, including **Eaton's** department store.

Government St itself is one long mall from *Humboldt St* north to *Johnson St.* **Munro's Books**, *1108 Government St; tel: (259) 382-2464; fax: (250) 382-2832*, originally the Royal Bank, has one of Victoria's best selections of Canadiana. **Murchie's Tea & Coffee**, *1110 Government St; tel: (250) 383-3112; fax: (250) 383-3255*, has been a BC fixture since 1894. Empress Afternoon Blend is the same mix of Ceylon, Keemun, Darjeeling and Assam teas served at The Empress every afternoon. The pastry, tea and coffee bar is one of the busiest budget eateries on *Government St.*

Beautiful British Columbia, *910 Government St (Harbour Centre); tel: (250) 384-7773*, specialises in made-in-BC gifts, crafts, souvenirs, clothing and food items. **Cowichan Trading Co.**, *1328 Government St; tel: (250) 383-0321*, and **James Bay Trading Co.**, *1102 Government St; tel: (250) 388-5477*, specialise in First Nations art as well as other Canadian-made items.

Market Square, *560 Johnson St; tel: (250) 386-2441*, is a collection of nine heritage buildings, most of them originally shops and storehouses, that have been redeveloped into an arcade for shopping, public art, eating, busking and gawking.

Just north is **Chinatown**, Canada's first Chinese community, dating from the 1840s and 1850s when Victoria was BC's only city. **Fan Tan Alley**, *Fisgard St–Pandora Ave*, is lined with small shops selling everything from antique parasols to New Age music in what were once gambling dens, opium parlours and brothels. **Antique Row**, *Fort St, Blanshard–Cook Sts*, has more than two dozen antique shops.

SIGHTSEEING

Nearly all of touristic Victoria lies within walking distance of the **Inner Harbour**, the carefully engineered remains of the natural harbour that lured Hudson's Bay Company trader James Douglas to the site in 1842. Douglas built Fort Victoria the next year on what is now *Bastion Square.* Envisaged as a refuge against expansionist Americans who were following the Oregon Trail into the Columbia River basin, Victoria became one of the richest and rowdiest cities in North America.

Three years later, the US-Canada border was set at the 49th Parallel. HBC moved its Pacific operations from Fort Vancouver, across the Columbia River from present-day Portland, Oregon, to Victoria. Fuelled by growing commerce and gold rushes on the Fraser River and the Kootenays, the city soon outgrew its origins.

What remained of the wooden fort was pulled down in 1862 to make way for commercial expansion. All that survives is a handful of rusted iron mooring rings buried beneath overgrown blackberry bushes along the Inner Harbour.

The original blockhouse stood at what became the corner of *View* and *Government Sts.* Canada's only surviving HBC bastion is in Nanaimo (see p. 297).

Coloured bricks along *View St* west to

279

Totem Poles

Totem poles, a combination of calling cards and advertisements, once stood outside every long house in coastal and riverine villages throughout BC. Poles often include real animals such as the orca, bear and raven, as well as supernatural creatures such as Thunderbird and Giant Woodpecker. The animals figure prominently in religion and legend, but the poles themselves were a form of story-telling or self-aggrandisement, not objects of worship as many early Christian missionaries believed.

Strangers could read the poles vertically to determine who lived in each house; the height of the poles gave the relative status of the family in the village. Figures normally depicted the family's clan allegiance and its traditional crests and history, but poles had other purposes as well. Memorial poles commemorate a great person by recounting his or her names and deeds. A mortuary pole holds the remains of an important elder or chief, usually in a box attached near the top of the pole. Commemorative poles recall some great event. Shame poles depict a person in a compromising position in order to embarrass him or her into repaying a debt.

Archaeological evidence suggests that coastal tribes have been carving totems for thousands of years. So have their inland relatives who settled along major rivers. Both enjoyed a similarly high standard of living with ample time and resources to create massive pieces of art.

Totem poles reached their zenith with the rise of the coastal fur trade in the late 18th–early 19th centuries. Traditional motifs became even grander and more complex as families and bands grew rich trading with the growing stream of ships from America, Britain, Russia and Spain. Clans which had significant dealings with Russian (double eagle) and Hudson's Bay Company (beaver) fur traders often added the foreign symbols to their existing clan names. The new names were translated into totem pole figures which proudly proclaimed profitable ties with the recent arrivals.

Eagle and beaver clan names survived, but trading profits disappeared as epidemics of smallpox, measles and other Western diseases decimated BC's Aboriginal population later in the 19th century. As the population shrank, Native art forms began to disappear. As Native culture shrivelled under the foreign onslaught, missionaries and government agents inveighed and legislated against the continued carving of totem poles as well as other expressions of traditional culture. The expressed goal of turning First Nations peoples into 'proper British subjects' very nearly succeeded. By the 1950s, totem carving was a lost art. Most surviving poles had long since been carted off to museums in Europe, America and Eastern Canada. The less impressive poles that remained in BC were decaying into lumps of wood.

The University of British Columbia hired carver Mungo Martin to copy as many of the surviving poles as possible. In the process, Martin and his fellow First Nations carvers sparked a renaissance of Native arts that has spread to tribes across North America. Although full-sized totem poles are again being carved throughout BC, the finest are being produced in Alert Bay (see p.308), just off Port McNeil on Vancouver island, and in the inland villages of Hazleton, Kispiox, Gitsegukla and Kitwanga (see p.331), off Hwy 16 between Terrace and Smithers.

BC's single largest collection of public poles decorate city streets in Duncan (see p.295), south of Nanaimo on Vancouver Island. Other significant collections can be seen at UBC's Museum of Anthropology in Vancouver (see p.233), the Royal British Columbia Museum and adjoining Thunderbird Park, both in Victoria (see p.281).

Bastion Sq., south along *Government St* to *Fort St,* then west toward the harbour, outline the original stockade. The imposing colonial buildings of **Old Town,** *Humboldt St–Pandora St, Inner Harbour–Government St,* date from the 1880s–1910s.

Architecture

Victoria's most imposing structures have nothing whatsoever to do with James Douglas. **Parliament Buildings**, *S. end of Inner Harbour; tel: (250) 387-3046,* and **The Empress Hotel**, *721 Government St; tel: (250) 384-8111,* were both built by British architect Francis Mawson Rattenbury. Rattenbury arrived in Victoria in 1892 at the age of 25 and promptly won an Empire-wide competition to design and build the province's new Parliament House.

When the Parliament Buildings opened in 1898, the only dignitary not in attendance was the builder himself. Ratz, as he preferred to be called, was in London trying to finance a scheme to transport miners and materials to the Yukon Gold Rush. The Yukon scheme came to naught, but Ratz built the Empress, perhaps the continent's most opulent Edwardian edifice, the Crystal Garden (see below), and dozens of other major buildings in Victoria.

Ratz also built a new life on a lurid divorce and remarriage. Stuffy Victorian society snubbed both the new wife, who was so unspeakably modern as to smoke cigarettes in public, and the man who so openly pursued her. The couple moved to England in 1930, where Ratz was murdered by his wife's young lover four years later.

Rattenbury's other great public project is the **Crystal Garden**, *713 Douglas St; tel: (250) 381-1277; fax: (250) 383-1218,* open daily 0800–2000 (July–Aug), 0900–1800 (Apr–June and Sept–Oct), 1000–1630 (Nov–Mar), adults $6.50, children 6–16 $4, an immense glass hall modelled on England's Crystal Palace. Crystal Garden held the largest indoor swimming pool in the British Empire when it opened in 1925. With ballrooms, tea rooms and an elegant promenade, it became one of the most famous landmarks in Canada. The building now houses tropical butterflies, a waterfall, monkeys and a somewhat parched rain forest.

First Nations Exhibits

Between the Crystal Garden and Parliament Buildings is the **Royal British Columbia Museum**, *675 Belleville St; tel: (800) 661-5411 or (250) 387-3701,* open daily 0900–1700, adults $7, children 6–11 $2.14, family $14. The immense museum has three floors of displays on the natural and human history of British Columbia.

The First Nations exhibit includes a full-sized Kwaktuil chief's house, complete with totems, carvings and chiefly regalia. Even more striking is the careful rendition of the full flowering of First Nations arts in the profitable decades after first contact and the even swifter collapse as smallpox and other diseases decimated the Native population between 1843 and 1885. A single outbreak of smallpox which began in Victoria in 1862 killed 20,000, 30% of the Native population.

In the 1940s, the museum donated a section of its grounds to **Thunderbird Park**, *Belleville and Douglas Sts,* to display totem poles. Chief Mungo Martin of the Kwagiulth band from Fort Rupert led a group of Thunderbird Park carvers in a successful attempt to rediscover what was a largely lost art. Replicas of Martin's original poles tower above the park; many originals are on display inside the museum.

The museum also sponsors outstanding environmental and historical excursions led by departmental curators or collectors Apr–Oct. Most are day trips in the Victoria area, featuring First Nations archaeology, sea kayaking, marine biology, bird watching, snorkelling with salmon, or local history. Prices range from $45 to $2300 for a sailing excursion to Haida Gwaii.

281

Historic Buildings

Immediately behind Thunderbird Park is **Helmcken House**; *tel: (250) 387-4697,* open 1100–1700 (May–Sept), 1200–1600 (Oct–Apr), adults $4, students $3, family $10. Dr. John Helmcken built the house in 1852 for his wife Cecilia, James Douglas' eldest daughter. Helmcken, Speaker of three colonial legislatures, is better remembered for reserving Beacon Hill as a public park. The squared logs of his original cabin are visible through a window set into one wall. An excellent tour describes life in early Victoria and explains the furnishings.

Next door is **St Ann's Schoolhouse**, built about 1845, Victoria's oldest surviving building. The site of James Douglas' house, which stood until 1906, is marked by a small plaque in **Cherry Tree Square**, *west side of the Museum.*

Inner Harbour

The **Royal London Wax Museum**, *470 Belleville St; tel: (250) 388-4461,* open 0900–2100 (July–Aug), 0930–1630 rest of the year, adults $7, students $6.25, children 6–12 $3, family $22, offers the usual collection of wax figures of the rich and infamous. The 1924 Beaux Arts-style Roman Temple was originally the Canadian Pacific Steamship Company terminal.

Undersea Gardens, *490 Belleville St; tel: (250) 382-5717,* open 0900–2100 (May–Sept), 0900–1700 the rest of the year, adults $7, children $3–$4.75, family $17.50, is an immense aquarium stocked with native marine life.

Broad walkways around the southern and eastern sides of the Inner Harbour provide ample room for buskers. A kilted bagpiper is a semi-permanent afternoon fixture at the harbourside corner of *Government* and *Belleville Sts.*

The **Tourism Victoria Visitor Info-Centre**, *812 Wharf St,* sits atop a collection of tourist shops, restaurants, public toilets, showers and a laundromat, all designed for travelling yachters moored nearby.

Just north along the waterfront is **Victoria Marine Adventure Centre**, *950 Wharf St; tel: (800) 995-2211 or (250) 995-1222,* booking and departure point for whale watching, marine wildlife tours, kayaking, scuba diving, sea plane tours and other outdoor activity companies.

Museums and Galleries

Just inland (east) is **Bastion Square** and the **Maritime Museum of British Columbia**, *28 Bastion Sq.; tel: (250) 385-4222,* open daily 0930–1630, adults $5, students $3, children $2, family $13. The museum includes ship models, figureheads, tools and naval uniforms. The museum is in the Victoria Law Courts building, used as a court 1889–1962. Its polished brass elevator is Canada's oldest working lift.

Market Square, *560 Johnson St; tel: (250) 386-2441,* dates from the same era. The collection of nine red-brick heritage buildings, now a shopping arcade, were originally shops and storehouses for the docks and industrial areas built to supply waves of gold miners, fishing fleets, sealskin hunters, coal ships and cargo vessels. Nearby streets, saloons, gambling dens and brothels were as wild as any on the Pacific coast, but strict law enforcement maintained a clear separation between the working classes who laboured and lived near the Inner Harbour and the moneyed classes who moved inland.

The ultimate docklands escapee was Robert Dunsmuir, a Scottish indentured labourer who built BC's largest fortune on coal, railways and the well-trampled backs of company employees. His **Craigdarroch Castle**, *1050 Joan Cres; tel: (250) 592-5323,* open 0900–1930 (June–Sept), 1000–1700 the rest of the year, adults

$7.50, students $5, children $2, was the tallest home atop the tallest hill in Victoria. Dunsmuir died before the house was completed in 1889, but his widow and daughters lived in the 39-room rough stone castle until 1909. His grandchildren squandered the family fortune.

Fisgard Lighthouse & Fort Rodd Hill National Historic Site, *603 Fort Rodd Hill Rd, west of Esquimalt off Hwy 1A; tel: (250) 478-6481; fax: (250) 478-8415.* The 1860 lighthouse is the oldest on Canada's West Coast. An automated light guides ships into Esquimalt, but the keeper's house has become a fine lighthouse and shipping museum. Fort Rodd Hill was part of Canada's marine defence system 1878–1956, protecting the naval base and coaling station at Esquimalt. Both sites temper history with excellent coastal views.

Point Ellice House, *2616 Pleasant St; tel: (250) 380-6506,* open 1000–1700 (May–Oct), a rambling Italianate villa, has Canada's most complete collection of Victoriana and a fine afternoon tea (advance booking required). **Craigflower Farmhouse and School**, *Admirals Rd and Hwy 1A; tel: (250) 387-4697,* open daily 1200–1600 (July–Sept), Thur–Mon (Sept–June), is a restored 1850s farmhouse originally built for the HBC. The property includes heirloom plantings and farm animals, with extremely knowledgeable and enthusiastic interpreters in period costume.

Emily Carr House, *207 Government St; tel: (250) 383-5843,* open 1000–1700 (May–Oct), is the birthplace of Canadian painter and writer Emily Carr.

The **Art Gallery of Greater Victoria**, *1040 Moss St; tel: (250) 384-4101; fax: (250) 361-3995,* open Mon–Sat 1000–1700, Thur 1000–2100, Sun 1300–1700, adults $5, students $3, free on Mon, is partially housed in an 1889 mansion. The Gallery specialises in contemporary artists

from Canada and Asia and historical art from Asia, Europe and North America.

Parks and Gardens
Government House Gardens, *1401 Rockland Ave,* open daily dawn–dusk, has 14 hectares of formal flower beds, shrubs, lawns, ivy, heather, azaleas and rhododendrons surrounding the Lt Governor's official residence (closed to the public).

Beacon Hill Park, *from Douglas and Dallas Sts,* is 74 hectares of formal gardens and playing fields sloping down to the sea. A seaside walkway is especially popular with runners, dog walkers and sightseers for its splendid views across the Strait of Juan de Fuca to the Olympic Peninsula. **Butchart Gardens**, *Brentwood Bay; tel: (250) 652-4422,* open daily 0900, closing varies with the season, adults $14.50, children $7.25, reduced admission Nov–Mar, is one of the most visited gardens in North America. Its 20 hectares, once a private estate, are divided into Rose, Japanese, Italian and Sunken Gardens plus other landscape features. The Gardens are spectacular all year and breathtaking in summer – as are the crowds. Try to arrive after 1530 to miss the worst of the crush.

Tours
Many tours leave from *Belleville* and *Menzies Sts,* along the Inner Harbour. **Gray Line**, *700 Douglas St, Victoria, BC V8W 2B3; tel: (800) 318-0818 (BC), (800) 663-8390 (US) or (250) 388-5248; fax: (250) 388-9461,* operate the most extensive schedule of coach tours in Victoria, including the bright red double-decker buses parked in front of The Empress Hotel. **Royal Blue Line**; *tel: (800) 663-1128* or *(250) 360-2249,* offer tours around the city and as far afield as The Butchart Gardens.

Victoria Harbour Ferry; *tel: (250) 480-0971,* offer harbour tours. The **SS**

283

Victoria Gardens

Victorians take their gardening seriously. It's not just the trademark flower baskets hanging from lamp posts along the Inner Harbour or the famed Butchart Gardens. The entire city is fixated on flowers. While the rest of Canada shivers beneath the arctic snows of Feb, hundreds of perfectly normal-seeming Victorians can be found stooped over their crocus beds, calculators in hand, or perched on precarious ladders to count individual blossoms on flowering fruit trees. The city-wide count is celebrated at the end of winter.

Victoria's passion for gardens began with the first White settlers. When Hudson's Bay Company factor James Douglas surveyed what would become the Inner Harbour in 1842, he wrote to a friend 'The place appears a perfect Eden in the midst of the dreary wilderness of North West Coast, and so different is its general aspect . . . that one might be pardoned for supposing it had dropped from the clouds.' Douglas himself was no gardener, but his son-in-law, Dr. John Helmcken, Victoria's first physician, was an ardent collector of native plants. The farmers and merchants who settled at the fort Douglas laid out in 1843 set about recreating the look of an England they had left behind. Hawthorn hedges, cowslips, primroses and roses soon replaced the trees and brush that once covered the rolling hills of Victoria.

As commerce grew and great houses began to appear, gardens became as crucial as any architectural detail. By the time an abandoned limestone quarry was transformed into Butcharts' famed Sunken Garden in 1917, Victoria had already established itself as the most beflowered city in Canada.

Beaver, *1002 C Wharf St; tel: (250) 384-8116; fax: (250) 384-8933,* has harbour tours and dinner cruises aboard a replica of the Hudson's Bay Company 1835 paddle-wheel steam ship of the same name.

Victoria Carriage Tours, *Belleville and Menzies Sts; tel: (250) 383-2207,* offer 15–60-min horse-drawn carriage tours.

Bird's Eye View offer historical walking tours of the inner harbour area leaving from the Tourism Victoria InfoCentre each evening at 1900 in summer.

Victoria Bobby; *tel: (250) 955-0233,* guide walking tours of the old town three times daily, also from the InfoCentre.

Another Way Adventures; *tel: (250) 385-2035,* stalk back alleys in search of murder, ghosts and mayhem at 1900 in summer; book both in advance.

Lantern Tours; *tel: (250) 598-8870,* offer lantern tours of the Old Burying Ground at 2130 (July–Aug).

The Old Cemetery Society; *tel: (250) 598-8870,* sponsor guided cemetery tours most Sundays throughout the year. The **Canadian Forces Base Esquimalt Naden**; *tel: (250) 363-4395,* is open for self-guided walking tours Mon–Fri 0800–1600 at the HMCS Naden–North Gate, off *Admirals Rd* in Esquimalt.

Victorian Garden Tours; *tel: (250) 721-2797,* offer guided garden tours at Government House, the Horticulture Center of the Pacific, Saxe Point Park/Point Ellice House and Hatley Park (Royal Roads University).

Western Forest Products Ltd; *tel: (250) 642-6351,* have free forestry tours leaving from Victoria, Colwood and Sooke (June–Sept).

Grand Circle Tour; *Box 57, Cowichan Bay, BC V0R 1N0; tel: (250) 480-7245 or (800) 665-7374; fax: (250) 748-6525,* have a summer-only circle tour combining **E&N Railway** to Duncan, the **Cowichan Native Village**, a 3-hr sail, walking tour of **Butchart Gardens** and coach back to Victoria.

VICTORIA CIRCUIT

Allow the better part of a day for this 125-km drive around Victoria. If time is short, eliminate the loops west to Fort Rodd Hill/Fisgard Lighthouse and north to Butchart Gardens. Visiting all of the museums and attractions could stretch to the better part of a week.

ROUTE: 125 KM

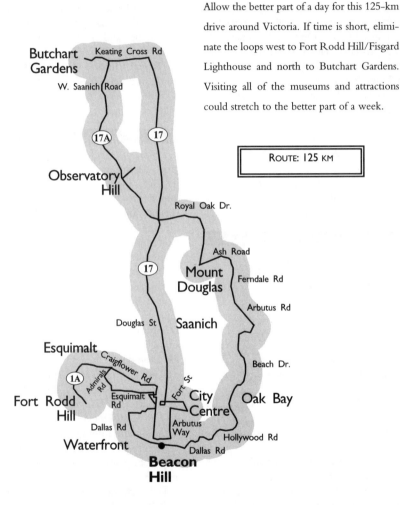

285

ROUTE

The circuit begins and ends at the southwest corner of Beacon Hill Park, *Douglas St* and *Dallas Rd*. These directions reduce left turns and take advantage of one-way streets. Avoid major arteries during rush hour, 0730–0900 and 1600–1800.

BEACON HILL

Follow *Dallas Rd* east from *Douglas St* through Beacon Hill Park along the Juan de Fuca Strait. **Beacon Hill** is named for the signal fire that once burned on the hilltop to guide ships around treacherous reefs guarding the harbour entrance.

A shoreline walking, running and cycling path is popular with photographers entranced by the Olympic Mountains rising across the strait. The totem pole on the left was once the tallest in the world. **Clover Point** has good views.

Dallas Rd continues by **Ross Bay Cemetery**, where most early Victorians can be found. There is parking and public access to a rocky beach below. *Dallas Rd* becomes *Hollywood Crescent* just beyond the cemetery, then *Hollywood Rd* as it curves around **Gonzales Bay**, better known as **Foul Bay** for seabird droppings. The fine sandy beach is busy in summer.

OAK BAY

Take *King George Terrace* to the right, following green Scenic Drive signs. The **King George Lookout**, part of **Trafalgar Park**, has Victoria's best sea level view. Port Angeles, WA is 37 km south. The view is even better from a small park atop Gonzales Hill, accessible via *Denison Rd,* just beyond Trafalgar Park.

King George Terrace ends at *Beach Dr.* Go right (east) on *Beach Dr.* along the shores of McNeil Bay to the **Municipality of Oak Bay**. Traditional English motifs are so popular that the municipal limit is called the Tweed Curtain. *Beach Dr.* swings north through the **Victoria Golf Club**, a popular place for a stroll.

Just north of the golf course is the **Oak Bay Beach Hotel**, *1175 Beach Rd; tel: (250) 598-4556; fax: (250) 598-6180,* and, directly opposite, the **Oak Bay Native Plant Park**. A few hundred metres north are **Haynes Park** and the **Oak Bay Marina**; *tel: (250) 598-3369.*

Continue north past **Willows Park** and

through the stone gates of **Uplands**. The posh 1912 housing estate was designed by the Olmsted brothers, who created New York's Central Park. Victoria's largest tract of undeveloped Garry Oak habitat, the entire park is a natural area except for two boat ramps and minimal shore development. Continue 5 km north to **Loon Bay**, the **Royal Victoria Yacht Club** and the northern boundary of Uplands. *Beach Dr.* becomes *Cadboro Bay Rd* at the Municipality of Saanich.

SAANICH

Continue past *Sinclair Rd* and a small shopping mall to curve right onto *Maynard Rd,* then left onto *Telegraph Rd* and a four-way stop at *Arbutus Rd.* Turn left (north) onto *Arbutus,* following the Scenic Route signs through increasingly rural countryside. Continue 2 km north to *Finnerty Rd* and bear right, remaining on *Arbutus* to the T-junction with *Gordon Head Rd,* 1 km north, and turn right. Continue 1 km around the left onto *Ferndale Rd* and a four-way stop. The entrance to **Mt Douglas Park** picnic grounds and beach are right. *Cedar Hill Rd* climbs the slopes of **Mt Douglas** to the left.

Take *Cedar Hill Rd* 1 km to the end of the forested section on the right. Turn right onto *Churchill Dr.,* a steep 1 km road up 229-m Mt Douglas. Short trails lead up to the summit from the car park.

Return to *Cedar Hill Rd* and the four-way stop. Turn left (north) onto *Ash Rd* and left (west) again onto *Royal Oak Dr.,* past the **Broadmead Village** shopping mall. Turn right (north) onto BC 17, following ferry signs for Sidney/Swartz Bay.

Follow BC 17 for 7 km, passing Beaver Lake, Elk Lake and *Sayward Rd* to go left onto *Keating Cross Rd,* often abbreviated on street maps as 'X Rd'. Climb 4 km through the low hills forming the spine of the peninsula. *Keating Cross Rd* becomes *Benvenuto Ave* at *West Saanich Rd*, BC 17A.

On the left (south) is **Victoria Butterfly Gardens**; *tel: (250) 652-3822;* open daily 0900–dusk, a tropical garden filled with butterflies. *Benvenuto* continues 2 km to **Butchart Gardens**. Return to *W. Saanich Rd* and turn right (south). The country road winds 6 km to **Observatory Hill** and the free **Dominion Astrophysical Observatory**, *507 W. Saanich Rd; tel: (250) 363-0012,* open all year Mon–Fri 0915–1630, Sat 0900–2300, Sun and holidays 0900–2000 (May–Aug).

The access road climbs around the hill to a car park at the base of the observatory dome. The 1.82-m reflecting telescope inside is still used.

Return to BC 17A and turn left (south) for 3 km to *Royal Oak Dr.* Turn left (east), following signs for BC 17 and Victoria. Just after the first traffic signal *(Elk Lake Rd),* turn right (south) onto BC 17. At the end of the dual carriageway, 4 km south, make a sharp left turn onto *Douglas St* at the **Town and Country Centre**.

Turn right 1 km later onto *Cloverdale Rd,* following signs and lane markings for 'Victoria by way of Douglas St'. At the second traffic signal, turn left onto *Douglas* to pass **Mayfair Shopping Centre**. **The Bay**, *1701 Douglas; tel: (250) 385-1311,* occupies the south-east corner *Douglas and Herald Sts.* The pink and grey brick **Victoria City Hall** is on the west side of Douglas at *Pandora St.*

ROCKLAND

Continue five blocks to *Broughton St* and turn right (west) at the red brick **St Peter's Presbyterian Church**, right again at *Broad St* and again onto *Fort St,* one-way eastbound. Follow *Fort St* 2 km past *Antique Row* to *Moss St.* Turn right (south), following green signs for the **Art Gallery**

of **Greater Victoria**. Turn right onto *Will Spencer Pl.,* left onto *Moss* and right onto *Fort St.* Take the next right turn into *Joan Crescent* to **Craigdarroch Castle**.

Exit onto *Joan Crescent* and turn right. Continue to *Rockland Ave,* turn right and then immediately left into **Government House Gardens**. Leave Government House to the left on *Rockland.* Homes are palatial to merely mansion-sized, hidden behind hedges and trees. Continue across *Moss St, Cook* and *Vancouver Sts,* where *Rockland* becomes *Courtney St,* to *Quadra St* and **Christ Church Anglican Cathedral**, *912 Vancouver St; tel: (250) 383-2714,* built in 13th-century Gothic style. Turn left (south) onto *Quadra,* which becomes *Arbutus Way* in Beacon Hill Park. Veer left onto *Bridge Way,* then right onto *Circular Dr.,* to follow *Park Way* to the top of **Beacon Hill**. Return to *Circular Dr.* and follow the circle left to *Douglas St,* then go left (south) onto *Douglas.* Go right (west) onto *Niagara St* two blocks to *Government St* and turn right (north). **Emily Carr House** is ahead on the right.

287

CITY CENTRE

Continue north past the **James Bay Inn** toward *Belleville St,* with the **Parliament Buildings** on the left and the **Royal BC Museum**, on the right. Across *Belleville,* the **Inner Harbour** is on the left and **The Empress Hotel** on the right. Move to the right lane following *Government St* north, passing the **Visitor InfoCentre** on the left.

Continue past *Fort St* with **Eaton Centre** on the right and **Munro's Books** on the left. At *View St,* **Bastion Square** and the **Maritime Museum** are to the left. Turn left (west) onto *Yates St.* Turn right (north) onto *Wharf St* one block later, and move into the left or middle lane. Turn left (west) and cross the sky-blue Johnson St Bridge over Victoria Harbour.

Market Square is to the north-east at the corner of *Johnson and Wharf Sts.*

ESQUIMALT

Johnson St becomes *Esquimalt Rd* across the bridge. **Songhees Park**, south, was named after the Songhees First Nations band which was evicted from Fort Victoria and moved across the harbour. *Esquimalt Rd* continues 4 km to *Admirals Rd*. Turn right (north) onto *Admirals,* following signs for BC 1A toward Sooke and Nanaimo.

At the railway tracks, turn left (west) into **HMCS Naden**, *tel: (250) 363-4395,* open Mon–Fri 0800–1600 for 30-min self-guided walking tours, including **Esquimalt Graving Dock**, the largest civilian dry-dock on North America's west coast.

Turn left (north) back onto *Admirals Rd,* originally a horse trail from the Admiral's residence at Esquimalt to **Craigflower House**, 3 km north at the intersection with BC 1A, the *Island Highway.* To visit **Craigflower**, continue through the intersection and take the first left turn. To continue on the circuit, turn left (west) onto BC 1A to the **City of Colwood**, a strip of auto dealers, fast-food outlets and small businesses. Turn left onto *Ocean Blvd* at the first traffic signal beyond the **Juan de Fuca Recreation Centre** (on the south side), following signs for **Fort Rodd Hill** and **Fisgard Lighthouse**. Continue straight for 2 km to visit the twin historic sites, or take the first right for the route to **Port Renfrew**.

Return to BC 1A and turn right (east) towards Victoria. At the intersection with *Admirals Rd,* continue straight onto *Craigflower Rd* past **Gorge Vale Golf Course**, on the right. *Craigflower* becomes *Skinner St* at **Banfield Park**, on the left. Turn right two blocks later onto *Catherine St,* then left onto *Langford St,* following signs for the Point Ellice Bridge. **Point Ellice House** is to the left immediately after the bridge.

THE WATERFRONT

Cross the bridge onto *Bay St* and turn right (south) onto *Government St* at the second set of traffic signals. The first drive on the right is **Vancouver Island Brewery**, *2330 Government St; tel: (250) 953-9000, ext 4722,* tours Mon–Fri and Sat in summer. Try Piper's Pale Ale.

Continue south on *Government St.* The ornamental gate over *Fisgard St* marks the entrance to **Chinatown**. Remain in the right-hand lane and turn right (west) onto *Yates St,* where *Government St* becomes one-way northbound. Move into the left-hand lane and turn left onto *Wharf St,* passing **Bastion Square** and **Wharfside** along the **Inner Harbour**. *Wharf St* curves east to meet *Government St* and the **Visitor InfoCentre** on the right. Turn right onto *Government St,* then right onto *Belleville* at the first traffic signal. **Parliament Buildings** are on the left, **Undersea Gardens** and **Royal London Wax Museum** on the right, with the ferry docks just beyond.

Follow the main road left onto *Pendra St,* then right onto *Cross St,* left onto *Montreal St,* right onto *Kingston St,* left onto *Lawrence St* and right into **Fisherman's Wharf Park**. Leave the park on *Dallas Rd,* which turns south toward the **Ogden Point Docks** and ferries to Seattle. Continue past the docks to *Douglas St.*

Colour section (i): Victoria (pp. 274–284): Inner Harbour, Parliament House after sunset and Historic City Hall.

(ii): Native cemetery portal, Alert Bay (p. 308); schoolhouse at Barkerville (p. 323); inset, Thunderbird totem pole, Campbell River (p. 302).

(iii): Prince Rupert harbour (p. 326–328); 108 Mile House (p. 323).

(iv): Big Bar Ranch teepee, Clinton (p. 324); sunset on Tofino Beach (p. 342).

VICTORIA–PORT RENFREW

BC 14, *Sooke Rd,* is more commonly called the *West Coast Rd.* By any name, it runs 95 km along the southern coast of Vancouver Island to the town of Sooke, then past a succession of ever-wilder beaches to Port Renfrew and the start of the West Coast Trail to Bamfield. Views south across the Strait of Juan de Fuca are mouthdropping in clear weather and thunderous during winter storms. Views across recent clear-cuts closer to the road are equally stunning, if for different reasons. Traffic can be slow at weekends or holidays. Allow at least a full day for the return trip. Better still, overnight in Sooke and Port Renfrew.

289

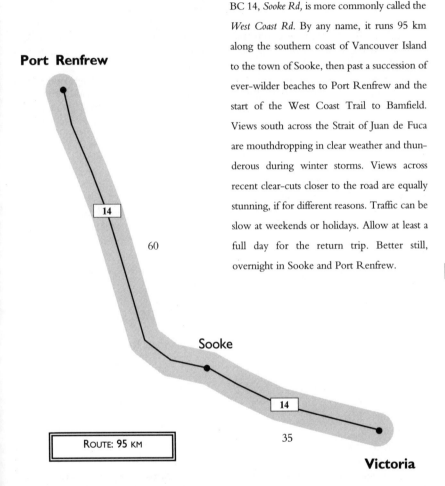

Port Renfrew

14

60

Sooke

14

35

Victoria

ROUTE: 95 KM

ROUTE

From the Empress Hotel, drive north on *Government St* to *Humboldt St.* Turn left, then right on *Wharf St* and left again over the *Johnston St Bridge* onto *Esquimalt Rd.*

Continue 4 km to *Admirals Rd.* Turn right onto *Admirals Rd* at the Tudor House Pub, pass the CFB Nanden Museum and go another 2 km to the Island Highway at Craigflower House. Turn left onto the

Island Highway, passing the Six Mile Pub and the town of **Colwood**. Just beyond the **Juan de Fuca Recreation Centre** (on the left), go left at the traffic signal onto *Ocean Blvd,* following signs for *Fort Rodd Hill.*

Continue straight 2 km to **Esquimalt Lagoon**. At the west end of the lagoon, turn right onto *Lagoon Rd.* At the top of the hill, turn left onto *Metchosin Rd.* Pass Albert Head Lagoon Park and Witty's Lagoon Regional Park, 3 km to **My-Chosen Café** and veer right onto *William Head Rd.* Turn right up the narrow avenue of *Lombard Poplars,* 2 km ahead, just past **Devonian Park**. Turn left onto *Rocky Point Rd,* then right after 3 km onto *Matheson Lake Park Rd* (Rocky Point continues straight to a military ammunition depot; visitors are emphatically unwelcome).

Continue past East Sooke Regional Park 6 km to *Gillespie Rd.* Turn right and follow *Gillespie Rd* north to BC 14 and turn west (left).

Pass *Sooke River Rd* and the Sooke Potholes, the Sooke River Hotel, the **Sooke Region Museum** and **Info-Centre** and continue into **Sooke**.

Take BC 14 west from Sooke past the Shearingham Light and Shirley, Point No Point and a string of undeveloped beaches and beach parks, the lumber town of Jordan, then drive another 42 km into **Port Renfrew**.

Backtrack to Victoria from Port Renfrew, or in good weather, follow unpaved logging roads to **Lake Cowichan** and **Douglas**, then continue south along the Island Highway to Victoria.

VICTORIA TO SOOKE

Esquimalt Lagoon offers a good view east toward the Fisgard Lighthouse. The lagoon attracts large flocks of waterfowl. To seaward is Royal Roads, a protected anchorage first used by the Spanish in 1790.

Albert Head Lagoon Park, just past the gravel pit, is a wildlife sanctuary and cobble beach with good views back to Victoria and across the Juan de Fuca Strait to the Olympic Peninsula in Washington State. The lagoon has a large wildlife population, including swans.

Witty's Lagoon Regional Park, *Capital Regional District Parks, 490 Atkins Ave, Victoria, BC V9B 2Z8; tel: (250) 478-3344; fax: (250) 478-5416,* 3 km beyond Albert Head, is a birders' paradise with luxuriant stands of Douglas-fir, sword fern, creeks running to Sitting Lady Falls, sandy beach and rocky beach. Look for seals and great blue herons along the water.

Metchosin Schoolhouse, *Happy Valley Rd,* was BC's first school after Confederation. A local Sun market is held across the street behind the Volunteer Fire Department, with takeaway breads, sausages and sweets from local producers. **My-Chosen Café,** *4492 Happy Valley Rd; tel: (520) 474-2333,* cheap–budget, is a local favourite.

Devonian Regional Park, *1 km east,* is a nature sanctuary with a 1-km trail past Sherwood Pond (excellent birding) to Perry Bay and good marine mammal viewing. Low tide exposes a 5-km trail east to Witty's Lagoon. The Lombard Poplar avenue just beyond was planted by Hans Helgesen, a Nordic traveller who settled the area in 1865.

East Sooke Regional Park, *490 Atkins Ave, Victoria, BC V9B 2Z8; tel: (250) 478-3344,* covers more than 1400 hectares along the Strait of Juan de Fuca. Untouched foreshore fringed with twisted arbutus and stunted shore pine gives way to stately Sitka spruce, red cedar, hemlock and Douglas-fir. Bald eagles wait at the edge of the forest as river otters and mink scurry through tangled driftwood and cormorants dive offshore. Sea lions are common Sept–May. A complex trail system runs from easy forest jaunts to an all-day 10-km trek along the entire shoreline, but it can be confusing without a map. Dozens of small beaches have offshore islands and spits, creating endless picnic spots.

Inland, **Galloping Goose Trail** follows an abandoned railroad line from Colwood to Sooke and the abandoned mining settlement of **Leechtown**. The park, popular with cyclists and equestrians, is 47 km long and just 30 m wide.

Sooke Potholes Provincial Park, *5 km north on Sooke River Rd,* a series of deep swimming holes in the Sooke River, is familiar to generations of local residents. The potholes are extremely popular in summer for swimming.

SOOKE

Tourist Information: Sooke Region Museum, *2070 Phillips Rd, Sooke, BC V0S 1N0; tel: (250) 642-6351,* open daily 0900–1800 summer, Tues–Sun autumn–spring. Get directions for the many undeveloped (and often unmarked) beaches to the west, including **Gordons**, **Sandcut**, **Mystic** and **Sombrio**. Beachcombing is best for driftwood, fishing floats and flotsam, directly after storms.

ACCOMMODATION AND FOOD

Choose from three dozen Bed and Breakfasts and the **Sooke Harbour House**, *1528 Whiffen Spit Rd, Sooke, BC V0S 1N0; tel: (250) 642-342; fax: (250) 642-6988.* The fine expensive hotel is better known for its very pricey restaurant that lures gourmands from around the world: BC cuisine only, caught fresh from the waters just offshore, grown by local farmers or plucked from the restaurant's own gardens.

Mom's Cafe, *2036 Shields Rd; tel: (250) 642-3314,* budget, is a busy local eatery.

SIGHTSEEING

Sooke began as a fishing and forestry town, the site of Vancouver Island's first successful steam-powered sawmill and one of the last of BC's commercial fish traps. Both stories are recounted in detail at the **Sooke Region Museum and Art Gallery**, *2070 Phillips Rd, Sooke, BC V0S 1N0; tel: (250) 642-6351,* open daily 0900–1800 in summer, Tues–Sun (autumn–spring).

Moss Cottage, built in 1870, is Sooke's oldest structure, built of lumber from the Muir Mill, opened in 1855 with a boiler salvaged from a shipwreck. In summer, costumed guides invite visitors into the cottage, furnished as a turn-of-the-century working class home. The cottage is open year round. The museum collection covers local First Nations as well as early settlement and the 1864 gold rush that turned 40 km of riverbank into gold mines and earned just $100,000.

Speculation continued with the Sooke Harbour Hotel, built in 1912 in anticipation of a land boom that never materialised. The hotel burned in 1934 but the riding stables were converted to an ever-popular roadside pub. City fish traps, immense nets and pilings sunk nearly 50 m deep, were built every summer to catch salmon returning to spawn and dismantled before winter storms swept up the Strait of Juan de Fuca. Faced with diminishing salmon runs, the traps were dismantled for the last time in 1954. Sooke remains a centre for sport salmon fishing.

Sooke Harbour is protected from the Strait by Whiffen Spit, a narrow gravel strip at the foot of *Whiffen Spit Rd,* a few metres from the Sooke Harbour House. Whiffen Spit was the site of the Muir Mill. Sooke's

291

first mill was opened in 1849 by Capt Walter Colquhoun Grant, a former military officer. Grant left the island after a few years but is still reviled for planting the first seeds of the brilliant yellow Scotch Broom that has become a prolific environmental scourge as far south as California.

Sooke Harbour stretches 5 km east from the Spit, then opens onto the Sooke Basin, an estuary twice the size of the harbour and a favourite with paddlers. Commercial fishermen frequently sell fresh fish from their boats at Government Wharf.

SOOKE TO PORT RENFREW

Shearingham Point Light, *17 km west of Sooke, 1 km south on Shearingham Point Rd*, a scenic red and white lighthouse, has been guiding ships along the coast since 1912. RVs should not take the dirt road due to limited turnaround space at the lighthouse.

French Beach Provincial Park, *2 km west of Shearingham Point Rd; tel: (250) 387-4363*, is a good spot to watch the grey whale migration early–mid April (northbound) and mid–late Dec (southbound). Up to twenty thousand whales pass the park yearly on a 16,000-km migration to Baja California. A few greys remain in the area all year. No one is sure why, but whales of all species spy-hop, or thrust themselves vertically from the water and look around, more than usual off French Beach. Other visitors include orcas, minke whales, Stellar sea lions, California sea lions, dolphins and seals. An easy paved path leads to the beach.

Point No Point Resort, *3 km west, 1505 West Coast Rd, RR 2, Sooke, BC V0S 1N0; tel: (250) 646-2020*, is a traditional stopping point on the way to Port Renfrew and a popular moderate seaside inn. The budget afternoon tea is a local classic worth twice the price. The point is named for confused cartographers in the

last century who saw the prominent headland from one direction but lost it from the other side.

Jordan River, *7 km west of Point No Point*, is a tiny logging town with some of the best surfing on the southern coast but no lodging. Western Forest Products Ltd., which has a large information sign on the beach, holds the local logging licence. Clear-cuts are obvious. Many of the most devastating clear-cuts were made over vocal local protests.

China Beach Provincial Park, *4 km west*, has a waterfall and sandy beach. The **Juan de Fuca Marine Trail** leads 47 km west to Botanical Beach at Port Renfrew. The shoreline wilderness trail takes 3–4 days, with sections cut off at high tide. Access points are **China Beach, Sombrio Beach, Parkinson Beach** and **Botanical Beach**.

Mystic Beach, *2 km west*, is a 20-min walk down a steep trail from the parking area. Best views are coming back up the trail, when drifting mists help obscure the clear-cut scars.

Sombrio Beach, *17 km west*, once had the last old-growth forest within a reasonable drive of Victoria. The hillsides were logged into a wasteland despite loud protests. Resulting erosion has made the rough access road dangerous for passenger vehicles in wet weather and impassable for RVs anytime. The 10-min walk down to the beach may be muddy, but the vista is worth the effort, from a picturesque creek across a shore battered by surf to sea caves at the other end. Continue 18 km to Port Renfrew.

PORT RENFREW

Tourist Information: Sooke Travel Infocentre (see p.290), or **West Coast Trail Information Centre**, *16 km west of Sombrio Beach*, open daily 0900–1700.

ACCOMMODATION

Most Port Renfrew lodging caters to backpackers starting or ending the tough trek along the West Coast Trail. The moderate **Arbutus Beach Lodge**, *5 Queesto Dr., Port Renfrew, BC, V0S 1K0; tel: (520) 647-5458*, is notably better than its competitors and has a stunning view over Port San Juan and the San Juan River.

EATING AND DRINKING

The budget–moderate **Arbutus Beach Lodge**, open for lunch and dinner in summer, weekends the rest of the year, is the best restaurant in town. **The Lighthouse Pub**; *tel: (520) 647-5543*, is a good alternative, budget–moderate.

SIGHTSEEING

Port Renfrew is textbook West Coast: wet weather, lush forests, rich wildlife and outdoor recreation on all sides. The entire area is used heavily by hikers, paddlers, anglers, beachcombers and hunters, depending on the season. May–Sept is the busiest season with thousands of West Coast Trail walkers pouring through town, but expect at least a few chance companions in any season and any weather.

Botanical Beach Provincial Park, *4 km south on a dirt road from the end of BC 4*, at the entrance to Juan de Fuca Strait, is one of the island's most intriguing beaches. Deep, clear tidepools are teeming with sea life, from the waving tentacles of green anemones to the sharp spines of red and green sea urchins, purple sea stars and innumerable fish. Pounding surf has carved sheer cliffs into coves, creating natural amphitheatres surrounded by dense forest. The same forces have eroded the headlands between the cliffs into twisting, swirling sculptures of sandstone capped with Sitka spruce and shore pine.

It's best not to visit Botanical Beach without a Tofino tide chart in hand. At high tide, both beach and tidepools disappear beneath the rough waters. The rising tide sweeps in much more quickly than most visitors expect, with occasional rogue waves washing far up what had been dry rock. The best – and safest – time to visit is near the end of a falling tide or at slack water. The Juan de Fuca Trail runs 47 km east to China Beach, a three- to four-day walk.

Red Creek Fir, *12 km from Port Renfrew*, was for years the largest Douglas-fir in Canada, 73m tall and 4m in diameter. Foresters estimate the tree to have been closer to 90m tall before the top broke off in a windstorm sometime during the past nine hundred years. The tall was left when loggers clear cut the area in 1987. Ask locally for directions and, more importantly, road conditions. The unpaved road is usually passable by passenger vehicles in good weather but can be extremely rough. It is not suitable for RVs.

A taller Douglas-fir was found in the upper Coquitlam watershed in the mid-1990s but not measured for the record book until 1996. The new tallest tree is 94m tall, 2.5m in diameter.

Unpaved **logging roads** lead from Port Renfrew inland to BC 117 at **Mesachie Lake** and **Lake Cowichan**, near the head of the Cowichan Valley, then 32 km east to Duncan and the Island Highway (see p.295).

The logging roads are not recommended for RVs, but the mainlines, the major arteries, are usually passable with caution by passenger vehicles. Check locally before setting out. Unannounced road closures are common due to active logging and driving conditions can change dramatically overnight. Some car and RV hire companies prohibit driving off paved highways.

293

VICTORIA–NANAIMO

The 110-km drive to Nanaimo takes less than 90 mins outside commuting hours, or several days with stops in the small towns that dot the Cowichan Valley north of the Malahat Hills. The Island Highway, Canada 1 or the Trans-Canada Highway, is never far away if time presses, but the scenic route is a taste of the rural side of Vancouver Island that Victoria has ignored from its inception.

Nanaimo

20

1 Ladysmith

20 Chemainus

35 Crofton

20 10

Duncan Genoa Bay

15 Scenic Route

35 Cowichan

Bay

Direct Route 24

Malahat Hills

25

Victoria

DIRECT ROUTE: 110 KM

Malahat Dr. becomes the **Island Highway**, running north through the agricultural Cowichan Valley to **Duncan**, **Ladysmith** and **Nanaimo**.

SCENIC ROUTE

The scenic route follows the direct route 50 km to *Cowichan Bay Rd*, 18 km north of the Malahat summit. Take *Cowichan Bay Rd* east through 6 km of rolling farmland to **Cowichan Bay**. Continue north. *Cowichan Bay Rd* becomes *Tzouhalem Rd* at a T-junction 1 km north of a historical marker on the west side of the road, commemorating the first English settlers in 1862. Another marker lauds poet Robert W Service, who worked and published locally in the early 1900s. *Tzouhalem Rd* continues 5 km to Maple Bay. Follow *Maple Bay Rd* north-east 6 km to *Genoa Bay Rd* and turn east. *Genoa*

ROUTES

DIRECT ROUTE

The direct route leaves the Empress Hotel going north four blocks along *Government St* to *Fort St*. Turn east (right) onto *Fort* and continue two blocks to *Douglas St*, TransCanada Hwy 1. Turn north (left) onto *Douglas* and follow Canada 1 signs through Greater Victoria, then west past Portage Inlet and Thetis Lake Park. The highway swings north at Goldstream Provincial Park and becomes *Malahat Dr.* through the **Malahat Hills**.

Bay Rd follows the shore of Maple Bay south to tiny **Genoa Bay**. Return 8 km to *Maple Bay Rd*. Turn north 1 km to Maple Bay. Take *Herd Rd* north and west 3 km to *Osborne Bay Rd* and turn north. Drive 5 km to *Chaplain St* and turn east into **Crofton**. Return up *Chaplain St* to *Crofton Rd* and turn north to *Chemainus Rd*, 2 km beyond the Fletcher Challenge pulp and paper mill. Follow *Chemainus Rd* across a wooden bridge and continue north 1 km to **Chemainus**. *Chemainus Rd* continues another 10 km to rejoin the Island Hwy. Turn north 13 km to *Cedar Point Rd*. Turn east through 3 km of farm country to *Yellowpoint Rd*. Turn east at the petrol station and pass the Yellowpoint Lodge. Continue north 11 km past Roberts Memorial Provincial Park, back onto *Cedar Point Rd*. At *MacMillan Rd*, turn right to visit the Harmac pulp mill or go straight 3 km to the **Island Hwy** and **Nanaimo**, just across the Cowichan River.

BUSES

Island Coach Lines run from Victoria to Nanaimo five times a day, taking 2 hrs. See OTT table 67.

MALAHAT HILLS

Malahat Mountain was a formidable barrier to land travel north from Victoria until well into this century. A crude road crossed the Malahat in 1861, more suited to cattle than wagons. Public pressure pushed another try in 1877, but it was still too steep for heavy traffic. It took a new century and a new survey to open the present route in 1911. A lay-by at the 352-m summit has a totem pole and view across to the Saanitch Peninsula. A second lay-by, 2 km north, has a spectacular view across the Gulf Islands and the snow-capped peak of Mt Baker in Washington.

DUNCAN

Tourist Information: Duncan–Cowichan Chamber of Commerce, *381 TransCanada Hwy (at Coronation Way), Duncan, BC V9L 3R5; tel: (250) 746-4636; fax: (250) 746-8222*, open daily 0900–1700 in summer, Mon–Fri 0900–1700 the rest of the year.

There's more to Duncan than the strip mall that girdles the highway. Three dozen totem poles dot city streets with one of Canada's greatest public concentrations of First Nations art. The **Cowichan Native Village**, *200 Cowichan Way, Duncan, BC V9L 4T8; tel: (250) 746-8119; fax: (250) 746-4143*, has a large collection of First Nations arts, crafts and books, a budget restaurant serving First Nations specialities and an excellent multimedia presentation. European immigrant history is covered at **Cowichan Valley Museum**, *120 Canada Ave; tel: (250) 746-6612*, Duncan's old train station.

Somenos Marsh, *2 km north, Box 711; tel: (250) 746-8383*, is 48 hectares of waterfowl nesting and wintering habitat. Wildlife viewing is best from a short trail 50 m north. The **British Columbia Forest Museum**, *RR #4; tel: (250) 715-1113; fax (250) 746-1487*, 1 km north of the marsh, open Apr–Oct, is the forestry industry's tribute to itself. A narrow-gauge steam train winds through a logging camp, homestead farm and forest May–Sept; environmental issues are ignored all year. The **Freshwater Eco-Centre**, *1080 Whamcliffe Rd; tel: (250) 746-6722*, explains the freshwater ecosystem of the Cowichan River, including a trout hatchery and walking trails along the Cowichan River dike.

COWICHAN BAY

The Cowichan River valley was already occupied when the Europeans arrived. In the 1850s, James Douglas sent several

295

Logging

The cutting and processing of trees was a major Western Canadian industry long before Europeans arrived. Native peoples turned trees into boats, bags, homes, clothing, weapons, sacred objects and toys. So did later immigrants from Europe and Eastern North America, who saw the seemingly endless forests as a treasure trove to be tapped.

Loggers call Capt George Vancouver the region's first timberman; his journal records the first detailed search for the straightest trees (Douglas-fir) and the effort involved in cutting and dragging them from the forest to the shore. Two centuries of technology have changed the scale of logging, but Vancouver's carpenters would likely recognise today's forest industry.

A **logger** works in the forest, often called the **woods**. **Fallers** fell, or cut, trees, a process now called **harvesting**. Felled trees are **yarded**, collected in a **yard**, from where they are hauled away to be sorted by size, quality and species. When possible, logs are sorted at a **dry-land sort** on the shores of a river, lake or estuary, then dumped into the water. The floating logs are **boomed**, or bound into bundles, and tied into **rafts** to be towed to a mill for processing. Inland mills sort logs at the mill, where they are turned into pulp, paper, or lumber.

Work that was once done by hand is now largely mechanised. Axes and saws have been replaced by chain saws, themselves giving way to mechanical harvesters that can grasp and clip a tree a metre in diameter as neatly as a gardener prunes a rose – and almost as quickly. Teams of oxen replaced rope and windlass, to be replaced in turn by steam engines and diesel power.

Because machinery is most efficient in open areas, **clear-cutting**, cutting every tree on a parcel, has become the norm. With no trees left to hold soil during the heavy rains that make Western forests so productive, mountainsides turn into churning masses of sliding mud and rock. Streams and rivers choke on debris, smothering fish habitat. Logging is a major cause of the decline in salmon and other fish populations throughout the Western North America.

Milling can be equally destructive. Pulp and paper mills traditionally dumped tonnes of poisonous wastes in the nearest waterway. Public pressure has forced changes, but the cloying stench of pulp and paper production still hangs heavy over many areas. Producers call it the 'smell of money'. Timber *has* fuelled much of the region's economic development. It took massive amounts of wood to lay railway tracks across Canada. Entire forests have been transformed into lumber for cities from the Canadian Prairies to San Francisco and Japan.

Reforestation is the industry solution: clear cut, replant, fertilise, thin and harvest every 30–80 years. In practice, clear cutting destroys the old growth forest that deer, elk, bear, many smaller species and birds need for survival. At the same time, a rubble of logging refuse is often left on the ground to add nutrients to the soil through decomposition, help anchor the soil, and provide habitat for some smaller species.

Timber companies are cutting trees far faster than they are replanting. The fate of what remains of the forests that once stretched from the Rockies to the Pacific is still being decided in courtrooms, legislatures and on logging roads on both sides of the Canadian-US border.

military expeditions from Victoria to subdue the 'fierce, treacherous and turbulent Cowichans' who objected to HBC plans for the warm, lush valley. What the military began, smallpox and other imported plagues soon finished. The shallow bay became the centre for fishing, timber and farming, with regular steam ship connections to Victoria. When the E&N Railway lured commerce to Duncan, Cowichan Bay turned to sport fishing and leisure pursuits. The local lawn tennis tournament is the second oldest in the world after Wimbledon, England.

Wooden Boat Society and Cowichan Maritime Centre; *tel: (250) 746-4955*, on the former Chevron fuel pier in the centre of town, has a fine local history museum with vintage photographs. **The Marine Ecology Station**, *RR1; tel: (250) 748-4522; fax: (250) 748-4410*, 100m north on Pier 66, offers marine displays to explain the cold water environment.

GENOA BAY

Drive the 8 km from Maple Bay to Genoa Bay soon. Much of the area is marked for development, which will displace what is barely more than a single track road through a succession of tiny valleys rimmed with sheer granite cliffs. **Genoa Bay** is a small marina in an exquisite cove surrounded by forbidding cliffs. **Grape Vine Café**; *tel: (250) 746-0797*, open daily summer and Thur–Mon autumn–spring, lures yachties from up and down the coast.

CROFTON

Tourist Information: Crofton Museum, *next to BC Ferries; tel: (250) 246-2456*, summer only. **Crofton** was built in 1902 as a smelter site. The smelter closed, but forest industries and BC Ferries to Salt Spring Island kept the town alive. The Museum covers the copper mine, smelter and local history.

CHEMAINUS

Tourist Information: Chemainus and District Chamber of Commerce, *Box 575, Chemainus, BC V0R 1K0; tel: (250) 246-3944, in the red caboose at Heritage Sq.*, in summer, **Arts and Business Council of Chemainus**, *across from the waterwheel; tel: (250) 246-4701*, all year. *Chemainus Accommodations* from the Chamber of Commerce lists more than a dozen inns and Bed and Breakfasts.

Chemainus calls itself 'the little town that did' for a successful switch from timber to tourism after the town's major mill closed in 1983. Local activists convinced artists to paint downtown murals showcasing regional history. Murals lure coachloads of tourists to Canada's largest permanent outdoor art collection. Mural walking tour maps are sold at the InfoCentre and at **Chemainus Valley Museum**, *Waterwheel Park; tel: (502) 246-2445*. **Chemainus Theatre**; *tel: (250) 246-9820*, has a year-round schedule of live theatre.

LADYSMITH

Tourist Information: Ladysmith Chamber of Commerce, *Box 598, Ladysmith, BC V0R 2E0; tel: (250) 245-2212*, InfoCentre open summer only. Ladysmith was founded by coal baron James Dunsmuir, who named the streets after English generals in the Boer War to curry favour with military clients. *First Ave* is lined with restored heritage buildings that are now art galleries and boutiques.

NANAIMO

Tourist Information: Nanaimo Tourist and Convention Bureau, (NTCB) *Beban House, 2290 Bowen Rd, Nanaimo, BC V9T 3K7; tel: (250) 756-0106 or (800) 663-7337*.

GETTING THERE

BC Ferries, *Departure Bay Ferry Terminal; tel: (250) 753-1261; fax: (250) 381-5452*, have regular sailings between Nanaimo and Vancouver's northern terminal at Horseshoe Bay. *Duke Point Terminal; tel: (888) 223-3779 or (250) 386-3431*, south end of Nanaimo Harbour, serves ferries from Tsawwassen. The **Island Highway** is the main road link north and south.

ACCOMMODATION AND FOOD

Chains include *BW, DI* and *TL*. Best value

297

is **Harbourview Days Inn**, *809 Island Highway South, Nanaimo, BC V9R 5K1; tel: (250) 754-8171 or (800) 329-7466,* moderate. Expensive **Yellow Point Lodge**, *RR 3, Ladysmith, BC V0R 2E0; tel: (250) 245-7422,* is an immense log lodge and rustic cabins on the ocean off *Yellowpoint Rd.* Bed and Breakfast guides are available from the NTCB.

Nanaimo has Vancouver Island's best eating and drinking selection outside Victoria. Fast-food outlets are concentrated in the malls along Island Highway north of town. The **Old City Quarter**, an arc of streets east of the Island Hwy, has a number of trendy shops and eateries. One of the better choices is **Phüong**, *428 Fitzwilliam St; tel: (250) 754-2523,* for moderate Vietnamese. **Pagliacci's**, *7 Old Victoria Rd (in the Old Firehall); tel: (250) 754-3443,* has some of the best budget–moderate Italian choices and friendliest service in town.

SIGHTSEEING

Nanaimo's sheltered channel and bay were a traditional meeting ground for Coast Salish bands until HBC explorers discovered coal along the harbour and paid local Salish workers the equivalent of one shirt per day to work the mines. When disputes erupted over land ownership, the HBC traded 688 blankets for 20 km of coast, imported Prince Rupert miners and erected a bastion to enforce their version of the bargain. Ten years later, HBC sold out to a competitor for £40,000. A detachment of 1850s naval guardsmen fire a cannon daily at noon in summer at the **Bastion**, *Bastion and Front Sts; tel: (250) 753-1821,* museum open July–Sept, the only HBC fortification to survive the ravages of time and commerce. Coalmines covered most of the waterfront, delving deep beneath the harbour and into Newcastle Island. Mine owners, including

former indentured labourer Robert Dunsmuir, got rich, got political power and got the better of their workers. Mine accidents were as frequent as labour actions. Owners regularly brought in strike-breakers and turned strikers out of company-housing in the dead of winter. When hard-headed miners demanded safer working conditions and more than $1 per tonne of coal, Chinese labourers were hired for a flat $1 per day. Mine owners created decades of racial tension but kept profits high until oil began to replace coal. Nanaimo's last major mine closed in 1950; the last one-man colliery shut in 1968.

The only remaining pit is a model mine at the **Nanaimo & District Museum**, *100 Cameron Rd; tel: (250) 753-1821.* The museum also has an excellent display of local First Nations artefacts as well as exhibits from *Main St,* circa 1900, and Chinatown, which burned in 1960. **Newcastle Island Provincial Park**; *tel: (250) 755-2483,* is a popular spot for picnicking, camping and exploring caves, quarries, beaches and forests. Access is by private boat or ferry from **Maffeo Sutton Park**, near the city centre; *tel: (250) 753-8244.*

Mainland coal docks have been replaced with a sparkling 4-km Harbourside Walkway from the boat basin to the Departure Bay Ferry Terminal. **Swyalana Lagoon Park**, once an abandoned industrial area, is now Canada's first artificial tidal lagoon.

Three **Heritage Walks** from The Bastion explore the harbour area, coal mining and development spurred by the arrival of the **E&N Railway**, *Selby and Fitzwilliam Sts; tel: (604) 383-4324 or (800) 561-8630.* **Petroglyph Park**, *east side of Island Hwy, 3 km south of Nanaimo,* one of about 20 local petroglyph, or rock carving, sites in the area, features carvings of humans, birds, wolves, sea monsters and supernatural creatures.

NANAIMO–CAMPBELL RIVER

The 160 km between Nanaimo and Campbell River are a gradual transition from gentle farmland to the rougher, resource-based North Island. The coastal plain that makes South Island life and travel easy narrows to the north, squeezing the strip of civilisation along the Island Highway into increasingly smaller pockets. Allow at least one long day for this route; three days are better, with overnights near Parksville/Qualicum Beach and Courtenay.

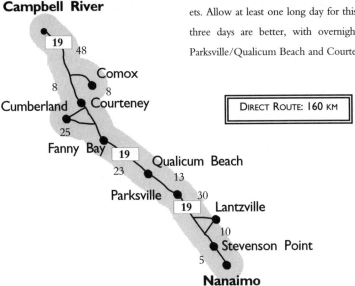

DIRECT ROUTE: 160 KM

ROUTES

DIRECT ROUTE

➡ Follow the Island Hwy, BC 19, north to **Parksville**, **Qualicum Beach**, **Courtenay** and Campbell River.

SCENIC ROUTE

The scenic route follows *Departure Bay Rd* north around the end of Departure Bay, past the Pacific Biological Station to *Stevenson Point Rd* and right onto *Hammond Bay Rd,* past Piper's Lagoon Park and right onto *Dickenson Rd* to **Lantzville**. Continue to BC 19 and turn

north (right) 16 km to the **Parksville and District Chamber of Commerce** and the adjoining **Craig Heritage Museum**. Drive another 3 km into **Parksville** and on to **Qualicum Beach**. Pass pleasant beaches to a brant-goose (brent-goose) viewing area and a succession of small settlements where playing children and grazing deer can slow traffic. Continue north to **Bowser**, **Fanny Bay**, the **Denman Island** ferry, **Union Bay**, **Royston** and the **Cumberland** turn-off. **Courtenay** is 4 km north.

Turn east (right) from BC 19 onto *17th Ave* toward **Comox** at the Riverside Mall, just past the Courtenay Travel InfoCentre. Go right again onto *Comox Rd*, to Comox. Turn right onto *Balmoral Ave* at the four-way stop, then right again onto *Croteau Rd* to the Comox Spit.

Return to *Comox Rd*, turn right to *Lazo Rd* and go left onto **Lazo**, following the blue and white 'scenic drive' signs. The road curves around **Pt Holmes** to the chainlink and barbed wire fence surrounding the Canadian Forces Base, Comox. Continue past the Comox Valley Regional Air Terminal to the Main Gate and Museum.

Go straight to the Griffen Pub sign and right onto *Kilmorley Rd*, then 1 km to *Astra Rd*. Turn left onto *Astra*, passing **Kin Beach** to a T-junction with *Prairie River Rd*. Turn right onto Prairie River and immediately left into **Wilkinson** for 1 km to *Eleanor Rd*.

Turn left for BC 19 (right for BC Ferries to Powell River), then veer right into *Anderton Rd*. Take a sharp left turn after 2 km into *Wavelander Rd* and left again after 1 km onto *Bates Rd*, following signs for BC 19 and Campbell River. Pass the **Seal Bay Nature Park** and continue 3 km to the stop sign at *Coleman Rd*. Turn left for the final 4 km back to BC 19. Turn north (right) to Campbell River.

BUSES

Island Coach Lines operate five trips a day from Nanaimo to Campbell River. Journey time: 3 hrs 20 mins. OTT table 67.

STEVENSON POINT

The blunt point forms the north side of Departure Bay and the ship channel to the Georgia Strait. Public beaches offer marine traffic view points.

Piper's Lagoon Park, *on the north side of the point*, is a local favourite for late afternoon walks.

LANTZVILLE

Lantzville's biggest attraction is a herd of 400 sea lions that winter near the waterfront. The broad, sandy shores of **Nanoose Harbour** are good for clam digging.

PARKSVILLE

Tourist Information: Parksville and District Chamber of Commerce, *Box 99, Parksville, BC V9P 2G3; tel: (250) 248-3613; fax: (250) 248-5210; InfoCentre on Hwy 19 at the south end of town, open daily.*

ACCOMMODATION

BW and *HI* are the only chains in the adjoining resort towns of Parksville/Qualicum Beach, but there are dozens of motels along BC 19. **Sandcastle Inn**, *374 Island Hwy W., Parksville, BC V9P 1K8; tel: (250) 248-2334 or (800) 335-7263*, is the newest, budget–moderate choice.

The Qualicum Beach Chamber of Commerce, *2711 W. Island Hwy, Qualicum Beach, BC V9K 2C4; tel: (250) 752-9532; fax: (250) 752-2923*, publishes a free list of Bed and Breakfasts.

EATING AND DRINKING

Hwy 19 is lined with malls and fast-food outlets. Two tastier alternatives are **India Curry House**, *261 E. Island Hwy; tel: (250) 954-3630*, budget, and the pricey summer dinner theatre at **Best Western Bayside**, *240 Dogwood St; tel: (250) 248-3424.*

SIGHTSEEING

Parksville and **Qualicum Beach** are a well-established holiday area. Every low tide exposes hundreds of hectares of flat beach filled with large shallow pools. **Rathtrevor Beach Provincial Park**; *tel: (250) 248-3931*, claims BC's warmest ocean water, 21°C in summer.

Craig Heritage Park Museum, *at the*

Tourist InfoCentre on BC 19; tel: (250) 248-6966, displays local artefacts in historic buildings moved to the museum grounds. A free *Guide to Studios and Galleries* introduces the nearly two dozen art galleries and studios in the area.

QUALICUM BEACH

Tourist Information: Qualicum Beach Chamber of Commerce, *2711 W. Island Hwy, Qualicum Beach, BC V9K 2C4; tel: (250) 752-9532; fax: (250) 752-2923.*

This retirement and tourist community is known for golfing, salmon fishing and beachcombing. The Chamber of Commerce publish a free area walking guide, including the village centre, 1 km inland. **The Power House Museum**, *587 Beach Rd; tel: (250) 752-5533*, open June–Sept, displays local artefacts in the town's original brick power house.

Horne Lake Caves Provincial Park, *16 km north on BC 19, then 15 km west on Horne Lake Rd; tel: (250) 248-3931*, has caves open for self-guided tours year-round and guided tours in summer. All caves require sturdy shoes and warm clothing for moderate climbing and at least two lights per person. Torches and hard hats *(highly* recommended) are $4 to hire per person.

Big Qualicum River Fish Hatchery, *west at the sign between Horne Lake Rd and the Big Qualicum River; tel: (250) 757-8412.* The salmon and trout hatchery is open year-round for self-guided tours.

DENMAN ISLAND AND HORNBY ISLAND

Tourist Information: Hornby–Denman Tourist Association, *c/o Sea Breeze Lodge, Hornby Island, BC V0R 1Z0; tel: (250) 335-2321.*

These small boat-accessible islands, just off the coast of **Buckley Bay**, are hugely popular for beachcombing, camping, hiking, fishing and relaxing. **Hornby** is more mountainous; constant pounding from the Georgia Strait has carved dramatic sea caves at **Tribune Bay** and several other sites.

CUMBERLAND

Tourist Information: Cumberland Chamber of Commerce, *2755 Dunsmuir Way, Box 250, Cumberland, BC V0R 1S0; tel: (250) 336-8313.*

Founded by coal baron Robert Dunsmuir, **Cumberland** had nearly 10,000 people in the 1910s. British, Italian, Chinese and Japanese miners lived in segregated neighbourhoods, each with its own bars, brothels, gambling houses, theatres and shops. Low wages and atrocious safety standards sparked a bitter 2-year island-wide coal strike in 1912. BC Premier WJ Bowser sent a thousand troops to 'keep the peace' by forcing Cumberland miners back to work. In 1918, police killed local pacifist and union organiser Ginger Goodwin, sparking more unrest. The BC government named a nearby section of the Island Highway *'Ginger Goodwin Way'* in 1995.

Cumberland's last mine closed in 1966, but slag heaps remain. So does **Cumberland Cultural Centre and Museum**, *First St and Dunsmuir Ave; tel: (250) 336-2445*, a splendid museum with restored storefronts and period façades. Its unvarnished look at life in the mines is stunning, as is the collection of photos of the local Japanese community destroyed by World War II internment.

COURTENAY

Tourist Information: Comox Valley Chamber of Commerce, *2040 Cliffe Ave, Courtenay, BC V9N 2L3; tel: (250) 334-3234; fax: (250) 334-4908*, **Info-Centre** *on BC 19 just south of the Comox turn-off.*

301

The Comox Valley is one of the few spots in Canada where it actually *is* possible to ski in the morning and play golf in the afternoon. **Forbidden Plateau**; *Strathcona Provincial Park; tel: (250) 334-2944*, and **Mt Washington Ski Area**; *tel: (250) 338-1386*, are also popular summer retreats.

The **Courtenay & District Museum**, *360 Cliffe Ave; tel: (250) 334-3611; fax: (250) 334-4277*, open Tues–Sat 1000–1630, is housed in the historic **Native Sons' Hall**, the largest vertical log building in the world. Inside is the fossilised skeleton of a 14-m Elasmosaur, the largest marine reptile ever found in Canada west of the Rocky Mountains.

COMOX

Tourist Information: Comox Valley Chamber of Commerce, *2040 Cliffe Ave, Courtenay; BC V9N 2L3; tel: (250) 334-3234; fax: (250) 334-4908.*

'Comox' is a First Nations word meaning 'place of abundance' for the rich harvest of berries and game the valley once provided. Extensive farmlands, nature preserves and public beaches remain, including **Seal Bay Regional Nature Park**; *tel: (250) 334-6000*, 700 hectares of peaceful forest and undeveloped beach. Tour **Filberg Lodge**, *61 Filberg at Comox Ave; tel: (250) 339-2715*, the former residence of local timber magnate Robert Filberg on 29 hectares of landscaped grounds. **Comox Air Force Museum**, *CFB Comox, Lazo, BC V0R 2K0; tel: (250) 339-8162*, traces the history of Canada's Air Forces.

CAMPBELL RIVER

Tourist Information: Campbell River & District Chamber of Commerce, *Box 400, Campbell River, BC V9W 5B6; tel: (250) 287-4636; fax: (250) 286-6990;* **InfoCentre**, *1235 Shoppers Row at Tyee Plaza*, open Mon–Fri 0900–1700.

ACCOMMODATION

Motel chains haven't come to Campbell River, but there are a dozen motels near BC 19. **The Town Centre Inn**, *1500 Elm St, Campbell River, BC V9W 3A6; tel: (250) 287-8866 or (800) 287-7107; fax: (250) 287-3944*, moderate, is good value.

EATING AND DRINKING

Seafood is always a good choice. **Panache**, *1090 Shoppers Row; tel: (250) 830-0025*, may be the best, and most expensive, restaurant along the Island Hwy. **Pier Street Café**, *207-871 Island Hwy; tel: (250) 287-2772*, has moderate prices and more basic preparation.

SIGHTSEEING

Some 60% of visitors come to fish the enormous shoals of salmon and other species moving through the narrow waters of **Discovery Passage**, connecting the Georgia and Johnstone Straits. Even non-boaters do well fishing off **Discovery Pier**, just south of the marina. The pier is also a good vantage point to watch cruise ships and ferries passing between Vancouver/Seattle and Alaska.

Discovery Passage scuba diving is spectacular for the rich underwater life, especially in the clear winter water, but ripping tidal currents make local guides a must. **Island Dive Connection**, *1621 N. Island Hwy, Campbell River, BC V9W 2E6; tel: (250) 830-0818; fax: (250) 830-0832*, are experienced, knowledgeable and friendly.

The Museum at **Campbell River**, *470 Island Hwy, Campbell River, BC V9W 4Z9; tel: (250) 287-3103*, covers local First Nations, contemporary and pioneer history. Best outdoor totems are in **Foreshore Park**, *just south of the BC Ferries terminal*, with new poles as well as a well-weathered eagle overlooking Quadra Island.

CAMPBELL RIVER– PORT HARDY

Drivers in a hurry can make the 245kms north to Port Hardy in three hours if traffic and weather co-operate, but allow at least one full day to absorb the vistas. There's still a frontier feeling beyond Campbell River, albeit a frontier where more mountainsides have been scalped than allowed to retain their original forest cover. Logging trucks and heavy equipment share the roads and the infrequent hamlets with hunters, fishermen and sightseers. Lodging, petrol and other services are rare along twisting canyons so narrow that even radio reception is problematic. Outside the frequent campsites, the only places to overnight en route are occasional Bed and Breakfasts on the side tracks to Sayward/Kelsey Bay and Zeballos, and basic motels at Telegraph Cove, Alert Bay and Port McNeill. Advance booking is essential, especially in summer.

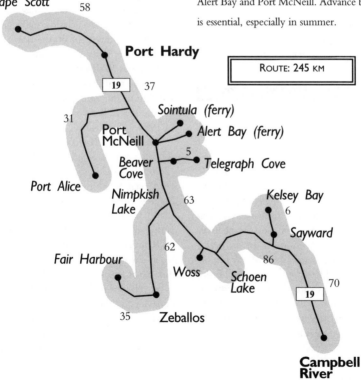

Cape Scott   58

Port Hardy

ROUTE: 245 KM

19   37

31   Sointula (ferry)

Port McNeill   Alert Bay (ferry)

Beaver Cove   5   Telegraph Cove

Port Alice   Nimpkish Lake   63   Kelsey Bay

6

Sayward

Fair Harbour   62   86

Woss   Schoen Lake   70

19

35   Zeballos

Campbell River

ROUTE

Take BC 19 north past the turn-off for Strathcona Provincial Park to Seymour Narrows. The road continues beyond a series of lakes to the **Sayward–Kelsey Bay** turn-off and into the twisting Nimpkish River canyon. Follow the shores of Nimpkish Lake to the **Telegraph Cove** turn-off, then north past turn-offs to **Port McNeill**, **Port Alice** and **Cape Scott** to the end of the road at **Port Hardy**. Traffic sometimes backs up through the scenic geologic jumble that makes up much of North Island. RV traffic is particularly heavy in summer with holidaymakers on their way to and from Prince Rupert (on the mainland) via the BC Ferries terminal at Port Hardy.

BUSES

Island Coach Lines operate one trip a day between Campbell River and Port Hardy, with an extra service in summer. See OTT table 67.

CAMPBELL RIVER TO WOSS

Strathcona Provincial Park, *District Manager, Box 1479, Parksville, BC V9P 2H4; tel: (250) 755-2483*, is 48 km west of Campbell River on BC 28. The 211,973-hectare park is a rough wilderness triangle straddling Vancouver Island. Highlights include 440-m **Della Falls**, the highest waterfall in Canada, 2200-m **Golden Hinde**, the tallest point on Vancouver Island and a collection of lesser peaks, meadows, forests and lakes. Mt Washington and Forbidden Plateau ski areas border the park. There are campsites scattered throughout the park and the moderate motel-like **Strathcona Park Lodge**, *Box 2160N, Campbell River, BC V9W 5C9; tel: (250) 286-8206; fax: (250) 286-8208*, just outside, as well as lodging in Campbell River or Courtenay.

Fletcher Challenge Elk Falls Pulp and Paper Mill, *4405 N. Island Hwy, Campbell River; tel: (250) 287-5594*, rises 7 km north of Campbell River, just beside BC 19. A large lay-by overlooking the mill, barge terminal and Quadra Island has signs explaining plant buildings and operations. Tours available Mon–Fri in summer, advance booking required.

Seymour Narrows, *7 km north of the mill*, is a perilous pass between Vancouver Island and Maude Island. The twin peaks of Ripple Rock once lay just beneath the surface of the Narrows, creating one of the most hazardous ship passages in the world. A government project, one of the largest non-nuclear explosions in history, removed Ripple Rock in 1958, but fierce currents and treacherous eddies still churn the Narrows into a boiling mass of white water at flood tide. Marine traffic passes a convenient viewpoint on the north (right) side of the highway. A moderate 8-km path climbs **Wilfred Pt**, overlooking the Narrows, from a trailhead 6 km north. The last ship to run aground on the remains of Ripple Rock, the *SS Sundancer*, hit bottom in 1984.

Link and Pin Logging Museum, *23 km north of Ripple Rock Overlook; tel: (250) 287-3931*, open daily (June–late Sept), claims the island's best collection of logging paraphernalia, from handsaws to stamp hammers, caulk boots, antique oil lamps and early North Island photographs.

Roberts Lake and rest area, *east (right) side of the hwy, 600m north*, is one of dozens of scenic fishing lakes off BC 19. Most hillsides within view of BC 19 have been logged repeatedly. The surrounding mountains are at their mysterious best when fog and mist hide the scars. Widespread replanting began in the 1950s under public and government pressure. Look for signs along the highway giving the cutting date(s), replanting year and next planned cut under the banner of 'Forests Forever'.

Most of Vancouver Island is owned by timber firms or controlled by the industry under licence from the provincial government. Timber companies have, however, opened thousands of square kilometres to recreational use and built dozens of highway rest areas – easily identified by signboards like the one at McNair Lake, 4 km north of the Link and Pin Logging Museum, extolling the virtues of clear cutting over the 'dying and diseased' state of old growth forests.

⬛ SIDE TRACK
⬛ TO SAYWARD AND
KELSEY BAY

Sayward is one of BC's few remaining company towns, entirely owned by the MacMillan Bloedel Ltd. Board Company. MacMillan's Kelsey Bay Lumber Operation and town are 10 km north (right) of BC 19. Kelsey Bay is 3 km beyond.

Turn north (right) 29 km north of McNair Lake, following signs for Sayward, and cross the single track bridge over the Salmon River. In addition to salmon, the 74-km river is reputed to hold the largest steelhead on the island. Just beyond the bridge on the left-hand side of the road is a steam donkey, or steam engine, once used to haul logs through the forest, now overgrown by moss and brush. The dense poplar trees just beyond are a tree farm.

Sayward is 8 km ahead, overshadowed by 1671-m **Hkusam Mountain**. A marsh and a small lake create the fog that frequently rings the peak. There are no public services.

The upper reaches of Kelsey Bay are a MacMillan Blodell log pond, protected by the rusting hulks of barges sunk as breakwaters. The Kelsey Bay wharf was once the southern terminus for BC Ferries' route to Prince Rupert that now ends at Port Hardy. Today, the small harbour is the domain of sailors, fishermen and charter boat captains. Return to BC 19 and turn north (right). ⬛

SCHOEN LAKE TO WOSS

Schoen Lake Provincial Park, *to the south (left) 54 km north of the Sayward/ Kelsey Bay road; tel: (250) 248-3931,* is a stunning wilderness park. The 1802-m peak of **Mt Schoen** reflects in the narrow, still waters of **Schoen Lake**, a 5 km stretch of canoeing waters. Hikers and campers can expect to see deer, bears, beavers, wolves, cougars and Roosevelt elk, or at least sign of their recent passing. The road is passable by passenger vehicles in good weather, but chains are required in winter to get to the **Mt Cain Ski Area**, *19 km off BC 19, Box 1225, Port McNeill, BC V0N 2R0; tel: (250) 956-2246,* 16 ski runs and 20 km of unmarked cross-country trails, open weekends and school holidays. Mt Cain probably gets more visitors in summer for its wildflowers, wild blueberries, alpine meadows and marshes.

Hoomac Lake, *4 km north of the Schoen Lake turn-off,* is a rest and recreation area maintained by Canadian Forest Products Ltd, better known as Canfor. A signboard clearly explains Canfor's forest cutting and replanting scheme to boost wood production by 80%, but the best reason to stop is a pleasant walking path down the lake. A few hectares of old growth forest have been left around the lake to provide habitat for elk and other creatures that don't prosper in farmed forests.

Woss, *7 km north and 2 km west of BC 19,* is another logging company town. Canfor keeps an antique steam locomotive engine on display. In summer, the railway is still used to haul tourists about 25 km through the **Nimpkish Valley** to the dry-land sort and booming grounds at **Beaver Cove**. The tour takes about five hours; *tel: (250) 281-2300*. Woss has one of the few petrol stations and restaurants between Campbell River and Port McNeill.

SIDE TRACKS FROM WOSS

ZEBALLOS

Zeballos, *21 km north of Woss, then 41 km south,* is a scenic village at the end of a rough gravel road that offers stunning mountain views. The road is open all year, but is too rugged for RVs and low-clearance passenger vehicles. The tiny settlement is a base for boat and kayak trips on the long inlets and waterways around Nootka Island.

ACCOMMODATION

Choices include the **Zeballos Hotel**; *tel: (250) 761-4275*, **Zeballos Inlet Lodge**; *tel: (250) 761-4294; fax: (250) 761-2060*, and the **Zeballos Mini-Motel**; *tel: (250) 761-4340,* all budget–moderate, and several campsites.

SIGHTSEEING

An even rougher unpaved road, not recommended in winter, continues 35 km north-west to **Fair Harbour**, a favourite launching point for kayakers putting into the **Kyuquot Sound** and the **Provincial Wilderness Recreation Area** on the Brooks Peninsula. Vancouver Island's last known indigenous sea otter was killed near Fair Harbour in 1929; otters transplanted from Alaska in the 1970s seem to be re-establishing themselves along the relatively deserted coast. Return to Zeballos

and BC 19 and turn north (left) toward Port McNeill.

NIMPKISH LAKE

Nimpkish Lake skirts the highway for 22km, finally flowing into the Queen Charlotte Strait just beyond the turn-off for Beaver Cove and Telegraph Cove.

SIDE TRACK TO BEAVER COVE AND TELEGRAPH COVE

Turn south (right) off BC19 just beyond the north end of Nimpkish Lake at the **North Island Forestry Centre**; *tel: (250) 956-3844* or *(800) 661-7177*. The centre is run by five forestry companies that offer tours. Most tours are summer only, with departures from Port Hardy, Port McNeill, Port Alice or Woss. Advance booking required.

The paved road ends at a T-junction 11 km from the highway. Turn left, following signs for the Telegraph Cove Resort. A fish hatchery just beyond the turn is sometimes open for self-guided tours. Fletcher Challenge's **Beaver Cove** facility is 1 km beyond. Continue another kilometre past the dryland sort to a lay-by on the left near the top of the hill.

Fletcher Challenge's facility below is the largest dryland sort in Canada, processing 1.4 million cubic metres of logs each year. Logs are sorted into 35 different categories by species, size and grade for lumber, shakes, shingles, plywood, pulp, poles and log homes. Once the logs are sorted, they are weighed, strapped together and dumped into the booming grounds, or ponds, to be 'stowed up', or chained together, into rafts 21m wide by 121m long. Tugs tow 12 rafts at once to mills in

Quadra Island

The large (276 square km) Quadra Island, off Campbell River which forms one side of Discovery Passage, is known for fishing, scuba diving and hiking, but mostly for the **Kwagiulth Museum and Cultural Centre**, *Cape Mudge Village, Box 8, Quathiaski Cove, BC V0P 1N0; tel: (250) 285-3733.* The museum was built to house part of a potlatch collection seized by federal officials in a 1922 crackdown on First Nation ceremonies. **Potlatch**, a ceremony in which tribal leaders distributed immense quantities of food, trade goods, clothing and household furnishings to their people, was banned in 1884.

The ceremony, usually held in winter, was a central part of First Nation life along the North West coast. It was a time to reinforce tradition and authority through performances of sacred rites and to establish political authority. The greater the wealth a leader was able to distribute to members of his own tribe as well as to neighbouring bands, the greater his power.

Christian missionaries and government agents condemned potlatch as part of a 'decrepit' culture. Complained one government agent in 1918, 'During these gatherings, they lose months of time, waste their substance, contract all kinds of diseases and generally unfit themselves for being British subjects in the proper sense of the word'.

The potlatch ban was quietly dropped in the 1950s. Most of the items seized, including masks, headdresses, blankets and other ceremonial regalia, were returned to this museum and a similar institution in Alert Bay (on Cormorant Island, off Port McNeill, see p.308) in 1988. The gift shop has an excellent selection of contemporary Kwagiulth masks, prints, wooden plaques, oil paintings and jewellery.

There are also accessible **petroglyphs** in a small park across from the museum as well as Wa Wa Kie Beach and Francisco Point.

307

Vancouver. Woods tours are usually available with advance booking; *tel: (250) 928-3023.*

Continue another kilometre to a stop sign and a second T-junction. Turn left and drive 2 km to Telegraph Cove. **Telegraph Cove Resorts**, *Telegraph Cove, BC V0N 3J0; tel: (250) 928-3131 or (250) 284-3426* (in winter); *fax (250) 928-3105,* open May–Oct, is one of BC's best-preserved boardwalk communities. The tiny town was built early in the century at the terminus of the first telegraph line to North Island, then grew into a thriving sawmill and fish salting community. The handful of surviving buildings, most built on stilts over the cove, have been absorbed into the budget–expensive resort. Other facilities include a small marina, general store, RV park and campsite.

The cove is as popular with environmental groups as it is with fishermen. Sixteen pods (family groups) of orcas, or killer whales, more than 200 individuals, congregate in the nearby Johnstone Strait in summer and autumn. An ecological preserve has been established at Robson Bight, about 20 km south, a shallow area off the mouth of the Tsitka River where orcas rub on gravel beaches. **Stubbs Island Whale Watching**, *Box 7, Telegraph Cove, BC V0N 3J0; tel: (250) 928-3185 or (800) 665-3066; fax: (250) 928-3102,* run whale watching trips daily (June–Oct). More than 90% of trips see whales (minke, humpback and grey as well as orcas) plus porpoises, seals, sea lions, bald eagles and other wildlife. Advance booking highly recommended. Return to BC 19 and turn north (right).

In the early years of the century, more than 10,000 sockeye salmon were caught in the Nimpkish River each year; by 1978, ocean fishing off the West Coast of Vancouver Island and habitat destruction from logging in the Nimpkish Valley had cut the annual run to fewer than 500 sockeye. The **Nimpkish Fish Hatchery**, *2 km north of the Telegraph Cove turn-off; tel: (250) 974-9556*, open daily 0900–1500 (Oct–May), is incubating, rearing and releasing several million fish each year in an attempt to restore the fishery. The Nimpkish facility does a better job than most explaining why salmon are important culturally as well as economically, why the runs have declined and how hatcheries and habitat restoration may help. And, unlike most hatcheries, this one has viewing windows as clean as any commercial aquarium, with entrancing views into swirling shoals of fish.

BC 4 crosses the Nimpkish River just north of the hatchery. On the east side of the road just over the river is an imposing totem pole carved in 1966 to commemorate the centennial of the political joining of Vancouver Island with the mainland. The Port McNeill exit is 6 km north to the right.

PORT MCNEILL

Tourist Information: Port McNeill Chamber of Commerce, *1558 Broughton Blvd, Box 129, Port McNeill, BC V0N 2R0; tel: (250) 956-3131 or (250) 956-4437; fax: (250) 956-4972.*

Most area lodging is in **Port Hardy**. Port McNeill choices include **HaidaWay Motor Inn**, *Box 399, Port McNeill, BC V0N 2R0; tel: (250) 956-3373; fax: (250) 956-4710*, the **Datewood Inn**, *Box 280, Port McNeill, BC V0N 2R0; tel: (250) 956-3304; fax: (250) 956-4351*, and the

McNeill Inn, *Box 999, Port McNeill, BC V0N 2R0; tel/fax: (250) 956-3466*, all moderate, with restaurants.

Port McNeill is a lumber and fishing town. **North Island Forestry Center**, *Box 130; tel: (250) 956-3844; fax: (250) 956-3848*, offer daily tours (June–Aug). Tours last about six hours, advance booking required. The **world's largest burl** is 1.5 km north of town on BC 19, 13.5 m around and weighing more than 20 tonnes. It was found at the head of the Benson River, about 40 km south.

The harbour is an active commercial and sport fishing port as well as the terminus for BC Ferries' route to Alert Bay and Sointula.

SIDE TRACK
TO ALERT BAY AND SOINTULA

Tourist Information: Alert Bay Tourist Information Centre, *118 Fir St, Alert Bay, BC V0N 1A0; tel: (250) 974-5213; fax: (250) 974-5470*, open daily (June–Sept), Mon–Fri (Sept–June).

GETTING THERE

BC Ferries *from Port McNeill; tel: (888) 223-3779 or (250) 956-4533*, daily.

SIGHTSEEING

Nowhere is Canada's mystical First Nations heritage more evident than at **Alert Bay**. The 'Namgis burial ground is guarded by a phalanx of totem poles towering above the beach, a sight more often seen in faded black and white museum photographs than in living colour through swirling ocean mists. The burial ground is not open to the public, but the poles are clearly visible from the road.

In the 1870s, missionaries convinced the 'Namgis band to move from the

Nimpkish Valley to Alert Bay on Cormorant Island, just off Port McNeill, to staff a salmon saltery. Today, the village is an ethnic mix, but the ethos is decidedly First Nations. The biggest draw is the **U'mista Cultural Centre**, *Box 253, Alert Bay, BC V0N 1A0; tel: (250) 974-5403; fax: (250) 974-5499,* open daily, home to half of a potlatch collection confiscated in 1922. The remainder of the collection is on display at the **Kwagiulth Museum and Cultural Centre** on Quadra Island (see p.307). The cultural centre also has temporary exhibitions of contemporary First Nations art and cultural events.

Sointula, on Malcom Island, is linked to Port McNeill and Alert Bay by BC Ferries. The tiny fishing village began in 1901 as a utopian retreat organised by Finnish philosopher and playwright Matti Kurrika. The colony collapsed in 1905, but Finnish is still heard on the streets. **Sointula Finnish Museum**; *left on First St after leaving the ferry; tel: (250) 973-6353,* reflects Finnish fishing and farming roots.

Misty Lake Rest Area, *17 km north of Port McNeill Rd,* is a scenic rest area on the east side of the road. The 2-m stumps are all that remains of the original forest cover. The road to **Port Alice** is 3 km north.

SIDE TRACK TO PORT ALICE
Tourist Information: Quatsino Chalet, *1061 Marine Dr., Port Alice, BC V0N 2N0; tel: (250) 284-3318,* open daily Mon–Fri.

SIGHTSEEING
The 33-km drive east from BC19 passes

Beaver Lake, beloved by locals for a thriving population of cutthroat and Dolly Varden trout, and two of North Island's few golf courses. The **Seven Hills Golf and Country Club**; *tel: (250) 949-9818,* has nine holes and a 1910 tractor that bogged down while hauling logs. Since the tractor was too heavy to move, the course was built around it. The **Port Alice Golf and Country Club**, another 9-hole course, is so steep it has a periscope at the second tee. Return to BC 19 and turn north (left) toward Port Hardy.

Beaver Harbour, *Fort Rupert Rd east (right) toward the airport, 3 km north of BC Hydro's Keogh Generating Station,* was the original Hudson's Bay Company settlement in the region. Today, the area is a Kwakwaka'wakw reserve. The only sign of the fort is a crumbling chimney. Several of BC's finest Native artists work, display and sell at **The Copper Maker**; *Box 755, Port Hardy, BC V0N 2P0; tel: (250) 949-8491; fax: (250) 949-7345,* open Mon–Sat. **Bear Cove**, *1 km north of Fort Rupert Rd, then 6 km east,* is the **BC Ferries** terminal for Prince Rupert; *tel: (250) 949-6722 or (800) 663-7600.* Ferries operate weekly in both directions (Oct–Apr), twice weekly (May–Sept). Advance bookings required all year. Artefacts from an 8000-year-old Bear Cove settlement are at the Port Hardy Museum. Port Hardy is 4 km north from the junction with BC19.

Tourist Information: Port Hardy & District Chamber of Commerce, *7250 Market St, Port Hardy, BC V0N 2P0; tel: (250) 949-7622; fax: (250) 949-6653,* open daily (June–late Sept), Mon–Fri (Oct–June).

Salmon Country

To the early inhabitants of the Pacific Northwest, the annual salmon migration was more than a mystery of life, it *was* life. The rich, meaty fish were so important that a delay in the annual migration could mean mass human starvation. Five species of salmon live in the rivers and streams of the Pacific Northwest, plus two species of migratory trout. All are *anadromous*, spawning (laying eggs) in fresh water but spending at least part of their lives in the ocean, and all are distinct from Atlantic salmon. Homing instincts draw adult fish back from the Pacific Ocean. Fat from 2–5 years of gorging at sea, the fish fight their way upstream through hordes of fishermen armed with hooks and nets, and rapids, waterfalls and dams to spawn in the same stream where they were born. By the time they arrive, the fish look ghastly, battered and tattered, thin, often missing fins or eyes, but determined to reproduce.

The fish pair off, the female digging a shallow nest, or *redd*, in the gravel and laying 3000–5000 eggs. The male fertilises the gelatinous mass of eggs with *milt*, and the female covers the mass with gravel to protect the eggs from predators and from washing downstream. Salmon spawn once and die, their bodies an important food source for bald eagles, bears and other animals. Seagoing trout, **steelhead** and **cutthroat**, spawn and return to the sea.

Chinook *(Onchorhynchus tshawytscha)* or **king** salmon are the largest and most highly valued. Adults average 20–25 pounds, but 40–50 pounders are common. Larger rivers have separate runs in spring, summer and autumn. Fish are silver until close to spawning when males turn a dark maroon or red; females become dark silver to black.

Coho *(O. kisutch)* or **silver** salmon average 6–12 pounds but grow to 25 pounds. Males turn brick red and females become a dull bronze during autumn migration.

Chum *(O. keta)* or **dog** salmon were named by early settlers who fed these fish to their dogs and saved the richer chinook and sockeye for their own tables. Autumn migration.

Pink *(O. gorbuscha)* or **humpback** salmon average 6–12 pounds; the males develop a pronounced humped back during the autumn migration.

310

ACCOMMODATION

Year-round ferry traffic means year-round business for local motels, inns and Bed and Breakfasts; book in advance, especially in summer. **North Islands Reservations**; *tel: (250) 949-7622*, book local lodging. **Pioneer Inn**, *Bying Rd, near the Bear Cove turn-off, Box 699, Port Hardy, BC V0N 2P0; tel: (250) 949-7271; fax: (250) 949-7334*, is the best budget–moderate value. **Thunderbird Inn**, *7050 Rupert St, Port Hardy, BC V0N 2P0; tel: (250) 949-7767; fax: (250) 949-7740*, moderate, is central.

SIGHTSEEING

Port Hardy is the commercial centre of North Island. BC19 comes to an end at a broad bayfront park with a bright orange wooden carrot and handcarved 'Welcome to Port Hardy' sign. The 'carrot at the end of the road' is a pointed reminder that a generation of provincial governments reneged on campaign pledges to extend BC19 to Port Hardy until 1979. A scenic harbour walkway is a favourite gathering place for bald eagles, Canada geese and other birds.

Buildings just up from the town dock are part of original Port Hardy, founded in 1925. The town's first community hall is now **Port Hardy Museum and Archives**, *7110 Market St, Port Hardy, BC V0N 2P0; tel: (250) 949-8143*, open Tues–Sat afternoons (Oct–May), daily in summer. Exhibits cover First Nations history

Sockeye (*O. nerka*) or **red** salmon average 3–7 pounds, but can reach 15 pounds. Normally a metallic blue-black, maturing fish turn bright red with green heads and tails as they move upriver mid-summer–autumn.

No one knows how many salmon once moved up North Western waterways. Early explorers wrote of walking across rivers atop shoals of migrating fish. Today, newspapers proclaim 10,000 chinook returning to the entire state of Washington.

The Hudson's Bay Company began exporting salmon from Fort Langley in 1835 and built its first Fraser River salmon cannery in 1876. By 1900, Canadian canneries were beginning to close for lack of fish. The story was similar in Washington and Oregon, where a fish and game magazine warned in 1894 that 'It is only a matter of a few years when the chinook of the Columbia will be as scarce as the beaver that once was so plentiful in our streams'.

Overfishing was compounded by dam building. Fifty-five major dams block salmon migrations on the Columbia River alone. Fish ladders allow some fish to make their way over smaller dams, but Chief Joseph and other dams are impassable. Fish migrating downstream are sucked into powerplant turbines and turned to fish paste. Reservoirs flood the shallow, fast-moving water salmon need for spawning.

Logging adds to the destruction. Clear cutting contributes to erosion, clogging gravel spawning beds with silt and smothering both eggs and young fish. Agricultural run-off, industrial waste and toxic drainage from roads and cities pollute streams and rivers.

Fish hatcheries release millions of fish each year to help replace the wild salmon and trout that have disappeared. But hatchery fish are less resistant to disease and less likely to escape predators than wild fish. Salmon are mired in controversy. In the end, the only way to restore salmon runs is to restore the habitat salmon need to reproduce and to limit the number of fish caught each year.

The argument, and the mythical romance that still attaches to salmon, are graphically illustrated in *Ray Troll's Shocking Fish Tales: Fish, Romance, and Death in Pictures*, by Bradford Matsen and Ray Troll, 1993, Ten Speed Press, Berkeley, CA.

311

(including excavations at Bear Cove) and European exploration and settlement.

The port is home to a commercial and sport fishing fleet, both benefiting from the **Quatse River Salmon Hatchery**, *5050 Hardy Bay Rd (across from the Pioneer Inn); tel: (250) 949-9022*, open Mon–Fri 0800–1630. The hatchery raises coho, chinook and chum salmon, with pleasant walking paths along the river.

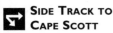
SIDE TRACK TO CAPE SCOTT

The only access into **Cape Scott Provincial Park** is by foot, but logging roads lead 63 km from Port Hardy to the trailhead. Cape Scott itself is a rugged 2-day return hike with stunning views of both sides of Vancouver Island from the lighthouse perched far above crashing waves rolling off the open Pacific Ocean. Less adventurous walkers generally opt for the 45-min walk along chip paths and boardwalks to the sandy shores of **San Josef Bay**.

Although the park is a wilderness area, loggers have long been working the mountains between Port Hardy and the Pacific. Gravel roads to **Holberg**, **Winter Harbour** and **Raft Cove** are well maintained and passable – with care – by passenger vehicles during the summer, but not recommended for large RVs because of occasional rough patches on the road and difficulty pulling over for logging trucks.

PORT HARDY– BELLA COOLA

This marine route from the north end of Hwy 19 on Vancouver Island through the Inside Passage to the west end of Hwy 20 twists through some of the most dramatic coastal scenery in North America. Snow-capped peaks drop precipitously into deep blue fjords lined with dense forests. There are more ghost towns than settlements along this corrugated coastline and no regular contact with the outside world save this summer-only ferry route. Don't expect slavish devotion to schedules. The 100m car ferry stops wherever a passenger wants to get on or off, and detours are the norm when the Captain spots a pod of orcas or a humpback whale.

ROUTE: 15 HOURS

312

Klemtu

Ocean Falls

Shearwater

Bella Coola

McLoughlin Bay

Namu

Ferry Route

Port Hardy

ROUTE

The *Queen of Chilliwack* sails the **Discovery Coast** between Port Hardy, at the north end of Vancouver Island, and Bella Coola, at the western end of Hwy 20, from late May–late Sept. Check the BC Ferries schedule for sailing dates and port calls. The voyage takes 15–33 hours in each direction, depending on how many of the five intermediate stops (**Namu, McLoughlin Bay, Shearwater, Klemtu** and **Ocean Falls**) the ship visits. A return trip takes about 50 hours. Allow $250 per person for a single journey and about the same for a passenger car. Motorcycles and bicycles cost less, RVs more.

For the *best maritime scenery*, take the *Queen* southbound from Bella Coola to Port Hardy to see all of **North Bentinck Arm** and the **Dean Channel** in daylight. For *easier driving* between Bella Coola and interior BC, sail northbound from Port Hardy to Bella Coola. It's safer to drive up The Hill, a hairpin dirt track section of Hwy 20 between Bella Coola and Williams Lake, than downhill (see p. 318).

Advance booking is required for vehicles and strongly recommended for foot passengers, **BC Ferries**, *1112 Fort St, Victoria, BC V8V 4V2; tel: (888) 223-2779 or (250) 386-3431; fax: (250) 381-5452.* Space for May and late Sept sailings *may* be available at the last minute, but book 4–6 months in advance for June, July and Aug. Bookings can be changed, subject to availability and a $50 per segment fee.

Port Hardy vehicles and passengers board at the Bear Cove ferry dock (see p. 309). In Bella Coola, foot passengers board at the dock, but vehicles must check in at the Cedar Inn parking lot to obtain a boarding pass before driving 2 km to the dock. Boarding begins one hour before sailing at both ports. Board as early as possible to claim a window seat. Most hotels and motels in both ports arrange transport to and from the dock for foot passengers.

Vehicle decks are supposed to remain locked while at sea to prevent pilferage and injury, but it is usually possible to visit your vehicle. Some passengers keep a change of clothing or a supply of soda pop handy. And since both passengers and vehicles use the same vehicle ramps to get on and off the ship, it's easy to grab something from your car while in port.

Although summer weather is usually fine, fog, rain and wind are no strangers to the mid-coast. Comfort is the rule, including flat shoes for walking about the deck, up and down stairs and on shore. Repeat

passengers eschew shorts and sandals for long pants and closed shoes in case of clammy fog or a chill rain. Bring jumpers and jackets with hoods (against wind and rain) even if the weather forecast calls for brilliant sun and 28°C for the next week.

The Norwegian-built *Queen* is no cruise ship. The ferry has no casino, no sauna and no fancy dress dinners. She *does* have complete facilities, including a cafeteria serving full meals and snacks, a licensed lounge, showers, laundry, video arcade, games, videos, gift shop, exercise machines, an enclosed solarium and elevators. There is ample outside deck space to watch the scenery and scan for orcas, whales, dolphins, bald eagles and passing ships. Bring cameras and binoculars.

There are no cabins on board, but reclining seats are quite comfortable for sleeping. Seats cannot be reserved, so most passengers drop an extra coat or backpack on the chair of their choice immediately after boarding. Window seats in the forward lounge go quickly. There is also space to pitch tents in the main cabins and in the solarium. Blankets, pillows and tents can be hired on board. It's also possible to overnight in Shearwater, Klemtu, or Ocean Falls and rejoin the ship on a later trip, but accommodation on shore is limited and must be booked well in advance.

Port calls last from 30 mins to 4 hrs. Arrival and departure times for the next port are posted near the Purser's Office, just forward of the cafeteria. Shore excursions are available in most ports, ranging from walking tours to traditional dancing demonstrations, feasts and canoe trips. The Purser's Office has information and tickets for all shore activities. Prices range from $15–$45 per person.

Passengers are also encouraged to explore the small towns on their own, but the ship doesn't wait for stragglers. The

313

only warning is a long blast from the ship's whistle 15 mins before departure.

Unlike most BC Ferries, the *Queen of Chilliwack* crew are encouraged to mingle with passengers. The bearded guitar player singing sea chanteys in the aft lounge is as likely to be one of the mates as a passenger. The chef passing out sausages and salmon steaks from the barbecue could be the captain as easily as one of the cooks. And the purser picks videos on passenger request.

Expect a calm passage no matter what the weather, though the ship occasionally rocks across the open waters of Queen Charlotte Sound, just north of Vancouver Island. The rest of the Inside Passage route is extremely well protected from storms and ocean swells by the maze of islands lying just off the BC coast.

Whatever the weather, don't miss the monument to Alexander Mackenzie, on the shores of **Dean Channel** about 60 km east of Bella Coola. Mackenzie painted his name and the date on a rock just above the waterline in 1793, marking the first overland crossing of North America north of Mexico. Mackenzie and his party paddled back to Bella Coola along the same route the *Queen* now follows.

BUSES

See OTT table 30 for details of services.

KLEMTU

Tourist Information: Kitasoo Band Council, *86 Klemtu St, Klemtu, BC V0V 1L0 tel: (250) 839-2346 or (250) 839-1255; fax: (250) 839-1256.*

The Kitasoo Band operate a campsite, a small Bed and Breakfast (advance booking required) and a café.

Most of Klemtu's 300 residents turn out for the *Queen's* arrival every eight days. *Main St* is one of the longest boardwalks in North America, connecting two sides of a

bay teeming with fish, bald eagles, dolphins, orcas and other wildlife. Guides offer a 3-hr walking tour of Klemtu that includes a busy wood carving shed. Highlight of the tour is a traditional feast and dancing. The Band offer a full schedule of boat charters for fishing, sightseeing and hikes on nearby islands. Visitors can also hire (or bring their own) sea kayaks for a personal exploration of nearby waters.

MCLOUGHLIN BAY

The principal town, **Bella Bella**, is 3 km from the BC Ferries dock, too far to walk during the short port call. Several fine First Nations artists set up shop at the dock, when the *Queen* comes to call, including silversmith Peter Gladstone. McLoughlin Bay is a familiar destination to kayakers, who disembark to paddle through the nearby Haki Pass archipelago.

If the weather is less than a full gale, walk the crushed shell beach to the traditional-style longhouse built by Helsiuk Band carver Frank Brown. Brown offers local history displays, First Nations art, a lunch of salmon roasted on cedar planks over an open fire and basic camping facilities. He also leads passengers on a 1-hr paddle in the *Glwa*, a traditional canoe carved from a 7-tonne cedar log, down a sheltered passage past a 200-year-old totem pole and several abandoned fish canneries. Expect to see bald eagles, herons, orcas, dolphins and perhaps bears or deer on shore. Paddlers meet the ferry at the next port, Shearwater Bay. On runs that only stop at Shearwater, Brown brings his hand-carved canoe out to meet the ship and take on paddlers. Canoe space is limited, so sign up for the paddle immediately after boarding the *Queen* in either Port Hardy or Bella Coola.

NAMU

The *Queen* stops at Namu only on request.

The faded white buildings of the Namu Cannery glimmer against the green shoreline, all but deserted since the plant was closed in 1970. Archaeological excavations have revealed at least 10,000 years of human habitation on the shores of this quiet cove, making Namu the oldest continuously occupied site on the BC coast. The original Namu cannery was built next to a Heiltsuk village in 1893.

OCEAN FALLS

Tourist Information: BC Ferries, *1112 Fort St, Victoria, BC V8V 4V2; tel: (888) 223-2779* or *(250) 386-3431; fax: (250) 381-5452,* have information on accommodation and dining.

Link Falls, the waterfall that gave Ocean Falls its name, still thunder into the deep waters of **Cousins Inlet**. The falls were dammed for hydroelectric power earlier in the century, power to run a pulp mill that became a peeling ruin.

More than 3000 people lived here in the 1950s, enough to support a hospital, high school, hotel and Olympic-sized indoor swimming pool. When the mill closed in 1980, most of the town closed, too. A handful of people remain at the old townsite spreading out from the ferry dock, another hundred in **Martin Valley**, just west. A few homes, a firehall, the skeleton of a hotel and a modern school remain, but most of the townsite is disappearing beneath a vibrant green sea of blackberry bushes. The most obvious sign of habitation is the occasional splash of blue hydrangea in what was once a front garden.

Those who remain in Ocean Falls like it that way. The *Queen* fills walking tours up to the dam and a handful of Bed and Breakfast rooms in summer, fishing offers steady work the rest of the year and the untouched scenery is hard to beat in any season.

SHEARWATER

The **Shearwater Resort**, *1 Shearwater Rd, Shearwater, BC V0T 1B0, tel: (250) 957-2366; fax: (250) 957-2422,* moderate–expensive, is geared to ferry and sport fishing traffic. There are also several Bed and Breakfasts nearby.

Shearwater, on **Denny Island** an hour from McLoughlin Bay and Bella Bella, was famous as a fish-packing plant around the turn of the century and almost unknown as a seaplane base during World War II. Packing plant and air base are long gone, but Shearwater has become the centre for mid-coast commerce and tourism. The bay is a favourite stopping spot for fishing boats, plush sailboats and extravagant yachts plying the Inside Passage. The *Queen* stops long enough for a meal or a drink at the Resort, or spend several days cycling and hiking the island and exploring nearby waterways.

BELLA COOLA

Tourist Information: Tourism Bella Coola, *Box 670, Bella Coola, BC V0T 1C0; tel: (250) 982-2504.*

ACCOMMODATION

Cedar Inn, *MacKenzie St, Box 183, Bella Coola, BC V0T 1C0; tel: (250) 799-5316; fax: (250) 799-5610,* moderate, is the best hotel in town and closest to the ferry dock. The alternative is the **Bella Coola Motel**, *Box 188, Bella Coola, BC V0T 1C0; tel: (250) 799-5323,* which is slightly less expensive. Bed and Breakfasts come and go in **Hagensborg**, 10 mins east on Hwy 20; check *BC Accommodations* for current listings.

SIGHTSEEING

Alexander Mackenzie reached the Pacific Ocean at Bella Coola in 1793, disappointed not to have found the Columbia

315

River. Gold seekers followed the Bella Coola River upstream in the 1850s and Norwegian colonists settled just east in Hagensborg 40 years later. The Bella Coola Band of the Nuxalk Nation has lived in the flat, narrow valley surrounded by soaring snow-capped peaks for millennia, fishing the rich waters and combing the warm valley for seasonal crops and game.

The setting is stunning, from the bald eagles as common as crows along the river to the pasture-like expanse of tidal meadows between the town and Government Wharf, 2 km west, and the vast glacier-carved mountains rising on all sides. The best view of North Bentinck Arm, the 100-km long arm of the Pacific Ocean that ends at Government Wharf, is from the gravel road that continues past the wharf to Clayton Falls Creek and beyond.

The surrounding mountains are filled with recreational opportunities from mountain climbing and mountain biking to easy walks, fishing and birding. **Dream Factory Adventures**, *Cedar Inn, Box 188, Bella Coola, BC V0T 1C0; tel: (800) 707-3363 or (250) 982-2312,* is the largest local outfitter for land-based adventures. **Bella Coola Outfitting Co**, *Box 336, Bella Coola, BC V0T 1C0; tel: (250) 982-2933; fax: (250) 982-2932,* specialises in fishing, whale watching and other water activities.

In town, don't miss the **totem poles** in front of the Bella Coola Band administrative headquarters, **The House of Noomyst Long House**, a traditional long house, and fine First Nations carvings and paintings on the outside of **Acwsalcta**, the School of the Nuxalk Nation, 4 km east off Hwy 20.

BELLA COOLA–KAMLOOPS

This 755 km trek is a microcosm of British Columbia, climbing from the temperate coast through the trackless Coast Mountains to the rolling vastness of the Chilcotin Plateau and down the Cariboo Gold Rush Trail into the semi-desert cattle ranching country of Kamloops. Allow time and energy for some of the most challenging and least-travelled highways in British Columbia, including major stretches of gravel road. The entire route can be driven in two frantic days, but try to allow at least four nights to absorb the expansive beauty of interior BC and explore the maze of side roads and walking paths leading off the major highways. Better still, take a week and add the highly recommended side track to the gold rush town of Barkerville.

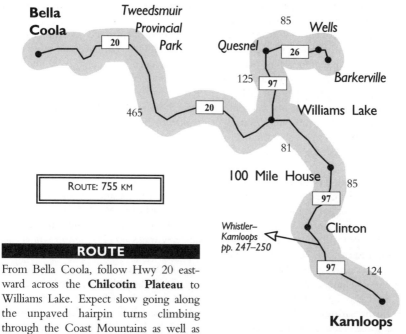

Bella Coola **Tweedsmuir Provincial Park** **20** **465** **20**

Quesnel **85** **Wells** **26** **125** **97** **Barkerville** **Williams Lake** **81** **100 Mile House** **85** **97** **Whistler–Kamloops pp. 247–250** **Clinton** **97** **124** **Kamloops**

ROUTE: 755 KM

317

ROUTE

From Bella Coola, follow Hwy 20 eastward across the **Chilcotin Plateau** to Williams Lake. Expect slow going along the unpaved hairpin turns climbing through the Coast Mountains as well as straighter gravel sections around Kleena Kleene. At Williams Lake, take Hwy 97 south along what was once the Cariboo Wagon Road to Cache Creek and eastward to Kamloops. Best stopping points are **Nimpo Lake/Anahim Lake**, **Riske Creek**, **Williams Lake**, **100 Mile House**, **Clinton** and **Cache Creek**.

Accommodation is limited throughout interior BC; advance booking is highly recommended May–Sept as well as hunting and fishing seasons and all holidays.

BUSES

There is no link between Bella Coola and Kamloops, but Greyhound Lines of Canada operate a service between Quesnel and Kamloops. See OTT table 100.

BELLA COOLA TO TWEEDSMUIR PROVINCIAL PARK

Hwy 20 east runs gently uphill through the Bella Coola Valley, the main trade route through the Coastal Mountains long before Alexander Mackenzie walked and paddled from Lake Athabasca in Northern Alberta to the Pacific Ocean at Bella Coola in 1793. Coastal First Nations – the Heiltsuk, Nuxalk and Kwakwaka'wakw – traded oil from the eulachon, a small anchovy-like fish, with inland Dakelh or Carrier tribes for obsidian and other interior products.

The best example of local First Nations art is the exterior of **Acwsalcta**, the Nuxalk Nation school, 4 km east of Bella Coola. For more traditional arts, turn onto *Thorsen Creek Rd,* 1.5 km beyond Acwsalcta, to a **petroglyph** site with more than a hundred glyphs. Ask for directions to the gravel road.

Snootli Creek Fish Hatchery, 6 km beyond Thorsen Creek, is an attempt to replenish local salmon and steelhead stocks hit hard by logging and habitat destruction. The Norwegian village of **Hagensborg** lies 2.5 km east of the hatchery. Many of the hand-cut square timbered log barns and houses are a century old. The valley narrows and twists upward east of Hagensborg. **Burnt Bridge** lies at the western edge of Tweedsmuir Provincial Park.

TWEEDSMUIR PROVINCIAL PARK

Tweedsmuir Provincial Park, *181 First Ave N., Williams Lake, BC V2G 1Y8; tel: (250) 799-5526.* The park is open all year,

The Grease Trail

Centuries of spilled oil created what came to be called the **Grease Trail**. Part of the Trail has been recreated as the **Alexander Mackenzie Heritage Trail/Nuxalk-Carrier Grease Trail**, 420 tough kilometres of track from Bella Coola to Quesnel, on the Fraser River. The track roughly parallels Hwy 20 from Burnt Bridge, 49 km east of Bella Coola, into Tweedsmuir Provincial Park. The **Alexander Mackenzie Trail Association**, *Box 425, Kelowna, BC V1Y 7P1*, publish an excellent free brochure to Mackenzie's route.

but park headquarters, 13 km east; *tel: (250) 398-4414,* campsites and other facilities only open in summer. A 90-min loop trail leads to excellent views of Bella Coola River and a mountain that Mackenzie named Stupendous (2700m). BC's largest park with 994,246 hectares, Tweedsmuir is a mountain wilderness. Outside the Hwy 20 corridor, the park is accessible only by foot, horseback or floatplane.

The best view of **Horsetail Falls**, 5 km inside the park, is just west of the highway bridge. **Fisheries Pool**, 5 km east of the falls, offers a fine picnic and camping area and easy walks along salmon spawning and rearing channels. **Atnarko River Spawning Channels**, 3 km east, offers more riverside paths. Black and grizzly bears frequent the same trails in search of an easy salmon meal. Bears *always* have the right of way. If trails are closed, stay out: hungry bears are extremely dangerous (see p.35).

The paved road ends abruptly 14 km east at the foot of **The Hill**, 19 km of single-track hairpin turns, with neither verges nor guard-rails. The gravel road twists 1000 m up the mountainside, drops

318

300m, then climbs another 600m to Heckman Pass at the eastern edge of Tweedsmuir Park.

Use low gear to crawl up the 18% grade. It's even more important to use low gear to creep downhill in order to spare brakes from boiling and failing. Views are stupendous, but there are no lay-bys. RVs can expect difficulties on tight turns.

Bella Coola is justly proud of The Hill, surveyed and built by local volunteers in the 1950s after Provincial engineers said the job was impossible. Hwy 20 remains one of only four highways between the BC coast and interior (the others are Hwy 16 to Prince Rupert, Hwy 99 to Squamish and Hwy 1 to Vancouver).

An easy 8-km trail climbs north 1 km east of the brake check area at the top of The Hill to overlook the **Rainbow Range**, a string of ancient volcanoes stained red, yellow and purple by minerals. Heckman Pass, 1524m, and the park boundary are 6 km east. Continue down toward the Tsulko River with good views back to the multi-coloured mountains. First Nations mined obsidian at **Tsitsutl Peak**, 2500m, the highest Rainbow peak.

TWEEDSMUIR PROVINCIAL PARK TO WILLIAMS LAKE

The paved highway begins just west of **Anahim Lake**, a small First Nations community. **A.C. Christensen general store**, *Christensen Rd; tel: (250) 742-3266*, has local information and one of the best stocks of general goods in the Chilcotin. Gravel roads lead north along the Dean River, noted for fine steelhead and trout fishing. Check locally for road conditions before setting out. Beyond the end of the road lies the Nuxalk-Carrier Grease Trail and the Home Ranch, popularised in *Grass Beyond the Mountains* and *The Rancher Takes*

a Wife, by Rich Hobson. Cattle drives once followed the Grease Trail east to Quesnel or Vanderhoof.

Hwy 20 crosses the Dean River 13 km east of Anahim Lake. A historical marker commemorates the 1864 **Chilcotin War**. Victoria merchant Albert Waddinton attempted to build a road from Bute Inlet (opposite Campbell River on Vancouver Island) across the Chilcotin to the Cariboo gold fields. Fearing the twin epidemics of smallpox and miners, Tsilhqo'tin warriors killed eighteen roadbuilders, packers and settlers. The Tsilhqo'tin war chief and four others were executed by colonial troops, but the road was abandoned. The five were given posthumous pardons and a memorial following a 1993 justice inquiry.

Just beyond is **Nimpo Lake** and several May–Sept fishing resorts. The best is **The Dean River Resort**, *Box 80, Nimpo Lake, BC V0L 1R0; tel/fax: (250) 742-3332*, with lakefront cabins or fly-in accommodation on remote mountain lakes. **Country Inn Motel**, *Box 50, Nimpo Lake, BC V0L 1R0; tel/fax: (250) 742-3331*, is open all year. Both are moderate. The 12-km lake offers excellent fishing, boating and hiking, but frequent floatplanes into Tweedsmuir and surrounding wilderness areas can make it a noisy spot.

The pavement ends again just east of Nimpo Lake. The well-maintained gravel highway winds southward through Coast Range foothills. Rusty-red conifers around the village of **Kleena Kleene** are infested with pine beetles. **Tatla Lake**, 31 km beyond, is the halfway point to Williams Lake and the western edge of the Chilcotin Plateau. The gently rolling grasslands, also called the Fraser Plateau, stretch east to the Fraser River. Summer weather is deceptively gentle. Winter temperatures regularly dip to -50°C. **Pollywog Marsh**, 12 km east, is a pleasant rest stop lakeside.

319

Best view of the entire Tatla Lake valley is from a lay-by 22 km beyond the lake.

Paved road begins again 15 km east, just west of **Chilanko Forks**. The highway east is dotted with stunning views back to the Coast Range. Look for the bright blue church steeple of **Redstone**, sometimes called Alexis Creek after a Tsilhqo'tin leader during the Chilcotin War. Redstone straggles along the highway for several kilometres to the cemetery, crowded with graves from the Tsilhqo'tin and other northern Dene tribes.

Bull Canyon Provincial Recreation Area, 26 km east of the cemetery, is a pleasant picnic and camping spot in an aspen forest along the grey-green Chilcotin River. The canyon was the site of an epic battle between the Tsilhqo'tin and Secwepemc bands, and a cattle round-up point. **Alexis Creek**, the chief settlement in the eastern Chilcotin, is 9 km east. Ten km beyond is the steepled church of the **Anahim Reserve**, the largest of six Chilcotin reserves. **Lee's Corner**, 12 km east, is named after an ill-fated attempt to drive 200 head of cattle 2500 km through the mountains to the Klondike gold fields in 1896. The cattle died, but drover Lee returned to the Chilcotin to found a successful ranching dynasty.

A gravel side road leads to **Hanceville**, named for Tom Hance, the first cattle rancher in the area. The road continues south and west to **Ts'yl-os Provincial Park**, *181 First Ave N., Williams Lake, BC V2G 1Y8; tel: (250) 799-5526*, created to protect traditional First Nations lands from logging. Tatlayoko and Chilko Lakes are popular for fishing, the rest of the park is accessible only by foot, horseback or air.

One of the best views of the Chilcotin is from a rest area at the top of a long grade 13 km east of Lee's Corner. A plaque details Lee's disastrous cattle drive. Several

fine examples of traditional wooden fences snake along the south side of the highway travelling east. Look for the golden log walls of the moderate **Chilcotin Lodge**, *Box 2, Riske Creek, BC V0L 1T0; tel/fax: (250) 659-5646*, 35 km beyond the rest area. The former hunting lodge has been reborn as a fine Bed and Breakfast, restaurant and campsite catering to outdoor enthusiasts. The town of **Riske Creek**, named for an early rancher, is 1.5 km east at the log cabins painted bright yellow on the north side of Hwy 20.

Another 1.5 km east is a good gravel road leading 16 km to **Farwell Canyon** and a wooden bridge across the Chilcotin River. The road follows the curves of the treeless plain before dropping into Farwell Canyon. Chilcotin River has cut deeply into golden limestone, leaving towering pinnacles and fairy-tale hoodoos topped with sand dunes. There are early rock paintings on the overhang south of the bridge and fish ladders beneath. Tsilhqot'in fishermen dip-net salmon in summer and fall, drying the catch on racks nearby. The area around the confluence of the Chilcotin and Fraser Rivers is the **Junction Sheep Range Provincial Park**, a reserve for California bighorn sheep, more than 40 butterfly species, birds, bears and other wildlife. Return to Riske Creek or continue the 50 km loop west to Hwy 20 at Lee's Corner.

The huge antennas 11 km east of Riske Creek are part of a long-range navigation system. The Loran-C station is sometimes open for tours; *tel: (250) 659-5611*, in advance. Continue east across **Becher's Prairie**, rolling grassland strewn with boulders deposited by retreating glaciers. Nesting boxes on fenceposts attract bluebirds and tree swallows which feast on the mosquitoes that can plague the small lakes and ponds dotting the Chilcotin.

The eastern edge of the plateau is the immense Fraser River trench. Watch for slow-moving logging trucks on the steep grades at both ends of the Sheep Creek Bridge over the river. The mouth of the Fraser River is 500 km south. Continue 25 km east into Williams Lake.

WILLIAMS LAKE

Tourist Information: Williams Lake and District Chamber of Commerce, *1148 S. Broadway (Hwy 97), Williams Lake, BC V2G 1A2; tel: (250) 392-5025; fax: (250) 392-4214*, open daily (July–Aug), Mon–Fri (Sept–June).

ACCOMMODATION

S8 is the only chain. Other choices include the **Fraser Inn**, *285 Donald Rd, Williams Lake, BC V2G 4K4; tel: (800) 452-6789; fax: (250) 398-8269*, and **Overlander Hotel**, *1118 Lakeview Crescent, Williams Lake, BC V2G 1A3; tel: (800) 663-6898; fax: (250) 392-3983*, both moderate.

SIGHTSEEING

Williams Lake missed the Cariboo gold rush bonanza because the local roadhouse owner refused a short-term loan to Cariboo Road builders. The miffed construction company built through 150 Mile House, where more obliging publicans grew wealthy on the new traffic. Williams Lake stagnated until the Great Pacific Eastern Railway arrived in 1920, rerouting traffic into what has become one of BC's fastest-growing towns.

Stampede, BC's largest rodeo, is held the first weekend in July. **Museum of the Cariboo Chilcotin**, *113 N. 4th Ave; tel: (250) 392-7404*, focuses on the ranching and rodeo history of the Chilcotin and the Cariboo region stretching east of the Fraser River. The former BC Rail station has become **The Station House Gallery**, *1*

Mackenzie Ave N.; tel: (250) 392-6113; fax: (250) 392-4051, specialising in BC artists. **Cariboo Friendship Society**, *99 S. Third Ave; tel: (250) 398-6831; fax: (250) 398-6115*, has the area's best selection of First Nations art and a good budget restaurant. **Scout Island Nature Centre**, *Scout Island, off Hwy 97 east of city centre; tel: (250) 398-8532*, has lakeside walking paths, wildlife viewing areas and a May–Aug Nature House exhibit centre.

⤵ SIDE TRACK
FROM WILLIAMS LAKE

This 210-km route follows the final leg of the Cariboo Gold Rush route to **Quesnel** and **Barkerville**. Take Hwy 97 north to Quesnel, paralleling the Fraser River, then go east on Hwy 26 to **Wells** and Barkerville.

The Cariboo Wagon Road ran from 150 Mile House to **Soda Creek**, the head of the upper Fraser canyon and the start of 650 km of navigable waters. The tiny town (estimated population 30) was once a booming terminal for steamboats that plied the Fraser north to Quesnel and Prince George. Trains replaced steamboats in the 1920s, but the bubbling creek, caused by carbonate of lime in the streambed, remains. **Xats'ull Heritage Village**, *Site 15, Comp. 2, RR#4, Williams Lake, BC V2G 4M8; tel: (250) 297-6323; fax: (250) 297-6300*, offers cultural and historical programmes at a recreated Shuswap Nation village above the Fraser River.

Marguerite Ferry, 32 km north, crosses the Fraser, guided by an overhead cable and powered by the river current. Four km north is the **Fort Alexandria Monument**, the limit of Alexander Mackenzie's river trip down the Fraser in 1793 and the site of an 1821 North West Company fur trading post. Mackenzie eventually took the advice of Carrier bands and returned upstream to Quesnel to follow the Grease Trail to Bella Coola.

QUESNEL

Tourist Information: Quesnel and District Visitor InfoCentre, *703 Carson Ave, Quesnel, BC V2J 2B6; tel: (250) 992-8716; fax: (250) 992-9606,* open daily (May–Sept), Mon–Fri (Sept–May).

ACCOMMODATION

There are no chain hotels. **Cascade Inn**, *383 Laurent Ave, Quesnel, BC V2J 2E1; tel: (800) 663-1581* or *(250) 992-5575; fax: (250) 992-2254,* and **Good Knight Inn**, *176 Davie St, Quesnel, BC V2J 2S7; tel: (800) 663-1585* or *(250) 992-2187; fax: (250) 992-1208,* are among the dozen moderate motels.

SIGHTSEEING

Quesnel is named after a member of Mackenzie's party, but the town attracted little attention until the Cariboo Gold Rush. Thousands of miners trekked the Cariboo Road to Soda Creek, boarded steamers for Quesnel, then walked east to Barkerville. There is still enough gold in rivers to keep prospectors busy. It's illegal to pan in staked, or claimed, territory, but the confluence of the Fraser and Quesnel Rivers within the city limits is set aside for public panning. The **Quesnel and District Museum and Archives,** *705 Carson Ave (in LeBourdais Park); tel: (250) 992-9580,* can suggest other places. The museum is a repository of local artefacts, including an outstanding collection of photographs from 1865 onwards.

Heritage Corner, *Carson and Front Sts,* where Hwy 97 turns north for Prince George, is the historical centre of

town. The 1929 bridge across the Fraser is now a footbridge. Oversized machinery in the riverside park is the remains of the gold rush steamer *Enterprise* and later mining equipment, including a wooden waterwheel. Quesnel's oldest building is the 1882 **Hudson's Bay Company Store**, *102 Carson St,* now a restaurant.

Quesnel has become a major timber, pulp, commercial and service centre for the north Cariboo. Forest and mill tours may be available through the Visitor Info Centre, or continue north 3 km on Hwy 97 to the **Quesnel Forest Industry Observation Tower**, overlooking four lumber mills, two pulp mills and related industries packed into the Two Mile Flat industrial park.

Turn east on Hwy 26, following signs for Barkerville and **Cottonwood House Historic Park**, *28 km east; tel: (250) 992-3997,* open May–Sept, adults $2, students $1, family $3, an 1864 roadhouse and farm built to serve Cariboo Road travellers. Costumed interpreters conduct tours and give period cooking and farming demonstrations. **Blessing's Grave Historic Park**, 11 km east of Cottonwood House, surrounds the isolated grave of one of the few miners murdered during the Cariboo Gold Rush.

WELLS

Tourist Information: Wells and District Chamber of Commerce, *Box 123, Wells, BC V0K 2R0; tel: (250) 994-2352.*

Wells was born of a second Cariboo Gold Rush in the 1930s. The Cariboo Gold Quartz Mining Co. closed its doors in 1967, but the town is slowly coming back to life as an arts and service centre for nearby Barkerville. The rebuilt **Wells Hotel**, *Box 39, Wells, BC*

V0K 2R0; tel: (800) 860-2299 or (250) 994-3427; fax: (250) 994-3494, moderate, is the best hotel in the Cariboo. Its **Pooley Street Cafe**, moderate–pricey, is one of BC's top-rated restaurants.

Birds, bears and other wildlife are common visitors to Wells, especially in the wetlands just east of town.

BARKERVILLE

Tourist Information: Barkerville Historic Town, *Box 19, Barkerville, BC V0K 1B0; tel: (250) 994-3332.* Adults $5.50, students $3.25, children $1, family $10.75, free mid Sept–late May. The town is open all year, but costumed interpreters offer demonstrations, theatre performances, wagon rides and more in summer.

In 1862, Billy Barker discovered gold on Williams Creek, sparking a gold rush that turned the Cariboo Road into the eighth wonder of the world. For the better part of a decade, Barkerville was the largest town in North America west of Chicago and north of San Francisco. The rough and tumble shanty town was so rich it very nearly outbid Victoria to become the capital of British Columbia. More than 125 heritage buildings remain, many restored. The bawdy houses remain shuttered, but theatres, restaurants, churches and Chinese groceries open for business.

For an even better sense of life in the 19th century, walk the last 1.6 km of the Cariboo Wagon Road from Barkerville to **Richfield** with *A Walk to Richfield*, a brochure keyed to eighteen historic sites. The brochure is available at the Barkerville entrance. The Wagon Road is open for Nordic skiing in winter. Return to Quesnel and follow Hwy 97 north to Prince George or south to Williams Lake and Kamloops.

WILLIAMS LAKE TO 100 MILE HOUSE

From Williams Lake, Hwy 97 winds through the forested hills of the Cariboo, broken by occasional agricultural areas. **150 Mile House**, 15 km south of Williams Lake, is a small local service centre. Like other mile house towns, it was named for the distance from Lillooet on the Cariboo Wagon Road. The vast wetlands south toward Lac la Hache are part of a waterfowl habitat restoration project.

Lac la Hache claims to be BC's longest town, a small settlement stretching along the shores of Lac la Hache. The lake was named for an axe dropped through winter ice by a French Canadian fur trapper early in the last century. **108 Mile House**, *Box 2002, 100 Mile House, BC V0K 2E0; tel: (250) 791-5288,* is a collection of heritage buildings from the area, including one of the largest log barns in Canada and the original 105 Mile Ranch house, now a museum: guided tours late May–late Sept.

100 MILE HOUSE

Tourist Information: South Cariboo Chamber of Commerce, *Box 2312, 100 Mile House, BC V0K 2E0; tel: (250) 395-5353; fax: (250) 395-4085*; **Visitor InfoCentre**, *Hwy 97 beside the giant skis.* The marsh behind the InfoCentre is a good spot for birding.

The Hills Guest Ranch, *C-26, 108 Mile Ranch, BC V0K 2Z0; tel: (250) 791-5225; fax: (250) 791-6384,* moderate–expensive, is the best-equipped accommodation in the area with a full restaurant, spa, horseback riding, walking, Nordic skiing and other activities spread across 8000 hectares. *BW* is the only chain in the area.

100 Mile House has grown from an isolated stopping point to become the service centre for the central Cariboo and a

323

major producer of log houses for North America and Japan. In winter, the town becomes a Nordic skiing mecca. **Mt Timothy Ski Hill,** *Box 33, 100 Mile House, BC V0K 2E0; tel/fax: (250) 395-3773,* is the largest alpine ski area in the Cariboo. Just south of town is the **100 Mile House Demonstration Forest.** Self-guided walking tour brochures from local forest companies are available at the Visitor InfoCentre as well as self-guided *Dry Belt Forestry Tour* driving brochures. Both tours take 2–3 hrs.

100 MILE HOUSE TO CLINTON

The countryside becomes progressively drier as Hwy 97 heads south and east. **93 Mile House** was the scene of the largest robbery in Cariboo history, $15,000 in gold dust, nuggets and bricks taken from the BX (British Columbia Express Company) stagecoach. The highwayman was captured, but his loot has never been found. **Chasm Provincial Park**, 41 km south of 93 Mile House, is a spectacular cleft through 120m of lava revealing brilliant reds and yellows from eruptions twelve to fifteen million years ago. Colours in the 1.5 km gorge, cut by glacial melt about 10,000 years ago, are best in late afternoon.

CLINTON

Tourist Information: Clinton and District Chamber of Commerce, *1522 Cariboo Hwy, Clinton, BC V0K 1K0; tel: (250) 459-2640.*

ACCOMMODATION

Clinton calls itself the Guest Ranch Capital of BC. Nearby valleys are dotted with budget–pricey ranches; accommodation ranges from tepees to posh cottages. **Big Bar Guest Ranch,** *Box 27, Jesmond, Clinton, BC V0K 1K0; tel/fax: (250) 459-2333,*

moderate, was one of the first and is still among the most complete ranches. Activities focus on range riding, backcountry horsepacking, river rafting and Nordic skiing, most pitched for beginners. **Nomad Motel,** *Box 142, Clinton, BC V0K 1K0; tel: (888) 776-6623* or *(250) 459-2214; fax: (250) 459-2189,* and **Round Up Motel,** *1214 Kelly Lake Rd, Clinton, BC V0K 1K0; tel: (250) 459-2226,* both budget–moderate, are top in-town choices.

SIGHTSEEING

Clinton was originally called Junction, for the wagon roads which met here and headed north for the gold fields. Queen Victoria changed the name to honour her Colonial Secretary. The town is something of a throwback, including a physician's advertisement on the short main street: 'Bones Set – Blood Let – Holes Patched – Babies Hatched'. The **South Cariboo Historical Museum,** *1419 Cariboo Hwy, Clinton, BC V0K 1K0; tel: (250) 459-2442,* chronicles area history from gold rush to cowboy country in an 1892 brick schoolhouse that was later used as a courthouse. Many of the early settlers are still in residence at the **Pioneer Cemetery** just north of town. The **Clinton Ball,** held in May each year since 1868, is the oldest continuous celebration in BC.

Several shallow lakes lie near the road south of Clinton. A gravel lay-by 22 km from town commemorates the BX, the British Columbia Express Company stage line that provided the fastest, safest link between the Cariboo gold fields and the rest of the world for half a century. Red and gold BX coaches originally started at Yale, head of navigation on the Fraser River, later from Ashcroft. The 450-km journey to Barkerville took four days.

Follow the last section of the Whistler–Kamloops route (see pp. 247–250).

PORT HARDY–PRINCE RUPERT

This fifteen-hour ferry journey is the single most popular cruise in British Columbia. The year-round marine route from the north end

Prince Rupert

Ferry Route

Port Hardy

of Hwy 19 on Vancouver Island through the Inside Passage to the west end of Hwy 16, the transcontinental Yellowhead Highway, passes some of the most dramatic coastal scenery in North America. In winter, the huge car ferry may be the only ship in sight between Port Hardy and Prince Rupert; in summer, expect to see a steady stream of ferries, fishing boats, pleasure craft and luxury cruise ships sailing between Vancouver and Alaska.

325

ROUTE: 15 HOURS

ROUTE

Two ships provide daily June–Sept sailings between Port Hardy and Prince Rupert. Ships depart both ports at 0730 to arrive at 2230 the same evening. In May, there are twice-weekly departures and one return trip each week Oct–Apr. Check BC Ferries schedules for off-season departure and arrival times.

Advance booking is required for vehicles all year and strongly recommended for foot passengers, especially in summer when tour groups fill ferries to capacity; **BC Ferries,** *1112 Fort St, Victoria, BC V8V 4V2; tel: (888) 223-2779* or *(250) 386-3431; fax: (250) 381-5452.* Space for May and Sept sailings *may* be available at the last minute, but book four–six months in advance for June, July and Aug. All bookings can be changed, subject to availability and a $50 per segment re-booking fee.

Port Hardy vehicles and passengers board at the **Bear Cove Ferry Dock** (see p.309). In Prince Rupert, follow *Second Ave* (Hwy 16) west from the city centre to the ferry docks. Boarding begins one hour before sailing at both ports. It's wise to board as early as possible to claim a window seat for the best views. Most hotels and motels in both ports can arrange transport to and from the dock for foot passengers. Allow about $350 for car and driver plus $120 per additional passenger for a single journey. Motorcycles and bicycles cost less, RVs more.

Unlike the Discovery Coast ferry route (see p.312), vehicle decks are locked while at sea, so be sure to bring adequate clothing onto the passenger decks. Summer weather is usually fine, but fog, rain and wind are no strangers to the mid-coast in every season. Comfortable clothing is the rule, including flat shoes for walking about the deck, up and down stairs and on shore. Coastal weather is as fickle as it is in the mountains. Repeat passengers eschew shorts and sandals for long pants and closed shoes in case of clammy fog or a chill rain. Bring jumpers and jackets with hoods (against wind and rain) even if the weather

forecast calls for brilliant sun and 28°C for the next week. In winter, expect rain, fog, cold and storms, but seldom snow.

BC Ferries are working vessels, not cruise ships. There are no casinos, no saunas and no fancy dress dinners. There *is* a fine moderate–pricey dining room, complete with white linen tablecloths, but most passengers opt for the cheap–budget cafeteria which serves full meals and snacks. There is also a licensed lounge, video arcade, games, free videos and a gift shop. Private cabins can be reserved at extra cost, but most passengers prefer the large public cabins equipped with tables and extremely comfortable reclining chairs.

The best view seats are along the windows in the forward cabin on **Promenade Deck**. Seats cannot be reserved, so board early for the best views. Crowding is seldom a problem Sept–May, but there is usually a scramble for seats in summer. Ferries also have ample outside deck space to watch the passing scenery and scan for orcas, whales, dolphins, bald eagles and passing ships. Cameras and binoculars are almost obligatory.

Expect a calm passage no matter what the weather, though the ship occasionally rocks across the open waters of Queen Charlotte Sound, just north of Vancouver Island. The remainder of the Inside Passage route is extremely well protected from storms and ocean swells by the maze of islands lying just off the BC coast. Prince Rupert is the rainiest city in BC, but storms usually pass quickly, especially in summer.

BUSES

For details of services, see OTT table 28.

PRINCE RUPERT

Tourist Information: Prince Rupert Travel InfoCentre, *100 1st Ave E., Prince*

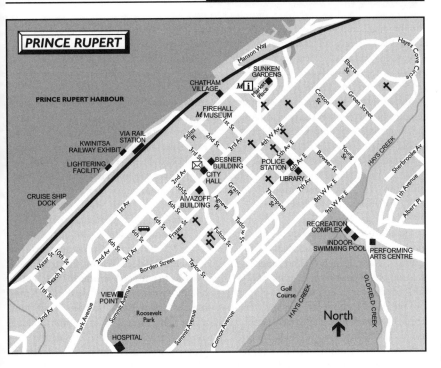

PRINCE RUPERT

PRINCE RUPERT HARBOUR

SUNKEN GARDENS

CHATHAM VILLAGE

M i

Market Place

Manson Way

Eberts St.

Hayes Cove Circle

Green Street

Cotton St.

FIREHALL
M MUSEUM

VIA RAIL STATION

KWINITSA RAILWAY EXHIBIT

Stiles Pl.

2nd St.

3rd Av E

4th W AV E

3rd Av E

5th Av E

Bowser St.

Young St.

HAYS CREEK

Sherbrooke Av

LIGHTERING FACILITY

3rd St.

BESNER BUILDING

POLICE STATION

2nd Av

5th St.

CITY HALL

LIBRARY

6th Av E

7th St.

8th W AV E

9th W AV E

11 th Avenue

Albert Pl

CRUISE SHIP DOCK

1st Av

ALVAZOFF BUILDING

6th St.

Agnew Pl

Grant

Thompson St.

Tatlo w St.

RECREATION COMPLEX

INDOOR SWIMMING POOL

PERFORMING ARTS CENTRE

Water St.

10th St.

Beach Pl

2nd Av

3rd Av

6th St.

Fraser St.

Taylor St.

Fulton St.

Borden Street

Golf Course

HAYS CREEK

OLDFIELD CREEK

11 th St.

2nd Av

VIEW POINT

Park Avenue

Summit Avenue

Roosevelt Park

Summit Avenue

Comox Avenue

North

HOSPITAL

Rupert, BC V8J 3S1; tel: (800) 667-1994 or *(250) 624-5637; fax: (250) 627-8009.*

ACCOMMODATION

The most central choice is the **Coast Prince Rupert Hotel**, *118 6th St, Prince Rupert, BC V8J 3L7; tel: (800) 663-1144 or (250) 624-6711; fax: (250) 624-3288,* moderate. Pricey **Crest Motor Hotel**, *222 W. First Ave, Prince Rupert, BC V8J 3P6; tel: (800) 663-8150 or (250) 624-6771; fax: (250) 627-7666,* has better views but is less convenient for the centre. Several motels are located on *2nd Ave* between the ferry dock and downtown.

EATING AND DRINKING

Fish, particularly halibut or salmon, is almost always a good choice in this busy fishing port. **Smile's Seafood Cafe**, *113 Cow Bay Rd; tel: (250) 624-3072,* is the oldest and best-known fish restaurant in town, budget–moderate. **Breakers Pub**, *117 George Hills Way; tel: (250) 624-5990,* budget–moderate, has equally tasty fish and a livelier atmosphere. **Cow Bay Café**, *205 Cow Bay Rd; tel: (250) 627-1212,* moderate, offers an eclectic mix of local fish and Trinidadian dishes. The finest choice is **The Waterfront**, *222 W. First St (Crest Motor Hotel); tel: (250) 624-6771,* for pricey fish and steaks with a stunning sunset view, or enjoy the same view for the price of a drink.

SIGHTSEEING

Prince Rupert is a speculator's dream come true. Charles Hays, president of the Grand Trunk Railway at the turn of the century, had visions of a second, more northerly transcontinental railway across Canada. In collusion with the BC government, he bought huge holdings on little-known Kaien Island facing an immense harbour 23 km long and nearly 2 km wide near the mouth of the Skeena River. The first surveyors arrived in 1906, ready to turn grandiose plans by Francis Rattenbury, designer of Victoria's Parliament Buildings and Empress Hotel, into Canada's greatest Pacific port.

Instead, Hays went down with the *Titanic* in 1912, taking his grandiose vision with him. The first transcontinental train finally pulled into Prince Rupert in 1914, just in time for World War I. The Grand Trunk Railway failed after the Great War and became part of the Canadian National Railway, while Prince Rupert languished as a remote fishing port. It took another half-century for transPacific shipping to turn the grand harbour into a major freight terminal. Almost two sailing days closer to Asia than Vancouver, cargo ships can dock at Prince Rupert, unload directly onto railway carriages, and have goods halfway across the continent before competitors even reach the docks in Vancouver. Grain, coal and container port facilities may be open for tours depending on season and workload; ask for hours and directions at the InfoCentre. Most area pulp mills have closed in recent years; those which have survived generally do not offer tours.

A statue of Hays stands next to **City Hall**, *3rd Ave and 3rd St*. The totem pole next to Hays is part of an extensive carved pole tour; the InfoCentre has self-guiding brochures. Also at the InfoCentre is the **Museum of Northern B.C.**, *100 1st Ave E., Prince Rupert, BC V8J 3S1; tel: (250) 624-3207; fax: (250) 627-8009,* the largest museum on the North Coast. Displays span ten thousand years, from the first human habitation of the area after the last Ice Age to 19th-century missionaries and fish canneries and modern First Nations

carvings. The museum also sponsors daily archaeological tours around the harbour in summer, visiting village sites two thousand years old. The number and variety of village sites suggest that Prince Rupert was once among the most heavily populated areas on the Pacific Coast. The Tsimshian Nation works closely with the museum to locate and protect heritage sites in the area.

Guided heritage walking tours of the town leave the museum and InfoCentre daily in summer; *tel: (250) 624-5637*. In the off-season, ask for a self-guiding brochure. Highlights include **City Hall**, the **Firehall Museum**, *200 1st Ave; tel: (250) 627-4475,* with a lovingly restored 1925 REO Speed-Wagon fire truck, and **Pacific Mariners Memorial Park** on the hillside overlooking the harbour. **Kinsmen's Linear Park** provides a circle tour of the city, from the ferry terminal along the waterfront past Cow Bay to the seaplane base at Seal Cove, up a creek to McClymont Park and back to the city centre by way of an ancient cedar forest along Hays Creek. Directions and detailed maps of the roads, paths and railway rights-of-way that make up the park are available at the InfoCentre.

One local landmark not on the tour (nor open to the public) is **BC Packers** fish cannery, the largest operating salmon cannery in the world. Prince Rupert also has BC's oldest fish cannery, the **North Pacific Cannery Village Museum**, *1889 Skeena Dr., Port Edward, BC V0V 1G0; tel: (250) 628-3538,* open daily (May–Sept), Wed–Sun (Oct–Apr), about 20 mins east of town. Built in 1889, the salmon cannery is being restored, complete with canning machinery, a waterfront boardwalk, docks and employee housing. North Pacific is the sole survivor of more than a dozen canneries that once lined the shores of Inverness Passage, part of the Skeena River estuary.

PRINCE RUPERT– VALEMOUNT

The northern interior of British Columbia is a series of plateaux separated by mountain ranges and cut with wild rivers, 760 km from the Pacific Ocean to the western slopes of the Rocky Mountains. The human population is so sparse that much of the land is little changed since Alexander Mackenzie paddled through in 1793. Deer, elk, moose, cougars, bear and wolves still roam the vast landscape. Rivers still teem with salmon, steelhead and trout. And even in the biggest of towns, the bush is never more than a few blocks away.

329

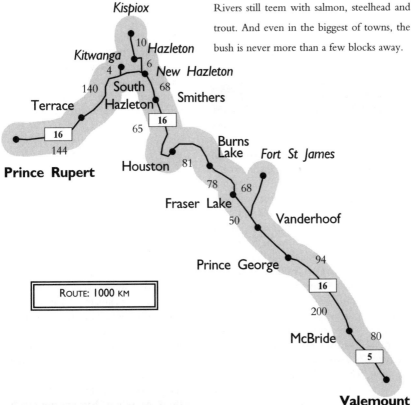

ROUTE: 1000 KM

ROUTE

From Prince Rupert, take Hwy 16, the Yellowhead Hwy, east through **Terrace**, **Smithers** and **Burns Lake** to **Prince George**. Continue south-east, paralleling the Fraser River between the Cariboo Mountains and the Rocky Mountains, to

Tête Jaune Cache. Turn south on Hwy 5 to **Valemount**. The drive can be made in two long days with an overnight in Prince George, but allow four to six days to enjoy the scenery and explore beyond the main route. Best stopping points are Terrace, Smithers, **Vanderhoof**, Prince George and **McBride**.

TRAINS AND BUSES

A VIA Rail service goes from Prince Rupert as far as Prince George three times a week, taking 12 hrs. See OTT table 7.

Greyhound Lines of Canada offer two bus trips a day, with a change in Prince George. Prince Rupert to Prince George takes 10½ hrs, Prince George to Valemount, 3½ hrs. OTT table 103.

PRINCE RUPERT TO TERRACE

Leave Prince Rupert via tidal **Butze Rapids**, which reverses directions with the tide. Foaming action is most spectacular on the falling tide. **Oliver Lake Park** protects 5 hectares of naturally stunted muskeg forest and insect-eating plants. Just beyond is Ridley Island Access Rd to coal and grain terminals. The Galloway Rapids bridge crosses from Kaien Island to the mainland.

At the mainland end of the bridge, turn right onto *Skeena Dr.* for Port Edward and **North Pacific Cannery Village Museum**; *tel: (250) 628-3538* (see p.328), or continue straight for Prince George. The highway passes gravel roads to **Diana Lake** and **Prudhomme Lake Provincial Parks**; *tel: (250) 847-7320*, with fishing, camping, hiking and stunning forest vistas, before meeting the broad **Skeena River**.

Skeena means 'river of mists' in the language of the Gitxsan and Tsimishian First Nations, who have inhabited the area since the last Ice Age. Swirling mists often obscure the distant riverbank. The river has long been a highway, first for 18-m cedar canoes, then for paddlewheel steamboats and now for Hwy 16 and a railway line. Harbour seals follow shoals of oily eulachon, candle fish, as well as coho, chinook, sockeye, pink and chum salmon 100 km upstream. Bald eagles, bears, ravens and other predators still hunt the forests and skies.

Best places to enjoy the scenery are **Basalt Creek Viewpoint**, 27 km east of Prudhomme Lake Park, and **Telegraph Point Rest Area,** 33 km beyond. **Exchamsiks River Provincial Park**; *tel: (250) 847-7320,* 30 km toward Terrace, has pleasant picnicking and camping and an easy nature trail beneath towering sitka spruce. **Shames River Flats** is a favourite local fishing area; 3 km east is the **Shames Mountain** turn-off; *tel: (250) 635-3773,* an alpine ski area with excellent summer hiking.

> ### SIDE TRACK TO RED SAND LAKE DEMONSTRATION FOREST
>
> Turn north on *West Kalum Rd,* a gravel logging road 18 km east of Shames Mountain. **The main forest,** *200-5220 Keith Ave, Terrace, BC V8G 1L1*; *tel: (250) 638-5100; fax: (250) 638-5734,* is 26 km from Hwy 16 in the transition zone between wet coastal and drier interior climates. Ancient volcanic eruptions created the red sand Kalum Lake beach at the main campsite. Three trails, all less than 4 km, cross managed and wild forest. A 1.66-km **Introduction Trail** is wheelchair accessible. The forest lies along trade routes used by Nisg'a and Kitsumkalum bands. Older trees are scarred where bark was stripped off to make clothing, rope and baskets in past decades. Look for early 20th-century farm homesteads.

TERRACE

Tourist Information: Terrace and District Chamber of Commerce, *4511 Keith Ave, Terrace, BC V8G 1K1; tel: (800) 499-1637 or (250) 635-0832; fax: (250) 635-2573.*

ACCOMMODATION AND FOOD

Top choice is **Coast Inn of the West**, *4620 Lakelse Ave, Terrace, BC V8G 1R1; tel: (800) 663-1144 or (250) 638-8141; fax: (250) 638-8999.* Other choices include **Alpine House Motel**, *4326 Lakelse Ave, Terrace, BC V8G 1N8; tel: (800) 663-3123 or (250) 635-7216; fax: (250) 635-4225,* and **Northern Motor Inn**, *3086 Hwy 16 E., Terrace, BC V8G 3N5; tel: (800) 663-3390 or (250) 635-6375; fax: (250) 635-6386,* all moderate.

Dante's Restaurante, *4606 Lazelle Ave; tel: (250) 635-7229,* serves good Italian dishes, budget–moderate.

SIGHTSEEING

Terrace is named for natural terraces cut by the Skeena River. The town was a major steamboat stop until the Grand Trunk Pacific Railway arrived in 1914. Today, Terrace lives on timber, sport fishing and tourism. **Skeena Sawmills**; *tel: (250) 635-6336,* offer tours.

Terrace is known for salmon and bears. Local First Nations legends tell of a white Spirit Bear that takes human form to punish evil-doers and rescue those in distress. The white bear is the **Kermode** (kermodie), a honey-blond to white subspecies of the black bear. The best place to spot Kermode, as well as its more common black and brown relatives, is the city dump.

The Skeena River and its tributaries offer some of the finest salmon fishing in North America. World record fish have been caught within walking distance of the city centre. Salmon also brought the Kitselas and Kitsumkalum Bands. The Kitsumkalum **House of Sim-Oi-Ghets**, *West Kalum Rd; tel: (250) 638-1629,* has the area's best supply of Native artworks. **Northern Light Studio & Gardens**, *4820 Halliwell Ave, Terrace, BC V8G 2J4; tel: (250) 638-1403; fax: (250) 638-0641,* offers a wide selection of arts as well as quiet Japanese-style outdoor gardens. **Heritage Park**, *Kerby Rd, Box 246, Terrace, BC V8G 4A6; tel: (250) 635-2508,* is an excellent collection of nine heritage buildings filled with regional artefacts and historic photographs. Look for a roadside rest and signpost 9 km beyond **Usk** detailing the steamboat traffic that once churned another 85 km inland to Hazleton.

SIDE TRACK TO KITWANGA

Seventy-two km from Usk, take Hwy 37 north across the Skeena River. Turn right into the Gitxsan village of **Gitwangak**. The name means 'place of rabbits', but keep a sharp eye out for children playing along the road near a line of totem poles carved as early as 1875. Tourist information may be available at **St. Paul's Anglican Church**, across from the totems. The English stained-glass windows are 400 years old; the wooden bell tower bears a resemblance to Norse stave churches.

Continue on Hwy 37 to the village of **Kitwanga**, 4 km north. Follow signs to **Kitwanga Fort National Historic Site**, *Fort St James National Historic Park, Box 1148, Fort St James, BC V0J 1P0; tel: (250) 996-7191.* The site is a tall rounded hill once surrounded by palisades and crowned by cedar plank redoubts.

The fort was a major strongpoint on the Grease Trail that linked Gitxsan villages to eulachon fisheries on the Nass

331

Boats and Islands

Unless Pacific Northwest drivers take to amphibious automobiles, much of British Columbia's coastline will remain inaccessible by land. Boat travel is a way of life. **BC Ferries**, *1112 Fort St, Victoria, BC V8V 4V2; tel: (888) 223-3779 or (250) 386-3431; fax: (250) 381-5452*, is one of the largest and busiest ferry systems in the world. Its 40 vessels serve 42 ports of call scattered along more than 1000 km of BC coastline. BC Ferries are sightseeing ships and basic transport, weaving between islands and threading narrow passages that are off limits to the immense cruise ships sailing the main channel of the **Inside Passage** (between Vancouver Island and the mainland) between Vancouver and Alaska.

The most popular ferry routes are Vancouver (Tsawwassen and Horseshoe Bay) to Vancouver Island (Swartz Bay, Nanaimo and Duke Point) and Vancouver to the Gulf Islands. One of the busiest summer circle routes is Vancouver to Nanaimo by ferry, by road to Port Hardy, ferry through the Inside Passage to Prince Rupert and road back to Vancouver.

Port Hardy–Prince Rupert summer sailings are booked months in advance. Advance vehicle bookings are required all year, although drive-on space is generally available in winter.

Advance bookings are required for both passengers and vehicles **Prince Rupert–Queen Charlotte Islands** and the summer-only **Discovery Coast Passage** route, **Port Hardy–Bella Coola**, on BC's mid-coast. The run twists through some of the most scenic islands in the Northwest. The flexible schedule has as many as seven stops, depending on the sailing date, taking between 15 and 30 hours.

Namu has BC's oldest archaeological site as well as an immense abandoned fish plant, both open for tours, and a Native art centre. **McLoughlin Bay** offers marine tours and some of the finest fishing along the coast. **Ocean Falls** and **Klemtu** provide historical walking tours. Isolation has helped **Bella Coola** preserve its First Nations/Norwegian history and charm. BC Ferries can provide lodging information for intermediate stops, or passengers can sleep on board in reclining seats. There are no cabins. BC Hwy 20 runs from Bella Coola through the interior of BC and south to Vancouver (see p. 226).

Alaska Marine Highway car and passenger ferries, *Box 25535, Juneau, AK 99802; tel: (800) 642-0066; fax: (907) 277-4829*, sail the Inside Passage between Bellingham, WA, Prince Rupert, BC and Alaska. Book staterooms and vehicle space as early as possible for summer sailings. Winter departures can be booked a few weeks before sailing.

Every coastal town on Vancouver Island has its own fleet of boats for local ferry service, fishing, scuba diving, whale watching and other water activities. The **MV Lady Rose** carries passengers as well as cargo to the Broken Group of Islands, Ucluelet and Bamfield from Port Alberni (p. 340). Advance bookings are required all year. The **MV Uchuck III**, *Box 57, Gold River, BC V0P 1G0; tel: (250) 283-2325; fax: (250) 283-7582; email: mvuchuck@goldrvr.island.net*, offers similar passenger, kayak and cargo service to Nootka Sound and Kyuquot Sound on the northwest coast of the island. The ship sails from Gold River, west of Campbell River.

Expect migrating grey whales in spring and autumn plus orcas, bears, seals, sea otters and flocks of sea birds. A summer-only day trip to Nootka Sound includes a stop at Resolution Cove, where Capt James Cook first landed on Vancouver Island in 1792. Trips last 1–2 days, with overnights in Bed and Breakfasts. Advance bookings are crucial, especially in summer.

Marine Link Tours, *Box 451, Campbell River, BC V9W 5C1; tel: (250) 286-337; fax: (250) 286-1149*, offer passage on the *MV Aurora Explorer*, a working freighter. The 30-m landing craft hauls general cargo and heavy equipment to lumber camps, fish farms, fly-in resorts, remote communities and isolated homesteads from its base in Campbell River. Destinations vary. Expect to spend two to six days wandering coastal inlets as far north as Bella Coola.

River, 100 km north. Kitwanga's last defender was Nekt, an immense warrior who wore a grizzly bear hide lined with slate tables for armour. Grease trails and fort lost importance as Native institutions were eroded by White encroachment in the early 1800s. 🔼

Back on Hwy 16, **Seeley Lake Provincial Park**, *3790 Alfred Ave, Bag 5000, Smithers, BC V0J 2N0; tel: (250) 847-7320*, has excellent Hazleton Mountain views. Continue past **South Hazleton** to the **Hazleton Area Visitor InfoCentre**, *Box 340, New Hazleton, BC V0J 2J0; tel: (250) 842-6071*, at the Hwy 16/Hwy 62 junction. Look for fibreglass statues of a mule packer, a miner and a logger.

🔼 **SIDE TRACK FROM NEW HAZLETON**
Take Hwy 62 left at the Visitor InfoCentre. Cross Hagwilget Bridge over the Bulkley River. Continue past *Kispiox Valley Rd* to **'Ksan** and **Hazleton**. Return to *Kispiox Valley Rd* and turn left 13 km to **Kispiox**.

South Hazleton is a modern village with food, accommodation and petrol. **New Hazleton** is an early 20th-century railway town. **Hazleton**, 6 km north-west, is the original riverside settlement. All three are dominated by **Mt Rocher Déboulé**, the 'mountain of rolling stone' named by French Canadian miners plagued by landslides. To the Gitxsan, it's **Stii Kyo Kin**, 'stands alone', their cultural heart, soul and capital. The Hazletons have the greatest concentration of standing totem poles in BC. Watch for *Hands of History* information plaques, a stylised hand with an eye in the palm.

The single-track **Hagwilget Bridge** hangs 100m above the foaming Bulkley

River. The Gitxsan and Wet'suwet'en peoples once swayed over the same gorge on a footbridge of poles lashed with cedar bark rope. Hwy 62 curves through rolling pasturelands to **'Ksan Indian Village**, *Box 326, Hazleton, BC V0J 1Y0; tel: (250) 842-5544; fax: (250) 842-6533*, open daily (mid Apr-Sept), a collection of heavily decorated longhouses, museum, carving shed and totems on a site that has been inhabited for seven thousand years.

Whites first appeared in significant numbers when steamboats began plying the Skeena to Hazleton in 1866. Miners, lumbermen and farmers followed. By 1910, sternwheelers were hauling equipment for Canada's second transcontinental railway, the Grand Trunk, which ended the riverboat era in 1914. Hazleton today could be a cinema set, from its Victorian-era buildings to a sternwheeler-style restaurant next to the town library and museum.

Hwy 62 parallels the Kispiox River north to **Kispiox**, an ancient Gitxsan village. Coho salmon run the famed fishing river Aug–Sept, steelhead Sept–Nov. The all-year attraction is 15 outstanding totem poles recording village history, with a rare weeping woman pole. **Bent Box Gallery** and **Hidden Place Gallery** sell fine local art. 🔼

The Bulkley River narrows to just 15m at **Moricetown**, 35 km east of New Hazleton. The Wet'suwer'en have fished the falls for at least 4000 years, gaffing salmon each autumn and drying them on nearby racks. Just south is **Adams Igloo**; *tel: (250) 847-3188*, a collection of mounted BC animals and birds.

333

SMITHERS
Tourist Information: Smithers and

The Queen Charlotte Islands

The **Queen Charlotte Islands**, *Queen Charlotte Islands Travel InfoCentre, 3922 Hwy 33, Box 337, Queen Charlotte City, BC V0T 1S0; tel: (250) 559-4742*, are as close to the British Columbia seen by Capt Cook and other early explorers as still exists. The hundred and fifty or so islands form an elongated triangle 250 km long some 90 km west of Prince Rupert. Early traders called them the Misty Islands for the two hundred days of fog, drizzle and rain that blanket the dense rain forest each year. The original **Haida** inhabitants called them 'Haida Gwaii', The Land of the People.

Legendary for their art, frequent raids and fierce domination up and down the coast, precious few of those People remain today. Smallpox and other epidemics introduced by White traders and missionaries killed more than 90% of the population. The rain forest has fared somewhat better, thanks largely to the 1988 creation of **Gwaii Haanas National Park,** *Box 37, Queen Charlotte City, BC V0T 1S0; tel: (250) 559-8818.*

The park, which was supported by the Haida over the fierce objections of timber and mining interests, covers 15% of the archipelago, including much of Moresby Island, the second largest in the archipelago, from development. The visual highlight is vast stretches of virgin rain forest with 1000-year-old trees whose 70-m tops disappear into the swirling mist most days. The park also protects several Haida villages that were abandoned during the epidemics of the last century.

The most famous – and the most scenic – is **Ninstints**, on **Anthony Island**. The village, which was abandoned in 1900 after 90% of the population died, was declared a UNESCO world cultural heritage site in 1981. The 200-year-old wooden buildings and towering totem poles are slowly disappearing beneath accumulating moss and crumbling back into the forest. Prior permission must be obtained from Parks Canada before visiting Ninstints and other First Nations sites.

One of the best places to explore Haida art and history is the **Queen Charlotte Islands Museum,** *RR1 Second Beach Rd, Skidegate, BC V0T 1S1; tel: (250) 559-4643.* The museum houses a number of historic totem poles as well as contemporary carvings in wood and stone, metal, glass and other media.

According to Haida legend, humanity first appeared on **Rose Spit**, which extends from the north-east corner of **Graham Island**, the largest of the group, ten thousand years ago. That was where Raven, the great trickster god, prised open a clamshell that contained the Haida people and released them to the earth. A wooden carving by Haida artist Bill Reid at the University of British Columbia's Museum of Anthropology in Vancouver recounts the legend.

Archaeological evidence suggests that the islands have been inhabited at least that long. When Capt Juan Josef Perez traded with the Haida in 1774, there were about 7000 Haida in the islands. By 1915, epidemics had reduced the Native population to about 600. The Haida community has grown to around a thousand, many of them living in **Old Masset** and **Skidegate**, both on Graham Island. The balance of the Islands' population of 6000 live in nearby Masset, Port Clements, Tlell and Queen Charlotte City.

The Queen Charlottes remain a naturalist's dream despite extensive logging. Tiny Sitka deer, immense brown bears and haughty bald eagles frequent the shores; seals, porpoises and whales haunt the many inlets.

Access to the islands is easy, if limited. There are regular flights from Prince Rupert and Vancouver and passenger/vehicle ferry service from Prince Rupert. There is a small road system on Graham Island, but sea kayaks remain the most popular way to explore the archipelago.

District Chamber of Commerce, *Box 2379, Smithers, BC V0J 2N0; tel: (800) 542-6673* or *(250) 847-9854; fax: (250) 847-3337;* **Visitor InfoCentre**, *railway parlour car, east side of Hwy 16,* open daily (July–Aug).

ACCOMMODATION

Top choice is **Hudson Bay Lodge**, *3251 E. Hwy 16, Smithers, BC V0J 2N0; tel: (800) 663-5040* or *(250) 847-4581; fax: (250) 847-4878,* moderate.

SIGHTSEEING

Smithers is the largest town in the Bulkley Valley, dwarfed by the classical symmetry of **Hudson Bay Mountain** (2621m), with kilometres of walking paths and **Ski Smithers**, *tel: (800) 665-4299* or *(250) 847-2058*. **Smithers Community Forest**, *10 km west of Smithers; tel: (250) 847-5072,* preserves 4620 hectares of Hudson Bay Mountain forest. The park opens for Nordic skiing in winter. The Chamber of Commerce publishes hiking guides to all nearby mountain areas.

For a pleasant backroad drive, follow *Driftwood Creek Rd* 11 km to **Driftwood Canyon Provincial Park**, *3790 Alfred Ave, Smithers, BC V0J 2N0; tel: (250) 847-7320,* a slate cliff filled with plant, insect and animal fossils surrounded by forest. The excellent gravel road continues 35 km to Hwy 16 at Moricetown. Watch for moose, especially late afternoon–early evening.

Central Park Building, *Hwy 16 and Main St,* houses **Bulkley Valley Museum**; *tel: (250) 847-5322,* **The Smithers Art Gallery**; *tel: (250) 847-3898,* and the **Chamber of Commerce**. To the east, *Main St* has been redone in Bavarian style, with red brick pavements and a statue of a man playing an alpenhorn. **Pacific Inland Resources**; *tel: (250) 847-2656,* offer summer tours of working woods and mill

with advance reservation. **Northern Lights Air**; *Box 850, Smithers, BC V0J 2N0; tel: (250) 847-4400; fax: (250) 847-4453,* sell sightseeing tours and fly-in, fly-out hiking, river rafting and other activities in the Hazleton and Babine Mountains.

HOUSTON

Tourist Information: Houston and District Chamber of Commerce, *Hwy 16 beneath the giant flyfishing rod, Box 396, Houston, BC V0J 1Z0; tel: (250) 845-7640.*

Houston began as a tie-cutting centre for the Grand Trunk Pacific Railway and still depends heavily on forest industries. The principal pastime is fishing, suggested by the 18-m flyrod cocked above the Travel InfoCentre. The town sits near the junction of the Morice and Bulkley Rivers, famous for steelhead fishing Aug–Nov.

The highest point on the Yellowhead Hwy is **Six Mile Summit**, 1423 m, 40km east of Houston.

335

BURNS LAKE

Tourist Information: Burns Lake and District Chamber of Commerce, *Box 339, Burns Lake, BC V0J 1E0; tel: (250) 692-3773; fax: (250) 692-3493.*

The town is the supply centre for the Lakes District, a region of lakes, meadows and second growth forests. Local guides claim 4828 km of fishing within a 100 km radius. Eleven km east is **Tintagel Cairn and Rest Area**, with a 45-kg chunk of wall from Tintagel Castle in Cornwall, England.

FRASER LAKE

Tourist Information: Fraser Lake Visitor InfoCentre, *65 Endako Ave, Box 430, Fraser Lake, BC V0J 1S0; tel: (250) 699-8841* or *(250) 699-6257; fax: (250) 699-6469,* open summer (June–late Sept) .

This pleasant lakeside town serves the

Lejac sawmill and Canada's largest molybdenum mine near Endako. A small InfoCentre museum recounts local history. Most area accommodation is in fishing resorts on Fraser, Francois and other lakes; among the best is **Stellako Lodge**, *Box 400, Fraser Lake, BC V0J 1S0; tel: (250) 699-6695*, moderate, with an excellent Swiss–Canadian restaurant.

⬆ SIDE TRACK
TO FORT ST JAMES

Follow Hwy 27 north for 68 km to Stuart Lake and the fort.

Tourist Information: Fort St James Chamber of Commerce, *Box 1164, Fort St James, BC V0J 1P0; tel: (250) 996-7023 or (250) 996-7063; fax: (250) 996-7047.*

Simon Fraser paddled into the Dakelh village of Nak'azdli in 1806 and named the region New Caledonia for its resemblance to Scotland. His North West Company fur post became the administrative centre between the Rocky and Coastal Mountains. When Hudson's Bay Company took over Fort St James in 1821, it became one of the most isolated posts in HBC's far-flung North American empire. Isolation eased as the Skeena River opened to steamboat traffic, but declining fur prices forced HBC to abandon the fort in the 1930s.

Forty years later, the site was restored to its 1896 appearance, including fully stocked warehouses, fish cache, officer and employee housing, trade store, kitchen garden, wooden fences and other features. **Fort St James National Historic Site**, *Box 1148, Fort St James, BC V0J 1P0; tel: (250) 996-7191*, open mid May–end Sept, puts interpreters in period costumes to explain the workings of a frontier fur trading post. The visitor centre has an excellent museum covering both the Dakelh, or Carrier, people and later arrivals. ⬛

VANDERHOOF

Tourist Information: Vanderhoof and District Chamber of Commerce, *2353 Burrard Ave, Box 126, Vanderhoof, BC V0J 3A0; tel: (250) 567-2124; fax: (250) 567-3316.*

Vanderhoof is 10 km west of the geographical centre of British Columbia. The town was created by Herbert Vanderhoof, a Chicago railway publicist who envisaged a luxurious riverside retreat for writers and artists. The retreat never materialised (nor did the writers), but cheap land lured lumbermen eager to clear the forests and ranchers equally eager to stock the newly opened acreages with herds of dairy and beef cattle. The **Vanderhoof Heritage Village Museum**, *Hwy 16 at West and Pine Sts, Box 1515, Vanderhoof, BC V0J 3A0; tel: (250) 567-2991*, open May–Sept, explores local history from the 1890s–1920s in eleven restored buildings.

The physical centre of BC is 10 km east. Look for a trailer court, then a cairn. For a quick overview of Dakelh history, stop at the **Cluculz Creek Rest Area** info panel, 16.5 km east on Hwy 16. Until a generation ago, Carrier families camped here at first frost to harvest white fish for the winter.

PRINCE GEORGE

Tourist Information: Tourism Prince George, *1198 Victoria St, Prince George, BC V2L 2L2; tel: (800) 668-7646 or (250) 562-3700; fax: (250) 563-3584;* **Visitor Info Centre**, *Hwys 16 and 97*, open May–Sept.

ACCOMMODATION

Top choice is **Coast Inn of the North**,

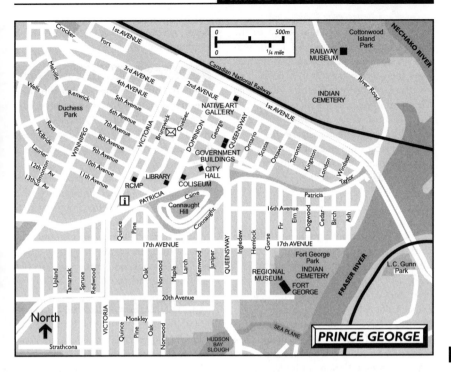

770 Brunswick St, Prince George, BC V2L 2C2; tel: (800) 663-1144 or (250) 563-0121; fax: (250) 563-1948, moderate–expensive. Chains include *Rm.*

EATING AND DRINKING

Galitas, *1148 7th Ave; tel: (250) 564-5951,* moderate, may be BC's best Spanish restaurant outside Vancouver. **Earl's Place**, *1440 E. Central; tel: (250) 562-1527,* serves moderate North Western dishes. Budget–moderate **Oodles Pasta House**, *1310 5th Ave; tel: (250) 563-5400,* is a popular Italian choice. **Bagel Street Café**, *1493 3rd Ave; tel: (250) 563-0071,* has great pastries.

SIGHTSEEING

Alexander Mackenzie paddled past the junction of the Fraser and Nechako Rivers in 1793. Simon Fraser built a tiny outpost named for King George III over the winter of 1807–1808. Fort George remained a village until the Grand Trunk Railway arrived on the way to Prince Rupert. The renamed town of Prince George began booming when road and rail construction linked the sleepy outpost with Vancouver, the Yukon and Alberta in 1952. A decade later, a trio of pulp mills helped turn Prince George into BC's northern capital. Advance booking is required for mill and forest tours through **Northern Forest Products Association**, *400-1488 Fourth Ave, Prince George, BC V2L 4Y2; tel: (250) 564-5135; fax: (250) 564-3588.*

The **University of Northern British Columbia (UNBC)**, *3333 University Way; tel: (250) 960-5678,* offers self-guided tours of its futuristic hilltop campus. Popular **Fort George Park**, *end of 20th*

Ave, site of Fraser's fort, is home to the **Fort George Railway**; *tel: (250) 562-6877,* $1 per person, Victoria Day–Labour Day, the shortest railway in Canada. The nearby **Fraser-Fort George Regional Museum**, *Box 1779, Prince Rupert, BC V2L 4V8; tel: (250) 562-1612; fax: (250) 562-6395,* concentrates on the history of transportation from dugout canoes to railways. **Prince George Railway and Forestry Museum**, *850 River Rd, Prince George, BC V2N 2S6; tel: (250) 563-7351,* open May–Sept, explores steam railroading and logging.

Next to **Cottonwood Island Nature Park** is a peaceful 32-hectare bird sanctuary on the Nechako River. **Connaught Hill Park**, *off Queensway,* is a volcanic plug with 360° views of city and river. Tourism Prince George has brochures for the 10-km **Heritage River Trail System** skirting the city centre. **Native Art Gallery**, *144 George St; tel: (250) 562-7385,* has the best selection of First Nations art in the region.

PRINCE GEORGE TO MCBRIDE

Hwy 16 crosses the Fraser River and climbs steeply onto a rolling forested plateau. A 1961 forest fire created prime moose habitat 29 km from Prince George. A **moose viewing** platform is a short walk from the north side of Hwy 16. To explore the forest itself, continue 5 km to the *Canadian Institute of Forestry's* **Willow River Interpretive Trail**, a series of 45-min to 2½-hr interpreted forest walks.

The 150 km stretch from **Purden Lake Provincial Park**, *57 km from Prince George; tel: (250) 565-6340,* crosses a broad belt of dense cedar and hemlock forests cut by numerous small streams and passes. There may be neither petrol nor food available, depending on season and time of day. Most convenient stop is the **Slim Creek Rest Area**, *south side of Hwy 16,* 61 km east of Purden Lake.

MCBRIDE

Tourist Information: McBride and District Chamber of Commerce, *Box 2, McBride, BC V0J 2E0; tel: (250) 569-3394; fax: (250) 569-3276;* **Visitor InfoCentre**, *Railway Caboose, south side Hwy 16,* open May–Sept.

This quiet market town is the commercial hub for a rural community that stretches several kilometres along Hwy 16. The narrow mountain valley is popular for wildlife viewing spring–autumn and Nordic skiing in winter. Best accommodation is the moderate **Scarecrow Inn** Bed and Breakfast; *tel/fax: (250) 565-0267.*

MCBRIDE TO VALEMOUNT

Hwy 16 turns west to Mt Robson Provincial Park, Jasper National Park and Jasper (see pp.219, 97–100) 63 km south-east of McBride. Continue south on Hwy 5 past **Tête Jaune Cache** (locally called 'Tay John'), Yellowhead Hwy and Yellowhead Pass (just east on Hwy 16), named after early 19th-century trapper Pierre Hatsinaton, called Tête Jaune, or Yellowhead, for his striking blond hair. Yellowhead was reputed to have cached a fortune of furs in the area, but died without reclaiming them. Man and legend came to life in Howard O'Haggan's 1939 classic film *Tay John.*

The town had its heyday as head of navigation on the Fraser River. Steamboats ran from Prince George to a landing about 5.5 km west on *Tête Jaune Cache Rd,* now marked only by the remains of abandoned pilings. The Fraser River runs emerald green as it exits the Rocky Mountains, turning silty yellow as it cuts through to the coast at Vancouver. Continue south on Hwy 5 to **Valemount**.

PARKSVILLE–TOFINO

This 180-km route cuts through the heart of Vancouver Island, from the sheltered waters of the Inside Passage on the east coast, through low, wet mountain ranges to the pounding surf of the unprotected Pacific coast. Along the way, small towns nestle between some of the oldest and tallest stands of Douglas-fir on the island and the more familiar patchwork of clear cutting. The West Coast and Pacific Rim National Park are wetter, wilder and even less developed than North Island. Until the road to Tofino was paved in 1972, the West Coast was almost a private preserve. Today, the return trip can be made in a day, but deserves at least one night each in Port Alberni, Ucluelet and Tofino.

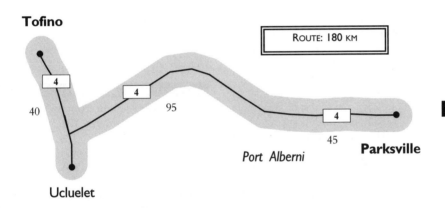

339

339

ROUTE

Take BC 4 west from Parksville past Englishman River Falls and the town of **Coombs** (look for goats grazing the rooftops) to **Cameron Lake, Cathedral Grove** and **Port Alberni**. The highway follows Sproat Lake, then swings southwest to a T-junction. **Ucluelet** is 7 km south (left), the Long Beach Unit of **Pacific Rim National Park**, and **Tofino** is 34 km north (right).

BUSES

Island Coach Lines operate services along this route. See OTT table 64. There are four trips a day from Parksville to Port Alberni and two trips a day from Port Alberni on to Tofino.

PARKSVILLE TO PORT ALBERNI

Emerald Forest Bird Garden, *1420 Alberni Hwy, Parksville, BC V9P 2G5; tel: (250) 248-7282; fax: (250) 248-7298,* open daily, is a welcome splash of brilliant colour. About 260 parrots, macaws, canaries and other tropical birds flutter and squawk in a recreated habitat. Many have been trained to perch on the nearest available arm, shoulder or head.

Englishman River Falls Provincial Park, *0.5 km W. of Emerald Forest to Arrington Rd, 7 km S.; tel: (250) 248-5212*, is a pleasant picnic spot with two small but photogenic waterfalls. Both falls are about 0.5 km through dark, mossy forest, a welcome relief from the island's usual stumps and tree farms.

On the way back to BC 4, turn right onto *Grafton Ave* (just before the highway), then left onto *Leffler Rd* at the end of the pavement, to the **North Island Wildlife Recovery Association Museum of Nature**, *1240 Leffler Rd, Errington, BC V0R 1V0; tel: (250) 248-8534; fax (250) 248-1274*. The museum recreates several forest environments; the recovery centre treats about 700 injured animals yearly. Animals too badly injured to be released back into the wild are sent to zoos or used for education programmes.

Coombs, 3 km west on BC 4, was a Salvation Army scheme that brought more than 250,000 poor English and Welsh to Canada. The tiny town is now a tourist trap and 1960s throwback. Goats graze the turf roof of the **Old Country Market** while tourists graze the fresh produce, ice-cream and wickerware inside. **Butterfly World**, *1 km west; tel: (250) 248-7026*, has hundreds of colourful butterflies fluttering in a semi-tropical environment.

Little Qualicum Hatchery, *8 km west of the junction with BC4A*, is one of the island's less impressive hatcheries. **Little Qualicum Falls Provincial Park**, *2 km west on BC 4; tel: (250) 752-6305*, includes the entire shoreline of **Cameron Lake**, on the north (right), 4 km west of the park entrance. There are a number of very pleasant picnic spots on the lakefront.

Cathedral Grove, part of **MacMillan Provincial Park**, lies just west of the lake. The park was named after Harvey Reginald MacMillan, BC's first provincial chief

forester (1909–1913) and later head of the timber company that became MacMillan Bloedel. Easy walking trails explore one of South Island's rare bits of virgin forest. Trees layered with 800 years worth of accumulated moss are among the largest Douglas-fir and red cedar left in BC. Smoking is not permitted in the 13-hectare park. **Port Alberni Summit**, 375m, is 7 km west.

Mt Arrowsmith Regional Park, *2 km west of the summit*, has winter skiing and ice climbing. The park is more popular in summer for hiking, wildflowers, fishing and expansive vistas from **Mt Arrowsmith** (1817m) and **Mt Cokely** (1616m). Carry chains in winter. Port Alberni junction is 5 km west. At the junction, go left into central Port Alberni or continue straight to Ucluelet and Tofino.

PORT ALBERNI

Tourist Information: Alberni Valley Chamber of Commerce, *RR 2, Site 215 C10, Port Alberni, BC V9Y 7L6; tel: (250) 724-6535*. **InfoCentre**, *Port Alberni Junction*, open Mon–Fri 0900–1700.

ACCOMMODATION AND FOOD

CS is the only area chain, but there are another 15 hotels/motels plus many Bed and Breakfasts and campsites. **Coast Hospitality Inn**, *3835 Redford St, Port Alberni, BC V9Y 3S2; tel: (250) 723-8111 or (800) 663-6677; fax: (250) 723-0088*, is the best in town, followed by **The Barclay**, *4277 Stamp Ave; tel: (250) 724-7171 or (800) 563-6590*. Both are moderate.

Seafood is always a safe bet in this long-time fishing port. **Paradise Café**, *4505 Gertrude St; tel: (250) 724-5050*, is a good choice. **Blue Door Café**; *tel: (250) 723-8811*, and **Steamers**; *tel: (250) 723-2211*, both at Alberni Harbour Quay, are local breakfast and lunch favourites.

SIGHTSEEING

Fishing and forestry have been economic mainstays since Port Alberni was established as a lumber town in 1860. Tourism is gaining quickly, especially near **Harbour Quay** at the foot of *Argyle St.* The **Observation Tower** has good views over Stamp Harbour and Alberni Inlet, stretching 40 km to the Pacific. **Forestry Information Centre**, *Harbour Quay; tel: (250) 724-7888,* arranges tours of local saw and pulp mills as well as lumbering operations. The Quay is also home to the *Lady Rose,* with passenger and freight service to Barkley Sound. Many commercial fishing boats now sell direct to the public at **Government Pier**. Others are moving to sport fishing, as Port Alberni disputes Campbell River for the 'Salmon Capital of the World' title.

Much of **Alberni Valley Museum**, *4255 Wallace St; tel: (250) 723-2181; fax: (250) 723-1035,* explores industrial history, including the **Alberni Pacific Railway**, a restored 1929 steam locomotive engine – carriages run summer weekends – and the **R.B. McLean Lumber Company**, a family-owned sawmill under restoration. Contact the museum for hours and tours. The museum also has a self-guided historic city walking tour brochure.

PORT ALBERNI TO UCLUELET

There are no services, including petrol, between Port Alberni and Ucluelet.

Roberson Creek Hatchery, *3 km beyond the Husky petrol station to Central Lake Rd, then 8 km north,* open daily 0800–1600, has an excellent series of displays. Bear, deer and other wildlife share the gravel road with vehicles.

Sproat Lake Provincial Park, *Box 1479, Parksville, BC V9P 2H4; tel: (250) 954-4600,* is busy in summer, almost deserted at other times. Loud aeroplane

sounds mean the Mars water bombers are dumping 27 tonnes of water on forest fires. These two converted military planes, the largest water bombers in the world, are based on the lake at **Flying Tankers**, *Bomber Base Rd; tel: (250) 723-6225.* No tours, but the base is open for visitors who keep out of the way.

The road west climbs past Sproat Lake, following the Taylor River into the **MacKenzie Range**. An extensive area around the road burned in 1967 when highway construction equipment sparked a major forest fire. Replanting began the same year. The high point is **Sutton Pass**, 175m, which leads to **Hydro Hill**, an 18% grade that runs straight into a recent 'clear-cut'. Graffiti on the guard rail, 'telephone poles – last of the old growth' reflects one side of local sentiment.

Continue 22 km to a T-junction and a summer-only **Travel InfoCentre**. Go left 7 km to Ucluelet.

341

UCLUELET

Tourist Information: Ucluelet Chamber of Commerce, *227 Main St, Ucluelet, BC V0R 3A0; tel: (250) 726-4641; fax: (250) 726-4611,* open Mon–Fri 1000–1500, daily (June–Sept).

Moderate–expensive **Canadian Princess Resort**, *1948 Peninsula Rd, Ucluelet, BC V0R 3A0; tel: (250) 726-7771; fax: (250) 726-7271,* a former hydrographic survey ship refitted as a resort, and the moderate–pricey **Snug Harbour Inn**, *460 Marine Dr., Ucluelet, BC V0R 3A0; tel: (888) 936-5222* or *(250) 726-2686; fax: (250) 726-2685,* are the best in town.

This scenic tourist, fishing and logging village is about a third of the way up Ucluelet Inlet from Barkley Sound and the open Pacific. Ucluelet is a local First Nations word for 'people of the sheltered bay'. The calm inlet is a sharp contrast to the pounding Pacific west of **Amphitrite Point**, 5 km south of the centre. The **lighthouse**, still operating, was built in 1906 after the *Line of Melfort* struck the point and sank with all hands.

Ha-tin-kis Park, *just before the lighthouse,* has an extensive boardwalk system through coastal forest and bogs. Park and lighthouse have stunning sunset views. The road ends in a housing estate just beyond the lighthouse. Return north through **Pacific Rim National Park** to Tofino.

TOFINO

Tourist Information: Tofino Chamber of Commerce, *Box 249, Tofino, BC V0R 2Z0; tel: (250) 725-3414; fax: (250) 725-3296,* open Mon–Fri 0900–1700.

ACCOMMODATION AND FOOD

BW is the only chain, but there are more than two dozen inns, Bed and Breakfasts and motels. Best in-town choice is moderate **Weigh West Marine Resort**, *634 Campbell St, Tofino, BC V0R 2Z0; tel: (250) 725-3277 or (800) 665-8922; fax: (250) 725-3922.* Best beach bet is **The Wickaninnish Inn**, *Box 250, Tofino, BC V0R 2Z0; tel: (800) 333-4604 or (250) 725-3100; fax: (250) 725-3310,* 5 km south on Chesterman Beach.

EATING AND DRINKING

The Blue Heron, *Weigh West Resort; tel: (250) 725-4266,* and **The Schooner**, *331 Campbell St; tel: (250) 725-3444,* are the pricey best. **Alleyway Café**, *305 Campbell St; tel: (250) 725-3105,* has the best vegetarian meals on the West Coast. The **Common Loaf Bakeshop**, *180 First St; tel: (250) 725-3915,* has shockingly good breads, pastries and light meals.

SIGHTSEEING

Government Dock at the foot of *First St*

is the end/beginning of the TransCanada Hwy and the entrance to **Clayoquot Sound**. Named after a 17th-century Spanish hydrographer, Tofino is better known as the land of the Nuu-chah-nulth First Nations, called Nootka by early Europeans. Commercial fishing is still important, but Tofino is growing as the supply town for the Pacific Rim National Park and has a flourishing outdoor recreation industry. Hiking, fishing, whale watching, sea kayaking and environmental activism are favourite pastimes. A 1993 provincial government decision to allow the logging of two-thirds of Clayoquot Sound, then among the largest surviving virgin temperate rain forests on the planet, sparked Canada's largest civil disobedience action. The industry-controlled **Rainforest Interpretive Centre**, *316 Main St; tel: (250) 725-2560; fax: (250) 725-1252,* is one of few local institutions to support logging.

Eagle Aerie, *350 Campbell St; tel: (250) 725-3235; fax: (250) 725-4466,* and **House of Himwitsa**, *300 Main St; tel: (250) 725-2017; fax: (250) 725-2361,* are Tofino's leading First Nations art galleries. Displays are the equal of anything shown in Vancouver and Victoria, as are the prices. Himwitsa operates popular **Sea Shanty Restaurant** and **Himwitsa Lodge**, both with broad views across Tofino Inlet.

Favourite Tofino spots to watch the sun drop are **Government Dock, Tonquin Park** and **Chesterman Beach**. **Meares**, an easy kayak paddle away, is known for virgin forests that have, so far, escaped the chain-saw. **Hot Springs Cove**, an all-day boat excursion to the island's only known hot springs, offers virgin forests and hot springs. The 50°C water cools as it plunges over a waterfall and flows through several pools toward the sea. Swimming costumes are optional, to the occasional delight of local mosquitoes.

Pacific Rim National Park

Pacific **Rim National Park Reserve**, *Box 280, Ucluelet, BC V0R 3A0; tel: (250) 726-7721* or *(800) 689-9025*, is three parks in one. The **West Coast Trail**, north from Port Renfrew, the **Broken Group Islands**, in Barkley Sound, and the **Long Beach Unit**, between Ucluelet and Tofino, encompass 510 square km of south-western Vancouver Island and some of the wildest scenery on Canada's Pacific Rim. The **Park Information Centre**, *BC 4, 3 km north of the Ucluelet-Tofino-Port Alberni junction; tel: (250) 726-4212*, is open mid Mar–mid Oct.

The **West Coast Trail** was originally a life-saving trail along the rugged coast between Port Renfrew and Bamfield. Spectacular virgin scenery is the norm, but generally wet weather and rugged topography make this 75-km, 6–7-day walk a challenge. The Trail is open 15 Apr–30 Sept; permits are required. Advance bookings begin 1 Mar; *tel: (604) 387-1642 or (800) 663-6000*, daily 0600–1800. The $25 booking fee can be paid by Visa or MasterCard. Space-available permits are available in Port Renfrew, Nitinat Lake (mid-way point) and Bamfield. The permit wait averages three days, but stretches longer each season.

The **Broken Group** is more than one hundred islands, most little more than rocks supporting a few windblown trees. Hundreds of ships have been wrecked on the outer edge of the Broken Group in the past two centuries, competing with the mouth of the Columbia River as the 'Graveyard of the Pacific'. Behind lies a maze of semi-protected islets and passages that harbour one of the richest concentrations of marine life off North America. Canoeists and kayakers come to view the wildlife as well as stunning untouched islands rising from pristine waters on every side. The only access is by water, usually aboard the *MV Lady Rose* from Port Alberni; *tel: (800) 663-7192*. Advance bookings required.

Road-building has transformed the **Long Beach Unit** from a seldom-seen island hideaway at the end of a tortuous logging road to one of the most popular parts of Vancouver Island. More than 800,000 people a year visit the 30 km of sandy beach, rocky headland, forest and bog between Ucluelet and Tofino. What were once empty beaches have sprouted busy parking lots with bright yellow payboxes – and wardens to enforce the $5 daily parking fee. Most visitors come for the day May–Oct. By late afternoon, the beaches are all but deserted except for sea gulls, sea lions and crabs hiding in the heaps of driftwood that wash up on every strip of sand.

Florencia Bay, or Wreck Beach, *S. off Long Beach Rd*, is a 5-km crescent pointing toward the **Wickaninnish Centre**, *end of Long Beach Rd; tel: (250) 726-7333*, open mid Mar–mid Oct, the main interpretive centre for the park. The restaurant, museum, and elevated walkways with broad vistas across Wickaninnish Bay are particularly busy July–Aug.

Centre and Bay are named after a Nootka chief who inadvertently sparked the fur trade. In June, 1788, Wickaninnish traded Capt John Meares fifty sea otter pelts for two copper kettles. Meares eventually sold the fur-bare pelts, used as bedding by his crew, for $2500 in China.

The surf-swept sand of Long Beach stretches 10 km north. **Combers Beach**, *5 km north on BC4*, is the north end of Long Beach. A well-marked trail explores the distinct ecological zones between salty, inhospitable sand and the dense, moss-draped forest a few hundred metres inland.

Radar Hill, *16 km north*, is the site of a 1954 radar base on the 'Pine Tree Line' built to defend the United States against nuclear attack from the Soviet Union. The Pine Tree Line followed the 49th Parallel, with the Mid-Canada Line running through Central Canada, and the DEW (Distant Early Warning) Line along the northern rim of the continent. Tofino is 12 km north on BC 4.

343

WEBSITES AND EMAIL ADDRESSES

Prices, opening hours and other details change as quickly in the Canadian Rockies as they do anywhere else in the world. Details in this volume were checked just before publication, but you can still expect to find changes that came too late for inclusion. For the absolutely latest updates, nothing beats the World Wide Web and Email. For details of **Thomas Cook** and its services around the world, visit their website on *http://www.thomascook.com.* (VA=Visitors Association; VB=Visitor Bureau; VCB=Visitor and Convention Bureau; CC=Chamber of Commerce; CVB=Convention and Visitor Bureau; CVC=Commerce and Visitors Centre.)

Aboriginal Tourism Authority:
http://www.aboriginalnet.com/tourism

Alaska Marine Highway:
http://www.dot.state.ak.us/external/amhs/home.html

Alberta Road Conditions:
http://www.ama.ab.ca/roadrep/roadrep.htm

Southwest Alberta: *http://www.albertasouth.com*

BC Ferries: *http://bcferries.bc.ca/ferries*

BC Rail: *http://www.bcrail.com/bcr*

BC Road Conditions:
http://www.bchighway.com/report

Tourism BC: *http://www.travel.bc.ca*

BC Transit: *http://transitbc.com*

British Columbia Bed and Breakfast Directory: *http://www.monday.com/tourism*

Canadian Pacific Hotels: *http://www.cphotels.ca*

Cascade Range Volcanoes:
http://vulcan.wr.usgs.gov/

Central Oregon VA: *cova@empnet.com*

Columbia River Gorge: *http://www.gorge.net*

The Dalles Area CC: *tolacc@gorbe.net*

Galiano Island CC:
http://www.islandnet.com/galiano

Gold Beach, OR, CC:
http://www.harborside.com/gb/

Harrison Hot Springs, BC, CC:
email: *harrison@uniserve.com*

HI American Youth Hostels:
http://www.hiayh.org

Hostelling International BC:
http://www.virtualynx.com/bchostels

La Grande-Union County, OR, CC:
http://www.ucinet.com/~lagrande/

Lane County CVA, OR: *http://www.cvalco.org*

Lynden CC: *http://www.pacificrim.net/~lynden*

Medford, Jackson County, OR, VCB:
MEDJACCC@Magick.Net

Tourism Nanaimo BC:
http://www.tourism.nanaimo.bc.ca/

Greater Newport CC:
http://www.newportnet.com

Ontario, OR, VCB: email: *ontvcb@micron.net*

Oregon, Washington & California Bed & Breakfast: *http://www.moriah.com/inns*

Oregon Caves National Monument:
http://www.nps.gov/orca/

Eastern Oregon:
http://www.eosc.osshe.edu/rec_poi.html

Southern Oregon coastal communities:
http://www.harborside.com/hs/online_comm/

Southern Oregon VA: *http://www.sova.org*

Oregon Online Highways:
http://www.ohwy.com:80/or/homepage.htm

Oregon Tourism: *http://www.traveloregon.com*

Osoyoos, BC: *http://alpha.ftcnet.com/~edoca/*

Portland Oregon VA: *http://www.pova.com*

Salem, OR, CVA:
http://www.oregonlink.com/~salem/scva/

San Juan Island, WA, CC:
http://www.pacificrim.net/~bydesign/chamber.html

Seaside, OR, CC: *seaside@aone.com*

Spokane, WA, Regional CV:
http://www.spokane-areacvb.org

Stubbs Island Whale Watching, Telegraph Cove, BC: *stubbs@north.island.net*

Tofino, BC, CC: *bnixon@lbmf.bc.ca*

Underground Onramp: email:
comments@underramp.com

Tourism Vancouver CVB:
http://www.travel.bc.ca/vancouver

Vancouver Island communities:
http://www.island.net/

Tourism Victoria: *http://www.travel.victoria.bc.ca/*

Canada-West Victoria Reservation Service: email: *canwest@netnation.com*

Wallowa County, OR, CC:
http://www.eosc.osshe.edu.~jkraft.wallowa.com

Washington State Tourism Division:
http://www.tourism.wa.gov

344

DRIVING DISTANCES AND TIMES

Approximate distances from major cities to surrounding places and main centres are given following the most direct routes. Driving times are meant as an average indication only, allowing for the nature of the roads but not for traffic conditions, which can be very variable (see the route descriptions throughout the book). They do not include allowance for stops or breaks en route. The journey times of the main ferry crossings are also shown.

	Kilometres	*Hours*
Banff to . . .		
Calgary	125	1½
Jasper	285	4
Kamloops	500	6¼
Lake Louise	60	1
Radium Hot Springs	125	3

	Kilometres	*Hours*
Calgary to . . .		
Banff	125	2
Drumheller	140	2
Edmonton	300	3½
Kananaskis	100	1½
Lethbridge	225	2½
Red Deer	145	2
Vancouver	975	12
Waterton Lakes National Park	275	4

	Kilometres	*Hours*
Edmonton to . . .		
Calgary	300	3½
Jasper	365	5
Prince Rupert	1475	17½
Red Deer	155	1½
Vancouver	1175	14

	Kilometres	*Hours*
Jasper to . . .		
Banff	285	4
Edmonton	365	5
Lake Louise	225	3
Kamloops	450	5¼

	Kilometres	*Hours*
Kamloops to . . .		
Banff	500	6¼
Bella Coola	755	15
Calgary	350	4½
Edmonton	625	7¼
Jasper	450	5¼
Kelowna	200	2½
Vancouver	350	4½

	Kilometres	*Hours*
Vancouver to . . .		
Calgary	975	12
Campbell River	ferry	3½
Cranbrook	850	11¼
Hope	150	2
Kamloops	350	4½
Osoyoos	400	5
Port Hardy (incl. ferry)	385	7
Victoria	ferry	1
Whistler	150	2½

	Kilometres	*Hours*
Victoria to . . .		
Campbell River	160	2½
Nanaimo	120	1¾
Port Hardy	500	7⅔
Tofino	315	5⅓
Vancouver	ferry	1

HOTEL CODES
AND CENTRAL BOOKING NUMBERS

The following abbreviations have been used throughout the book to show which chains are represented in a particular town. Cities and large towns have most except *HI*. Central booking numbers are shown in bold – use these numbers whilst in North America to make reservations at any hotel in the chain. Where available, numbers that can be called in your own country are also noted. (Aus = Australia, Can = Canada, Ire = Ireland, NZ = New Zealand, SA = South Africa, UK = United Kingdom, WW = Worldwide number).

BW **Best Western**
(800) 528 1234
Aus *(1 800) 222 422*
Ire *(800) 709 101*
NZ *(09) 520 5418*
SA *(011) 339 4865*
UK *(0800) 393130*

CI **Comfort Inn**
(800) 228 5150
Aus *(008)090 600*
Can *(800) 888 4747*
Ire *(800) 500 600*
NZ *(800) 808 228*
UK *(0800) 444444*

CM **Courtyard by Marriott**
(800) 321 2211

CP **Canadian Pacific**
(800) 441 1414

CS **Coast Hotels**
(800) 663 1144

DI **Days Inn**
(800) 325 2525
UK *(01483) 440470*

EL **Econolodge**
(800) 424 6423
WW *(800) 221 2222*

ES **Embassy Suites**
(800) 362 2779
Aus *02 959 3922*
Can *416 626 3974*
NZ *09 623 4294*
SA *11 789 6706*
UK *(01992) 441517*

FS **Four Seasons**
(800) 332 3442

Hd **Holiday Inn**
(800) 465 4329
Aus *(800) 221 066*
Ire *(800) 553 155*

NZ *(0800) 442 222*
SA *(011) 482 3500*
UK *(0800) 897121*

HI **Hostelling International**
202 783 6161
(information only)
Can/US *(800) 444 6111*
UK *(0171) 248 6547*

HJ **Howard Johnson (HoJo)**
(800) 654 2000
Aus *02 262 4918*
UK *(0181) 688 1418*

Hn **Hilton**
(800) 445 8667
Aus *(800) 222 255*
NZ *(800) 448 002*
SA *(011) 880 3108*
UK *(0345) 581595*

Hy **Hyatt**
(800) 233 1234
Aus *(800) 131 234*
Ire *(800) 535 500*
NZ *(800) 441 234*
SA *(011) 773 9888*
UK *(0345) 581666*

Ma **Marriott**
(800) 228 9290
Aus *(800) 251 259*
NZ *(800) 441 035*
UK *(800) 221222*

M6 **Motel 6**
(800) 437 7486

PP **Pan Pacific**
(800) 663 1515

QI **Quality Inn**
(800) 228 5151

Rd **Radisson**
(800) 333 3333

Ire *(800) 557 474*
NZ *(800) 443 333*
UK *(800) 191991*

RI **Residence Inn**
(800) 331 3131
Aus *(800) 251 259*
Ire *(800) 409929*
NZ *(800) 441035*

Rm **Ramada**
(800) 228 2828
Aus *(800) 222 431*
Can *(800) 854 7854*
Ire *(800) 252 627*
NZ *(800) 441 111*
UK *(800) 181737*

Rn **Renaissance**
as Ramada

Sh **Sheraton**
(800) 325 3535 or
(800) 325 1717
(hearing impaired)
Aus *(008) 073 535*
Ire *(800) 535 353*
NZ *(0800) 443 535*
UK *(0800) 353535*

S8 **Super 8**
WW *(800) 800 8000*

TL **Travelodge**
(800) 578 7878
Aus *(800) 622 240*
Ire *(800) 409 040*
NZ *(800) 801 111*
SA *(011) 442 9201*
UK *(0345) 404040*

VI **Vagabond Inn**
(800) 522 1555

WT **Westin**
(800) 228 3000

CONVERSION TABLES

DISTANCES (approx. conversions)
1 kilometre (km) = 1000 metres (m) 1 metre = 100 centimetres (cm)

Metric		Imperial/US		Metric		Imperial/US		Metric	Imperial/US	
	1 cm		3/8 in	9 m	(10 yd)	29 ft		0.75 km	½ mile	
1 m	0 cm	3 ft	3 in	10 m	(11 yd)	33 ft		1 km	5/8 mile	
2 m	0 cm	6 ft	6 in	20 m	(22 yd)	66 ft		5 km	3	miles
3 m	0 cm	10 ft	0 in	50 m	(54 yd)	164 ft		10 km	6	miles
4 m	0 cm	13 ft	0 in	100 m	(110 yd)	330 ft		20 km	12½	miles
5 m	0 cm	16 ft	6 in	200 m	(220 yd)	660 ft		30 km	18½	miles
6 m	0 cm	19 ft	6 in	250 m	(275 yd)	820 ft		50 km	31	miles
7 m	0 cm	23 ft	0 in	300 m	(330 yd)	984 ft		75 km	46	miles
8 m	0 cm	26 ft	0 in	500 m	(550 yd)	1640 ft		100 km	62	miles

24-HOUR CLOCK
(examples)

0000 = Midnight	1200 = Noon	1800 = 6.00 p.m.
0600 = 6.00 a.m.	1300 = 1.00 p.m.	2000 = 8.00 p.m.
0715 = 7.15 a.m.	1415 = 2.15 p.m.	2110 = 9.10 p.m.
0930 = 9.30 a.m.	1645 = 4.45 p.m.	2345 = 11.45 p.m.

TEMPERATURE
Conversion Formula: $°C \times 9 \div 5 + 32 = °F$

°C	°F	°C	°F	°C	°F	°C	°F
-20	-4	-5	23	10	50	25	77
-15	5	0	32	15	59	30	86
-10	14	5	41	20	68	35	95

WEIGHT
1 kg = 1000 g 100 g = 3½ oz

Kg	Pounds	Kg	Pounds	Kg	Pounds
1	2¼	5	11	25	55
2	4½	10	22	50	110
3	6½	15	33	75	165
4	9	20	45	100	220

FLUID MEASURES
1 litre(l) = 0.88 Imperial quarts = 1.06 US quarts

Litres	Imp.gal.	US gal.	Litres	Imp.gal.	US gal.
5	1.1	1.3	30	6.6	7.8
10	2.2	2.6	35	7.7	9.1
15	3.3	3.9	40	8.8	10.4
20	4.4	5.2	45	9.9	11.7

MEN'S CLOTHES

UK	Europe	US
36	46	36
38	48	38
40	50	40
42	52	42
44	54	44
46	56	46

MENS' SHOES

UK	Europe	US
6	40	7
7	41	8
8	42	9
9	43	10
10	44	11
11	45	12

LADIES' CLOTHES

UK	France	Italy	Rest of Europe	US
10	36	38	34	8
12	38	40	36	10
14	40	42	38	12
16	42	44	40	14
18	44	46	42	16
20	46	48	44	18

MEN'S SHIRTS

UK	Europe	US
14	36	14
15	38	15
15½	39	15½
16	41	16
16½	42	16½
17	43	17

LADIES' SHOES

UK	Europe	US
3	36	4½
4	37	5½
5	38	6½
6	39	7½
7	40	8½
8	41	9½

AREAS
1 hectare = 2.471 acres
1 hectare = 10,000 sq metres
1 acre = 0.4 hectares

INDEX

INDEX

350

READER SURVEY

If you enjoyed using this book, or even if you didn't, please help us improve future editions by taking part in our reader survey. Every returned form will be acknowledged, and to show our appreciation we will give you £1 off your next purchase of a Thomas Cook guidebook. Just take a few minutes to complete and return this form to us.

When did you buy this book?

Where did you buy it? (Please give town/city and if possible name of retailer)

When did you/do you intend to travel in the Canadian Rockies?

For how long (approx.)?
How many people in your party?

Which cities, national parks and other locations did you/do you intend mainly to visit?

351

Did you/will you:
☐ Make all your travel arrangements independently?
☐ Travel on a fly-drive package?
Please give brief details:

Did you/do you intend to use this book:
☐ For planning your trip?
☐ During the trip itself?
☐ Both?

Did you/do you intend also to purchase any of the following travel publications for your trip?
Thomas Cook Travellers: *Vancouver & British Columbia*
A road map/atlas (please specify)
Other guidebooks (please specify)

Have you used any other Thomas Cook guidebooks in the past? If so, which?

Please rate the following features of Touring the Canadian Rockies for their value to you (Circle VU for 'very useful', U for 'useful', NU for 'little or no use'):

The 'Travel Essentials' section on pages 20–47	VU	U	NU
The 'Driving in Western Canada' section on pages 48–56	VU	U	NU
The 'Touring Itineraries' on pages 59–63	VU	U	NU
The recommended driving routes throughout the book	VU	U	NU
Information on towns and cities, National Parks, etc	VU	U	NU
The maps of towns and cities, parks, etc	VU	U	NU
The colour planning map	VU	U	NU

Please use this space to tell us about any features that in your opinion could be changed, improved, or added in future editions of the book, or any other comments you would like to make concerning the book:

Your age category: ☐ 21-30 ☐ 31-40 ☐ 41–50 ☐ over 50

Your name: Mr/Mrs/Miss/Ms
(First name or initials)
(Last name)

Your full address: (Please include postal or zip code)

Your daytime telephone number:

Please detach this page and send it to: The Project Editor, Touring the Canadian Rockies, Thomas Cook Publishing, PO Box 227, Peterborough PE3 6PU, United Kingdom.

We will be pleased to send you details of how to claim your discount upon receipt of this questionnaire.

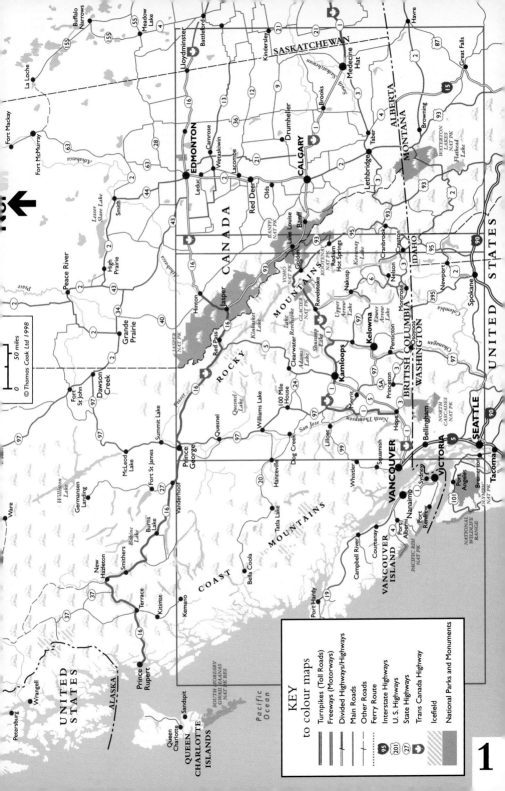

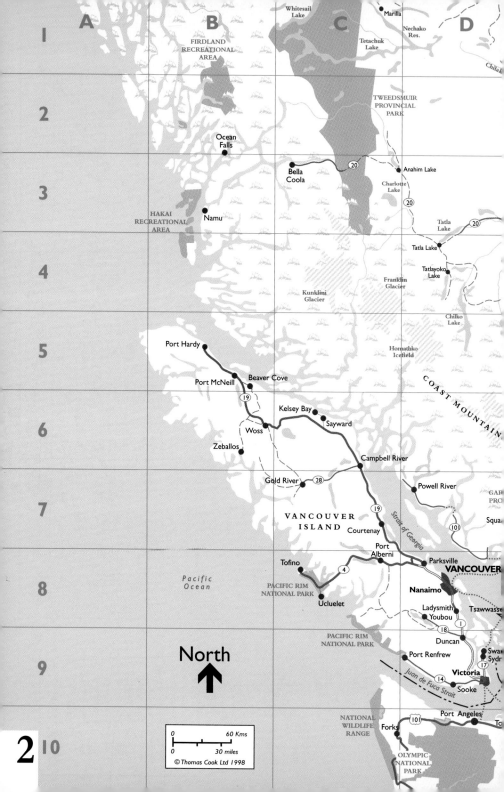

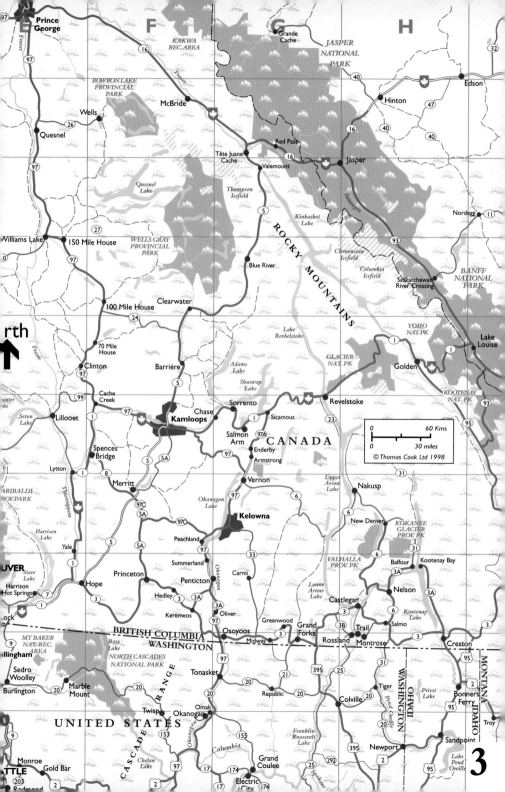

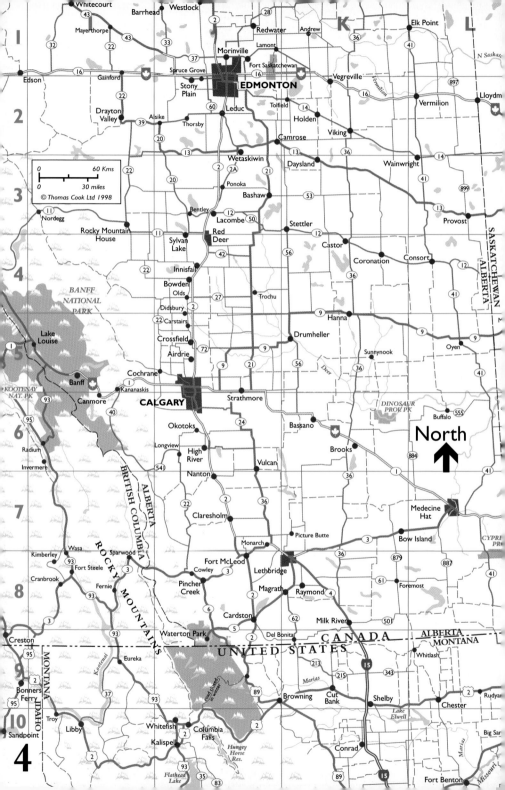